lonely planet

Budapest
& Hungary

Northern
Hungary
p240

The Danube Bend &
Western Transdanubia
p163

Budapest
p42

The Great Plain
p215

Lake Balaton
& Southern
Transdanubia
p187

Steve Fallon, Anna Kaminski

Contents

ON THE ROAD

ROMAS_PHOTO/SHUTTERSTOCK ©

MZPHOTO.CZ/GETTY IMAGES ©

BIRDWATCHING P285

Contents

MUSEUM OF APPLIED ARTS P89, BUDAPEST

WILL SANDERS/LONELY PLANET ©

GUIDE TO THERMAL BATHS & SPAS P35

Welcome to Budapest & Hungary

Stunning architecture, vital folk art, thermal spas and Europe's most exciting city after dark are the major drawcards of Hungary and its capital, Budapest.

Super Structures

The beauty of both Hungary and Budapest is not all God-given; humankind has played a role in shaping these pretty faces too. Architecturally, Hungary is a treasure trove, with everything from Roman ruins and medieval townhouses to baroque churches, neoclassical public buildings and art nouveau bathhouses and schools. And you won't just find all that in Budapest. Stroll through Szeged or Kecskemét, Debrecen or Sopron and you'll discover an architectural gem at virtually every turn.

In Hot Water

Hungarians have been 'taking the waters' supplied by an estimated 300 thermal springs since togas were all the rage and Aquincum (Roman Budapest) was the Big Smoke. They still do – for therapeutic, medicinal and recreational purposes – but the venues have changed somewhat. Today they range from authentic bathhouses dating from the Turkish occupation and art nouveau palaces to clinical sanatoriums straight out of a Thomas Mann novel. More and more popular are ultra-modern wellness centres offering myriad treatments.

Eat, Drink & Be Magyar

Hungarian food remains the most sophisticated in Eastern Europe. Magyars even go so far as to say there are three essential world cuisines: French, Chinese and their own. That may be a bit of an exaggeration, but Hungary's – and especially Budapest's – cuisine is, despite a fallow period under communism, once again commanding attention. So too are the nation's world-renowned wines, from the big-bodied reds of Eger and Villány and white *olaszrizling* from Badacsony to honey-sweet Tokaj.

Folk Culture

Hungary has one of the richest folk traditions still alive in Europe. With exquisite folk paintings found in the tiny wooden churches of the Bereg region and the wonderful embroidery that the women of Hollókő stitch to decorate smocks, skirts and slippers, this is often where the country comes to the fore artistically. Traditional music, played on a five-tone diatonic scale on a host of unusual instruments, continues to thrive as well, especially at *táncházak* (dance houses) – peasant 'raves' take place regularly in Budapest and other cities, where you'll hear Hungarian folk music and learn to dance too.

Why I Love Budapest & Hungary

By Steve Fallon, Writer

I love both Budapest and Hungary for so many reasons that it's impossible to put them into any order. Is it the capital's art nouveau architecture or the Turkish-era baths that are God-given cures for too much *pálinka* (fruit brandy)? Is it the gentle landscape, the rolling hills of the north or the sight- and fun-filled cities like Budapest, Szeged and Debrecen? Maybe it's the Jókai-style bean soup... But taking pride of place with all those reasons is Hungarian itself. When I sing a song of Hungary today it may be in a beautiful language that I once considered impenetrable, but no longer do.

For more about our writers, see p320

Above: Fishermen's Bastion (p60), Budapest

Hungary

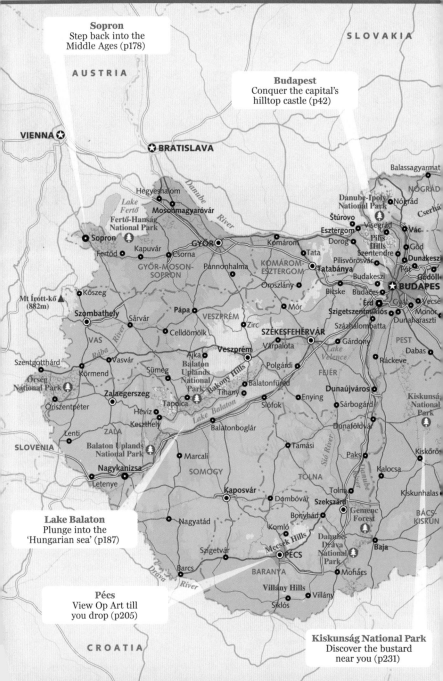

Sopron
Step back into the Middle Ages (p178)

Budapest
Conquer the capital's hilltop castle (p42)

Lake Balaton
Plunge into the 'Hungarian sea' (p187)

Pécs
View Op Art till you drop (p205)

Kiskunság National Park
Discover the bustard near you (p231)

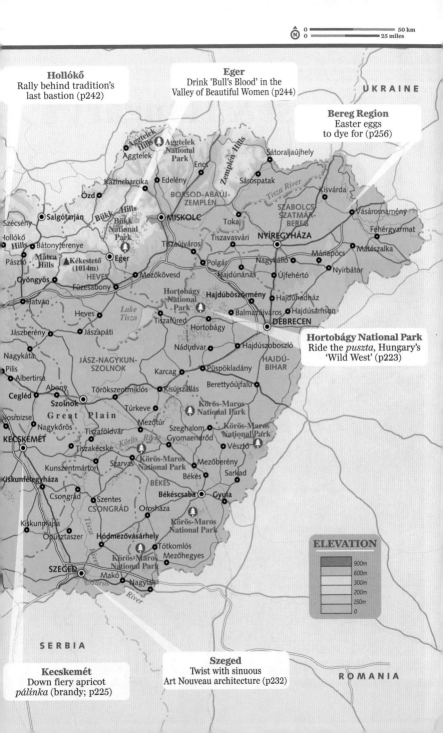

0 — 50 km
0 — 25 miles
Ⓝ

Hollókő
Rally behind tradition's
last bastion (p242)

Eger
Drink 'Bull's Blood' in the
Valley of Beautiful Women (p244)

UKRAINE

Bereg Region
Easter eggs
to dye for (p256)

Aggtelek Hills
Aggtelek
Aggtelek National Park
Encs
Sátoraljaújhely
Zemplén Hills
Kazincbarcika
Edelény
Sárospatak
Tisza River
Ózd
BORSOD-ABAÚJ-ZEMPLÉN
Kisvárda
Szécsény
Salgótarján
Bükk Hills
Bükk National Park
MISKOLC
Tokaj
SZABOLCS-SZATMÁR-BEREG
Vásárosnamény
Hollókő Hills
Bátonyterenye
Tiszaújváros
Tiszavasvári
NYÍREGYHÁZA
Fehérgyarmat
Pásztó
Mátra Hills
▲ Kékestető (1014m)
Eger
Polgár
Hajdúnánás
Nagykálló
Máriapócs
Mátészalka
Gyöngyös
HEVES
Mezőkövesd
Újfehértó
Nyírbátor
Hatvan
Füzesabony
Hortobágy National Park
Hajdúböszörmény
Hajdúhadház
Heves
Lake Tisza
Balmazújváros
Hajdúsámson
Jászberény
Tiszafüred
Hortobágy
DEBRECEN
Jászapáti
Nádudvar
Hajdúszoboszló
Nagykáta
JÁSZ-NAGYKUN-SZOLNOK
HAJDÚ-BIHAR
Pilis
Karcag
Püspökladány
Albertirsa
Berettyóújfalu
Cegléd
Abony
Törökszentmiklós
Kisújszállás
Szolnok
Túrkeve
Körös-Maros National Park
Great Plain
Nagykőrös
Mezőtúr
Szeghalom
Körös-Maros National Park
KECSKEMÉT
Tiszaföldvár
Körös River
Gyomaendrőd
Lakitelek
Tiszakécske
Vésztő
Kunszentmárton
Szarvas
Körös-Maros National Park
Mezőberény
Kiskunfélegyháza
Békés
Sarkad
BÉKÉS
Csongrád
Szentes
Békéscsaba
Gyula
CSONGRÁD
Orosháza
Kiskunmajsa
Körös-Maros National Park
Ópusztaszer
Hódmezővásárhely
Tótkomlós
Tisza River
Mezőhegyes
SZEGED
Körös-Maros National Park
Makó
Nagylak
Maros River

Hortobágy National Park
Ride the *puszta*, Hungary's
'Wild West' (p223)

SERBIA

ELEVATION

	900m
	600m
	300m
	200m
	150m
	0

Kecskemét
Down fiery apricot
pálinka (brandy; p225)

Szeged
Twist with sinuous
Art Nouveau architecture (p232)

ROMANIA

Budapest & Hungary's
Top 15

Budapest's Nightlife

1 Budapest can now claim to be the number-one nightlife destination (p137) in Europe. Alongside its age-old cafe culture and hallowed music halls, it offers a magical blend of unique drinking holes, fantastic wine, home-grown firewaters and emerging craft beers, all served up with a warm Hungarian welcome and a wonderful sense of fun. Unique are the *romkocsmák* (ruin bars) and *kertek* (gardens) that pop up all over town in the warmer months. Bottom left: Ruin bar Szimpla Kert (p143)

Eger

2 Everyone loves Eger (p244), and it's immediately apparent why. Beautifully preserved baroque architecture gives the town a relaxed, almost Mediterranean feel; it is flanked by two of northern Hungary's most beautiful ranges of hills (Bükk and Mátra), and it is the home of some of Hungary's best wines, including the celebrated Bull's Blood, which can be sampled at cellars in the evocatively named Valley of the Beautiful Women, a mere stroll away from the centre. Bottom right: Minorite Church of St Anthony of Padua (p244)

Thermal Baths

3 With more than 300 thermal hot springs (p35) in public use across Hungary, it's not hard to find a place to take the waters. Some of the thermal baths, like the Rudas and Király Baths in Budapest and part of the Turkish Bath in Eger, date back to the 16th century. Increasingly popular are wellness spas and water parks, which cater to a wider audience. Among the most unusual spa experiences: floating on a thermal lake at Hévíz. Top left: Rudas Baths, Budapest (p99)

Szeged

4 The cultural capital of the Great Plain and Hungary's third-largest city, Szeged (p232) is filled with eye-popping art nouveau masterpieces, students, open-air cafes and green spaces, straddling the ever-present Tisza River. Theatre, opera and all types of other classical and popular music performances abound, culminating in the Szeged Open-Air Festival in summer. Szeged is also justly famed for its edibles, including the distinctive fish soup made with local paprika and Pick, Hungary's finest salami. Top right: Gróf Palace (p233)

Budapest's Castle Hill

5 Budapest boasts architectural gems in spades, but the limestone plateau of Castle Hill (p60) towering over the Danube River's west bank is the Hungarian capital's most spectacular sight. Enclosed within medieval castle walls, numerous attractions vie for your attention, from the treasures in the Hungarian National Gallery and Castle Museum to the claustrophobic Hospital in the Rock and the show-stopping view of Parliament across the river in Pest from Fishermen's Bastion.

Lake Balaton's Northern Shore

6 Hungary's 'sea' (and Continental Europe's largest lake) is where people come to sun and swim in summertime. The quieter side of Lake Balaton (p190) mixes sizzling beaches and oodles of fun on the water with historic waterside towns like Keszthely and Balatonfüred. Tihany, on a peninsula jutting 4km into the lake, is home to a stunning abbey church.

Top: Tihany (p194)

Hollókő

7 It may consist of a mere two streets, but Hollókő (p242) is the most beautiful of Hungary's villages. Its 67 whitewashed houses, little changed since their construction in the 17th and 18th centuries, are pure examples of traditional folk architecture and have been on Unesco's World Heritage list since 1987. Most importantly, it is a bastion of traditional Hungarian culture, holding fast to the folk art of the ethnic Palóc people and some of their ancient customs.

Pécs

8 This gem of a city (p205) is blessed with rarities: Turkish architecture and early Christian and Roman tombs. Its Mosque Church is the largest Ottoman structure still standing in Hungary, while the Hassan Jakovali Mosque has survived the centuries in excellent condition. Pécs is exceptionally rich in art and museums. What's more, the climate is mild – almost Mediterranean-like – and you can't help noticing all the almond trees in bloom or in fruit here. Top left: Mosque Church (p205)

Hortobágy National Park

9 Hungarians view the *puszta* – the Great Plain – romantically, as a region full of hardy shepherds fighting the wind and snow in winter and trying not to go stir-crazy in summer as the notorious *délibábak* (mirages) rise off the baking soil. It's a nostalgic notion, but the endless plains can be explored in the Hortobágy National Park (p223). You can also watch as Hungarian cowboys ride with five horses in hand in a spectacular show of skill and horsemanship.

Folkloric Northeast

10 Preserved through generations, Hungary's folk-art traditions bring everyday objects to life. Differences in colours and styles easily identify the art's originating region. You'll find exquisite detailed embroidery, pottery, hand-painted or carved wood, dyed Easter eggs and graphic woven cloth right across the country, but the epicentre is in the Bereg region (p256). The culture of the tiny villages of this region in the far northeast of Hungary has much to do with their neighbours to the east, including their brightly dyed Easter eggs.

BOTOND HORVATH/SHUTTERSTOCK ©

Kecskemét

11 This city (p225) on the Southern Plain holds some surprises. Hidden behind its ring of vineyards and apricot orchards are fine examples of art nouveau, such as the Ornamental Palace, Otthon Cinema and Town Hall, and if you look hard enough you'll even find a yellow brick road. It can also boast among the richest arrays of museums in Hungary, with everything from musical instruments and toys to naive art on display. Above left: Decorated house in Kecskemét's old town

Wine & Pálinka

12 Hungarian wines (p279), produced here for millennia, are celebrated the world over. Honey-sweet Tokaj and crimson-red Bull's Blood from Eger are the best known, but travel around and meet (and taste) a few other of the fine wines available here. Punching much higher in the alcohol stakes is *pálinka*, a strong brandy flavoured with fruit (think apricots, plums and even raspberries) that kicks like a mule. Above top right: *Pálinka* bottles on display

Sopron

13 Sopron (p178) has the most intact medieval centre in Hungary, its cobbled streets lined with one Gothic or colourful early-baroque facade after another. A wander though the backstreets here is like stepping back in time. The icing on the cake is the town's Roman ruins. But architecture aside, the small border city beckons with its many vineyards and cellars in which to sample the local wine. Above bottom right: Fő tér (p179)

Paprika

14 Paprika (p32), the sine qua non of Hungarian cuisine, may not be exactly what you expect. All in all, it's pretty mild stuff; a taco with salsa or a chicken vindaloo from the corner take-away will taste more 'fiery' to you. But the fact remains that many Hungarian dishes wouldn't be, well, Hungarian (or dishes for that matter) without the addition of the 'red gold' spice grown for the most part around Szeged that comes in varying degrees of piquancy. It's a culinary and culturally Magyar essential.

Birdwatching

15 With a full 250 resident species, several of them endangered and many rare, birds (p287) are plentiful in Hungary and you don't have to go out of your way to spot our feathered friends. Head to the Hortobágy on the Great Plain to see autumn migrations, or to Lake Balaton to see aquatic birdlife. Bustards proliferate in Kiskunság National Park near Kecskemét. And white storks nesting atop chimneys in eastern Hungary are quite a sight between May and October. Bottom: Great bustard, Hortobágy National Park (p223)

Need to Know

For more information, see Survival Guide (p289)

Currency
Hungarian forint (Ft; international currency code HUF)

Language
Hungarian

Visas
Citizens of all European countries and Australia, Canada, Israel, Japan, New Zealand and the USA don't require visas for visits of up to 90 days. Check current visa requirements on the Ministry of Foreign Affairs website (http://konzulis zolgalat.kormany.hu/).

Money
ATMs widely available. Credit and debit cards accepted in many hotels and restaurants.

Mobile Phones
It is relatively cheap to use a mobile from another EU country in Hungary. Local SIM cards can be used in European, Australian and some North American phones. Other phones must be set to roaming (can be pricey).

Time
Central European Time (GMT plus one hour)

When to Go

Danube Bend
GO May, Jun & Oct

Northern Hungary
GO Jul–Aug, Sep–Oct

Budapest
GO May–Jun, Sep–Oct

Lake Balaton
GO Jul–Aug

Great Plain
GO Apr–May, Sep–Oct

Warm to hot summers, cold winters

High Season
(Jul–Aug)

➡ Summer is warm, sunny and unusually long everywhere.

➡ Resorts at Lake Balaton and in the northern Hungary hills book out; expect long queues at attractions and high prices everywhere.

➡ Many cities grind to a halt in August.

Shoulder
(Apr–Jun, Sep–Oct)

➡ Holidaymakers have gone home; prices drop.

➡ Spring is glorious everywhere, though it can be pretty wet in May/early June.

➡ Autumn is particularly special in the hills (eg Bükk and Mátra); festivals mark the *szüret* (grape harvest).

Low Season
(Nov–Mar)

➡ November is rainy; winter is cold and often bleak.

➡ Many sights reduce their hours sharply or close altogether.

➡ Prices are rock-bottom.

Useful Websites

Hungarian National Tourist Office (www.gotohungary.com) The single best website on Hungary; make it your first portal of call.

Tourinform (www.tourinform.hu) Good for visitor-centre locations.

Lonely Planet (www.lonelyplanet.com/hungary) Destination information, hotel bookings, traveller forum and more.

Hungary Museums (www.museum.hu) A list of every museum in the land currently open to the public.

Budapest by Locals (www.budapestbylocals.com) Excellent and very useful expat-driven site full of both glaringly obvious information and bits and pieces that impress even us.

Important Numbers

Hungary's country code	☑36
Ambulance	☑104
Europe-wide emergency number	☑112
Fire	☑105
Police	☑107

Exchange Rates

Australia	A$1	213Ft
Canada	C$1	208Ft
Europe	€1	308Ft
Japan	¥100	268Ft
New Zealand	NZ$1	201Ft
Switzerland	Sfr1	286Ft
UK	UK£1	341Ft
USA	US$1	279Ft

For current exchange rates, see www.xe.com.

Daily Costs

Budget:
Less than 12,000Ft

➡ Dorm bed: 3000–6500Ft

➡ Meal at a cheap or self-service restaurant: 1500–2500Ft

➡ Ticket to national museum or other attraction: 700Ft

Midrange:
12,000–35,000Ft

➡ Single/double private room: from 7500/10,000Ft

➡ Two-course meal with drink: 3500–7500Ft

➡ Cocktail: from 1500Ft

Top End:
More than 35,000Ft

➡ Double room in superior hotel: from 16,500Ft

➡ Dinner for two with wine at a good restaurant: from 12,500Ft

➡ All-inclusive ticket at a spa/water park: adult/child 3600/1600Ft

Opening Hours

With rare exceptions, opening hours (*nyitvatartás*) are posted on front doors of businesses; *nyitva* means 'open', *zárva* 'closed'.

Banks 7.45am–5pm Monday to Thursday, to 4pm Friday

Bars 11am–midnight Sunday to Thursday, to 2am Friday and Saturday

Businesses 9am–6pm Monday to Friday, to 1pm Saturday

Clubs 4pm–2am Sunday to Thursday, to 4am Friday and Saturday; some only open weekends

Grocery stores and supermarkets 7am–7pm Monday to Friday, 7am–3pm Saturday; some also 7am–noon Sunday

Restaurants 11am–11pm; breakfast venues open by 8am

Shops 10am–6pm Monday to Friday, to 1pm Saturday

Arriving in Hungary

Ferenc Liszt International Airport (Budapest; p298) Buses run around the clock from the airport to the Kőbánya-Kispest metro station. The airport shuttle does door-to-door drop-offs (around €22 to central Budapest), while a taxi costs around 5650Ft.

Keleti, Nyugati & Déli train stations (Budapest) All three stations are on metro lines of the same name; trams and/or night buses call when the metro is closed.

Népliget & Stadionok bus stations (Budapest) Both are on the M3 metro line and served by trams 1 and 1A.

Getting Around

Hungary's domestic transport system is efficient, comprehensive and inexpensive. Towns are covered by a system of frequent buses, trams and trolleybuses.

The majority of Hungary's towns and cities are easily negotiated on foot. There are no scheduled flights within Hungary; it's small enough to get everywhere by train or bus within a day.

EU citizens over the age of 65 travel for free on all public transport.

Menetred (www.menetrendek.hu) has links to all the timetables: bus, train, public transport and boat.

Train Reasonably priced, with extensive coverage of the country.

Car Handy for exploring the wilder corners of Hungary.

Bus Cheaper and often faster than trains. Useful for more remote destinations not served by trains.

For much more on **getting around**, see p298

First Time Budapest & Hungary

For more information, see Survival Guide (p289)

Checklist

➡ Check the validity of your passport

➡ Make any necessary bookings (for sights, accommodation and/or travel)

➡ Check your airline's baggage restrictions

➡ Inform your credit-/debit-card company you're going abroad

➡ Arrange travel insurance

➡ Check to see if you can use your mobile (cell) phone away from home

What to Pack

➡ Phrasebook

➡ Money belt

➡ Mobile phone charger

➡ Adapter plug

➡ Small kettle or coil immersion heater for hot drinks

➡ Hat/cap and sunscreen

➡ Swimsuit and towel

➡ Thongs/flip-flops

➡ Umbrella

➡ Padlock

➡ Torch (flashlight)

➡ Pocketknife

➡ Clothes pins/pegs

➡ Small pair of binoculars

Top Tips for Your Trip

➡ Make sure you pack a bathing suit even if you're travelling in winter. Many baths and spas are now co-ed and require you to be suited up.

➡ Remember that while trains across Hungary are often more expensive than buses, they can be faster and more comfortable.

➡ Eat your main meal at lunch when set meals at most restaurants – including high-end ones – cost a fraction of what they do at dinner.

➡ If you're using public transport a lot (especially in Budapest), buy a pass. It'll keep you safe from inspectors and usually works out cheaper.

➡ When tipping in a restaurant, never leave money on the table. Instead, tell waiters how much you intend to leave and they'll give the change accordingly.

What to Wear

In general, Hungarian dress is casual; many younger people attend classical-music concerts and even the opera in jeans. Men needn't bother bringing a tie, as it will be seldom (if ever) used. There are no items of clothing to remember, apart from a warm hat in winter. A swimsuit for use in the mixed-sex thermal spas and pools is important, as are plastic sandals or thongs (flip-flops). The summer fashions and beachwear here can be daringly brief, even by Western standards.

Sleeping

Hungary has a wide range of accommodation. Book a couple of months in advance if you're planning on visiting Budapest, Lake Balaton or the Danube Bend in July or August.

➡ **Camping** These range from private sites with few facilities to large caravan campgrounds with swimming pools.

➡ **Hostels** Inexpensive and with lots of backpacker facilities.

➡ **Hotels** Anything from socialist-era brutalist architecture to elegant five-star places, quirky boutique hotels and converted castles.

➡ **Pensions, inns and B&Bs** Many are cosy, family-run places with all the facilities of a small hotel.

➡ **Private homes and apartments** Book a room or the whole place (usually) with English-speaking hosts.

Money

Credit and debit cards can be used almost everywhere. Visa and MasterCard are the most popular options; American Express is less often accepted. Chip-and-pin is the norm for card transactions though business establishments will accept signatures as an alternative if the card is chipless. ATMs are everywhere, but be warned that those at branches of OTP, the national savings bank, dispense 20,000Ft notes, which can be hard to break. Hungary's value-added (or sales) tax on goods and services of between 5% and 27% is one of Europe's highest. Visitors are not exempt, but non-EU residents can claim refunds (p295).

Bargaining

It's OK to bargain at markets and it may be possible to negotiate a discount if you're staying in lower or midrange accommodation for several nights, but otherwise you have to pay the set price.

Tipping

➡ **Bars** Tip 30Ft to 50Ft per drink at the bar; if drinks are brought to your table, 10% of total.

➡ **Hairdressers** Ten percent of haircut price is appropriate.

➡ **Hotels** Tip 500Ft for luggage, 200Ft to 300Ft per day for housekeeping.

➡ **Petrol stations and thermal spas** Attendants expect some loose change.

➡ **Restaurants** For decent service 10%, up to 15% in more upmarket places; 12.5% service often included in the bill.

➡ **Taxis** Round up the fare.

Language

Hungarians like to boast that their language ranks with Japanese and Arabic as among the world's most difficult to master. All languages are challenging for non-native speakers, but it is true: Hungarian is very difficult to learn well. However, this should not put you off attempting a few words and phrases.

Things are changing, and many millennials speak English, particularly in Budapest. Older generations tend to speak only Hungarian (and perhaps German). Attempt a few words in Hungarian (Magyar) and they will be impressed and be extremely encouraging. For more, see our Language chapter, p305.

Etiquette

Hungarians are almost always extremely polite in their social interactions, and the language can be very courtly – even when doing business with the butcher or having one's hair cut.

➡ **Greetings** Young people's standard greeting to their elders is *Csókolom* ('I kiss it' – 'it' being the hand, of course). People of all ages, even close friends, shake hands when meeting up.

➡ **Asking for help** Say *legyen szíves* (be so kind as) to attract attention; say *bocsánat* (sorry) to apologise.

➡ **Eating and drinking** If you're invited to someone's home, bring a bunch of flowers or a bottle of good local wine.

➡ **Name days** As much as their birthday, Hungarians celebrate their name day, which is usually the Catholic feast day of their patron saint (all Hungarian calendars list them). Flowers, sweets or a bottle of wine are the usual gifts.

Eating

Hungary has an ever-increasing range of eating options, particularly in Budapest. In most places, it's fine to book on the day or not book at all; for fine dining in Budapest, book a week or two ahead.

➡ **Restaurants** Range from cheap Hungarian to refined sushi and Michelin-starred fine-dining establishments.

➡ **Vendéglő** Regional restaurants typically serving inexpensive homestyle cooking.

➡ **Cafes** Open during the daytime, these are great for coffee, cake and light (and sometimes substantial) meals.

➡ **Csárda** Typically rustic places serving large portions of Hungarian cuisine, often accompanied by Gypsy music.

If You Like...

Architecture

Hungary's architectural waltz through history begins with the Romans in Budapest and Sopron, moves to the early Christian sites in Pécs, climbs up to the castles of the Northern Uplands, and into the many splendid baroque churches across the land. Neoclassicism steps in with some fine public buildings in Debrecen. But taking centre stage is the art nouveau/Secessionism found in abundance in Budapest, Szeged and Kecskemét.

Budapest Wander through Budapest's historical heart and see how many different architectural styles you can spot within several blocks. (p42)

Pécs Home to the most significant architectural relics of Turkish rule, an early-Christian World Heritage Site and baroque structures. (p205)

Kecskemét This city claims a stunning assemblage of art nouveau and Secessionist buildings on its leafy squares. (p225)

Synagogues There are some fine example of Jewish houses of worship, especially in Szeged, and places like Pécs, Eger and Esztergom. (p233)

Castles Some of the best castles can be found in northern Hungary, at Hollókő and Eger. (p242)

Cuisine

Hungary boasts Eastern Europe's finest cuisine. It's very meaty, that's true, but big on flavour. Try one of the staples like paprika-laced *pörkölt* (a stew not unlike what we call goulash) or *gulyás* (or *gulyásleves*), a thick beef soup cooked with onions and potatoes. And don't overlook specialties such as *libamaj* (goose liver prepared in an infinite number of ways) and *halászlé*, a rich fish soup.

Budapest Choose between Hungarian-style cafes, trendy cellar eateries, Michelin-starred restaurants and everything in between. (p115)

Fish Locally caught fish at Lake Balaton is a must-try. The most popular varieties are pike-perch, catfish and carp. (p192)

Sopron Sample locally produced red *kékfrankos* and white *tramini* in a town known for its wine since Roman times. (p184)

Szeged The city's famed *halászlé* with several kinds of Tisza River fish is a meal in itself. (p237)

Bereg The deep-purple *szilva* (plums) of this region are used to make the finest *lekvár* (jam) and *pálinka* (brandy). (p256)

Patisseries Every town offers *cukrászdák* (cake shops) selling rich, sweet creations; the grandaddy is Budapest's Gerbeaud. (p139)

Thermal Spas

Since the time of the Romans in the 2nd century AD, people here have enjoyed Hungary's abundant thermal waters. The choice of venues is enormous and much varied, but the trend today is for extra large spas with a wellness centre offering services from A to Z for the adults and a huge water park attached for the kids.

Hévíz Gyógy-tó, Europe's largest thermal lake, is therapeutic, medicinal and filled with lotuses. (p203)

Budapest From *hammams* (Turkish baths) and palace-like baths to outdoor whirlpools, you are completely spoiled for choice in the capital. (p35)

Eger A massive renovation of a Turkish bath dating to 1617 has added six pools, saunas, a steam room and *hammam*. (p247)

Szeged The lovely Anna Baths were built in 1896 to imitate the tilework and soaring dome of a Turkish bath. (p235)

Kecskémet Thermal baths, swimming pools, full spa

facilities and every wellness treatment you could imagine are at the Kecskémet Baths. (p228)

Folk Art

Hungary has one of the richest folk traditions in Europe. Folk art and fine art are inextricably linked; the music of Béla Bartók and the ceramic sculptures of Szentendre's Margit Kovács, for example, are deeply rooted in traditional culture.

Budapest Check out the work of artisans from all over Hungary at the mid-August Budapest Festival of Folk Arts. (p102)

Sopron Folk art and crafts are on display at the handicraft fair during Sopron Festival Weeks from mid-June to mid-July. (p182)

Hollókő This tiny village is a treasure trove of Hungarian folk art and crafts. Visit during the Easter Festival in March/April. (p242)

Bereg region This area is the last bastion of folk life and famed for its needlework, wooden churches filled with naive murals and painting. (p256)

Szentendre A museum here is dedicated to Margit Kovács, a ceramicist who combined Hungarian folk, religious and modern themes. (p167)

Festivals

Hungary paints the town red year-round nowadays; the days when nothing got scheduled in August during the 'cucumber-growing season' are well and truly over. Choose from among themed festivals that celebrate things like Jewish culture and folklore, classical music or jazz, and new crops of grapes (or cherries or apples).

Top: New Synagogue, Szeged (p233)
Bottom: Traditional Hungarian embroidery

Sopron Celebrate Sopron's Grape Harvest in September by sampling its fine wines, accompanied by music and folk dancing. (p182)

Mohács The Busójárás carnival in February or March brings out masked creatures, lively processions, folk music and dancing. (p214)

Budapest Immerse yourself in Budapest's distinguished Jewish heritage during the eight-day Jewish Cultural Festival in September. (p102)

Szeged The Szeged Open-Air Festival in July and August is the country's most important and showcases every branch of the performing arts. (p236)

Hollókő Easter in this folkloric village is a special time, with women in colourful traditional costumes parading through the streets. (p242)

Debrecen The Flower Carnival here in August is arguably Hungary's most colourful festival. (p219)

Scenery

Hungary cannot claim any point higher than 1000m, and it's nowhere near the sea. Yet the country has an amazingly varied topography. There's the low-lying salty grasslands of the Great Plain, a half-dozen ranges of hills to the north and northeast, and two major (and very scenic) rivers: the Danube and the Tisza. Hungary also has well over 1000 lakes, of which the largest and most famous is Balaton.

Őrség Drive past peaceful meadows and through the hills of Őrség National Park for a glimpse of traditional village life. (p186)

Pannonhalma Head for the hilltop abbey for the all-encompassing views of the surrounding countryside. (p183)

Tihany This 80m-high peninsula is home to wild and vineyard-filled swaths of green and the most dramatic views across Lake Balaton. (p194)

Hortobágy The real Hortobágy on the Great Plain and the one in paintings and poems get mixed up, but it remains stunningly beautiful. (p223)

Bereg region This land of thatched peasant cottages, horse-drawn hay wagons and fruit trees is the Hungarian countryside at its most gentle. (p256)

Visegrád The view from the mighty fortress completed in 1259 will convince you that the Danube does 'bend'. (p171)

Month by Month

January

Hungary is still festive after the Christmas holidays. It is cold but the skies are bright blue. There may be a light dusting of snow on church spires and also possibly ice floes in the Danube and Tisza Rivers (although this is increasingly less likely).

☆ New Year's Gala Concert

This annual gala concert (www.hungariakoncert.hu), which is usually held in Budapest's Pesti Vigadó on 1 January, ushers in the new year and is the favourite of the capital's glitterati.

February

By February winter has hung on a bit too long for most people and the cold days are shorter and bleaker. Many attractions will remain closed (or keep shortened hours) until mid-March.

Busójárás

This pre-Lenten carnival of Busójárás (www.mohac-sibusojaras.hu) involves anthropomorphic costumes and is held in Mohács on the weekend before Ash Wednesday.

March

This is an excellent month to visit Hungary. Women have put their furs back in the closet, and it's the start of the concert and theatre season in many cities.

Pécs Spring Festival

This month-long 'everything but the kitchen sink' event (www.pecsi-tavaszifesztival.hu) takes place throughout Pécs in late March.

April

In April the brief interval between winter and summer looks, feels and smells like an old-fashioned spring.

Budapest Spring Festival

The capital's largest and most important cultural festival (www.springfesti-val.hu) takes place over two weeks at dozens of venues across the city.

Hollókő Easter Festival

Traditional costumes and folk traditions welcome in spring at this World Heritage–listed village's Easter Festival (www.holloko.hu).

May

The selection of fresh vegetables and fruit is not great in winter, but in spring a cycle of bounty begins, starting with asparagus.

National Gulyás Competition & Shepherd's Meeting

The National Gulyás Competition & Shepherd's

Meeting (www.hnp.hu) sees Hortobágy cattle herdsmen testing their skills in competition, with a *gulyás*-cooking competition thrown in for good measure.

June

Late spring is wonderful but the month of June can be pretty wet, especially early in the month. Beware the start of the holiday crowds.

◉ Museums Night

For Museums Night (https://muzej.hu), hundreds of museums across the country mark the summer solstice in mid-June by re-opening their doors at 6pm on a Saturday and not closing them till the wee hours (as late as 2am).

🍷 Kecskemét Apricot Brandy & Wine Festival

Vintners and distillers from around the country set up tasting booths on the squares of Kecskemét (www.hirosagora.hu).

🎭 Sopron Festival Weeks

All manner of concerts, theatrical performances, plus arts and crafts exhibitions are held in Sopron's squares from mid-June (www.prokultura.hu).

July

School's out for the summer, so now you're competing not only with foreign visitors but local ones too. Book early for Balaton and the hills of northern Hungary.

🎭 Szeged Open-Air Festival

The most celebrated open-air festival in Hungary (www.szegediszabadteri.hu) is held in July and August; includes opera, ballet, classical music and folk dancing.

☆ Balaton Sound Festival

This lakeside adjunct of Budapest's hugely popular Sziget Festival, held at Zamárdi, near Balatonfüred, over five days in July, boasts almost as impressive a lineup of bands (www.sziget.hu/balatonsound).

🍷 Eger Bikavér Festival

Four days devoted to Bull's Blood, Eger's iconic wine (www.eger.hu).

☆ Anna Ball

Even if you don't attend the Anna Ball (www.annabal.hu) on 26 July it's worth joining the crowds to watch the beautifully attired guests. On the following day the ball queen parades around Balatonfüred in an elaborate horse and carriage. Concerts accompany the days around the ball.

August

Hungary used to come to a grinding halt in what was called the 'cucumber-growing month', but that's all changed now and August is festival month.

☆ Formula 1 Hungarian Grand Prix

Hungary's prime sporting event (www.hungaroring.hu), held in early August in Mogyoród, 24km northeast of the capital.

🎭 Debrecen Flower Carnival

A week-long spectacular (www.iranydebrecen.hu/info/flower-carnival) in Debrecen kicked off by a parade of flower floats on St Stephen's Day (20 August).

🎭 Hortobágy Bridge Fair

This century-old fair (www.hnp.hu) held in Hortobágy around St Stephen's Day (20 August) has dance, street theatre, folklore performances and the occasional horse and pony.

☆ Sziget Festival

One of the biggest and most popular music festivals in Europe, with half a million revellers at last sighting, the Sziget Festival (http://szigetfestival.com) is held on Budapest's Hajógyár (Óbuda) Island.

September

September brings summer to a close. It's a good time to visit as there's still a lot going on, wine is starting to flow and peak-season prices are over.

🍷 Grape Harvest Festivals

Festivals celebrating the grape harvest are held in late September in all wine-producing areas of Hungary, including Tokaj, Eger and Sopron. The Budapest International Wine Festival (www.aborfesztival.hu), held in the Castle District, is when Hungary's foremost vintners introduce their vintages to the public.

🍷 Valley of the Beautiful Women Weekend

Three days of wine, women and song at the celebrated Valley of the Beautiful Women Weekend in Eger (www.eger.hu).

October

Though the days are getting shorter and everyone is back into their routines, autumn is beautiful, particularly in the Buda Hills and the hills of northern Hungary.

🏃 Budapest International Marathon

Eastern Europe's most celebrated race (www. budapestmarathon.com)

runs along the Danube and across its bridges in mid-October.

November

The month kicks off immediately with a public holiday: All Saints' Day on 1 November. After that the winter season begins, with many museums and other tourist attractions around the country sharply curtailing their hours or closing altogether.

🛍 Budapest Christmas Fair & Winter Festival

Budapest kicks off the start of the holiday season in mid-November with Christmas markets opening in V Vörösmarty tér and in

front of the basilica in V Szent István tér (http://budapestchristmas.com).

December

The build-up to Christmas intensifies as the month moves on, and the arrival of decorations, trees and coloured lights is a welcome sight.

⭐ New Year Gala & Ball

The annual calendar's most coveted ticket is this gala concert and ball held at the Hungarian State Opera House (www.opera.hu) in Budapest on 31 December.

Itineraries

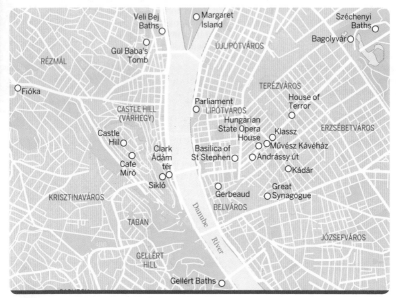

Budapest in Four Days

Spend most of the first day on **Castle Hill**, taking in the views, visiting a museum or two and perhaps having lunch at **Cafe Miró**. In the afternoon, ride the **Siklό** down to **Clark Ádám tér** and make your way to the **Gellért Baths**. In the evening, head to Liszt Ferenc tér for drinks and then to **Klassz** for dinner.

On the second day take a morning walking up **Andrássy út**, stopping off at the **House of Terror** and **Művész Kávéház**. Take the waters at the **Széchenyi Baths**, then have dinner at **Bagolyvár**.

On the third day, concentrate on the two icons of Hungarian nationhood and the places that house them: the Crown of St Stephen in **Parliament** and the saint-king's mortal remains in the **Basilica of St Stephen**. Have a cake break at **Gerbeaud** and catch a performance at the **Hungarian State Opera House**.

On day four visit the **Great Synagogue** and lunch at **Kádár**. In the afternoon, cross over to idyllic **Margaret Island**. On the other side of Margaret Bridge and up the hill is **Gül Baba's Tomb**, still a Muslim place of pilgrimage. Spend the rest of the afternoon at **Veli Bej Bath**, and go for dinner at nearby **Fióka**.

Top: Castle Hill Sikló (funicular), Budapest (p60)

Bottom: Hévíz Thermal Lake (p203)

BOTOND HORVATH/SHUTTERSTOCK ©

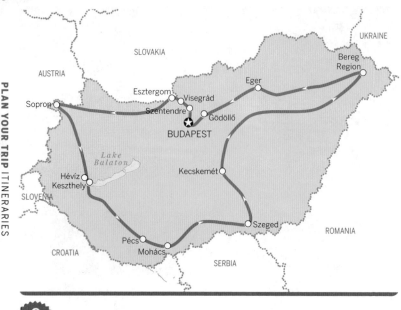

10 DAYS Essential Hungary

This itinerary offers you the best of Hungary and will give you a taste of the country's historical wealth and natural beauty. It takes in all four corners of the land, from the Danube Bend and Sopron to Pécs, Szeged and Eger, plus the Bereg region, Hungary's last bastion of folk culture.

From **Budapest**, make your way north to the towns of the Danube Bend: picture-postcard **Szentendre**, royal **Visegrád** and holy **Esztergom**. The road continues west along the Danube past some stunning scenery to **Sopron**, Hungary's finest medieval city, replete with worthwhile museums and churches. Travel south to Lake Balaton and recharge your batteries at lovely **Keszthely** and nearby **Hévíz**, which boasts its own thermal lake where you can bathe year-round. **Pécs**, Hungary's 'Mediterranean' town, is south; it's a treasure trove of early Christian and Turkish sites.

From there carry on east to **Mohács**, the site of Hungary's famous defeat at the hands of the Ottomans in 1526. A car ferry will take you to the right bank of the Danube and the road eastward to **Szeged**, the university town that is forever young. Should you pass though in July or August, catch a performance at the Szeged Open-Air Festival. **Kecskemét**, city of apricots and art nouveau architecture, is to the north.

Had enough of the flatlands of the Great Plain? Head for the northeast and the **Bereg region**. This is the richest area for folk traditions left in Hungary and is well worth a detour off the beaten track. From there head southwest to delightful **Eger**, a much-loved city, celebrated for its Bull's Blood (the region's ruby-red wine), baroque architecture and dramatic hilltop castle (from where the good folk of Eger were able to repel the Turks, at least for a while).

Head west back to Budapest, stopping at **Gödöllő**, the summer retreat of Emperor Franz Joseph and his beloved consort Elizabeth, whose renovated private apartments are now open to the public.

Plan Your Trip
Travel with Children

Hungary is a good destination for travellers with children. The little 'uns receive discounts on public transport and entry to museums and attractions, with some museums specifically geared towards kids. Many thermal parks across the country have slides, wave pools and designated kiddie pools, and some restaurants offer children's menus.

Budapest & Hungary for Kids

Dining Out

Some restaurants – particularly in Budapest – offer children's menus. Those that don't are usually happy to provide half-portions of adult dishes for kids.

Entertainment

Budapest has the lion's share of children's entertainment. This ranges from puppet theatres that transcend language barriers to folk music and dance evenings in which kids can participate if they want to.

Parks & Playgrounds

There is no shortage of green spaces in Hungary, and playgrounds are common in Hungarian towns. Budapest reigns supreme on this front, with City Park (p91) due to feature a brand-new amusement park by 2019, excellent playgrounds on Margaret Island, on Óbuda (Hajógyári) Island and in Szent István Park (p83), and smaller playgrounds dotted about the city.

Best Regions for Kids

Budapest
Children's attractions galore, from museums to thermal parks, but the costs can add up.

The Danube Bend & Western Transdanubia
Boat cruises up the Danube are reliable family-pleasers.

The Great Plain
Colourful traditional costumes and the chance to meet farm animals are popular with small children.

Lake Balaton & Southern Transdanubia
The shallow waters of Lake Balaton and plentiful cycle lanes are great for active families.

Northern Hungary
Hiking in the Bükk Hills and splashing in water parks is fun for outdoorsy kids.

Children's Highlights

Thermal Baths & Pools

Aquaworld, Budapest (p100) One of Europe's largest water parks, with a dozen slides and a wave pool.

Adventure Spa & Waterslide Park, Kecskemét (p228) Huge water park with pools and slides.

Széchenyi Baths, Budapest (p99) There's a fun whirlpool in one of several outdoor pools.

Napfényfürdő Aquapolis, Szeged (p235) Enormous water park with plenty of indoor and outdoor pools.

Meet the Animals

Máta Stud Farm, Hortobágy (p223) Riding a horse-drawn wagon across the prairie, spotting sheep and grey cattle on the way.

Budapest Zoo (p94) Hungary's most exotic collection of the furred and feathered kind.

Puszta Animal Park, Hortobágy (p224) The place to meet the animals of the *puszta* (literally 'deserted'; another name for the Great Plain): grey cattle, the mangalica (curly-haired pig) and the *racka* (sheep with distinctive corkscrew horns).

Cowboy Show, Kiskunság National Park (p232) Watch *csikósok* (cowboys) race each other bareback, while their horses perform all sorts of tricks.

Museums & Art Galleries

Museum of Fine Arts, Budapest (p59) Children's program that lets them create their own works of art.

Aquincum Museum, Budapest (p53) Interactive exhibits in the basement, including virtual gladiator fights.

Model Railway Museum, Keszthely (p201) Stunning model railway sets, with Austrian mountains, tunnels, snowy forests and minute train stations.

Toy Museum, Keszthely (p199) An incredible collection of dolls, trains, toy cars, teddy bears and play sets through the ages.

Toy Museum & Workshop, Kecskemét (p227) Spooky 19th- and 20th-century dolls, board games and wooden trains.

Rainy-Day Fun

Magic Tower, Eger (p245) Eighteenth-century astronomical equipment, a camera obscura and a planetarium for young star-gazers.

Tropicarium, Budapest (p103) Vast aquarium with Hungarian fish species and a non-Hungarian shark tunnel.

Palace of Wonders, Budapest (p103) 'Smart' toys, puzzles, and lots of interactive elements, such as the 'wind tunnel'.

Outdoor Activities

Children's Railway, Budapest (p98) Ride the rails through the Buda Hills on a train operated by children.

Boat Cruise, Szeged (p235) See the old town of Szeged from the river.

Sail & Surf, Tihany (p195) Have a go at stand-up paddleboarding on the calm waters of Lake Balaton.

River Ride, Budapest (p100) Explore Budapest by road and river on this amphibious bus.

Castles & Caves

Buda Castle Labyrinth (p61) Get lost in the dry-ice fog of this creepy underground world.

Minaret, Eger (p247) Winding steps followed by great views of the city.

Eger Castle (p244) Check out the armour, uniforms and models in this 13th-century castle.

Pálvölgy Cave, Budapest (p73) Spectacular stalactites and stalagmites await brave cave explorers.

Planning

Babysitting An ever-growing number of hotels in Budapest offer babysitting services, but try to book at least six hours beforehand.

Car hire Most car-hire firms have children's safety seats for hire at a nominal cost; book in advance.

Hotels and restaurants High chairs and cots (cribs) are standard equipment in many restaurants and hotels, but numbers can be limited; request them when booking.

Plan Your Trip
Eat & Drink Like a Local

It's not difficult to live like a local while travelling in Hungary. The natives are friendly, the food is excellent (and never too strange) and the wine even better. And there are lots of things here that many people everywhere like: fresh produce, sweet cakes and fruit-flavoured brandy that kicks like a mule.

Food Experiences

There is so much fresh produce in Hungary and so many interesting and unusual specialities that you might need some guidance. Fine-tune your culinary radar with the following edible musts:

Meals of a Lifetime

➡ **Ikon, Debrecen** (p220) Arguably the most inventive restaurant in provincial Hungary; unforgettable foie gras and rabbit cooked in *lecsó* (savoury mix of peppers, tomatoes and onions).

➡ **Padlizsán, Esztergom** (p176) A dramatic setting below a cliff, soft music at night and modern, very imaginative Hungarian dishes.

➡ **Macok Bistro & Wine Bar, Eger** (p250) An award-winning, very stylish eatery at the foot of Eger Castle with a top-notch menu and wine list.

➡ **Zeller Bistro, Budapest** (p132) Enlightened traditional dishes of meat, fish and produce sourced from the Lake Balaton area, served in a lovely candlelit cellar.

➡ **Zsolnay Restaurant, Pécs** (p212) Flawless service, an award-winning menu of creative Hungarian dishes and an emphasis on local ingredients.

➡ **Baraka, Budapest** (p123) Beautifully presented seafood dishes with Asian, French and Hungarian elements, along with a stellar bar and wine list.

The Year in Food

Food festivals take place year-round, celebrating everything from asparagus and honey to the lowly pumpkin and, of course, the grape.

Winter (Dec–Feb)

The selection of fresh vegetables and fruit is not great but the hunting season is on, and mushrooms and nuts have been collected. Budapest's Christmas markets are excellent places to nosh.

Spring (Mar–May)

A late-winter menu of preserved foods is consigned to the rubbish heap as the spring begins, starting with lettuces, *spárga* (asparagus) and then all the soft fruits. Ham figures largely at events like the Hollókő Easter Festival (p242).

Summer (Jun–Aug)

The bounty continues with strawberries, raspberries and cherries, then plums. Count on lots of grills and *gulyás* (a thick beef soup) cooked in a *bogrács* (cauldron) at the Hortobágy Bridge Fair (p224).

Autumn (Sep–Nov)

Dozens of wine festivals occur during the harvest. The most important one is the Budapest International Wine Festival (p102).

Cheap Treats

Some *hentesáru boltok* (butcher shops) have a *büfé* (snack bar) selling boiled or fried *kolbász* (sausage), *virsli* (frankfurters), *hurka* (blood sausage/black pudding), roast chicken and pickled vegetables. Point to what you want; the staff will weigh it and hand you a slip of paper with the price. You usually pay at the *pénztár* (cashier) and hand the stamped receipt back to the staff for your food. You pay for bread, mustard – even water.

Food stalls sell the same sorts of things, as well as fish when located near lakes or rivers. One of the more popular snacks is *lángos*, deep-fried dough with various toppings (usually cheese and sour cream), available at food stalls throughout Hungary. *Pogácsa*, a kind of dry, savoury scone introduced by the Turks, is the favoured snack among beer drinkers.

Dare to Try

Hungarians will happily consume *libamáj* (goose liver) and, to a lesser extent, *kacsamáj* (duck liver) whenever the opportunity presents itself, be it cold *zsírjában* (in its own fat), *roston sült* (pan-fried) with apples, or as *pástétom* (pâté), but they generally eschew other forms of offal. The most unusual Hungarian dishes are meatless and quite inviting. Cold fruit soups such as *meggyleves* (sour cherry soup) or less-common *fahéjas-almaleves* (cinnamon apple soup) are a positive delight on a warm summer's evening. Dishes such as *makós metélt* (vermicelli topped with poppy seeds) may look bizarre and fall neither in the savoury nor sweet category, but you won't soon forget the taste. Clean your teeth afterwards!

Local Specialities

Bread, Dumplings & Noodles

There's a saying that Hungarians 'eat bread with bread'. Since the reign of King Matthias Corvinus in the 15th century, leftover *kenyér* (bread) has been used to thicken soups and stews; *kifli* (crescent-shaped rolls) gained popularity during the Turkish occupation. Uniquely Magyar are the flour-based *galuska* (dumplings) and *tarhonya* (barley-shaped egg pasta) served with *pörkölt* and *paprikás* dishes.

Soups

A Hungarian meal always starts with *leves* (soup). This is usually something relatively light like *gombaleves* (mushroom soup) or *húsgombócleves* (tiny liver dumplings in bouillon). More substantial soups are *gulyás* (or *gulyásleves*), a thick beef soup, and *bableves*, a hearty bean soup usually made with meat. Another big favourite is *halászlé* (fisherman's soup), a rich soup of fish stock, poached carp or catfish, tomatoes, green peppers and paprika.

Meat & Stews

Hungarians eat an astonishing amount of meat. Pork, beef, veal and poultry are the meats most commonly consumed, and they can be breaded and fried, baked, simmered in *lecsó* (savoury mix of peppers, tomatoes and onions) and turned into paprika-flavoured creations.

The most popular dish prepared with paprika, the sine qua non of Hungarian cuisine, is the thick beef soup *gulyás* (or *gulyásleves*), usually eaten as main course. *Pörkölt* (stew) is closer to what foreigners

---

PAPRIKA: HUNGARY'S RED GOLD

Paprika, the *piros arany* (red gold) so essential in Hungarian cuisine, is cultivated primarily around the cities of Szeged and Kalocsa on Hungary's Great Plain. Between 8000 and 10,000 tonnes of the spice are produced annually, over half of which is exported. Hungarians each consume about 500g of the red stuff annually – it is richer in vitamin C than citrus fruits. Not only is paprika used when preparing dishes but it also appears on restaurant tables as a condiment beside the salt and pepper shakers.

There are many types of fresh or dried paprika available in Budapest markets and shops, including the rose, apple and royal varieties. But as a ground spice it is most commonly sold as *csípős* (hot), *erős* (strong) or *édes* (sweet) paprika.

Gulyás (thick beef soup)

call 'goulash'; the addition of sour cream, a reduction in paprika and the use of white meat such as chicken makes the dish *paprikás*.

Goose legs and livers and turkey breasts – though not much else of either bird – make an appearance on most menus. But lamb, mutton and rabbit are rarely seen.

Fish

Freshwater fish, such as *fogas* (great pikeperch) and the younger, smaller and more prized *süllő* (both indigenous to Lake Balaton), and *ponty* (carp) from the nation's rivers and streams, are plentiful (but often overcooked by Western standards).

Vegetable Dishes

Fresh salad (sometimes still called *vitamin saláta* here) is widely available, but more commonly eaten is *savanyúság* (sour things), which can be anything from mildly sour-sweet cucumbers and pickled peppers to very acidic sauerkraut. Such things go surprisingly very well with heavy meat dishes.

The traditional way of preparing *zöldség* (vegetables) is in *főzelék*, Hungary's unique 'twice-cooked' vegetable dishes. Here peas, green beans, lentils, vegetable marrow or cabbage are fried or boiled and then mixed into a *roux* with milk. This dish is sometimes topped with a few slices of meat and eaten at lunch.

In restaurants, vegetarians can usually order any number of types of *főzelék*, as well as *gombafejek rántva* (fried mushroom caps) and pasta and noodle dishes with cheese, such as *túróscsusza* and *sztrapacska*. Other meatless dishes include *gombaleves* (mushroom soup), *gyümölcsleves* (fruit soup) in season, *rántott sajt* (fried cheese) and *sajtoskenyér* (sliced bread with soft cheese). *Bableves* (bean soup) usually – but not always – contains meat. *Palacsinta* (pancakes) may be savoury and made with *sajt* (cheese) or *gomba* (mushrooms), or sweet and prepared with *dió* (nuts) or *mák* (poppy seeds).

Sweets & Desserts

Hungarians love sweets. Desserts eaten at the end of a meal include *Somlói galuska* (sponge cake with chocolate and whipped cream) and *Gundel palacsinta* (flambéed pancake with chocolate and nuts). More complicated pastries – such as *Dobos torta* (layered chocolate and cream cake with a caramelised brown-sugar top), and the wonderful *rétes* (strudel), filled with poppy seeds, cherry preserves or *túró* (curd or cottage cheese) – are usually consumed mid-afternoon in a *cukrászda* (cake shop or patisserie).

How to Eat & Drink
When to Eat

For the most part Hungarians are not big eaters of *reggeli* (breakfast), preferring a cup of tea or coffee with a plain bread roll at the kitchen table or on the way to work. *Ebéd* (lunch), eaten at around 1pm, is traditionally the main meal in the countryside and can consist of two or even three courses, but this is no longer the case for working people in the cities and towns. Still, many sit down to a meal with colleagues in a restaurant. *Vacsora* (dinner or supper)

DRINKING À LA MAGYAR

Hungarians love their wine and take it seriously. In summer spritzers (or wine coolers) of red or white wine mixed with mineral water are consumed in large quantities; knowing the hierarchy and the art of mixing a spritzer to taste is important and will definitely win you the badge of 'honorary local'. A *kisfröccs* (small spritzer) is 10cL (100mL) of wine and the same amount of mineral water; a *nagyfröccs* (big spritzer) doubles the quantity of wine. A *hosszúlépés* (long step) is 10cL of wine and 20cL (200mL) of water while a *házmester* (janitor) trebles the amount of wine. Any bar in town will serve you these but don't expect one at a *borozó*, a traditional 'wine bar' – usually a dive – serving rotgut.

Stronger libations include the fruit-flavoured brandy called *pálinka* and Unicum, a bitter aperitif nicknamed the 'Hungarian national accelerator'.

---

is less substantial when eaten at home: often just sliced meats, cheese and some pickled vegetables.

Where to Eat

An *étterem* is a restaurant with a large selection of dishes, sometimes including international options. A *vendéglő* (or *kisvendéglő*) is smaller and is supposed to serve inexpensive regional dishes or 'home cooking', but the name is now 'cute' enough for a lot of large places to use it.

An *étkezde* or *kifőzde* is something like a diner, smaller and cheaper than a *kisvendéglő* and often with seating at a counter. The term *csárda* originally signified a country inn with a rustic atmosphere, Gypsy music and hearty local dishes, but now any place that puts dried peppers and a couple of painted plates on the wall calls itself one. Most restaurants offer an excellent-value *menü* (set menu) of two or three courses at lunch, but make sure to book ahead at top-shelf places.

A *bisztró* is a much cheaper sit-down place that is often *önkiszolgáló* (self-service). A *büfé* is cheaper still and has a very limited menu. Food stalls, known as *Lacikonyha* (literally 'Larry's kitchen') or *pecsenyesütő* (roast ovens), can be found near markets, parks or train stations. At these you eat while standing at counters.

A *kávéház* (coffee house; cafe) is the best place to get something hot or nonalcoholic and cold. An *eszpresszó*, along with being a type of coffee, is essentially a coffee house too, but it usually also sells alcoholic drinks and light snacks.

Other useful words include *élelmiszer* (grocery store), *csemege* (delicatessen) and *piac* (market).

Menu Decoder

Restaurant menus are often translated into German, English and sometimes French with mixed degrees of success; a certain freshwater fish called 'crap' regularly appears on many. Two very important words on a menu to note include *készételek* ('ready-made', including dishes like *gulyásleves* and *pörkölt*) and *frissensültek* (dishes 'made to order').

Széchenyi Baths (p99), Budapest

Plan Your Trip

Thermal Baths & Spas

Budapest lies on the geological fault separating the Buda Hills from the Great Plain, and more than 30,000 cu metres of warm to scalding (21°C to 76°C) mineral water gush forth daily from some 123 thermal and more than 400 mineral springs. As a result, the city is a major spa centre.

Need to Know

Opening hours Opening times and whether everybody/men/women are welcome depend on the day of the week, but most baths are now completely mixed. Many open on weekend nights.

Costs Admission starts at 2400Ft; in theory this allows you to stay for 1½/two hours on weekends/weekdays, though this is seldom enforced nowadays.

Useful websites Budapest Spas and Hot Springs (www.spasbudapest.com) has excellent and up-to-date information.

What to Bring

➡ Fewer and fewer baths have male- and female-only days, so pack a bathing suit or be prepared to rent one (1350Ft to 2000Ft).

➡ Though some of the baths look a little rough around the edges, they are clean and the water is changed regularly. However, you might consider taking along a pair of plastic sandals or flip-flops/thongs.

➡ Sandals/flip-flops are also useful on slippery surfaces (especially at the Rudas Baths), and at some of the pools (eg Palatinus Strand), where the abundant concrete reaches scorching point in hot weather.

➡ Many places require the use of a bathing cap; bring your own or wear the disposable ones provided or sold for 700Ft.

➡ Bring a towel, otherwise most pools have them for rent (1000Ft).

History of a Spa Town

Remains of two sets of baths found at Aquincum (on the site of present-day Budapest) – both for the public and the garrisons – indicate that the Romans took advantage of Budapest's thermal waters almost two millennia ago. But it wasn't until the Turkish occupation of the 16th and 17th centuries that bathing became an integral part of everyday Budapest life. In the late 18th century, Habsburg Empress Maria

Theresa ordered that Budapest's mineral waters be analysed/recorded in a list at the Treasury's expense. By the 1930s Budapest had become a fashionable spa resort.

Healing Waters

Of course, not everyone goes to the baths for fun and relaxation. The warm, mineral-rich waters are also meant to relieve a number of specific complaints, ranging from arthritis and pains in the joints and muscles, to poor blood circulation and post-traumatic stress. And they are a miracle cure – we can vouch for this – for that most unpleasant affliction, the dreaded hangover.

What's Inside

The layout of most of Budapest's baths, both old and new, follows a similar pattern: a series of indoor thermal pools, where temperatures range from warm to hot, with steam rooms, saunas, ice-cold plunge pools and rooms for massage. Some have outdoor pools with fountains, wave machines and whirlpools.

Most baths offer a full range of serious medical treatments plus more indulgent services such as massage (5500/7500Ft for 20/30 minutes) and pedicure (4500Ft). Specify what you want when buying your ticket.

Depending on the time and day, a few baths can be for men or women only. There are usually mixed days and nowadays most baths – including the Széchenyi (p99), Gellért (p99) and Király Baths (p99) – are always for men and women together. On single-sex days or in same-sex sections, men are usually handed drawstring loincloths and women apron-like garments to wear, though the use of bathing suits is on the increase even on single-sex days.

Choosing a Bathing Experience

Which bath you decide to visit is a matter of choice, but certainly consider one of our four favourites:

Rudas Baths (p99) These renovated baths are the most Turkish of all in Budapest, built in 1566, with an octagonal pool, domed cupola with coloured glass and eight massive pillars. They're

Thermal Baths & Spas

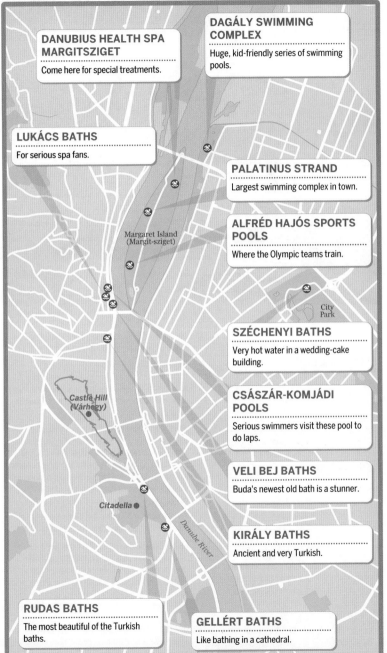

DANUBIUS HEALTH SPA MARGITSZIGET
Come here for special treatments.

DAGÁLY SWIMMING COMPLEX
Huge, kid-friendly series of swimming pools.

LUKÁCS BATHS
For serious spa fans.

PALATINUS STRAND
Largest swimming complex in town.

ALFRÉD HAJÓS SPORTS POOLS
Where the Olympic teams train.

Margaret Island
(Margit-sziget)

City Park

SZÉCHENYI BATHS
Very hot water in a wedding-cake building.

Castle Hill
(Várhegy)

CSÁSZÁR-KOMJÁDI POOLS
Serious swimmers visit these pool to do laps.

VELI BEJ BATHS
Buda's newest old bath is a stunner.

Citadella ●

Danube River

KIRÁLY BATHS
Ancient and very Turkish.

RUDAS BATHS
The most beautiful of the Turkish baths.

GELLÉRT BATHS
Like bathing in a cathedral.

Gellért Baths (p99), Budapest

THERMAL LIFE BEYOND BUDAPEST

Budapest is not the only place in Hungary where you can take the waters; in fact there are more than 300 thermal hot springs in public use across the country. Some, like the Turkish Bath (p247) in Eger and the Anna Baths (p235) in Szeged, have historical pedigrees, while others – the Aquaticum Thermal Baths (p218) in Debrecen and the Kecskemét Baths (p228) – are much more modern affairs. Probably the most unusual spa is the thermal lake (p203) at Hévíz.

The advent of massive water parks for kids with giant wellness centres attached for adults has broadened the fan base of spas in recent years.

The Hungarian National Tourist Office puts out a booklet called *Hungary: A Garden of Well-Being* and has listings online (http://gotohungary.com/spas-of-hungary).

mostly men-only during the week but turn into a real zoo on mixed weekend nights.

Gellért Baths (p99) Soaking in these art nouveau baths, now open to both men and women at all times, has been likened to taking a bath in a cathedral. The indoor swimming pools are the most beautiful in the city.

Széchenyi Baths (p99) The gigantic 'wedding-cake' building in City Park houses the Széchenyi Baths, which are unusual for three reasons: their immensity (a dozen thermal baths and three outdoor swimming pools); the bright, clean atmosphere; and the high temperature of the water (up to 40°C).

Veli Bej Baths (p99) This venerable (1575) Turkish bath in Buda has got a new lease of life after having been forgotten for centuries.

Other baths also have their special features. The waters of the Lukács Baths (p99) are meant to cure just about everything from spinal deformation and vertebral dislocation to calcium deficiency. The four small Turkish pools at Király Baths (p99), while begging for renovation, are the real McCoy and date to 1570. The facilities at the Danubius Health Spa Margitsziget (p99) on Margaret Island are soulless but modern and the choice of special treatments is enviable.

Regions at a Glance

Budgapest

Nightlife
Spas
Jewish Heritage

On the Town

Budapest's nightlife simply has no rival among other European cities. Along with bars, pubs, dance halls and classic concert venues, Budapest has unique *romkoc-smák* (ruin pubs) and *kertek* (gardens) that pop up all over town in the warmer months.

Taking the Waters

The 'city of healing waters' has enough thermal baths to satisfy the most wanton of appetites for wet fun. Some date back to the Turkish occupation, others are likened to swimming in a cathedral. If you want to splash in an outdoor whirlpool, there's plenty of that too.

Under the Star

Besides being home to Europe's largest and most splendid synagogue, Budapest has seen a resurgence of Jewish culture, music and cuisine. On the sombre end of the spectrum, the Jewish ordeal of WWII is well documented in the Holocaust Memorial Center.

p42

The Danube Bend & Western Transdanubia

Wine
Churches
The Danube

The Red & White

Western Transdanubia's climate is ideal for making wine and this age-old art is still widely practised here, particularly around Sopron, where you can sample fine reds and equally good whites.

Prayer Time

If ecclesiastical architecture is your thing, head north. As the seat of Roman Catholicism in Hungary, Esztergom boasts its largest church, and Szentendre is filled with Serbian Orthodox houses of worship.

River Cruising

The Bend is where you get to look the Danube right in the face. Depending on the time of year you can reach Szentendre, Visegrád and even Esztergom by ferry and/or hydrofoil from Budapest.

p163

Lake Balaton & Southern Transdanubia

Architecture
Activities
Wine

From Folk to Baroque

A diverse wealth of architecture styles resides here, from Tihany's baroque Benedictine abbey and Hungary's most celebrated mosque church in Pécs to delightful rural villages with open-air museums of folk architecture.

In Hot Water

The great outdoors beckon here: play and unwind in the medicinal thermal lake at Hévíz, paddleboard or windsurf on Hungary's 600-sq-km 'sea' or opt to hike in the wilds of the Tihany peninsula.

Vine Results

The Balaton-skimming Badacsony region produces the exquisite *olaszrizling*, one of the country's memorable dry white wines, while further south you'll find the tannin-rich rustic reds of Villány and ample cellars offering tastes of rich, pack-a-punch varieties such as *cabernet franc* and *merlot*.

p187

The Great Plain

Activities
Architecture
Museums

Ride 'em Cowboy

The Hortobágy is where to watch the most ambitious riding show on earth, with cowboys riding five-in-hand. And if you can't beat 'em, join 'em and saddle up yourself.

Sinuous Curves

Get a look up close at Hungary's most extravagant and colourful architecture (art nouveau/Secessionism) in Szeged and Kecskemét, both of which have superb examples of these related styles from the late 19th and early 20th centuries.

What's on Show

This region is overly endowed with great museums, exhibiting everything from fine art to peasant handicrafts. Some have been around for years (Szeged's Ferenc Móra Museum) while others are new (Debrecen's Centre of Modern & Contemporary Art) or have reopened after renovation (Kecskemet's Borzsó Collection).

p215

Northern Hungary

Folk Art
Wine
Castles

Northeastern Folkloric Heritage

The Bereg region of the northeast is Hungary's folkloric 'corner'. Come here to see traditional architecture, particularly the tiny wooden churches decorated with fabulous religious murals, and some wonderful embroidery and other needlework.

Overflowing Glass

This region can claim honey-sweet Tokaj wine. Need we say more? Well, we will. There's also Eger's famed red Bull's Blood and the new blended white wine dubbed Egri Csillag (Star of Eger).

Capture the Castle

Many of Hungary's most picturesque and historic castles and fortresses can be found in the hilly region to the north, including those at Eger and Hollókő.

p240

On the
Road

**Northern
Hungary**
p240

**The Danube Bend &
Western Transdanubia**
p163

★ **Budapest**
p42

The Great Plain
p215

**Lake Balaton
& Southern
Transdanubia**
p187

Budapest

🔊 1 / POP 1.7 MILLION

Best Places to Eat

➡ Borkonyha (p128)

➡ Baraka (p123)

➡ Mandragóra (p116)

➡ Múzeum (p136)

➡ Klassz (p133)

➡ Rosenstein (p135)

Best Places to Sleep

➡ Four Seasons Gresham Palace Hotel (p110)

➡ Pest-Buda Bistro & Hotel (p103)

➡ Gerlóczy (p108)

➡ Continental Hotel Budapest (p112)

➡ Brody House (p114)

➡ Bohem Art Hotel (p108)

Why Go?

There's no other city in Hungary like Budapest; everything of importance either starts or ends here. But it is the beauty of Budapest that makes it stand apart. Straddling a gentle curve in the Danube, it is flanked by the Buda Hills to the west and what is the start of the Great Plain to the east. Architecturally, it is a gem, with enough baroque, neoclassical, Eclectic (a style popular in Hungary in the Romantic period, drawing from sources both indigenous and foreign) and art nouveau (Secessionist) to satisfy anyone.

Besides the heady mix of museums and shopping streets to keep you busy, in the warmer months outdoor clubs called *kertek* (literally 'gardens') and 'ruin pubs' heave with party-makers and there are numerous thermal baths in which to pamper yourself.

Like any capital city, Budapest does have a gritty side. But come spring (or summer, or a brisk autumn day, or dusk), cross the Danube on foot and see why unique, passionate, vibrant Budapest remains so unmissable.

When to Go
Budapest

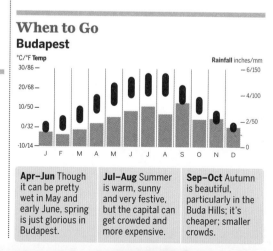

Apr–Jun Though it can be pretty wet in May and early June, spring is just glorious in Budapest.

Jul–Aug Summer is warm, sunny and very festive, but the capital can get crowded and more expensive.

Sep–Oct Autumn is beautiful, particularly in the Buda Hills; it's cheaper; smaller crowds.

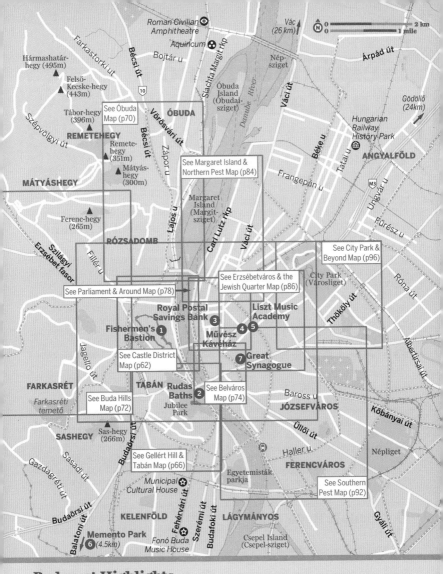

Budapest Highlights

1 Fishermen's Bastion
(p60) Taking in the views of the Danube and the rest of the city from atop Castle Hill.

2 Rudas Baths (p99)
Soaking the afternoon away in a thermal bath dating from the days of the Turkish occupation.

3 Royal Postal Savings Bank (p77) Ogling the sinuous curves and asymmetrical

forms of the city's incomparable art nouveau architecture.

4 Művész Kávéház (p146)
Enjoying a slice of something sweet at a traditional cafe like this one in Pest.

5 Liszt Music Academy
(p85) Taking in an evening of music at this august concert hall.

6 Memento Park (p52)
Sizing up the monumental socialist mistakes on display at this well-manicured rubbish heap of history.

7 Great Synagogue (p57)
Exploring Budapest's Jewish culture with a visit to one of Judaism's most important houses of worship.

Neighbourhoods at a Glance

❶ Castle District (p60)

The Castle District encompasses Castle Hill (Várhegy) – nerve centre of Budapest's history and packed with many of the capital's most important museums and other attractions – as well as ground-level Víziváros (Watertown). What the latter lacks in sights it makes up for in excellent restaurants, many of them around Széll Kálmán tér, a major transport hub and the centre of urban Buda. Major changes are afoot, as the government aims to consolidate Castle Hill as the seat of power, and the Hungarian National Gallery is due to move to City Park by 2019.

❷ Gellért Hill & Tabán (p65)

Standing atop Gellért Hill and proclaiming freedom throughout the city is the lovely Liberty Monument, Budapest's most visible statue. She looks down on the Tabán, a leafy neighbourhood dating to the 17th century. The main thoroughfare, Bartók Béla út, is fast laying claim to being the 'happening' part of south Buda – around here you'll find trendy cafes, a wine bar and even a vegan eatery.

❸ Óbuda & Buda Hills (p69)

Óbuda is the oldest part of Buda and retains a lost-in-the-past village feel. The narrow streets here hide excellent museums and some legendary eateries, while the remains of the Roman settlement of Aquincum lie further north. The Buda Hills offer great walking, the loftiest views of the city and forms of transport that will delight kids of all ages.

❹ Belváros (p73)

The 'Inner Town' is just that – the centre of Pest's universe, especially when it comes to tourism. This is where you'll find Váci utca, with its luxury shops, restaurants and bars, and Vörösmarty tér, home to the city's most celebrated *cukrászda* (cake shop) and one of its three Michelin-starred restaurants. The centre is Deák Ferenc tér, the main square where three metro lines converge.

❺ Parliament & Around (p77)

To the north of Belváros is Lipótváros (Leopold Town), with the landmark Parliament facing the Danube to the west and the equally iconic Basilica of St Stephen to the east. This is prime sightseeing territory; along with those two icons you'll also discover great museums and exhibits, some lovely squares and art nouveau buildings. We've also included part of Terézváros (Teresa Town), a busy after-dark district named in honour of Empress Maria Theresa, in this neighbourhood.

❻ Margaret Island & Northern Pest (p82)

Leafy Margaret Island is neither Buda nor Pest, but its shaded walkways, large swimming complexes, thermal spa and gardens offer refuge to the denizens of both sides of the river. Northern Pest in this section means Újlipótváros (New Leopold Town). Vaguely reminiscent of New York's Upper West Side, it has tree-lined streets, boutiques and cafes.

❼ Erzsébetváros & the Jewish Quarter (p83)

You'll probably be spending the bulk of your time in this neighbourhood, which takes in Erzsébetváros (Elizabeth Town) and most of Terézváros, including well- and high-heeled Andrássy út, the long, dramatic and very chic boulevard that slices through Terézváros. In this neighbourhood you'll find a large percentage of Budapest's accommodation, restaurants and the city's hottest nightspots.

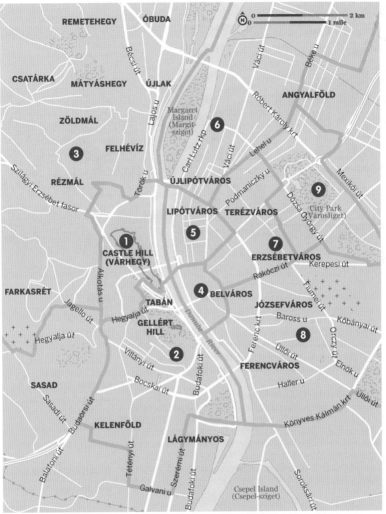

8 Southern Pest (p89)

The colourful districts of Józsefváros (Joseph Town) and Ferencváros (Francis, or Franz, Town) are traditionally working class and full of students. It's a lot of fun wandering the backstreets, peeping into courtyards and small, often traditional, shops. Both are ever-changing and developing areas, with new shops, bars and restaurants popping up constantly.

9 City Park & Beyond (p91)

City Park, at the northern end of epic Andrássy út, is the largest park in Budapest and its main entrance, Heroes' Sq, is ringed by important museums and monuments. The streets around the park boast impressive art nouveau and Secessionist architecture. Five new museums are due to be constructed in City Park by 2019.

TOP SIGHT
ROYAL PALACE

The enormous Royal Palace (Királyi Palota) has been razed and rebuilt six times over the past seven centuries. Béla IV established a residence here in the mid-13th century and subsequent kings added to it. The palace was levelled in the battle to rout the Turks in 1686. Today the palace contains two important museums and numerous statues and monuments.

Hungarian National Gallery

The **Hungarian National Gallery** (Nemzeti Galéria; Map p62; ☑1-201 9082; www.mng.hu; I Szent György tér 2, Bldgs A-D; adult/concession 1800/900Ft, audio guide 1000Ft; ⊘10am-6pm Tue-Sun) is an overwhelming collection spread across four floors that traces Hungarian art from the 11th century to the present day. The largest collections include medieval and Renaissance stonework, Gothic wooden sculptures and panel paintings, late Gothic winged altars and late Renaissance and baroque art. The museum also has an important collection of Hungarian paintings and sculpture from the 19th and 20th centuries.

The museum was formed in 1957 from a collection started in the mid-19th century that was previously exhibited at the Museum of Fine Arts and the Hungarian National Museum, and moved to this site in 1975. The permanent collection is, for the most part, exhibited in Buildings B, C and D, with A and the 3rd floor of all four buildings usually reserved for temporary exhibits. Much of the gallery was closed for renovations at the time of writing and by 2019, the collection is due to move to a purpose-built gallery in City Park.

DON'T MISS

➡ Late Gothic altarpieces

➡ Csontváry's works

➡ Rippl-Rónai's *Father and Uncle Piacsek Drinking Red Wine*

➡ Gothic statues and heads

➡ Renaissance door frame

PRACTICALITIES

➡ Királyi Palota

➡ Map p62

➡ I Szent György tér

➡ 🚌 16, 16A, 116

Gothic Works

The winged altarpieces in the so-called Great Throne Room on the 1st floor of Building D date from the 15th and early 16th centuries and form one of the greatest collections of late Gothic painting in the world. The almost modern *Visitation* (1506) by Master MS is both lyrical and intimate, but keep an eye open for the monumental Annunciation Altarpiece (1510–20) and the intense, almost Renaissance face of John the Baptist in a series of four paintings (1490) of scenes from his life.

Renaissance & Baroque Works

The finest 18th-century baroque painters in Hungary were actually Austrians, including Franz Anton Maulbertsch (1724–96; *Death of St Joseph*) and his contemporary Stephan Dorfmeister (1725–97; *Christ on the Cross*). Other greats of the period with more of a Magyar pedigree include Jakob Bogdány (1660–1724), whose *Two Macaws, a Cockatoo and a Jay, with Fruit* is a veritable Garden of Eden; and Ádám Mányoki (1673–1757), court painter to Ferenc Rákóczi II. You'll find their works in the galleries adjoining the Great Throne Room on the 1st floor.

Nineteenth-Century Works

Move into Building C for examples of the saccharine National Romantic School of heroic paintings, whose most prolific exponents were Bertalan Székely (1835–1910; *Women of Eger*) and Gyula Benczúr (1844–1920; *Recapture of Buda Castle, The Baptism of Vajk*). This style of painting gave way to the realism of Mihály Munkácsy (1844–1900), the 'painter of the Great Plain' *(Storm in the Puszta)* and of intense religious subjects *(Golgotha, Christ Before Pilate)*, whose works are in Building B. Here too are works by Pál Szinyei Merse (1845–1920), the country's foremost impressionist painter *(Picnic in May, The Skylark)*.

Twentieth-Century Works

The greatest painters working in the late 19th and early 20th centuries were Tivadar Kosztka Csontváry (p49), 1853–1919, who has been compared to Van Gogh, and József Rippl-Rónai (1861–1927), the key exponent of Secessionist painting in Hungary. Among the latter's greatest works (Building C, 2nd floor) are *Father and Uncle Piacsek Drinking Red Wine* and *Woman with Bird Cage*. Don't overlook the harrowing depictions of war and the dispossessed by WWI artist László Mednyánszky (1852–1919; *In Serbia, Soldiers Resting*) and the colourful, upbeat paintings of carnivals and celebrations by Vilmos Aba-Novák (1894–1941; *Procession, The Fair at Csíkszereda*). On the 3rd floor in Building C, you'll find the impressive new Shifts, the totally revamped permanent exhibition of Hungarian art since WWII.

ENTERING THE PALACE

There are three ways to enter. The first is via the Habsburg Steps and through an ornamental gateway dating from 1903. The second way in is via Corvinus Gate, with its big black raven symbolising King Matthias Corvinus. Either is good for the museums. Finally, you can take the escalator or steps from the Garden Bazaar below the south end of Castle Hill.

Facing the Royal Palace's large courtyard to the northwest is the Romantic-style **Matthias Fountain** (Mátyás kút; Map p62), portraying the young king Matthias Corvinus in hunting garb. To the right below him is Szép Ilona (Beautiful Helen). The middle one of the king's three dogs was blown up during the war; canine-loving Hungarians quickly had an exact copy made.

ILONA

Ilona, the girl featured prominently in the Matthias Fountain, is the protagonist of a Romantic ballad by poet Mihály Vörösmarty: she fell in love with a dashing 'hunter' – King Matthias – and, upon learning his true identity and feeling unworthy, died of a broken heart.

HUNGARIAN NATIONAL GALLERY

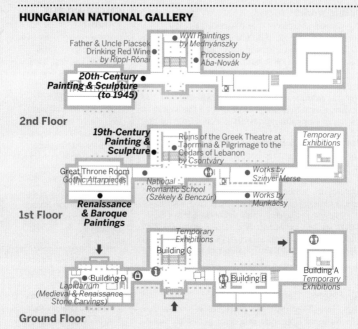

2nd Floor

Father & Uncle Piacsek
Drinking Red Wine
by Rippl-Rónai

WWI Paintings
by Mednyánszky

Procession by
Aba-Novák

**20th-Century
Painting & Sculpture
(to 1945)**

1st Floor

**19th-Century
Painting &
Sculpture**

Ruins of the Greek Theatre at
Taormina & Pilgrimage to the
Cedars of Lebanon
by Csontváry

Temporary
Exhibitions

Great Throne Room
Gothic Altarpieces

National
Romantic School
(Székely & Benczúr)

Works by
Szinyei Merse

Works by
Munkácsy

**Renaissance
& Baroque
Paintings**

Ground Floor

Temporary
Exhibitions

Building C

Building D

Lapidarium
(Medieval & Renaissance
Stone Carvings)

Building B

Building A
Temporary
Exhibitions

Castle Museum

The **Castle Museum** (Vármúzeum; Map p62; ☏1-487 8800; www.btm.hu; I Szent György tér 2, Bldg E; adult/concession 2000/1000Ft; ☺10am-6pm Tue-Sun Mar-Oct, to 4pm Nov-Feb), part of the multibranched Budapest History Museum, explores the city's 2000-year history over three floors. Restored palace rooms dating from the 15th century can be entered from the basement, where there are three vaulted halls. One of the halls features a magnificent Renaissance door frame in red marble bearing the seal of Queen Beatrix and tiles with a raven and a ring (the seal of her husband, King Matthias Corvinus), leading to the Gothic and Renaissance Halls, the Royal Cellar and the vaulted Tower Chapel (1320) dedicated to St Stephen.

On the ground floor, exhibits showcase Budapest during the Middle Ages, with dozens of important Gothic statues, heads and fragments of courtiers, squires and saints, discovered during excavations in 1974. There are also artefacts recovered from a well in 1999 that date back to the Middle Ages, notably a 14th-century tapestry of the Hungarian coat of arms with the fleur-de-lis of King Charles Robert's House of Anjou.

A wonderful exhibit on the 1st floor called '1000 Years of a Capital' traces the history of Budapest from the arrival of the Magyars and the Turkish occupation to modern times in 10 multimedia sections. The excellent audioguide is 1200Ft.

National Széchenyi Library

The **National Széchenyi Library** (Országos Széchenyi Könyvtár; Map p62; ☏1-224 3700; www.oszk.hu; I Szent György tér 4-6, Bldg F; ☺9am-8pm, stacks to 7pm Tue-Sat) contains codices and manuscripts, a large collection of foreign newspapers and a copy of everything published in Hungary or the Hungarian language. It was founded in 1802 by Count Ferenc Széchenyi, father of the heroic István, who endowed it with

TIVADAR KOSZTKA CSONTVÁRY

Many critics consider Tivadar Kosztka Csontváry – a symbolist artist whose tragic life is sometimes compared to van Gogh's – Hungary's greatest painter. Csontváry produced his major works in just a few years, starting in 1903 when he was 50. His first exhibition (Paris, 1907) met with praise, but critics panned his showing in Budapest the following year. He died penniless just after WWI. View works including *Ruins of the Greek Theatre at Taormina* (1905) and *Pilgrimage to the Cedars of Lebanon* (1907), on the 1st floor of the Hungarian National Gallery's Building C.

15,000 books and 2000 manuscripts. This library allows members (adult/student annual 6500/3500Ft, per six months 3500/2000Ft, daily per person 1200Ft) to do research, peruse the general stacks and read the large collection of foreign newspapers and magazines.

Statues Around the Royal Palace

To the east of the Habsburg Steps entrance to the palace is a bronze statue from 1905 of the **Turul** (Map p62), an eagle-like totemic bird that supposedly impregnated Emese, the grandmother of Árpád, the chief military commander who led the Magyar tribes into the Carpathian Basin in about AD 895. To the southeast, just in front of Building C, stands a statue of **Eugene of Savoy** (Map p62), the Habsburg prince who wiped out the last Turkish army in Hungary at the Battle of Zenta in 1697. Designed by József Róna 200 years later, it is considered to be the finest equestrian statue in Budapest. In the middle of the square is a statue by György Vastagh of a **Hortobágyi csikós** (Map p62), a Hungarian cowboy in full regalia breaking a mighty *bábolna* steed.

The Gothic statues found in the outer bailey of the Royal Palace in 1974 are a treasure trove for social historians. They total almost 80 and portray both commoners and aristocrats of both sexes. They are invaluable tools in the research of medieval dress, hairstyles and personal effects.

TOP SIGHT
PARLIAMENT

Hungary's largest building, Parliament stretches for some 268m along the Danube in Pest from Kossuth Lajor tér. The choice of location was not by chance. As a counterweight to the Royal Palace high on Buda Hill on the opposite side of the river, the placement was meant to signify that the nation's future lay with popular democracy and not royal prerogative.

Architecture

Designed by Imre Steindl in 1885 and completed after his death in 1902, this iconic structure is thought to have been inspired by London's rebuilt Palace of Westminster, which had opened in 1860. The building is a blend of many architectural styles (neo-Gothic, neo-Romanesque, neobaroque). Sculptures of the great and the good – kings, princes and historical figures – gaze out onto the river from the western facade, while the main door, the Lion Gate, gives on to revamped V Kossuth Lajos tér. The original structure was surfaced with a porous form of limestone that did not resist pollution very well. Due to its extensive surface and detailed stonework, the building has been under constant renovation, though new technology seems to have alleviated the problem. The entire building is dramatically lit up at night.

Interior

The interior contains just short of 700 sumptuously decorated rooms, but you'll only get to see a handful on a guided tour of the North Wing. From the **Parliament Visitors' Centre** (Map p78; ☎1-441 4415; http://hungarianparliament.com/visitor-centre-in-the-hungarian-parliament; ⊗8am-6pm Mon-Fri, to

DON'T MISS

➡ Crown of St Stephen
➡ Domed Hall
➡ Grand Staircase
➡ Congress Hall
➡ In Memoriam: 1956 Revolution memorial

PRACTICALITIES

➡ Országház
➡ Map p78
➡ ☎1-441 4904
➡ www.hungarian parliament.com
➡ V Kossuth Lajos tér 1-3
➡ adult/student EU citizen 2200/1200Ft, non-EU citizen 5400/2800Ft
➡ ⊗8am-6pm Mon-Fri, to 4pm Sat, to 2pm Sun
➡ Ⓜ M2 Kossuth Lajos tér, 🚋2

4pm Sat & Sun Apr-Oct, 8am-4pm daily Nov-Mar) on the north side you ascend the 132 steps of the highly decorated Golden Staircase and walk through a hallway with a frescoed ceiling and statues representing various trades, from mining to viticulture. Next is the centrepiece: the 16-sided, 66m-high Domed Hall where the Crown of St Stephen, the nation's most important national icon, is on display, along with the 15th-century ceremonial sword, an orb (1301) and the oldest object among the coronation regalia: the 10th-century Persian-made sceptre, with a large crystal head depicting a lion. The honour guard here stands duty 24 hours a day. The sweeping 96-step Grand Staircase, with frescoes by Károly Lotz and stained glass by Miksa Róth, descends to the Lion Gate, but you'll move on to one of the vaulted loges, where political discussions take place (check out the cool cigar rests no longer in use), and the 400-seat Congress Hall, where the House of Lords of the one-time bicameral assembly sat until 1944. It is almost identical to the National Assembly Hall, where parliamentary sessions are now held, in the South Wing.

Crown of St Stephen

Legend tells us that it was Asztrik, the first abbot of the Benedictine monastery at Pannonhalma in western Hungary, who presented a crown to Stephen as a gift from Pope Sylvester II around AD 1000, thus legitimising the new king's rule and assuring his loyalty to Rome over Constantinople. It's a nice story but has nothing to do with the object on display in the Domed Hall. The two-part crown here, with its characteristic bent cross, pendants hanging on either side and enamelled plaques of the Apostles, dates from the late 12th century. Its provenance notwithstanding, the Crown of St Stephen has become the very symbol of the Hungarian nation. The crown has disappeared several times over the centuries – purloined or otherwise – only to later reappear. It was damaged when placed in its carrying case in the 17th century, giving it a slightly skewered look. In 1945 Hungarian fascists fleeing ahead of the Soviet army took the crown to Austria. Eventually it fell into the hands of the US army, which transferred it to Fort Knox in Kentucky. In January 1978 the crown was returned to Hungary with great ceremony – and relief. Because legal judgments had always been handed down 'in the name of St Stephen's Crown' it was considered a living symbol and thus to have been 'kidnapped'!

➡ You can join a 45-minute tour in any of eight languages; the English-language ones are usually at 10am, noon and then hourly till 4pm (and maybe at 9.15am and 9.45am as well). Book ahead, online through Jegymester (www.jegymester.hu).

➡ There are no tours while the National Assembly is in session.

➡ The ceremonial guards in the Domed Hall are on duty 24 hours; the guards at the flagpole outside change every hour between 8am and 7pm (earlier in winter).

PARLIAMENT BY NUMBERS

➡ Rooms: 691 (including 200 offices and 20 workshops)

➡ Roof area: 1.8 hectares

➡ Gates: 27

➡ Courtyards: 10

➡ Staircases: 29

➡ Lifts: 13

➡ Light bulbs: 8730

➡ Clocks: 108

➡ Statues: 242 (90 outside, 152 inside)

➡ Decorative gold: 40kg

➡ Employees: 700

TOP SIGHT
MEMENTO PARK

The socialist Disneyland of Memento Park, 10km southwest of the city centre, has more than 40 statues, busts and plaques of Lenin, Marx, Engels, home-grown heroes such as Béla Kun, superhuman workers and others whose likenesses have ended up in dustbins or on rubbish heaps in other countries of the region.

The Monuments

Ogle the socialist realism and try to imagine that at least four of these monstrous relics were erected as recently as the late 1980s; a few of them, including the Béla Kun memorial of 'our hero' in a crowd by fence-sitting sculptor Imre Varga, were still in place as late as 1992.

Old Barrack Exhibition

An exhibition centre in an old barracks – Hungary was called 'the happiest barrack in the camp' under communism – has displays on the events of 1956 and the changes since 1989, as well as documentary film with rare footage of secret agents collecting information on 'subversives'. The Communist Hotline allows you to listen in on the likes of Lenin, Stalin and even Che Guevara.

Stalin's Boots

Excellent selfie ops include the reproduced remains of Stalin's boots (left after a crowd pulled the statue down from its plinth on XIV Dózsa György út during the 1956 Uprising) and an original two-stroke Trabant 601, the 'people's car' produced in East Germany.

The Shop

We normally don't recommend museum gift shops, but this one is a treasure trove of kitsch communist memorabilia: pins, CDs of revolutionary songs, books and posters.

DON'T MISS

➡ Monuments of superhuman socialist works

➡ Communist Hotline

➡ Photo ops sitting in a Trabant 601 car

PRACTICALITIES

➡ ☎ 1-424 7500

➡ www.mementopark.hu

➡ XXII Balatoni út & Szabadkai utca

➡ adult/student 1500/1000Ft

➡ ⊙ 10am-dusk

➡ 🚌 101, 150

TOP SIGHT
AQUINCUM

Aquincum, dating from the end of the 1st century AD and the most complete Roman civilian town in Hungary, had paved streets and sumptuous single-storey houses, complete with courtyards, fountains and mosaic floors, as well as sophisticated drainage and heating systems. It's not all immediately apparent as you explore the ruins in the open-air archaeological park, but the museum puts it in perspective.

Aquincum Museum

The museum, next to the entrance to the Roman town, contains an impressive collection of household objects: pottery, weaponry, grooming implements, a military discharge diploma... In the basement there are some hokey virtual games for kids, such as battling with a gladiator. Look out for the replica of a 3rd-century portable organ called a hydra, the mock-up of a Roman bath and a road map of the Roman Empire (*Tabula Peutingeriana*).

Painter's House & Mithraeum

Just opposite the museum is the wonderful Painter's House, a recreated, furnished Roman dwelling from the 3rd century AD. Behind it is the Mithraeum, a temple dedicated to the god Mithra, the chief deity of a religion that once rivalled Christianity.

Main Thoroughfare

Just north of the museum, the arrow-straight main thoroughfare leads you past ruins of the large public baths, the *macellum* (market) and the *basilica* (courthouse). Most of the large stone sculptures and sarcophagi are in the old museum building to the east.

DON'T MISS

➡ Aquincum's main thoroughfare

➡ Painter's House

➡ Hydra (portable organ)

➡ *Tabula Peutingeriana* (Roman road map)

PRACTICALITIES

➡ ☏ 1-250 1650

➡ www.aquincum.hu

➡ III Szentendrei út 133-135

➡ adult/concession museum & park 1600/800Ft, archaeological park only 1000/500Ft

➡ ◷ museum 10am-6pm Tue-Sun Apr-Oct, to 4pm Nov-Mar, park 9am-6pm Tue-Sun Apr-Oct

➡ ▣ 34, 106, ▣ HÉV to Aquincum

Roman Civilian Amphitheatre

Across III Szentendrei út to the northwest and close to the HÉV stop is the **Roman Civilian Amphitheatre** (Római polgári amfiteátrum; Zsófia utca & Szentendrei ut) FREE, about half the size of the amphitheatre reserved for the garrisons in Óbuda and seating 3000. Lions were kept in the small cubicles, while slain gladiators were carried through the 'Gate of Death' to the west.

TOP SIGHT
BASILICA OF ST STEPHEN

The Basilica of St Stephen is the most sacred Catholic church in all of Hungary, if for no other reason than that it contains the nation's most revered relic: the mummified right hand of the church's patron, King St Stephen. The church is also the Budapest seat of the shared Metropolitan Archdiocese of Esztergom-Budapest.

History

The neoclassical cathedral, the largest in Hungary, is in the form of a Greek cross and can accommodate 8000 worshippers. It was originally designed by József Hild, and though work began in 1851, the structure was not completed until 1905. Much of the interruption had to do with the fiasco in 1868 when the dome collapsed during a storm. The building then had to be demolished and rebuilt from the ground up by Hild's successor, Miklós Ybl.

The Dome

The facade of the basilica is anchored by two large bell towers, one of which contains a bell weighing 9.25 tonnes, a replacement for one looted by the Germans during WWII. Behind the towers is the 96m-high **dome** (Panoráma kilátó; Map p78; ☑1-269 1849; adult/child 500/400Ft; ⊙10am-4.30pm Oct-Jun, to 6.30pm Jul-Sep), with statues of the four Evangelists filling its niches. The top of the dome can be reached by a lift and 42 steps (or 302 steps if you want to walk all the way) – it offers one of the best views in the city.

DON'T MISS

➡ Holy Right Chapel
➡ Views from the dome
➡ Treasury
➡ Dome interior mosaics
➡ Organ concert

PRACTICALITIES

➡ Szent István Bazilika
➡ Map p78
➡ ☑1-311 0839, 06 30 703 6599
➡ www.basilica.hu
➡ V Szent István tér
➡ requested donation 200Ft
➡ ⊙ 9am-7pm Mon-Sat, 7.45am-7pm Sun
➡ Ⓜ M3 Arany János utca

The Interior

The basilica's interior is rather dark and gloomy, Károly Lotz's golden mosaics on the inside of the dome notwithstanding. Noteworthy items include Alajos Stróbl's statue of the king-saint on the main altar and Gyula Benczúr's painting of St Stephen dedicating Hungary to the Virgin Mary and Christ Child, to the right of the main altar.

Behind the altar and to the left is the basilica's major drawcard: the **Holy Right Chapel** (Szent Jobb kápolna; Map p78; ☺9am-5pm Mon-Sat, 1-5pm Sun Apr-Sep, 10am-4pm Mon-Sat, 1-4pm Sun Oct-Mar). It contains what is also known as the Holy Dexter, the mummified right hand of St Stephen and an object of great devotion here. It was restored to Hungary by Habsburg empress Maria Theresa in 1771 after it was discovered in a monastery in Bosnia. Like the Crown of St Stephen, it was snatched after WWII but was soon returned home.

As you enter the basilica there is a small lift to the right that will bring you to the 2nd-floor **treasury** (Szent István Bazilika kincstár; Map p78; www.bazilika.biz/kincstar/kincstar; adult/child 400/300Ft; ☺10am-5.30pm mid-Mar–Jun, to 6.30pm Jul-Sep, to 4.30pm Oct–mid-Mar) of ecclesiastical objects, including censers, chalices, ciboria and vestments. Don't miss the art deco double monstrance (1938). Otherwise, the treasury is a veritable shine to Cardinal Mindszenty, including his clothing, devotional objects and death mask.

Tours

English-language guided tours of the basilica (2000/1500Ft with/without dome visit) usually depart at 9.30am, 11am, 2pm and 3.30pm on weekdays and at 9.30am and 11am on Saturday, but phone or check the website to confirm.

CONCERTS

Organ concerts (from adult/concession 4500/4200Ft) are held here at 8pm, usually on Tuesday, Thursday and Friday (more often in summer).

HOLY RIGHT

If you want a good look at the Holy Right (St Stephen's mummified right hand) put 200Ft in the slot to illuminate the hand for closer inspection. (And view it from the right-hand side to see the knuckles.)

BUDAPEST BASILICA OF ST STEPHEN

TOP SIGHT
VÁCI UTCA & VÖRÖSMARTY TÉR

Váci utca is the capital's premier shopping street, a pedestrian strip crammed largely with chain stores, touristy restaurants and a smattering of shops and notable buildings worth seeking out. It was the total length of Pest in the Middle Ages.

Exploring Váci Utca

A good place to start is at the Párisi Udvar, built in 1909. It was under renovation at the time of writing, but you should be able to get a glimpse of the interior and its ornately decorated ceiling once it opens as a luxury hotel in 2017. Váci utca is immediately to the west.

Head first to **Philanthia** (Map p74; V Váci utca 9; ☉10am-7pm Mon-Thu, to 8pm Fri & Sat, 11am-6pm Sun; Ⓜ M1/2/3 Deák Ferenc tér, 🚊2), which has an original (and very rare) art nouveau interior from 1906. **Thonet House** (Map p74; V Váci utca 11/a; Ⓜ M1/2/3 Deák Ferenc tér, 🚊2) is a masterpiece built by Ödön Lechner in 1890, and to the west, at Régi Posta utca 13, there's a relief of an old postal coach by the ceramicist Margit Kovács of Szentendre.

Just off the top of Váci utca in Kristóf tér is the little **Fishergirl Fountain** (Map p74; V Kristóf tér), dating from the 19th century and complete with a ship's wheel that actually turns. A short distance to the northwest is the sumptuous **Bank Palace** (Bank Palota; Map p74; V Deák Ferenc utca 3-5; Ⓜ M1 Vörösmarty tér), built in 1915 and once the home of the Budapest Stock Exchange. It has since been converted into a shopping gallery called **Váci 1** (Map p74; ☎1-424 4398; www.vaci1.hu; ☉10am-7pm; Ⓜ M1 Vörösmarty tér).

Váci utca empties into **Vörösmarty tér** (Map p74; Ⓜ M1 Vörösmarty tér), a large square of smart shops, galleries, cafes and an artist or two, who will draw your portrait or caricature. In the centre is a **statue of Mihály Vörösmarty** (Map p74), the 19th-century poet after whom the square is named. At the northern end is Gerbeaud (p139), Budapest's fanciest and most famous cafe and cake shop. A pleasant way to return to Ferenciek tere is along the Duna korzó (p77), the riverside 'Danube Promenade' between Chain and Elizabeth Bridges.

DON'T MISS

➡ Párisi Udvar

➡ Philanthia

➡ Gerbeaud

➡ Bank Palace

PRACTICALITIES

➡ Map p74

➡ 🚊 7, Ⓜ M1 Vörösmarty tér, Ferenciek tere, 🚊 2

TOP SIGHT
GREAT SYNAGOGUE

Budapest's stunning Great Synagogue, with its crenellated red-and-yellow glazed-brick facade and two enormous Moorish-style towers, is the largest Jewish house of worship in the world outside New York City, seating 3000 worshippers. Built in 1859, the copper-domed Conservative (not Orthodox) synagogue contains both Romantic-style and Moorish architectural elements. It is also called the Dohány utca Synagogue (Dohány utcai Zsinagóga).

Rose Window
Because some elements of the synagogue recall Christian churches – including the central rose window with an inscription from the second book of Moses – the synagogue is sometimes referred to as the 'Jewish cathedral'. It was renovated in the 1990s largely due to private donations, including US$5 million from the cosmetic magnate Estée Lauder, who was born in New York to Hungarian Jewish immigrants.

Interior Fittings
Don't miss the decorative carvings on the Ark of the Covenant by National Romantic architect Frigyes Feszl, who also did the wall and ceiling frescoes of multicoloured and gold geometric shapes. Both Franz Liszt and Camille Saint-Saëns played on the rebuilt 5000-pipe organ dating back to 1902. Concerts are held here in summer.

DON'T MISS
➡ Ark of the Covenant
➡ Rose window
➡ Hungarian Jewish Museum & Archives
➡ Holocaust Tree of Life Memorial

PRACTICALITIES
➡ Nagy Zsinagóga
➡ Map p86
➡ ☎1-462-0477
➡ www.dohany-zsinagoga.hu
➡ VII Dohány utca 2
➡ adult/concession incl museum 3000/2000Ft
➡ ⊙10am-6pm Sun-Thu, to 4pm Fri Mar-Oct, 10am-4pm Sun-Thu, to 2pm Fri Nov-Feb
➡ Ⓜ M2 Astoria, 🚋 47, 49

Hungarian Jewish Museum & Archives
The **Hungarian Jewish Museum & Archives** (Magyar Zsidó Múzeum és Levéltár; Map p86; ☎1-343 6756; www.milev.hu; VII Dohány utca 2; incl in synagogue entry adult/concession 3000/2000Ft; ⊙10am-6pm Sun-Thu, to 4pm Fri Mar-Oct, 10am-4pm Sun-Thu, to 2pm Fri Nov-Feb; Ⓜ M2 Astoria, 🚋 47, 49), upstairs in an annexe of the synagogue, contains objects related to religious and everyday life. Interesting items include 3rd-century Jewish headstones from Roman Pannonia discovered in 1792 in Nagykanizsa in southwestern Hungary, a vast amount of liturgical items in silver, and manuscripts, including a handwritten book of the local Burial Society from the late 18th century.

Holocaust Tree of Life Memorial
In Raoul Wallenberg Memorial Park on the synagogue's north side and opposite VII Wesselényi utca 6, the **Holocaust Tree of Life Memorial** (Map p86; Raoul Wallenberg Memorial Park, opp VII Wesselényi utca 6; Ⓜ M2 Astoria, 🚋 47, 49), designed by Imre Varga in 1991, stands over the mass graves of those murdered by the Nazis in 1944–45. On the leaves of the metal 'tree of life' are the family names of some of the hundreds of thousands of victims. Nearby is a new stained-glass memorial to Nicholas Winton (1909–2015), the 'British Schindler' who rescued 700 Jewish children just before WWII.

 TOP SIGHT
HUNGARIAN NATIONAL MUSEUM

The Hungarian National Museum houses the nation's most important collection of historical relics. It traces the history of the Carpathian Basin from the Stone Age and that of the Magyar people and Hungary from the 9th-century conquest to the end of communism. The museum was founded in 1802 when Count Ferenc Széchényi donated his personal collection to the state.

Front Steps

Less than a year after it moved into its new premises, an impressive neoclassical building designed by Mihály Pollack in 1847, the museum was the scene of a momentous event. On 15 March a crowd gathered to hear the poet Sándor Petőfi recite his 'Nemzeti Dal' (National Song) from the front steps, sparking the 1848–49 revolution.

Archaeological Exhibition

Exhibits on the 1st floor trace the history of the Carpathian Basin and its peoples from earliest times to the end of the Avar period in the early 9th century. Don't miss the Golden Stag, a hand-forged Iron Age figure from the 6th century BC once part of a Scythian prince's shield. On the lower level just beyond the entrance is a stunning 2nd-century Roman mosaic from Balácapuszta, near Veszprém.

Coronation Mantle

In its own room to the left on the 1st floor, you'll find King Stephen's beautiful crimson silk coronation mantle, stitched by nuns in 1031. It was refashioned in the 13th century and the much-faded cloth features an intricate embroidery of fine gold thread and pearls.

DON'T MISS

➡ Coronation mantle

➡ Celtic gold and silver jewellery

➡ Socialist memorabilia

➡ 2nd-century Roman mosaic

➡ Broadwood piano used by Beethoven and Liszt

PRACTICALITIES

➡ Magyar Nemzeti Múzeum

➡ Map p92

➡ ☑1-338 2122

➡ www.hnm.hu

➡ VIII Múzeum körút 14-16

➡ adult/concession 1600/800Ft

➡ ⏰10am-6pm Tue-Sun

➡ 🚌 47, 49, Ⓜ M3/4 Kálvin tér

TOP SIGHT
MUSEUM OF FINE ARTS

The Museum of Fine Arts, in a neoclassical building on the northern side of Heroes' Sq, houses the city's most outstanding collection of foreign works of art dating from antiquity to the 21st century. The nucleus of the collection dates back to 1870, when the state purchased the private collection of Count Miklós Esterházy. The museum has been closed for renovation and is due to reopen in early 2018.

The Old Masters

The Old Masters collection is the most complete, with 3000 works from the Dutch and Flemish, Spanish, Italian, German, French and British schools between the 13th and 18th centuries, including seven paintings by El Greco. Among the most famous of all the works on display is the Esterházy Madonna, painted by Raphael, the supreme High Renaissance painter, around 1508. It's unfinished but still manages to achieve the beauty and harmony for which the paragon of classicism is acclaimed. It was among the 700-odd works that formed the original Esterházy collection.

Egyptian & Classical Exhibits

Especially fine – and a real hit with children because of a programme that allows them to handle original artefacts and works of art from the period – is the collection of Egyptian artefacts, including decorated sarcophagi and mummy portraits. Up a level on the ground floor, the classical section contains Greek, Etruscan and Roman works. The collection of Greek vases and urns ranks among the finest and most complete in Europe.

Other Exhibits

Other sections include 19th-century paintings, watercolours, graphics and sculpture, including some important impressionist works. Pieces from the second half of the 19th century are due to move to the Hungarian National Gallery-Ludwig Museum in the middle of City Park once it is constructed. The museum's collection of prints and drawings is among the largest in Europe, with upwards of 10,000 prints and 10 times as many drawings. At the very top of the building, the European sculpture room holds some wonderful pieces, including the fascinating work of Franz Xaver Messerschmidt.

DON'T MISS

➡ Mummy sarcophagus of Dihoriaut

➡ *Esterházy Madonna* by Raphael

➡ *The Penance of St Mary Magdalene* by El Greco

➡ *Water Carrier* by Goya

➡ Messerschmidt sculptures

PRACTICALITIES

➡ Szépmüvészeti Múzeum

➡ Map p96

➡ ☎ 1-469 7100

➡ www.mfab.hu

➡ XIV Dózsa György út 41

➡ Ⓜ M1 Hősök tere

History

Strictly speaking, the story of Budapest began only in 1873, when hilly Buda and historic Óbuda, on the western bank of the Danube, merged with industrial Pest on the flat eastern side, to form what was at first called Pest-Buda.

Until the Huns forced them to flee in the mid-5th century, the Romans had an important colony here named Aquincum. The Magyars arrived five centuries later, but Buda and Pest remained no more than villages until the 12th century, when foreign merchants and tradespeople settled here. King Béla IV built a fortress in Buda in the late 13th century, but it was King Charles Robert (Károly Róbert) who moved the court from Visegrád to Buda 50 years later.

The Mongols burned Buda and Pest to the ground in 1241, beginning a pattern of destruction and rebuilding that would last until the mid-20th century. Under the Turks, both towns lost most of their populations, and when they were defeated by the Habsburgs in the late 17th century, Buda Castle was in ruins. The 1848–49 revolution, WWII and the 1956 Uprising all took their toll, but in the late 20th century Budapest emerged from under the communist yoke as a vibrant, cosmopolitan capital.

☉ Sights

Budapest's most important museums are found on Castle Hill, in City Park, along Andrássy út in Erzsébetváros and in Southern Pest. The area surrounding the parliament is home to the splendid Parliament building, as well as Budapest's most iconic church; both Parliament and Belváros feature some of the city's best art nouveau architecture. Margaret Island and City Park are the city's most appealing green spaces, while the Buda Hills is a veritable playground for hikers, cavers and bikers. Óbuda is home to extensive Roman ruins and quirky museums, and Gellért Hill gives you some of the best views of the city.

☉ Castle District

No other place in Budapest can rival Castle Hill for the sheer number of heavyweight attractions crammed into such a compact space. These include Budapest's best history museum, best gallery of national art and one of the city's top churches, with a supporting cast of lesser museums. Víziváros also has a couple of museums well worth seeking out. By 2019, the Hungarian National Gallery is due to move into its new home in City Park.

★ Royal Palace   PALACE
See p46.

★ Castle Hill   HILL
(Várhegy; Map p62; ☐ 16, 16A, 116, Ⓜ M2 Batthyány tér, Széll Kálmán tér;, ☐ 19, 41;) Castle Hill is a kilometre-long limestone plateau towering 170m above the Danube. It contains some of Budapest's most important medieval monuments and museums, and is a Unesco World Heritage Site. Below it is a 28km-long network of caves formed by thermal springs.

The walled area consists of two distinct parts: the Old Town, where commoners once lived, and the Royal Palace, the original site of the castle built by Béla IV in the 13th century and reserved for the nobility.

The easiest way to reach Castle Hill from Pest is to take bus 16 from Deák Ferenc tér to Dísz tér, more or less the central point between the Old Town and the Royal Palace. Much more fun, though, is to stroll across Széchenyi Chain Bridge and board the Sikló, a funicular railway built in 1870 that ascends steeply from Clark Ádám tér to Szent György tér near the Royal Palace.

Alternatively, you can walk up the Király lépcső (Royal Steps) leading northwest off Clark Ádám tér.

Another option is to take metro M2 to Széll Kálmán tér, go up the stairs in the southeastern part of the square and walk up Várfok utca to Vienna Gate. This medieval entrance to the Old Town was rebuilt in 1936 to mark the 250th anniversary of the castle being taken back from the Turks. Bus 16A follows the same route from the start of Várfok utca.

★ Fishermen's Bastion   MONUMENT
(Halászbástya; Map p62; I Szentháromság tér; adult/concession 800/400Ft; ☺9am-8pm Mar–mid-Oct; ☐ 16, 16A, 116) The bastion, a neo-Gothic masquerade that looks medieval and offers some of the best views in Budapest, was built as a viewing platform in 1905 by Frigyes Schulek, the architect behind Matthias Church. Its name was taken from the medieval guild of fishermen responsible for defending this stretch of the castle wall. The seven gleaming white turrets represent the Magyar tribes that entered the Carpathian Basin in the late 9th century.

⭐**Matthias Church** CHURCH
(Mátyás templom; Map p62; ☑1-355 5657; www.
matyas-templom.hu; I Szentháromság tér 2; adult/
concession 1500/1000Ft; ⊙9am-5pm Mon-Sat,
1-5pm Sun; ☐16, 16A, 116) Parts of Matthias
Church date back 500 years, notably the carvings above the southern entrance. But basi-
cally Matthias Church (so named because
King Matthias Corvinus married Beatrix here
in 1474) is a neo-Gothic confection designed
by the architect Frigyes Schulek in 1896.

Music History Museum MUSEUM
(Zenetörténeti Múzeum; Map p62; ☑1-214 6770;
www.zti.hu/museum; I Táncsics Mihály utca 7;
adult/6-26yr 600/300Ft; ⊙10am-4pm Tue-Sun;
☐16, 16A, 116) Housed in an 18th-century
palace with a lovely courtyard, this wonderful little museum traces the development
of music in Hungary from the 18th century
to the present day in a half-dozen exhibition rooms. There are rooms devoted to the
work of Béla Bartók, Franz Liszt and Joseph
Haydn, with lots of instruments and original
scores and manuscripts.

Buda Castle Labyrinth CAVE
(Budavári Labirintus; Map p62; ☑1-212 0207;
www.labirintusbudapest.hu; I Úri utca 9 & Lovas út 4/a; adult/under 12yr/senior & student
2000/600/1500Ft; ⊙10am-7pm; ☐16, 16A, 116)
This 1200m-long cave system, located some
16m under the Castle District, contains a
motley collection of displays in its joined-
up labyrinths encompassing 10 halls. Expect
the history of Dracula, dry-ice mist and displays of figures from different operas, with
music carrying eerily underground. It's all
good fun and a relief from the heat on a
hot summer's day – it's always 20°C down
here. If you dare, step into the tunnel where
you're confronted with complete darkness.

Hospital in the Rock MUSEUM
(Sziklakórház; Map p62; ☑06 70 701 0101; www.
sziklakorhaz.eu; I Lovas út 4/c; adult/concession
4000/2000Ft; ⊙10am-8pm; ☐16, 16A, 116) Part
of the Castle Hill caves network, this subterranean hospital was used extensively during
the WWII siege of Budapest and during the
1956 Uprising. It contains original medical
equipment as well as some 200 wax figures
and is visited on a guided one-hour tour,
which includes a walk through a Cold War-
era nuclear bunker and an eight-minute in-
troductory video.

Museum of Military History MUSEUM
(Hadtörténeti Múzeum; Map p62; ☑1-325 1600;
www.militaria.hu; I Tóth Árpád sétány 40; adult/6-
26yr 1500/750Ft; ⊙10am-6pm Tue-Sun; ☐16,
16A, 116) Loaded with weaponry dating from
before the Turkish conquest, this museum
also does a good job with uniforms, medals,
flags and battle-themed fine art, though the
text explanations are a bit dense. Exhibits
focus particularly on the 1848–49 War of Independence and the Hungarian Royal Army
under the command of Admiral Miklós Horthy (1918–43). Outside in the back courtyard
is a mock-up of the electrified fence that
once separated Hungary from Austria.

Medieval Jewish Prayer House JEWISH SITE
(Középkori Zsidó Imaház; Map p62; www.btm.hu;
I Táncsics Mihály utca 26; adult/child 800/400Ft;
⊙10am-6pm Tue-Sun; ☐16, 16A, 116) With
sections dating from the late 14th century,
this tiny, ancient house of worship contains
documents and items linked to the Jewish
community of Buda, as well as Gothic stone
carvings and tombstones. Closed for renovation at the time of writing.

Golden Eagle Pharmacy MUSEUM
(Arany Sas Patika; Map p62; ☑1-375 9772; www.
semmelweis.museum.hu; I Tárnok utca 18; adult/con-
cession 500/250Ft; ⊙10.30am-6pm Tue-Sun; ☐16,
16A, 116) Just north of Dísz tér, on the site of
Budapest's first pharmacy (1681), this small,
entertaining museum contains a mock-up of
an alchemist's laboratory, with dried bats and
stuffed crocodiles suspended from the ceiling,
a small 'spice rack' used by 17th-century travellers for their daily fixes of curative herbs,
mysterious jars, curiously shaped glassware
and a blackened mummy head.

Széchenyi Chain Bridge BRIDGE
(Széchenyi lánchíd; Map p62; ☐16, ☐19, 41) One
of the most striking bridges in Budapest,
Széchenyi Chain Bridge is particularly beautiful when lit up at night.

Clark Ádám tér SQUARE
(Adam Clark Sq; Map p62; ☐19, 41) Víziváros begins at this square named after the 19th-cen-
tury Scottish engineer who supervised the
building of the Széchenyi Chain Bridge
and who designed the all-important tunnel
(alagút) under Castle Hill, which took just
eight months to carve out of the limestone
in 1853.

BUDAPEST SIGHTS

BUDAPEST

Castle District

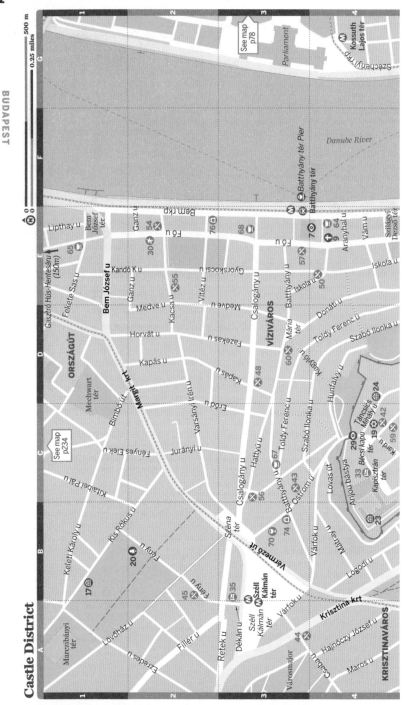

500 m
0.25 miles

See map p78

Parliament

Kossuth
Lajos tér

Széchenyi rkp

Danube River

Battyány tér Pier

Battyány tér

Bem rkp

Lipthay u

Bem József tér

Ganz u

54

Fő u

76

68

30

Szilágyi Dezső tér

Vám u

Aranyhal u

9 64

7

57

Gasztró Hús-Hentesáru (150m)

65

Bem József u

Fekete Sas u

Kandó K u

Ganz u

Medve u

Kacsa u

55

Gyorskocsi u

Vitéz u

Medve u

Csalogány u

Iskola u

Fő u

Mária Battyány u

50

Iskola u

ORSZÁGÚT

Horvát u

Kapás u

Fazekas u

Kapás u

48

VÍZIVÁROS

Mária tér

60

Donáti u

Toldy Ferenc u

Szabó Ilonka u

Mechwart tér

Bimbó út

Margit krt

Erdő u

Varsányi Irén u

Erdő u

Csalogány u

Hattyú u

67

Toldy Ferenc u

Szabó Ilonka u

Kapu u

Hunfalvy u

Tóth Árpád

See map p234

Fényes Elek u

Jurányi u

Batthyány u

56

Ostrom u

43

Lovas út

Anjou bástya

29

Bécsi kapu tér

33

Kapisztrán tér

Táncsics Mihály u

19 42

59

Kard u

24

23

Kis Rókus u

Szena tér

70

74

Várfok u

Mátray u

Logodi u

Keleti Károly u

Fény u

20

17

35

45

Fény u

Széll Kálmán tér

Széll Kálmán tér

Vérmező út

Várfok u

Krisztina krt

Marczibányi tér

Lövőház u

Ercedes u

Fillér u

Retek u

Dékán u

44

Hajnóczy József u

Csaba u

Maros u

Városmajor u

KRISZTINAVÁROS

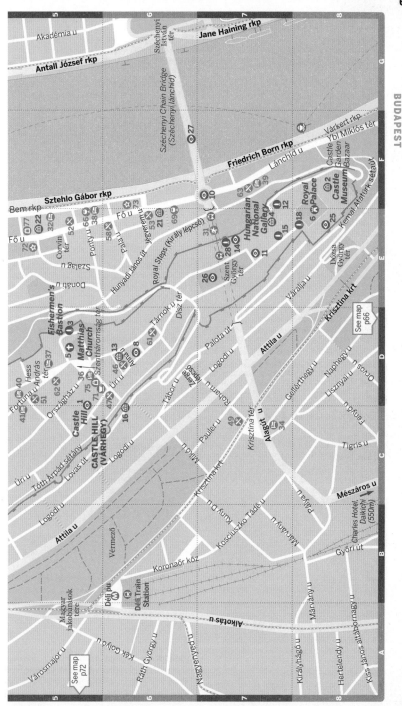

Akadémia u

Jane Haining rkp

Antall József rkp

Széchenyi István tér

Széchenyi Chain Bridge (Széchenyi lánchíd)

27

Friedrich Born rkp

Lánchíd u

Várkert rkp

Ybl Miklós tér

Sztehlo Gábor rkp

Castle Garden Bazaar

Bem rkp

Fő u

77
22
32

52

66
38

73

Fő u

63
39

Hungarian National Gallery

Castle Museum

2

Kemal Atatürk sétaút

72

Corvin tér

58

Ponty u

Palota u

53
21

69

10

31

Royal Palace

4

12

Royal

6
25

15

18

Szalag u

Hunyadi János út

Jegyerem u

Jegyps

Royal Steps (Király lépcső)

14

28

11

Dózsa György tér

Donáti u

Szent György tér

26

Váralja u

Fishermen's Bastion

3

Matthias Church

Szentháromság tér

Tárnok u

Dísz tér

Palota út

Krisztina krt

See map p66

Hess András tér

5

37

13

8

61

Anna u

Úri u

46

Logodi u

Attila u

Fortuna u

40

Országház u

36

75

71

47

16

Tábor u

Zerge lépcső

Roham u

Gellérthegy u

Naphegy u

Lisznyai u

Órcos u

Fény u

Castle Hill
51

62

Úri u

Palcza u

Krisztina tér

49

34

Tigris u

Castle Hill

1

Úri u

Tóth Árpád sétány

Lovas út

CASTLE HILL
(VÁRHEGY)

Logodi u

Miklós u

Pauler u

Krisztina krt

Alagút u

Mészáros u

Charles Hotel, Dalkich
(550m)

Logodi u

Attila u

Vérmező

Kúny u

Kosciuszko Tádéu

Márvány u

Győri út

Magyar jakobinusok tere

Déli pu

Déli Train Station

Koronaőr köz

Alkotás u

Kék Golyó u

See map p72

Városmajor u

Ráth György u

Nagyenyed u

Királyhágó u

Hertelendy u

Kiss János altábornagy u

Castle District

Batthyány tér SQUARE

(Map p62; Ⓜ M2 Batthyány tér, 🚋 19, 41) The centre of Víziváros, Batthyány tér is the best place to take pictures of the photogenic Parliament building across the Danube. In the square's centre is the entrance to both the M2 metro and the HÉV suburban line to Szentendre.

On the southern side is the 18th-century baroque Church of St Anne (Szent Ana templom; Map p62; ☎ 1-201 6364; http://archivum.piar.

hu/melte; I Batthyány tér 7; ⊙ mass 5pm Mon-Fri, 11am Sun), with one of the most eye-catching interiors of any baroque church in Budapest, including a magnificent late 18th-century pulpit and organ.

Museum of Applied Hungarian Folk Art MUSEUM

(Map p62; ☎ 1-201 8734; www.heritagehouse.hu; II Fő utca 6; adult/concession 600/300Ft; ⊙ 10am-6pm Tue-Sat; 🚋 19, 41) This absorbing museum focuses on folk art from around the country. There are impressive collections of fine textiles and embroidery, wood and bone carvings, leatherwork, pottery, metalwork and dolls dressed in traditional costume. Don't miss the wonderful devil masks, traditionally worn during the Busójárás festival in Mohács. Temporary exhibitions are held in a separate building three blocks north, at Szilágyi Dezső tér 6 (Map p62; ☑1-201 8734; www.heritagehouse.hu; ⑈ Szilágyi Dezső tér 6; adult/concession 600/300Ft; ⊙9am-4pm Mon-Thu, to 1pm Fri; ⛴19, 41).

Millennium Park   PARK

(Millenáris Park; Map p62; ☑1-336 4000; www.millenaris.hu; ⑈ Kis Rókus utca 16-20; ⊙6am-1am; Ⓜ M2 Széll Kálmán tér, ⛴4, 6) Millennium Park is an attractive landscaped complex comprising fountains, ponds, little bridges, a theatre, a playground and a gallery containing the Invisible Exhibition (Lathatatlan Kiállítás; Map p62; ☑06 20 771 4236; www.lathatatlan.hu; ⑈ Kis Rókus utca 16-20, Millenáris B Bldg; adult/student weekdays 1700/1400Ft, weekends 1900/1700Ft; ⊙10am-8pm Sat-Thu, to 11pm Fri).

👁 Gellért Hill & Tabán

These districts are not overly endowed with things to see and do. Come here for the unparalleled views of Buda, Pest and the Danube dividing them from the top of Gellért Hill and the leafy promenade that runs along the river in the Tabán neighbourhood.

★ Memento Park   PARK

See p52.

★ Liberty Monument   MONUMENT

(Szabadság-szobor; Map p66; ⛴27) The Liberty Monument, the lovely lady with the palm frond proclaiming freedom throughout the city, is to the east of the Citadella. Some 14m high, she was raised in 1947 in tribute to the Soviet soldiers who died liberating Budapest in 1945. The victims' names in Cyrillic letters on the plinth and the soldiers' statues were removed in 1992 and sent to Memento Park. The inscription reads: 'To those who gave up their lives for Hungary's independence, freedom and prosperity'.

★ Citadella   FORT

(Citadel; Map p66; ⛴27) The Citadella is a fortress that never saw a battle. Built by the Habsburgs after the 1848–49 War of Independence to defend the city from further insurrection, the structure was obsolete by the time it was ready in 1851 due to the change in political climate. Today the fortress contains some big guns peeping through the loopholes, but the interior has now been closed to the public while its future is decided.

Castle Garden Bazaar   HISTORIC SITE

(Várkert Bazár; Map p66; ☑1-225 0554; www.varkertbazar.hu; Ybl Miklós tér 6; ⛴86, ⛴19, 41) The reopening of this renovated pleasure park (dating from 1893) has added a whole new dimension to Tabán district. The complex comprises over a dozen neo-Gothic and neo-Renaissance structures, including a theatre, convention centre and, in the Southern Palaces, a large gallery with cutting-edge exhibitions. A staircase and lift from Lánchíd utca lead to the Neo-Renaissance Garden, and stairs, lifts and an escalator take you up to Castle Hill. The huge Foundry Courtyard boasts a restaurant with terrace and large performance space.

Liberty Bridge   BRIDGE

(Szabadság-híd; Map p66; Ⓜ M4 Szent Gellért tér, ⛴47, 49) Liberty Bridge, with its fin de siècle cantilevered span, was opened in time for the Millenary Exhibition in 1896. The bridge was originally named after Habsburg Emperor Franz Joseph, and each of its posts is topped by a mythical *turul* (an eagle-like totem of the ancient Magyars and now a national symbol) ready to take flight. It was rebuilt immediately after WWII.

Cave Church   CHURCH

(Sziklatemplom; Map p66; ☑06 20 775 2472; www.sziklatemplom.hu; XI Szent Gellért rakpart 1/a; adult/child 600/500Ft; ⊙9.30am-7.30pm Mon-Sat; Ⓜ M4 Szent Gellért tér, ⛴47, 49, 18, 19) This chapel is on a small hill directly opposite the landmark Danubius Hotel Gellért. It was built into a cave in 1926 and was the seat of Hungary's Pauline order until 1951, when the priests were imprisoned by the communists and the cave sealed off. It was reopened and reconsecrated in 1992. Behind the chapel is a monastery with neo-Gothic turrets that are visible from Liberty Bridge.

Queen Elizabeth Statue   STATUE

(Erzsébet királyné-szobor; Map p66; ⑈ Döbrentei tér; ⛴19, 41) To the northwest of Elizabeth Bridge is a statue of Elizabeth, Habsburg empress and Hungarian queen. Consort to Franz Joseph, 'Sissi' was much loved by the Magyars because, among other things, she learned to speak Hungarian. She was assassinated by

Gellért Hill & Tabán

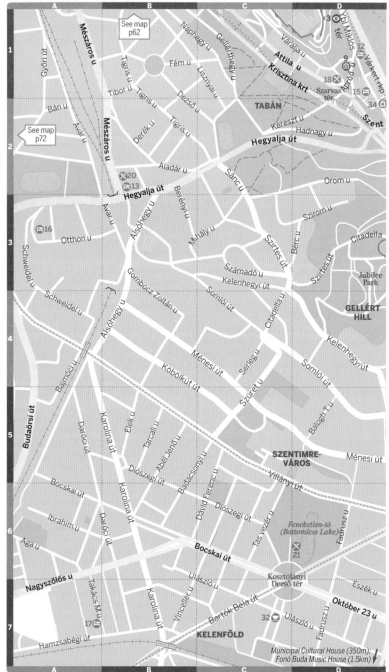

See map p62

See map p72

Municipal Cultural House (350m);
Fonó Buda Music House (1.5km)

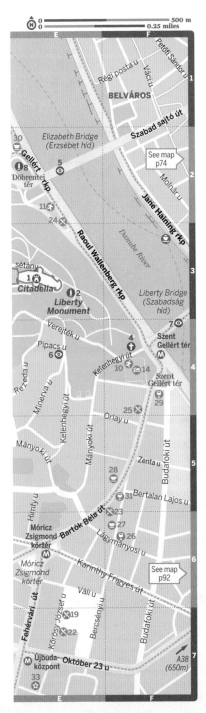

Gellért Hill & Tabán

an Italian anarchist in Geneva in 1898 with a sharpened needle file. What a brute.

Elizabeth Bridge   BRIDGE
(Erzsébet-híd; Map p66; 🚊7, 86, 🚃19) Elizabeth Bridge enjoys a special place in the hearts of many Budapesters, as this gleaming white suspension bridge (1964) was the first newly

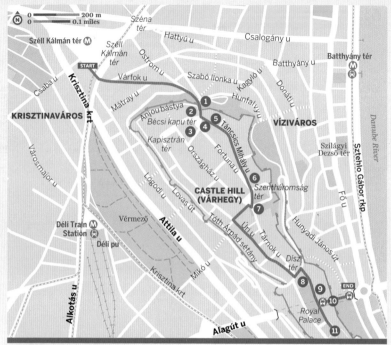

Neighbourhood Walk
Castle Hill

START II SZÉLL KÁLMÁN TÉR
END I CLARK ÁDÁM TÉR
LENGTH 1.2KM; TWO HOURS

Walk up Várfok utca from Széll Kálmán tér to ❶ **Vienna Gate**, the medieval entrance to the Old Town. The large building to the west with the superbly coloured maiolica-tiled roof contains the ❷ **National Archives** (Országos Levéltár; 1920). To the west of Bécsi kapu tér (Vienna Gate Sq) – a weekend market in the Middle Ages – is an attractive group of ❸ **burgher houses**.

Narrow ❹ **Táncsics Mihály utca** is full of little houses painted in lively hues and adorned with statues. In many courtyard entrances you'll see *sedilia* (13th-century stone niches perhaps used as merchant stalls). Further along the road to the southeast, at Táncsics Mihály utca 9, is the ❺ **former prison** where the leader of the 1848–49 War of Independence, Lajos Kossuth, was held from 1837 to 1840.

The architecturally controversial ❻ **Hilton Budapest** (p104), incorporating parts of a medieval Dominican church and a baroque Jesuit college, is further south. To the southeast, in the centre of ❼ **I Szentháromság tér**, is a replica statue of the Holy Trinity (Szentháromság szobor), a 'plague pillar' erected by grateful (and healthy) Buda citizens in the early 18th century.

Walking along Úri utca south to Dísz tér you'll come face to face with the bombed-out ❽ **former Ministry of Defence**, a casualty of WWII, and NATO's supposed nuclear target for Budapest during the Cold War. It's getting a long-overdue renovation.

Further south on the left is the restored ❾ **Sándor Palace**, now housing the offices of the president of the republic. A rather low-key guard change takes place in front hourly between 9am and 6pm.

Just south of the upper station of the ❿ **Sikló** funicular, which descends to I Clark Ádám tér, are the ⓫ **Habsburg Steps**, a 1903 ornamental gateway with steps leading to the Royal Palace.

designed bridge to reopen after WWII (the original span, erected in 1903, was too badly damaged in the war to rebuild). Boasting a higher arch than the other bridges spanning the Danube, it offers dramatic views of both Castle and Gellért Hills and, of course, the river.

Semmelweis Museum of Medical History MUSEUM

(Semmelweis Orvostörténeti Múzeum; Map p66; ☑ 1-375 3533, 1-201 1577; www.semmelweis.museum.hu; I Apród utca 1-3; adult/child 700/350Ft; ☺ 10am-6pm Tue-Sun Mar-Oct, 10am-4pm Tue-Fri, to 6pm Sat & Sun Nov-Feb; ☒ 86, ☒ 19, 41) This quirky (and sometimes grisly) museum traces the history of medicine from Graeco-Roman times through medical tools and photographs; inevitably in Hungary, another antique pharmacy makes an appearance. Featured are the life and works of Ignác Semmelweis (1818–65), the 'saviour of mothers', who discovered the cause of puerperal (childbirth) fever. He was born in this house.

◉ Óbuda & Buda Hills

Attractions in Óbuda and Buda Hills are diverse in character: they range from the lofty green expanse of the Buda Hills, best explored by foot or mountain bike, to several caves, Budapest's most extensive Roman site, and a clutch of quirky museums and galleries.

★ Aquincum ARCHAELOGICAL SITE
See p53.

★ Vasarely Museum GALLERY

(Map p70; ☑ 1-388 7551; www.vasarely.hu; III Szentlélek tér 6; adult/6-26yr 800/400Ft; ☺ 10am-5.30pm Tue-Sun; ☒ 29, 109, ☒ Szentlélek tér) Installed in the imposing Zichy Mansion (Zichy kastély), built in 1757, this museum contains the works of Victor Vasarely (or Vásárhelyi Győző, as he was known before he emigrated to Paris in 1930), the late 'father of op art'. The works, especially *Keek* and *Ibadan-Pos*, are excellent and fun to watch as they 'swell' and 'move' around the canvas. Closed for renovation until late 2017.

★ Kiscell Museum MUSEUM

(Kiscelli Múzeum; Map p70; ☑ 1-250 0304; www.kiscellimuzeum.hu; III Kiscelli utca 108; adult/concession 1600/800Ft; ☺ 10am-6pm Tue-Sun Apr-Oct, to 4pm Tue-Sun Nov-Mar; ☒ 29, 109, ☒ 17, 19, 41) Housed in an 18th-century monastery, this museum contains three excellent sections. Downstairs you'll find a complete 19th-

century apothecary brought from Kálvin tér; a wonderful assembly of ancient signboards advertising shops and other trades; and rooms dressed in empire, Biedermeier and art nouveau furniture.

An impressive collection of works by contemporary artists József Rippl-Rónai, Lajos Tihanyi, István Csók and Béla Czóbel is upstairs. The juxtaposition of the stark Gothic church shell against the temporary multimedia and art exhibits is visually arresting.

★ Hungarian Museum of Trade & Tourism MUSEUM

(Magyar Kereskedelmi és Vendéglátó-ipari Múzeum; Map p70; ☑ 1-375 6249; www.mkvm.hu; III Korona tér 1; adult/student 1000/500Ft; ☺ 10am-6pm Tue-Sun; ☒ 29, 109, ☒ Tímár utca) This excellent little museum traces Budapest's catering and hospitality trade through the ages, including the dramatic changes post-WWII, with restaurant items, tableware, advertising posters, packaging and original shop signs. Go upstairs for an intimate look at the lives of various tradespeople – from bakers and publicans to launderers. The lovely cafe is lit by antique lamps. A gem.

Imre Varga Collection GALLERY

(Varga Imre Gyűjtemény; Map p70; ☑ 1-250 0274; www.budapestgaleria.hu; III Laktanya utca 7; adult/student & senior 800/400Ft; ☺ 10am-6pm Tue-Sun Apr-Oct, to 4pm Tue-Sun Nov-Mar; ☒ 29, 109, ☒ Szentlélek tér) This collection includes sculptures, statues, medals and drawings by Imre Varga (b 1923), one of Hungary's foremost sculptors. Like others before him, notably Zsigmond Kisfaludi Strobl, Varga seems to have sat on both sides of the fence politically for decades – sculpting Béla Kun and Lenin as dexterously as he did St Stephen, Béla Bartók and even Imre Nagy. But his work always remains fresh and is never derivative. Note the fine bust of Winston Churchill (2003) near the entrance.

A very short distance to the southwest of the museum you'll see a group of outdoor sculptures by Varga. They portray four rather worried-looking women holding umbrellas in the middle of the street.

Gül Baba's Tomb ISLAMIC TOMB

(Gül Baba türbéje; Map p70; ☑ 1-237 4400; www.museum.hu/budapest/gulbabaturbe; II Türbe tér 1; ☺ 10am-6pm; ☒ 4, 6, 17) **FREE** This reconstructed tomb contains the mortal remains of Gül Baba, an Ottoman dervish who took part in the capture of Buda in 1541 and is

Óbuda

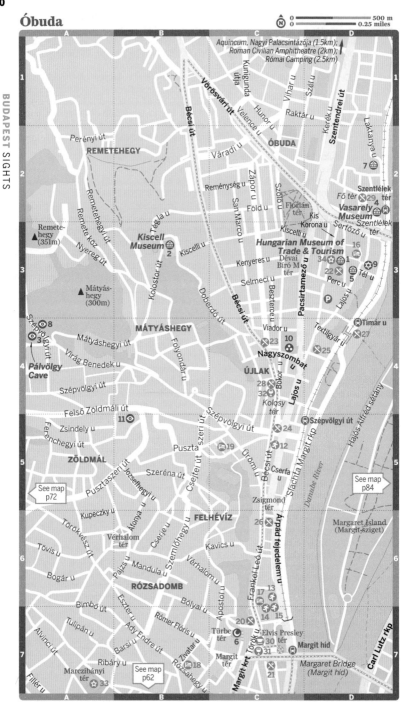

N 0 ———————— 500 m
0 ———————— 0.25 miles

Aquincum, Nagyi Palacsintázója (1.5km);
Roman Civilian Amphitheatre (2km);
Római Camping (2.5km)

REMETEHEGY

Remete-
hegy
(351m)

Kiscell
Museum

Mátyás-
hegy
(300m)

MÁTYÁSHEGY

Pálvölgy
Cave

ZÖLDMÁL

ÓBUDA

Fő tér

Szentlélek
tér

Vasarely
Museum

Szentlélek
tér

Hungarian Museum of
Trade & Tourism

Nagyszombat

ÚJLAK

Szépvölgyi út

FELHÉVÍZ

RÓZSADOMB

Danube River

Margaret Island
(Margit-sziget)

Türbe
tér

Margit
tér

Elvis Presley
tér

Margit híd

Margaret Bridge
(Margit híd)

See map
p72

See map
p62

See map
p84

Marczibányi
tér

Carl Lutz rkp

Óbuda

known in Hungary as the 'Father of Roses'. The tomb and mosque are a pilgrimage place for Muslims, especially from Turkey, and you must remove your shoes before entering. From Török utca, walk up steep Gül Baba utca to the set of steps just past No 16. Closed for renovation at the time of writing.

Óbuda Synagogue   SYNAGOGUE
(Óbudai zsinagóga; Map p70; ☑1-268 0183; www.zsido.com; III Lajos utca 163; 🚌29, 109, 🚋Szentlélek tér) Next to the landmark Aquincum Hotel, the Óbuda Synagogue was built in 1821. For many years it housed Hungarian TV (MTV) sound studios because the much-reduced post-WWII Jewish population couldn't afford the upkeep, but it is now functioning at least part time as a *súl* (Jewish prayer house). Under renovation at the time of writing.

Goldberger Textile Museum   MUSEUM
(Goldberger Textilipari Gyűjtemény; Map p70; ☑1-250 1020; www.textilmuzeum.hu; Lajos utca 136-138; adult/concession 1400/700Ft; ⊙10am-6pm Tue-Sun; 🚻; 🚌29, 109, 🚋Tímár utca) Housed in the former home of the Goldberger family, this excellent museum tells the story of Hungary's textile industry, and that of the textile factory founded by Jewish entrepreneur Ferenc Goldberger in 1784, which dominated Hungary's clothing industry until the

late 20th century and supplied fine fabrics to the Habsburgs in its heyday. Learn about blue-dying and screen-printing through interactive exhibits, check out the machinery that was revolutionary for its time and marvel at the gorgeous fabric samples.

**Roman Military
Amphitheatre**   ARCHAEOLOGICAL SITE
(Római Katonai Amfiteátrum; Map p70; III Pacsirtamező utca; 🚌9, 109, 🚋Tímár utca) **FREE** Built in the 2nd century for the Roman garrisons, this amphitheatre, about 800m south of Flórián tér, could accommodate 6000 spectators. The rest of the military camp extended north to Flórián tér. Archaeology and classical-history buffs taking bus 9 to Flórián tér should get off at III Nagyszombat utca.

Elizabeth Lookout   VIEWPOINT
(Erzsébet kilátó; Erzsébet kilátó utca; ⊙8am-8pm; 🚋Children's Railway) High up on Buda's highest hill, János-hegy (527m), is this tower. Take the 134 steps up to the top for remarkable views of Budapest in the distance and the surrounding countryside. On a clear day, you can see the Tatra Mountains in Slovakia. To get here, take the Children's Railway to János-hegy, the fourth stop, or else the nearby **chairlift** (Libegő; www.bkv.hu; 1 way/return adult 1000/1400Ft, 6-26yr 600/800Ft; ⊙10am-7pm May-Aug; 🚌291).

Buda Hills

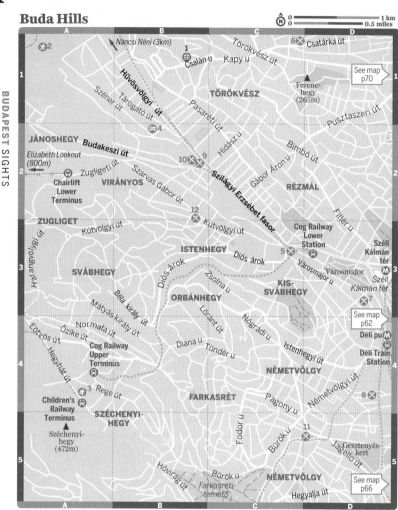

Buda Hills

Béla Bartók Memorial House　MUSEUM
(Bartók Béla Emlékház; Map p72; ☎1-394 2100; www.
bartokmuseum.hu; II Csalán út 29; 1500Ft; ◎10am-

5pm Tue-Sun; 🚌5, 29, 🚃61) North of Szilágyi
Erzsébet fasor, this house (1924) is where the
great composer resided from 1932 until 1940,

when he emigrated to the US. Visits are by guided tour and include seeing the old Edison recorder (complete with wax cylinders) that Bartók used to record Hungarian folk music in Transylvania, as well as his beloved hand-carved dining-room furniture and even half a cigarette he smoked! Chamber-music concerts take place here throughout the year; see the website for details.

★**Pálvölgy Cave** CAVE
(Pálvölgyi-barlang; Map p70; ☑1-325 9505; www.palvolgyi.atw.hu; II Szépvölgyi út 162/a; adult/concession 1400/1100Ft, joint ticket with Szemlőhegy Cave 2000/1600Ft; ☉10am-5pm Tue-Sun; ☒65) The second-largest in Hungary, this 29km-long cave discovered in 1904 is noted for both its spectacular stalactites and rock formations. Tours last 45 minutes and depart from 10.15am (last tour at 4.15pm) from the lowest level, taking you through dank, claustrophobia-inducing passages and up several hundred steps. Highlights include John's Lookout in the largest of chambers, as well as Radium Hall, reminiscent of Dante's *Inferno*. The temperature is a constant 11°C so wear a jacket or jumper. Alight the bus at the Pálvölgyi-cseppkőbarlang stop.

Mátyáshegy Cave CAVE
(Mátyáshegyi-barlang; Map p70; ☑06 20 928 4969; www.barlangaszat.hu; II Szépvölgyi út; adult/8-14yr 7000/6000Ft; ☉tours 4.30pm Mon, Wed & Fri, 10am Tue & Thu, 2pm Sat; ☒65) Of Budapest's 200 caves, several are accessible to the public and can be visited on walk-through guided tours; prices depend on group size. This one, left in its natural state, throws down a gauntlet to would-be speleologists, keen on crawling through narrow passages and climbing cave walls. Caving equipment is provided; email ahead. Alight the bus at the Pálvölgyi-cseppkőbarlang stop.

A number of hostels in Budapest also offer adventurous 2½- to three-hour caving excursions to this cave, which is opposite to and links up with Pálvölgy Cave.

Szemlőhegy Cave CAVE
(Szemlőhegyi-barlang; Map p70; ☑1-325 6001; www.dunaipoly.hu/hu/helyek/bemutatohelyek/szemlo-hegyi-barlang; II Pusztaszeri út 35; adult/concession 1300/1000Ft, joint ticket with Pálvölgy Cave 2000/1600Ft; ☉10am-4pm Wed-Mon; ☒29, 111) A beautiful cave about 1km southeast of Pálvölgy and Mátyáshegy Caves, and the most accessible of the three. The temperature at Szemlőhegy is 12°C and the cave has no sta-

lactites or stalagmites; instead, it's notable for its peculiar grapelike formations. The tour lasts 35 to 45 minutes. The lower part of the cave is used as a respiratory sanatorium due the exceptional quality of its air.

◉ Belváros

With the exception of Váci utca (Budapest's premier shopping street), Belváros' main attraction lies in wandering its streets and admiring the fine architecture around its main square, Vörösmarty tér, and along the river. There are also several niche museums and private art galleries.

★**Váci utca** STREET
See p56.

★**Vörösmarty tér** SQUARE
See p56.

★**Pesti Vigadó** NOTABLE BUILDING
(Map p74; www.pestivigado.hu; V Vigadó tér 1; adult/concession 2500/2000Ft; ☉10am-7.30pm; Ⓜ M1 Vörösmarty tér, ☒2) This Romantic-style concert hall, built in 1864 and badly damaged during WWII, faces the river to the west of Vörösmarty tér. Reopened in 2014 after reconstruction, the building has been fully restored to its former grandeur. Floors five and six have been set aside for temporary exhibitions and there's now a fantastic terrace affording expansive views over the Danube. It's a fantastic place to catch a classical concert in glamorous surrounds. English-language guided tours available (2900Ft); check the website for schedule.

★**Trapéz** GALLERY
(Map p74; ☑06 30 210 3120; www.trpz.hu; V Henszlmann Imre utca 3; ☉noon-6pm Tue-Fri; Ⓜ M3 Ferenciek tere, M3/4 Kálvin tér) Exciting new contemporary art gallery showcasing installations, sculpture, photography and other media by up-and-coming international artists.

Károly Garden GARDENS
(Károlyi kert; Map p74; V Ferenczy István utca; Ⓜ M3/4 Kálvin tér, ☒47, 48, 49) A pleasant place to take a breather, the flora-filled Károlyi kert was built for the Károly Palace, which now houses the **Petőfi Museum of Literature** (Petőfi Irodalmi Múzeum; Map p74; ☑1-317 3611; www.pim.hu; V Károlyi utca 16; adult/6-26yr 600/300Ft, temporary exhibitions 800/400Ft; ☉10am-6pm Tue-Sun). Frequented by locals, many with families (it has a

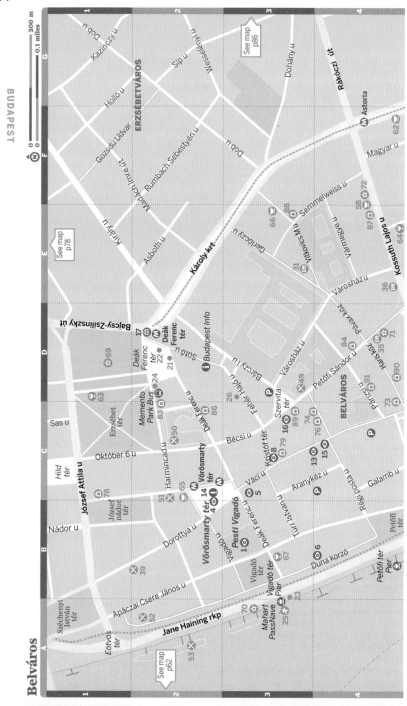

Belváros

0 0.1 miles
0 200 m

See map p86

See map p78

See map p62

ERZSÉBETVÁROS

BELVÁROS

Rákóczi út

Astoria

Magyar u

Kossuth Lajos u

Károly krt

Bajcsy-Zsilinszky út

Deák Ferenc tér

Budapest Info

Vörösmarty tér

Pesti Vigadó

József Attila u

Hild tér

József nádor tér

Nádor u

Széchenyi István tér

Eötvös tér

Jane Haining rkp

Mahart PassNave

Apáczai Csere János u

Vigadó tér

Duna korzó

Petőfi tér

Pier

Dohány u

Síp u

Kazinczy u

Holló u

Dob u

Wesselényi u

Gozsdu Udvar

Madách Imre út

Rumbach Sebestyén u

Király u

Asboth u

Semmelweis u

Gerlóczy u

Vármegye u

Vitkovics M u

Városháza u

Városház u

Hársfa köz

Petőfi Sándor u

Párizsi u

Régi posta u

Galamb u

Aranykéz u

Türr István u

Deák Ferenc u

Váci u

Kristóf tér

Bécsi u

Deák Ferenc u

Fehér Hajó u

Szervita tér

Harmincad u

Október 6 u

Sas u

Erzsébet tér

Deák Ferenc tér

Harris köz

Pilvax köz

Petőfi tér

Memento Park Bus

Dorottya u

Vigadó u

Sütő u

Balázsi I u

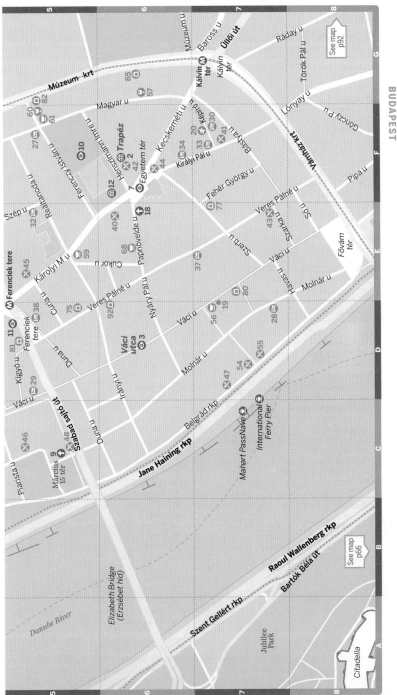

Belváros

lovely little playground), the garden is a riot of colourful flower beds in the summer months, and there are plenty of shady benches. **Csendes Társ** (Map p74; ☑1-727 2100; www.facebook.com/csendestars; Magyar utca 18; ☉11am-11pm; Ⓜ M2 Astoria, 🚊4, 6) is an atmospheric spot for a sundowner or snack, with a little terrace of tables crowded round the park's pretty, wrought-iron entrance gate.

Egyetem tér SQUARE
(University Sq; Map p74; M M3/4 Kálvin tér) Boasting new seating, water features, abstract sculpture and shade sails, 'University Sq' takes its name from the branch of the prestigious Loránd Eötvös Science University located here. Attached to the main university building to the west is the lovely baroque 1742 **University Church** (Egyetemi templom; Map p74; ☑ 1-318 0555; V Papnövelde utca 5-7; ⊙ 7am-7pm). Over the altar is a copy of the Black Madonna of Częstochowa so revered in Poland.

Underground Railway Museum MUSEUM
(Földalatti Vasúti Múzeum; Map p74; www.bkv.hu; Deák Ferenc tér metro station; adult/concession 350/280Ft; ⊙ 10am-5pm Tue-Sun; M M1/2/3 Deák Ferenc tér) In the pedestrian subway beneath V Deák Ferenc tér, next to the main ticket window, the small, revamped Underground Railway Museum traces the development of the capital's underground lines. Much emphasis is put on the little yellow metro (M1), continental Europe's first underground railway, which opened for the millenary celebrations in 1896. The museum is atmospherically housed in a stretch of tunnel and station, and features wonderfully restored carriages.

Duna korzó AREA
(Map p74; M M1 Vörösmarty tér, ☑ 2) An easy way to cool down on a warm afternoon (and enjoy views of Castle Hill) is to stroll along the Duna korzó, the riverside promenade between Széchenyi Chain Bridge and Elizabeth Bridge. Full of cafes, musicians and handicraft stalls by day, it leads into **Petőfi tér**, named after the poet of the 1848-49 War of Independence. **Március 15 tér**, which marks the date of the outbreak of the 1989 revolution, abuts it to the south.

Inner Town Parish Church CHURCH
(Belvárosi plébániatemplom; Map p74; www.belvarosiplebania.hu; V Március 15 tér 2; ⊙ 9am-7pm; ☑ 2) A Romanesque church was first built on the eastern side of Március 15 tér in the 12th century, within a Roman fortress. The present church was rebuilt in the 14th century and again in the 18th century, and you can easily spot Gothic, Renaissance, baroque

---

BUDAPEST SIGHTS

DON'T MISS

SECESSIONIST ARCHITECTURAL GEMS

Southeast of Szabadság tér are two of the most beautiful buildings in Pest. The former **Royal Postal Savings Bank** is a Secessionist (architectural style similar to art nouveau) extravaganza of colourful tiles and folk motifs built by Ödön Lechner in 1901. It is now part of the **National Bank of Hungary** (Magyar Nemzeti Bank; Map p78; V Szabadság tér 9; ☑ 15, 115) next door, which has terracotta reliefs that illustrate trade and commerce through history: Arab camel traders, African rug merchants, Chinese tea salesmen – and the inevitable solicitor witnessing contracts.

and even Turkish – eg the mihrab (prayer niche) in the eastern wall – elements.

⊙ Parliament & Around

This district is overly endowed with important museums such as the Ethnography Museum and cultural venues like the Hungarian State Opera House. But it also contains the two most important landmarks in the capital: the Parliament, facing along the Danube, and the Basilica of St Stephen, both of which can be visited.

★ Parliament HISTORIC BUILDING
See p50.

★ Basilica of St Stephen CATHEDRAL
See p54.

★ Hungarian State Opera House NOTABLE BUILDING
(Magyar Állami Operaház; Map p78; ☑ 1-332 8197; www.operavisit.hu; VI Andrássy út 22; adult/concession 2990/1990Ft; ⊙ tours in English 2pm, 3pm & 4pm; M M1 Opera) The neo-Renaissance Hungarian State Opera House was designed by Miklós Ybl in 1884 and is among the most beautiful buildings in Budapest. Its facade is decorated with statues of muses and opera greats such as Puccini, Mozart, Liszt and Verdi, while its interior dazzles with marble columns, gilded vaulted ceilings, chandeliers and near-perfect acoustics. If you cannot attend a performance, join one of the three daily tours. Tickets are available from the souvenir shop inside the lobby.

Parliament & Around

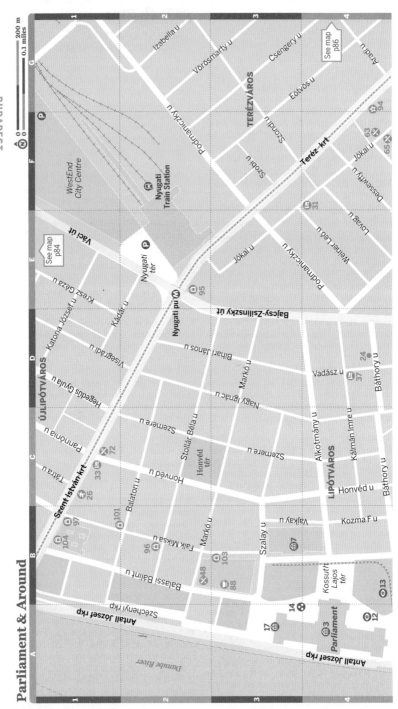

Danube River

Antall József rkp

Szécheny rkp

Antall József rkp

WestEnd
City Centre

Nyugati
Train Station

Szent István krt

Váci út

See map
p84

See map
p86

UJLIPÓTVÁROS

TERÉZVÁROS

LIPÓTVÁROS

Parliament

Kossuth
Lajos
tér

Honvéd
tér

Nyugati
tér

Podmaniczky u

Izabella u

Vörösmarty u

Csengery u

Eötvös u

Szondi u

Szobi u

Teréz krt

Jókai u

Dessewffy u

Jókai u

Podmaniczky u

Weiner Leó u

Lovag u

Aradi u

Vadász u

Báthory u

Alkotmány u

Kálmán Imre u

Honvéd u

Báthory u

Kozma F u

Nagy Ignác u

Markó u

Bihari János u

Stollár Béla u

Semmere u

Semmere u

Szalay u

Valkay u

Markó u

Balaton u

Falk Miksa u

Honvéd u

Balassi Bálint u

Pannónia u

Tátra u

Hegedűs Gyula u

Visegrádi u

Katona József u

Kresz Géza u

Kádár u

Bajcsy-Zsilinszky út

Nyugati pu

200 m
0.1 miles

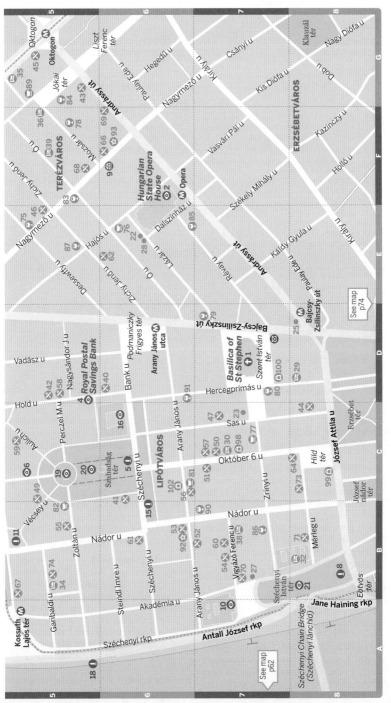

Oktogon

Oktogon 45

89 35

Jókai tér

Jókai 84 43

Andrássy út

36 78 69

39 Ó u 66 93

TERÉZVÁROS

Zichy Jenő u

Nagymező u

9

Hungarian State Opera House 2

M Opera

83

75 Nagymező u

Hajós u 76 22

87 62 28

Zichy Jenő u

Ó u Lázár u

Dalszínház u 85

Andrássy út

CSÁNYI u

Hegedű u

Paulay Ede u

Nagymező u

Király u

Kis Diófa u

Klauzál tér

Nagy Diófa u

Dob u

ERZSÉBETVÁROS

Kazinczy u

Holló u

Vasvári Pál u

Székely Mihály u

Rékay u

Káldy Gyula u

Paulay Ede u

Király u

Bajcsy-Zsilinszky út

49 25

Bajcsy-Zsilinszky út

See map p74

Vadász u

Nagysándor J u

4 Royal Postal Savings Bank

58 40

Bank u

Podmaniczky Frigyes tér

Arany János utca

Hercegprímás u

91

Basilica of St Stephen 1

Szent István tér

100

29

80

Hold u

42

Vécsey u

82 49

59

Auln u

6

19 20

Szabadság tér

5

16

Arany János u

47 23

Sas u

57 50 30 98

Október 6 u

77

44

József Attila u

Erzsébet tér

József nádor tér

LIPÓTVÁROS

Széchenyi u

15 41

102 56

81 51

90

Nádor u

Zrínyi u

Hild tér

73 64

99

11

55 61

53 52

92

Nádor u

54 60

27

86

71 32

Mérleg u

67

74 34

Garibaldi u

Zoltán u

Steindl Imre u

Széchenyi u

Arany János u

Vigyázó Ferenc u

38

Akadémia u

10

Széchenyi István tér 21

8

Eötvös tér

Jane Haining rkp

Kossuth Lajos tér

M

18

Széchenyi rkp

Antall József rkp

Széchenyi Chain Bridge (Széchenyi lánchíd)

See map p62

Parliament & Around

Szabadság tér SQUARE
(Liberty Square; Map p78; ☐15, Ⓜ M2 Kossuth Lajos tér) This square, one of the largest in Budapest, is a few minutes' walk northeast of Széchenyi István tér. As you enter you'll pass a delightful fountain that works on optical sensors and turns off and on as you approach or back away from it, as well as the controversial Antifascist Monument placed here in 2014. At the northern end is a **Soviet Army memorial** (Map p78; V Szabadság tér; Ⓜ M2 Kossuth Lajos tér), the last of its type still standing in the city.

On the eastern side is the fortress-like US Embassy, now cut off from the square by high steel fencing and concrete blocks. It was here that Cardinal József Mindszenty sought refuge after the 1956 Uprising, staying for 15 years until his departure for Vienna in 1971. The embassy backs onto Hold utca (Moon St), which, until 1990, was named Rosenberg házaspár utca (Rosenberg Couple St) after the American husband and wife Julius and

Ethel Rosenberg who were executed as Soviet spies in the US in 1953. Today a statue of the late US President Ronald Reagan graces the northern end of the park.

A controversial **statue** (Horthy Miklós-szobor; Map p78; V Szabadság tér 2; ☐15, 115) of Hungary's intrawar leader Miklós Horthy, called a hero by the right wing but reviled as a fascist dictator by many others, stands in front of the Homecoming Presbyterian Church in the square's southwest corner.

Antifascist Monument MONUMENT
(Antifasiszta emlékmű; Map p78; V Szabadság tér; ☐15, 115, Ⓜ M2 Kossuth Lajos tér) This memorial dedicated to the 'victims of the German occupation' appeared at the southern end of V Szabadság tér in July 2014. It remains extremely controversial (and has yet to be official dedicated) as many people believe that the puppet government of Arrow Cross Party leader Ferenc Szálasi fully supported the Nazis when installed in 1944, as did many local

citizens. An alternative (and poignant) memorial of candles, letters and personal memorabilia has been set up by protesters.

Kossuth Lajos tér
SQUARE

(Map p78; Ⓜ M2 Kossuth Lajos tér) Northwest of Szabadság tér, this square is the site of Parliament, Budapest's most photographed building, and the Ethnography Museum, the country's best collection of traditional arts and crafts. The square reopened in 2014 after being restored to its original prewar plans. It is now a traffic-free zone with a sustainable park, sculptures of the great and the good, an underground **lapidary** (kőtar; Map p78; V Kossuth Lajos tér; ⊙ 10am-5pm; Ⓜ M2 Kossuth Lajos tér) FREE and a **memorial** (V Kossuth Lajos tér; Map p78; ⊙ 10am-5pm) FREE to the victims of the Kossuth Lajos tér massacre on 25 October 1956.

Ethnography Museum
MUSEUM

(Néprajzi Múzeum; Map p78; ☑ 1-473 2400; www.neprajz.hu; V Kossuth Lajos tér 12; adult/concession 1000/500Ft, with temporary exhibitions 1400/700Ft; ⊙ 10am-6pm Tue-Sun; Ⓜ M2 Kossuth Lajos tér) Visitors are offered an easy introduction to traditional Hungarian life at this sprawling museum opposite Parliament, with thousands of displays in a dozen rooms on the 1st floor. The mock-ups of peasant houses from the Őrség and Sárköz regions of west and southwest Hungary are well done, and there are some priceless objects, which are examined through institutions, beliefs and stages of life.

On the ground floor, most of the excellent temporary exhibitions deal with other peoples of Europe and further afield: Africa, Asia, Oceania and the Americas. The building itself was designed in 1893 by Alajos Hauszmann to house the Supreme Court;

note the ceiling fresco in the lobby of Justice by Károly Lotz. At the time of writing, the museum was scheduled to move to a new location in City Park at a date still unknown.

Imre Nagy Statue
STATUE

(Map p78; V Vértanúk tere; M M2 Kossuth Lajos tér) Southeast of V Kossuth Lajos tér is an unusual statue of Imre Nagy standing in the centre of a small footbridge. Nagy was the reformist Communist prime minister executed in 1958 for his role in the uprising two years earlier. The statue was unveiled with great ceremony in the summer of 1996.

Bedő House (House of Hungarian Art Nouveau)
NOTABLE BUILDING, MUSEUM

(Bedő-ház (Magyar Szecesszió Háza); Map p78; ☑1-269 4622; www.magyarszecessziohaza.hu; V Honvéd utca 3; adult/concession 2000/1500Ft; ☺10am-5pm Mon-Sat; M M2 Kossuth Lajos tér) Just around the corner from Kossuth Lajos tér, the stunning art nouveau Bedő-ház apartment block was designed by Emil Vidor in 1903. It is now a shrine to Hungarian Secessionist interiors, its three levels crammed with furniture, porcelain, ironwork, paintings and objets d'art. But only true art nouveau fans will shell out the admission fee to enter. The lovely Ëgoist Cafe (Map p78; ☑06 70 643 2331; http://egoistcafe.hu; ☺9am-7pm) is on the ground floor.

House of Hungarian Photographers
GALLERY

(Magyar Fotográfusok Háza; Map p78; ☑1-473 2666; www.maimano.hu; VI Nagymező utca 20; adult/student 1500/700Ft; ☺2-7pm Mon-Fri, 11am-7pm Sat & Sun; ☐trolleybus 70, 78, M M1 Opera) An extraordinary venue in the city's theatre district, the House of Hungarian Photographers has top-class photo exhibitions. It is in Mai Manó Ház, which was built in 1894 as a photo studio. Don't miss the extraordinary Daylight Studio (Napfényműterem) on the top floor, which was used to take studio photographs in natural light.

Széchenyi István tér
PLAZA

(Map p78; ☐16, 105, ☐2) For decades known as Roosevelt tér after the long-serving (1933–45) American president, this square has now been renamed to honour the statesmen and developer of Chain Bridge, which it faces. The square offers one of the best views of Castle Hill in Pest.

The Hungarian Academy of Sciences (Magyar Tudományos Akadémia; Map p78; V

Széchenyi István tér 9; ☐15, 115, ☐2), founded by Count István Széchenyi in 1825, is at the northern end of the square.

The art nouveau building with the gold tiles to the east is Gresham Palace (Map p78), built by an English insurance company in 1907. It now houses a luxury hotel.

On the southern end of Széchenyi István tér is a statue of Ferenc Deák (Map p78), the Hungarian minister largely responsible for the Compromise of 1867, which brought about the dual monarchy of Austria and Hungary.

Shoes on the Danube
MONUMENT

(Cipők a Dunapartján; Map p78; V Antall József rakpart; ☐2) Along the banks of the river between Széchenyi István tér and Parliament is a monument to Hungarian Jews shot and thrown into the Danube by members of the fascist Arrow Cross Party in 1944. Entitled *Shoes on the Danube* by sculptor Gyula Pauer and film director Can Togay, it's a simple but poignant display of 60 pairs of old-style boots and shoes in cast iron, tossed higgledy-piggledy on the bank of the river.

⊙ Margaret Island & Northern Pest

Margaret Island and northern Pest feature a motley collection of mostly low-key sights.

Margaret Bridge
BRIDGE

(Margit híd; Map p84; ☐2, 4, 6) Margaret Bridge, which has finally emerged from a massive three-year reconstruction, introduces the Big Ring Rd to Buda. It's unique in that it doglegs in order to stand at right angles to the Danube where it converges at the southern tip of Margaret Island. The bridge was originally built by French engineer Ernest Gouin in 1876; the branch leading to the island was added in 1901.

Water Tower & Open-Air Theatre
ARCHITECTURE

(Víztorony és Szabadtéri Színpad; Map p84; ☑06 20 383 6352; Lookout Gallery adult/concession 600/300Ft; ☺Lookout Gallery 11.30am-7pm May-Oct; ☐26) Erected in 1911 in the north-central part of Margaret Island, the octagonal water tower rises 66m above the open-air theatre *(szabadtéri színpad),* which is used for concerts and plays in summer. The tower contains the Lookout Gallery (Kilátó Galéria). Climbing the 153 steps will earn you a pleasant 360-degree view of the island, consisting mostly of treetops. En route you'll see a recent exhibition of Budapest landscapes being projected on to bare walls.

Dominican Convent   RUINS
(Domonkos kolostor; Map p84; 🚌26) A ruin is all that remains of the 13th-century convent built by Béla IV where his daughter St Margaret (1242–71) lived. According to the story, the king promised to commit his daughter to a life of devotion in a nunnery if the Mongols were driven from the land. They were and she was – at nine years of age. A red-marble sepulchre cover surrounded by a wrought-iron grille marks her original resting place and there's a viewpoint overlooking the ruins.

Canonised in 1943, St Margaret commands something of a cult following in Hungary. A short distance southeast of the sepulchre there's a much-visited brick shrine with votives thanking her for various favours and cures.

Premonstratensian Church   CHURCH
(Premontre templom; Map p84; 🚌26) This reconstructed Romanesque Premonstratensian Church, dedicated to St Michael by the order of White Canons, dates back to the 12th century. Its 15th-century bell mysteriously appeared one night in 1914 under the roots of a walnut tree knocked over in a storm. It was probably buried by monks during the Turkish invasion.

Japanese Garden   GARDENS
(Japánkert; Map p84; 🚌26) This attractive garden at the northwestern end of the island has koi carp and lily pads in its ponds, as well as bamboo groves, Japanese maples, swamp cypresses, a small wooden bridge and a waterfall.

Musical Fountain   FOUNTAIN
(Zenélőkút; Map p84) Just north of the Japanese Garden, on a raised gazebo, is the revamped Musical Fountain. A replica of one in Transylvania, it plays children's songs at 11am and 4pm daily in summer, as well as the likes of 'Pretty Woman' by Roy Orbison and 'Time to Say Goodbye' by Andrea Bocelli in the evenings between 9pm and 10pm.

Szent István Park   PARK
(Szent István körút; Map p84; Újpesti rakpart; ⊙8am-8pm; 🚊15, 🚊trolleybus 75, 76) St Stephen Park contains a **statue of Raoul Wal-**

lenberg (Map p84) doing battle with a snake (evil). Erected in 1999 and titled *Kígyóölő* (Serpent Slayer), it is a copy of the one created by sculptor Pál Pátzay that was removed by the communist regime in 1949. Facing the river is a row of Bauhaus apartments, which were the delight of modernists when they were built in the late 1920s. Enter from the southern end.

Lehel Market   MARKET
(Lehel Csarnok; Map p84; XIII Lehel tér; ⊙6am-6pm Mon-Fri, to 2pm Sat, to 1pm Sun; 🚇M3 Lehel tér) This is a great traditional market housed in a hideous boatlike structure designed by László Rajk, son of the communist minister of the interior executed for 'Titoism' in 1949. They say this building is his revenge.

Hungarian Railway History Park   MUSEUM
(Magyar Vasúttörténeti Park; 🕿1-450 1497; www.vasuttortenetipark.hu; XIV Tatai utca 95; adult/4-18yr 1600/700Ft; ⊙10am-6pm Tue-Sun Apr-Oct; 🚌30, 30A, 🚊14) This mostly outdoor museum contains more than 50 locomotives (a dozen or so still working) and an exhibition on the history of the railway in Hungary. There's a wonderful array of hands-on activities – mostly involving getting behind the wheel – for kids. Riding the miniature locomotive is a real treat.

◉ Erzsébetváros & the Jewish Quarter

You'll find a tremendous number of worthy sights in Erzsébetváros and the Jewish Quarter, from museums and galleries to such important houses of worship as the Great Synagogue. But these districts were made for exploring on foot, and a surprise, usually in the form of art nouveau/Secessionist architecture, awaits around every corner.

★Great Synagogue   SYNAGOGUE
See p57.

★House of Terror   MUSEUM
(Terror Háza; Map p86; 🕿1-374 2600; www.terrorhaza.hu; VI Andrássy út 60; adult/concession 2000/1000Ft, audioguide 1500Ft; ⊙10am-6pm Tue-Sun; 🚇M1 Oktogon) The headquarters of the dreaded secret police is now the startling House of Terror, focusing on the crimes and atrocities of Hungary's fascist and Stalinist regimes in a permanent exhibition called Double Occupation. But the

Margaret Island & Northern Pest

Margaret Island & Northern Pest

BUDAPEST SIGHTS

years after WWII leading up to the 1956 Uprising get the lion's share of the exhibition space (almost three-dozen spaces on three levels). The reconstructed prison cells in the basement and the Perpetrators' Gallery, featuring photographs of the turncoats, spies and torturers, are chilling.

The tank in the central courtyard makes for a jarring introduction and the wall outside displaying metallic photos of the many victims speaks volumes. The building has a ghastly history – it was here that activists of every political persuasion before and after WWII were taken for interrogation and torture. The walls were apparently of double thickness to muffle the screams.

Liszt Music Academy NOTABLE BUILDING
(Liszt Zeneakadémia; Map p86; ☑1-462 4600; www.zeneakademia.hu; VI Liszt Ferenc tér 8; adult/concesssion 7500/3750Ft; ⊙daily tours 1.30pm; Ⓜ M1 Oktogon, ☐4, 6) The art nouveau Liszt Music Academy, built in 1907, attracts students from all over the world and is a top concert venue (p150). The renovated interior, which has five concert halls and is richly embellished with Zsolnay porcelain and frescoes, is worth visiting on a guided tour if you're not attending a performance.

Hungarian Electrical Engineering Museum MUSEUM
(Magyar Elektrotechnikai Múzeum; Map p86; ☑1-322 0472; http://elektromuzeum.hu/hu/; VII Kazinczy utca 21; adult/student 800/400Ft; ⊙10am-5pm Tue-Fri, to 4pm Sat; ☐trolleybus 74, Ⓜ M2 Astoria) This place might not sound like everyone's cup of tea, but some of the exhibits are unusual (and quirky) enough to warrant a visit. The staff will also show you how the alarm system of the barbed-wire fence between Hungary and Austria once worked, and there's also an exhibit on the nesting platforms that the electric company kindly builds for storks throughout the country, so they won't interfere with the wires and electrocute themselves.

There are tons of old household appliances (many still work), and colourful communist-era neon shop signs adorn the outside courtyard. The weirdest display is the collection of electricity-consumption meters, one of the largest in the world, which includes one installed in the apartment of 'Rákosi Mátyás elvtárs' (Comrade Mátyás Rákosi), the Communist Party secretary, on his 60th birthday in 1952, and another recalling Stalin's 70th birthday in 1948.

Erzsébetváros & the Jewish Quarter

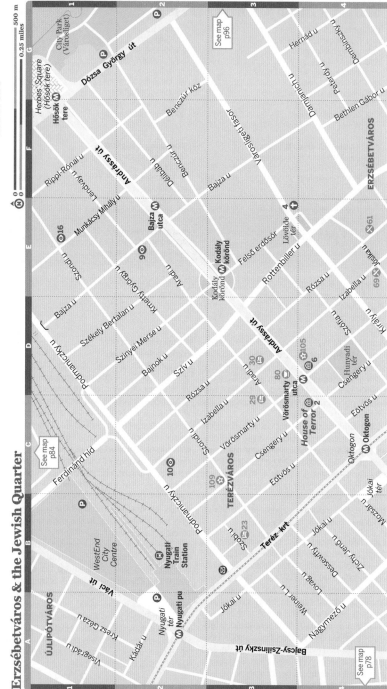

See map p96

See map p84

See map p78

ÚJLIPÓTVÁROS

TERÉZVÁROS

ERZSÉBETVÁROS

Heroes' Square
(Hősök tere)

Hősök tere

City Park
(Városliget)

Dózsa György út

House of
Terror 2

Nyugati
Train
Station

Nyugati pu

Nyugati
tér

WestEnd
City
Centre

Kodály
Körönd

Bajza
utca

Vörösmarty
utca

Oktogon

Lövölde
tér

0.25 miles
500 m

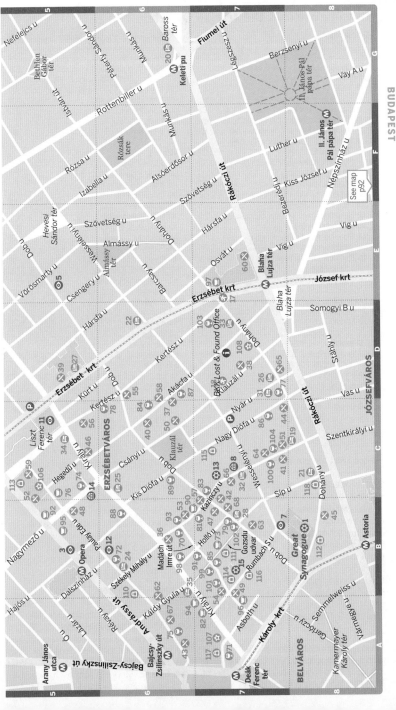

BUDAPEST

Erzsébetváros & the Jewish Quarter

Ferenc Liszt Memorial Museum   MUSEUM
(Liszt Ferenc Emlékmúzeum; Map p86; ☑1-322 9804; www.lisztmuseum.hu; VI Vörösmarty utca 35; adult/child 1500/750Ft; ⊙10am-6pm Mon-Fri, 9am-5pm Sat; ⓂM1 Vörösmarty utca) This wonderful little museum is housed in the Old Music Academy, where the great composer lived in a 1st-floor apartment for five years until his death in 1886. The three rooms are filled with his pianos (including a tiny glass one), portraits and personal effects – all original. Concerts (adult/child 1500/750Ft or 2200/1000Ft with a museum visit) are usually held in the Chamber Hall at 11am on Saturday.

Orthodox Synagogue   SYNAGOGUE
(Ortodox zsinagóga; Map p86; ☑1-351 0524; www.kazinczyutcaizsinagoga.hu; VII Kazinczy utca 29-31; 1000Ft; ⊙10am-6pm Sun-Thu, to 4pm Fri Apr-Oct, 10am-4pm Sun-Thu, to 2pm Fri Nov-Mar; ⓂM2 As-

toria, 🚊47, 49) Once one of a half-dozen synagogues and prayer houses in the Jewish Quarter, the Orthodox Synagogue was built in 1913 in what was at the time a very modern design. It has late art nouveau touches and is decorated in bright colours throughout. The stained-glass windows in the ceiling were designed by Miksa Róth, although what you see today are reconstructions, as the originals were bombed during WWII.

Rumbach Sebestyén Utca Synagogue   SYNAGOGUE
(Rumbach Sebestyén utcai zsinagóga; Map p86; ☑1-343 0420; http://enmilev.weebly.com; VII Rumbach Sebestyén utca 11-13; adult/child 500/300Ft; ⊙10am-6pm Sun-Thu, to 4pm Fri Mar-Oct, 10am-4pm Sun-Thu, to 2pm Fri Nov-Feb; ⓂM2 Astoria, 🚊4, 6) The Moorish Rumbach Sebestyén utca Synagogue was built in 1872 by Aus-

trian Secessionist architect Otto Wagner for the Status Quo Ante (moderate Conservative) community. The interior decorations are superb though it badly needs a facelift.

Robert Capa Contemporary Photography Center GALLERY
(Robert Capa Kortárs Fotográfiai Központ; Map p86; ☏1-413 1310; www.capacenter.hu; VI Nagymező utca 8; adult/concession 1500/800Ft; ⏰2-7pm Mon-Fri, 11am-7pm Sat & Sun; 🚎trolleybus 70, 78, Ⓜ M1 Opera) Named after the Hungarian-born photographer and Magnum Photos cofounder Robert Capa (born Endre Friedmann; 1913–54), and housed in a renovated cultural centre dating back 100 years, the centre seeks to show the best in contemporary visual arts in changing exhibitions.

👁 Southern Pest

Southern Pest contains an abundance of not-to-be-missed attractions, including half a dozen important museums, the Holocaust Memorial Center and a cemetery whose list of occupants reads like a Hungarian who's who. For students of history it is also the area where much of the fighting in October 1956 took place when the Uprising broke out.

⭐**Hungarian National Museum** MUSEUM
See p58.

⭐**Museum of Applied Arts** MUSEUM
(Iparművészeti Múzeum; Map p92; ☏1-456 5107; www.imm.hu; IX Üllői út 33-37; adult/student 2000/1000Ft, with temporary exhibitions 3500/1750Ft; ⏰10am-6pm Tue-Sun; Ⓜ M3 Corvin-negyed, 🚋4, 6) The Museum of Applied

Arts, housed in a gorgeous Ödön Lechner–designed building (1896) decorated with Zsolnay ceramic tiles, has two permanent collections. One contains Hungarian and European furniture from the 18th and 19th centuries, art nouveau and Secessionist artefacts, and objects relating to trades and crafts (glassmaking, bookbinding, goldsmithing). The other consists of Islamic art and artefacts from the 9th to the 19th centuries.

Among the Collectors and Treasures exhibits, it's worth keeping an eye out for the Herend and Zsolnay porcelain as well as the 300 pieces recently donated by Magda Bácsi, a Hungarian violinist whose treasures date across five millennia. The museum's stunning central hall of white marble was supposedly modelled on the Alhambra in Spain.

★ **Kerepesi Cemetery** CEMETERY
(Kerepesi temető; Map p92; ☑ 06 30 331 8822; www.nemzetisirkert.hu; VIII Fiumei út 16; ⊗ 7am-8pm May-Jul, to 7pm Apr & Aug, to 6pm Sep, to 5pm Mar & Oct, 7.30am-5pm Nov-Feb; Ⓜ M2/4 Keleti train station, ⬛ 24) **FREE** Budapest's equivalent of London's Highgate or Père Lachaise in Paris, this 56-hectare necropolis was established in 1847 and holds some 3000 gravestones and mausoleums, including those of statesmen and national heroes Lajos Kossuth, Ferenc Deák and Lajos Batthyány. Maps indicating the location of noteworthy graves are available free at the entrance. Plot 21 contains the graves of many who died in the 1956 Uprising.

Ervin Szabó Central Library LIBRARY
(Fővárosi Szabó Ervin Könyvtár; Map p92; ☑ 1-411 5000; www.fszek.hu; VIII Reviczky utca 1; ⊗ 10am-8pm Mon-Fri, to 4pm Sat; Ⓜ M3/4 Kálvin tér) **FREE** Southeast of the Hungarian National Museum is the main repository of Budapest's public library system, which holds 2.4 million books and bound periodicals and upwards of 250,000 audiovisual and digital items. Completed in 1889 and exquisitely renovated, the public reading room has gypsum ornaments, gold tracery and enormous chandeliers. It's worth quickly registering (with photo ID) to gain access, but you can just visit the ground-floor cafe to get a sense of the building.

Zwack Museum & Visitors' Centre MUSEUM
(Zwack Múzeum és Látogatóközpont; Map p92; ☑ 1-476 2383; www.zwack.hu; IX Dandár utca 1; adult/under 18yr 2000/1000Ft; ⊗ 10am-5pm Mon-Fri; ⬛ 2, 24) Unicum, the thick medicinal-tasting aperitif made from 40 herbs and spices, is as bitter as a loser's tears and a favourite drink in Hungary. To delve into its history, head for this small museum, which starts with a rather schmaltzy video, has an enormous collection of 17,000 miniatures from across the globe and concludes with an educated tasting session. You can buy more from the adjacent shop. A combined ticket with the Holocaust Memorial Center costs adult/concession 2800/1000Ft.

Holocaust Memorial Center JEWISH SITE
(Holokauszt Emlékközpont; Map p92; ☑ 1-455 3333; www.hdke.hu; IX Páva utca 39; adult/concession 1400/700Ft; ⊗ 10am-6pm Tue-Sun; Ⓜ M3 Corvin-negyed, ⬛ 4, 6) Housed in a striking modern building, the Holocaust Memorial Center opened in 2004, on the 60th anniversary of the start of the Holocaust in Hungary. The thematic permanent exhibition traces the rise of anti-Semitism in Hungary and follows the path to genocide of Hungary's Jewish and Roma communities. A sublimely restored synagogue in the central courtyard (1924), designed by Leopold Baumhorn, hosts temporary exhibitions, while an 8m wall nearby bears the names of Hungarian victims of the Holocaust.

The exhibits consist of a series of maps, photographs, personal effects and graphic videos. The music is festive to begin with, but the exhibits are accompanied by the sounds of a pounding heartbeat and marching as the doomed are deprived of their freedom and dignity and deported to German death camps. The films of the camps, taken by the liberators, are particularly harrowing, featuring piles of corpses and emaciated survivors.

A combined ticket with the Zwack Museum and Visitors' Centre (p90) costs adult/concession 2800/1000Ft.

National Theatre THEATRE
(Nemzeti Színház; Map p92; ☑ 1-476 6800; www.nemzetiszinhaz.hu; IX Bajor Gizi Park 1; ⬛ 2, 24, Ⓡ HÉV 7 Közvágóhíd) Hard by the Danube in southwestern Ferencváros, the National Theatre (2002) remains controversial for its architecture. Designed by Mária Siklós, it is supposedly 'Modern Eclectic', mirroring other great Budapest buildings (Parliament, Opera House). The overall effect, however, is a pick-and-mix of classical and folk motifs, porticoes, balconies and columns. Some say it looks like a typewriter. The ziggurat structure outside offers good views of the river.

Former Hungarian
Radio Headquarters ARCHITECTURE

(Magyar Rádió; Map p92; VIII Bródy Sándor utca 5-7; M M3 Kálvin tér, 47, 49) The renovated former headquarters of Hungarian Radio was where shots were first fired on 23 October 1956; a memorial plaque marks the spot.

Hungarian Natural
History Museum MUSEUM

(Magyar Természettudományi Múzeum; Map p92; 1-210 1085; www.nhmus.hu; VIII Ludovika tér 2-6; adult/child 1600/800Ft, with temporary exhibits 2200/1200Ft; 10am-6pm Wed-Mon; M M3 Klinikák) The skeleton of a finback whale greets you at this science museum, which houses a confusing raft of interactive displays over three floors. Interesting exhibits focus on the biodiversity of coral reefs and the natural resources of the Carpathian Basin, insects and minerals. Noah's Ark, part of the Variety of Life exhibit on the 3rd floor, is fun but the big plastic dinosaurs of the Lost World exhibit (adult/child 400/300Ft) in the garden are a joke. Good temporary exhibitions.

Ludwig Museum of
Contemporary Art MUSEUM

(Ludwig Kortárs Művészeti Múzeum; Map p92; 1-555 3444; www.ludwigmuseum.hu; IX Komor Marcell utca 1; adult/student & child 1600/1000Ft, with temporary exhibitions 2400/1200Ft; 10am-8pm Tue-Sun; 2, 24, HÉV 7 Közvágóhíd) Housed in the architecturally controversial Palace of Arts north of Rákóczi Bridge, the Ludwig Museum holds Hungary's most important collection of international contemporary art. Works by Hungarian, American, Russian, German and French artists span the past half-century, while works by Central and Eastern European artists largely date from the 1990s. The museum's temporary exhibitions are invariably well received.

New Municipal Cemetery CEMETERY

(Új Köztemető; 1-433 7300; X Kozma utca 8-10; 8am-5pm Aug-Apr, to 8pm May-Jul; 28, 37) **FREE** This huge 207-hectare cemetery, easily reached by tram from Blaha Lujza tér, is where Imre Nagy, prime minister during the 1956 Uprising, and 2000 others were buried in unmarked graves (plots 298–301) after executions in the late 1940s and 1950s. The area has been turned into a moving National Pantheon and is about a 30-minute walk from the entrance; follow the signs pointing the way to '298, 300, 301 parcela'.

◉ City Park & Beyond

City Park is a heavyweight when it comes to Budapest's top sights. Apart from one world-class art museum and a smaller one dedicated to contemporary art, there's also Budapest's most impressive square, not to mention the zoo and a fine 19th-century castle. By 2019 City Park's roster of attractions is due to include a biodome, a new amusement park, a new art gallery to house the Hungarian National Art collection and a revamped Transport Museum.

★ Museum of Fine Arts
See p59.

★ Heroes' Square SQUARE

(Hősök tere; Map p96; 105, M M1 Hősök tere) Heroes' Sq is the largest and most symbolic square in Budapest, and contains the Millenary Monument (Ezeréves emlékmű), a 36m-high pillar topped by a golden Archangel Gabriel. Legend has it that he offered Stephen the crown of Hungary in a dream. At the column's base are Prince Árpád and other chieftains. The colonnades behind the pillar feature various illustrious leaders of Hungary. It was designed in 1896 to mark the 1000th anniversary of the Magyar conquest of the Carpathian Basin.

★ Palace of Art MUSEUM

(Műcsarnok; Map p96; www.mucsarnok.hu; XIV Dózsa György út 37; adult/concession 1800/900Ft; 10am-6pm Tue, Wed & Fri-Sun, noon-8pm Thu; 20, 30, M M1 Hősök tere) The Palace of Art, reminiscent of a Greek temple, is among the city's largest exhibition spaces. It focuses on contemporary visual arts, with some three to four major exhibitions staged annually; recent exhibitions comprised cutting-edge photography, sculpture and installations by home-grown and international artists. Go for the scrumptious venue and the excellent museum shop. Concerts are sometimes staged here as well.

City Park PARK

(Városliget; Map p96; 20E, 30, M M1 Hősök tere, Széchenyi fürdő) City Park is Pest's green lung, an open space measuring almost a square kilometre that hosted most of the events during Hungary's 1000th anniversary celebrations in 1896. In general, museums lie to the south of XIV Kós Károly sétány, while activities of a less cerebral nature, including the

BUDAPEST SIGHTS

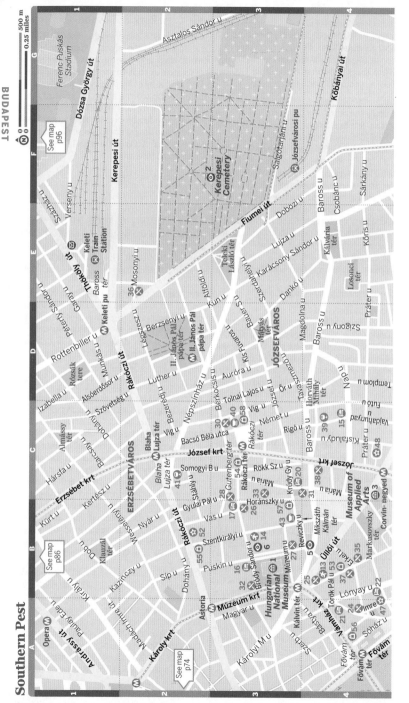

Southern Pest

See map p96

See map p86

See map p74

Opera

Andrássy út

Károly krt

Erzsébet krt

ERZSÉBETVÁROS

Rákóczi út

Blaha Lujza tér

József krt

JÓZSEFVÁROS

Keleti Train Station

Keleti pu

Rákóczi út

Kerepesi út

Fiumei út

Kőbányai út

Kerepesi Cemetery

Ferenc Puskás Stadium

Dózsa György út

Astoria

Hungarian National Museum

Múzeum krt

Kálvin tér

Vámház krt

Museum of Applied Arts

Corvin-negyed

Fővám tér

Üllői út

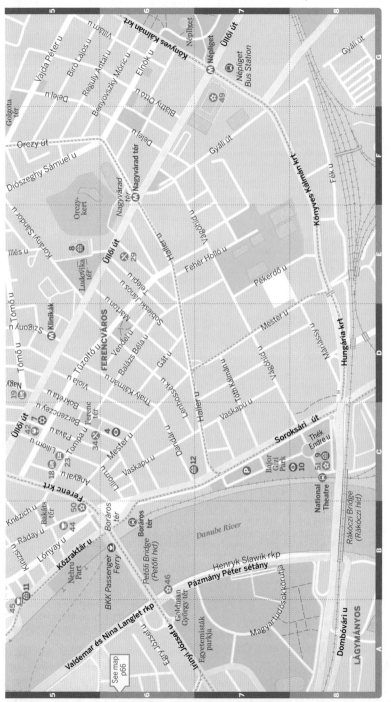

Southern Pest

Municipal Great Circus and the Széchenyi Baths (p99), are to the north. At the time of writing, there was much public protest over unpopular government plans to cut down trees and build controversial new venues.

Budapest Zoo   ZOO
(Budapesti Állatkert; Map p96; ☑1-273 4900; www.zoobudapest.com; XIV Állatkerti körút 6-12; adult/2-14yr/family 2500/1800/7300Ft; ☺9am-6pm Mon-Thu, to 7pm Fri-Sun; ⏸; ⏸trolleybus 72, Ⓜ︎M1 Széchenyi fürdő) This zoo, which opened with 500 animals in 1866, has an excellent collection of big cats, hippopotamuses, bears and giraffes, and some of the themed houses

(eg Madagascar, wetlands, nocturnal Australia) are well-executed, though water in ponds could be less stagnant. Have a look at the Secessionist animal houses built in the early part of the 20th century, such as the **Elephant House** with Zsolnay ceramics, and the **Palm House** with an aquarium erected by the Eiffel Company of Paris.

The Varázshegy (Magic Mountain) is an interactive exhibition inside the Great Rock, covering the earth's evolution and diversity through 3D film, live animal demonstrations, games and all manner of simple and fun educational tools.

Hungarian Agricultural Museum MUSEUM
(Magyar Mezőgazdasági Múzeum; Map p96; ☑1-422 0765; www.mezogazdasagimuzeum.hu; Vajdahunyad Castle, XIV Vajdahunyadvár; adult/concession 1200/600Ft, combo ticket with Apostles' Tower 1700/1100Ft; ☉10am-5pm Tue-Sun Apr-Oct, to 4pm Tue-Fri, to 5pm Sat & Sun Nov-Mar; Ⓜ︎M1 Hősök tere) This rather esoteric island museum is housed in the stunning baroque wing of Vajdahunyad Castle (Map p96; Ⓜ︎M1 Széchenyi fürdő). Scattered across several grand halls, the museum showcases Europe's largest collection of things agricultural, from centuries-old butter churns to livestock breeding in the 15th century, and Hungary's prodigious grain yields in the 19th century. Farming, hunting and fishing equipment abound. Don't miss the 275-year-old dugout carved from a single tree trunk.

Apostles' Tower TOWER
(Apostolok Tornya; Map p96; www.mezogazdasagimuzeum.hu; Vajdahunyadvár; 600Ft; ☉10am-5pm Tue-Sun; Ⓜ︎M1 Széchenyi fürdő) Accessed via the Hungarian Agricultural Museum, the Apostles' Tower stands 30m tall and looks down on the beautiful Jak Chapel below, as well as giving you a bird's-eye view of the Széchenyi Baths. The 150 steps to the viewing platform take you past frescoes depicting hunting scenes. Entry is by hourly guided tour only, though the 'tour' consists of the guide accompanying you and not saying anything unless prompted.

Ják Chapel CHURCH
(Jáki kápolna; Map p96; ☑1-251 1359; XIV Vajdahunyadvár; 100Ft; ☉10am-1pm & 4-6pm Mon, Wed & Fri; Ⓜ︎M1 Hősök tere) The little church with the jungly, overgrown cloister opposite Vajdahunyad Castle is called Ják Chapel because its intricate, many-layered portal was copied from the 13th-century Abbey Church in Ják in western Hungary. The interior is far less impressive.

Miksa Róth Memorial House MUSEUM
(Róth Miksa Emlékház; Map p96; ☑1-341 6789; ww.facebook.com/rothmiksaemlekhaz; VII Nefelejcs utca 26; adult/child 750/375Ft; ☉2-6pm Tue-Sun; Ⓜ︎M2/4 Keleti pályaudvar) This fabulous museum exhibits the work of the eponymous art nouveau stained-glass maker Róth (1865–1944) over two floors of the house and workshop where he lived and worked from 1911 until his death. Róth's dark-brown living quarters stand in sharp contrast to the lively, Technicolor creations that emerged from his workshop. His stunning mosaics are less well known than his stained glass.

Postal Museum MUSEUM
(Postamúzeum; Map p96; ☑1-269 6838; www.postamuzeum.hu; VI Benczúr utca 27, Benczúr Ház; adult/student 500/250Ft; ☉10am-6pm Tue-Sun; Ⓜ︎M1 Bajza utca) The exhibits at the Postal Museum – original 19th-century post-office counters, old uniforms and coaches, some big brass horns – probably won't do much for you. But the museum is housed in Egyed Palace (now Benczúr House), built at the end of the 19th century and beautifully preserved. Even the communal staircase and hallway are richly decorated with fantastic murals.

Ferenc Hopp Museum of East Asian Art MUSEUM
(Hopp Ferenc Kelet-Ázsiai Művészeti Múzeum; Map p96; ☑1-322 8476; http://hoppmuseum.hu; VI Andrássy út 103; adult/child 1000/500Ft; ☉10am-6pm Tue-Sun; Ⓜ︎M1 Bajza utca) The Ferenc Hopp Museum of East Asian Art is housed in the former villa of its benefactor and namesake. Founded in 1919, the museum shows cracking temporary exhibitions from its collection of Chinese and Japanese ceramics, porcelain, textiles and sculpture, Indonesian wayang puppets and Indian statuary as well as lamaist sculpture and scroll paintings from Tibet.

🏃 Activities

Budapest is a city with plenty of outdoor pursuits. Apart from its many thermal baths for soaking there are plenty of swimming complexes, and cycling is a terrific way to explore parts of the city. If you're looking for something more specialised, the Buda Hills are honeycombed with caves, three of which are open to visitors and one of which involves serious caving. Kayaking and canoeing on the Danube is perhaps of less interest to the casual visitor, but if that's your passion, then kayaks and canoes are available to rent.

Canoeing & Kayaking

The best place for canoeing and kayaking in Budapest is on the Danube from the Buda side at Rómaifürdő. To get there, take the HÉV suburban line to the Rómaifürdő stop and walk east towards the river. Rent kayaks or canoes from the rowing clubs about 5km north of the Árpád Bridge.

City Park & Beyond

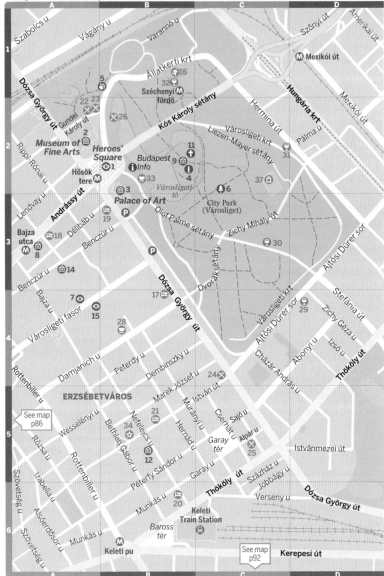

Caving

If you like to get down and dirty, head for the hills and visit one of Buda's underground caverns: Mátyáshegy Cave, Pálvölgy Cave or Szemlőhegy Cave (p73).

Cycling

Cycling has become popular in the city, with an ever-growing network of designated cycle lanes and numerous places to rent bicycles. The most cycle-friendly parts of town are City

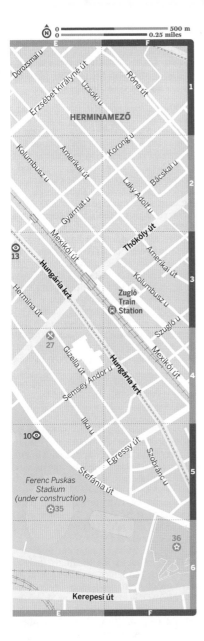

City Park & Beyond

Park and Margaret Island, while the trails in Buda Hills tend to be for mountain bikers.

Escape Rooms

Budapest is the undisputed European capital of live escape (or exit) games, in which teams of between two and six people willingly lock themselves in a set of rooms to spend 60 minutes working through numerous riddles that will eventually unlock the door back to freedom.

Like the city's ruin pubs, the games are often set in empty and disused apartment blocks, especially their dank and atmospheric basements. Each game has a distinct theme and story – from ancient Egypt and medieval to Cold War and sci-fi – and involves not only the solving of puzzles but, crucially, the ability to identify the puzzles in the first place.

Inspired by escape-the-room video games, the game is claimed by some to be unique to the city, although a similar idea was developed in Japan in 2007. Mentally challenging (teams frequently get 'locked in'), the games are incredibly addictive and popular with tourists and locals alike; Budapest now counts over 100 of them.

Parapark
ESCAPE GAME

(Map p92; ☑ 06 20 626 2471; http://parapark.hu; VIII Vajdahunyad utca 4; per team of 2/6 7000/10,000Ft; ⊙ 1-11pm; ▣ 4, 6) The city's very first escape game, with three different themes, is set in the basement of the Bujdosó Kert (p148) ruin pub. Teams of two to six players can test their puzzling skills on scenarios that will have you riding an elevator, summoning spirits or picking through a crime scene to riddle your way free.

Mystique Room
ESCAPE GAME

(Map p78; ☑ 06 30 799 5679; www.mystiqueroom. hu; Szent István körút 9; per team of 2/3/4 11,990/14,970/19,960Ft; ⊙ 9am-10.30pm; ▣ 4, 6) Very high-end exit games with four rooms themed around feudal Japan, the construction of a massive cathedral, the inevitable Egyptian tomb and a virtual-reality game involving weightlessness called Cosmos.

Claustrophilia
ESCAPE GAME

(Map p86; http://claustrophilia.hu; VII Erzsébet körút 8; per team of 2/4/5 8000/10,000/12,000Ft; ⊙ 10am-10pm; Ⓜ M2 Blaha Lujza tér, ▣ 4, 6) A skillfully choreographed escape game that begins the moment you step through the entrance of this intricate set of puzzle rooms. Search through the treasures from Lord Wicklewood's travels to reveal the riddles required to unlock the final door. A second location offers the chance to save a voodoo priestess, and the world, from an evil sorcerer.

MindQuest
ESCAPE GAME

(Map p86; ☑ 06 20 354 8778; http://mindquest.hu; VII Klauzál utca 19; per team of 2-3/5 6000/10,000Ft; ⊙ 1pm-midnight; Ⓜ M2 Blaha Lujza tér, ▣ 4, 6) Set above the ruin pub Füge

Udvar (p144), MindQuest offers four escape rooms: there's a Cold War bomb to diffuse, a diamond to steal, a matrix to outwit and a South American god-beast called Noo'zaca to destroy. Drop-ins are possible, although it's usually fully booked at the weekend.

Hiking

Buda Hills
HIKING

(Map p72) With 'peaks' rising up to 500m, a comprehensive system of trails and no lack of unusual conveyances to get you around, the Buda Hills are the city's playground and a welcome respite from Pest's heat in summer. If you're planning to do some serious hiking here, get Cartographia's 1:25,000 *A Budai-hegység* map (No 6). It's a popular destination for Budapest's mountain bikers too.

With all the unusual transport options, getting to/from the hills is half the fun. From Széll Kálmán tér metro station on the M2 line in Buda, walk westward along Szilágyi Erzsébet fasor for 10 minutes (or take tram 59 or 61 for two stops) to the circular Hotel Budapest at II Szilágyi Erzsébet fasor 47. Directly opposite is the terminus of the Cog Railway (Fogaskerekű vasút; www.bkv.hu; XII Szilágyi Erzsébet fasor 14-16; admission 1 BKV ticket or 350Ft; ⊙ 5am-11pm). Built in 1874, the Cog climbs for 3.7km in 14 minutes twice to four times an hour to Széchenyi-hegy (427m), one of the prettiest residential areas in Buda.

At Széchenyi-hegy you can stop for a picnic in the attractive park south of the old-time station or board the narrow-gauge Children's Railway, two minutes to the south on Hegyhát út. The railway was built in 1951 by Pioneers (socialist Scouts) and is now staffed entirely by schoolchildren aged 10 to 14 (except for the engineer). The little train chugs along for 11km, through eight stops, terminating at Hűvösvölgy. Departure times vary widely, depending on the day, week and season; consult the website.

There are walks fanning out from any of the stops along the Children's Railway line, or you can return to Széll Kálmán tér on tram 61 from Hűvösvölgy. Much more fun, however, is to get off at János-hegy, the fourth stop on the Children's Railway and the highest point (527m) in the hills. About 700m to the east is the chairlift (p71), which will take you down to Zugligeti út.

Thermal Baths & Swimming

For more details see Thermal Baths & Spas (p35).

★**Gellért Baths** BATHHOUSE
(Gellért gyógyfürdő; Map p66; ☑1-466 6166; www.
gellertbath.hu; XI Kelenhegyi út 4, Danubius Hotel
Gellért; with locker/cabin Mon-Fri 5100/5500Ft, Sat
& Sun 5300/5700Ft; ☺6am-8pm; ☐7, 86, Ⓜ M4
Szent Gellért tér, ⓔ18, 19, 47, 49) Soaking in the
art nouveau Gellért Baths, open to both men
and women in mixed sections (so bring a
swimsuit), has been likened to taking a bath
in a cathedral. The eight thermal pools (one
outdoors) range in temperature from 19°C
to 38°C, and the water is said to be good for
pain in the joints, arthritis and blood circulation.

★**Rudas Baths** BATHHOUSE
(Rudas Gyógyfürdő; Map p66; ☑1-356 1322; www.
rudasfurdo.hu; I Döbrentei tér 9; with cabin Mon-
Fri/Sat & Sun 3200/3500Ft, morning/night ticket
2500/4600Ft; ☺men 6am-8pm Mon & Wed-Fri,
women 6am-8pm Tue, mixed 10pm-4am Fri, 6am-
8pm & 10pm-4am Sat, 6am-8pm Sun; ☐7, 86,
ⓔ18, 19) Built in 1566, these renovated baths
are the most Turkish in Budapest, with an
octagonal pool, domed cupola with coloured
glass and massive columns. It's a real zoo on
mixed weekend nights, when bathing costumes (rental 1300Ft) are compulsory. You
can enter the lovely swimming pool (Map
p66; ☑1-356 1322; www.rudasfurdo.hu; with locker
Mon-Fri/Sat & Sun 2900/3200Ft, with thermal bath
3800/4200Ft; ☺6am-8pm daily, plus 10pm-4am
Fri & Sat; ☐7, 86, ⓔ18, 19) separately if you're
more interested in swimming than soaking.

★**Veli Bej Baths** BATHHOUSE
(Veli Bej Fürdője; Map p70; ☑1-438 8500; www.
irgalmas.hu/veli-bej-furdo; II Árpád fejedelem útja
7 & Frankel Leó út 54; 6am-noon 2240Ft, 3-7pm
2800Ft, after 7pm 2000Ft; ☺6am-noon & 3-9pm;
☐9, 109, ⓔ4, 6, 17, 19) One of the oldest (1575)
and most beautiful Ottoman-era baths in
Budapest, with five thermal pools of varying
temperatures – the central pool lies under
a beautiful cupola. The water is high in so-
dium, potassium and calcium and good for
joint ailments, chronic arthritis and calcium
deficiency. There's also a cluster of saunas
and steam rooms; massage available.

★**Széchenyi Baths** BATHHOUSE
(Széchenyi Gyógyfürdő; Map p96; ☑1-363 3210;
www.szechenyibath.hu; XIV Állatkerti körút 9-11; tickets incl locker/cabin Mon-Fri 4700/5200Ft, Sat & Sun
4900/5400Ft; ☺6am-10pm; Ⓜ M1 Széchenyi fürdő)
These thermal baths are particularly popular

with visitors and have helpful, English-speaking attendants. Its mix of indoor and outdoor
pools includes 12 thermal pools (water temperatures up to 40°C), a swimming pool and
an activity pool with whirlpool. The baths
are open year-round, and it's quite a sight
to watch men and women playing chess on
floating boards when it's snowing.

Király Baths BATHHOUSE
(Király Gyógyfürdő; Map p62; ☑1-202 3688; www.
kiralyfurdo.hu; II Fő utca 84; daily tickets incl locker/
cabin 2400/2700Ft; ☺9am-9pm; ☐109, ⓔ4, 6,
19, 41) The four pools for soaking here, with
water temperatures of between 26°C and
40°C, are genuine Turkish baths erected
in 1570. The largest has a wonderful skylit
central dome (though the place is begging
for a renovation); the other three are small.
There's also a steam room and sauna. The
Király is open to both men and women daily.

Lukács Baths BATHHOUSE
(Lukács Gyógyfürdő; Map p70; ☑1-326 1695;
www.spasbudapest.com; II Frankel Leó út 25-29;
with locker/cabin Mon-Fri 3300/3700Ft, Sat & Sun
3400/3800Ft; ☺6am-9pm; ☐9, 109, ⓔ4, 6, 17, 19)
Housed in a sprawling 19th-century complex
popular with medical patients, these baths
consist of thermal pools (temperatures 24°C
to 40°C) and three swimming pools, including an unheated one. The baths are always
mixed and a bathing suit is required. Could
be cleaner.

Danubius Health Spa Margitsziget SPA
(Map p84; ☑1-889 4737; www.danubiushotels.com;
Mon-Fri 5300Ft, Sat & Sun 6400Ft; ☺6.30am-9pm;
ⓔ26) Among the most modern (but least atmospheric) of all Budapest bathhouses, this
thermal spa is in the Danubius Grand Hotel Margitsziget (p111). The baths are open
to men and women in separate sections
weekdays and mixed at the weekend. A daily
ticket includes entry to the swimming pools,
sauna and steam room, as well as use of the
fitness machines.

★**Palatinus Strand** SWIMMING
(Map p84; ☑1-340 4505; www.palatinusstrand.hu;
XIII Margit-sziget; adult/child Mon-Fri 2800/2100Ft,
Sat & Sun 3200/2300Ft; ☺9am-7pm May-Sep;
ⓔ26) The largest and best series of outdoor
pools in the capital, the 'Palatinus Beach'
complex has upward of a dozen pools (two
with thermal water), wave machines, water
slides and kids' pools.

Dagály Swimming Complex SWIMMING
(Map p84; ☑ 1-452 4500; www.dagalyfurdo.hu; XIII Népfürdő utca 36; adult Mon-Fri 2000Ft, Sat & Sun 2400Ft, concession 1700Ft; ☺ outdoor pools 6am-7pm May-Sep, indoor pools 6am-8pm; Ⓜ M3 Árpád híd, ☒ 1) This huge postwar complex has a total of 10 pools, including two thermal ones (open year-round), a whirlpool and a children's pool. Spa services include massage and solarium. Could be cleaner.

Aquaworld AMUSEMENT PARK
(☑ 1-231 3760; www.aqua-world.hu; Íves út 16; 2hr/day adult 2990/5890Ft, 3-14yr 1490/2990Ft, student & senior 2390/4690Ft; ☺ 6am-10pm; ☒ 30) In northern Pest, this is one of Europe's largest water parks, with an adventure centre covered by a 72m dome, pools with whirlpools and a dozen slides, and an array of saunas to keep the whole family gainfully at play. A free shuttle bus departs from in front of the Palace of Art in Heroes' Sq (M1 Hősök tere) at 9.30am, 1.30pm, 5.30pm and 7.30pm.

🍳 Courses

Chefparade COOKING
(Map p70; ☑ 1-210 6042; www.chefparade.hu; II Bécsi út 27; ☺ 8am-6pm Mon-Thu, to 4pm Fri; ☒ 17, 19, 41) Branch of a popular cooking school for those wishing to learn to cook Hungarian dishes.

Debreceni Nyári Egyetem LANGUAGE
(Map p74; ☑ 1-320 5751; www.nyariegyetem.hu/bp; V Váci utca 63, 2nd fl; Ⓜ M2 Kossuth Lajos tér) The Budapest branch of the most prestigious Hungarian-language school in the land offers intensive courses lasting three weeks (60 hours) for 95,000Ft and regular evening classes of 60/84 hours for 72,000/95,500Ft.

👉 Tours

If you can't be bothered making your own way around Budapest or don't have the time, a guided tour can be a great way to learn the lie of the land.

Boat Tours

River Ride BOATING
(Map p78; ☑ 1-332 2555; www.riverride.com; V Széchenyi István tér 7-8; adult/child 8500/6000Ft; ☒ 2) This strange and hugely entertaining 1½-hour tour in a bright-yellow amphibious bus takes you overland and then into the Danube. Three to four departures daily year-round; check the website for the timetable with live commentary in English and Ger-

man (recorded in seven other languages). Departure is from Széchenyi István tér 7-8.

Legenda BOATING
(Map p74; ☑ 1-266 4190; www.legenda.hu; V Vigadó tér, pier 7; adult/student/child day 3900/3500/2400Ft, night 5500/4400/2750Ft; ☒ 2) This long-established operator has both day and night cruises on the Danube, with taped commentary in 30 languages. The night lights of the city rising to Buda Castle, Parliament, Gellért Hill and the Citadella make the evening trip far more attractive than the afternoon one. Check Legenda's website for the exact schedule.

Silverline Cruises CRUISE
(Map p74; ☑ 06 20 332 5364; www.silver-line.hu; Jane Haining rakpart, Pier 11; per person €52) Highly recommended three-hour dinner cruises aboard a luxurious catamaran, complete with folkloric dancers and operetta songs; 7pm departures April to October. Silverline also run trips to Szentendre from May to September, departing at 9am and 12.40pm.

Bus Tours

Program Centrum BUS
(Map p74; ☑ 1-317 7767; www.programcentrum.hu; V Erzsébet tér 9-11, Le Meridien Hotel; adult/0-8yr €22/free; Ⓜ M1/2/3 Deák Ferenc tér, ☒ 47, 49) This company runs sightseeing tours. Tickets valid for two bus routes (one taped in 25 languages, one with live commentary in English and German), a one-hour river cruise and a walking tour for 48 hours.

Cityrama Gray Line BUS
(Map p78; ☑ 1-302 4382; www.cityrama.hu; V Báthory utca 22; adult/concession 8500/4250Ft; ☒ 15, 115, Ⓜ M3 Arany János utca) If you prefer to stay on the bus without getting off and on, this operator offers three-hour city tours with several photo stops and live commentary in five languages.

Tuk Tuk Taxi TOURS
(Map p74; ☑ 06 20 465 5600; www.tuktuktaxi.hu; V Fehér Hajó utca 8-10; 2 people €50; Ⓜ M1/2/3 Deák Ferenc tér) Popular two-hour tours that take place in Hungary's only tuk-tuk taxi. From your open-air vantage point you get to see Castle Hill, Heroes' Square, Gellért Hill, Parliament and other popular sites.

Cycling Tours

Most bike-hire companies offer tours for around 5000Ft to 5500Ft per person, but itineraries often depend on the whim of the group leader. See p160.

Walking Tours

Free Budapest Tours
WALKING

(Map p74; ☑ 06 70 424 0569; www.freebudapest-tours.eu; V Deák Ferenc tér; ◷ 10.30am & 2.30pm) **FREE** Innovative walking tours organised by an outfit whose name is as descriptive as it is, er, pedestrian; the guides work for tips only, so dig deep. The 2½-hour tour of Pest leaves from V Deák Ferenc tér daily at 10.30am and the 2½-hour tour of Buda departs from the front of Gerbeaud (p139), in V Vörösmarty tér, daily at 2.30pm.

Absolute Walking Tours
WALKING

(Map p78; ☑ 1-269 3843; www.absolutetours.com; VI Lázár utca 16, Absolute Tours Centre; adult/student/child €34/32/17; ◷ 10am year-round, plus 2.30pm Mon, Wed, Fri & Sat Apr-Oct; Ⓜ M1 Opera) A 3½-hour guided walk through City Park, central Pest and Castle Hill run by the people behind Yellow Zebra Bikes. Tours depart daily from the Absolute Tours Centre behind the Opera House.

They also offer several specialist tours, including the popular 3½-hour Hammer & Sickle Tour (adult/student/child €54/50/27) of Budapest's communist past.

Special Interest Tours

Tasting Table
WINE

(Map p92; ☑ 06 30 551 9932; www.tastingtablebu-dapest.com; VIII Bródy Sándor utca 9; ◷ noon-8pm; Ⓜ M3 Kálvin tér, ☐ 47, 49) Should you be looking for a painless crash course in Hungarian wine, this attractive cellar with two tasting rooms is the place to come. Order a flight of three wines (in 100mL glasses) for 3900Ft or a five-wine flight with a sumptuous cheese and charcuterie plate for 9900Ft. A knowledgable sommelier will walk you through and explain all.

There is special wine course available, and every other Thursday they host a themed three-course, six-wine dinner (9900Ft) with a special guest. The shop on site has the largest collection of Tokaj wines available in Budapest. Also ask them about their themed walks, including a four-hour culinary tour of Budapest (€85 per person).

Jewish Heritage Tours
CULTURAL

(Map p74; ☑ 1-317 1377; www.ticket.info.hu; Deák Ferenc tér; Ⓜ M1/2/3 Deák Ferenc tér, ☐ 47, 49) Recommended tours delve into the culture and history of Budapest's Jewish community. The Essential Tour (adult/student 6900/6500Ft, 2½ hours) takes in the two most important synagogues, as well as the

streets of the Jewish Quarter, while the Grand Tour (adult/student 11,400/10,400Ft, 3½ to 4 hours) includes all the stops of the Essential Tour, as well as the Memorial Park, the Godzsu Passage and a third synagogue.

Budapest Underguide
CULTURAL

(Map p78; ☑ 06 30 908 1597; www.underguide.com; Sas utca 15; per person from 9250Ft; Ⓜ M1 Bajcsy-Zsilinszky út) This outfit gets rave reviews from visitors for its themed private four-hour tours. Themes include fashion and design, art nouveau, communism, Budapest's best bars, contemporary art and Buda Castle for kids.

Hungária Koncert
CULTURAL

(☑ 1-317 1377; www.ticket.info.hu) Concerts, Jewish heritage tours, Segway tours, Danube cruises and sightseeing by helicopter can be arranged here.

✳ Festivals & Events

January

New Year's Gala Concert
MUSIC

(www.hungariakoncert.hu; ◷ 1 Jan) This is an annual event usually held in the Pest Vigadó to herald the new year.

February

Budapest Dance Festival
DANCE

This annual 10-day festival (www.budapest-tancfesztival.hu), held in five different venues across town from late February, features an array of styles from ballet and contemporary to folk.

March

VinCE Budapest
WINE

The primary focus of this three-day event (http://vincebudapest.hu/en), usually held at the Corinthia Hotel Budapest, is wine (vin) in Central Europe (CE), with over 100 wineries from Hungary and neighbouring countries offering master classes, workshops and, of course, lots of tastings.

April

Budapest Spring Festival
PERFORMING ARTS

(www.springfestival.hu; ◷ mid-Apr) The capital's largest and most important cultural festival, with 200 events, takes place over two weeks in mid-April at 60 venues across the city.

National Dance
House Festival
PERFORMING ARTS

(www.tanchaztalalkozo.hu/eng; ◷ late Apr) Hungary's biggest táncház (evening of folk music and dance), with performances by folk artists and dance bands, plus traditional crafts, held over two days in late April at the Buda Concert Hall and other venues.

May

Jewish Art Days ART
(http://zsidomuveszetinapok.hu; ⊘ late May–mid-Jun) New festival that celebrates the best of Jewish culture, from gastronomy to music, theatre and film, with events taking place in a variety of venues, including the Franz Liszt Academy of Music, Millenáris Theater, Urania National Film Theater, Átrium Movie Theater, A38 Ship and BMC.

June

Danube Carnival
International Multicultural
Festival Budapest PERFORMING ARTS
(http://dunakarneval.hu/en/; ⊘ Jun) Pan-Hungarian international 10-day carnival of folk dance, world music and modern dance, held from mid-June in Vörösmarty tér and on Margaret Island.

Craft Beer Festival BEER
(Főzdefeszt; http://visitbudapest.travel/budapest-events/craft-beer-festival/; ⊘ mid-Jun) Held in City Park on a weekend in mid-June, the craft-beer festival brings together 60 Hungarian microbreweries that showcase their wares alongside guest breweries from Germany and the Czech Republic.

Budapest Pride PARADE
(www.budapestpride.com; ⊘ late Jun) Budapest's exuberant, weeklong gay festival is at the end of June, with numerous events and a parade.

July

Formula 1 Hungarian Grand Prix SPORTS
(www.hungaroring.hu; ⊘ late Jul) The Formula 1 Hungarian Grand Prix takes place at the Hungaroring, in late July. The qualifying warm-up is on Saturday and the race begins at 2pm on Sunday. The best seats are Super Gold that cost €360 for the weekend; cheaper are Gold (€235 to €275), Silver (€140 to €155) and standing room (€75 for the weekend, €65 for Sunday).

August

★ Sziget Festival MUSIC
(http://szigetfestival.com; ⊘ mid-Aug) One of the biggest and most popular music festivals in Europe, held in mid-August on Budapest's Hajógyár (Óbuda) Island, with some 500,000 revellers (in 2016) and a plethora of Hungarian and international bands.

Budapest Festival of Folk Arts CULTURAL
(Budapest Craft Days; http://hungarianfolk.com/hungarian-folk-festival; ⊘ mid-Aug) Check out the work of artisans from all over Hungary at Budapest's Craft Days festival, held in and around Buda Castle for three days in mid-August.

September

Jewish Cultural Festival CULTURAL
(Zsidó Kultuális Fesztivál; www.zsidokulturalisfesztival.hu/en; ⊘ Sep) Immerse yourself in Budapest's distinguished Jewish heritage during an eight-day extravaganza of culture and music.

★ Budapest International
Wine Festival WINE
(www.aborfesztival.hu; ⊘ mid-Sep) Hungary's foremost winemakers introduce their wines at this ultrapopular event in the Castle District. The tipples are accompanied by a cornucopia of edibles along the Gastro Walkway.

October

Budapest International Marathon SPORTS
(www.budapestmarathon.com; ⊘ mid-Oct) Eastern Europe's most celebrated race goes along the Danube and across its bridges.

★ CAFE Budapest PERFORMING ARTS
(Contemporary Art Festival; www.budapestbylocals.com/event/budapest-autumn-festival; ⊘ Oct) Contemporary art takes on many forms during this two-week-long festival: poetry slams, contemporary fashion design, modern theatre, a jazz marathon and the 'Night of the Contemporary Galleries', to name a few. Design Week, the Art Market Budapest and the Mini Festival of Contemporary Music in Várkert Bazaar are all part of the celebrations.

November

Wine and Cheese Festival FOOD & DRINK
(http://visitbudapest.travel/budapest-events/new-wine-and-cheese-festival/; Vajdahunyad Castle, City Park; ⊘ late Nov) New festival, with winemakers from all over Hungary introducing their tipples alongside artisanal cheeses over the last weekend in November. The 2000Ft day pass includes entry to the Agricultural Museum.

December

New Year's Gala & Ball MUSIC
(www.opera.hu; ⊘ 31 Dec) The annual calendar's most coveted ticket is this gala concert and ball, held at the Hungarian State Opera House.

WORTH A TRIP

SOUTH BUDA SIGHTS

Nagytétény Castle Museum (Nagytétényi Kastélymúzeum; ☑ 1-207 0005; www.nagytet-enyi.hu; XXII Kastélypark utca 9-11; adult/child 1500/800Ft; ☉ 10am-6pm Tue-Sun; ☑ 33 from XI Móricz Zsigmond körtér in south Buda) Housed in the huge Száraz-Rudnyánszky baroque mansion in deepest south Buda, this branch of the Museum of Applied Arts traces the development of European furniture – from Gothic (1450) to Biedermeier styles (1850) – with some 300 items on display in more than two dozen rooms over two floors. On no account miss the collection of clocks and watches dating from the 17th to 19th centuries – each piece is genuine and fully functional.

Palace of Wonders (Csodák Palotája; ☑ 06 30 210 5569, 1-814 8050; www.csopa.hu; ll Nagytétényi út 37-43, 1st fl, Campona Shopping Mall; adult/student & child 2500/1900Ft; ☉ 9am-7pm Mon-Fri, 10am-8pm Sat & Sun; ☑ 33 from XI Móricz Zsigmond körtér in south Buda) Subtitled the Centre of Scientific Wonder, this playhouse for children of all ages in a shopping mall in south Buda has 'smart' toys and puzzles, most with a scientific bent, and lots of interactive stuff, such as a playing a 'velvet harp', lying on a 'fakir' bed' and shooting an 'air cannon'. Count on spending three hours here. There's also a branch in Óbuda.

Tropicarium (☑ 1-424 3053; www.tropicarium.hu; XXII Nagytétényi út 37-45, Ground fl, Campona Shopping Mall; adult/child 2500/1800Ft; ☉ 10am-8pm; ☑ 33 from XI Móricz Zsigmond körtér in south Buda) The vast aquarium complex Tropicarium is apparently the largest in Central Europe. The place prides itself on its local specimens – though there's an 11m-long 'shark zoo' (cápás állatkert) containing all manner of beasties. Feeding time is between 3pm and 4pm Thursdays.

🛏 Sleeping

Accommodation in Budapest runs the gamut from hostels in converted flats and private rooms in far-flung housing estates to luxury guesthouses in the Buda Hills and five-star properties charging upwards of €350 a night. In general, accommodation is more limited in the Buda neighbourhoods than on the other side of the Danube River in Pest.

🛌 Castle District

Bed & Beers Inn GUESTHOUSE $
(Map p62; ☑ 06 30 964 9155; www.bedandbeers.hu; Gellérthegy utca 1; r from €39, apt €190; ☎; ☑ 56, 56A) The name says it all: we're talking about lodgings above a cellar bar. It's a colourful three-bedroom apartment with a compact double and two larger rooms with bunk beds and convertible sofas; rooms can be rented separately. The beer in question is cheap, as is the bar food, available until the wee hours. Great for groups. Helpful owner.

BiBi Panzió PENSION $$
(Map p62; ☑ 1-786 0955; www.bibipanzio.hu; ll Dékán utca 3; r/tr from €65/67; P ✳ ☎; Ⓜ M2 Széll Kálmán tér) Just a block off the northern side of Széll Kálmán tér, this pension under new management may look ordinary from the outside, but it has 10 comfortable, though small, rooms. Decor is the basic 'just off the assembly line' look. We love the wall map with pins indicating where all the guests hail from.

Charles Hotel APARTMENT $$
(Map p66; ☑ 1-212 9169; www.charleshotel.hu; l Hegyalja út 23; studio €45-80, apt €75-155; P ☎; ☑ 8, 112, 178) On the Buda side and somewhat on the beaten track (a train line runs right past it), the Charles has 70 'studios' (larger-than-average rooms) with kitchens, as well as good-sized two-room apartments. Rental bikes cost 2000Ft a day.

★**Pest-Buda Bistro & Hotel** BOUTIQUE HOTEL $$$
(Map p62; ☑ 1-225 0377; www.pest-buda.com; Fortuna utca 3; r/ste from €120/194; ☎) There's a lot to love about this fantastic, 10-room boutique hotel that has opened on the site of Hungary's oldest hotel. Each room is individually designed, with oak floors, excellent bedding and quirky touches: red fridges, designer lamps, contemporary pieces by Hungarian graphic artists. We love the free-standing tubs in the atelier suites. The restaurant and service are terrific.

★ **Baltazár**   BOUTIQUE HOTEL **$$$**

(Map p62; ☑ 1-300 7051; http://baltazarbudapest.
com/; I Országház utca 31; r/ste from €135/214;
✿ 🛇; ⬚ 16, 16A, 116) This family-run boutique
hotel at the northern end of the Castle Dis-
trict has 11 individually decorated rooms
decked out with vintage furniture and strik-
ing wallpaper. Nods to more recent times
include street art on the walls and a rain
shower in the bathrooms. One of the rooms
has a lovely little balcony with views to the
castle. Excellent value.

★ **Lánchíd 19**   BOUTIQUE HOTEL **$$$**

(Map p62; ☑ 1-419 1900; www.lanchid19hotel.hu; I
Lánchíd utca 19; r €110-325; ✿ 🛇; ⬚ 19, 41) This
award-winning boutique number facing the
Danube has the wow factor. Each of the 45
rooms and three 'panoramic' suites is different, with distinctive artwork and unique
chairs designed by art-college students. You
can't lose with the views from the floor-to-
ceiling windows: to the front is the Danube
and to the back Buda Castle; 5th floor and
above is best.

St George Residence   BOUTIQUE HOTEL **$$$**

(Map p62; ☑ 1-393 5700; www.stgeorgehotel.hu; I
Fortuna utca 4; ste from €129; 🛇; ⬚ 16, 16A, 116)
Housed in a venerable 700-year old building
right in the heart of the Castle District, this
somewhat over-the-top boutique hotel is all
period grandeur, its four classes of suites
featuring such touches as green marble in
the decor, imported Italian furniture and ja-
cuzzis (which are a welcome anachronism).

Hilton Budapest   HOTEL **$$$**

(Map p62; ☑ 1-889 6600; www.budapest.hilton.
com; I Hess András tér 1-3; r/ste from €210/260;
P ✿ 🛇; ⬚ 16, 16A, 116) Perched above the
Danube on Castle Hill, the Hilton was carefully built in and around a 14th-century
church and baroque college. Its rooms are
somewhat sombre, but you can't beat the
ambience in the Danube River–view rooms,
and we particularly like the split-level Baroque suite with wrought-iron railings.
Creature comforts include quality bedding,
hypoallergenic pillows and rain showers.

Hotel Victoria   HOTEL **$$$**

(Map p62; ☑ 1-457 8080; www.victoria.hu; I Bem
rakpart 11; r from €124; P ✿ 🛇; ⬚ 19, 41) This
rather elegant hotel has 27 comfortable and
spacious rooms with million-dollar views
of parliament and the Danube. Despite
its small size it gets special mention for its
friendly service and contemporary facilities,

including plasma-screen TVs in all rooms.
Attached to the hotel is the 19th-century
Jenő Hubay Music Hall (Map p62; ☑ 1-457
8080; www.hubaymusichall.com), which serves
as a small concert venue and theatre.

Art'otel Budapest   HOTEL **$$$**

(Map p62; ☑ 1-487 9487; www.artotels.com/buda-
pest☐; I Bem rakpart 16-19; r/ste from €109/169;
P ✿ 🛇; ⬚ 19, 41) The Art'otel is a minimalist establishment that would not look out
of place in London or New York. But what
makes this 165-room place unique is that
it cobbles together a seven-storey modern
building and an 18th-century baroque building, linking them with a leafy courtyard-
atrium. We love the gaming theme throughout. Rooms with Danube views cost extra.

Burg Hotel   HOTEL **$$$**

(Map p62; ☑ 1-212 0269; www.burghotelbuda-
pest.com; I Szentháromság tér 7-8; s/d/ste from
€105/115/134; P ✿ 🛇; ⬚ 16, 16A, 116) This
small hotel with all the mod cons has 26
spacious rooms with floral bedspreads, com-
fortable beds and not much else. But, as they
say, location is everything – it's just opposite
Matthias Church. Very helpful staff.

🛏 Gellért Hill & Tabán

★ **Shantee House**   HOSTEL **$**

(Map p66; ☑ 1-385 8946; www.backpackbudapest.
hu; XI Takács Menyhért utca 33; beds in yurt €10-
13, dm small/large from €12/16, d €38-52; P @ 🛇;
⬚ 7, 7A, 🚋 19, 49) Budapest's first hostel (orig-
inally known as the Back-Pack Guesthouse),
the Shantee has added two floors to its col-
ourfully painted suburban 'villa' in south
Buda. It's all good and the fun (and sleeping
bodies in high season) spills out into a lovely
landscaped garden, with hammocks, a yurt
and a gazebo. Two of the five doubles are en
suite.

The upbeat attitude of friendly,
much-travelled owner-manager Attila and
his staff seems to permeate the place, and
the welcome is always warm. Ask about ex-
cursions to the Pilis Mountains and other
activities. Vegan breakfasts are 1500Ft; bikes
rent for 3000Ft a day.

Art Hostel Gallery   HOSTEL **$**

(Map p66; ☑ 06 30 911 2986; http://arthostelgal-
lery.hu; Döbrentei út 2-4; d 6000Ft; @ 🛇; ⬚ 5, 178,
🚋 18, 19, 41) Basic dormitory accommodation
(rickety metal bunk beds) in three spotless-
ly clean, colourful and bright rooms by the
river, with a small but complete kitchen. An

easy walk to the Castle Garden Bazaar and the Castle District.

05

Kisgellért Vendégház GUESTHOUSE $

(Map p66; ☑06 30 933 2236, 1-279 0346; www.kisgellert.hu; XI Otthon utca 14; s/d/tr 7000/9000/12,500Ft; P🖥; 🖥8, 112, 🖪61) This cute little guesthouse with 11 rooms is named after the 'Little Gellért' hill to the west of the more famous larger one and sits dreamily on 'At Home St'. It's away from the action but leafy and quiet and easily reached by bus.

Hotel Orion Várkert HOTEL $$

(Map p66; ☑1-356 8583; www.hotelorion.hu; I Döbrentei utca 13; s €40-90, d €50-100; 🖥@; 🖥18, 19, 41) Hidden away in the Tabán district, the Orion is a cosy place with a relaxed atmosphere within easy walking distance of the Castle Garden Bazaar and the Castle District. The 30 rooms are bright and of a good size, and there's a small sauna for guests' use.

Danubius Hotel Gellért HOTEL $$$

(Map p66; ☑1-889 5500; www.danubiushotels.com/our-hotels-budapest/danubius-hotel-gellert; XI Szent Gellért tér 1; s/d/ste from €84/170/268; P🖥@🖥; Ⓜ M4 Szent Gellért tér, 🖥18, 19, 47, 49) Buda's grande dame is a 234-room four-star hotel with loads of character. Completed in 1918, the hotel contains examples of the late art nouveau, notably the thermal spa's entrance hall and Zsolnay ceramic fountains. Prices depend on which way your room faces and what sort of bathroom it has. Use of the thermal baths is free for hotel guests.

🛏 Óbuda & Buda Hills

Zen House HOSTEL $

(Map p70; ☑06 30 688 7599; www.zenhouse-budapest.com; III Repkény utca 11; r/tr €27/32; 🖥; 🖥29, 🖥17, 19, 41, 🖪Szépvölgyi út) In a quiet cluster of streets, within a stone's throw of Óbuda's limited nightlife, this peaceful, family-run hostel welcomes travellers with its clutch of spacious, stylish private rooms with shared bathroom facilities. Buddha images and plants are scattered throughout and there's a chill-out area and garden. Zen indeed.

Római Camping CAMPGROUND $

(☑1-388 7167; www.romaicamping.hu; III Szentendrei út 189; campsites for 1/2/camper vans/caravans 4720/6000/5665/7220Ft, bungalows for 2/4 people 6000/12,000Ft; ⊙year-round; P🖥; 🖪Rómaifürdő) Located in a leafy park north of the city, opposite the popular Rómaifürdő

swimming-pool complex, this is the city's largest camping ground. It gets very crowded in summer. Rómaifürdő station is almost opposite the site.

Hotel Császár HOTEL $

(Map p70; ☑1-336 2640; www.csaszarhotel.hu; II Frankel Leó út 35; s/d/q €39/49/69; 🖥🖥🖥; 🖥9, 109, 🖥17, 19, 41) The huge yellow building in which the 'Emperor' is located was built in the 1850s as a convent, which might explain the size of the 45 cell-like rooms. Request one of the superior rooms, which are larger and look on to the nearby outdoor Olympic-size pools of the huge Császár-Komjádi swimming complex (Map p70; ☑1-212 2750; http://mnsk.hu; II Árpád fejedelem útja 8; adult/concession 1800/1100Ft; ⊙6am-7pm; 🖥9, 109, 🖥17, 19, 41). For a quiet night, go for rooms 001 to 010.

★Hotel Papillon HOTEL $$

(Map p70; ☑1-212 4750; www.hotelpapillon.hu; II Rózsahegy utca 3/b; s/d/tr €44/54/69, apt €39-99; P🖥🖥🖥; 🖥4, 6) This cosy hotel in Rózsadomb (Rose Hill) has a delightful back garden with a small swimming pool, and some of the 20 rooms have balconies. There are also four apartments available in the same building, one boasting a lovely roof terrace, as well as more apartments (studio to three-bedroom) next door. The staff are on the ball and helpful.

Aquincum Hotel SPA HOTEL $$

(Map p70; ☑1-436 4100; www.aquincumhotel.com; II Árpád fejedelem útja 94; s/d/ste from €99/108/250; 🖥🖥🖥; 🖥26, 106, 🖪Árpád híd) Handy for exploring the old streets of Óbuda, this large spa hotel is big on relaxation facilities. Guests have access to two thermal pools, Finnish and infrared saunas, steam rooms and a hot tub, and the on-site restaurant serves decent Hungarian dishes. Our only quibble is that the rooms are rather dated and could use dragging into the 21st century.

Beatrix Panzió Hotel GUESTHOUSE $$

(Map p72; ☑1-275 0550; www.beatrixhotel.hu; II Széher út 3; s/d €55/60, apt €65-80; P🖥; 🖥5, 🖪61) On the way up to the Buda Hills, but still easily accessible by frequent public transport, this is an attractive, award-winning pension with 15 rooms and four apartments. Surrounding the property is a lovely pine-shaded garden with sun terraces and a grill; a barbecue might even be organised during your stay.

BUDAPEST SLEEPING

1. Szimpla Farmers' Market (p155) **2.** Nagycsarnok (p156)
3. Gouba (p156) **4.** Old military jackets at a Budapest flea market

SARAH COGHILL/LONELY PLANET ©

GONEWITHTHEWIND/SHUTTERSTOCK ©

Budapest's Markets

From grand 19th-century food halls bursting with a rainbow of fruit and veg, rows of dangling cured meats and fresh-from-the-farm jams and honey, to communist-era flea markets and cutting-edge design markets, Budapest's markets provide the perfect opportunity to see a slice of local life and bag some great souvenirs into the bargain.

Food Markets

The best place to soak up the sights, smells and sounds of a Budapest produce market is at the grandaddy of them all, Nagycsarnok (p156). This is the place to pick up some potted foie gras or paprika, or head upstairs for a whole world of Hungarian souvenirs. For something more low-key, try Rákóczi tér (p157) or the Szimpla Farmers' Market (p155), held in a ruin pub every Sunday. The newly renovated Belvárosi Piac (p124) near Parliament is a delight.

Flea Markets

Jostling with locals shopping for bargains at Ecseri Piac (p156), one of Central Europe's largest flea markets, is a fabulous way to spend a Saturday morning. Lose yourself amid a cornucopia of gramophones, rocking horses, uniforms, violins and even suits of armour. If you can't make it here, the smaller PECSA Bolhapiac (p157) offers a less impressive jumble of vintage knick-knacks.

Design Markets

A regular fair that takes place roughly once a month, WAMP, held in various locations throughout the city, showcases the latest of Hungary's hippest designers. Clothes, bags and jewellery are hung alongside artworks, prints and photos, and coffee and cakes sweeten the shopping. It's a great place to buy one-of-a-kind souvenirs you may not find in stores. More frequent Gouba (p156) offers a smaller selection of local arts and crafts.

📇 Belváros

⭐ Loft Hostel
HOSTEL $

(Map p74; 📋 1-328 0916; www.lofthostel.hu; V Veres Pálné utca 19; dm/d 5600/7000Ft; @ 🛜; 🚇 5, 7, Ⓜ M3/4 Kálvin tér) This hostel may well succeed in its loft-y aspirations to be the hottest backpacker magnet in town. Travellers end up lingering longer than expected, seduced by the wonderful atmosphere; it feels like staying at a friend's house. The homemade decorations are a nice touch and staff are super helpful.

Maverick Hostel
HOSTEL $

(Map p74; 📋 1-267 3166; www.mavericklodges. com; V Ferenciek tere 2; dm/d from €17/52; @ 🛜; Ⓜ M3 Ferenciek tere) A clean, well-run hostel with 19 rooms over three floors in a splendid old building, the Maverick has a kitchen on each floor, a comfortable common room, private doubles and four- to 10-bed dorms (no bunks). Two dorms and one double share bathrooms. It attracts a range of travellers, including families, and hosts relaxed evening events such as wine tastings.

11th Hour Cinema Hostel
HOSTEL $

(Map p74; 📋 06 70 620 4479; www.11thhourcinemahostel.com; V Magyar utca 11; dm €25-30, apt €75-100; @ 🛜; Ⓜ M2 Astoria) Its cinematic decor appealing to film fans, this excellent hostel is set in its very own three-storey town house, with en-suite dorms sleeping four to 10, as well as private apartments. Five hundred movies are available in its projection room, and there are relaxed communal areas as well as table football.

Gingko Hostel
HOSTEL $

(Map p74; 📋 1-266 6107; www.gingko.hu; V Szép utca 5; dm/d/tr €15/44/60; @ 🛜; Ⓜ M2 Astoria) In an old apartment block, this homely, hippyesque hostel has six rooms, with two doubles and seven-bed dorms, all sharing bathrooms. It has a relaxed, sociable vibe, with the feel of a big, friendly shared house, without being a crush-a-beer-can-against-your-forehead party hostel.

⭐ Bohem Art Hotel
BOUTIQUE HOTEL $$

(Map p74; 📋 1-327 9020; www.bohemarthotel.hu; V Molnár utca 35; r/ste incl breakfast from €95/118; P 🌀 🛜; Ⓜ M4 Fővám tér, M3/4 Kálvin tér, 🚇 47, 48, 49) Though the rooms at this delightful small hotel are a little on the compact side, each one is decorated in its own individual style (the suites done by local artists – we particularly like Room 302), with giant prints, bold touches of colour amid monochrome decor and ultramodern furnishings present throughout. Indulgent buffet breakfast.

⭐ Katona Apartments
APARTMENT $$

(Map p74; 📋 06 70 221 1797; www.katonaapartments.hu; V Petőfi Sándor utca 6; studios for 2/4 €54/74, 2-room apt for 2/4/6 €84/104/124; 🌀 🛜; Ⓜ M3 Ferenciek tere) Simply furnished and cleverly arranged apartments in a quiet old block, right in the heart of Belváros. Additional twin beds pull out from under each double, making these fantastic for families. Each is equipped with kitchen, TV, fan or aircon, washing machine, hairdryer and iron. The owners are exceptionally helpful and a font of knowledge on the latest city news.

Butterfly Home
HOTEL $$

(Map p74; 📋 06 30 964 7287; www.butterflyhome.hu; V Képíró utca 3; s/d/ste incl breakfast €58/75/112; 🌀 🛜; Ⓜ M3/4 Kálvin tér) In a quiet little backstreet close to Kálvin tér, this small and welcoming hotel has a large, sweeping staircase leading to spacious, plainly decorated rooms. It's professionally run, with lots of friendly advice from the cheerful owner.

Gerlóczy
BOUTIQUE HOTEL $$

(Map p74; 📋 1-501 4000; www.gerloczy.hu; V Gerlóczy utca 1; r €69-94; 🌀 🛜; Ⓜ M2 Astoria) Gerlóczy hits the mark with an excellent combination of good value, decor and atmosphere. Set over four floors of an 1890s building on an attractive square, the individually designed and well-proportioned rooms all have king-sized beds. The winding wrought-iron staircase and domed stained-glass skylight are wonderful touches. Staff run the cafe downstairs and hotel service can be lacking. Wi-fi intermittent. Of the 19 rooms, two have balconies overlooking the square and four are in the attic with exposed wooden beams.

Hotel Art
HOTEL $$

(Map p74; 📋 1-266 2166; www.threecorners.com; V Király Pál utca 12; s/d from €73/80; 🌀 🛜; Ⓜ M3/4 Kálvin tér) Part of a small Belgian chain, this orderly corner hotel has art deco touches (including a pink facade) in the public areas, a small fitness centre and sauna, and 36 clean and well-kept guestrooms, including four apartments with separate sitting and sleeping areas.

Leo Panzió
PENSION $$

(Map p74; 📋 1-266 9041; www.leopanzio.hu; V Kossuth Lajos utca 2/a; s/d/tr €69/75/86; 🌀 🛜; Ⓜ M3 Ferenciek tere) At this very centrally located place, a dozen of the 14 immaculate rooms look down on busy Kossuth Lajos utca, but they all have double glazing and are quiet. Two rooms face an internal courtyard. It's well run, well kept and traditionally furnished.

★ **Buddha Bar Hotel** BOUTIQUE HOTEL $$$
(Map p74; ☑ 1-799 7300; www.buddhabarhotel-budapest.com; V Váci utca 34; d €150-300; ✳ ☎; Ⓜ M3/4 Kálvin tér, ⌂ 2, 47, 48, 49) This glamorous five-star hotel inhabits impressive neo-baroque Klotild Palace, which retains some of its period features, such as the original staircase, but is kitted out throughout in a modern, Asian style. Choose between opulent, crimson doubles and themed suites; all come with rain showers and multimedia hubs. There's an excellent cocktail bar, a spa and an Asian restaurant (p123) downstairs.

★ **Hotel Rum** DESIGN HOTEL $$$
(Map p74; ☑ 1-424 9060; www.hotelrumbudapest. com; V Királyi Pál utca 4; s/d from €109/115; ✳ ☎; Ⓜ M3/4 Kálvin tér, ⌂ 47, 48, 49) Conceived by Budapest designers, the 38 rooms at this whimsical design hotel fall into four categories, each named after a different rum, the Black Rums being the largest. Blonde wood, capsule espresso machines and a cream-and-charcoal colour scheme are present throughout. Boons include the on-site Urban Tiger restaurant, with its Asian flavours, as well as the rooftop bar for chilling out...

🛏 **Parliament & Around**

Home-Made Hostel HOSTEL $
(Map p78; ☑ 06 30 200 4546, 1-302 2103; www. homemadehostel.com; VI Teréz körút 22; dm €10-18, d €48-52; @ ☎; Ⓜ M1 Oktogon, ⌂ 4, 6) This homey, extremely welcoming hostel with 20 beds in four rooms has recycled tables hanging upside down from the ceiling and old valises under the beds that serve as lockers. The whole idea is to use forgotten objects from old Budapest homes in a new way. The old-style kitchen is museum quality. Dorms have four to eight beds.

Central Backpack King Hostel HOSTEL $
(Map p78; ☑ 06 30 200 7184; www.centralbackpack-king.hostel.com; V Október 6 utca 15; dm €12-18, d €30-70; @ ☎; ⌂ 15, 115, Ⓜ M3 Arany János utca) This upbeat place in the heart of Lipótváros has dorm rooms with seven or eight beds on one floor and doubles, triples and quads on another. There's a small but scrupulously clean kitchen and a large common room.

Retox Party Hostel HOSTEL $
(Map p78; ☑ 06 20 455 6220; http://budapestpar-tyhostels.com/hostels/retox-party-hostel; VI Ó utca 41; dm €7-10, d €35; ☎; Ⓜ M1 Oktogon) With a dozen rooms occupying a one-time nursing home, this place makes no secret of the fact that it is the 'partiest' of the Budapest Party Hostels' four properties. It's built around a courtyard with a central and all-important bar and decorated from top to bottom with crazy and risqué street art.

Full Moon Design Hostel HOSTEL $$
(Map p78; ☑ 1-792 9045, 06 30 326 6888; www. fullmoonhostel.com; V Szent István tér 11; dm/d €12/60; ℗ ✳ ☎; ⌂ 4, 6) With oversized portraits of Joplin and Hendrix in the lobby and an upbeat party atmosphere this is a hostel for the 21st century. There's a fabulous eat-off-the-floor kitchen, a huge breakfast bistro and generous-sized laundry. Dorms have between six and eight beds.

Hotel Medosz HOTEL $$
(Map p78; ☑ 1-374 3000; www.medoszhotel.hu; VI Jókai tér 9; s/d/ste €69/79/119; ℗ ☎; Ⓜ M1 Oktogon) One of the most central cheaper hotels in Pest, the Medosz is just opposite the restaurants and bars of Liszt Ferenc tér. All of the 74 rooms have now been refitted and boast parquet floors, double glazing and small but up-to-the-minute bathrooms. Choose a room with a balcony or terrace (such as 903, 1001 or 1003).

Garibaldi Guesthouse & Apartments GUESTHOUSE, APARTMENT $$
(Map p78; ☑ 06 30 951 8763, 1-302 3457; www.gar-ibaldiguesthouse.hu; V Garibaldi utca 5; s €28-36, d €44-68, 2-/4-person apt €54/116; ☎; Ⓜ M2 Kossuth Lajos tér, ⌂ 2) This welcoming guesthouse has four rooms with shared bathroom and two kitchens in a flat just around the corner from Parliament. In the same building, there are a half-dozen apartments available on four floors; one large one has a balcony overlooking Garibaldi utca. Central and comfortable.

Hotel Parlament HOTEL $$
(Map p78; ☑ 1-374 6000; www.parlament-hotel. hu; V Kálmán Imre utca 19; r €95-170; ℗ ✳ @ ☎; ⌂ 15, 115, Ⓜ M2 Kossuth Lajos tér) This minimalist delight in Lipótváros has 65 beautifully designed rooms. Bonuses are the nonallergenic white pine floors, the self-service bar off the lobby, the dedicated ironing room, the adorable wellness centre with its own private

dressing room, sauna and jacuzzi, and the free tea and coffee at 5pm daily.

Cotton House Budapest HISTORIC HOTEL **$$**
(Map p78; ☑06 30 184 1128; http://cottonhouse-budapest.hu; Jókai utca 26; r €65-110; ☀@☎; ⬛4, 6) This 23-room place has a jazz/speak-easy theme that gets a bit tired after a while (though the vintage telephones actually do work). Prices vary widely depending on the season, and rooms have shower, tub or jacuzzi. Enter from Weiner Leó utca 19.

★ Aria Hotel HOTEL **$$$**
(Map p78; ☑1-445 4055; www.ariahotelbudapest.com; V Hercegprímás utca 5; r €200-320; P☀☎; ⬛15,115, Ⓜ M1 Bajcsy-Zsilinszky út) Our favourite new hotel in Budapest, the Aria is a music-themed hostelry built around an old townhouse, with Jazz, Opera, Classical and Pop Wings. Each of the 49 rooms has a balcony and bears the name of a musician or composer – they are also filled with portraits of, books about and CDs by the same. There's a fabulous wellness centre in the basement.

From the delightful lobby, where there's live piano music (and free wine and cheese for guests) from 5pm to 7pm, follow the black and white piano keys on the lobby floor to the lift and the stupendous High Note Roof Bar (p141). More great extras are the fully loaded multimedia library and the small cinema with films and more music off the lobby.

★ Four Seasons
Gresham Palace Hotel HOTEL **$$$**
(Map p78; ☑1-268 6000; www.fourseasons.com/budapest; V Széchenyi István tér 5-6; r/ste from €295/815; P☀@☎☒; ⬛16, 105, ⬛2) This one-of-a-kind 179-room hotel was created out of the long-derelict art nouveau Gresham Palace (1907) and a lot of blood, sweat and tears. No expense was spared to piece back together the palace's Zsolnay tiles, mosaics, and celebrated wrought-iron Peacock Gates leading north, west and south from the enormous lobby – the hotel is truly worthy of its name.

The spa on the 5th floor, with a smallish infinity lap pool and iced towels at the ready, is among the most beautiful in the city. Some rooms (eg twin 325) have heart-stopping views of the Danube and Buda Castle.

Prestige Hotel Budapest HOTEL **$$$**
(Map p78; ☑1-920 1000; www.prestigehotelbudapest.com; Vigyázó Ferenc utca 5; s/d €180/280; P☀☎; ⬛15, 115, ⬛2) With its enormous chandeliers, gold and white cloud mosaics and sofas in rust-coloured crushed velvet, this hotel is almost slipping into the kitsch category. But the light and the inspired design save the day. There are 85 rooms spread over six floors in a lovely neoclassical building. Standard rooms face the atrium courtyard while superior ones look to the street. A major plus: Michelin-starred Costes Downtown (p129) is the in-house eatery.

📛 Margaret Island & Northern Pest

★ Groove HOSTEL **$**
(Map p84; ☑1-786 8038; www.groovehostel.hu; Szent István krt 1; dm €17-21; ☎; ⬛4, 6) There's a real sense of traveller camaraderie at this friendly hostel inside a beautiful art nouveau building. The dorms are huge and individually decorated, and perks include large lockers, orthopaedic mattresses and individual reading lights. Staff organise outings too. So take Madonna's advice and, erm, get into the Groove.

Aventura Boutique Hostel HOSTEL **$**
(Map p84; ☑1-239 0782; www.aventurahostel.com; XIII Visegrádi utca 12; dm/d/apt from €15/40/57; @☎; Ⓜ M3 Nyugati pályaudvar, ⬛4, 6) This has got to be the most chilled hostel in Budapest. A family-run haven, it has four themed rooms (India, Africa, Japan and – our favourite – Space). We love the colours and fabrics, the in-house massage, and the dorms with loft sleeping for four to eight. There's also a double and three nearby apartments available as well.

NH Budapest HOTEL **$$**
(Map p84; ☑1-814 0000; www.nh-hotels.com; XIII Vígszínház utca 3; r from €96; P☀☎; ⬛4, 6) There are 160 rooms spread out over this eight-floor hotel, and two or three rooms on each floor have a balcony. We especially like the hotel's location behind the Comedy Theatre, the minimalist but welcoming and very bright atrium lobby, and the flash fitness centre on the 8th floor. It's tucked away from the main road, so not too noisy.

Boat Hotel Fortuna HOTEL **$$**
(Map p84; ☑1-288 8100; www.fortunahajo.hu; XIII Szent István Park, Carl Lutz rakpart; s/d with bathroom from €65/75, with washbasin from €38/48; ☀☎; ⬛trolleybus 76) Sleeping on a former river ferry anchored in the Danube is an 'experience'. This 'boatel' has 42 single and double rooms with shower and toilet at wa-

ter level. Below deck, an additional 14 rooms with one, two or three beds and washbasin are not unlike old-fashioned hostel accommodation. The air-con struggles in summer and service, though friendly, can be erratic.

**Danubius Grand
Hotel Margitsziget** HOTEL $$$
(Map p84; ☑1-889 4700; www.danubiushotels.com; XIII Margit-sziget; s/d/ste from €100/110/190; P❄️🏊; ☐26) Constructed in the late 19th century, this comfortable (but not grand) and tranquil hotel has 164 rooms that boast all the mod cons. It's connected to the Danubius Health Spa Margitsziget (p99) via a heated underground corridor, and the cost of taking the waters is included in the hotel rate.

🛏 Erzsébetváros & the Jewish Quarter

Bazaar Hostel HOSTEL $
(Map p86; ☑1-787 6420; http://bazarhostel.com; VII Dohány utca 22-24; dm €8-14, d €39-59; ❄️@📶; ⓂM2 Astoria, ☐47, 49) This very central, colourful (think yellow, orange and burgundy) and purpose-built hostel counts five rather luxurious doubles (three of them en suite) and six six-bed dorms, one of which is for women only. The common room and large open kitchen are modern and clean, and – just think of the convenience! – it sits above a 24-hour laundry. Helpful and friendly staff.

Wombat's HOSTEL $
(Map p86; ☑1-883 5065; www.wombats-hostels.com/budapest; Király utca 20; dm €13-21, d €50-65; 📶; ⓂM1/2/3 Deák Ferenc tér) Directly opposite the Király utca entrance to buzzing Gozsdu udvar, this slick and well-equipped hostel can accommodate a whopping 465 guests in its 120 rooms. Choose from four- to eight-bed dorms or doubles, all of which are en suite. There's a clean, cool design throughout and a large common area set in a colourful glass-roofed atrium.

Maverick City Lodge HOSTEL $
(Map p86; ☑1-793 1605; www.mavericklodges.com; Kazinczy utca 24-26; dm from €10-22, d €40-70; @📶; ⓂM2 Astoria) Sister to the Maverick Hostel (p108), the more comfortable Maverick City Lodge has three floors of dorms and private rooms, decorated in a modern, warehouse style with white wood, bold colours and beanbags. Each bed has a locker, curtain and reading light; private rooms with mezzanines are good for families. Common areas, including the kitchen, are well thought out and equipped.

Big Fish Hostel HOTEL $
(Map p86; ☑06 70 302 2432; www.bigfishhostel.com/budapest; VII Erzsébet körút 33; dm €14-20, d €40-50; @📶; ⓂM2 Blaha Lujza tér, ☐4, 6) If you like your music, you'll want to stay in this not-so-small pond where visiting bands lay their heads and the sound-engineer owner is a nightlife encyclopedia. There are five rooms – dorms (one of them a loft) with four to eight beds and a private double – plus a separate apartment available in summer. Great kitchen; huge TVs.

Avail Hostel APARTMENT $
(Map p86; ☑06 30 299 0870; huqwerty@yahoo.com; VII Kazinczy utca 5; s/d from €29/44; 📶; ⓂM2 Astoria, ☐47, 49) Formerly the Blue Danube Hostel, this place offers a series of rooms in self-contained flats in two locations side by side on very central VII Kazinczy utca. Some rooms have shared bathroom, others are en suite. Super knowledgable host Sándor always makes guests feel welcome, equipping them with maps and advice and even picking them up at ungodly hours.

Unity Hostel HOSTEL $
(Map p86; ☑06 20 801 4822, 1-413 7377; www.unityhostel.com; VI Király utca 60, 3rd fl; dm €10-12, d €47-56; ❄️@📶; ⓂM1 Oktogon, ☐4, 6) This hostel's location in the heart of party town would be draw enough, but add to that a roof terrace with breathtaking views of the Liszt Music Academy and the amiable, relaxed atmosphere and you have a winner. It sleeps 54 people over two levels in dorms of six to eight beds and doubles.

Marco Polo Top Hostel HOSTEL $
(Map p86; ☑1-413 2555; www.marcopolohostel.com; VII Nyár utca 6; dm/tw €10-25, d €45-69; @📶; ⓂM2 Blaha Lujza tér, ☐4, 6) The Mellow Mood Group's very central flagship hostel is a long-established, pastel-painted 47-room place with TVs in all the rooms (except the dorms) and a lovely courtyard. Even the four spotless 12-bed dorms are 'private', with the dozen beds separated by lockers and curtains. Efficiently run and a great place to meet people.

Carpe Noctem Original HOSTEL $
(Map p86; ☑06 70 670 0384; http://budapest-partyhostels.com; VI Szobi utca 5; dm 5400-6500Ft; @📶; ⓂM3 Nyugati pályaudvar, ☐4, 6) The most subdued property in the Budapest

Party Hostels stable, this chilled place offers a smaller, more laid-back option than its sister establishments and is slightly off the beaten track. With just three rooms of six- to eight-bed dorms, it has an intimate, easygoing atmosphere. It's right at the top of an apartment block – so expect quite a climb.

★ Hive Hostel
HOSTEL **$$**

(Map p86; ☑06 30 826 6197; www.thehive.hu; VII Dob utca 19; dm €15-25, d €60-100; @ ☎; Ⓜ M1/2/3 Deák Ferenc tér) This enormous and very central place with more than 50 rooms of all sizes and shapes over several levels is for the slightly better-heeled budget traveller. There's a big common area and kitchen and a wonderful rooftop bar that looks down on a courtyard with two large chestnut trees and a popular ruin garden. A wonderful place, with equally great staff.

★ Kapital Inn
B&B **$$**

(Map p86; ☑06 30 915 2029; www.kapitalinn.com; VI Aradi utca 30, 4th fl; r €89-129, ste €199; ✱ @ ☎; Ⓜ M1 Vörösmarty utca) A stylishly decorated and well-run guesthouse with five luxurious rooms and a two-bed suite on the 4th floor of a beautiful 1893 building. The sleek, recently revamped and massive kitchen has a fridge stocked with goodies that can be raided at any time, and the 56-sq-metre terrace is a great place to take breakfast or just relax in the sun. Guests can also use an adjoining office with its own laptop. The less-expensive rooms share a bathroom, and there's no lift.

Casati Budapest Hotel
HOTEL **$$**

(Map p86; ☑1-343 1198; www.casatibudapesthotel. com; VI Paulay Ede utca 31; r €90-140; P ✱ ☎; Ⓜ M1 Opera) ✐ The art-adorned reception area sets the tone at this classy hotel, set in a made-over 18th-century building that has tastefully retained a number of original features. Its 25 rooms come in a variety of cool and contemporary styles and breakfast is served in a funky covered courtyard. There's a small gym and sauna in the cellar.

Connection Guest House
GUESTHOUSE **$$**

(Map p86; ☑1-267 7104; www.connectionguest-house.com; VII Király utca 41; s €30, d €50-90; @ ☎; Ⓜ M1 Opera, ☒ 4, 6) A very central gay-friendly guesthouse above a leafy courtyard with nine en-suite bedrooms. It attracts guests of all ages and has super helpful owners. Larger rooms have sofas and loft levels. Breakfast is available.

Baross City Hotel
HOTEL **$$**

(Map p86; ☑1-461 3010; www.barosshotel.hu; VII Baross tér 15; s/d/tr/q/apt €60/70/90/110/160; ✱ @ ☎; Ⓜ M2/4 Keleti pályaudvar) Part of the local Mellow Mood group of hotels, the Baross is an exceptionally comfortable *caravanserai* conveniently located directly opposite Keleti train station. The 52 rooms are simply and uniformly furnished, and the reception, on the 5th floor, is clean and bright. The large, two-room apartments sleeping up to six are good for families or sharers. There's a lift.

★ Mamaison
Residence Izabella
APARTMENT **$$$**

(Map p86; ☑1-475 5900; www.residence-izabella. com; VI Izabella utca 61; 1-bed apt €110-150, 2-bed apt €240-280, 3-bed apt €350-380; P ✱ @ ☎; Ⓜ M1 Vörösmarty utca) This fabulous conversion of a 19th-century Eclectic building has 38 apartments measuring between 45 and 97 sq metres just off swanky Andrássy út. The apartments surround a delightful and very tranquil central courtyard garden and are set off by terracotta-toned decor. The lobby/reception area is warm and welcoming, with comfortable sofas and bold original art.

Continental Hotel Budapest
HOTEL **$$$**

(Map p86; ☑1-815 1000; www.continentalhotel-budapest.com; VII Dohány utca 42-44; r/ste from €130/200; P ✱ @ ☎ ☒; Ⓜ M2 Blaha Lujza tér, ☒ 4, 6) A sympathetic renovation of the glorious Hungária Fürdő (Hungaria Bath), the Continental has atmosphere and style in spades. With 272 large and beautifully furnished rooms and a huge atrium lobby retaining some of the original 19th-century building's features, the major draw here is the wellness centre on the top floor and the panoramic garden with swimming pool.

Corinthia Hotel Budapest
HOTEL **$$$**

(Map p86; ☑1-479 4000; www.corinthia.com/en/ hotels/budapest; VII Erzsébet körút 43-49; r/ste from €150/390; P ✱ @ ☎ ☒; Ⓜ M1 Oktogon, ☒ 4, 6) The erstwhile Royal Hotel is now the very grand, 440-room five-star Corinthia. Its lobby – a double atrium with massive marble staircase – is among the most impressive in the capital. The restored Royal Spa, dating back to 1886 and incorporated into the hotel, is now as modern as tomorrow, with a 15m-long pool and a dozen treatment rooms.

Soho Hotel
BOUTIQUE HOTEL **$$$**

(Map p86; ☑1-872 8292; www.sohohotel.hu; VII Dohány utca 64; s/d/ste €109/119/159; P ✱ @ ☎; Ⓜ M2 Blaha Lujza tér, ☒ 4, 6) This delightfully

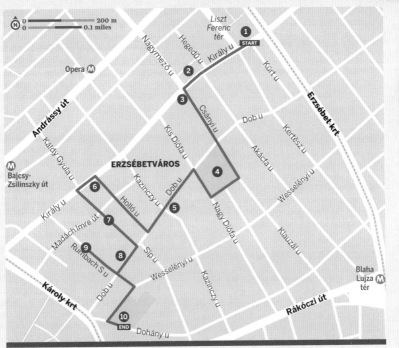

Neighbourhood Walk
Erzsébetváros & the Jewish Quarter

START VI LISZT FERENC TÉR
END VII DOHÁNY UTCA
LENGTH 1KM; ONE TO TWO HOURS

Begin the walk in restaurant- and cafe-packed VI Liszt Ferenc tér, and poke your head into the sumptuous ❶ **Liszt Music Academy** (p85). Walking southwest along Király utca you'll pass the ❷ **Church of St Teresa**, built in 1811 and containing a massive neoclassical altar designed by Mihály Pollack in 1822. At Király utca 47 (and directly opposite the church) is an interesting ❸ **neo-Gothic house** built in 1847, with a delightful oriel window.

Turning into Csányi utca, head southeast over Dob utca to the heart of the old Jewish Quarter, ❹ **Klauzál tér**. The square still has a feeling of prewar Budapest. A continued Jewish presence is still evident in the surrounding streets – with several kosher restaurants, the wonderful Fröhlich Cukrászda cake shop and cafe, and a butcher just next to the ❺ **Orthodox Synagogue** (p88).

Walk up Holló utca and turn left. If the gate at Király utca 15 is open, walk to the courtyard's rear to see a 30m-long piece of the original ❻ **ghetto wall**, rebuilt in 2010. Votive lamps and stones stand before it in tribute to Holocaust victims. The next turning on the left is the passageway called ❼ **Gozsdu udvar** (1901); now the district's number-one nightlife destination, it's lined with bars, cafes and restaurants and pulses with music and merrymakers come evening.

At Dob utca 12 is an unusual antifascist ❽ **monument to Carl Lutz**, a Swiss consul who, like Raoul Wallenberg, provided Jews with false papers in 1944. It portrays an angel on high sending down a long bolt of cloth to a victim. Just around the corner, bordering a car park, are two large ❾ **murals**. The one on the left (2013) commemorates the 60th anniversary of the football victory of Hungary's 'Golden Team', the first time a continental team beat England at Wembley (6–3). The one on the right is an oversized Rubik's Cube, the frustratingly difficult 3D puzzle invented in 1974 by Hungarian sculptor and architecture professor Ernő Rubik.

Retrace your steps and you'll find the **Great Synagogue** (p57) at the end of the street.

stylish boutique hotel with 68 rooms and eight suites is not far from the New York Palace, and we know which one feels more like the Big Apple. We adore the glass-and-tile lobby, the nonallergenic rooms with bamboo matting on the walls and parquet floors, and the music/film theme throughout.

🛏 Southern Pest

★ KM Saga Guest Residence   GUESTHOUSE $
(Map p92; 🕿 1-217 1934; www.km-saga.hu; IX Lónyay utca 17, 3rd fl; r from €35; ❈ 🛜; MM4 Fővám tér) This unique place has five themed rooms, an eclectic mix of 19th-century furnishings, and hospitable, multilingual Hungarian-American owner Shandor. It's essentially a gay B&B, but everyone is welcome. Two rooms share a bathroom.

Casa de la Musica   HOSTEL $
(Map p92; 🕿 06 70 373 7330; www.casadelamusicahostel.com; VIII Vas utca 16; dm €9-26, d €28-32; @🛜🖂; MM4 Rákóczi tér, 🚋 4, 6) This colourful place has 100 beds, including dorm rooms with four to 12 beds (two are for women only) and twins and doubles. There's a great kitchen and common room, as well as a terrace with bar, a summer kitchen and a pool with its own little 'beach' if you fancy a splash about.

★ Brody House   BOUTIQUE HOTEL $$
(Map p92; 🕿 1-266 1211; http://brodyhouse.com; VIII Bródy Sándor utca 10; r €75-140; ❈ @🛜; MM3 Kálvin tér, 🚋 47, 49) Offering retro chic at its hippest, this one-time residence of the prime minister when parliament sat at No 8 (now the Italian Cultural Centre) has been refurbished but not altered substantially, with antique furnishings and modern art blending seamlessly in its eight unique guestrooms dedicated to local and international artists. A minor drawback is the lack of a lift.

Fraser Residence   APARTMENT $$
(Map p92; 🕿 1-872 5900; http://budapest.frasershospitality.com/en; Nagy Templom utca 31; studios €70-80, 1-bed apt €95-120, 2-bed apt €140-160; ❈ @🛜; MM3 Corvin-negyed) Part of an international chain, the 51 apartments here attract both long- and short-staying guests. Some of the clean, modern flats come with balconies and all have kitchens, large beds and L'Occitane toiletries. All but the studios have washer/dryers too. Love the little sun terrace with garden.

Bo18 Hotel   HOTEL $$
(Map p92; 🕿 1-468 3526; www.bo18hotelbudapest.com; Vajdahunyad utca 18; d incl breakfast €60-100; P 🛜; MM3 Corvin-negyed, 🚋 4, 6) An independent hotel on a quiet street, Bo18 has 50 simply yet stylishly decorated rooms in a range of colours, a small sauna and gym, super clean tiled bathrooms and a tiny garden area. Generous breakfast buffet.

Kálvin House   HOTEL $$
(Map p92; 🕿 1-216 4365; www.kalvinhouse.hu; IX Gönczy Pál utca 6; s/d/ste from €68/89/109; @🛜; MM3/4 Kálvin tér, 🚋 47, 49) The 36 rooms in this atmospheric old apartment block range over four storeys and have original wooden floors, enormously high ceilings (particularly room 109), plants, and vintage furniture dating to the early 20th century. Some of the rooms have balconies and bathtubs; those facing the inner courtyard are cooler in summer, and happily there's a lift.

Thomas Hotel   HOTEL $$
(Map p92; 🕿 1-218 5505; www.hotelthomas.eu; IX Liliom utca 44; s/d €48/56; P❈@🛜; MM3 Corvin-negyed) A brightly coloured place, the Thomas has 37 rooms that are a real bargain for such a central location. Some rooms have balconies looking onto an inner courtyard. The goofy-looking kid in the logo is the owner as a young 'un, we're told. There's a restaurant on site.

Corvin Hotel Budapest   HOTEL $$
(Map p92; 🕿 1-218 6566; http://corvinhotelbudapest.hu; IX Angyal utca 31; s €74-90, d €79-100, apt €110; P❈@🛜; MM3 Corvin-negyed, 🚋 4, 6) What were once two separate hotels have come together to form a very comfortable 91-room place on a quiet street in Ferencváros. The four-star Corvin wing has 42 sleek, minimalist and renovated rooms. But equally comfortable is the 44-room Sissi wing. There are also five apartments with small kitchens and balconies in a separate building on the same street.

★ Hotel Palazzo Zichy   HISTORIC HOTEL $$$
(Map p92; 🕿 1-235 4000; www.hotel-palazzo-zichy.hu; VII Lőrinc pap tér 2; r/ste from €125/150; P❈@🛜; MM3 Corvin-negyed, M3/4 Kálvin tér, 🚋 4, 6) Once the sumptuous 19th-century residence of the aristocratic Zichy family, the 'palace' has been transformed into a lovely hotel, with its original features such as wrought-iron bannisters blending seamlessly with the ultramodern decor. The 80 rooms, all charcoals and creams, are en-

livened by red-glass-topped desks, and the showers are terrific. There's a sauna and fitness room in the cellar crypt.

🛏 City Park & Beyond

Baroque Hostel HOSTEL **$**
(Map p96; ☑1-788 3718; www.baroquehostel.hu; Dózsa György út 80/a; dm/s/d from €11/24/34; 🛜; 🚌30) Just across the street from City Park and a five-minute walk from Heroes' Sq, this hostel is run by travellers, for travellers. The dorms and private rooms are super clean and there are lots of nice extra touches: reading lights, laundry service, trips organised for guests, chill-out room with games console. The dorms with windows facing the corridor get hot in summer.

Royal Park Boutique Hotel BOUTIQUE HOTEL **$$**
(Map p96; ☑1-872 8805; www.royalparkboutiquehotel.hu; XIV Nefelejcs utca 6; s/d from €69/81; 🚌5, 7, 110, Ⓜ M2 Keleti pályaudvar) Handy for the Keleti train station, this smart brick building hides equally smart rooms, livened up with crimson accents and pieces of contemporary art. Boons? Rain showers in every bathroom, capsule espresso machines in every room, good beds, attentive staff. Banes? Some rooms are rather noisy due to the close proximity of a main road.

Mirage Medic Hotel HOTEL **$$**
(Map p96; ☑1-462 7070; www.miragehotelbudapest.com; XIV Dózsa György út 88; s/d from €80/95; 🛜; 🚌30, Ⓜ M1 Hősök tere) The location couldn't be grander – mere steps from Heroes' Sq and City Park – at this hotel boasting 37 well-kitted-out rooms over three floors, plus a suite. The building dates from the 1820s and four front rooms come with access to impressive stone balconies, with views over the square. Its faux-Burberry decor lends it a classical look. Can be noisy.

Star City Hotel HOTEL **$$**
(Map p96; ☑1-479 0420; www.starhotel.hu; VII István utca 14; s/d from €60/75; ✳@🛜; 🚌trolleybus 74, 79, Ⓜ M2 Keleti pályaudvar) Another member of the Mellow Mood Group is this brightly coloured midrange hotel a few minutes' walk north of Keleti train station. Most of the 48 guestrooms are doubles spread over four floors, though there are apartments for up to four people too. The ground-floor lobby is quite spacious; a glass 'bubble' lift links it with the other floors and guestrooms.

⭐**Mamaison Hotel**
Andrassy Budapest BOUTIQUE HOTEL **$$$**
(Map p96; ☑1-462 2100; www.mamaisonandrassy.com; Andrássy út 111; s/d/ste from €330/355/508; ✳🛜; Ⓜ M1 Hősök tere) This sleek boutique hotel features contemporary, well-appointed rooms decked out in warm shades. Plasma-screen TVs and showers are de rigueur in standard rooms; the seven suites come with their own jacuzzis. Staff are friendly and professional and pluses include an extensive breakfast and excellent on-site dining (French and Hungarian) – all this just a couple of minutes' walk way from Heroes' Sq.

🍴 Eating

The dining scene in Budapest has undergone a sea change in recent years. Hungarian food has 'lightened up', offering the same wonderfully earthy and spicy tastes but in less calorific dishes. The number of vegetarian (or partially meatless) restaurants has gone up, and the choice of eateries with cuisines other than Magyar is greater than ever before.

🍴 Castle District

⭐**Budavári Rétesvár** HUNGARIAN **$**
(Strudel Castle; Map p62; ☑06 70 408 8696; www.budavariretesvar.hu; I Balta köz 4; strudel 310Ft; ⊗8am-7pm; 🚌16, 16A, 116) Strudel in all its permutations – from poppyseed with sour cherry to dill with cheese and cabbage – is available at this hole-in-the wall dispensary in a narrow alley of the Castle District.

Artigiana Gelati GELATERIA **$**
(Map p62; ☑1-212 2439; www.etterem.hu/8581; XII Csaba utca 8; scoops 380Ft; ⊗11am-8pm Tue-Sun; Ⓜ M2 Széll Kálmán tér) This place sells some of the best shop-made ice cream and sorbet in Buda; its 27 unusual flavours include fig, pomegranate, Sachertorte and Gorgonzolawalnut. The lactose intolerant are catered for with flavours made using soya and rice milk.

Ildikó Konyhája HUNGARIAN **$**
(Ildikó's Kitchen; Map p62; ☑1-201 4772; www.ildiko-konyhaja.hu; I Fő utca 8; dishes 510-1850Ft; ⊗11.30am-10pm; 🚌19, 41) This spick-and-span *étkezde* (canteen that serves simple dishes) with checked tablecloths has traditional Hungarian favourites (goulash, stews...) at rock-bottom prices just below the Castle District.

Vár Cafe
HUNGARIAN $

(Map p62; ☑06 30 237 0039; I Dísz tér 8; mains 1700-2900Ft; ⊙8am-9pm; ☐16, 16A, 116) This cheap self-service restaurant straddles the Royal Palace and the Old Town and is an OK choice if you're looking for something fast and low priced. Gourmet it ain't, and there's a two-course fixed 'tourist' menu for 1500Ft.

Auguszt Cukrászda
CAFE $

(Map p62; ☑1-316 3817; www.auguszt1870.hu; II Fény utca 8; cakes 340-750Ft; ⊙10am-6pm Tue-Fri, 9am-6pm Sat; ☑; Ⓜ M2 Széll Kálmán tér, ☐4, 6) Tucked away behind the Fény utca market and Mammut shopping mall complex, this is the original and smallest Auguszt (there are two newer branches in Pest), which sells its own shop-made cakes, pastries and biscuits.

Nagyi Palacsintázója
HUNGARIAN $

(Map p62; www.nagyipali.hu; I Batthyány tér 5; pancakes 190-680Ft; ⊙24hr; ☑; Ⓜ M2 Batthyány tér, ☐19, 41) Riverside branch of the popular round-the-clock pancake minichain that serves them up with sweet and savoury fillings. Baked potatoes also on offer.

Édeni Vegán
VEGETARIAN $

(Map p62; ☑06 20 337 7575; www.facebook.com/edeni.vegan; I Iskola utca 31; mains 1100-1690Ft; ⊙8am-9pm Mon-Thu, to 7pm Fri, 11am-7pm Sun; ☑; Ⓜ M2 Batthyány tér, ☐19, 41) Located in an early 19th-century town house just below Castle Hill, this self-service place offers stodgy vegetarian and vegan platters, salad and pasta bowls and ragouts without a single no-no (fat, preservatives, MSG, white sugar etc). In warmer months, sit in the atrium courtyard or terrace.

Fortuna Önkiszolgáló
HUNGARIAN $

(Fortune Self-Service Restaurant; Map p62; ☑1-375 2401; I Fortuna utca 4; mains 2200-4400Ft; ⊙11.30am-2.30pm Mon-Fri; ☐16, 16A, 116) You'll find cheapish and quick weekday lunches in a place you'd least expect to – on Castle Hill – at this basic, clean and cheerful self-service restaurant. Reach it via the stairs on the left side as you enter the Fortuna Passage – and note the *sedile* (medieval stone niche) to the right as you go in.

Toldi Konyhája
HUNGARIAN $

(Map p62; ☑1-214 3867; I Batthyány utca 14; mains 1200-1490Ft; ⊙11am-4pm Mon-Fri; ☑; ☐11, 111, Ⓜ M2 Batthyány tér) This little eatery west of Fő utca is the place to come if you're in search of Hungarian comfort food at lunch-time on weekdays. Unusually for this kind of place, 'Toldi's Kitchen' has on offer about a half-dozen *real* vegetarian dishes.

Gasztró Hús-Hentesáru
HUNGARIAN $

(Map p70; ☑1-212 4159; II Margit körút 2; dishes from 350Ft; ⊙7am-6pm Mon, 6am-7pm Tue-Fri, 6am-1pm Sat; ☐4, 6) Opposite the first stop of trams 4 and 6 on the Buda (west) side of Margaret Bridge, this traditional butcher's shop also serves cooked sausages and roast chicken to be eaten in or taken away.

Nagyi Palacsintázója
HUNGARIAN $

(Granny's Crepe Place; Map p62; www.nagyipali.hu; I Hattyú utca 16; pancakes 190-680Ft; ⊙24hr; ☑; Ⓜ M2 Széll Kálmán tér, ☐4, 6) This small eatery serves Hungarian pancakes – both savoury and sweet – round the clock and is often packed. Peckish night owls may also wish to consider the baked-potato range (650Ft to 750Ft).

★ Baltazár Grill & Wine Bar
STEAK $$

(Map p62; ☑1-300 7050; www.baltazarbudapest.com; I Országház utca 3; mains 2760-8960Ft; ⊙noon-11pm; ☐16, 16A, 116) Free-range chickens, ducks, Styrian pork and juicy rib eyes, Wagyu steaks and *onglets* (a French cut of beef)sizzle on the charcoal grill at this excellent restaurant. Hungarian classics are also well represented, with several vegetarian dishes completing the picture. If you're not peckish, you can make your way to the atmospheric wine bar instead to sample tipples from the Carpathian Basin.

★ Mandragóra
HUNGARIAN $$

(Map p62; ☑1-202 2165; www.mandragorakavehaz.hu; II Kacsa utca 22; mains 2000-4200Ft; ⊙11am-11pm Mon & Tue, to midnight Wed-Sat; ☐11, 111, ☐19, 41) With a hint of black magic in its name and a cosy location in the basement of a residential block, this family-run restaurant has earned loyal local fans with its excellent takes on Hungarian classics. Feast on slow-cooked duck with red cabbage, grey-cattle sausage or pearl-barley risotto. The weekly specials are a bargain.

★ Csalogány 26
INTERNATIONAL $$

(Map p62; ☑1-201 7892; www.csalogany26.hu; I Csalogány utca 26; mains 3800-5300Ft; ⊙noon-3pm & 7-10pm Tue-Sat; ☐11, 111) Definitely one of the better restaurants in town, this intimate place with spartan decor turns its creativity to its superb food. Try the suckling *mangalica* (a kind of pork) with savoy cabbage (4900Ft) or other meat-heavy dishes that make the most of local ingredients. A three-course set lunch is a budget-pleasing 2900Ft.

Zóna
INTERNATIONAL $$

(Map p62; ☑06 30 422 5981; www.zonabudapest.com; I Lánchíd utca 7-9; mains 3400-6800Ft; ⏱noon-midnight Mon-Sat; ☐19, 41) Where the beautiful set eat and sup, Zóna is as much an architectural triumph as a foodie magnet. The menu is succinct and nicely executed; we particularly like the wild duck with vanilla-potato dumplings and the selection of Hungarian cheeses paired with pear ice cream. There are burgers, too, if all you want is a quick bite.

Déryné
BISTRO $$

(Map p62; ☑1-225 1407; www.bistroderyne.com; I Krisztina tér 3; mains 2980-3980Ft; ⏱7.30am-midnight Mon-Thu, to 1am Fri, 9am-1am Sat, to midnight Sun; ☐16, 105, ☐56, 56A) What used to be a traditional cafe near the entrance to the Alagút (the tunnel under Castle Hill), established the year WWI broke out, has metamorphosed into a beautiful bistro with excellent breakfasts and more substantial meals (risotto, slow-braised beef cheek) throughout the day. Great horseshoe-shaped bar plus music, a lovely terrace, an open kitchen and always a warm welcome.

Cafe Miró
INTERNATIONAL $$

(Map p62; ☑1-201 2375; www.cafemiro.hu; I Úri utca 30; mains 2990-4990Ft; ⏱9am-midnight; 🛜☑; ☐16, 16A, 116) Its interior inspired by the art of Joan Miró, this cafe/bistro is great for enormous fruit smoothies in summer and a fabulous selection of teas, coffees and soups on colder days, as well as imaginative dishes such honey-chilli duck with noodles, and baby mozzarella salad with homemade pesto. Efficient service, too.

21 Magyar Vendéglő
HUNGARIAN $$

(Map p62; ☑1-202 2113; www.21restaurant.hu; I Fortuna utca 21; mains 2760-5760Ft; ⏱11am-midnight; ☐16, 16A, 116) This place with a less-than-inspiring name has some wonderfully innovative modern takes on traditional Hungarian dishes such as veal stew and chicken *paprikás* (a variation of stew with sour cream, a reduction in paprika and white meat). There's super old/new decor and friendly service, and it bottles its very own wine.

Pavillon de Paris
FRENCH $$

(Map p62; ☑1-225 0174; www.pavillondeparis.hu; II Fő utca 20-22; mains 3500-6900Ft; ⏱noon-midnight Tue-Sat; ☐19, 41) A regular haunt of staff from the French Institute across the road (who *should* know *la cuisine française*), the Pavillon is housed in a wonderful old town house abutting an ancient castle wall. The back garden ablaze in fairy lights is a delight in summer. The food is imaginative French (black cod with beetroot, foie gras with poached pear). Excellent service.

Daikichi
JAPANESE $$

(Map p66; ☑1-225 3965; http://daikichihu.wixsite.com/daikichi; I Mészáros utca 64; mains 2200-4800Ft; ⏱noon-3pm & 5-10pm Tue-Sat, noon-9pm Sun; ☐27, 110, 112) This snug little Japanese eatery, in a nondescript area on the Buda side, serves up authentic Japanese cuisine including decent soba noodles (hot and cold), sushi, teriyaki-style grilled meats, and seafood and pork dishes.

Kacsa
HUNGARIAN $$

(Map p62; ☑1-201 9992; www.kacsavendeglo.hu; II Fő utca 75; 3-course menus lunch/dinner 3500/6000Ft; ⏱noon-midnight; ☐19, 41) The 'Duck' is the place to go, well, 'quackers', though you need not restrict yourself to the dishes with a bill (homestyle crispy duck with red cabbage, duck in pastry with dill sauce); it also does a couple of dishes prepared from Hungarian grey-horned cattle, for example. This elegant place dates back over a century, with Gypsy music every evening.

Horgásztanya Vendéglő
SEAFOOD $$

(Fisherfarm Restaurant; Map p62; ☑1-212 3780; www.horgasztanyavendeglo.hu; II Fő utca 20; mains 1490-3450Ft; ⏱noon-midnight; ☐19, 41) A classic fish restaurant by the Danube where soup is served in bowls, pots or kettles, and your carp, catfish or trout might be prepared Baja-, Tisza- or more spicy Szeged-style.

★ Arany Kaviár Étterem
RUSSIAN $$$

(Map p62; ☑1-201 6737; www.aranykaviar.hu; I Ostrom utca 19; mains 4900-18,900Ft; ⏱noon-3pm & 6pm-midnight Tue-Sun; 🛜; ☐16, 16A, 116) Accompanied by stellar service and beautiful presentation, this is Russian food like you've never seen it before. We can't fault the flavours – the home-smoked fish, the wild-boar *pelmeni* (dumplings), the selection of caviars – or the wine selection. The three-course lunch menu (5000Ft) is excellent value, but it's well worth splurging on the multicourse dinner (14,900Ft) for a real treat.

★ **Pierrot**   INTERNATIONAL **$$$**
(Map p62; ☑ 1-375 6971; www.pierrot.hu; I Fortuna utca 14; mains 3840-7640Ft; ⊙ 11am-midnight; 🚊 16, 16A, 116) This very stylish and long-established restaurant, housed in what was a bakery in the Middle Ages, specialises in dishes of the Austro-Hungarian Empire, revamped for the 21st century. Expect the likes of lamb tartare, quail stuffed with foie gras and mushrooms, and duck breast with caramelised apple. Presentation is faultless; eat in the vaulted dining room or in the garden.

Vár: a Speiz   INTERNATIONAL **$$$**
(Castle: The Pantry; Map p62; ☑ 1-488 7416; www.varaspeiz.hu; I Hess András tér 6; mains 3900-9200Ft; ⊙ noon-midnight; 🚊 16, 16A, 116) Michelin may have taken its 'bib' away, but we still love this romantic bistro. Vár: a Speiz takes its food very seriously indeed and most of the dishes (including venison with thyme-blueberry polenta, duck leg with savoy cabbage) tend to be satisfying and memorable. Service can be patchy, though.

✖ Gellért Hill & Tabán

Vegan Love   VEGAN **$**
(Map p66; www.veganlove.hu; Bartók Béla út 9; mains 1490-1590Ft; ⊙ 11am-8pm Mon-Sat, noon-8pm Sun; ☑; Ⓜ M4 Móricz Zsigmond körtér, 🚊 18, 19, 47, 49) Vegan fast (sorry, street) food doesn't get much better than at this hole-in-the-wall eatery on up-and-coming Bartók Béla út. Try the likes of sweet potato or curry lentil burgers, or the vegan chilli tofu hotdog. Small/large servings from the salad bar cost 590/1120Ft.

Marcello   ITALIAN **$**
(Map p66; ☑ 06 30 243 5229, 1-466 6231; www.marcelloetterem.hu; XI Bartók Béla út 40; mains 1500-4000Ft; ⊙ noon-10pm Sun-Wed, to 11pm Thu-Sat; 🚊 6) A perennial favourite with students from the nearby university since it opened more than a quarter-century ago, this family-owned operation just down the road from XI Szent Gellért tér offers reliable Italian fare at affordable prices. The pizzas (1280Ft to 1900Ft) and the salad bar are good value, as is the lasagne (1600Ft), which is legendary in these parts.

Cserpes Tejivó   CAFE **$**
(Map p66; www.cserpestejivo.hu; Kőrösy József utca, Allee Shopping Centre; sandwiches & salads 230-760Ft, menus 760-1190Ft; ⊙ 7.30am-10pm Mon-Fri, 9am-8pm Sat, 9am-6pm Sun; Ⓜ M4 Móricz Zsigmond körtér, 🚊 6, 47) This modern version of the traditional Hungarian *tejivó* (milk bar) is sponsored by the country's number-one producer of dairy products so it's just got to be good. One of four branches, this one is in the flash Allee Shopping Centre near XI Móricz Zsigmond körtér, handy to the M4 metro.

★ **Rudas Restaurant & Bar**   INTERNATIONAL **$$**
(Map p66; ☑ 06 20 921 4877; www.rudasrestaurant.hu; Döbrentei tér 9, Rudas Baths; mains 2450-4350Ft; ⊙ 11am-10pm; 🚊 7, 86, 🚊 18, 19) We love, love, love this place with its turquoise interior and stunning views of the Danube and bridges. It sits above the Rudas Baths Wellness Centre (ask about inclusive packages) so it's just the ticket after a relaxing massage or treatment. The smallish outside terrace is a delight in summer (though it can be noisy).

Leroy Cafe   INTERNATIONAL **$$**
(Map p66; ☑ 06 70 333 2035; http://leroyujbuda.hu; Kőrösy József utca 7-9, Allee Shopping Centre; mains 2590-5590Ft; ⊙ 11am-10pm Mon-Sat, to 7.30pm Sun; Ⓜ M4 Móricz Zsigmond körtér, 🚊 6, 47) This attractive cafe-restaurant serves international cuisine that is not especially inspired but is of a certain standard – and it's there in the Allee Shopping Centre when you've ordered one too many craft beers in the neighbourhood. Sandwiches and wraps (3000Ft) too. The large terrace fills up (and stays that way) very early when the weather's warm.

Hemingway   INTERNATIONAL **$$**
(Map p66; ☑ 1-381 0522, 06 30 488 6000; http://hemingway-etterem.hu; XI Kosztolányi Dezső tér 2; mains 3400-4200Ft; ⊙ noon-midnight Mon-Sat, to 4pm Sun; 🚊 19, 47, 49) This very stylish eatery, in a fabulous location in a small park overlooking Feneketlen-tó (Bottomless Lake) in south Buda, has a varied and ever-changing menu and a wonderfully spacious terrace. There are lots of vegie dishes (1490Ft to 2750Ft) should you want something light and easy, and Sunday brunch (4600Ft; with unlimited drinks 5950Ft) is a crowd-pleaser.

Aranyszarvas   HUNGARIAN **$$**
(Map p66; ☑ 1-375 6451; www.aranyszarvas.hu; I Szarvas tér 1; mains 2750-3600Ft; ⊙ noon-11pm Tue-Sat; 🚊 86, 🚊 18) Set in an 18th-century inn literally down the steps from the southern end of Castle Hill (views!), the 'Golden Stag' serves up some very meaty and unusual dishes (try the venison in fruity game sauce, the saddle of boar with dried tomatoes or the duck breast with Savoy cabbage). The covered outside terrace is a delight in summer.

✗ Óbuda & Buda Hills

Pastrami
INTERNATIONAL $

(Map p70; ☑1-430 1731; www.pastrami.hu; III Lajos utca 93-99; mains 1900-3900Ft; ☺8am-11pm; 🚇17, 19, 41, 🚊Tímár utca) In Óbuda's Újlak district, this light, bright bistro-meets-New-York-style-deli does indeed serve its namesake in its many guises, including the celebrated Reuben sandwich (2900Ft). But come here also for breakfast, and more complicated mains, such as pumpkin risotto or duck confit with horseradish potatoes.

Nagyi Palacsintázója
HUNGARIAN $

(http://nagyipali.hu; III Szentendrei út 13; pancakes 190-680Ft; ☺24hr; ☑; 🚊HÉV Aquincum) One of the city's four round-the-clock pancake joints serving oodles of doughy delights with sweet and savoury fillings, from marzipan to chicken stew.

★ Sushi Sei
JAPANESE $$

(Map p70; ☑1-240 4065; www.sushisei.hu; III Bécsi út 58; mains 2000-6300Ft; ☺noon-10pm Sun-Thu, to 11pm Fri & Sat; 🚇17, 19, 41) This stylish restaurant is one of the best spots in Budapest for a wide spectrum of authentic Japanese cuisine. Apart from beautifully presented nigiri, sushi and tempura sets, you can feast on cold soba noodles, yakitori, tonkatsu and grilled fish. The bento boxes (1900Ft to 2200Ft) are particularly good value.

Okuyama no Sushi
JAPANESE $$

(Map p70; ☑1-250 8256; http://okuyamanosushi. uw.hu/; III Kolosy tér 5-6, basement; sushi 1400-5000Ft, mains 1400-7000Ft; ☺1-10pm Tue-Sun; 🚌9, 109, 🚇17, 19, 41) This tiny hole-in-the-wall restaurant in the courtyard of a mini shopping mall in Óbuda serves some of the best Japanese food in town, including seasonal sashimi. There's a special daily menu of five dishes for 4500Ft.

Fióka
HUNGARIAN $$

(Map p72; ☑1-426 5555; www.facebook.com/ fiokavarosmajor; XII Városmajor utca 75; mains 2460-5900Ft; ☺11am-midnight Wed-Sun; 🚌56, 59, 61) This light, bright bistro and wine bar has a succinct, imaginative menu, featuring such treats as smoked goose carpaccio and bone marrow on toast. The great selection of wines is not just from Hungary but the whole Carpathian Basin, and there's a supporting cast of *pálinkas* (fruit brandies).

Pata Negra
SPANISH $$

(Map p70; ☑1-438 3227; www.patanegra.hu; III Frankel Leó út 51; tapas 380-1850Ft, plates 840-2200Ft; ☺11am-midnight; 🚇17, 19, 41) The 'Black Foot' (a type of Spanish cured ham) is a lovely Spanish tapas bar and restaurant that serves such standards as *calamares a la romana* (fried calamari) and *pimiento de padrón* (padrón pepper with sea salt), as well as more sophisticated offerings. The floor tiles and ceiling fans help create a mood *à la Valenciana* and of the 30 wines, most are available by the glass.

Szép Ilona
HUNGARIAN $$

(Map p72; ☑1-275 1392; www.szepilonavende-glo.hu; II Budakeszi út 1-3; mains 1800-4500Ft; ☺noon-11pm; 🚌56, 59, 61) This refined Buda Hills spot is a good place to come for hearty indigenous fare, such as duck leg in orange sauce, at modest prices. The name refers to the 'Beautiful Helen' in the ballad by poet Mihály Vörösmarty: she falls in love with a dashing 'hunter', who turns out to be the young King Matthias Corvinus. Alas...

Symbol
ITALIAN $$

(Map p70; ☑1-333 5656; www.symbolbudapest.hu; III Bécsi út 56; mains 1880-4890Ft; ☺11.30am-midnight; ☑; 🚇17, 19, 41) Part of Óbuda's ambitious Symbol complex of bars and restaurants, and built in and around a late 18th-century town house, this large restaurant serves relatively reasonably priced 'Italian fusion' (meaning they Magyarise the pasta) as well as simpler fare like wood-fired pizza (1680Ft to 2980Ft). There's live music and a good kids' menu. Prepare for a leisurely meal.

Földes Józsi Konyhája
HUNGARIAN $$

(Map p70; ☑1-438 3710; www.foldesjozsikonyha-ja.hu; II Frankel Leó út 30-34; mains 1350-3800Ft; ☺11.30am-3.30pm Mon, to 10pm Tue-Sat, noon-3.30pm Sun; 🚌4, 6, 17) This rustic little place just opposite the Lukács Baths was established by former hotel chef Joe Earthy – hey, that's what his name means! – some years back and still serves excellent Hungarian homestyle dishes, including veal stew with dumplings and a good range of *főzelék* (vegetables in a roux).

Mezzo Music Restaurant
INTERNATIONAL $$

(Map p72; ☑1-356 3565; www.mezzorestau-rant.hu; XII Maros utca 28; mains 2900-4800Ft; ☺8am-midnight Mon-Fri, noon-midnight Sat, noon-10pm Sun; 🚌128, Ⓜ M2 Széll Kálmán tér) A glamorous bistro between Széll Kálmán

LIKE A LOCAL

It's not difficult to live like a local in Budapest. The natives are friendly, the food is excellent (and never too strange) and the wine even better. And there are lots of things here that many people everywhere like: hot mineral baths, sweet cakes and diamonds-and-rust flea markets.

Eating Like a Local

While in Budapest, learn to like meat. Hungarians are big carnivores, and 'meat-stuffed meat' is actually a dish here. For stick-to-the-ribs fare on the hoof try Belvárosi Disznótoros (p122), a butcher-caterer who satisfies the ravenous daily. Still popular are retro-style étkezdék, diner-like eateries that serve traditional Hungarian fare and comfort dishes like főzelék (vegetables fried or boiled and then mixed into a roux with milk). The most local of these are Kádár (p132) in Erzsébetváros, Kisharang (p124) near Parliament in Pest, and Toldi Konyhája (p116) in Buda's Víziváros. The best places for traditional fish soup are Horgásztanya Vendéglő (p117) in Víziváros or Új Sípos Halászkert (p121) in Óbuda.

Drinking Like a Local

Drinking establishments in the city run the gamut from quirky pubs and bohemian bars to much more refined wine and cocktail bars. If you want to sample the local beer (most commonly Dreher, Kőbányai and Arany Ászok) head for a söröző, a 'pub' with draught beer (csapolt sör) served in a pohár (0.3L) or korsó (0.4L or 0.5L). Many pubs and bars now also serve a range of craft beers from microbreweries across the country.

Entertaining Like a Local

No self-respecting Budapester ever clubs indoors in the warm summer months; that's what kertek (outdoor garden clubs) and rough-and-ready romkocsmák (ruin pubs) are for. As for more high-brow entertainment, while the Liszt Music Academy (p150) and Palace of Arts (p151) are incomparable for their acoustics and talent, many Budapesters prefer to hear music in smaller, more intimate venues such as the Óbuda Society (p149) or organ recitals in one of the city's many fine churches.

If you want to see Budapest down and dirty on the playing field, attend a Ferencváros football match at the new €40-million Groupama Arena (p152).

Shopping Like a Local

The Nagycsarnok (p156) is a great market for shopping, but don't expect to see peasant women fresh in from the countryside selling snowdrops in spring or homemade tomato juice in summer. For that sort of thing head for the Rákóczi tér Market (p157) or even the covered Lehel Market (p83) in Újlipótváros. And have a look at the newly renovated Belvárosi Piac (p124) off V Szabadság tér. Locals never go to the Ecseri Piac (p156), the largest flea market in Central Europe, during the week but head out as early as they can make it on Saturday morning to see what treasures are coming in from the countryside or being flogged by amateurs.

---

tér and Déli train station, Mezzo has upmarket international and Hungarian dishes – and jazz from 7.30pm Monday to Saturday. Beef tartare and goose breast stand out. Service could be more congenial.

Vendéglő a KisBíróhoz   BISTRO $$
(Map p72; ☑1-376 6044; http://vendegloakisbirohoz.hu; XII Szarvas Gábor út 8; mains 3400-5400Ft; ◕noon-11pm Tue-Sun; ◻61) Sister restaurant to Bock Bisztro, this almost-luxurious place in the Buda Hills caters to the well-heeled denizens of district XII. The tapas (from 1400Ft) make the most of local produce, and we par-

ticularly like the retro-style ox cheek and the bizarre sausage-flavoured ice cream.

Náncsi Néni   HUNGARIAN $$
(Auntie Nancy; ☑1-397 2742; www.nancsineni.hu; II Ördögárok út 80; mains 850-3450Ft; ◕noon-11pm Mon-Fri, 9am-11pm Sat & Sun; ◻63, 157) Auntie Náncsi (Hungarian for any loopy old lady) is a favourite with locals and expats alike, and she's very much of sound mind. Located up in Hűvösvölgy, this restaurant specialises in game in autumn and winter, plus goose-liver dishes. In summer it's the lighter fare –

lots of stuff cooked with grapes and morello cherries – and garden seating that attracts.

Kéhli Vendéglő
HUNGARIAN $$

(Map p70; ☑ 1-368 0613; www.kehli.hu; III Mókus utca 22; mains 1490-6990Ft; ☺ noon-midnight; ☒ 29, 109, ⌨ Szentlélek tér, Tímár utca) Self-consciously rustic, Kéhli has some of the best traditional Hungarian food in town. One of Hungary's best-loved writers, the novelist Gyula Krúdy (1878–1933), who lived in nearby Dugovics Titusz tér, moonlighted as a restaurant critic and enjoyed Kéhli's *forró velőscsont fokhagymás pirítóssal* (bone marrow on toast; 980Ft) so much that he included it in one of his novels.

Remíz
HUNGARIAN $$

(Map p72; ☑ 06 30 999 5131; www.remiz.hu; II Budakeszi út 5; mains 1480-4380Ft; ☺ noon-11pm; ⌨ 56, 59, 61) Next to a tram depot *(remíz)* in the Buda Hills, this veritable institution remains popular for its reliable food (try the meats cooked on hot lava stones, especially the ribs; from 3380Ft) and verdant garden terrace. We love the catfish stew with chanterelles and curd cheese pasta. Portions are huge, service flawless.

Új Sípos Halászkert
HUNGARIAN $$

(New Piper Fisher's Garden; Map p70; ☑ 1-388 8745; www.ujsipos.hu; III Fő tér 6; mains 1590-3890Ft; ☺ noon-10pm Sun-Thu, to 11pm Fri, to midnight Sat; ☑; ☒ 29, 109, ⌨ Szentlélek tér) This old-style eatery faces (and, in the warmer weather, has outside seating in) Óbuda's most beautiful and historical square. Try the signature *halászlé* (fish soup; 1190Ft), which comes in various guises. As the restaurant's motto says: *Halászlében verhetetlen* (You can't beat fish soup). Several vegetarian options too, plus a children's menu.

Rozmaring
HUNGARIAN $$

(Map p70; ☑ 1-367 1301; www.rozmaringkertvendeglo.hu; III Árpád fejedelem útja 125; mains 1100-4900Ft; ☺ noon-11pm Mon-Thu, to midnight Fri & Sat, to 9pm Sun; ⌨ Tímár utca) You wouldn't want to come all the way up to this part of Óbuda just for the food (average Hungarian). But the flower-bedecked, covered terraces at this 'garden restaurant', which look out on to the Danube and the western side of Margaret Island, with the water tower visible above the trees, are a delight in warm weather and worth the schlep.

Mongolian Barbecue
ASIAN $$

(Map p72; ☑ 1-356 6363; www.mongolianbbq.hu/hu/; XII Márvány utca 19/a; buffet before 5pm/after 5pm/weekends 3890/4990/5490Ft; ☺ noon-5pm & 6-11pm; ⌨ 105, ☒ 61) This is one of those average all-you-can-eat Asian(ish) places where you choose the raw ingredients and legions of cooks stir-fry it for you. The difference here is that as much beer, house wine and sangria as you can sink is included in the price.

Maharaja
INDIAN $$

(Map p70; ☑ 1-250 7544; www.maharaja.hu; III Bécsi út 89-91; mains 2190-3990Ft; ☺ noon-11pm; ☑; ☒ 17, 19, 41) This Óbuda institution was the first Indian restaurant to open in Budapest. It specialises in northern Indian dishes, especially tandoori ones. The original is not necessarily the best, but it does manage some decent samosas and butter chicken.

★ Fuji Japán
JAPANESE $$$

(Map p72; ☑ 1-325 7111; www.fujirestaurant.hu; II Csatárka út 54; mains 2800-11,900Ft; ☺ noon-11pm; ☒ 29) It's well worth travelling into the hills of posh district II for the most authentic Japanese food in town. Apart from super fresh sashimi sets and imaginative sushi rolls, repeat clients come for hotpots, yakitori and more. For a special occasion, opt for tatami seating and blow your budget on a 10-course *kaiseki* menu (18,500Ft). Set weekday lunch is just 2290Ft.

★ Tanti
FUSION $$$

(Map p72; ☑ 06 20 243 1565; www.tanti.hu; XII Apor Vilmos tér 11-12; 3-course lunch/dinner 4700/12,000Ft; ☺ noon-3pm & 6-11pm Mon-Sat, noon-4pm Sun; ☏; ☒ 59, 59A, 59B) If you come to 'Auntie' expecting solid, home-style cooking, you won't find it. Instead, you'll find an atrium-like dining room, brightened by dozens of hanging lamps, and beautifully presented, innovative dishes that draw on Hungarian and French influences and ingredients. The newest recipient of Budapest's share of Michelin stars is informal and particularly affordable at lunchtime.

✕ Belváros

Csendes M
VEGAN $

(Map p74; ☑ 06 30 948 1488; www.csend.es; V Henszlmann Imre utca 1; 2-/3-course menus 1290/1690Ft; ☺ 10am-8.30pm Wed-Sat; ☑; Ⓜ M2 Astoria, M3/4 Kálvin tér) An unlikely outpost in a country of carnivores, Csendes M appreciates that there's more to vegetarian and vegan food than boiling the heck out of vegetables. Expect creative and varied daily dishes, such as Middle Eastern salad with lentil loaf, baked pumpkin with chocolate glaze and chilli sin carne.

Nagyi Palacsintázója HUNGARIAN $

(Map p74; www.nagyipali.hu; V Petőfi Sándor utca 17-19; pancakes 160-680Ft; ⊙24hr; M M3 Ferenciek tere) The most central branch of 'Granny's Palacsinta Place', Budapest's popular chain selling both savoury and sweet Hungarian-style pancakes to night owls and insomniacs.

Hummus Bar MIDDLE EASTERN $

(Map p74; ☑ 06 70 932 8284; www.hummusbar.hu; V Kecskeméti utca 1; mains 1190-1990Ft; ⊙11am-10pm Mon-Fri, noon-10pm Sat & Sun; 🛜🍴; M M3/4 Kálvin tér) A handy branch of the Middle Eastern chain that's taken Budapest by storm. There are reliable, good vegie dishes such as *shakshuka* (eggs cooked in a tomato-based sauce), couscous salad with roasted vegetables, falafel, *labneh* (savoury yoghurt for dipping) and pitta stuffed with *sabich* (fried aubergine). Jerusalem mix awaits the meat-eaters. It's cheap, cheerful and a nice alternative to the ubiquitous Hungarian dishes.

Belvárosi Disznótoros HUNGARIAN $

(Map p74; ☑ 06 70 602 2775; V Károlyi utca 17; dishes 500-1600Ft; ⊙7am-8pm Mon-Fri, to 3pm Sat; M M3/4 Kálvin tér, 🚊47, 48, 49) If your level of hunger could be described as ravenous, visit this butcher-caterer (a *disznótor* is where the animal is turned into sausages and other comestibles) that does every type of Hungarian meat dish known to humankind, and whose name could be loosely translated as 'Inner Town Feast'. Take away or eat standing up at the counters inside and out.

★Paris Budapest Restaurant INTERNATIONAL $$

(Map p74; ☑1-235 1230; www.parisbudapest.hu; V Széchenyi István tér 2; mains 3600-12,500Ft; ⊙11am-11pm; 🛜; M M1 Vörösmarty tér, 🚊2) One of Budapest's loveliest restaurants hides inside the Sofitel Hotel. The decor is minimalist, the service is some of the best we've come across anywhere in Budapest, and the dishes are imaginative without being pretentious (truffled chicken breast, wild-mushroom risotto, seared butterfish). Add to that an excellent wine list and you're on your way to a perfect evening.

★Monk's Bistrot HUNGARIAN $$

(Map p74; ☑ 06 30 789 4718; www.monks.hu; V Piarista köz 1; mains 3980-5780Ft, 3-course lunches 2980Ft; ⊙11am-midnight; 🛜; 🍴2) With its vaguely industrial decor, an open kitchen and young serving staff, this ambitious new restaurant specialises in bold pairings of ingredients that nevertheless seem to work, alongside contemporary reimaginings of Hungarian dishes. The peach gazpacho with mackerel really shines, as does the beef cheek with Dijon mustard. Weekday lunch is a welcome bargain.

★Magyar QTR HUNGARIAN $$

(Map p74; ☑ 06 70 329 7815; www.magyarqtr.com; V Belgrád rakpart 18; mains 2750-4750Ft; ⊙noon-midnight; M M3 Ferenciek tere, 🍴2) It's difficult not to love this bistro, for three reasons: the excellent Hungarian wine (more than 100 vintages), the food and the fabulous river views. The succinct menu includes such inspired takes on Hungarian dishes as duck with marrow ragout and chanterelles, and *mangalica* pork with truffle and blackberries. Weekly specials are based on seasonal ingredients.

★Kárpátia HUNGARIAN $$

(Map p74; ☑1-317 3596; www.karpatia.hu; V Ferenciek tere 7-8; mains 4100-7700Ft; ⊙11am-11pm Mon-Sat, 5-11pm Sun; 🛜🍴; M M3 Ferenciek tere) A palace of fin-de-siècle design dating from 1877, the 'Carpathia' serves almost-modern Hungarian and Transylvanian specialities in both a palatial restaurant in the back and a less-expensive *söröző* (brasserie). The mostly meaty dishes are expertly prepared and the Hungarian wine list is solid. This is one place to hear authentic *csárdás* (Gypsy-style folk music), played from 6pm to 11pm.

Kiosk INTERNATIONAL $$

(Map p74; ☑ 06 70 311 1969; www.kiosk-budapest.hu; V Március 15 tér 4; mains 2950-4950Ft; ⊙noon-midnight; M M3 Ferenciek tere, 🍴2) With a large outdoor terrace and a cavernous interior, Kiosk wears many hats. It's a casual place to grab an imaginative lunch dish or two, the excellent bar attracts the young and the trendy in the evenings with its 25 signature cocktails, there's live music on weekends and the place is also a confectioner: get your classic Hungarian sweets here.

Halkakas SEAFOOD $$

(Map p74; ☑ 06 30 226 0638; www.halkakas.hu; V Veres Pálné utca 33; mains 2150-5850Ft; ⊙noon-10pm Mon-Sat, to 5pm Sun; M M4 Fővám tér)

Charming corner restaurant on a quiet street close to Váci utca that throws back its doors on sunny days, when diners spill onto the pavement outside. Fresh, simple and great-value fish dishes (sturgeon with couscous, grilled carp with Dijon mustard) are served from the kitchen directly behind the service counter on mismatched plates to happy punters.

Borssó Bistro
HUNGARIAN $$

(Map p74; ☑1-789 0975; www.borsso.hu; V Királyi pál utca 14; mains 2900-7500Ft; ☺noon-11pm Wed-Sun, 6-11pm Tue; Ⓜ M3/4 Kálvin tér) Cosy, classy and welcoming corner restaurant set over two levels, with dark-wood furniture and romantic candlelight come evening. There's clear attention to detail in the French-influenced Hungarian dishes (confit duck with cassoulet, pasta with wild mushrooms) as well as in other touches, such as the homemade bread and courteous service.

Taverna Dionysos
GREEK $$

(Map p74; ☑1-328 0958; www.taverna-dionysos.hu; V Belgrád rakpart 16; mains 3500-6990Ft; ☺noon-midnight; ☑2) All faux Greek columns and a blue-and-white colour scheme, this taverna facing the river packs diners in on its three floors. Expect all the usual Greek favourites – from tzatziki and souvlaki to fresh grilled fish – and more. We particularly like the feta-stuffed burger.

Buddha Bar
ASIAN $$

(Map p74; ☑1-799 7300; www.buddhabarhotel.hu; V Váci utca 34; mains 3400-11,900Ft; ☺7-11pm Sun-Wed, to midnight Thu-Sat; Ⓜ M3 Ferenciek tere) It's difficult to say whether this is an Asian restaurant or a temple. The focal point in the dimmed lighting is a giant golden Buddha, the furnishings create the illusion of colonial opulence, the music is ambient lounge and the menu stampedes from gyoza to sushi, tempura and Thai curry. The food's overpriced but we love the ambience.

Trattoria Toscana
ITALIAN $$

(Map p74; ☑1-327 0045; www.toscana.hu; V Belgrád rakpart 13; mains 1990-4990Ft; ☺noon-midnight; ☑15, 115, ☑2, 47, 48, 49) Hard by the Danube, this trattoria serves rustic and very authentic Italian and Tuscan food, including *pappardelle al ragú alla Toscana* (pappardelle with a hearty Tuscan meat ragout) and a wonderful Tuscan farmer's platter of prepared meats. The pizza and pasta dishes are excellent.

★ Baraka
FUSION $$$

(Map p74; ☑1-200 0817; www.barakarestaurant.hu; V Dorottya utca 6; mains 7200-17,500Ft, 3-course lunches 6900Ft, 7-course tasting menus 27,000Ft; ☺11am-3pm & 6-11.30pm Mon-Sat; ☎; Ⓜ M1 Vörösmarty tér) If you only eat in one fine-dining establishment while in Budapest, make it Baraka. You're ushered into the monochrome dining room, where chef Norbert Bíró works his magic in the half-open kitchen. Seafood features heavily, with French, Asian and Hungarian elements to the beautifully presented dishes. The bar, with its vast array of Japanese whiskies and pan-Asian tapas, is a treat.

Onyx
HUNGARIAN $$$

(Map p74; ☑06 30 508 0622; www.onyxrestaurant.hu; V Vörösmarty tér 7-8; 4-/6-course lunches 19,900/24,900, tasting menus from 29,900Ft; ☺noon-2.30pm Tue-Fri, 6.30-11pm Tue-Sat; ☎; Ⓜ M1 Vörösmarty tér) This Michelin-starred eatery adjacent to (and owned by) Gerbeaud (p139) has taken it upon its own lofty shoulders to modernise Hungarian cuisine, and its six-course 'Hungarian Evolution' tasting menu (29,900Ft) suggests it's well on its way to achieving that goal. Expect seamless service and the quiet tinkling of a piano in the background. One for romancing your sweetie.

Nobu
JAPANESE $$$

(Map p74; ☑1-429 4242; www.noburestaurants.com/budapest; V Erzsébet tér 7-8, Kempinski Hotel Corvinus; sashimi per piece 900-3800Ft, dishes 1300-12,900Ft; ☺noon-3.30pm & 6-11.45pm; ☎; Ⓜ M1 Vörösmarty tér) Budapest knew it had arrived when it got a branch of a favourite canteen of the London glitterati. As elsewhere, Nobu is minimalist in decor and anonymously efficient in service, but can be surprisingly disappointing: some of the exquisitely presented sushi, sashimi and tartare offerings work better than others. Spoil yourself with a seven-course menu (25,000Ft) if you can.

Spoon
INTERNATIONAL $$$

(Map p74; ☑1-411 0933; www.spoonrestaurants.hu; off V Vigadó tér 3; mains 3990-8500Ft; ☺noon-midnight; ☑; ☑2) If you like the idea of dining on a two-level boat but still remaining tethered to the bank, Spoon is for you. The choice of seating is legion: cafe, lounge, winter garden or breezy terrace. The dishes? Creative international (veal with bone-marrow sauce, scallop and black pudding ravioli). You can't beat the views of the castle and Chain Bridge.

✕ Parliament & Around

Baotiful
ASIAN $

(Map p78; ☑06 30 505 3632; www.facebook.com/baotiful; V Szabadság tér 17; bao 690-890Ft, dumplings 990-2790Ft; ☺noon-10pm Mon-Fri, to midnight Sat, to 8pm Sun; ☒15, 115, Ⓜ M2 Kossuth Lajos tér) Should you have a craving for Asian dumplings or *bao* (steamed, filled rice-flour buns), head for this informal eatery in what was for many years the sumptuous headquarters of Magyar Televízió (Hungarian Television). The pork and Korean barbecue dumplings are excellent; the *gua bao* of cured pork belly with five-spice powder out of this world. The lunch menu is 1590Ft.

Pizzica
PIZZA $

(Map p78; ☑06 30 993 5481; www.facebook.com/pizzicapizza; VI Nagymező utca 21; pizza slices 290-490Ft, for 2 1690Ft; ☺11am-midnight Mon-Thu, to 3am Fri & Sat; Ⓜ M1 Oktogon) If there is better pizza in Budapest, we don't know where to find it. Owned and operated by an Italian named Paolo, Pizzica serves the real McCoy, with such toppings as potato and sage and mortadella. It's a tiny place but there's more seating in the art gallery upstairs.

Kisharang
HUNGARIAN $

(Map p78; ☑1-269 3861; www.kisharang.hu; V Október 6 utca 17; mains 1000-2350Ft; ☺11.30am-10pm; ☒15, 115) Centrally located 'Little Bell' is an *étkezde* (canteen serving simple Hungarian dishes) that's top of the list with students and staff of the nearby Central European University. The daily specials are something to look forward to and the retro decor is fun. *Főzelék* (370Ft to 490Ft), the traditional Hungarian way of preparing vegetables and sometimes served with meat, is always a good bet.

Butterfly
ICE CREAM $

(Map p78; ☑1-311 3648; http://butterflycukraszda.hu; VI Teréz körút 20; ice cream per scoop 220Ft; ☺10am-10pm; Ⓜ M1 Oktogon) This place – and not the pastry shop next door – is where to head for some of Pest's best ice cream, as you'll be able to deduce from the queues. In winter, its cakes (465Ft to 525Ft) are an appealing choice.

Belvárosi Piac
MARKET $

(Downtown Market; Map p78; ☑1-353 1110; www.facebook.com/belvarosipiac; V Hold utca 13; ☺6.30am-5pm Mon, to 6pm Tue-Fri, to 4pm Sat; Ⓜ M3 Arany János utca) What used to be called the Hold utca Market has been given a to-

tal facelift. It remains a true-blue purveyor of meat and produce, but we come here for the dozen or so eateries on the upper gallery, which serve everything from *főzelék*, the traditional Hungarian way of preparing vegetables sometimes served with meat, and Vietnamese *pho* (noodle soup)to paella and lobster.

Artizán
CAFE $

(Map p78; ☑06 30 856 5122; www.artizan.hu; Hold utca 3; salads & sandwiches 690-1390Ft; ☺7am-7pm Mon-Fri, 8am-4pm Sat; Ⓜ M3 Arany János utca) A new-style cafe with gallery seating upstairs, Artizán serves whole food only with no additives and bakes its own sourdough bread on the premises. The soup-and-sandwich menus (1150Ft to 1500Ft) are excellent value.

Gelateria Pomo d'Oro
ICE CREAM $

(Map p78; ☑06 70 390 7885; www.viaitalia.hu; V Arany János utca 12; 2/3/4 scoops 790/1190/1500Ft; ☺11.30am-9pm; ☒15, 115, ☒2) This small shop sells genuine gelato. It's located on a street that has become known as 'Via Italia' because of all its Italian restaurants and other businesses.

Padthai Wokbar
THAI $

(Map p78; ☑1-784 5079; http://padthaiwokbar.com; Október 6 utca 4; dishes 1380-1880Ft; ☺11am-10.30pm; ☒15, 115, ☒2) This Thai eatery on two levels offers dishes with a base of rice or noodles (1090Ft) with accompanying toppings (290Ft to 790Ft), and sauces free of charge. Hugely popular with students of the Central European University, who like the communal wooden tables and the too-clever-by-half aphorisms etched into the glass walls.

Culinaris
INTERNATIONAL $

(Map p78; ☑1-373 0028; www.culinaris.hu; XIII Balassi Bálint utca 7; mains 1990-2490Ft; ☺8am-3pm Mon-Sat; ☒2) Is it a restaurant? A cafe? A gourmet food shop? Apparently all three, and we love it for its welcoming colours and chaotic selection (pork vindaloo, Mexican beef chilli, Moroccan lamb pita, etc) but not its bankers' hours. Still, the shop section opens till 8pm (6pm on Sunday), so self-catering remains an option.

Roosevelt Étterem
HUNGARIAN $

(Map p78; ☑06 30 460 8706; www.facebook.com/roosevelttetterem; V Széchenyi István tér 7-8; mains 1200Ft; ☺8am-4pm Mon-Fri; ☒15, 115, ☒2) This brightly coloured caf that *used* to be on Roosevelt tér is a modern take on a Hungarian *önkiszolgáló* (self-service restaurant) where, along with light meals available throughout the day, main dishes are sold by weight (430Ft per 100g).

Duran SANDWICHES $
(Map p78; ☑1-332 9348; www.duran.hu; V Október 6 utca 15; sandwiches 230-390Ft; ⊙8am-5pm Mon-Fri, 9am-1pm Sat; ▣15) This branch of the popular sandwich bar is by the Central European University and is always rammed with penny-pinching students. It's branched out into serving mini pizzas as well.

Ring Cafe BURGERS $
(Map p78; ☑1-331 5790; www.ringcafe.hu; VI Andrássy út 38; burgers 1990-3390Ft; ⊙10am-midnight Mon-Thu, to 1am Fri & Sat, to 10pm Sun; ☎; ⓜM1 Oktogon) Excellent burgers, with lots of different varieties, are served in this small, modern joint that also does snacks, salads and breakfast till 1pm.

Gastronomia Pomo d'Oro ITALIAN $
(Map p78; ☑1-374 0288; www.pomodorobudapest. com; V Arany János utca 9; dishes 1700-2490Ft; ⊙9am-10pm Mon-Sat; ▣15, 115, ▣2) Next door to a much more extravagant trattoria bearing the same name on a street locals call 'Via Italia', this Italian delicatessen-caterer has a little dining area on the 1st floor where you can choose from a small selection of dishes or sample cheese and prepared meats in 100g measures (550Ft to 1800Ft). Sandwiches are 1590Ft to 1990Ft.

Salaam Bombay INDIAN $
(Map p78; ☑1-411 1252; V Mérleg utca 6; mains 1490-3100Ft; ⊙noon-3pm & 6-11pm; ☎; ▣15, 115, ▣2) If you're hankering for a fix of authentic Indian curry or tandoori in a bright, upbeat environment, look no further than this attractive eatery just east of Széchenyi István tér. There's an endless choice of breads and rice to go with your chicken tikka (2590Ft) and there are a dozen vegetarian dishes (1200Ft to 1990Ft) available too.

Pick Ház HUNGARIAN $
(Map p78; ☑1-331 7783; www.pick.hu; V Kossuth Lajos tér 9; mains 425-820Ft; ⊙8am-3pm Mon-Fri; ⓜM2 Kossuth Lajos tér) Next to the Kossuth Lajos tér metro station, this self-service eatery sits above the famous salami manufacturer's central showroom and shop (open 6am to 7pm Monday to Thursday, to 6pm Friday). It's convenient for lunch if you're visiting

Parliament, which is opposite, or for any of the sights in the area. The set menu is 990Ft.

Momotaro Metélt NOODLES $
(Map p78; ☑06 30 670 5184, 1-269 3802; www. momotaroramen.com; V Széchenyi utca 16; mains 2000-4900Ft; ⊙11am-10.30pm Tue-Sun; ☎; ▣15, 115, ▣2) This is a favourite pit stop for noodles – especially the soup variety – and dumplings (1000Ft to 2350Ft) when *pálinka* (fruit brandy), Unicum and other libations have been a-flowin' the night before. It's also good for dim sum and more substantial dishes.

Veggie Nyers Vegan Bisztró VEGETARIAN $
(Veggie Raw Vegan Bistro; Map p78; ☑06 30 625 5665; http://veggiebisztro.hu; V Garibaldi utca 5; mains 1200-1900Ft; ⊙11.30am-8pm Mon-Sat, to 3.30pm Sun; ☎; ⓜM2 Kossuth Lajos tér, ▣2) The second part of Veggie's name says it all: raw, vegan and a bistro. Of the eight or nine main courses available daily, all are also gluten-, lactose- and sugar-free. It has cakes (400Ft to 500Ft) too.

Napos Oldal VEGETARIAN $
(Map p78; ☑1-354 0048; VI Jókai utca 7; dishes 690-990Ft, set meals 1050-1490Ft; ⊙9am-8pm Mon-Fri, 11am-6pm Sat; ☎; ⓜM1 Oktogon, ▣4, 6) This tiny cafe-restaurant inside a health-food shop on the 'Sunny Side' of the street serves fresh salads, pastries and soups.

Szeráj KEBAB $
(Map p78; ☑1-311 6690; XIII Szent István körút 13; mains 700-1700Ft; ⊙9am-4am Mon-Sat, to midnight Sun; ▣4, 6) A very inexpensive self-service Turkish place good for *lahmacun* (Turkish 'pizza'; 650Ft), falafel (700Ft) and kebabs (from 1300Ft), with up to a dozen varieties on offer. It heaves after midnight, so whoever you were cruising in the pub or on the dance floor probably got here before you did.

Govinda VEGETARIAN $
(Map p78; ☑1-473 1310; www.govinda.hu; V Vigyázó Ferenc utca 4; dishes 250-1200Ft; ⊙11.30am-9pm Mon-Fri, noon-9pm Sat; ☎; ▣15, 115, ▣2) This basement restaurant northeast of the Chain Bridge serves wholesome salads, soups and desserts as well as daily set-menu plates (one/two/three courses for 1200/2000/3800Ft).

★**Borkonyha** HUNGARIAN $$
(Wine Kitchen; Map p78; ☑1-266 0835; www. borkonyha.hu; V Sas utca 3; mains 3150-7950Ft; ⊙noon-4pm & 6pm-midnight Mon-Sat; ▣15, 115, ⓜM1 Bajcsy-Zsilinszky út) Chef Ákos Sárközi's ap-

Budapest's Coffee Houses

My Cafe, My Castle

Cafe life has a long and colourful history in Budapest. The Turks introduced what the Magyars nicknamed *fekete leves* (black soup) to Hungary in the early 16th century, and the coffee house was an essential part of the social scene here long before it had even made an appearance in, say, Vienna or Paris. In the final decades of the Austro-Hungarian Empire, Budapest counted 600 cafes.

Budapest cafes of the 19th century were a lot more than just places to drink coffee. They embodied the progressive ideal that people of all classes could mingle under one roof, and acted as an incubator for Magyar culture and politics. Combining the neighbourliness of a local pub, the bonhomie of a gentlemen's club and the intellectual activity of an open university, coffee houses were places in which to relax, gamble, work, network, do business and debate. As the writer Dezs Kosztolányi put it in his essay 'Budapest, City of Cafés': *'Az én kávéházam, az én váram'* (My cafe is my castle).

Different cafes catered to different groups. Actors preferred the Pannónia, artists the Café Japán and businessmen the Orczy, while cartoonists frequented the Lánchíd and stockbrokers the Lloyd. But the two most important cafes in terms of the city's cultural life were the still-extant New York and the Centrál.

The literary New York Café (1891; p143) hosted virtually every Hungarian writer of note at one time or another. Indeed, the playwright Ferenc Molnár famously threw the key into the Danube the night the cafe opened so that it would never close. And it remained open round the clock 365 days a year

1. Centrál Kávéház (p140)
2. New York Café (p143)
3. *Rétes* (strudel)

for decades. The Centrál Kávéház (p140) attracted the same literary crowd, and two influential literary journals – *Nyugat* (West) and *A Hét* (The Week) – were edited here.

But the depression of the 1930s, the disruption of WWII and the dreary days of communism conspired against grand old cafes in favour of the cheap (and seldom cheerful) *eszpresszó* (coffee shop). By 1989 and the return of the Republic of Hungary only about a dozen traditional cafes remained.

Nowadays, though, you're more likely to find young Budapesters drinking a beer or a glass of wine at one of the new modern cafes serving smoothies and flat whites. The cafe is, in fact, very much alive in Budapest. It's just reinvented itself.

WHAT TO ORDER WHERE

Hungarians drink a huge amount of coffee (*kávé*), generally as a single black (*fekete*), a double (*dupla*) or with milk (*tejes kávé*). Most cafes now serve some variation of cappuccino and latte. Decaffeinated coffee is *koffeinmentes kávé*.

Pastries such as *Dobos torta* (a layered chocolate and cream cake with a caramelised-brown-sugar top) and the wonderful *rétes* (strudel), filled with poppy seeds, cherry preserves or *túró* (curd or cottage cheese), are usually eaten not as desserts but mid-afternoon in one of Budapest's ubiquitous *kávézók* (cafes) or *cukrászdák* (cake shops), including our favourites: Auguszt Cukrászda (p116), Szalai Cukrászda (p142) and Gerbeaud (p139).

proach to Hungarian cuisine at this Michelin-starred restaurant is contemporary, and the menu changes every week or two. Go for the signature foie gras appetiser wrapped in strudel pastry and a glass of sweet Tokaj wine. If *mangalica* (a special type of Hungarian pork) is on the menu, try it with a glass of dry *furmint*.

★ Pesti Disznó
HUNGARIAN $$

(Map p78; ✆1-951 4061; www.pestidiszno.hu; VI Nagymező utca 19; mains 2690-4490Ft; ⏱11am-midnight Sun-Wed, to 1am Thu-Sat; 🖋; Ⓜ M1 Oktogon) Punters would be forgiven for thinking that the 'Pest Pig' was all about pork. In fact, of the 10 main courses more than half are poultry, fish or vegetarian. It's a wonderful space, loftlike almost, with high tables and charming, informed service. The wine card is very, very good and most wines are available by the glass, too.

★ Kispiac
HUNGARIAN $$

(Map p78; ✆1-269 4231; www.kispiac.eu; V Hold utca 13; mains 2300-3950Ft; ⏱noon-10pm Mon-Sat; Ⓜ M3 Arany János utca) This hole-in-the-wall retro-style restaurant next to the Belvárosi Piac market on Hold utca serves *seriously* Hungarian things like stuffed *csülök* (pig's trotter – and way better than it sounds), roast *malac* (piglet) and an infinite variety of *savanyúság* (pickled vegetables). There's a warm welcome, and you probably won't eat again for a week.

Liberté
HUNGARIAN $$

(Map p78; ✆06 30 715 4635; www.libertebudapest.com; V Aulich utca 8; mains 2890-4950Ft; ⏱8am-11pm; Ⓜ M2 Kossuth Lajos tér) Established in 1902 (but not at this location), Liberté looks and feels more like a cafe and bar than a restaurant, and that's what people seem to use it for during the week. But it serves some finely prepared dishes and the daily specials alone – *sólet* (bean stew), Hungarian fish soup, lamb's knuckle – are worth a visit.

bigfish
SEAFOOD $$

(Map p78; ✆1-269 0693; www.thebigfish.hu; VI Andrássy út 44; fish at market prices, sides 670-1100Ft, other mains 980-5900Ft; ⏱noon-10pm; Ⓜ M1 Oktogon) Select your seafood type from the ice trays, choose the cooking method and a side or two, and then sit back and wait for super fresh fish and shellfish to be delivered to your table. This simply decorated restaurant has plenty of tables inside as well as on a terrace along busy Andrássy út. And there

are bibs for you messy eaters. Pasta and rice dishes also available for ichthyophobes.

Da Mario
ITALIAN $$

(Map p78; ✆1-301 0967; www.damario.hu; V Vécsey utca 3; mains 2000-6000Ft; ⏱11am-midnight; 🚊15, 115, Ⓜ M2 Kossuth Lajos tér) Owned and operated by a southern Italian, Da Mario can't put a foot wrong in our book. While the cold platters, soups, and meat and fish mains all look good, we stick to the house-made pasta dishes (2000Ft to 3500Ft) and pizzas (2000Ft to 4200Ft) from the wood-burning stove.

Mák
INTERNATIONAL $$

(Map p78; ✆06 30 723 9383; www.mak.hu; V Vigyázó Ferenc utca 4; mains 3400-6800Ft; ⏱noon-3pm & 6pm-midnight Tue-Sat; 🚊15, 115, 🚊2) The award-winning 'Poppy' serves inventive international dishes that lean in the direction of Hungary from a chalkboard menu that changes daily. Casual surrounds and seamless and very friendly service, with good advice on wine. At lunch the menu's two/three courses are a budget-friendly 3200/3800Ft.

Parázs Presszó
THAI $$

(Map p78; ✆06 30 371 5035, 1-950 3770; www.parazspresszo.com; VI Jókai utca 8; mains 2150-3950Ft; ⏱noon-11pm; Ⓜ M1 Oktogon, 🚊4, 6) This branch of a small chain serves Thai food just off the Big Ring Rd and has all the favourites – from *tom yum gung* (1400Ft) and *pad thai* (from 2150Ft) to the full range of green, red, Penang and Massaman curries. It has a very loyal following.

Café Bouchon
FRENCH $$

(Map p78; ✆1-353 4094; www.cafebouchon.hu; VI Zichy Jenő utca 33; mains 2590-4980Ft; ⏱11am-11pm Mon-Sat; 🚊trolleybus 70, 78, Ⓜ M3 Arany János utca) It's a little bit pricey for what and where it is, but *Ooh la la, c'est si bon!* A family-run *bouchon* (small restaurant) with a warm welcome and an art nouveau–style interior, it serves provincial French food stirred with a little Hungarian inspiration and the occasional Italian dish making an appearance. The four-course tasting menu without/with wine is 6690/8990Ft.

Kashmir
INDIAN $$

(Map p78; ✆1-354 1806; www.kashmiretterem.hu; V Arany János utca 13; mains 1390-2990Ft; ⏱6-10pm Tue-Sat, noon-6pm Sun; 🖋; Ⓜ M3 Arany János utca) One of our favourite subcontinentals in Pest, this places serves the cuisine of its namesake, which is always a bit sweeter than other Indian food, as well as a variety of tandoori cooked meats. There are lots of vegetarian choices and a Sunday buffet lunch for 1390Ft.

Első Pesti Rétesház HUNGARIAN $$
(Map p78; ☑1-428 0134; www.reteshaz.com; V Október 6 utca 22; mains 3390-6990Ft; ☺9am-11pm; ☑15, 115) It may be a bit overdone, with 'olde-worlde' counters, painted plates stuck on the walls and old letters and curios embedded in plexiglas, but the 'First Strudel House of Pest' is just the place to taste this Hungarian stretched and filled pastry (from 350Ft), with or without a full meal preceding it. Fillings include apple, cheese, poppy seed or sour cherry. Breakfast (from 890Ft) is served till noon. The weekday set lunch is 1550Ft.

Café Kör INTERNATIONAL $$
(Map p78; ☑1-311 0053; www.cafekor.net; V Sas utca 17; mains 2490-4790Ft; ☺10am-10pm Mon-Sat; ☑15, 115, Ⓜ️M3 Arany János utca) Just around the corner from the Basilica of St Stephen, the 'Circle Café' is a long-standing favourite for lunch or dinner but a great place for a light meal at any time, including breakfast (190Ft to 880Ft), which is available till noon. Service is welcoming and helpful, and there are lots of daily specials.

Most Kortárs Bistro INTERNATIONAL $$
(Now Contemporary Bisto; Map p78; ☑06 70 248 3322; http://mostbisztro.hu; VI Zichy Jenő utca 17; mains 2290-4590Ft; ☺noon-midnight Sun-Wed, to 1am Thu, to 2am Fri & Sat; Ⓜ️M3 Arany János utca) This place with the mouthful of a name is a restaurant-bistro-cafe-bar with a 'lived-in' look that clearly wants to be everything to everyone. And it almost succeeds. There is a small bar, a stage and roof terrace, a large indoor dining room and a big back garden. Food from the 'newspaper' menu is a mixed bag (burgers, tandoori and/or stir-fry dishes, anyone?). We mostly come for the brunch menu (1890Ft) though, available from 10am to 4pm on Saturday and Sunday. There's live music (jazz and blues) from 8pm to 10pm on Monday and noon to 4pm on Saturday.

Iguana MEXICAN $$
(Map p78; ☑1-331 4352; www.iguana.hu; V Zoltán utca 16; mains 1860-4890Ft; ☺11.30am-11pm Sun-Thu, to midnight Fri & Sat; ☑15, 115, Ⓜ️M2 Kossuth Lajos tér) Iguana serves decent enough Mexican food, with such dishes as enchilada and burrito combination *platos* and fajitas. There's a two-course lunch for just 1490Ft and a brunch menu at the weekend. The bar is busy.

Costes Downtown INTERNATIONAL $$$
(Map p78; ☑1-920 1015; www.costesdowntown. hu; V Vigyázó Ferenc utca 5; mains 7300-9300Ft; ☺6.30am-midnight; ☑15, 115, ☑2) The fifth restaurant in Budapest to be awarded a Michelin star and the second Costes one, Costes Downtown calls itself a fine-dining bistro and has added a new dimension to Budapest's restaurant scene. Watch the two chefs at work in the open kitchen and, nibbling on squid-ink chips, order such delectable offerings as swordfish ceviche and pan-seared duck with grapefruit and fennel.

With a brick vaulted ceiling and wine on display throughout, the feeling here is one of a cellar. But the floor-to-ceiling windows and 'living wall' dispel any feeling of being submerged. Weekday business lunches are 6900Ft. Tasting dinner menus of four/five/six courses are 22,000/25,000/30,000Ft, or 32,000/37,500/45,000Ft with wine pairings.

Tigris HUNGARIAN $$$
(Map p78; ☑1-317 3715; www.tigrisrestaurant.hu; V Mérleg utca 10; mains 4300-7900Ft; ☺noon-midnight Mon-Sat; ☑15, 115, ☑2) This upbeat, modern Hungarian restaurant, with its white linen tablecloths and antique-looking cupboards, has links to the Gere family of wine fame. Count on faultless service, a sommelier who will take you on a giddy tour of Hungary's major wine regions, and as many variations on goose liver as you can imagine.

🗡 Margaret Island & Northern Pest

★ Oriental Soup House VIETNAMESE $
(Map p84; ☑06 70 617 3535; www.facebook.com/ orientalsouphouse; XIII Hollán Ernő utca 35; mains 750-1990Ft; ☺11.30am-10pm Sun-Thu, to 11pm Fri & Sat; ☑; ☑trolleybus 75, 76) Though it's far away from central Budapest, this authentic Vietnamese joint is regularly packed. Customers squeeze around the communal tables beneath paper lanterns and tuck into several kinds of *pho* (rice noodle soup), as well as *mien ga* (chicken noodle soup) and *bun cha* (grilled pork and noodles).

★ Édesmindegy CAFE $
(Map p84; ☑06 30 502 9358; www.facebook.com/ Edesmindegy; XIII Pozsonyi út 16; cakes 1090Ft; ☺9am-9pm; ☑4, 6) Come here for some of Budapest's best and most imaginative cakes.

Temptations include poppyseed cheesecake with almond and sea buckthorn, strawberry cheesecake with Sichuan pepper, chocolate tart with salted caramel and probably the best *pasteis de nata* (custard tarts) outside Portugal.

Sarki Fűszeres
CAFE $

(Grocery Store on Corner; Map p84; ☑1-238 0600; www.facebook.com/sarkifuszeres; XIII Pozsonyi út 53-55; breakfast & sandwiches 790-2300Ft; ⏱8am-8pm Mon-Fri, to 3pm Sat; ☐trolleybus 75, 76) This delightful retro-style cafe on tree-lined Pozsonyi út is the perfect place for brunch, a late breakfast, a specialty coffee or just a quick sandwich. Doubles as a deli/wine shop.

Donut Library
BREAKFAST $

(Map p84; www.thedonutlibrary.com; XIII Pozsonyi út 22; doughnuts 320Ft; ⏱10am-8pm; ☐trolleybus 75, 76, ☐2, 4, 6) Budapest's first bona fide doughnut outlet sells dozens of varieties of both coated and filled fried dough. Great place for a quick hit of sugar and caffeine and there are comfy armchairs and window seats for perusing the book exchange.

Dunapark
CAFE $

(Map p84; ☑1-786 1009; www.dunaparkkavehaz. com; XIII Pozsonyi út 38; cakes 450-800Ft; ⏱8am-11pm Mon-Fri, 10am-11pm Sat, 10am-10pm Sun; ☑; ☐trolleybus 75, 76) Built in 1938 as a cinema, this art deco place with a lovely upstairs gallery, outdoor terrace and views of Szent István Park is also a restaurant. But we still think of – and use – it as a *cukrászda* (cake shop); its cakes are among the best this side of the Danube.

Café Panini
SANDWICHES $

(Map p84; ☑06 70 946 8072; www.cafepanini. hu; XIII Radnóti Miklós utca 45; sandwiches & salads 930-1600Ft; ⏱11am-10pm Mon, 8am-10pm Tue-Fri, 9am-10pm Sat & Sun; ☐trolleybus 75, 76) With an enviable location overlooking the Danube, this upbeat and very casual venue is worth a visit for the tasty views of Margaret Island alone. But come for great panini, stuffed bagels, wraps, salads, and breakfasts (1290Ft to 2390Ft) ranging from Parisian to full English.

Pozsonyi Kisvendéglő
HUNGARIAN $

(Map p84; ☑1-787 4877; XIII Radnóti Miklós utca 38; mains 1200-2800Ft; ⏱9am-midnight; ☐trolleybus 75, 76, ☐2, 4, 6) Visit this neighbourhood restaurant on the corner of Pozsonyi út for the ultimate local Budapest experience:

gargantuan portions of Hungarian classics (don't expect gourmet), rock-bottom prices and a cast of local characters. There's a bank of tables on the pavement in summer and a weekday set menu for 900Ft.

★Laci! Konyha!
HUNGARIAN $$

(Map p84; ☑06 70 370 7475; www.lacikonyha.com; XIII Hegedűs Gyula utca 56; mains 3400-4500Ft; ⏱noon-3pm & 6-11pm Mon-Fri; ☐15, 115, Ⓜ M3 Lehel tér) One of the most ambitious eateries in Budapest, this self-styled 'boutique restaurant' in the unlikely wilds of northern Pest is under the watchful gaze of chef Gábor Mogyorósi, who puts an eclectic spin on old favourites (expect the likes of pak choi with guinea fowl and Japanese mushrooms with oxtail). The daily two-course lunch is a snip at 2500Ft.

★Firkász
HUNGARIAN $$

(Map p84; ☑1-450 1118; www.firkasz.hu; XIII Tátra utca 18; mains 2390-7990Ft; ⏱noon-midnight; ☐15, 115, ☐4, 6) Set up by former journalists, retro-style restaurant 'Hack' has been one of our favourite Hungarian 'nostalgia' eateries for years, thanks to the lovely old mementoes on the walls, great homestyle dishes such as roast goose leg in red wine and Karpati-style pikeperch, a good wine list and nightly piano music.

Kiskakukk
HUNGARIAN $$

(Map p84; ☑1-450 0829; www.kiskakukk.hu; XIII Pozsonyi út 12; mains 1750-4990Ft; ⏱noon-midnight; ☐75, 76, ☐2, 4, 6) This ever-so-traditional Hungarian eatery with a retro shop sign in front has been serving up classic *gulyásleves* (hearty beef soup; 990Ft), veal stew with *spaetzle* (noodles; 3750Ft) and goose-liver medallions (4450Ft) for over a century. It's tried and tested and true.

Okay Italia
ITALIAN $$

(Map p84; ☑1-349 2991; www.okayitalia.hu; XIII Szent István körút 20; mains 1050-5490Ft; ⏱11am-midnight Mon-Fri, noon-midnight Sat & Sun; ☑; ☐4, 6) A perennially popular eatery started by Italians more than 20 years ago, Okay Italia does a full range of dishes, but most people come for the imaginative pasta and pizza, which is more than just 'okay'. The terrace on the Big Ring Rd is a lively place to meet in summer.

Mosselen
BELGIAN $$

(Map p84; ☑1-452 0535; www.mosselen.hu; XIII Pannónia utca 14; mains 3190-6290Ft; ⏱noon-midnight; ☐15, 115, Ⓜ M4 Nyugati pu) This pleasant

'Belgian beer cafe' in Újlipótváros serves Belgian (and some Hungarian) specialities, including its namesake, those much-loved bivalves, prepared in several different ways. There's a wide selection of Belgian beers, including some two dozen fruit-flavoured ones.

Trófea Grill
BUFFET $$

(Map p84; ☑ 06 20 949 4206; www.trofeagrill. net; XIII Visegrádi utca 50/a; lunch weekdays/ weekends 4399/5999Ft, dinner Mon-Thu 5999Ft, dinner Fri-Sun 6599Ft; ☺ noon-midnight Mon-Fri, 11.30am-midnight Sat, 11.30am-8.30pm Sun; ☷; ◨ 15, 115, ⓂM3 Lehel tér) This is the place to head when you really could eat a horse (which may or may not be on one of the serving tables). It's an enormous buffet of more than 100 cold and hot dishes over which appreciative diners swarm like bees. Children under 12 eat free on weekends.

✖ Erzsébetváros & the Jewish Quarter

★ Igen
PIZZA $

(Map p86; ☑ 06 20 348 0132; www.facebook.com/ igenitalia; VII Madách Imre út 5; slices 380-580Ft, pizzas 1520-2320Ft; ☺ noon-midnight Tue-Thu, to 2am Fri & Sat, to 10pm Sun; ⓂM1/2/3 Deák Ferenc tér) We'll always say 'Yes' (the meaning of *igen*) to this tiny pizzeria near Gozsdu udvar that features four regular pizzas (margherita, marinara, potato and truffle) and four 'guest' ones. It's Italian-owned and -operated, and the pizzas are as authentic as you'd find in Naples.

★ Bors Gasztro Bár
SANDWICHES $

(Map p86; www.facebook.com/BorsGasztroBar; VII Kazinczy utca 10; soups 600Ft, baguettes 670-890Ft; ☺ 11.30am-midnight; ☷; ⓂM2 Astoria) We love this thimble-sized place, not just for its hearty, imaginative soups (how about sweet potato with coconut or tiramisu?) but for its equally good grilled baguettes: try 'Bors Dog' (spicy sausage and cheese) or 'Brain Dead' (pig's brains are the main ingredient). It's not a sit-down kind of place; most chow down on the pavement outside.

Fröhlich Cukrászda
CAFE, JEWISH $

(Map p86; ☑ 06 20 913 2595, 1-266 1733; www. frohlich.hu; VII Dob utca 22; items 330-780Ft; ☺ 9am-6pm Mon-Thu, to 2pm Fri, 10am-6pm Sun; ⓂM1/2/3 Deák Ferenc tér) This kosher cake shop and cafe in the former ghetto, dating back to 1953, makes and sells old Jewish favourites such as *flódni* (a three-layer cake

with apple, walnut and poppy-seed fillings; 480Ft) and *mákos kifli* (crescent-shaped biscuits stuffed with poppy seed; 330Ft).

Naspolya Nassolda
VEGAN $

(Map p86; ☑ 06 70 380 8407; http://naspolya.hu; VI Káldy Gyula utca 7; dishes & snacks 780-940Ft; ☺ 10am-8pm Mon-Sat; ☷; ⓂM1 Bajcsy-Zsilinszky utca) This cafe serves sweets and savoury snacks that are raw, vegan, and gluten- and dairy-free. Try the chocolate cake with tonka-bean foam, a citrus granola bar or one of the healthy breakfasts. You might just be won over. The name refers to the medlar, a fruit rarely seen or eaten nowadays.

Desszert Neked
DESSERTS $

(Dessert for You; Map p86; ☑ 06 20 253 1519; www. desszertneked.hu; VI Paulay Ede utca 17; cakes 300-980Ft, ice cream per scoop 300Ft; ☺ 11am-9pm Mon-Fri, 10am-9pm Sat & Sun; ⓂM1 Bajcsy-Zsilinszky utca) This pretty place, all pastel colours (including the macaroons) and sweet things, serves ice cream and cakes to eat in or take away.

Abszolút Pho
VIETNAMESE $

(Map p86; ☑ 06 70 551 7630; www.facebook.com/ AbszolutPho; VII Kazinczy utca 52/c; mains 1390-2500Ft; ☺ 11.30am-10pm; ⓂM1/2/3 Deák Ferenc tér) There's nothing faux about this cubby hole of a Vietnamese place at the top of Kazinczy utca. But as its name suggests, don't expect to find much more here than the pungent noodle soup with herbs and beef or chicken and a few dumplings. Real Sriracha sauce too.

Zing Burger
BURGERS $

(Map p86; ☑ 06 20 424 9099; www.zingburger.hu/ en; VI Király utca 60; burgers 1150-1790Ft; ☺ 11am-11pm Sun-Wed, to 1am Thu-Sat; ⓂM1 Oktogon, ◨ 4, 6) Widely acclaimed as having the best burgers in Budapest, Zing has the full range – from basic to fancy (loads of vegetables and goat cheese added). For noncarnivores there are such offerings as grilled cheese sandwiches with peppers or mushrooms, onion rings and jalapeño peppers with chilli sauce.

Hokedli
VEGETARIAN $

(Map p86; ☑ 06 70 604 1869; www.facebook.com/ hokedli; Nagymező utca 10; soups & dishes 480-890Ft; ☺ 11.30am-7pm; ☷; ⓂM1 Opera) This charming little eatery that is mostly geared up for takeaways serves vegetarian, vegan and gluten-free soups and potages in pots. It also does some excellent homemade cakes.

Szimpla Farmers' Cafe
CAFE **$**

(Map p86; ☑06 20 511 7414; http://szimpla.hu/szimpla-farm-shop; VII Kazinczy utca 7; sandwiches 500-690Ft; ☺8am-10pm; ☑; Ⓜ M2 Astoria) Sourcing its ingredients from the farmers selling their wares at the Szimpla Farmers' market (p155) across the road on Sundays, this lovely, rustic cafe has a daily menu using seasonal ingredients for 1590Ft (soup and a main course), sandwiches, pastries, fresh fruit juices and Has Bean coffee.

Bangla Büfé
BANGLADESHI **$**

(Map p86; ☑1-266 3674; www.banglabufe.com; VII Akácfa utca 40; mains 1090-1790Ft; ☺noon-11pm Sat-Thu, 2.30-11pm Fri; ☑; 🚋4, 6) This place, owned and operated by a Bangladeshi expat, has as authentic samosas (550Ft), vegetarian, chicken and lamb biryani (from 1090Ft) and dhal as you'll find in Budapest. Simple but tasty.

Kádár
HUNGARIAN **$**

(Map p86; ☑1-321 3622; X Klauzál tér 9; mains 1000-2500Ft; ☺11.30am-3.30pm Tue-Sat; 🚋4, 6) Located in the heart of the Jewish district, Kádár is one of the most popular and authentic *étkezdék* you'll find in town and attracts the hungry with its ever-changing menu. Here you pay for everything: slices of bread, glasses of fizzy water from the seltzer bottle on the table etc.

Bollywood
VEGETARIAN **$**

(Map p86; ☑06 70 541 3812; www.bollywoodbudapest.com; VII Akácfa utca 50; mains 990-1995Ft; ☺noon-11pm Mon-Wed, to midnight Thu-Sat, to 10pm Sun; ☑; 🚋4, 6) There aren't a lot of top Indian actors to be found in this little Indian eatery just off the Big Ring Rd, but it is the place to got for a cheap fix of South Indian vegetarian and vegan dishes.

Montenegrói Gurman
BALKAN **$**

(Map p86; ☑06 70 673 0585; www.mnggurman.com; VII Rákóczi út 54; dishes 1590-4990Ft; ☺24hr; 🚋7, Ⓜ M2 Blaha Lujza tér) When we're famished, broke and it's well past the bewitching hour, we head for this South Slav eatery and join all the taxi drivers chomping on grills like *csevapcsicsa* (spicy meatballs), *pljeskavica* (spicy meat patties) or *razsnyics* (shish kebab). Breakfast is 1390Ft.

Erdélyi-Magyar Étkezde
HUNGARIAN **$**

(Map p86; ☑06 20 938 6352; www.erdelyimagyar.lapunk.hu; VII Nagy Diófa 3; daily menu 690-1250Ft; ☺11am-4pm Mon-Fri; Ⓜ M2 Astoria, 🚋4, 6) This little *étkezde* serves Transylvanian and Hungarian specialities to appreciative diners but, alas, keeps bankers' hours. If you can do any better than this for the price, though, let us know. Seating on two levels.

Kis Parázs
THAI **$**

(Map p86; ☑06 30 733 7760; www.parazspresszo.com; VII Kazinczy utca 7; soup 950-1450Ft; wok dishes 1680-2080Ft; ☺noon-11pm Sun-Tue, to 3am Wed-Sat; Ⓜ M2 Astoria) This little Thai eatery, with simple dishes on busy Kazinczy utca, has become a pre- or postclub nosh spot of choice in central Pest.

Napfényes
VEGAN **$**

(Map p86; ☑06 20 313 5555; www.napfenyeseterem.hu; VII Rózsa utca 39; mains 1800-2200Ft; ☺noon-10.30pm; ☑; Ⓜ M1 Kodály körönd) 'Sunny' is a titch out of the way (though not if you're staying on or near Andrássy út), but the friendly welcome, cute cellar space and wholesome vegan foods are worth the trip. There is an organic shop where you can stock up on both packaged and baked goods, including excellent cakes. Live entertainment too, including jazz concerts.

Frici Papa Kifőzdéje
HUNGARIAN **$**

(Map p86; ☑1-351 0197; www.fricipapa.hu; VI Király utca 55; mains 790-900Ft; ☺11am-11pm Mon-Sat; Ⓜ M1 Oktogon, 🚋4, 6) 'Papa Frank's Canteen' is larger and more modern than most *étkezdék* in Budapest. Excellent *főzelék* (traditionally prepared vegetable) dishes and soups are around 600Ft. We love the funny old murals of Pest in the days of yore.

★Zeller Bistro
HUNGARIAN **$$**

(Map p86; ☑1-321 7879, 06 30 651 0880; VII Izabella utca 38; mains 2900-5400Ft; ☺noon-3pm & 6-11pm Tue-Sat; Ⓜ M1 Vörösmarty utca, 🚋4, 6) You'll receive a very warm welcome at this lovely candlelit cellar where the attentive staff serve food sourced largely from the owner's family and friends in the Lake Balaton area. The Hungarian home cooking includes some first-rate dishes such as grey beef, duck leg, oxtail and lamb's knuckle. Superb desserts too. Popular with both locals and expats; reservations are essential.

★Barack & Szilva
HUNGARIAN **$$**

(Map p86; ☑1-798 8285; www.barackesszilva.hu; VII Klauzál utca 13; mains 3200-5500Ft; ☺6pm-midnight Mon-Sat; Ⓜ M2 Blaha Lujza tér) This is the kind of perfectly formed restaurant that every neighbourhood wishes it could boast. Run by a husband-and-wife team, the 'Peach & Pear' serves high-quality and exceptionally well-prepared Hungarian provincial food in a bistro setting. Try the duck pâté with dried plums and the red-wine beef *pörkölt* (goulash). Lovely terrace in summer too.

★ Kőleves
JEWISH **$$**

(Map p86; ☑ 06 20 213 5999; www.kolevesvendeglo.hu; VII Kazinczy utca 37-41; mains 2120-4920Ft; ☺ 8am-1am Mon-Fri, 9am-1am Sat & Sun; ☎ ☑ ; Ⓜ M1/2/3 Deák Ferenc tér) Always buzzy and lots of fun, the 'Stone Soup' attracts a young crowd with its Jewish-inspired (but not kosher) menu, lively decor, great service and reasonable prices. Good vegetarian choices. Breakfast (890Ft to 1250Ft) is served from 8am to 11.30am. The daily lunch is just 1250Ft, or 1100Ft for the vegetarian version.

★ M Restaurant
HUNGARIAN **$$**

(Map p86; ☑ 06 70 633 3460, 1-322 3108; www.metterem.hu; VII Kertész utca 48; mains 2200-3200Ft; ☺ 6pm-midnight; ☎ ; Ⓜ M1 Oktogon, ☒ 4, 6) A small, romantic spot with laid-back vibe, brown-paper-bag decor and a short but very well thought-out menu of Hungarian dishes with a French twist. Recommended.

★ Klassz
INTERNATIONAL **$$**

(Map p86; www.klasszetterem.hu; VI Andrássy út 41; mains 2990-4990Ft; ☺ 11.30am-11pm; Ⓜ M1 Oktogon) Permanent fixtures on the menu include foie gras in its various avatars and native *mangalica* pork. More unusual (and fleeting) dishes are lamb and vegetable ragout and orange-glazed duck. The food is of a very high standard. Reservations are not accepted; just show up and wait. Owned by the local wine society, Klassz is mostly about wine, however – Hungarian, to be precise.

Here you can order wine by the 10cL (100mL) measure from an ever-changing list of up to four dozen wines to sip and compare.

Konyha
HUNGARIAN **$$**

(Map p86; ☑ 1-322 5274; www.facebook.com/konyhabudapest; VII Madách Imre út 8; mains 2700-4500Ft; ☺ 9am-11pm Mon-Fri, 10am-midnight Sat; Ⓜ M1/2/3 Deák Ferenc tér) A new breed of Hungarian restaurant, 'Kitchen' is all about that, with the emphasis entirely on what is being prepared and put on the table. The menu is brief – four starters and a half-dozen mains – and sous-vide cooking dominates. Try the barbecue pork ribs or the *lecsó* eggs in a scrumptious tomato and pepper sauce.

Mazel Tov
ISRAELI **$$**

(Map p86; ☑ 06 70 626 4280; http://mazeltov.hu/en; VII Akácfa utca 47; mains 1990-4190Ft; ☺ 6pm-2am Mon-Fri, noon-2am Sat, noon-midnight Sun; ☑ ; ☒ 4, 6) An Israeli restaurant with an enormous courtyard that comes into its own in the warmer months, 'Good Luck' serves lots of grilled meats like *merguez* sausages and chicken *shawarma* that would not go amiss on a menu in Tel Aviv. But as there, lots of vegetarian options make an appearance too. It's always busy; book ahead – even on weekdays.

Tábla
HUNGARIAN **$$**

(Map p86; ☑ 06 20 360 0394; www.facebook.com/tablabudapest; VII Dohány utca 29; ☺ 11.30am-10pm Mon-Fri, to 2.30pm Sat & Sun; Ⓜ M2 Blaha Lujza tér, ☒ 4, 6) Less well-heeled sister restaurant of the expensive Esca next door, 'Blackboard' (yes, it has one of them) has some tasty offerings that change daily. Smoked trout sits happily with spicy Thai chicken soup and there is a preponderance of poultry dishes (especially duck and goose) served with lots of vegetables and fruit. Warm welcome and friendly service.

Tel Aviv Cafe
JEWISH **$$**

(Map p86; ☑ 06 30 438 7884; www.facebook.com/Cafe.Tel.Aviv.Budapest; VII Kazinczy utca 28; mains 1490-3400Ft; ☺ 8am-8.30pm Sun-Thu, to 3pm Fri; ☒ 4, 6) This cute, spick-and-span cafe in the heart of the Jewish district serves Israeli-style kosher food, from couscous and *shakshuka* to hummus and pasta dishes (1390Ft to 2500Ft). It's essentially a place for breakfast and lunch; come early on a Friday.

Bock Bisztró
HUNGARIAN **$$**

(Map p86; ☑ 1-321 0340; www.bockbisztropest.hu; VII Erzsébet körút 43-49; mains 3400-5400Ft; ☺ noon-midnight Mon-Sat; ☎ ; Ⓜ M1 Oktogon, ☒ 4, 6) An elegant and upmarket place to try a good range of traditional Hungarian delicacies and wines from around the country. It's formal and the tables are too closely set to one another, but the dishes are very well prepared and the staff helpful and friendly. Reservations recommended.

La Bodeguita del Medio
CUBAN **$$**

(Map p86; www.labodeguitadelmedio.hu; VII Dob utca 55; mains 2290-7590Ft; ☺ noon-1am Mon-Thu & Sun, to 3am Fri & Sat; ☒ 4, 6) Anchor tenant of the Fészek Club, meeting place of artists and intellectuals since 1901, La Bodeguita del Medio is a Cuban restaurant with such favourites as banana and yucca chips, *mantanzas* (a dish of grilled meats) and *ropa vieja* (beef jerky). It's in the city's most beautiful leafy courtyard, and there's live Cuban music from 8pm Tuesday to Saturday.

Cirkusz HUNGARIAN $$
(Map p86; ☑1-786 4959, 06 70 623 1616; www.facebook.com/cirkuszbudapest; VII Dob utca 25; mains 2200-3200Ft; ☺9am-10pm Mon-Sat, to 5pm Sun; ☎; Ⓜ M1/2/3 Deák Ferenc tér) One of the more interesting choices along Dob utca, colourful Cirkusz serves traditional Hungarian dishes with some international touches. But it is more of a cafe than a restaurant. Come for breakfast (750Ft to 1700Ft) – late (served till 4pm) or otherwise. Try the Turkish eggs.

Spinoza Café HUNGARIAN $$
(Map p86; ☑1-413 7488; www.spinozacafe.hu; VII Dob utca 15; mains 1950-4650Ft; ☺8am-midnight Mon-Fri, 9am-11.30pm Sat & Sun; Ⓜ M2 Astoria) This attractive cafe-restaurant includes an art gallery and theatre, where *klezmer* (Jewish folk music) concerts are staged at 7pm on Fridays (9500Ft with three-course meal), along with a coffee house and restaurant where there's live piano music nightly. The food is mostly Hungarian and Jewish comfort food, not kosher but no pork. The all-day breakfast (1500Ft) is a steal.

Menza HUNGARIAN $$
(Map p86; ☑1-413 1482; www.menzaetterem.hu; VI Liszt Ferenc tér 2; mains 2590-4990Ft; ☺10am-midnight; Ⓜ M1 Oktogon) This stylish restaurant on one of Budapest's more lively squares takes its name from the Hungarian for a school canteen – something it is anything but. It's always packed with diners, who come for its simple but well-prepared Hungarian classics with a modern twist, in trendy, mid-century-styled dining rooms. Weekday two-course set lunches are 1290Ft.

Vak Varjú HUNGARIAN $$
(Map p86; ☑1-268 0888; http://vakvarju.com; VI Paulay Ede utca 7; mains 2250-4390Ft; ☺noon-midnight; Ⓜ M1 Bajcsy-Zsilinszky utca) The 'Blind Crow' is a favourite among local young professionals who like the large spaces, long wooden tables and quality food served in huge portions. This is where you can try things like sweet potato cream soup, pig's brain on toast with red onion salad, and chicken breast with pumpkin and pear risotto. It's a party atmosphere most nights.

Vintage Garden BISTRO $$
(Map p86; ☑06 30 790 6619; www.facebook.com/vintagegardenbudapest; VII Dob utca 21; mains 1990-6990Ft; ☺8am-midnight; Ⓜ M1/2/3 Deák Ferenc tér) Described by a friend as the perfect place for a first date, Vintage Garden is a bit, well, romantic, with a lovely covered back terrace and bleached wooden floors, chandeliers, mirrors and flowers throughout. Mains such as jambalaya are worth considering, or stick to burgers, sandwiches and salads (2490Ft to 2990Ft) if you're working fast.

Macesz Bistro JEWISH $$
(Map p86; ☑1-787 6164; http://maceszbistro.hu; VII Dob utca 26; mains 2490-4590Ft; ☺noon-4pm & 6-11pm Sun-Thu, to midnight Fri & Sat; Ⓜ M1/2/3 Deák Ferenc tér) A marriage of modern and traditional, the Macesz serves up Hungarian Jewish dishes in a swish bistro-style dining room, handsomely dressed up with lace tablecloths, flock wallpaper and rocking horses. The Jewish-style eggs (1290Ft) and matzo-ball soup (1490Ft) are good starters, and goose and duck feature heavily on the list of excellent main courses.

Hanna JEWISH $$
(Map p86; ☑1-342 1072; VII Dob utca 35; mains 2800-3600Ft; ☺11am-10pm Sun-Thu, to 11pm Fri, noon-3pm Sat; ☒4, 6) Housed upstairs in an old school in the Orthodox Synagogue complex, this eatery is pretty basic and informal but is an option for glatt kosher meals. On the Sabbath you order and pay for meals in advance. Set three-course menu from 5900Ft.

Fausto's ITALIAN $$$
(Map p86; ☑1-269 6806, 06 30 589 1813; www.fausto.hu; VII Dohány utca 3; mains osteria 2400-4800Ft, restaurant 4900-8200Ft; ☺noon-3pm & 7-11pm Mon-Sat; Ⓜ M2 Astoria) Elegant Fausto's offers a top-class dining room in its *ristorante* and a cheaper *osteria* just up from the Great Synagogue. It does excellent and innovative pasta dishes, daily specials and desserts. There's also a well-chosen range of Italian and Hungarian wines. Three-/four-course lunches in the *osteria* are 3200/4200Ft. Impeccable service.

✖ Southern Pest

Curry House INDIAN $
(Map p92; ☑1-264 0297; www.curryhouse.hu; VIII Horánszky utca 1; mains 1700-3100Ft; ☺11am-10pm Tue-Sun; ☒; Ⓜ M4 Rákóczi tér) This richly decorated and well-run Indian restaurant offers a warm welcome, attentive service and a wide range of authentic dishes. There are lots of options for vegetarians (1300Ft

to 2200Ft) as well as lunchtime thalis (trays with a variety of tasting-size dishes), succulent tandoori (1700Ft to 3000Ft) and accomplished curries.

Hanoi Xua
VIETNAMESE $

(Map p92; ☑ 1-314 6736; www.facebook.com/hanoixuarestaurant; IX Ernő utca 30-34; mains 1390-2290Ft; ⊙ 11am-10pm; Ⓜ M3 Nagyváradtér) A little out of the way, but handy for the Hungarian Natural History Museum, this spacious, functional-looking restaurant has an extensive, excellent-value and authentic menu of *pho* (noodle soup), *bún* (rice noodles), *bánh mì* (sandwiches) and other Vietnamese favourites, and attracts a loyal following.

African Buffet
AFRICAN $

(Map p92; 06 30 443 2437; VIII Bérkocsis utca 21; dishes from 1300Ft; ⊙ 10am-11pm Mon-Sat; Ⓜ M4 Rákóczi tér, ☒ 4, 6) We love the food, the colourful decor and and the warm welcome at this little African oasis just round the corner from the Rákóczi tér market. It's family run and the food's homemade; try the spicy goat soup and the Zanzibar rice studded with good things.

Macska
VEGETARIAN $

(Map p92; ☑ 1-786 8370; www.facebook.com/macska23; VIII Bérkocsis utca 23; dishes 1400-2800Ft; ⊙ 4pm-midnight Mon-Thu, to 2am Fri; ☑; Ⓜ M4 Rákóczi tér, ☒ 4, 6) 'Cat' is a peculiar little cafe-bar, with vegie and vegan dishes like enchiladas and burritos on the menu and, as befitting its name, felines in various guises as part of its eclectic decor. Chilled atmosphere and good music.

Pink Cadillac
PIZZA $

(Map p92; ☑ 1-216 1412; www.pinkcadillac.hu; IX Ráday utca 22; pizzas 1340-2450Ft, pasta 1550-2450Ft; ⊙ 10am-midnight; Ⓜ M3/4 Kálvin tér) Ráday utca has been Southern Pest's most important restaurant strip for nigh on two decades now. If you don't like the surrounds at the Pink Cadillac, have your pizza delivered to Paris Texas (p148), which is the bar next door (not some one-horse town with ambitions in the Lone Star State).

★ Rosenstein
HUNGARIAN $$

(Map p92; ☑ 1-333 3492; www.rosenstein.hu; VIII Mosonyi utca 3; mains 2900-6500Ft; ⊙ noon-11pm Mon-Sat; Ⓜ M2/4 Keleti train station, ☒ 24) A top-notch and cosy Hungarian restaurant in an unlikely location, with Jewish tastes and super service. Family-run – the owner is also the chef – it has been here for years,

so expect everyone to know each other. The extensive menu features some interesting game dishes as well as good-value daily lunch specials (2200Ft to 3200Ft).

Matrjoska Bisztró
RUSSIAN $$

(Map p92; ☑ 1-796 8496; www.matrjoskabisztro.com; VIII Lőrinc pap tér 3; mains 2800-4900Ft; ⊙ noon-midnight Mon-Sat; Ⓜ M3/4 Kálvin tér, ☒ 4, 6) Set on a cute little square, this Russian-influenced bistro, with high ceilings, a contemporary forest theme and waiters buzzing between tables, does great caviar, borscht, *pelmeny* (dumplings) and of course serves a wide selection of vodka. Book ahead at weekends or perch on a stool at the enormous shared barrel-shaped table.

Petrus
FRENCH $$

(Map p92; ☑ 1-951 2597; www.petrusrestaurant.hu; IX Ferenc tér 2-3; mains 2990-4190Ft; ⊙ noon-3.30pm & 6-11pm Tue-Sat; Ⓜ M3 Klinikák, ☒ 4, 6) Owned by prominent chef Zoltán Feke, Petrus offers French bistro cooking: boeuf bourguignon, duck confit and snails done in a profusion of ways. The restaurant artfully balances modern and traditional decor, but the Deux Chevaux car in the middle of the dining room does nothing but take up space. The wine list is good, though service could be better.

Padrón
TAPAS $$

(Map p92; ☑ 06 30 900 1204; www.facebook.com/padrontapas; VIII Horánsky utca 10; tapas 690-1490Ft; ⊙ 5-11pm Mon-Fri, 9am-11pm Sat; ☎; Ⓜ M4 Rákóczi tér) An authentic slice of Spain in the backstreets of Budapest, Padrón is passionately run by well-informed staff and expertly trained chefs. There's a great range of tapas such as tortilla, *jamón iberico* (cured ham), *gambas al pil-pil* (garlic and chilli prawns), lots of *bacalao* (dried salted cod) dishes and *morcilla* (blood sausage). Seasonal options, too.

Építész Pince
HUNGARIAN $$

(Map p92; ☑ 1-266 4799; www.epiteszpince.hu; VIII Ötpacsirta utca 2; mains 2050-4250Ft; ⊙ 11am-10pm Mon-Thu, to midnight Fri & Sat; Ⓜ M3/4 Kálvin tér) This basement restaurant behind the Hungarian National Museum is stunningly designed, and why wouldn't it be? It's in the neoclassical headquarters of the Magyar Építész Kamara (Chamber of Hungarian Architects). The food is mostly enlightened Hungarian favourites; come here for the decor, the artsy crowd and the gorgeous paved courtyard that's candlelit come dusk. The weekday set lunch is just 1150Ft.

Borbíróság
HUNGARIAN $$

(Map p92; ☐1-219 0902; www.borbirosag.com; IX Csarnok tér 5; mains 2250-4650Ft; ☺noon-11.30pm Mon-Sat; Ⓜ M4 Fővám tér, ☐47, 49) The simple, classy 'Wine Court', where almost 100 Hungarian wines are available by the glass and the food – especially duck – is taken pretty seriously, is just by Nagycsarnok market (p156). The terrace on a quiet square is a delight in the warmer months.

Fülemüle
HUNGARIAN $$

(Map p92; ☐06 70 305 3000, 1-266 7947; www.fulemule.hu; VIII Kőfaragó utca 5; mains 2900-5500Ft; ☺noon-10pm Sun-Thu, to 11pm Fri & Sat; Ⓜ M4 Rákóczi tér, ☐4, 6) This quaint Hungarian restaurant with long wooden tables and old photos on the wall is quite a find in deepest Józsefváros and well worth the search. Dishes mingle Hungarian and international tastes with some old-style Jewish favourites, including six kinds of *sólet*, a traditional Hungarian-Jewish stew made with kidney beans, barley, onions, paprika and (usually) meat. The picture menu helps.

Soul Café
INTERNATIONAL $$

(Map p92; ☐1-217 6986; www.soulcafe.hu; IX Ráday utca 11-13; mains 2490-6200Ft; ☺noon-midnight; Ⓜ M3/4 Kálvin tér) One of the better choices along a street heaving with so-so restaurants and overpriced cafes, the Soul Café has inventive continental food and decor, and a great terrace on both sides of the street. The three-course daily menu is 1490Ft.

Stex Ház
HUNGARIAN $$

(Map p92; ☐1-318 5716; www.stexhaz.hu; VIII József körút 55-57; mains 2790-5290Ft; ☺8am-4am Mon-Sat, 9am-2am Sun; ☎; Ⓜ M3 Corvin-negyed, ☐4, 6) A big, noisy place that's open almost around the clock, Stex offers soups, sandwiches, pasta, fish and meat dishes, including massive mixed platters for one/two 3590/5990Ft. It transforms into a lively bar at night and it also serves breakfast (760Ft to 1690Ft).

★ Múzeum
HUNGARIAN $$$

(Map p92; ☐1-267 0375; www.muzeumkavehaz.hu; VIII Múzeum körút 12; mains 3600-7200Ft; ☺6pm-midnight Mon-Sat, noon-3pm Sun; Ⓜ M3/4 Kálvin tér) This cafe-restaurant is the place to come if you like to dine in old-world style with a piano softly tinkling in the background. It's still going strong after 130 years at the same location. The goose-liver parfait (3400Ft) is to die for, the goose leg and cabbage (3900Ft) iconic. There's also a good selection of Hungarian wines.

Costes
HUNGARIAN, FUSION $$$

(Map p92; ☐1-219 0696; www.costes.hu; IX Ráday utca 4; mains 9000-13,000Ft; ☺6.30pm-midnight Wed-Sun; ☎; Ⓜ M3/4 Kálvin tér) The first Hungarian restaurant to gain a Michelin star, Costes is the carefully orchestrated high-end dining experience you might expect. The service is scrupulous yet friendly, the setting – chocolate and cream – is sleek, and the beautifully presented food is expertly created using top-quality ingredients. The menu changes regularly to reflect what's in season. Book ahead.

Four-/five-/six-course set meals are 40,500/46,500/53,000Ft.

✖ City Park & Beyond

Kilenc Sárkány
CHINESE $

(Map p96; www.kinaietterem.hu/etterem/kilenc-sarkany; VII Dózsa György út 56; mains 1200-3600Ft; ☺11.30am-11.30pm; ☐79) We asked friends at the Chinese Embassy where they go for their fix of pork dumplings and fried rice, and the unanimous verdict was Nine Dragons at the southwestern end of City Park. Bearing the same name as Kowloon, it's not surprising the restaurant also does that Cantonese favourite, dim sum.

★ Olimpia
HUNGARIAN $$

(Map p96; ☐1-321 0680; www.alparutca5.hu; VII Alpár utca 5; 2-/3-course lunches 2850/2990Ft, 4-/5-/6-/7-course dinners 7500/8600/9500/9900Ft; ☺noon-3pm Tue-Fri, 7-10pm Tue-Sat; ☎; ☐5, 7, Ⓜ M2 Keleti pályaudvar) Traditional Hungarian with a twist is on offer at this brilliant restaurant that offers a table d'hôte set-lunch menu of one to three courses and a dinner menu of up to seven; the set lunches are a steal. Book ahead.

★ Bagolyvár
HUNGARIAN $$

(Map p96; ☐1-889 8127; www.bagolyvar.com; XIV Gundel Károly út 4; mains 3900-5900Ft; ☺noon-midnight; ☎; Ⓜ M1 Hősök tere) With reworked Hungarian classics that make it a winner, the 'Owl's Castle' attracts the Budapest cognoscenti, who leave its sister restaurant, **Gundel** (Map p96; ☐1-889 8111; www.gundel.hu; XIV Gundel Károly út 4; mains 5500-59,000Ft; set lunch menus 5900-7500Ft, Sun brunch adult/child 7900/3950Ft; ☺noon-midnight; ☎; Ⓜ M1 Hősök tere), next door, to the expense-account brigade. There are excellent three-course set menus for 4700Ft, and 2500Ft mains at lunch on weekends, all served in a pleasantly old-fashioned dining room or on a sunny terrace.

Wang Mester   CHINESE $$

(Map p96; ☑1-251 2959; www.kinaikonyha.hu; XIV Gizella út 46/a; dishes 2890-5590Ft; ☺noon-11pm; � ; ☐5, 7, ☐1) A short walk from the southeastern corner of City Park, this minimalist, authentic restaurant serves dishes from across China with an emphasis on Sichuanese classics, such as fish in chilli broth and *mapo tofu* (tofu in a spicy sauce). Brick walls and dark-wood furniture make for an elegant atmosphere, with a counter kitchen where the chefs work magic. Popular with local Chinese.

Robinson   INTERNATIONAL $$$

(Map p96; ☑1-422 0222; www.robinsonrestaurant. hu; XIV Városligeti tó; mains 4000-13,700Ft; ☺11am-11pm, restaurant noon-3pm & 6-11pm; ☏ ; Ⓜ M1 Hősök tere) Located within leafy City Park, informal yet stylish Robinson is the place to secure a table on the lakeside terrace on a warm summer's evening. Starters include beef tartare (4400Ft), while mains feature grilled *fogas* (Balaton pike-perch; 5400Ft) and various meats cooked over charcoal (4900Ft to 13,900Ft). It's pricey, but – as ever – it's all about location, location, location.

🍷 Drinking & Nightlife

In recent years Budapest has justifiably gained a reputation as one of Europe's top nightlife destinations. Alongside its age-old cafe culture, it offers a magical blend of unique drinking holes, fantastic wine, home-grown firewaters and emerging craft beers, all served up with a warm Hungarian welcome and a wonderful sense of fun. www.wheretraveler.com/budapest is useful for nightlife listings.

🍷 Castle District

★**Kávé Műhely**   COFFEE

(Map p62; ☑06 30 852 8517; www.facebook.com/ kavemuhely; II Fő utca 49; ☺7.30am-6.30pm Mon-Fri, 9am-5pm Sat & Sun; Ⓜ M2 Batthyány tér, ☐19, 41) This tiny coffee shop is one of the best in the city. These guys roast their own beans, and their cakes and sandwiches are fantastic. Too hot for coffee? They've got craft beers and homemade lemonades, too. The attached gallery stages vibrant contemporary art exhibitions.

Belga Söröző   BAR

(Belgian Brasserie; Map p62; ☑1-201 5082; www.belgasorozo.com/fooldal; II Bem rakpart 12; ☺noon-midnight; ☐19, 41) Dark, wood-panelled, underground bar specialising in an extensive range of Belgian beers. There are only six on tap, but there's a much more inspiring bottled selection, as well as Belgian nibbles such as *moules marinière* (mussels in white wine) to keep hunger at bay.

Bereg Cafe & Bar   CAFE

(Map p62; ☑06 70 296 9411; II Batthyány utca 49; ☺8am-10pm Mon-Wed, to 10.30pm Thu & Fri, 10.30am-10pm Sat; ☐16, 16A, 116) Housed in the Swan House, a remarkable example of Hungarian organic architecture, this friendly place welcomes 'wanderers, lovers, artists' and more. There's a peaceful garden for lingering over a craft beer, a glass of Hungarian wine or a coffee, and you may well be visited by the pet pygmy rabbit and cat.

Oscar American Bar   BAR

(Map p62; ☑06 20 214 2525; www.oscarbar.hu; I Ostrom utca 14; ☺5pm-2am Mon-Thu, to 4am Fri & Sat; Ⓜ M2 Széll Kálmán tér) The decor is cinema-inspired (Hollywood memorabilia on the wood-panelled walls, leather directors' chairs) and the beautiful crowd often act like they're on camera. Not to worry: the potent cocktails (950Ft to 2250Ft) – from daiquiris and cosmopolitans to champagne cocktails and mojitos – go down a treat. There's music most nights.

Lánchíd Söröző   BAR

(Chain Bridge Pub; Map p62; ☑1-214 3144; www. lanchidsorozo.hu; I Fő utca 4; ☺11am-midnight; ☐16, 16A, ☐19, 41) As its name implies, this pub near the Chain Bridge head has a wonderful retro Magyar feel to it, with old movie posters and advertisements on the walls and red-checked cloths on the tables. A proper local place with friendly service.

Ruszwurm Cukrászda   CAFE

(Map p62; ☑1-375 5284; www.ruszwurm.hu; I Szentháromság utca 7; ☺10am-7pm Mon-Fri, to 6pm Sat & Sun; ☐16, 16A, 116) This diminutive cafe dating from 1827 is the perfect place for coffee and cakes (420Ft to 750Ft) in the Castle District. In high season it's almost always impossible to get a seat.

Angelika Kávéház   CAFE

(Map p62; ☑1-225 1653; www.angelikacafe.hu; I Batthyány tér 7; ☺9am-11pm; Ⓜ M2 Batthyány tér) Attached to an 18th-century church,

BUDAPEST DRINKING & NIGHTLIFE

GARDEN CLUBS & RUIN BARS

During the long and often very hot summers, so-called *kertek* (literally 'gardens', but in Budapest any outdoor spot that has been converted into an entertainment zone) empty out even the most popular indoor bars and clubs. These vary enormously, from permanent bars with an attached garden, and clubs with similar outdoor sections, to totally al fresco spaces only frequented in good weather.

Ruin pubs (*romkocsmák*) began to appear in the city from the early 2000s, when entrepreneurial free thinkers took over abandoned buildings and turned them into pop-up bars. At first a very word-of-mouth scene, the ruin bars' popularity grew exponentially and many have transformed from ramshackle, temporary sites full of flea-market furniture to more slick, year-round fixtures with covered areas to protect patrons from the winter elements.

Many garden clubs and ruin pubs have DJs, live music or jam sessions. Table football, table tennis, pool and other pub games are frequently a fixture, and a number of places offer street food; some also host escape games.

Angelika is as much a restaurant as a cafe, with a raised outside terrace. The more substantial dishes are just so-so; come here for the cakes and the views across the square to the Danube and parliament.

Bambi Eszpresszó CAFE
(Map p62; ☑1-213 3171; www.facebook.com/bambieszpresszo; II Frankel Leó út 2-4; ⊗7am-10pm Mon-Fri, 9am-10pm Sat & Sun; ☐19, 41) The words 'Bambi' and 'modern' do not make comfortable bedfellows; little about this place (named after a communist-era local soft drink) has changed since the 1960s. And that's just the way the crowd here likes it. Friendly though set-it-down-with-a-crash service completes the picture.

🍴 Gellért Hill & Tabán

★ Szatyor Bár és Galéria BAR
(Carrier Bag Bar & Gallery; Map p66; ☑1-279 0290; www.szatyorbar.com; XIII Bartók Béla út 36-38; ⊗noon-1am; Ⓜ M4 Móricz Zsigmond körtér, ☐18, 19, 47, 49) Sharing the same building as the cafe Hadik Kávéház and separated by just a door, the Szatyor is the funkier of the twins, with cocktails, street art on the walls and a Lada driven by the poet Endre Ady. Cool or what? There's food here, too (mains 1900Ft to 2400Ft).

B8 Craft Beer & Pálinka Bar CRAFT BEER
(B8 Kézműves Sör és Pálinkabár; Map p66; ☑1-791 3462; www.facebook.com/b8pub; Bercsényi utca 8; ⊗4-11pm Mon, noon-11pm Tue-Fri, 5-11pm Sat; Ⓜ M4 Móricz Zsigmond körtér, ☐18, 19, 47, 49) Our favourite new watering hole in Buda, this pint-sized place (though there are three

floors) has more than two-dozen craft beers available from Hungary's 52 (at last count) breweries. Look for the names Legenda, Monyo and Etyeki and try the last's Belga Búza (Belgian Wheat). Harder stuff? Some 10 types of *pálinka* (fruit brandy), from Japanese plum to Gypsy cherry.

Kelet Cafe & Gallery CAFE
(Kelet Kávézó és Galéria; Map p66; ☑06 20 230 0094; www.facebook.com/keletkavezo; Bartók Béla út 29; ⊗7.30am-11pm Mon-Fri, 9am-11pm Sat & Sun; Ⓜ M4 Móricz Zsigmond körtér, ☐18, 19, 47, 49) This really cool cafe moonlights as a used-book exchange on the ground floor and a large, bright gallery with seating upstairs. There are foreign newspapers to read and soups (780Ft to 990Ft) and sandwiches (850Ft to 1100Ft) should you feel peckish. Try the super hot chocolate.

Tranzit Art Café CAFE
(Map p66; ☑1-209 3070; www.tranzitcafe.com; XI Bukarest utca & Ulászló utca; ⊗9am-11pm Mon-Fri, 10am-10pm Sat; ☐7, ☐19, 49) As chilled a place to drink and nosh as you'll find in south Buda, the Tranzit made its home in a small disused bus station, put art on the walls and filled the leafy courtyard with hammocks and comfy sofas. Breakfast (1190Ft) and sandwiches (from 1590Ft) are available.

Two-/three-/four-course lunches or dinners (including a vegie one) can be had for 1390/1690/1990Ft during the week.

Palack Borbár WINE BAR
(Bottle Wine Bar; Map p66; ☑06 30 997 1902; http://palackborbar.hu; Szent Gellért tér 3; ⊗noon-11pm Mon, to midnight Tue-Sat, to 10pm Sun; ☐7,

86, MM4 Szent Gellért tér, 🚋18, 19, 47, 49) While we are pleased to see a real wine bar open on the Buda side, with well over 100 types from 16 Hungarian regions available by the 1.5dL (150mL) glass (600Ft to 1800Ft), we hope they do something about the service and the quality of sliced meats and cheese plates (1490Ft to 2290Ft) that traditionally act as blotter here.

Hadik Kávéház CAFE
(Map p66; ☏1-279 0291; www.hadikkavehaz.com; XIII Bartók Béla út 36; ☺noon-1am; MM4 Móricz Zsigmond körtér, 🚋18, 19, 47, 49) This place has brought history back to Bartók Béla út. The Hadik is a revived old-world cafe that pulled in the punters for more than four decades before being shut down in 1949. It's now back, as relaxed and atmospheric as ever. Excellent daily lunch menu for 1490Ft.

Café Ponyvaregény CAFE
(Map p66; ☏06 30 920 2470; www.cafeponyvaregeny.hu; XI Bercsényi utca 5; ☺10am-midnight Mon-Sat, 2-10pm Sun; MM4 Móricz Zsigmond körtér, 🚋18, 19, 47, 49) The 'Pulp Fiction' is a quirky little basement cafe that has a loyal following despite all the competition in this part of south Buda. The old books and fringed lampshades are a nice touch, and the coffee (350Ft to 660Ft) is excellent.

Platán Eszpresszo CAFE
(Map p66; ☏06 20 361 2287; Döbrentei tér 2; ☺10am-10pm Sun-Thu, to 11pm Fri & Sat; 🚋18, 19, 41) There's not much to recommend this place, with its rather dark interior and lacklustre grills (1790Ft to 2390Ft). But we've always enjoyed sitting under the plane tree (the giveaway name) out in front supping Dreher in the warmer months, especially after a session at the nearby Rudas Baths.

🍴 Óbuda & Buda Hills

Barako Kávéház COFFEE
(Map p70; ☏06 30 283 7065; www.barakokavehaz.com; II Török utca 3; ☺8am-8pm Mon-Sat, 9am-6pm Sun; 🚋4, 6, 19, 41) Run by a tattooed Filipino, this thimble-sized coffee house aims to spread the fame of Liberica Baraco coffee from the Philippines. While arabica tastes sour when cold, Liberica Baraco retains its sweetness. In addition to latte, ristretto and other standards, you can also fortify yourself with ice drip Dutch coffee here.

Calgary Antik Bár BAR
(Map p70; ☏1-316 9087; www.etterem.hu/669; II Frankel Leó út 24; ☺4pm-4am; 🚋4, 6) This teensy bar just over Margaret Bridge hides an Aladdin's Cave. It's filled to bursting with antiques and a host of loyal regulars who stay up all night playing cards, drinking and gossiping with owner Viky Szabó, model turned junk-shop proprietor.

Puskás Pancho Sports Pub PUB
(Map p70; ☏06 30 806 3109; www.symbolbudapest.hu; III Bécsi út 56; ☺7.30am-midnight Mon-Fri, 11.30am-midnight Sat & Sun; 🚋17, 19, 41) In Óbuda's sprawling Symbol entertainment complex, this popular sports pub is named after Ferenc Puskás (1927–2006), Hungary's greatest football player, who emigrated to Spain after the 1956 Uprising and played for Real Madrid. Ferenc in Hungarian and Pancho in Spanish are the same name: Frank. See the statue of him outside III Bécsi út 61.

🍴 Belváros

★**Marionett Craft Beer House** CRAFT BEER
(Marionett Kézműves Sörház; Map p74; ☏06 30 832 0880; www.marionettcraftbeer.house; V Vigadó tér; ☺3pm-midnight; MM1/2/3 Deák Ferenc tér, 🚋2) Minimalist on the inside, yet livened up by the colourful hanging marionettes, this elegant newcomer on the craft-beer scene has been winning accolades for its great selection of local brews. If you're hungry, you can nibble on sausages and pastrami sandwiches, and the drinks selection doesn't stop with beer: the wine list is excellent. Small summer terrace, too.

★**Gerbeaud** CAFE
(Map p74; ☏1-429 9001; www.gerbeaud.hu; V Vörösmarty tér 7-8; ☺noon-10pm; MM1 Vörösmarty tér) Founded on the northern side of Pest's busiest square in 1858, Gerbeaud has been the most fashionable meeting place for the city's elite since 1870. Along with exquisitely prepared cakes and pastries, it serves continental/full breakfast and a smattering of nicely presented Hungarian dishes with international touches. A visit is mandatory.

Táskarádió Eszpresszó CAFE
(Map p74; ☏1-266 0413; V Papnövelde utca 8; ☺9am-midnight; MM3/4 Kálvin tér, 🚋47, 49) With its whirl of colourful retro lamps,

nostalgic black-and-white photos of ye olde Budapest, psychedelic works of art, the communist pioneer credo and a collection of old radios, Táskarádió captures the essence of the '60s and '70s. Come here for an assortment of dishes straight from the communist barracks, or knock back a glass of wine or two to kick-start your night.

Fekete COFFEE

(Map p74; ☎1-787 7503; http://feketekv.hu; V Múzeum körút 5; ⌚7.30am-6pm Mon-Fri, 9am-6pm Sat & Sun; 📶; Ⓜ M2 Astoria) Squeeze into this minute coffee shop (there's just a bar to perch at and tables in the quiet open-air inner courtyard), where you can sample well-poured, Budapest-roasted espresso macchiato or ristretto in cool, monochrome surrounds.

Kontakt CAFE

(Map p74; http://kontaktcoffee.com; V Károly körút 22, Röser udvar; ⌚8am-7pm Mon-Fri, 10am-2pm Sat; 📶; Ⓜ M2 Astoria) Design-led decor, excellent locally roasted coffee and delicious breakfasts make this little cafe, down a tiny pedestrian passage, a great place to pause. It serves sandwiches, cakes and fantastic home-toasted muesli.

Csendes BAR

(Map p74; ☎06 30 727 2100; www.facebook.com/csendesvintagebar; V Ferenczy István utca 5; ⌚10am-midnight Mon-Wed, to 2am Thu & Fri, 2pm-2am Sat, noon-midnight Sun; 📶; Ⓜ M2 Astoria) A quirky cafe just off the Little Ring Rd with junkyard chic decorating the walls and floor space, the 'Quietly' is just that until the regular DJ arrives and cranks up the volume.

Habroló GAY

(Map p74; ☎1-950 6644; www.habrolo.hu; V Szép utca 1; ⌚5pm-late; Ⓜ M3 Ferenciek tere) Named after a flaky pastry, this welcoming neighbourhood gay bar on 'Beautiful St' (could it be anywhere else?) is a cafe with a tiny mezzanine space upstairs and a small stage.

Auguszt Cukrászda CAFE

(Map p74; ☎1-337 6379; www.auguszteukraszda.hu; V Kossuth Lajos utca 14-16; ⌚9am-9pm Tue-Fri, 11am-6pm Sat; Ⓜ M2 Astoria, M3 Ferenciek tere, 🚋47, 48, 49) Not the original branch of the splendid 1870 institution, but the most central and convenient one. Take a seat within the opulent interior and choose one (or more!) of the delectable cakes on display (550Ft to 820Ft), and wash it down with a selection of loose-leaf or fresh herbal teas. Other branches at XI Sasadi út 190 and II Fény utca 8.

1000 Tea TEAHOUSE

(Map p74; ☎1-337 8217; www.1000tea.hu; V Váci utca 65; ⌚noon-9pm Mon-Thu, to 10pm Fri & Sat, 2-9pm Sun; 📶; 🚌15, 115, 🚋2, 47, 48, 49) In a small courtyard off lower Váci utca, this is the place to go if you want to sip a soothing blend made by tea-serious staff and relax in a Japanese-style tearoom. You can also sit in the bamboo-filled courtyard. There's a shop here too.

Centrál Kávéház CAFE

(Map p74; ☎1-266 2110; www.centralkavehaz.hu; V Károlyi utca 9; ⌚9am-11pm; 📶; Ⓜ M3 Ferenciek tere) This grande dame of a traditional cafe dates back to 1887. Awash with leather and dark wood inside, it's also a great spot for pavement people-watching. It serves meals as well as breakfast until 11.45am (990Ft to 2950Ft), plus cakes and pastries (750Ft to 1150Ft).

Action Bar GAY

(Map p74; ☎1-266 9148; www.action.gay.hu; V Magyar utca 42; 1000Ft; ⌚9pm-4am; Ⓜ M3/4 Kálvin tér, 🚋47, 48, 49) Action is where to head if you want just that (though there's a strip show at 1am on Friday and 'oral academy' on Saturday, which may distract). Take the usual precautions and don't forget to write home. Men only. Entrance fee includes a drink.

Fröccsterasz BAR

(Map p74; ☎06 30 419 5040; www.facebook.com/froccsterasz; V Erzsébet tér 13; ⌚noon-4am; Ⓜ M1/2/3 Deák Ferenc tér) In what was once a bus terminal, this popular open-air bar heaves in summer, when young crowds flock here to drink *fröccs* (wine spritzer), meet friends and catch up beneath fairy-lit trees. Great for the location, but the drinks are made of cheap ingredients and it shows.

Funny Carrot BAR

(Map p74; ☎1-782 5502; V Szép utca 1/b; ⌚7pm-5am; Ⓜ M2 Astoria, M3 Ferenciek tere, 🚋47, 48, 49) Cavernous decor and comfy lounge seats at one of Budapest's oldest gay bars are perfect for a quiet tête-à-tête. There is also some space upstairs for more privacy. Try not to snigger at the name.

🍷 Parliament & Around

⭐ DiVino Borbár   WINE BAR
(Map p78; ☑06 70 935 3980; www.divinoborbar.
hu; Ⓥ Szent István tér 3; ⊙4pm-midnight Sun-Wed,
to 2am Thu-Sat; Ⓜ M1 Bajcsy-Zsilinszky út) Central
and always heaving, DiVino is Budapest's
most popular wine bar, as the crowds spilling
out onto the square in front of the Basilica of
St Stephen in the warm weather will attest.
Choose from more than 140 wines produced
by 36 winemakers under the age of 35, but be
careful: those 0.15dL (15mL) glasses (650Ft
to 3500Ft) go down quickly. The glass depos-
it is 500Ft.

⭐ Instant   CLUB
(Map p78; ☑1-311 0704, 06 30 830 8747; www.in-
stant.co.hu; Ⅶ Akácfa utca 51; ⊙4pm-6am; Ⓜ M1
Opera) We still love this 'ruin bar' on one of
Pest's most vibrant nightlife strips and so do
all our friends. It has 26 rooms, seven bars,
seven stages and two gardens with underground DJs and dance parties. It's always
heaving.

High Note Roof Bar   ROOFTOP BAR
(Map p78; ☑1-445 4055; www.ariahotelbudapest.
com; Ⓥ Hercegprímás utca 5; ⊙11am-midnight;
🚊15, 115, Ⓜ M1 Bajcsy-Zsilinszky út) If you need
to impress someone – even yourself – lead
them up to this rooftop bar above the Aria
Hotel (p110). With your noses stuck into the
dome of the basilica and virtually every landmark in Budapest within your grasp, you'll
only be able to utter 'Wow!'. Great cocktails
and friendly staff. What's not to love?

Tütü Bar   GAY
(Map p78; ☑06 70 353 4074; http://tutubudapest.
hu; Ⓥ Hercegprímás utca 18; ⊙10pm-5am Thu-Sat;
Ⓜ M3 Arany János utca) Budapest's newest gay
club is a basement bar that serves up a lot
more than just drinks and attitude. From
pole-dancers and acrobats to drag and fashion shows, they are out to entertain you. A
barrel of laughs.

Suttogó Piano Bar   BAR
(Map p78; ☑06 20 455 7329; http://suttogopi-
anobar.hu; Ⅵ Hajós utca 27; ⊙9.30pm-5am Tue-
Sat; Ⓜ M1 Oktogon) Camp as a caravan park
– agreed – but we always have fun at this romantic spot near the Hungarian State Opera
House. Music starts at around 10pm, with a
different pianist nightly. Cocktails are especially good (if a titch pricey) and you won't
lack for nibbles.

Caledonia   BAR
(Map p78; ☑1-311 7611; www.kaledonia.hu; Ⅵ
Mozsár utca 9; ⊙2pm-midnight Mon-Thu, to 1am Fri,
noon-1am Sat, noon-midnight Sun; Ⓜ M1 Oktogon,
🚊4, 6) Think anything Scottish and the Cal-
edonia does it – whisky (140 types) with or
without Irn-Bru, plus smoked salmon, breakfast (with or without haggis), not to mention
big-screen sports coverage and so on. It's all
good fun and something of an expat magnet.

Morrison's 2   CLUB
(Map p78; ☑1-374 3329; www.morrisons2.hu; Ⓥ Szent István körút 11; ⊙5pm-4am; 🚊4, 6) Far and
away Budapest's biggest party venue, this
cavernous club attracts a younger crowd
with its six dance floors and as many bars
(including one in a covered courtyard and
one with table football). Great DJs. The cover charge is 500Ft.

Impostor   COCKTAIL BAR
(Map p78; ☑06 30 505 3632; Ⓥ Szabadság tér
17; ⊙5pm-1am Tue-Thu, to 2am Fri, 1pm-2am Sat,
5pm-midnight Sun; 🚊15, 115, Ⓜ M2 Kossuth Lajos
tér) This excellent bar occupies a ruin space
and courtyard in what used to be Magyar
Televizió (Hungarian Television) headquarters. Try one of the mixologist's prize creations, such as the Midnight Espresso with
coffee and tequila or the Crystal Jam with
lots of booze and plum preserves (1780Ft).

Bad Girlz   BAR
(Map p78; ☑06 30 665 6666; www.facebook.com/
badgirlzbudapest; Ⓥ Széchenyi István tér 11; ⊙9pm-
5am Thu-Sat; 🚊15, 115, 🚊2) Raunchy bar-cum-
club with bad-ass dancers with a sense of
humour. Friendly staff and good drinks
prices too. It never takes itself too seriously,
which is why it attracts such a motley crowd.

Espresso Embassy   CAFE
(Map p78; ☑06 20 445 0063; http://espressoem-
bassy.hu; Ⓥ Arany János utca 15; ⊙7.30am-7pm
Mon-Fri, 9am-6pm Sat, 9am-5pm Sun; Ⓜ M3 Arany
János utca) Some people say that this upbeat
cafe just south of Szabadság tér has the
best espressos, flat whites, cappuccinos and
lattes in town (430Ft to 730Ft). Try the excellent cold brewed coffee.

Farger Kávé   CAFE
(Map p78; ☑06 20 237 7825; www.farger.hu; Ⓥ
Zoltán utca 18; ⊙7am-9pm Mon-Fri, 9am-6pm Sat
& Sun; Ⓜ M2 Kossuth Lajos tér) This modern
cafe is among the leafiest in Pest thanks to
an ingenious 'urban gardening' plan and has
first-rate views of Szabadság tér through the

foliage from the window seats and terrace. Gotta love the mug collection in the window and the two-course lunch for 990Ft.

Ötkert
CLUB

(Map p78; ☑ 06 70 333 2121; www.otkert.hu; V Zrínyi utca 4; ☺ 11am-midnight Sun-Wed, to 5am Thu-Sat; ☐ 15, 115, ☐ 2) A popular drinking spot in the week with indoor and outdoor spaces (including a cool central courtyard), the 'Five Garden' ('five' as in district V) transmogrifies into one of the district's most popular dance clubs from Thursday into the weekend.

Terv Presszó
BAR

(Map p78; ☑ 1-781 9625; www.facebook.com/tervpresszo; V Nádor utca 19; ☺ 11am-10pm Sun-Thu, to midnight Fri & Sat; ☐ 15, 115, Ⓜ M3 Arany János utca) Dating back to 1854, 'Plan' (as in the communist five-year variety) is a retro-style cafe-bar on two levels, decorated with photographs of Hungarian athletes, politicians, actors etc from the 1950s and '60s. Unlike a lot of such places, the theme doesn't get old in a half-hour. It's slightly off the beaten track and never rammed.

Alterego
GAY

(Map p78; ☑ 06 70 565 1111; www.alteregoclub. hu; VI Dessewffy utca 33; ☺ 10pm-5am Fri, to 6am Sat; ☐ 4, 6) Still Budapest's premier gay club, Alterego has the chicest crowd and the best dance music on offer. Don't miss the drag shows by Lady Dömper and the Alterego Trans Company. Always a hoot.

Morrison's Pub
CLUB

(Map p78; ☑ 1-269 4060; http://morrisonspub.hu; VI Révay utca 25; ☺ 7pm-4am Thu-Sat; Ⓜ M1 Opera) A basement music pub that draws a more mature crowd, with two dance floors, weekly karaoke and a signature red telephone booth brought all the way from Londontown.

Teaház a Vörös Oroszlánhoz
TEAHOUSE

(Map p78; ☑ 1-269 0579; www.vorosoroszlanteahaz.hu; VI Jókai tér 8; ☺ 2-10pm; Ⓜ M1 Oktogon) This serene place with quite a mouthful of a name (it means 'Teahouse at the Sign of the Red Lion') just north of Liszt Ferenc tér is quite serious about its teas (760Ft to 1670Ft). It's on two levels, with a shop (open from 10am) on the ground floor and some magnificent Asian-inspired tearooms above.

Ballett Cipő
CAFE

(Map p78; ☑ 06 70 639 4076; www.facebook.com/balettterem; VI Hajós utca 14; ☺ 10.30am-midnight Mon-Sat; Ⓜ M1 Opera) The pretty little 'Ballet Slipper' in the theatre district – just behind the Hungarian State Opera House – is a delightful place to stop for a rest and refreshment or to have a snack or meal (dishes 800Ft to 3000Ft).

Szalai Cukrászda
CAFE

(Map p78; ☑ 1-269 3210; http://szalaicukraszda.hu; V Balassi Bálint utca 7; ☺ 9am-7pm Wed-Mon; ☐ 2) This humble cake shop in Lipótváros just north of Parliament and dating back to 1917 probably has the best cherry strudel (450Ft) in the capital. It does mean apple and *túrós* (cheese curd) ones too.

Captain Cook Pub
PUB

(Map p78; ☑ 1-269 2357; www.cookpub.hu; VI Bajcsy-Zsilinszky út 19/a; ☺ 10am-1.30am Mon-Sat, to 2pm Sun; Ⓜ M3 Arany János utca) There's not much to say about the Cook except that it enjoys an enviable location diagonally opposite the Basilica of St Stephen, the terrace is a delight in the warm weather, there are four beers on tap and the staff are welcoming and friendly. Enough said?

Kiadó Kocsma
PUB

(Map p78; ☑ 1-331 1955; www.facebook.com/kiadokocsma; VI Jókai tér 3; ☺ 10am-1am Mon-Fri, 11am-1am Sat & Sun; Ⓜ M1 Oktogon) The 'Pub for Rent' is a great place for a swift pint and a quick bite (sandwiches from 1590Ft, salads from 1890Ft) just a stone's throw – and light years – away from flashy VI Liszt Ferenc tér. Breakfast is served till noon and there's a bargain weekday set lunch for 1050Ft.

Café Montmartre
CAFE

(Map p78; ☑ 06 20 511 9177, 06 70 643 2331; www. facebook.com/CafeMontmartreBudapest; V Zrínyi utca 18; ☺ 9am-1am; Ⓜ M3 Arany János utca, Ⓜ 15) This very unpretentious cafe/art gallery in full splendid view of the Basilica of St Stephen is always fun, and the music (retro rock and metal – Manowar posters all over the place) always a surprise.

Margaret Island & Northern Pest

★ Double Shot
COFFEE

(Map p84; ☑ 06 70 674 4893; www.facebook. com/doubleshotspecialtycoffee; XIII Pozsonyi út 16; ☺ 7am-8pm Mon-Thu, to 9pm Fri, 8am-9pm Sat, 8am-7pm Sun; ☐ 4, 6) With an unfinished, grungy look, and break-your-neck stairs to the small seating area upstairs, this thimble-sized coffee shop is the brainchild of two expats. The artisan coffee from around the globe is excellent.

Raj Ráchel Tortaszalon
CAFE

(Map p84; ☑06 20 492 7062; http://raj-rachel-blog.torta.hu; XIII Hollán Ernő utca 25; ☺10am-6pm Mon-Fri; ☐trolleybus 75, 76) What is probably the first kosher cake shop–cafe to open in Újlipótváros since WWII serves all the usual favourites, including killer *flódni* (a substantial three-layer cake with apple, walnut and poppy-seed fillings; 750Ft). It may have changed its name, but not the quality.

L.A. Bodegita
COCKTAIL BAR

(Map p84; ☑1-789 4019; www.labodegita.hu; XIII Pozsonyi utca 4; cocktails1400-1900Ft; ☺11am-midnight Mon-Wed, to 2am Thu-Sat, to 6pm Sun; ☐trolleybus 75, 76, ☐2, 4, 6) The Cuban-style food here is missable, but you should definitely taste master mixologist András Lajsz' incomparable American-style (hi, LA!) cocktails; he does a mean Cosmo and we also like Chameleon, the house special. Live Cuban music on Friday night.

Blue Tomato
BAR

(Map p84; ☑1-339 8099; www.bluetomato.hu; XIII Pannónia utca 5-7; ☺11.30am-midnight Mon & Tue, to 2am Wed & Thu, to 4am Fri & Sat, to 11pm Sun; ☐15, 115) This big boozer is like something out of the old American sitcom *Cheers,* especially the upstairs bar. It's been a popular feature of the district for a decade and a half and the food – mostly Med-Hungarian, with mains from 1390Ft to 7980Ft – is more than just the usual bar or pub blotter.

Holdudvar
CLUB

(Map p84; ☑1-236 0155; www.facebook.com/holdudvaroldal; XIII Margit-sziget; ☺11am-2am Sun-Wed, to 4am Thu, to 5am Fri & Sat; ☐4, 6) Trying to be all things to all people – restaurant, bar, gallery, seasonal outdoor club, disco and *kert* (outdoor garden club) – is not always advisable, but the 'Moon Court', occupying a huge indoor and outdoor space on Margaret Island, is pretty good at the nightlife aspect. Food is forgettable and continents may drift before you get served.

Briós
CAFE

(Map p84; ☑1-789 6110; www.brioskavezo.hu; XIII Pozsonyi út 16; ☺7.30am-10pm; ☐trolleybus 75, 76) Kids in tow? This place is for you, with toys and games and other things to keep the ankle-biters at bay while you tuck into breakfast, the set lunch or just a reviving *kávé* (coffee).

🍷 Erzsébetváros & the Jewish Quarter

★Szimpla Kert
RUIN PUB

(Map p86; ☑06 20 261 8669; www.szimpla.hu; VII Kazinczy utca 14; ☺noon-4am Mon-Thu & Sat, 10am-4am Fri, 9am-5am Sun; ☐M2 Astoria) Budapest's first *romkocsmák* (ruin pub), Szimpla Kert is firmly on the drinking-tourists' trail but remains a landmark place for a drink. It's a huge complex with nooks filled with bric-a-brac, graffiti, art and all manner of unexpected items. Sit in an old Trabant car, watch a film in the open-air back courtyard, down shots or join in an acoustic jam session.

★Léhűtő
BAR

(Map p86; ☑06 30 731 0430; www.facebook.com/lehuto.kezmuvessorozo; VII Holló utca 12-14; ☺4pm-midnight Mon, to 2am Tue-Thu, to 4am Fri & Sat; ☎; ☐M1/2/3 Deák Ferenc tér) Drop into this very friendly basement bar if you fancy a craft beer, of which it does a large Hungarian and international range, with staff willing to advise and let you try before you buy. Coffee-based craft beer? Yep. There's also above-ground seating amid an often-buzzing crowd that gathers at this crossroads on warm nights.

★Doblo
WINE BAR

(Map p86; www.budapestwine.com; VII Dob utca 20; ☺1pm-2am Sun-Wed, to 4am Thu-Sat; ☐M1/2/3 Deák Ferenc tér) Brick-lined and candlelit, Doblo is where you go to taste Hungarian wines, with scores available by the 1.5cL (15mL) glass for 900Ft to 2150Ft. There's food too, such as meat and cheese platters.

★Lotz Terem Book Cafe
CAFE

(Map p86; ☑1-461 5835; www.lotzterem.hu; VI Andrássy út 39; ☺10am-8pm; ☐M1 Opera, ☐4, 6) On the 1st floor of a branch of Alexandra (p156), one of Budapest's best bookshops, this glitzy cafe in the revamped decorative hall of the one-time Paris Department Store shows off frescoes by Károly Lotz and other wonderful touches of opulence. It's a great spot for a light lunch (salads and sandwiches; 1290Ft to 2590Ft) or for coffee pre- or postbrowse.

★Boutiq' Bar
COCKTAIL BAR

(Map p86; ☑06 30 554 2323; www.boutiqbar.hu; V Paulay Ede utca 5; ☺6pm-1am Tue-Thu, to 2am Fri & Sat; ☐M1 Bajcsy-Zsilinszky utca) A low-lit 'speakeasy' serving expertly mixed cocktails (2250Ft to 5950Ft) using fresh juices and an educated selection of craft spirits. For something specifically Hungarian, try a creation that includes Unicum like Die Kaiser, or plum *pálinka* (fruit brandy) such as Positive Drinking. The gin-based Budapest BBQ is something else. Informed, charming service; reservations are advised.

★ New York Café
CAFE

(Map p86; ☑1-886 6167; www.newyorkcafe.hu; VII Erzsébet körút 9-11; ⊙8am-midnight; ⓂM2 Blaha Lujza tér, ⊠4, 6) Considered the most beautiful cafe in the world when it opened in 1894, this Renaissance-style place on the ground floor of the Boscolo Budapest Hotel has been the scene of many a literary gathering. Some say it lacks the warmth and erudite crowd of most traditional cafes but the opulence and history will impress. It's a great place for breakfast (2400Ft to 7500Ft; 9am to noon).

360 Bar
ROOFTOP BAR

(Map p86; ☑06 70 259 5153; www.360bar.hu; VI Andrássy út 39, 8th fl, Alexandra bookshop; ⊙2pm-midnight Mon-Wed, to 2am Thu & Fri, noon-midnight Sun May-Sep; ⓂM1 Oktagon, ⊠4, 6) This bar on the roof of the Alexandra (p156) bookshop eight floors above Andrássy út 39 offers nothing extraordinary in the way of libations (some craft beer, wine, lower-shelf cocktails), but the views – literally all around you – are out of this world. Come up here of an evening and you've done all the Budapest sightseeing you need to do.

Füge Udvar
RUIN PUB

(Fig Court; Map p86; ☑1-782 6990; VII Klauzál utca 19; ⊙4pm-4am; ⓂM2 Blaha Lujza tér, ⊠4, 6) This enormous ruin pub has a large covered courtyard with a large (and eponymous) fig tree in the centre. There are lots of side rooms and great street art to lose yourself in. Here you'll also find the MindQuest (p98) escape game.

Kisüzem
BAR

(Map p86; ☑06 20 957 2291, 1-781 6705; www.facebook.com/Kisuzem; VII Kis Diófa utca 2; ⊙noon-2am Sun-Wed, to 3am Thu-Sat; ☎; ⊠4, 6) The bare-brick interior of this relaxed corner bar gives it a bohemian vibe. A mixed-age crowd mingles at the bar or on the pavement outside, or chats at the tables ranged around the interior. It hosts live music such as jazz, folk and experimental (usually at 9pm Thursday and Sunday), and serves bar food and locally roasted coffee.

Café Zsivágó
CAFE

(Map p86; ☑06 30 212 8125; http://cafezsivago.hu; VI Paulay Ede utca 55; ⊙10am-midnight Mon-Fri, noon-midnight Sat, 2-10pm Sun; ⓂM1 Oktogon, ⊠4, 6) A little Russian living room with lace tablecloths, wooden dressers, mismatched tea sets, hat stands and vintage lamps provides a relaxing daytime coffee stop that morphs into a hopping bar at night offering cocktails, champagne and vodka. If you can, bag a seat in the little gallery alcove upstairs.

Csak a Jó Sör
CRAFT BEER

(Map p86; ☑1-950 2788, 06 30 251 4737; www.csakajosor.hu; VII Kertész utca 42-44; ⊙2-9pm Mon-Sat; ⓂM1 Oktogon, ⊠4, 6) True to its name (which translates as 'Only the Good Beer'), this expanded shop has shelves stacked high with brown bottles containing an extensive selection of international and local bottled craft beer. About six beers are usually also available on draught, including the owner's own quality brews.

Grandio
CLUB

(Map p86; ☑06 70 670 0390; http://budapestparty-hostels.com/hostels/grandio-party-hostel; VII Nagy Diófa utca 8; ⊙11am-3am; ☎; ⓂM2 Blaha Lujza tér, ⊠4, 6) A large *kert* (outdoor garden club) in a courtyard below Grandio Party Hostel. What sets Grandio apart are the hearty urban weeds that have taken back their share of space and created not a 'garden' but a 'forest club'. The big, long bar dispenses copious drinks to enthusiastic punters.

Mika Tivadar Mulató
CLUB

(Map p86; ☑06 20 965 3007; www.mikativadarmulato.hu; VII Kazinczy utca 47; ⊙4pm-midnight Sun-Wed, to 3am Thu-Sat; ⓂM1/2/3 Deák Ferenc tér) This grand one-time copper factory dating from 1907 sports a chilled ground-floor bar, a small venue downstairs and a fantastic garden courtyard, among our favourite *romkertek* (ruin gardens) in Budapest. Most nights there are DJs and live music (all sorts, including jazz, swing, punk and funk). Great toilets.

Kőleves Kert
CAFE

(Map p86; www.kolevesvendeglo.hu; VII Kazinczy utca 37-41; ⊙1pm-midnight Mon-Wed, to 1am Thu & Fri, 11am-1am Sat, 11am-midnight Sun; ⓂM1/2/3 Deák Ferenc tér) Lie back in a hammock at this large, brightly decorated garden club, popular with diners from parent restaurant Kőleves (p133) next door.

Yellow Zebra Pub
BAR

(Map p86; www.yellowzebrapub.com; VII Kazinczy utca 5; ⊙10am-midnight Sun-Thu, to 3am Fri & Sat; ⓜM2 Astoria) Owned by the tour agency of the same name, the Yellow Zebra cellar pub is the only bar in Budapest for cyclists. It has a half-dozen Czech and Hungarian craft beers on tap, a fabulous old-style open kitchen serving up stick-to-the-ribs Hungarian dishes (mains 1500Ft to 2400Ft), and live jazz and blues from 9pm on Wednesday, Thursday and Saturday.

Rumpus Tiki Bar
COCKTAIL BAR

(Map p86; ☏06 20 624 0085; http://rumpus.hu; VII Király utca 19; ⊙6pm-2am Sun-Thu, to 3am Fri & Sat; ⓜM1/2/3 Deák Ferenc tér) OK, so what's not to love about a tiki bar, with those fake coconut trees, palm-frond huts, colourful idols and mai tais that go down like water after a run? Rumpus has all of the above plus a long bamboo bar with totem-like stools, the occasional ukulele concert and waitresses in grass skirts.

Központ
BAR

(Map p86; ☏1-783 8405; www.facebook.com/kozpontbudapest; VII Madách Imre út 5; ⊙8am-1am Mon-Wed, to 2am Thu & Fri, 6pm-2am Sat; ⓜM1/2/3 Deák Ferenc tér) At the time of writing, 'Centre' was the hipster meeting place in Budapest, where every bearded young man with a top knot breakfasted and gathered by night to drink, chat and listen to canned music. It just might still be hot.

Hopaholic
CRAFT BEER

(Map p86; ☏1-611 2415; www.facebook.com/hopaholicpub; VII Akácfa utca 38; ⊙4pm-midnight Mon-Wed, to 2am Thu-Sat; ⓑ4, 6) This tiny premises has lots of craft beer that's available from Csak a Jó Sör, plus 10 more on tap.

Tuk Tuk Bar
COCKTAIL BAR

(Map p86; ☏1-343 1198; www.tuktukbar.hu; VI Paulay Ede utca 31; ⊙4pm-midnight; ⓜM1 Opera) This 'Shanghai-inspired bar' – aren't *tuk-tuks* (like the one on the pavement outside) from Bangkok, we cry? – is an ever-so-Asian gay-friendly hang-out at the Casati Budapest Hotel (p112). There's art on the walls, great cocktails, a DJ on Thursday and live jazz on Friday. Friendly staff.

Vicky Barcelona
CLUB

(Map p86; ☏06 30 465 9505; www.facebook.com/vickybarcelonatapas; VII Gozsdu udvar, Dob utca 16; ⊙noon-5am Mon & Thu-Sat, 4pm-5am Tue & Wed, 1pm-midnight Sun; ⓜM1/2/3 Deák Ferenc tér) This Spanish restaurant/bar/club at the southern end of the Gozsdu udvar is a one-stop-shopping night out in Budapest. Arrive mid-evening and grab a seat either inside the long narrow restaurant or on a bar stool outside right on the Gozsdu udvar. Have drinks and tapas (950Ft to 2100Ft) and at about 11pm watch the place transform into one big salsa music and dance party.

Fekete Kutya
BAR

(Map p86; ☏06 20 580 3151; www.facebook.com/feketekutja; VII Dob utca 31; ⊙5pm-2am Mon-Sat, to midnight Sun; ⓜM1/2/3 Deák Ferenc tér) The 'Black Dog' is a tiny bar, popular with a local expat crowd who come to drink craft beer in a casual setting.

Spíler
BAR

(Map p86; ☏1-878 1309; http://spilerbp.hu; VII Gozsdu udvar; ⊙9am-midnight Sun-Wed, to 2am Thu-Sat; ⓜM1/2/3 Deák Ferenc tér) A big, bold and bustling bistro bar on nightlife-central Gozsdu udvar, Spíler serves craft beer, wine, cocktails and full meals to an up-for-it crowd. Sit under the awnings on the jam-packed street or at one of the bars inside. Nightly DJs and a street-food menu too.

Anker't
RUIN PUB

(Map p86; www.facebook.com/ankertbar; VI Paulay Ede utca 33; ⊙2pm-2am Mon-Wed & Sun, to 4am Thu-Sat; ⓢ; ⓜM1 Opera) Sister bar to the Anker Klub (p147), this achingly cool, grown-up courtyard pub surrounded by seriously ruined buildings has monochrome decor and lighting that sets off the impressive surrounds to great effect. There's a vast garden, numerous bars, food, a long drinks list, DJs and live music. A great dance venue.

Kadarka
WINE BAR

(Map p86; ☏06 30 297 4974, 1-266 5094; www.facebook.com/kadarkabar; VII Király utca 42; ⊙4pm-midnight; ⓢ; ⓜM1 Opera) A buzzy, modern wine bar that serves a dizzying array of varieties (mostly Hungarian) in a range of volumes to suit all appetites and tastes. The staff are on hand to advise on the wines, as well as the great selection of *pálinka* (fruit brandy).

Ecocafe
CAFE

(Map p86; ☏06 70 333 2116; http://ecocafe.hu; VI Andrássy út 68; ⊙7am-8pm Mon-Fri, 8am-8pm Sat & Sun; ⓜM1 Vörösmarty utca) A welcome stop along Andrássy út, this simple cafe serves great coffee alongside smoothies, juices, teas, sandwiches (590Ft to 890Ft) and cakes

(250Ft to 690Ft), which are almost all organic. There's also a great salad bar (1590Ft), and tables on the pavement outside.

Gozsdu Manó Klub
CLUB

(GMK; Map p86; ☑06 20 779 1183; www.gozsdumano.hu; VII Gozsdu udvar, cnr Madách Imre út; ☺4pm-2am Sun-Wed, to 5am Thu-Sat; Ⓜ M1/2/3 Deák Ferenc tér) There's an upstairs bar and restaurant here, but the real draw is the basement club, which puts on excellent live music and DJs in a cavernous space with a quality sound system, an unpretentious vibe and a devoted local following.

Bordó Bisztró
WINE BAR

(Map p86; ☑06 70 359 8777; www.facebook.com/bordobisztro; VI Nagymező utca 3; ☺10am-midnight; Ⓜ M1 Opera) This bistro at the end of Budapest's 'Broadway' takes wine very seriously indeed. About the only funny thing about the place is its cheesy name – a clumsy pun on Bordeaux and *bor* ('wine' in Hungarian). The food is a hotchpotch of fish cakes, ginger spare ribs and four-cheese penne; come for the midweek set lunch (1050Ft to 1300Ft) or a winey weekend brunch.

Mozaik
TEAHOUSE

(Map p86; ☑1-266 7001; VI Király utca 18; ☺9am-10.30pm; ☎; Ⓜ M1/2/3 Deák Ferenc tér) A calm little teahouse on a busy street, with a lovely upper level where you can grab a piece of chalk and leave your mark while you sup one of the 120 types of tea on offer. Homemade cakes, booze in the bar upstairs and a wonderful mosaic – thus the name – of Bacchus.

Fogas
RUIN PUB

(Map p86; ☑06 70 638 5040; www.fogashaz.hu; VII Akácfa utca 49-51; ☺6pm-4am; ☎; 🚊4, 6) This huge tree-filled complex, with eight bars and four dance floors in two buildings, hides a warren of good times, including live music and nightly DJs, plus art, film clubs and workshops. There is plenty of indoor space for inclement weather and you can always climb the stairs to club Lärm (p147) for something more hardcore.

400 Bar
BAR

(Map p86; ☑06 20 776 0765; www.400bar.hu; VII Kazinczy utca 52/b; ☺11.30am-1am Sun-Wed, to 2am Thu, to 4am Fri & Sat; ☎; Ⓜ M1/2/3 Deák Ferenc tér) One of the most popular cafe-bars in Pest, the 'Négyszáz' is a big space, with outside seating in a no-car zone near Gozsdu udvar. Come just to relax over a drink, or

try the daily lunch menu (1090Ft). Serbian grilled dishes too, and there's a great terrace.

Művész Kávéház
CAFE

(Map p86; ☑06 70 333 2116; www.muveszkavehaz.hu; VI Andrássy út 29; ☺9am-10pm Mon-Sat, from 10am Sun; Ⓜ M1 Opera) Almost opposite the Hungarian State Opera House, the Artist Coffeehouse is an interesting place to people-watch (especially from the shady terrace), though some say its cakes (550Ft to 890Ft) are not what they used to be (though presumably they're not thinking as far back as 1898, when the cafe opened).

Vittula
BAR

(Map p86; www.vittula.hu; VII Kertész utca 4; ☺6pm-late; ☎; Ⓜ M2 Blaha Lujza tér, 🚊4, 6) A great studenty cellar bar covered in graffiti, where hedonistic folk and bearded men drink late into the night accompanied by alternative music and plenty of fun. Cheap drinks, funky decor, great parties.

CoXx Men's Bar
GAY

(Map p86; ☑06 30 949 1650, 1-344 4884; www.coxx.hu; VII Dohány utca 38; ☺9pm-4am Sun-Thu, to 5am Fri & Sat; Ⓜ M2 Blaha Lujza tér, 🚊4, 6) Probably the cruisiest gayme in town, this place with the in-your-face name has 400 sq metres of hunting ground, three bars and some significant play areas in back. Don't bring dark glasses.

Fat Fairy
CAFE

(Map p86; ☑06 20 378 8467; www.facebook.com/TheFatFairyBudapest; VI Király utca 18; ☺8am-8pm Mon-Thu, to 10pm Fri & Sat, 9am-6pm Sun; Ⓜ M1/2/3 Deák Ferenc tér) OK, we'll admit it: we come to this little greener-than-green (as in the colour) cafe because of the name. But it does some excellent waffles (790Ft) and cakes (590Ft to 790Ft), and there's always a queue waiting to be served. She is kinda plump.

Blue Bird Cafe
CAFE

(Map p86; www.facebook.com/bluebirdcafehungary; VII Gozsdu udvar, Dob utca 16; ☺9am-3am Mon-Thu, to 5am Fri-Sun; ☎; Ⓜ M1/2/3 Deák Ferenc tér) A warmly decorated cafe with a small terrace on busy Gozsdu udvar serving own-roast coffee, cakes and all-day breakfasts, including crêpes. It turns into a raucous karaoke bar by night.

My Little Melbourne & Brew Bar
CAFE

(Map p86; ☑06 70 394 7002; http://mylittlemelbourne.hu; VII Madách Imre út 3; ☺7am-7pm; ☎;

Ⓜ M1/2/3 Deák Ferenc tér) A Budapest couple who fell in love with Melbourne have recreated a little slice of Australia here. With shop-roasted coffee from London (Workshop) and Italy (Danesi), they serve a mean flat white, as well as pastries and cakes – including Australian lamington (chocolate and coconut sponge) – in this tiny space over two floors. There's an adjoining cafe too.

Telep　　　BAR
(Map p86; ☑1-784 8911; www.facebook.com/Telep-Galeria; VII Madách Imre út 8; ⊙noon-2am Mon-Fri, 4pm-2am Sat; 🕾; Ⓜ M1/2/3 Deák Ferenc tér) A small art gallery and upstairs exhibition space that also holds gigs and hosts DJs, this hipster haunt is steps away from busy Gozsdu udvar on a pedestrian street, where drinkers hang out late into the evening.

Lärm　　　CLUB
(Map p86; http://larm.hu; VII Akácfa utca 51; ⊙11pm-6am Fri & Sat Sep-May; 🕾; 🚊4, 6) This intimate club with two small bars overlooks the courtyard of ruin pub Fogas and is dedicated to techno music.

Ellátó Kert　　　RUIN PUB
(Map p86; ☑06 30 628 9136; VII Kazinczy utca 48; ⊙5pm-4am; 🕾; Ⓜ M1/2/3 Deák Ferenc tér) A perennially popular and huge ruin pub, Ellátó is ranged over several rooms full of plants and paper lanterns. Table tennis, billiards, table football and Mexican tacos keep everyone amused and happy.

Anker Klub　　　CLUB
(Map p86; ☑06 70 621 0741; VI Anker köz 1-3; ⊙9am-1am Mon-Fri, 10am-3am Sat; Ⓜ M1/2/3 Deák Ferenc tér) A cafe that turns into a hipster hang-out with DJs in the evening, the Anker is spacious, minimalist and about as central as you'll find.

🍷 Southern Pest

★**Corvin Club & Roof Terrace**　　　CLUB
(Map p92; ☑06 20 474 0831; www.corvinteto.hu; VIII Blaha Lujza tér 1; ⊙10pm-6am Wed-Sat; Ⓜ M2 Blaha Lujza tér) On top of the former Corvin department store, this excellent club, with stunning views from its open-air dance floor, holds a variety of nights from techno to rooftop cinema. If you can't face the stairs, once you've paid (cover 500Ft to 2000Ft) head 100m south to the Cafe Mundum at Somogyi Béla utca 1 and ride the goods lift to the roof.

Nándor Cukrászda　　　CAFE
(Map p92; ☑1-215 8776; www.nandori.hu; IX Ráday utca 53; ⊙7.30am-7pm Mon-Sat; 🚊4, 6) This tiny place with excellent biscuits and cakes (350Ft to 650Ft) has apparently been here since 1957. A sign advising clients to take a number and join the queue is an indication of its popularity.

Élesztő　　　CRAFT BEER
(Map p92; www.facebook.com/elesztohaz; IX Tűzoltó utca 22; ⊙3pm-3am; Ⓜ M3 Corvin-negyed, 🚊4, 6) This ruin pub, set in a former glass-blowing workshop, has three sections: a cafe, a wine bar with tapas (690Ft to 1390Ft) and the reason we come...a bar with an unrivalled selection of craft beer. With a brewery on-site and a name meaning 'yeast', 20 brews on tap, beer cocktails and brewing courses, this is a hophead's dream.

Lumen　　　CAFE
(Map p92; www.facebook.com/lumen.kavezo; VIII Mikszáth Kálmán tér 2-3; ⊙8am-midnight Mon-Fri, 10am-midnight Sat, 10am-10pm Sun; 🕾; Ⓜ M3/4 Kálvin tér, 🚊4, 6) A relaxed cafe and bar with a little terrace on Mikszáth Kálmán tér, this plant-bedecked joint roasts its own coffee and serves wine and Hungarian craft beer like Stari. In the evenings it fills with an arty crowd who come for the eclectic program of live music and DJ nights.

Jelen Bisztró　　　BAR
(Map p92; ☑06 20 344 3155; www.facebook.com/jelenbisztro; VIII Blaha Lujza tér 1-2; ⊙10am-midnight; 🚊5, 7, Ⓜ M2 Blaha Lujza tér) We love this enthusiastic, spacious and bohemian cafe-bar tucked down a backstreet off Rákóczi út. Food is available, from breakfast to evening grills (1290Ft to 2490Ft), and it also hosts local live music at 7pm, with open-mic night on Monday from 8pm to 11pm. Enter from Stáhly utca 12.

Café Csiga　　　CAFE
(Map p92; ☑06 30 613 2046; www.facebook.com/cafecsiga; VIII Vásár utca 2; ⊙9am-midnight; 🕾; Ⓜ M4 Rákóczi tér, 🚊4, 6) The Snail is a very popular, welcoming place alongside the Rákóczi tér market. The relaxed space on two levels, with battered wooden floorboards, copious plants and wide-open doors on sunny days, attracts a boho crowd. It does food, too, including lots of vegie options (salads from 1950Ft), breakfast (750Ft to 1190Ft) and an excellent set lunch for 1100Ft.

Zappa Caffe
CAFE

(Map p92; ☏06 20 972 1711; www.zappacaffe.hu; VIII Mikszáth Kálmán tér 2; ⊘11am-midnight Mon-Thu, to 2am Fri, noon-2am Sat, noon-midnight Sun; ⓂM3/4 Kálvin tér, ⛟4, 6) An anchor tenant in a car-free square loaded with students and locals, this large, laid-back cafe (and bar and restaurant) has one of the largest terraces in the area. Good music, too.

Paris Texas
BAR

(Map p92; ☏1-218 0570; www.facebook.com/parizs.kavehaz; IX Ráday utca 22; ⊘noon-3am Mon-Sat, to midnight Sun; ⓂM3 Kálvin tér) One of the original bars on the IX Ráday utca nightlife strip, this place has a coffeehouse feel to it with old sepia-tinted photos on the walls and pool tables downstairs. Nurse a cocktail from the huge list and order a pizza from Pink Cadillac (p135) next door.

Tamp & Pull
CAFE

(Map p92; ☏06 30 456 7618; www.facebook.com/tamppull; IX Czuczor utca 3; ⊘7am-7pm Mon-Fri, 9am-5pm Sat, noon-4pm Sun; ⓂM4 Fővám tér) The original venture of Attila Molnár, four-times Hungarian National Barista Champion, Tamp & Pull is a small, bare-brick, rather earnest cafe with a few tables inside and out, and coffee-related art on the walls. It serves the UK's Has Bean coffee, plus delicious cakes and biscuits, juices and sandwiches.

Bujdosó Kert
RUIN PUB

(Map p92; www.facebook.com/bujdosokert; VIII Vajdahunyad utca 4; ⊘4pm-2am Mon-Sat, to midnight Sun; ⛟4, 6) What was the laid-back ruin pub Gondozót in a former social-care home has reopened as Bujdosó Kert, with grilled cuisine, snooker, live music and a giant screen. The city's first escape game, Parapark (p98), is still here in the basement.

🍷 City Park & Beyond

Kertem
BEER GARDEN

(Map p96; ☏06 30 225 1399; www.facebook.com/kertemfesztival; XIV Olof Palme sétány 1; ⊘11am-4am; ⓂM1 Hősök tere) In a new location in the south of City Park, Kertem is a wonderful beer garden, filled with multicoloured chairs and trees strung with fairy lights. By day it's an easygoing oasis full of families; by night it's a great place to grab a beer and a burger and listen to live music (hosted on weekend evenings).

Varosliget Café
CAFE

(Map p96; ☏06 30 869 1426; www.varosligetcafe.hu; XIV Olof Palme sétány 5; ⊘noon-10pm; ⓂM1 Hősök tere) This popular cafe by the edge of the lake in City Park is a great place to relax, watch rowers on the lake and have a coffee or sundowner. If you're peckish, you can go for something more substantial, such as crispy duck with braised cabbage, lamb ragout or grilled sheep's cheese with roast vegetables.

Dürer Kert
CLUB

(Map p96; ☏1-789 4444; www.durerkert.com; XIV Ajtósi Dürer sor 19-21; ⊘5pm-5am; 🛜; 🚎trolleybus 74, 75, ⛟1) A very relaxed open space and club on the southern edge of City Park, Dürer Kert boasts some of the best DJs on the 'garden' circuit.

Sparty
CLUB

(Map p96; www.spartybooking.com; XIV Állatkerti út 1; from €35; ⊘10.30pm-3am Sat; ⓂM1 Széchenyi fürdő) Sparty (see what they did there?) organises a variety of weekly club nights in the Széchenyi Baths (p99) combining drinking, a light show, house and funk DJs, VJs, acrobatics and bathing with a very up-for-it and underdressed crowd. Don't forget your goggles.

Cat Cafe
CAFE

(Map p96; ☏1-792 4549; www.catcafe.hu; VII Damjanich utca 38; all you can drink 1590Ft; ⊘2-10pm Tue-Sun; ⛟30) In a purrfect cellar location on a quiet street, this cat cafe seeks to amuse you by introducing you to its three adorable cats. The idea is that you pay a set fee (which includes a slice of cake and unlimited teas), then play with the cats or just chill out with a board game.

Pántlika
BAR

(Map p96; ☏06 70 376 9910; www.pantlika.hu; XIV Városligeti körút; ⊘noon-midnight Sun-Thu, to 2am Fri & Sat; 🚎trolleybus 72, 74, ⓂM1 Széchenyi fürdo, ⛟1, 1A) For a place housed in a communist-era kiosk dating back to the 1970s with a bizarre flyaway roof, this DJ bar and cafe is very hip and has a great terrace. Food – soups, stews and hamburgers from 1100Ft – emerges from a tiny kitchen, and the selection of *pálinka* (fruit brandy) is extensive. It's opposite XIV Hermina út 47.

☆ Entertainment

For a city of its size, Budapest has a huge choice of things to do and places to go after dark, from opera and folk dancing to live jazz and films screened in palatial cinemas. It's usually not difficult getting tickets or getting in; the hard part is deciding what to do and where to go.

☆ Castle District

Buda Concert Hall   DANCE
(Budai Vigadó; Map p62; ☑1-225 6049; www.hagyomanyokhaza.hu; I Corvin tér 8; performances 3600-6200Ft; ☐19, 41) The artistes of the Hungarian State Folk Ensemble (Magyar Állami Népi Együttes) perform at this venue, also known as the Hagyományok Háza (House of Traditions), at 8pm on Tuesday and Friday from June to October, with occasional performances at other times during the rest of the year.

Budavár Cultural Centre   LIVE MUSIC
(Budavári Művelődési Háza; Map p62; ☑1-201 0324; www.bem6.hu; Bem rakpart 6; programs 800-1000Ft; ☐19, 41) This cultural centre just below Buda Castle has frequent programs for children and adults, including the excellent Sebő Klub és Táncház at 7pm on the second Saturday of every month and the Regejáró Misztrál Folk Music Club at the same time on the last Sunday.

☆ Gellért Hill & Tabán

Fonó Buda Music House   LIVE MUSIC
(Fonó Budaio Zeneház; ☑1-206 5300; www.fono.hu; XI Sztregova utca 3; ⊘box office 9am-5pm Mon-Fri; ☐41, 56) This venue has táncház (folk music and dance) programs several times a week (especially on Wednesday) at 6.30pm or 8pm, as well as concerts by big-name bands (mostly playing world music) throughout the month; it's one of the best venues in town for this sort of thing.

Municipal Cultural House   LIVE MUSIC
(Fővárosi Művelődési Háza (FMH); ☑1-203 3868; www.fmhnet.hu; XI Fehérvári út 47; ⊘box office 3-7pm Mon & Thu, to 6pm Tue & Wed, 4-6pm Fri; ☐41, 56) There's folk music and dance at what is also called the FMH at 7pm on alternate Mondays, Fridays and Saturdays (see the website). A children's dance house hosted by the incomparable folk group Muzsikás runs every Tuesday from 5pm to 7pm.

A38   LIVE MUSIC
(Map p92; ☑1-464 3940; www.a38.hu; XI Pázmány Péter sétány 3-11; ⊘11am-midnight Sun-Thu, to 3am Fri & Sat; ☐212, ☐4, 6) Moored on the Buda side south of Petőfi Bridge, the 'A38 Ship' is a decommissioned Ukrainian stone hauler from 1968 that has been recycled as a major live-music venue. It's so cool that Lonely Planet readers once voted it the best bar in the world. The ship's hold rocks throughout the year. Terraces open in the warmer weather.

Mu Színház   DANCE
(Map p66; ☑1-209 4014; www.mu.hu; XI Kőrösy József utca 17; ⊘box office 10am-6pm Mon-Fri; ☐4, 6) Virtually everyone involved in the Hungarian modern-dance scene got their start at this landmark place in south Buda, where excellent performances can be enjoyed.

☆ Óbuda & Buda Hills

Óbuda Society   CONCERT VENUE
(Óbudai Társaskör; Map p70; ☑1-250 0288; www.obudaitarsaskor.hu; III Kis Korona utca 7; tickets 1000-4500Ft; ☐86, ☐Tímár utca) This very intimate venue in Óbuda takes its music seriously and hosts recitals and some chamber orchestras. Highly recommended.

Marczibányi tér Cultural Centre   LIVE MUSIC
(Marczibányi téri Művelődési Központ; Map p70; ☑1-212 2820; www.marczi.hu; II Marczibányi tér 5/a; performances 800-3200Ft; ⊘from 7pm Thursday; ☐4, 6) This venue has Hungarian, Moldavian and Slovakian dance and music by Guzsalyas every Thursday at 7pm.

☆ Belváros

Akvárium Klub   LIVE MUSIC
(Map p74; ☑06 30 860 3368; www.akvariumklub.hu; V Erzsébet tér; ⊘noon-1am Mon-Thu, to 4.30am Fri & Sat; Ⓜ M1/2/3 Deák Ferenc tér) The Akvárium Klub delivers a varied program of Hungarian and international live music, from indie, rock, world and pop to electronica and beyond. The main hall has capacity for 1500, the smaller for 700. There are also regular club nights here, and a bar and bistro. A carpet of drinkers layers the surrounding steps in warm weather.

Pesti Vigadó   CONCERT VENUE
(Map p74; www.vigado.hu; V Vigadó tér 1; ⊘box office 10am-7.30pm; Ⓜ M1 Vörösmarty tér, ☐2) Pesti Vigadó, the Romantic-style concert hall built in 1864, hosts classical concerts in opulent surrounds.

Puskin Art Mozi   CINEMA
(Map p74; ☑1-459 5050; www.puskinmozi.hu; V Kossuth Lajos utca 18; ☐7, Ⓜ M2 Astoria) The long-established 'Pushkin Art Cinema'

shows a healthy mix of art-house and popular releases.

Columbus Club
LIVE MUSIC

(Map p74; ☑1-266 9013; www.columbuspub.hu; V Vigadó tér, pier no 4; ☺noon-midnight; Ⓜ M1 Vörösmarty tér, ☑2) On a boat moored on the Danube off the northern end of V Vigadó tér, this club features nightly live music, including jazz, with big-name local and international bands. Music starts at 7.30pm and there are usually two concerts lasting 45 minutes.

József Katona Theatre
THEATRE

(Katona József Színház; Map p74; ☑1-266 5200; www.katonajozsefszinhaz.hu; V Petőfi Sándor utca 6; tickets free-4200Ft; ☺box office 11am-7pm Mon-Fri, 3-7pm Sat & Sun; Ⓜ M3 Ferenciek tere) The József Katona Theatre is the best known in Hungary, hosting a varied repertoire of performances, from Shakespeare plays and *Waiting for Godot* to home-grown productions. Its studio theatre, Kamra, hosts some of the best troupes in the country.

☆ Parliament & Around

★ Hungarian State Opera House
OPERA

(Magyar Állami Operaház; Map p78; ☑1-814 7100, box office 1-353 0170; www.opera.hu; VI Andrássy út 22; ☺box office 10am-8pm; Ⓜ M1 Opera) The gorgeous neo-Renaissance opera house is worth a visit as much to admire the incredibly rich decoration inside as to view a performance and hear the perfect acoustics.

Aranytíz House of Culture
TRADITIONAL MUSIC

(Aranytíz Kultúrház; Map p78; ☑1-354 3400; www.aranytiz.hu; V Arany János utca 10; ☺box office 2-9pm Mon & Wed, 9am-3pm Sat; ☑15) At this cultural centre in Lipótváros, the wonderful Kalamajka Táncház has programs from 7pm on Saturday that run till about midnight. Bring the kids in earlier (about 5pm) for the children's version. Check the website for all the other programs and events.

Budapest Operetta
OPERA

(Budapesti Operettszínház; Map p78; ☑1-312 4866; www.operettszinhaz.hu; VI Nagymező utca 17; tickets 1000-13,000Ft; ☺box office 10am-7pm Mon-Fri, 1-7pm Sat & Sun; Ⓜ M1 Opera) This theatre presents operettas, which are always a riot, especially campy ones like *The Gypsy Princess* by Imre Kálmán or Ferenc Lehár's *The Merry Widow*, with their over-the-top staging and costumes. Think baroque Gilbert and Sullivan – and then some. There's an interesting bronze statue of Kálmán outside the main entrance.

Művész Art Mozi
CINEMA

(Map p78; ☑1-459 5050; www.artmozi.hu; VI Teréz körút 30; tickets adult/student 1550/1150Ft; Ⓜ M1 Oktogon, ☑4, 6) The 'Artist Art Cinema' shows, appropriately enough, art and cult films, but not exclusively so.

☆ Margaret Island & Northern Pest

Budapest Jazz Club
JAZZ

(Map p84; ☑1-798 7289; www.bjc.hu; XIII Hollán Ernő utca 7; ☺10am-midnight Sun-Thu, to 2am Fri & Sat; ☑trolleybus 75, 76) A very sophisticated venue – now pretty much the most serious one in town – for traditional, vocal and Latin jazz by local and international talent. Past international performers have included Terrence Blanchard, the Yellowjackets and Liane Carroll. Concerts most nights at 8pm or 9pm, with jam sessions at 10pm or 11pm on Friday, Saturday and Monday.

Comedy Theatre
THEATRE

(Vígszínház; Map p84; ☑1-329 2340; http://vigszinhaz.hu/; XIII Szent István körút 14; ☑4, 6) The attractive little building on Szent István körút, roughly halfway between the Danube and Nyugati tér, is where comedies (including Shakespearean ones in translation) and musicals are staged. When it was built in 1896 it was criticised for being too far out of town.

☆ Erzsébetváros & the Jewish Quarter

★ Liszt Music Academy
CLASSICAL MUSIC

(Liszt Zeneakadémia; Map p86; ☑1-462 4600, box office 1-321 0690; www.zeneakademia.hu; VI Liszt Ferenc tér 8; ☺box office 10am-6pm; Ⓜ M1 Oktogon, ☑4, 6) Performances at Budapest's most important concert hall are usually booked up at least a week in advance, but more expensive (though still affordable) last-minute tickets can sometimes be available. It's always worth checking.

Gödör
LIVE MUSIC

(Map p86; ☑06 20 201 3868; www.godorklub.hu; VI Király utca 8-10, Central Passage; ☺6pm-late; ☎; Ⓜ M1/2/3 Deák Ferenc tér) In the bowels of the Central Passage shopping centre on Király utca, Gödör has maintained its reputation for scheduling an excellent variety of indie, rock, jazz, electronic and experimental music, as well as hosting quality club nights in its spare, industrial space. Exhibitions and movies in summer too.

Pótkulcs
LIVE MUSIC

(Map p86; ☑1-269 1050; www.potkulcs.hu; VI Csengery utca 65/b; ☺5pm-1.30am Sun-Wed, to 2.30am Thu-Sat; Ⓜ M3 Nyugati pályaudvar) The 'Spare Key' is a fine little drinking venue with a varied menu of live music most evenings and occasional *táncház* (Hungarian music and dance). The small central courtyard is a wonderful place to chill out in summer.

Giero Brasserie
LIVE MUSIC

(Map p86; VI Paulay Ede utca 58; ☺1pm-late; Ⓜ M1 Oktogon) This basement bar, presided over by Gizi néni (Aunt Gizi), is *the* place to come to listen to Gypsy music, as Roma musicians play from about 10pm when they're off duty after playing saccharine junk at top-end hotels. Expect a warm welcome but no frills.

Ladó Café
LIVE MUSIC

(Map p86; ☑06 70 350 3929; www.ladocafe.hu; VII Dohány utca 50; ☺8am-11.30pm; Ⓜ M2 Blaha Lujza tér) An unassuming place by day with decent food and excellent service, the Ladó comes into its own at 8pm most nights when it hosts live entertainment – usually jazz and swing.

Budapest Puppet Theatre
PUPPET THEATRE

(Budapest Bábszínház; Map p86; ☑1-321 5200, box office 1-342 2702; www.budapest-babszinhaz.hu; VI Andrássy út 69; tickets 1300-1900Ft; ☺box office 9am-6pm; Ⓜ M1 Vörösmarty utca) The city's puppet theatre presents shows designed for children at 10am or 10.30am, and 2.30pm or 3pm. Performances usually don't require fluency in Hungarian. Consult the website for program schedules and exact times.

☆ Southern Pest

★ Palace of Arts
CONCERT VENUE

(Művészetek Palotája; Map p92; ☑1-555 3300; www.mupa.hu; IX Komor Marcell utca 1; ☺box office 10am-6pm; ☎; ☐2, 24, ☐HÉV 7 Közvágóhíd) The two concert halls at this palatial arts centre by the Danube are the 1700-seat **Béla Bartók National Concert Hall** (Bartók Béla Nemzeti Hangversenyterem) and the smaller **Festival Theatre** (Fesztivál Színház), accommodating up to 450 people. Both are purported to have near-perfect acoustics. Students can pay 500Ft one hour before all performances for a standing-only ticket.

Budapest Music Center
CONCERT VENUE

(BMC; Map p92; ☑1-216 7894; http://bmc.hu; IX Mátyás utca 8; tickets from 1300Ft; ☺library 9am-4.30pm Mon-Fri; ☎; Ⓜ M4 Fővám tér) Hosting a fantastic line-up of mainly Hungarian jazz and classical performances, the Budapest Music Center comprises a classy 350-capacity concert hall, the **Opus Jazz Club** with concerts at 9.30pm Thursday to Saturday (and restaurant), and a library and recording studios. Head here on Tuesday or Wednesday when there are free concerts.

Jedermann Cafe
LIVE MUSIC

(Map p92; ☑06 30 406 3617; www.jedermann.hu; XI Ráday utca 58; ☺8am-1am; ☎; ☐4, 6) This lovely and uberchilled old-style cafe and restaurant at the southern end of Ráday utca turns into a great music venue at night, focusing on jazz, world and folk. Gigs (500Ft) are at 9pm on Monday, Wednesday, Friday and/or Saturday, depending on the season. There's an eclectic, changing food menu, from breakfast and grilled-meat mains (1390Ft to 1990Ft) to salads and cake. The daily set lunch on weekdays is 990Ft.

Trafó House of Contemporary Arts
DANCE

(Trafó Kortárs Művészetek Háza; Map p92; ☑bookings 1-215 1600; www.trafo.hu; IX Liliom utca 41; ☺box office 4-8pm; ☎; Ⓜ M3 Corvin-negyed, ☐4, 6) This ultrahip stage in Ferencváros presents a mixture of music, theatre and especially dance, including a good pull of international acts. It also has a gallery and a club.

National Theatre
THEATRE

(Nemzeti Színház; Map p92; ☑bookings 1-476 6868; www.nemzetiszinhaz.hu; IX Bajor Gizi Park 1; tickets 1300-3800Ft; ☺box office 10am-6pm Mon-Fri, 2-6pm Sat; ☐2, ☐HÉV 7 Közvágóhíd) This rather eclectic venue is the place to go if you want to brave a play in Hungarian or just check out the theatre's bizarre architecture.

Corvin Cinema
CINEMA

(Corvin Mozi; Map p92; ☑1-459 5050; www.corvin.hu; VIII Corvin köz 1; Ⓜ M3 Corvin-negyed, ☐4, 6) A restored art deco building, the Corvin sits in the middle of a square flanked by Regency-like houses. Note the two wonderful reliefs outside the main entrance to the cinema and the monument to the *Pesti srácok,* the heroic 'kids from Pest' who fought and died in the neighbourhood during the 1956 Uprising.

Uránia National Cinema
CINEMA

(Uránia Nemzeti Filmszínház; Map p92; ☑1-486 3400; www.urania-nf.hu; VIII Rákóczi út 21; ☐7) This art deco/neo-Moorish extravaganza is a tarted-up film palace. It has an excellent cafe with balcony on the 1st floor overlooking busy Rákóczi út.

Groupama Arena FOOTBALL
(Map p92; www.groupamaarena.com; IX Üllői út 129; ⓜM3 Népliget) Brand-new Groupama Arena, rebuilt on the site of the Flórián Albert Stadium opposite Népliget bus station, is home to Ferencvárosi Torna Club (www.fradi.hu), the country's loudest, brashest and most popular team. You either love the Fradi boys in green and white or you hate 'em. With room for 23,700 spectators, it's the second-largest stadium in Hungary after Ferenc Puskás Stadium.

☆ City Park & Beyond

Ferenc Puskás Stadium FOOTBALL
(Stadion Puskás Ferenc; Map p96; ☑1-471 4221; www.stadiumguide.com/puskasferencstadion; XIV Istvánmezei út 1-3; ⓜM2 Puskás Ferenc Stadion) This stadium, home to Hungary's national football team, was undergoing massive reconstruction at the time of research. When completed in 2019, it will accommodate upwards of 70,000 fans. But don't expect any miracles if things continue as they have been.

**László Papp Budapest
Sportaréna** LIVE MUSIC
(Map p96; ☑1-422 2600; www.budapestarena.hu; XIV Stefánia út 2; ⊙box office 9am-5pm Mon-Fri; ⓜM2 Puskás Ferenc Stadion) This purpose-built 15,000-seat arena named after a local boxing great is where big local and international acts (eg Jean-Michel Jarre, Placebo, Rihanna) perform.

Bethlen Square Theatre THEATRE
(Bethlen Téri Színház; Map p96; ☑1-342 7163; www.bethlenszinhaz.hu; VII Bethlen Gábor tér 3; tickets 1500-2500Ft; ⓜM2/4 Keleti pályaudvar) This small and atmospheric theatre puts on drama, dance and puppet shows, as well as stand-up comedy (if your Hungarian's up to it). There's a good cafe, a gallery and the Central European Dance Theatre (Közép-Európa Táncszínház) is also based here. Enter from VII István út 4.

🔒 Shopping

Budapest is a fantastic city for shopping, whether you're in the market for traditional folk craft with a twist, cutting-edge designer goods, the latest in flash headgear or honey-sweet dessert wine. Traditional markets stand side by side with mammoth shopping malls, and old-style umbrella-makers can still be found next to avant-garde fashion boutiques.

🔒 Castle District

Mester Porta MUSIC
(Map p62; ☑06 20 232 5614; www.facebook.com/mesterporta.galeria; I Corvin tér 7; ⊙10.30am-6pm Tue-Sat; ☒19, 41) This wonderful shop has CDs and DVDs of Hungarian and other folk music as well as musical instruments, scores, books and now even folk costumes.

Herend CERAMICS
(Map p62; ☑1-225 1051; www.herend.com; I Szentháromság utca 5; ⊙10am-6pm Mon-Fri, to 4pm Sat & Sun Apr-Oct, closes 2pm Sat & Sun Nov-Mar); ☒16, 16A, 116) For both contemporary and traditional fine porcelain, there is no other place to go but Herend, Hungary's answer to Wedgwood. Among the most popular motifs produced by the company is the Victoria pattern of butterflies and wildflowers, designed for the British queen during the mid-19th century.

Bortársaság WINE
(Map p62; ☑1-289 9357; www.bortarsasag.hu; I Batthyány utca 59; ⊙10am-9pm Mon-Sat, to 7pm Sun; ⓜM2 Széll Kálmán tér, ☒4, 6) Once known as the Budapest Wine Society, this place has a dozen or so retail outlets in the capital with an exceptional selection of Hungarian wines. No one, but no one, knows Hungarian wines like these guys do.

Herend Village Pottery CERAMICS
(Map p62; ☑1-356 7899; www.herendimajolika.hu; II Bem rakpart 37; ⊙10am-6pm Tue-Fri, to 1pm Sat; ⓜM2 Batthyány tér, ☒19, 41) An alternative to delicate Herend porcelain is the hard-wearing Herend pottery and dishes sold here, decorated with bold and colourful fruit and flower patterns.

🔒 Gellért Hill & Tabán

Prezent DESIGN
(Map p66; www.prezentshop.hu; Döbrentei utca 16; ⊙10.30am-6pm Wed-Mon; ☒18, 19, 41) This shop specialising in 'sustainable Hungarian design' sells fashion and accessories as well as natural cosmetics. Earnest and admirable, and good stuff too!

🔒 Belváros

★**Le Parfum Croisette** PERFUME
(Map p74; ☑06 30 405 0668; www.leparfum.hu; V Deák Ferenc utca 18; ⊙10am-7pm Mon-Fri, to 5pm Sat & Sun; ⓜM1/2/3 Deák Ferenc tér, ☒47, 48, 49) ✐ Hungary's only *parfumier*, Zsolt

Zólyomi, creates scents at his atelier-shop, as well as selling cutting-edge, animal-friendly perfumes from around the globe, such as Romano Ricci's Juliette Has a Gun range of cognac scents, whose recipes go back 750 years. Zólyomi, who foresees a renaissance in the once-great Hungarian perfume industry, holds perfume-making workshops here too.

★ **Rózsavölgyi Csokoládé** CHOCOLATE
(Map p74; ☑ 06 30 814 8929; www.rozsavolgyi. com; V Királyi Pál utca 6; ⊘ 10.30am-1pm & 1.30-6.30pm Mon-Fri, noon-6pm Sat; M M3/4 Kálvin tér) Tiny, low-lit boutique selling delicious and artfully packaged, award-winning bean-to-bar chocolate. The range of handmade chocolates includes such interesting flavours as coffee and balsamic vinegar, and star anise with red peppercorn.

★ **Bomo Art** ARTS & CRAFTS
(Map p74; ☑ 1-318 7280; www.bomoart.hu; V Régi Posta utca 14; ⊘ 10am-6.30pm Mon-Fri, to 6pm Sat; M M3 Ferenciek tere) This tiny shop just off Váci utca sells some of the finest paper and paper goods in Budapest, including leather-bound notebooks, photo albums and address books.

Wonderlab FASHION & ACCESSORIES
(Map p74; ☑ 06 20 314 2058; www.facebook.com/ wonderLABconcept; V Veres Pálné utca 3; ⊘ noon-8pm Tue-Sat; ☑ 5, 7, 110, M M2 Astoria, ☑ 2) Hip and very wearable fashion by a collection of up-and-coming Hungarian designers who are sometimes on hand to discuss their work. Interesting items, including handbags, jewellery, graphic-design pieces, furniture and some exquisite ceramics.

Paloma FASHION & ACCESSORIES
(Map p74; ☑ 06 20 961 9160; www.facebook. com/PalomaBudapest/; V Kossuth Lajos utca 14; ⊘ 11am-7pm Mon-Fri, to 3pm Sat; M M2 Astoria/ M3 Ferenciek tere, ☑ 47, 49) Combining fashion and art, Paloma showcases the work of a couple of dozen up-and-coming Hungarian designers, as well as staging contemporary art exhibitions.

Je Suis Belle FASHION & ACCESSORIES
(Map p74; ☑ 1-951 1353; www.jesuisbelle.hu; V Ferenciek tere 11, Párisi udvar; ⊘ noon-4pm Thu & Fri; M M3 Ferenciek tere) Striking ladies' threads by Dalma Devenyi and Tibor Kass, the founders of one of Hungary's leading fashion brands.

Nanushka FASHION & ACCESSORIES
(Map p74; ☑ 1-202 1050; www.nanushka.hu; V Deák Ferenc utca 17; ⊘ 10am-8pm Mon-Sat, noon-6pm Sun; M M1/2/3 Deák Ferenc tér) Flagship store of Budapest-born designer Nanushka (aka Sandra Sandor), whose inspired retail space, with log floor and all-white canvas drapes, sets off the cutting-edge and covetable ladies' fashions inside.

Hecserli FOOD
(Map p74; www.hecserli.hu; V Szerb utca 15; ⊘ 8am-7pm Mon-Fri, 9am-3pm Sat; M M3/4 Kálvin tér) A world of Hungarian cuisine awaits in Hecserli, where helpful staff wax lyrical about the freshly pressed, potted, homemade and home-grown products. Ham, salami, cheese, syrups, tea and fresh bread are available. The place doubles as an organic cafe and wine bar.

Rozsnyai Shoes SHOES
(Map p74; ☑ 06 30 247 7340; www.rozsnyaishoes. com; V Haris Köz 3; ⊘ 10am-6pm Mon & Sat, to 7pm Tue-Fri; M M3 Ferenciek tere) Bespoke shoes for men and women, handmade by a team of experienced craftspeople. It takes two weeks to create a pair from scratch; international delivery offered.

Rododendron GIFTS & SOUVENIRS
(Map p74; ☑ 06 70 419 5329; www.rododendron. hu; V Semmelweis utca 19; ⊘ 10am-7pm Mon-Fri, to 5pm Sat; M M2 Astoria) This delightful shop presents the work of numerous local designers, with everything from jewellery and cuddly toys to handbags and a range of beautiful and quirky prints on offer.

Herend CERAMICS
(Map p74; ☑ 1-317 2622; www.herend.com; V József nádor tér 11; ⊘ 10am-6pm Mon-Fri, to 2pm Sat; M M1/2/3 Deák Ferenc tér, ☑ 2) A central branch of the iconic Hungarian porcelain brand. Herend makes an excellent – though pricey – souvenir or gift.

Cadeau CHOCOLATE
(Map p74; ☑ 06 30 299 2919; www.cadeaubonbon. hu; V Veres Pálné utca 8; ⊘ 10am-6pm Mon-Fri; M M3 Ferenciek tere) 'Death by chocolate' has arrived in Budapest by way of Gyula, a city in Hungary's southeast where the delectable handmade bonbons sold here are made and served at the celebrated Százéves Cukrászda (Century Cake Shop). Also serves delicious ice cream (250Ft a scoop).

Szamos Marcipán   FOOD

(Map p74; ☑ 1-275 0855; www.szamosmarcipan.hu;
V Párizsi utca 3; ⊙ 10am-7pm; Ⓜ M3 Ferenciek tere)
'Many Kinds of Marzipan' sells just that – in
every shape and size imaginable. It also does
a delectable array of cakes (500Ft to 750Ft),
including a Hungarian flag marzipan cake.

Balogh Kesztyű Üzlet   FASHION & ACCESSORIES

(Map p74; ☑ 1-266 1942; V Haris köz 2; ⊙ noon-
6pm Mon, 11am-6pm Tue, 11.30am-6pm Wed &
Thu, to 5pm Fri, to 1pm Sat; Ⓜ M3 Ferenciek tere)
If he can have a pair of bespoke shoes from
Vass Shoes, why can't she have a pair of
custom-made gloves lined with cashmere?
You'll find them here at the 'Balogh Gloves
Shop' – and there's any number of materials
to choose from for men too, including shear-
ling-lined leather gloves.

Rózsavölgyi és Társa   MUSIC

(Map p74; www.rozsavolgyi.hu; V Szervita tér 5;
⊙ 10am-10pm Mon-Sat; Ⓜ M1/2/3 Deák Ferenc
tér) Housed in Béla Latja's Rózsavölgyi
House, a wonderful example of early mod-
ernist architecture, this is a great choice for
CDs and DVDs of traditional folk and classical music, with a good selection of sheet music, too. Also sells concert tickets and hosts
performances in its upstairs cafe.

Központi Antikvárium   BOOKS

(Map p74; ☑ 1-317 3514; www.kozpontiantikvarium.
hu; V Múzeum körút 13-15; ⊙ 10am-6pm Mon-Fri, to
2pm Sat; Ⓜ M2 Astoria) For antique maps and
antique and secondhand books in Hungarian, German and English, try the 'Central
Antiquarian'. Established in 1891, it is the
largest (and oldest) antique bookshop, not
just in Budapest, but in Eastern Europe.

Vass Shoes   SHOES

(Map p74; ☑ 1-318 2375; www.vass-cipo.hu; V Haris
köz 2; ⊙ 10am-7pm Mon-Fri, to 4pm Sat; Ⓜ M3
Ferenciek tere) A traditional shoemaker that
stocks ready-to-wear shoes and cobbles to
order, Vass has a reputation that goes back
to 1896; some people travel to Hungary just
to have their footwear made here.

Folkart Kézművésház   ARTS & CRAFTS

(Map p74; ☑ 1-318 5143; www.folkartkezmuveshaz.
hu; V Régi Posta utca 12; ⊙ 10am-6pm Mon-Fri, to
3pm Sat & Sun; Ⓜ M3 Ferenciek tere) This is a
large shop where everything Magyar (all of
it made here) is available, from embroidered
waistcoats and tablecloths to painted eggs
and rustic-chic pottery. The staff are helpful.

Magma   HOMEWARES

(Map p74; ☑ 1-235 0277; www.magma.hu; V Petőfi
Sándor utca 11; ⊙ 10am-7pm Mon-Fri, to 3pm Sat;
Ⓜ M3 Ferenciek tere) This showroom in the
heart of the Inner Town focuses on Hungarian design and designers exclusively, with
everything from glassware, porcelain and
toys to textiles and furniture.

Intuita   ARTS & CRAFTS

(Map p74; ☑ 1-266 5864; www.intuitashop.com;
V Váci utca 67; ⊙ 10am-6pm Mon-Fri, to 4pm Sat;
Ⓜ M4 Fővám tér, ☒ 2) Specialising in Hungarian artisanship, this place is chock-a-block
with contemporary hand-crafted items such
as jewellery, ceramics, notebooks and locally
designed, funky handbags.

Inmedio   STATIONERY

(Map p74; ☑ 06 30 509 9503; V Váci utca 10;
⊙ 8am-8pm; Ⓜ M1 Vörösmarty tér) The best
place in Budapest for foreign-language
newspapers and magazines.

Múzeum Antikvárium   BOOKS

(Map p74; ☑ 1-317 5023; www.muzeumantikvar-
ium.hu; V Múzeum körút 35; ⊙ 10am-6pm Mon-
Fri, to 2pm Sat; Ⓜ M3/4 Kálvin tér) Just opposite the Hungarian National Museum, this
well-stocked bookshop has both used and
antique volumes in a Babel of languages,
including English. It's our favourite of the
many bookshops on this street.

🏛 Parliament & Around

★ Bestsellers   BOOKS

(Map p78; ☑ 1-312 1295; www.bestsellers.hu; V Október 6 utca 11; ⊙ 9am-6.30pm Mon-Fri, 11am-6pm
Sat, noon-6pm Sun; Ⓜ M1/2/3 Deák Ferenc tér)
Our favourite English-language bookshop
in town, with fiction, travel guides and lots
of Hungarica, as well as a large selection
of newspapers and magazines overseen by
master bookseller Tony Láng. Helpful staff
are at hand to advise and recommend.

Moró Antik   ANTIQUES

(Map p78; ☑ 1-311 0814; www.moroantik.hu; Falk
Miksa utca 13; ⊙ 10am-6pm Mon-Fri, to 1pm Sat;
☒ 2, 4, 6) A considerable collection of antique swords and pistols, as well as porcelain, paintings and other items from China,
Japan and other parts of Asia.

Memories of Hungary   ARTS & CRAFTS

(Map p78; ☑ 1-780 5844; www.memoriesofhungary.
hu; V Hercegprímás utca 8; ⊙ 10am-10pm; Ⓜ M1
Bajcsy-Zsilinszky út) One of our favourite places

to buy souvenirs and gifts, this shop has (mostly genuine) Hungarian handicrafts as well as a good selection of local foodstuffs and wine. It's also useful as an information point.

Alexandra   BOOKS
(Map p78; 1-428 7070; www.alexandra.hu; V Nyugati tér 7; 10am-10pm Mon-Sat, to 8pm Sun; M M3 Nyugati pályaudvar) A large branch of the nationwide chain of bookshops, opposite Nyugati train station.

Originart Galéria   ARTS & CRAFTS
(Map p78; 1-302 2162; www.originart.hu; V Arany János utca 18; 10am-6pm Mon-Fri; 15, 115, M M3 Arany János utca) Hungarian handicrafts guaranteed to put a smile on your face, from brightly painted ceramic figures to jewellery boxes, mugs and acryllic paintings. All very playful and with kiddie appeal too.

BÁV   ANTIQUES
(Bizományi Kereskedőház és Záloghitel; Map p78; 1-473 0666; www.bav.hu; XIII Szent István körút 3; 10am-7pm Mon-Fri, to 2pm Sat; 4, 6) This chain of pawn and second-hand shops, with a number of branches around town, is a fun place to comb for trinkets and treasures, especially if you don't have time to get to the Ecseri Piac market (p156). Check out this branch for china, textiles, artwork and furniture.

Pintér Galéria   ANTIQUES
(Map p78; 1-311 3030; www.pinterantik.hu; V Falk Miksa utca 10; 10am-6pm Mon-Fri, to 2pm Sat; 2, 4, 6) With a positively enormous antique showroom (some 2000 sq metres) in a series of cellars near the Parliament building, Pintér has everything – from furniture and chandeliers to oil paintings and china – and is the best place on Falk Miksa utca for browsing.

Malatinszky Wine Store   WINE
(Map p78; 1-317 5919; www.malatinszky.hu; V József Attila utca 12; 10am-6pm Mon-Sat; M M1/2/3 Deák Ferenc tér, 2, 47, 49) Owned and operated by a one-time sommelier at the Gundel restaurant, this shop has an excellent selection of high-end Hungarian wines, including three vintages from his own organically farmed vines. Ask the staff to recommend a bottle.

Szőnyi Antikváriuma   BOOKS
(Map p78; 1-311 6431; www.szonyi.hu; V Szent István körút 3; 10am-6pm Mon-Fri, 9am-1pm Sat; 2, 4, 6) This long-established antiquarian bookshop has, in addition to old tomes, an excellent selection of antique prints and

maps. Just open the drawers in the chests at the back and have a browse.

Anna Antikvitás   ANTIQUES
(Map p78; 1-302 5461; www.annaantikvitas.eu; V Falk Miksa utca 18-20; 10am-6pm Mon-Fri, to 1pm Sat; 2, 4, 6) Anna is the place to go if you're in the market for embroidered antique tablecloths and bed linen. They're stacked up all over the shop and are of very good quality.

🏠 Margaret Island & Northern Pest

Mountex   SPORTS & OUTDOORS
(Map p84; 1-239 6050; www.mountex.hu; XIII Váci út 19; 10am-8pm Mon-Sat, to 6pm Sun; M M3 Lehel tér) This huge emporium on two levels with branches throughout the city carries all the gear you'll need for camping, hiking, trekking and climbing.

Mézes Kuckó   FOOD
(Honey Nook; Map p84; XIII Jászai Mari tér 4; 10am-6pm Mon-Fri, 9am-1pm Sat; 2, 4, 6) This hole-in-the-wall shop is the place to go if you have the urge for something sweet; its nut-and-honey cookies, 240Ft per 100g, are to die for. A colourfully decorated *mézeskalács* (honey cake; 330Ft to 750Ft) in the shape of a heart makes a lovely gift.

🏠 Erzsébetváros & the Jewish Quarter

Garden Studio   FASHION & ACCESSORIES
(Map p86; 06 30 848 6163; www.thegarden studio.hu; VI Paulay Ede utca 18; 10am-8pm Mon-Sat; M M1 Bajcsy-Zsilinszky utca) This great designer-owned shop stocks an enviable supply of clothing and accessories from young contemporary Hungarian designers: Tomcsányi retro and vintage styles from the '70s and '80s, Kele knitwear and VYF scarves.

Szimpla Farmers' Market   MARKET
(Map p86; http://szimpla.hu; VII Kazinczy utca 14; 9am-2pm Sun; ; M M2 Astoria) Every Sunday, ruin pub Szimpla Kert (p143) holds a charming farmers' market where you can buy all manner of locally produced jam, honey, yoghurt, cheese and bread. Also available are paprika, vegetables, fruit, cured meat and fruit juice.

Massolit Budapest   BOOKS
(Map p86; 1-788 5292; www.facebook.com/ MassolitBudapest; VII Nagy Diófa utca 30; 8am-

DON'T MISS

ECSERI PIAC

One of the biggest flea markets in Central Europe, **Ecseri** (Ecseri Market; www.piaconline.hu; XIX Nagykőrösi út 156; ⊙8am-4pm Mon-Fri, 5am-3pm Sat, 8am-1pm Sun; 🚌54, 84E, 89E 94E) sells everything from antique jewellery and Soviet army watches to Fred Astaire–style top hats. Take bus 54 from Pest's Boráros tér, or for a quicker journey, express bus 84E, 89E or 94E from the Határ út stop on the M3 metro line in Pest and get off at the Fiume utca stop. Early Saturday is the best time to go for those diamonds in the rough.

7.30pm Mon-Sat, 10am-7.30pm Sun; Ⓜ M2 Astoria) A branch of the celebrated bookshop in Kraków, Massolit is one of Budapest's best, with new and secondhand English-language fiction and nonfiction, including Hungarian history and literature in translation. It has a beautiful shady garden and tables set among the shelves, so you can enjoy coffee, sandwiches, cakes and bagels as you browse the volumes.

Gouba　　　　　　　　　　　MARKET
(Map p86; www.gouba.hu; VII Gozsdu udvar; ⊙10am-7pm Sun; Ⓜ M1/2/3 Deák Ferenc tér) A weekly arts and crafts market along Gozsdu udvar, where you can pick up some interesting pieces from local artists and designers. It's a good place to shop for souvenirs, too.

Szputnyik Shop　　　FASHION & ACCESSORIES
(Map p86; ☎1-321 3730; http://szputnyikshop. hu; VII Dohány utca 20; ⊙10am-8pm Mon-Sat, to 6pm Sun; Ⓜ M2 Astoria) A bright, open space, stuffed with vintage fashion like US college jackets and Converse sneakers, plus a selection of new alternative lines from international designers.

Retrock　　　　　FASHION & ACCESSORIES
(Map p86; ☎06 30 472 3636; www.retrock.com; VI Anker köz 2; ⊙11am-9pm Mon-Thu, to 10pm Fri & Sat, to 8pm Sun; Ⓜ M1/2/3 Deák Ferenc tér) A large, hip store with a vast collection of vintage clothing, bags, jewellery and shoes, and a small line in Hungarian streetwear designers.

Printa　　　　　　FASHION & ACCESSORIES
(Map p86; ☎06 30 292 0329; www.printa.hu; VII Rumbach Sebestyén utca 10; ⊙11am-7pm Mon-Sat; Ⓜ M1/2/3 Deák Ferenc tér) This wonderful, hip

silkscreen studio, design shop and gallery focuses on local talent and sells bags, leather goods, prints, T-shirts, stationery and jewellery. There's both recycled and upcycled clothing too.

Alexandra　　　　　　　　　　　BOOKS
(Map p86; ☎1-322 1645; www.alexandra.hu; VI Andrássy út 39; ⊙10am-8pm; Ⓜ M1 Opera, 🚋4, 6) In what was originally opened as the Grande Parisienne department store in 1911 you'll now find a branch of the Alexandra bookshop chain. The foreign-language section is on the 1st floor, and there's a range of souvenirs and wine on the ground floor. Don't leave before checking out the fantastic Lotz Terem Book Cafe (p143).

Írók Boltja　　　　　　　　　　BOOKS
(Writers' Bookshop; Map p86; ☎1-322 1645; www. irokboltja.hu; VI Andrássy út 45; ⊙10am-7pm Mon-Fri, 11am-1pm Sat; Ⓜ M1 Oktogon) For a very large selection of Hungarian authors in translation, the 'Writers' Bookshop' is the place to go in Budapest.

Hollóháza Porcelain Shop　　HOMEWARES
(Hollóházai Márkabolt; Map p86; ☎06 20 592 5676; www.hollohazi.hu/markaboltok.php; VII Dohány utca 1/c; ⊙9am-5pm Mon-Fri, to 1pm Sat; Ⓜ M2 Astoria) This chinaware and crystal shop sells Hungarian-made Hollóháza dinnerware, which is much more affordable than Herend and Zsolnay.

Ludovika　　　　　FASHION & ACCESSORIES
(Map p86; http://ludovika-shop.tumblr.com; VII Rumbach Sebestyén utca 15; ⊙noon-8pm Mon-Fri, to 6pm Sat; Ⓜ M1/2/3 Deák Ferenc tér) A small vintage clothes shop stocking carefully selected pieces for women from a range of eras over two floors. Great handbags.

🔒 Southern Pest

★**Nagycsarnok**　　　　　　　　MARKET
(Great Market Hall; Map p92; ☎1-366 3300; www. piaconline.hu; IX Vámház körút 1-3; ⊙6am-5pm Mon, to 6pm Tue-Fri, to 3pm Sat; Ⓜ M4 Fővám tér) This is Budapest's biggest market, though it has become a tourist magnet since its renovation for the millecentenary celebrations in 1996. Still, plenty of locals come here for fruit, vegetables, deli items, fish and meat. Head up to the 1st floor for Hungarian folk costumes, dolls, painted eggs, embroidered tablecloths, carved hunting knives and other souvenirs.

Gourmets will appreciate the Hungarian and other treats available here for less than they'd pay in the shops on nearby Váci utca: shrink-wrapped and potted foie gras, garlands of dried paprika, souvenir sacks and tins of paprika powder, and as many kinds of honey as you'd care to name.

Magyar Pálinka Háza DRINKS
(Hungarian Pálinka House; Map p92; ☑ 06 30 421 5463; www.magyarpalinkahaza.hu; VIII Rákóczi út 17; ☉ 9am-7pm Mon-Sat; ☑ 7) This large shop stocks hundreds of varieties of *pálinka* (fruit brandy). Szicsek and Prekop are premium brands. *Pálinka*-filled chocolates make for an unusual gift.

Portéka GIFTS & SOUVENIRS
(Map p92; ☑ 06 70 313 0348; www.portekabolt.hu; Horánszky utca 27; ☉ noon-6pm Mon-Fri, to 2pm Sat; Ⓜ M3/4 Kálvin tér, ☑ 4, 6) Just off Krúdy Gyula utca, Portéka is a little treasure chest of national delicacies and design. It has a good selection of honey, jam, syrups, spices and organic wine, as well as jewellery, bags, notebooks and postcards. Best of all is the fine range of Tibor Szántó's bean-to-bar chocolate.

Babaház ARTS & CRAFTS
(Dollhouse; Map p92; ☑ 1-213 8295; http://dollhouse.uw.hu; IX Ráday utca 14; ☉ 11am-7pm Mon-Sat; Ⓜ M3/4 Kálvin tér) Dolls and their fabulous period outfits are made in-house here. The friendly owner does a nice line of teddy bears and fabric flowers too.

Rákóczi tér Market MARKET
(Map p92; ☑ 1-476 3921; www.piaconline.hu; VIII Rákóczi tér 7-9; ☉ 6am-4pm Mon, to 6pm Tue-Fri, to 1pm Sat; Ⓜ M4 Rákóczi tér, ☑ 4, 6) Rákóczi tér has sported this handsome blue-and-yellow market hall since 1897. Renovated in the early 1990s after a fire, the market contains all the usual staples: fruit, veg, cured meats, pasta, cheese and baked goods, as well as branches of chains Spar (supermarket) and Rossman (beauty products).

Liszt Ferenc Zeneműbolt MUSIC, BOOKS
(Map p92; ☑ 1-267 5777; www.lisztbolt.hu; VIII Kölcsey utca 1, Libra Books; ☉ 8am-7pm Mon-Fri, 9am-2pm Sat; Ⓜ M4 Rákóczi tér) The Ferenc Liszt Music Shop, with mostly classical CDs as well as sheet music and books of local interest, has moved from A VI Andrássy út and now shares space in Southern Pest with a Libra Books branch.

Bálna MALL
(Map p92; ☑ 06 30 790 2187; www.balnabudapest. hu; IX Fővám tér 11-12; ☉ 10am-8pm Sun-Thu, to 10pm Fri & Sat; Ⓜ M4 Fővám tér) Best appreciated from the opposite side of the Danube, the 'Whale', a striking glass structure, was

designed by Dutch architect Kas Oosterhuis and built around two existing warehouses on the riverbank. It houses the **New Budapest Gallery** (Új Budapest Galéria; Map p92; ☑ 1-388 6784; http://budapestgaleria.hu; IX Fővám tér 11-12; adult/child 1000/500Ft; ☉ 10am-6pm Tue-Sun; Ⓜ M4 Fővám tér, ☑ 2), hosts events and has a range of shops, restaurants and cafes. Great views from the upper levels.

City Park & Beyond

PECSA Bolhapiac FLEA MARKET
(Map p96; www.bolhapiac.com; XIV Zichy Mihály utca 14; admission 150Ft; ☉ 7am-2pm Sat & Sun; ☑ trolleybus 72, 74, ☑ 1) If you don't have the time for Ecseri Piac, the next best thing is this Hungarian flea market held next to the Petőfi Csarnok concert venue. There's everything from old records and draperies to candles and honey on offer. Sunday is the better day.

ℹ️ Information

DANGERS & ANNOYANCES
➡ Do not even think of riding 'black' (without paying a fare) on public transport – you will be caught and severely fined.

➡ Avoid at all costs taxis with no company name on the door and only a removable taxi light box on the roof; these are just guys with cars and likely to rip you off.

➡ Excessive billing of customers still occasionally happens in some bars and restaurants, so check your bill carefully.

➡ Pickpocketing is quite common in busy public places.

BKV Lost & Found Office (Map p86; ☑ 1-325 5255; VII Akácfa utca 18; ☉ 8am-8pm Mon, to 5pm Tue-Thu, to 3pm Fri; Ⓜ M2 Blaha Lujza tér) If you've left something behind on any form of public transport in Budapest, contact the BKK Lost & Found Office.

DISCOUNT CARDS
Budapest Card (1-438 8080; www. budapestinfo.hu; per 24/48/72 hours 4655/7505/9405Ft) Free admission to selected museums and other sights in and around the city; unlimited travel on all forms of public transport; two free guided walking tours; and discounts for organised tours, car rental, thermal baths, and at selected shops and restaurants. Available at tourist offices but cheaper online.

EMERGENCIES
District V Police Station (☑ 1-373 1000; V Szalay utca 11-13; Ⓜ M2 Kossuth Lajos tér) Any crime must be reported at the police station of the district you are in. In the centre of Pest

this is the Belváros-Lipótváros Police Station. If possible, bring along a Hungarian-speaker.

INTERNET ACCESS

Wireless (wi-fi) access is available at most hostels and hotels; fewer and fewer hotels charge for the service. Many restaurants, cafes and bars offer wi-fi, usually free to paying customers.

Some hostels and hotels have at least one computer terminal available to guests either free or for a nominal sum. Internet cafes are rapidly going the way of the dodo, due to the proliferation of smartphones and wi-fi hotspots.

Electric Cafe (☑1-781 0098; www.electric-cafe.hu; VII Dohány utca 37; per hr 300Ft; ⏱9am-midnight; 🛜; Ⓜ M2 Blaha Lujza tér) Large place with attached laundrette (!).

Vist@netcafe (☑06 70 585 3924; http://vistanetcafe.com; XIII Váci út 6; per hour 250Ft; ⏱24hr; Ⓜ M3 Nyugati pályaudvar) One of the very few internet cafes open round the clock.

MEDICAL SERVICES

Consultations and treatment are very expensive in private clinics catering to foreigners. Dental work is usually of a high standard and fairly cheap by European standards.

Clinics

FirstMed Centers (☑1-224 9090; www.firstmedcenters.com; I Hattyú utca 14, 5th fl; ⏱8am-8pm Mon-Fri, to 2pm Sat, urgent care 24hr; Ⓜ M2 Széll Kálmán tér)

SOS Dent (☑1-269 6010, 06 30 383 3333; www.sosdent.hu; VI Király utca 14; ⏱8am-8pm Mon-Sat; Ⓜ M1/2/3 Deák Ferenc tér) Dental consultations from 5000Ft, with extractions 9000Ft to 22,000Ft, fillings 15,000Ft to 35,000Ft and crowns from 42,000Ft.

Pharmacies

Each of Budapest's 23 districts has a rotating all-night pharmacy; a sign on the door of any pharmacy will help you locate the nearest 24-hour place.

Déli Gyógyszertár (☑1-355 4691; www.deli-gyogyszertar.hu; XII Alkotás utca 1/b; ⏱24hr; Ⓜ M2 Déli pályaudvar)

Teréz Patika (☑1-311 4439; www.terezpatika.hu; VI Teréz körút 41; ⏱8am-8pm Mon-Fri, to 2pm Sat, with 24hr window; Ⓜ M3 Nyugati pályaudvar)

MONEY

ATMs are everywhere, including at the airport and train and bus stations. Visa, MasterCard and American Express widely accepted in many hotels and restaurants.

K&H Bank (V Deák Ferenc utca 1; ⏱8am-5pm Mon, to 4pm Tue-Thu, to 3pm Fri; Ⓜ M1 Vörösmarty tér) Bank with ATM just west of the main shopping drag.

OTP Bank (V Deák Ferenc utca 7-9; ⏱8am-6pm Mon, to 5pm Tue-Thu, to 4pm Fri; Ⓜ M1 Vörösmarty tér) The national savings bank (with ATM) offers among the best exchange rates for cash and travellers cheques.

POST

Main post office (Map p78; V Bajcsy-Zsilinsky út 16; ⏱8am-8pm Mon-Fri; Ⓜ M1/M2/M3 Deák Ferenc tér) In the centre of town.

Nyugati train station branch (Map p86; VI Teréz körút 51-53; ⏱7am-8pm Mon-Fri, 8am-6pm Sat; Ⓜ M3 Nyugati pályaudvar) Just south of the station.

Keleti train station branch (Map p92; VIII Baross tér 11/a-11/c; ⏱24hr; Ⓜ M2 Keleti pályaudvar) Most easily reached from platform 6.

TELEPHONE

Hungary's three main mobile-phone providers are: **Telenor** (www.telenor.hu; II Lövőház utca 2-6, Mammut I, 2nd fl, shop 203; ⏱10am-9pm Mon-Sat, to 6pm Sun; Ⓜ M2 Széll Kálmán tér, 🚃4, 6), **T-Mobile** (www.t-mobile.hu; V Petőfi Sándor utca 12; ⏱9am-7pm Mon-Fri, 10am-5pm Sat; Ⓜ M3 Ferenciek tere) and **Vodafone** (www.vodaphone.hu; VI Váci út 1-3, WestEnd City Center, 1st fl; ⏱10am-9pm Mon-Sat, to 6pm Sun; Ⓜ M3 Nyugati pályaudvar). It is now relatively inexpensive to use a mobile from another EU country in Hungary. Local SIM cards can be used in European and Australian phones, as well as most North American smartphones. Other phones must be set to roaming to work, which can be pricey (check with your service provider).

TOURIST INFORMATION

Budapest Info (Map p74; ☑1-438 8080; www.budapestinfo.hu; V Sütő utca 2; ⏱8am-8pm; Ⓜ M1/2/3 Deák Ferenc tér) Budapest Info is about the best single source of information about Budapest, but it can get hopelessly crowded in summer, and the staff are not very patient. Less crowded is the City Park branch (Map p96; ☑1-438 8080; www.budapestinfo.hu; Olof Palme sétány 5, City Ice Rink; ⏱9am-7pm; Ⓜ M1 Hősök tere). There are also information desks in the arrivals sections of Ferenc Liszt International Airport.

TRAVEL AGENCIES

Ibusz (☑1-501 4910; www.ibusz.hu; V Aranykéz utca 4-6; ⏱9am-6pm Mon-Fri, to 1pm Sat; Ⓜ M1 Vörösmarty tér, 🚃2) Ibusz books all types of accommodation and sells transport tickets.

Vista (☑1-429 9999; www.vista.hu; VI Andrássy utca 1; ⏱9.30am-6pm Mon-Fri, 10am-2.30pm Sat; Ⓜ M1/2/3 Deák Ferenc tér) Excellent for all your travel needs, both outbound (air tickets, package tours) and incoming (room bookings, organised tours).

Wasteels (☎1-210 2802; www.wasteels.hu; VIII Kerepesi út 2-6, Keleti train station; ⊙8am-8pm Mon-Fri, to 6pm Sat; Ⓜ M2/M4 Keleti pályaudvar) Sells all train tickets, including discounted ones of up to 60% off to those 26 years and under. Next to platform 9 at Keleti train station.

ⓘ Getting There Away

AIR

Budapest's **Ferenc Liszt International Airport** (p298) has two modern terminals side by side 24km southeast of the city centre.

Terminal 2A deals with departures and arrivals from Schengen countries. Flights to and from non-Schengen destinations (USA, UK, Israel, Russia, Gulf States...) use Terminal 2B, which is next door. There are no scheduled flights within Hungary. The airport website lists which airlines use which terminal. The new SkyCourt connects the two terminals.

At both terminals and in the SkyCourt you'll find currency-exchange desks operated by **Interchange** (⊙8am-1am) and ATMs. In Terminal 2A there are half a dozen car-hire desks. Luggage lockers are available around the clock on the ground floor of the SkyCourt.

BOAT

➡ A hydrofoil service on the Danube River between Budapest and Vienna (5½ to 6½ hours) is run by **Mahart PassNave** (p299) from late April to late September.

➡ Boats leave from Budapest at 9am Tuesday, Thursday and Saturday; from Vienna they depart at the same time on Wednesday, Friday and Sunday.

➡ Adult one-way/return fares are €99/125. (Children between two and 12 years of age travel half-price.) Taking a bicycle costs €25 one way.

➡ In Budapest, hydrofoils arrive at and depart from the **International Ferry Pier** (Nemzetközi hajóállomás; Map p74; ☎1-484 4013; www.mahartpassnave.hu; V Belgrád rakpart; ⊙9am-4pm Mon-Fri; 🚊2), which is between Elizabeth and Liberty Bridges on the Pest side.

BUS

All international buses and domestic ones to/from western Hungary arrive at and depart from **Népliget bus station** (Map p92; ☎1-219 8030; IX Üllői út 131; Ⓜ M3 Népliget) in Pest. The international ticket office is upstairs. Eurolines (www.eurolines.hu) is represented here, as is its Hungarian associate, **Volánbusz** (p299). There are left-luggage lockers on the ground floor.

Népliget is on the blue metro M3 (station: Népliget). Stadion bus station generally serves cities and towns in eastern Hungary. The ticket office and left-luggage lockers are on the ground floor.

Stadion is on the red metro M2 (station: 2 Stadionok).

TRAIN

Budapest has three train stations.

Keleti Train Station

MÁV (p299) links up with the European rail network in all directions. Most international trains (and domestic traffic to/from the north and northeast) arrive at **Keleti train station** (Keleti pályaudvar; VIII Kerepesi út 2-6; Ⓜ M2/M4 Keleti pályaudvar).

➡ The station has left-luggage lockers, a post office and a grocery store that is open late.

➡ Avoid queues by buying your tickets in advance online and either printing them out at your accommodation, or collecting them from ticket machines at the station by inputting the 10-digit reference number.

➡ Keleti is on two metro lines: the green M4 and the blue M3.

➡ Night buses serve the station when the metro is closed.

Nyugati Train Station

Trains from some international destinations (eg Romania) and from the Danube Bend and Great Plain arrive at **Nyugati train station** (Western Train Station; VI Nyugati tér).

➡ Amenities include left-luggage lockers.

➡ The station is on the blue M3 line.

➡ Night buses serve the station when the metro is closed.

Déli Train Station

Trains from some destinations in the south, eg Osijek in Croatia and Sarajevo in Bosnia, as well as some trains from Vienna, arrive at **Déli train station** (Déli pályaudvar; I Krisztina körút 37; Ⓜ M2 Déli pályaudvar).

➡ Amenities include left-luggage lockers.

➡ The station is on the red M2 line.

➡ Night buses serve the station when the metro is closed.

ⓘ Getting Around

Travel passes valid for one day to one month are valid on all trams, buses, trolleybuses, HÉV suburban trains (within city limits) and metro lines.

➡ **Metro** The quickest but least scenic way to get around. Runs 4am to about 11.15pm.

➡ **Bus** Extensive network of regular buses runs from around 4.15am to between 9pm and 11.30pm; from 11.30pm to just after 4am a network of 41 night buses (three digits beginning with '9') kicks in.

➡ **Tram** Faster and more pleasant for sightseeing than buses; a network of 30 lines. Tram 6 runs overnight.

Trolleybus Mostly useful for getting to and around City Park in Pest.

TO/FROM THE AIRPORT

Bus & Metro The cheapest (and most time-consuming) way to get into the city centre from the airport is to take bus 200E (350Ft, on the bus 450Ft; 4am to midnight) – look for the stop on the footpath between terminals 2A and 2B – which terminates at the Kőbánya-Kispest metro station. From there take the M3 metro into the city centre. The total cost is 700Ft to 800Ft. Between midnight and 4am night bus 900 makes the run.

Shuttle The **MiniBUD** (☑1-550 0000; www.minibud.hu; one way from 1900Ft) airport shuttle carries passengers from both terminals directly to their hotel, hostel or residence in nine-seat vans. Tickets are available at a clearly marked desk in the arrivals halls, though you may have to wait while the van fills up. You need to book your journey back to the airport at least 12 hours in advance.

Taxi Reputable **Fő Taxi** (p296) has the monopoly on picking up passengers at the airport. Fares to most locations in Pest are about 6000Ft, and in Buda about 7000Ft.

BICYCLE

More and more cyclists can be seen on the streets of Budapest, taking advantage of the city's ever-growing network of dedicated bike paths. Some of the main roads might be a bit too busy for enjoyable cycling, but the side streets are fine and there are some areas (eg City Park, Margaret Island) where cycling is positively ideal. You can hire bicycles from **Yellow Zebra Bikes** (Map p78; ☑1-269 3843; www.yellow zebrabikes.com; VI Lázár utca 16; tours adult/student/3-12yr €28/26/12; ☺9am-8.30pm Apr-Oct, to 7pm Nov-Mar; Ⓜ M1 Opera) as well as the following:

Bubi Bikes (www.molbubi.bkk.hu; access fee per 24hr/72hr/week 500/1000/2000Ft, hire per 1/2/3hr 500/1500/2500Ft) Budapest's bicycle-sharing scheme has 1286 bikes available at 112 docking stations across the city. You can collect your bike at any docking station and return it at any of the others. The first 30 minutes are free. Hire is available for a maximum of 24 hours at a time – you must allow five minutes between each access. The scheme is sponsored by oil and gas group MOL.

Bike Base (☑06 70 625 8501; www.bikebase. hu; VI Podmaniczky utca 19; per 1/2/3 days 3200/5500/7800Ft; ☺9am-7pm Apr-Oct; Ⓜ M3 Nyugati pályaudvar) Bike Base has bikes available from April to October.

Budapest Bike (☑06 30 944 5533; www. budapestbike.hu; VII Wesselényi utca 13; day/24hr/3 days 2500/3500/9000Ft; ☺9am-

---

❶ Fares & Travel Passes

➡ To ride the metro, trams, trolleybuses, buses and the HÉV as far as the city limits, you must have a valid ticket (which you can buy at kiosks, news stands, metro entrances, machines and, in some cases, on the bus for an extra charge) or travel pass.

➡ Life will most likely be simpler if you buy a travel pass, and you won't have to worry about validating your ticket each time you board. The most central place to buy them is the ticket office at the Deák Ferenc tér metro station, open from 6am to 11pm daily.

➡ Children aged under six and EU seniors over 65 travel free.

➡ Bicycles can be transported only on the HÉV.

➡ The basic fare for all forms of transport is a 350Ft ticket (3000Ft for a block of 10), allowing you to travel as far as you like on the same metro, bus, trolleybus or tram line without changing/transferring. A 'transfer ticket' allowing unlimited stations with one change within one hour costs 530Ft. On the metro exclusively, the base fare drops to 300Ft if you are just going three stops within 30 minutes. Tickets bought on the bus and all night buses cost 450Ft.

➡ You must always travel in one continuous direction on any ticket; return trips are forbidden. Tickets have to be validated in machines at metro entrances and aboard other vehicles – inspectors will fine you for not doing so.

➡ A 24-hour travel card is poor value at 1650Ft, but the 72-hour one for 4150Ft and the seven-day pass for 4950Ft are worthwhile for most people. You'll need to input your name if purchasing the 15-day/monthly pass (6300/9500Ft).

➡ Travelling without a valid ticket or pass is foolhardy; with what seems like constant surveillance (especially in the metro), there's an excellent chance you'll get caught. The on-the-spot fine is 8000Ft, which doubles if you pay it at the **BKK office** (Budapesti Közlekedési Központ, Centre for Budapest Transport; 1-258 4636; www.bkk.hu) up to 30 days later. After that date it goes up to 32,500Ft.

➡ If you've left something on any form of public transport, contact the **BKV lost & found office** (p157).

6pm; Ⓜ M2 Astoria, 🚊 4, 6) Budapest Bike has bikes available year-round.

Dynamo Bike & Bake (Map p74; 📞 06 30 868 1107; www.dynamobike.com; V Képíró utca 6; bike rental per 24/48/72hr 6800/6800/10,000Ft; ⏱ 8.30am-7pm Mon-Fri, 9.30am-7pm Sat & Sun; Ⓜ M3/4 Kálvin tér, 🚊 47, 49) A fantastic little cake shop–bike-hire place, Dynamo is run by a keen cycling guide who appreciates the value of good equipment. The hybrid urban bikes and mountain bikes are brand new and meticulously maintained; rental includes safety gear.

BOAT

Throughout most of the year passenger ferries run by **BKK** (www.bkk.hu) depart from alongside the **A38** (p149) club boat in south Buda up to 10 times a day, Monday to Saturday, and head for IV Árpád út in north Pest, a one-hour trip with eight stops along the way. Tickets (adult/under 15 years 179/110Ft) are sold on board. The ferry stop closest to the Castle District is I Batthyány tér, and V Petőfi tér is not far from the pier just west of Vörösmarty tér. Transporting a bicycle costs 170Ft.

BUS

An extensive system of buses running on some 260 routes day and night serves greater Budapest. On certain bus lines the same bus may have an 'E' after the number, meaning it is express and makes limited stops.

Buses run from around 4.15am to between 9pm and 11.30pm, depending on the line. From 11.30pm to just after 4am a network of 40 night buses (always with three digits and beginning with 9) operates every 15 to 60 minutes, again depending on the route.

Following are bus routes (shown with blue lines on most Budapest maps) that you might find useful:

7 Cuts across a large swath of central Pest from XIV Bosnyák tér and down VII Rákóczi út before crossing Elizabeth Bridge to southern Buda. The 7E makes limited stops on the same route.

15 Takes in most of the Inner Town from IX Boráros tér to XIII Lehel tér north of Nyugati train station.

105 Goes from V Deák Ferenc tér to XII Apor Vilmos tér in central Buda.

CAR & MOTORCYCLE

Driving in Budapest can be a nightmare: ongoing roadworks reduce traffic to a snail's pace; there are more serious accidents than fender benders; and parking spots are near impossible to find in some neighbourhoods. The public-transport system is good and very inexpensive. Use it.

For information on traffic and road conditions in the capital, check the Főinform website (http://kozut.bkkinfo.hu).

Hire

All the international car-hire firms have offices in Budapest, and online rates, particularly if you choose the 'pay now' option, are very reasonable. A Suzuki Swift from **Avis** (p302), for example, costs €41/195 per day/week, with unlimited kilometres, collision damage waiver (CDW) and theft protection (TP) insurance.

Parking

Parking, should you be lucky enough to find a spot, costs between 175Ft and 440Ft per hour on the streets of Budapest (more on Castle Hill), generally between 8am and 6pm (sometimes 8pm) Monday to Friday and 8am and noon Saturday. Illegally parked cars are usually clamped or towed.

METRO & HÉV

Budapest has four underground metro lines. Three of them converge at Deák Ferenc tér (only): the little yellow (or Millennium) line designated M1 that runs from Vörösmarty tér to Mexikói út in Pest; the red M2 line from Déli train station in Buda to Örs vezér tere in Pest; and the blue M3 line from Újpest-Központ to Kőbánya-Kispest in Pest. The green M4 metro runs from Kelenföldi train station in southern Buda to Keleti train station in Pest, where it links with the M2. It links with the M3 at Kálvin tér. All four metro lines run from about 4am and begin their last journey at around 11.15pm.

The HÉV suburban train line, which runs on four lines (north from Batthyány tér in Buda via Óbuda and Aquincum to Szentendre, south to both Csepel and Ráckeve, and east to Gödöllő), is almost like a fifth, above-ground metro line.

TAXI

Taxis in Budapest are cheap by European standards, and are – at long last – fully regulated, with uniform flagfall (450Ft) and per-kilometre charges (280Ft).

Be careful when hailing a taxi on the street, though. Avoid at all costs 'taxis' with no name on the door and only a removable taxi light on the roof. Never get into a taxi that does not have a yellow licence plate and an identification badge displayed on the dashboard (as required by law), plus the logo of one of the reputable taxi firms on the outside of the side doors and a table of fares clearly visible on the right-side back door.

Reputable taxi firms:

Budapest Taxi (p296)

City Taxi (📞 1-211 1111; www.citytaxi.hu)

Fő Taxi (p296)

Taxi 4 (📞 1-444 4444; www.taxi4.hu)

TRAM

BKK (www.bkk.hu) runs 34 tram lines. Trams are often faster and generally more pleasant for sightseeing than buses.

Important tram lines (always marked with a red line on a Budapest map) are as follows:

2 Scenic tram that travels along the Pest side of the Danube from V Jászai Mari tér to IX Boráros tér and beyond.

4 and 6 Extremely useful trams that start at XI Fehérvári út and XI Móricz Zsigmond körtér in south Buda, respectively, and follow the entire length of the Big Ring Rd in Pest before terminating at II Széll Kálmán tér in Buda. Tram 6 runs every 10 to 15 minutes round the clock.

18 Runs from southern Buda along XI Bartók Béla út through the Tabán to II Széll Kálmán tér before carrying on into the Buda Hills.

19 Covers part of the same route as 18, but then runs along the Buda side of the Danube to I Batthyány tér.

47, 48 and 49 Link V Deák Ferenc tér in Pest with points in southern Buda via the Little Ring Rd.

61 Connects XI Móricz Zsigmond körtér with Déli train station and II Széll Kálmán tér in Buda.

TROLLEYBUS

Trolleybuses on 15 lines go along cross streets in central Pest and so are usually of little use to visitors, with the sole exception of the ones to, from and around City Park (70, 72 and 74) and down to Puskás Ferenc Stadion (75 and 77). A broken red line on a map indicates a trolleybus route.

AROUND BUDAPEST

Gödöllő

◉ Sights

Gödöllő Royal Palace   PALACE
(Gödöllői Királyi Kastély; ☑ 28-410 124; www.kiralyikastely.hu; Szabadság tér 1; adult/child 2500/1250Ft; ⊙ 10am-4pm Mon-Fri, to 5pm Sat & Sun) Gödöllő Royal Palace, the largest baroque manor house in Hungary, was designed by Antal Mayerhoffer for Count Antal Grassalkovich (1694–1771), confidante of Empress Maria Theresa, and completed in the 1760s. It was enlarged as a summer retreat for and gifted to Emperor Franz Joseph in the 1870s and soon became the favoured residence of his consort, the much-loved Habsburg empress and Hungarian queen Elizabeth (1837–98), affectionately known as Sissi (or Sisi). It opened to the public in 1996.

Between the two world wars the regent, Admiral Miklós Horthy, also used it as a summer residence, but after the communists came to power part of it was used as a barracks for Soviet and Hungarian troops and as an old people's home. The rest was left to decay.

Partial renovation of the palace began in the mid-1980s and it reopened a decade later. Today 32 rooms can be visited on the ground and 1st floors. They have been restored to the period when the imperial couple was in residence, and Franz Joseph's suites and Sissi's private apartments on the 1st floor are impressive. Check out the Ornamental Hall, all gold tracery, stucco and chandeliers. Also see the Queen's Reception Room, with an oil painting of Sissi repairing the coronation robe of King Stephen with needle and thread; the Queen Elizabeth Memorial Exhibit, which looks at the queen's assassination by Italian anarchist Luigi Lucheni, who stabbed her to death with a needle file; and the Grassalkovich Era Exhibition, which offers a glance at the palace during its first century. The Chapel and its Oratory are also impressive.

You can also visit the Baroque Theatre (adult/concession 1600/900Ft; ⊙ 10.20am, 11.30am, 2.30pm & 3.30pm Sat & Sun) as well as the WWII-vintage Horthy's Bunker (adult/concession 900/750Ft; ⊙ 10.30am & 2pm Mon & Fri, 11am, noon, 2pm & 3pm Sat & Sun) with a guide. Be aware that the permanent exhibition is by guided tour (three to five a day) during the week in winter. Audioguides cost 800Ft.

✖ Eating

Pizza Palazzo   PIZZA **$**
(☑ 28-420 688; www.pizzapalazzo.hu; Szabadság tér 2; pizza & pasta 1120-1590Ft; ⊙ 11am-10pm Sun-Thu, to 11pm Fri & Sat) This popular pizzeria, with more substantial pasta dishes as well, is conveniently attached to Gödöllő's Szabadság tér HÉV station.

Solier Cafe   HUNGARIAN **$$**
(☑ 06 20 396 5512; www.solier.hu; Dózsa György utca 13; mains 2490-4590Ft, set lunch 1250Ft; ⊙ 8am-10pm Mon-Sat, 9am-9pm Sun) In the centre of Gödöllő next to the post office is this upbeat cafe, with a wonderful *cukrászda* (cake shop) and a lovely restaurant on top.

ℹ Information

Tourinform (☑ 28-415 402; www.gkrte.hu; Gödöllő Royal Palace; ⊙ 9am-6pm Wed-Sun Apr-Oct, to 5pm Wed-Sun Nov-Mar) Helpful tourist office just inside the entrance to the Gödöllő Royal Palace.

ℹ Getting There & Away

To get here from Budapest take an hourly 45-minute bus from Stadion bus station, or one of the frequent 45-minute HÉV trains from Örs vezér tere to Gödöllő's Szabadság tér station.

The Danube Bend & Western Transdanubia

Best Places to Eat

➡ Sopronbánfalvi Pálos-Karmelita Kolostor (p184)

➡ Mjam (p170)

➡ Erhardt (p183)

➡ Koriander (p175)

➡ Kovács-kert (p173)

Best Places to Sleep

➡ Pauline-Carmelite Monastery of Sopronbanfalva (p182)

➡ Szent Kristóf Panzió (p175)

➡ Hotel Wollner (p182)

➡ Bükkös Hotel & Spa (p170)

➡ Hotel Silvanus (p172)

Why Go?

The Danube Bend is a region of peaks and picturesque river towns to the north of Budapest. The name is quite literal: this is where hills on both banks force the river to turn sharply and flow southward. It is the most beautiful stretch of the Danube along its entire course, where several historical towns vie for visitors' attention. Szentendre has its roots in Serbian culture and became an important centre for art early in the 20th century. Round the bend is tiny Visegrád, Hungary's 'Camelot' in the 15th century and home to Renaissance-era palace ruins and a forbidding hilltop fortress. Esztergom, once the pope's 'eyes and ears' in Hungary, is now a sleepy town with the nation's biggest cathedral. The Danube meanders towards Western Transdanubia where you find Sopron, a historic city that's been around since the Roman Empire. South of Sopron are the beautiful, remote forests and villages of Őrség National Park.

When to Go

Vac

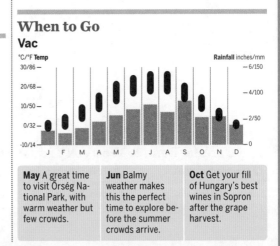

May A great time to visit Őrség National Park, with warm weather but few crowds.

Jun Balmy weather makes this the perfect time to explore before the summer crowds arrive.

Oct Get your fill of Hungary's best wines in Sopron after the grape harvest.

The Danube Bend & Western Transdanubia Highlights

1 **Szentendre** (p166) Strolling the cobbled backstreets, where life remains largely untouched by the town's tourist tumult.

2 **Citadel** (p171) Climbing up Visegrád's medieval hilltop and enjoying the wonderful views of the Danube.

3 **Pannonhalma Abbey** (p183) Exploring a 1000-year-old abbey, the architecturally splendid spiritual heart of Hungary, in a lofty hilltop location.

SLOVAKIA

Danube-Ipoly National Park

NÓGRÁD

Komárno
Komárom
Szob
Štúrovo
Esztergom
Tokod
Szentendre Island
Visegrád
Vác

Danube River

Dunaszentmiklós
Bajna
Dorog
Gõd
Pilis Park Forest

Tata
Tarján
Piliscsaba
Pilisvörösvár
Danube-Ipoly National Park
Dunakeszi

KOMÁROM-ESZTERGOM
Szentendre
Tatabánya
Nagykovácsi
M2

Pannonhalma Abbey
Kisbér
Budakeszi
BUDAPEST

Oroszlány
Bicske
M1

Mór
Érd

Zirc
Százhalombatta
Dunaharaszti
Csepel Island

Várpalota
SZÉKESFEHÉRVÁR
Lake Velence
Gárdony
PEST
Ráckeve

Veszprém
FEJÉR

Balatonfűzfő
Polgárdi
M6

Balatonalmádi

Balatonfüred

Tihany
Siófok
Dunaújváros
BÁCS-KISKUN

Tab
Sárbogárd

Tamási
Dunaföldvár

SOMOGY
TOLNA
Paks

Danube River

4 Sopron (p178)
Wandering the cobbled streets and peeking into the picturesque hidden courtyards of the medieval Inner Town.

5 Őrség National Park
(p186) Exploring a region of unspoilt rural beauty, where three countries meet.

THE DANUBE BEND

ℹ️ Getting There & Away

Regular buses serve towns on the west bank of the Danube, but trains only go as far as Szentendre, with a separate line running to Esztergom. For Visegrád, you can take one of the regular trains from Budapest to the opposite bank of the river and then take a ferry across (timings linked to train arrivals).

Regular **Mahart PassNave** (📞1-484 4013; www.mahartpassnave.hu; ⊗8am-4pm Mon-Fri) boats run to and from Budapest over the summer months.

Szentendre

📞26 / POP 25,542

Szentendre ('St Andrew') is the southern gateway to the Danube Bend but has none of the imperial history or drama of Visegrád or Esztergom. As an art colony turned lucrative tourist centre, and easily accessible from Budapest just 19km south, Szentendre strikes many travellers as a little too 'cute', and is crowded most of the year. Still, it's an easy trip from the capital, and the town's dozens of art museums, galleries and churches are well worth the trip. Just try to avoid it on summer weekends.

History

Szentendre was home first to the Celts and then the Romans, who built an important border fortress here. The Magyars colonised the region in the 9th century; by the 14th century Szentendre was a prosperous estate under the supervision of Visegrád.

Serbian Orthodox Christians came here from the south in advance of the Turks in the 15th century, but the Turkish occupation of Hungary over the next two centuries brought the town's peaceful coexistence to an end, and by the end of the 17th century the town was deserted. Though Hungary was soon liberated from the Ottomans, fighting continued in the Balkans and a second wave of Serbs fled to Szentendre. Believing they would return home, but enjoying complete religious freedom under the Habsburgs, Orthodox clans built their own churches and gave the town its unique Balkan feel.

Szentendre's delightful location began to attract day trippers and painters from Budapest early last century; an artists colony was established here in the 1920s and the town is still known for its art and artists.

◉ Sights

★ Art Mill
GALLERY

(Művészet Malom; Map p168; 📞26-301 701; www.muzeumicentrum.hu; Bogdányi utca 32; adult/6-26yr 2000/1200Ft; ⊗10am-6pm) This enormous gallery, spread over three floors of an old mill, exhibits cutting-edge photography, light and sound installations, sculpture, paintings and works in other media by both local and national artists, and it underscores Szentendre's renewed commitment to being a centre for serious art. It was the centrepiece of the 2016 Art Capital festival (p169), and featured a particularly arresting display of wicker and wire sculpture among its many offerings.

Fő tér
SQUARE

(Main Square; Map p168) Colourful Fő tér, the town's main square, contains many buildings and monuments from the 18th and 19th centuries, including the Memorial Cross in its centre – the town's way of thanking the plague epidemic for passing Szentendre by in 1763. The pedestrian lanes surrounding the square are filled with shops selling gift items and folk craft.

Blagoveštenska Church
CHURCH

(Blagoveštenska templom; Map p168; 📞26-310 554; Fő tér; 400Ft; ⊗10am-5pm Tue-Sun) The highlight of Fő tér is the Blagoveštenska Church, built in 1752. The church, with fine baroque and rococo elements, hardly looks 'Eastern' from the outside, but once you are inside, the ornate iconostasis and elaborate 18th-century furnishings immediately give the game away. Szentendre had a large Serbian population between the 14th and 19th centuries, with refugees fleeing various regional conflicts.

Castle Hill
VIEWPOINT

(Vár-domb; Map p168) Castle Hill, reached via Váralja lépcső, the narrow steps between Fő tér 8 and 9, was the site of a fortress in the Middle Ages. From here you get splendid views of the town.

Belgrade Cathedral
CHURCH

(Belgrád Székesegyház; Map p168; 📞26-312 399; Pátriárka utca 5; admission incl art collection 700Ft; ⊗10am-6pm Tue-Sun) Just north of Castle Hill is the red tower of Belgrade Cathedral, completed in 1764 and seat of the Serbian Orthodox bishop in Hungary, when Hungary had a large Serbian population. It's worth peeking inside at the beautiful interior furnished with New Testament icons.

Serbian Ecclesiastical Art Collection   MUSEUM

(Szerb Egyházművészeti Gyüjtemény; Map p168; ☑ 26-312 399; Pátriárka utca 5; 700Ft; ⏲10am-6pm Tue-Sun) This is a treasure trove of icons, vestments and other sacred objects in precious metals. A 14th-century glass painting of the crucifixion is the oldest item on display; a 'cotton icon' of the life of Christ from the 18th century is unusual. Look at the defaced portrait of Christ on the wall upstairs – the story goes that a drunken *kuruc* (anti-Habsburg) mercenary slashed it and, when told the next morning what he had done, drowned himself in the Danube.

Margit Kovács Ceramic Collection   MUSEUM

(Kovács Margit Kerámiagyüjtemény; Map p168; ☑ 26-310 244; www.muzeumicentrum.hu; Vastagh György utca 1; adult/concession 1200/600Ft; ⏲10am-6pm) Descend Görög utca from the main square and turn right on to Vastagh György utca to reach this museum (in an 18th-century salt house) dedicated to the work of Szentendre's most famous artist. Margit Kovács (1902–77) was a ceramicist who combined Hungarian folk, religious and modern themes to create Gothic-like figures. Some of her works are overly sentimental, but many others are very powerful, especially the later ones in which mortality is a central theme.

Ferenczy Károly Museum   MUSEUM

(Ferenczy Károly Múzeum; Map p168; ☑ 26-779 6657; www.muzeumicentrum.hu; Kossuth Lajos utca 5; adult/concession 1500/1000Ft; ⏲10am-6pm Tue-Sun) The first museum you come across when walking up from the HÉV or bus station is this one, in the former home of the prolific Ferenczy family. Károly Ferenczy (1862–1917) is credited with introducing impressionism to Hungary, and many of his works are displayed in the Hungarian National Gallery, as well as here. His works aside, you'll also find expressionist paintings by his son Valér, sculpture by Beni, his other son, and tapestries and socialist-themed works by his daughter Noemi.

Szanto Memorial Home & Synagogue   SYNAGOGUE

(Szanto Emlékház és Imaház; Map p168; ☑ 06 30 932 2900; Hunyadi utca 2; entry by donation; ⏲11am-2pm Tue-Sun) The relics inside Europe's tiniest synagogue are a loving tribute to Szentendre's 250-strong Jewish community, devastated by the Holocaust.

Hungarian Open-Air Ethnographical Museum   MUSEUM

(Magyar Szabadtéri Néprajzi Múzeum; ☑ 26-502 537; www.skanzen.hu; Sztaravodai út; adult/6-26yr 2000/1000Ft; ⏲9am-5pm Tue-Sun) Just 5km northwest of Szentendre is Hungary's most ambitious *skanzen* (open-air folk museum displaying village architecture), with farmhouses, churches, bell towers, mills and so on set up in eight regional divisions. Craftspeople and artisans do their thing on random days (generally on weekends) from Easter to early December, and the museum hosts festivals throughout the season. Reach it on bus 230 from bay 7 at the bus station.

Ámos-Anna Museum   MUSEUM

(Ámos-Anna Múzeum; Map p168; ☑ 26-310 790; www.muzeumicentrum.hu; Bogdányi utca 10-12; adult/concession 700/400Ft; ⏲10am-6pm Thu-Sun) The excellent Ámos-Anna Museum displays the surrealist and expressionist paintings of husband-and-wife team Margit Anna and Imre Ámos. Imre Ámos' dark *Apocalypse* series seems to have been a foreshadowing of his death in a concentration camp in 1944.

National Wine Museum   MUSEUM

(Nemzeti Bormúzeum; Map p168; ☑ 26-317 054; www.bor-kor.hu; Bogdányi utca 10; admission 300Ft, 5/9 tastings 2000/3000Ft; ⏲10am-10pm) The National Wine Museum, in the cellar beneath Labirintus restaurant, traces the development of winemaking in Hungary and offers wine tastings of between five and nine vintages.

Szamos Marzipan Museum   MUSEUM

(Marcipán Ház; Map p168; ☑ 26-310 545; www.szamosmarcipan.hu; Dumtsa Jenő utca 12; 500Ft; ⏲9am-7pm) Attached to the cafe (p170) of the same name, this cute little museum shows off elaborate marzipan creations. Highlights include a tasty model of the Budapest Parliament and a likeness of Princess Diana, immortalised in ground-almond confectionery.

Church of St John the Baptist   CHURCH

(Keresztelő Szent János Templom; Map p168; Templom tér, Vár-domb; ⏲10am-5pm Tue-Sun) **FREE** This baroque church at Castle Hill is all that's left of the site of a fortress built in the Middle Ages. Note the frescoes painted by members of the artists colony in the 1930s, among them Béla Czóbel.

Szentendre

Požarevačka Church CHURCH
(Map p168; ☑26-310 554; Kossuth Lajos utca 1; 300Ft; ☉noon-4pm) Dedicated in 1763, this late-baroque Serbian Orthodox church has a lovely iconostasis dating from 1742. The church is on the way into town from the bus and train stations and a good introduction to Szentendre's predominant architecture. It's sometimes inexplicably closed.

Kmetty Museum MUSEUM
(Map p168; ☑26-310 244; www.muzeumicentrum. hu; Fő tér 21; adult/concession 700/400Ft; ☉2-

6pm Wed-Sun) The Kmetty Museum, on the southwestern side of Fő tér, displays the work of the cubist János Kmetty (1889–1975), as well as sculptures by Jenő Kerényi.

Czóbel Museum GALLERY
(Map p168; ☑26-310 244; www.muzeumi-centrum.hu; Templom tér 1; adult/concession 700/400Ft; ☉10am-6pm Tue-Sun) The Czóbel Museum contains the works of the impressionist Béla Czóbel (1883–1976), a friend of Pablo Picasso and student of Henri Matisse.

Szentendre

THE DANUBE BEND & WESTERN TRANSDANUBIA SZENTENDRE

★ Festivals & Events

★ **Art Capital**   ART
(www.artcapital.hu; ☉ Aug & Sep) In 2016 Szentendre held a high-profile, two-month-long art festival that the city hopes to turn into a biannual event. A dozen museums took part, with themed art exhibitions and installations by Hungarian and international artists displayed at the Art Mill, the Ferenczy Károly Museum, and other venues.

⊨ Sleeping

With Budapest so close, the only reason to stay here is if you want to enjoy the quiet streets after the day trippers have gone or if you plan to push on to the rest of the Danube Bend. There are at least a dozen *panzió* (pension or guesthouse) accommodations to choose from, as well as a decent hotel.

Ilona Panzió   GUESTHOUSE $
(Map p168; ☑ 26-313 599; www.ilonapanzio.hu; Rákóczi Ferenc utca 11; s/d 5800/8000Ft; ☏) A spiffy little guesthouse with six rooms, Ilona has plenty going for it: superb central location, secure parking, inner courtyard for breakfast and rooms in very good nick (although they're of the can't-swing-a-cat variety). This place almost feels rural.

Pap-Sziget Camping   CAMPGROUND $
(☑ 26-310 697; www.camping-budapest.com; small/large campsites for 2 people 4000/4600Ft, bungalows from 8600Ft; ☉ May–mid-Oct; ☏☷) This

big, leafy camping ground takes up most of Pap Island, some 2km north of Szentendre. Motel (6400Ft per double) and hostel (4800Ft per double) rooms are very basic, though the 'comfort bungalows' are slightly more, well, comfortable. Facilities include a small supermarket, a snack bar and a restaurant.

Buses heading north on Rte 11 to Visegrád and Esztergom will stop nearby; ring the bell after you pass the Hotel Danubius (Ady Endre utca 28) on the left.

Mathias Rex Panzió   GUESTHOUSE $$
(Map p168; ☑ 26-505 570; www.mathiasrexhotel. hu; Kossuth Lajos utca 16; s/d 10,000/15,000Ft, studio from 20,000Ft; ☷☏) This very central *panzió* (pension or guesthouse) has a dozen rooms so clean they border on sterile, but of a good size. The decor is modern and minimalist, there's a pretty courtyard and an inexpensive cellar-restaurant occupies the basement. English and German spoken.

Hotel Centrum Panzió   HOTEL $$
(Map p168; ☑ 26-302 500; www.hotelcentrum. hu; Bogdányi utca 15; s/d 10,000/12,000Ft; ☷☏) 'Hotel' is a bit of a misnomer, but this town house is a stone's throw from the Danube and the location couldn't be more central. Its seven large, bright rooms are filled with interesting old furniture, but the walls are on the thin side, so you may feel as if you're in bed with your neighbours.

⭐ **Bükkös Hotel & Spa** HOTEL $$$
(Map p168; ☑ 26-501 360; www.bukkoshotel.hu; Bükkös part 16; r from €85; 🅿🛜🌊) Overlooking the canal, just a couple of minutes' walk from Szentendre's main square, this small but perfectly formed hotel blends a rustic stone exterior with thoroughly modern carpeted rooms. Besides satellite TV, powerful showers and views of Old Town, perks include the on-site spa with a full roster of massages and treatments, plus a Jacuzzi and sauna. One for a romantic getaway.

✕ Eating

Adria BALKAN $
(Map p168; ☑ 06 20 448 8993; www.facebook.com/adriaszentendre; Kossuth Lajos utca 4; mains 850-1500Ft; ⊙noon-10pm) This funky little spot by the canal has a cosy interior bedecked in bright colours and a tree-shaded terrace. Expect soulful music served alongside your choice of coffee, tea and cake, and Balkan grilled dishes. Our only quibble is with the service; no Mr/Miss Congeniality prizes awarded here.

Levendula ICE CREAM $
(Map p168; www.levendulafagylaltozo.hu; Fő tér 8; scoops 250Ft; ⊙10am-9pm; ☑) Szentendre has now opened its own branch of the artisanal ice-cream joint from Budapest. Flavours include the signature dark chocolate and lavender, lemon-basil, chia seed and caramelised fig. No artificial flavours and the fruity ones don't contain milk.

⭐ **Mjam** FUSION $$
(Map p168; ☑ 06 70 440 3700; Városház tér 2; mains 2600-4750Ft; ⊙11am-10pm Tue-Thu, to 11pm Fri & Sat, to 5pm Sun) These guys bill themselves as a Caribbean restaurant, but while there are Caribbean-ish elements to what they do, we think that they're far more experimental than that. Besides seafood curry, you may find yourself facing such dishes as duck breast smoked with tea leaves and noodle bird's nest. The service is young and friendly and the homemade lemonades are wonderful thirst quenchers.

Aranysárkány INTERNATIONAL $$
(Golden Dragon; Map p168; ☑ 26-301 479; www.aranysarkany.hu; Alkotmány utca 1/a; mains 2900-4300Ft) The fashionable 'Golden Dragon' may sound Chinese but it actually serves up mains like Angus steak and goose liver with rose petal jam. It was Hungary's first private restaurant (established in 1977) and is still considered groundbreaking in the local food scene.

Promenade INTERNATIONAL $$$
(Map p168; ☑ 26-312 626; www.promenade-szentendre.hu; Futó utca 4; mains 2300-4250Ft; ⊙11am-11pm Tue-Sun) Vaulted ceilings, whitewashed walls, a huge cellar for tasting wine and a wonderful terrace overlooking the Danube are all highlights at the Promenade, one of Szentendre's best restaurants.

🍷 Drinking & Nightlife

⭐ **Teddy Beer** CRAFT BEER
(Map p168; ☑ 06 20 318 7599; www.facebook.com/TeddyBeerSzentendre; Péter Pál utca 2; ⊙4.30pm-midnight Tue-Thu, noon-midnight Fri-Sun) There are two reasons to love this place: they know their craft beers and you can sample three dozen beers from around Hungary, as well as a good Belgian selection. Plus, the bar food is seriously above par: excellent burgers, pulled pork and gourmet hot dogs.

Jovialis CAFE
(Map p168; ☑ 06 30 939 4779; www.jovialis.hu; Görög utca 2; ⊙10am-6pm; 🛜) Our favourite cafe in Szentendre is an ultramodern and very comfortable affair attached to the Margit Kovács Ceramic Collection (p167). The staff are fonts of information and they know their doppio from their ristretto.

Szamos Marzipan Museum Cafe CAFE
(Map p168; ☑ 26-311 931; www.szamosmarcipan.hu; Dumtsa Jenő utca 14; ⊙9am-7pm) This cafe, next door to the marzipan museum (p167), is a good place to stop for cake (420Ft to 650Ft) and ice cream.

☆ Entertainment

Danube Cultural Centre PERFORMING ARTS
(Dunaparti Művelődési Ház; Map p168; ☑ 26-312 657; www.szentendreprogram.hu; Duna korzó 11/a) This centre stages theatrical performances, concerts and folk-dance gatherings, and can also tell you what's on elsewhere.

ℹ Information

OTP Bank (Dumtsa Jenő utca 6) Equipped with an ATM.

Main Post Office (Map p168; Kossuth Lajos utca 23-25; ⊙9am-5pm Mon-Fri, to noon Sat)

Touformrin (Map p180; ☑ 99-517 560; http://turizmus.sopron.hu; Liszt Ferenc utca 1, Ferenc Liszt Conference & Cultural Centre; ⊙9am-5pm Mon-Fri, to 1pm Sat year-round,

9am-1pm Sun Mar-Sep only) Lots of information about Szentendre and the Danube Bend.

ℹ Getting There & Away

BOAT

Mahart PassNave (p299) runs daily boats from Budapest to Szentendre between late March and late October, departing Budapest at 10am, arriving in Szentendre at 11.30am, and leaving for Budapest at 5pm (one-way/return 2000/3000Ft). On weekends in July and August the boats continue to Visegrád.

BUS

Buses from Budapest's Újpest-Városkapu train station, which is on the M3 blue metro line, run to Szentendre at least once an hour (310Ft, 25 minutes, 15km). Onward service to Visegrád (465Ft, 45 minutes, 21km, hourly) and Esztergom (930Ft, 1½ hours, 48km, hourly) is frequent.

TRAIN

The easiest way to reach Szentendre from Budapest is to catch the HÉV suburban train from Batthyány tér in Buda (630Ft, 40 minutes, every 10 to 20 minutes). Remember that a yellow city-bus/metro ticket is good only as far as the Békásmegyer stop. Buy the 310Ft Békásmegyer-Szentendre supplement ticket from a ticket machine at Batthyány tér, or at Szentendre if travelling the other way. Also, many HÉV trains run only as far as Békásmegyer, where you must cross the platform to board the train for Szentendre. The last train leaves Szentendre for Budapest just after 11pm.

Visegrád

🎵 26 / POP 1842

Soporific, leafy Visegrád (from the Slavic words for 'high castle') has the most history of the four main towns on the Danube Bend. While much of it has crumbled to dust over the centuries, reminders of its grand past can still be seen in its Renaissance palace and 13th-century citadel, which offers spectacular views from high above a curve in the river.

History

The Romans built a border fortress just north of the present castle in the 4th century, and it was still being used by Slovak settlers 600 years later. After the Mongol invasion in 1241, King Béla IV began work on a lower castle by the river and then on the hilltop citadel. Less than a century later, embattled King Charles Robert of Anjou moved the royal household to Visegrád.

For almost 200 years, Visegrád was Hungary's 'other' (often summer) capital and an important diplomatic centre. But Visegrád's real golden age came during the reign of King Matthias Corvinus (r 1458–90) and Queen Beatrix, who had Italian Renaissance craftsmen rebuild the Gothic palace. The sheer size of the residence, and its stonework, fountains and gardens, were the talk of 15th-century Europe.

The destruction of Visegrád came first with the Turks and later in 1702, when the Habsburgs blew up the citadel to prevent Hungarian independence fighters from using it as a base. All trace of it was lost until the 1930s, when archaeologists uncovered the ruins.

◉ Sights

★**Citadel**   FORTRESS
(Fellegvár; ☎26-598 080; www.parkerdo.hu; Várhegy; adult/concession 1800/900Ft; ☺9am-5pm mid-Mar-Apr & Oct, to 6pm May-Sep, to 3pm Nov-mid-Mar) The 13th-century citadel looms over Visegrád atop a 350m hill and is surrounded by moats hewn from solid rock. The real highlight is just walking along the ramparts of this eyrie and admiring what is arguably the best view of the Börzsöny Hills and the Danube. Take the steep 'Fellegvár' trail from the back gate of Solomon's Tower (40 minutes), the shorter 'Kálvária sétány' (Calvary Promenade) trail behind the Catholic church on Fő tér (20 minutes) or the City-Bus minibus.

Completed in 1259, the citadel was the repository for the Hungarian crown jewels until 1440, when Elizabeth of Luxembourg, the daughter of King Sigismund, stole them with the help of her lady-in-waiting and hurried off to Székesfehérvár to have her infant son László crowned king. (The crown was returned to the citadel in 1464 and held here – under a stronger lock, no doubt – until the Turkish invasion.)

There's a small pictorial exhibit in the residential rooms on the west side of the citadel and two smaller displays near the east gate on hunting, falconry and traditional occupations in the region, like stone cutting and beekeeping.

Royal Palace   PALACE
(Királyi Palota; ☎26-597 010; www.visegrad.hu; Fő utca 29; adult/concession 1100/550Ft; ☺9am-5pm Tue-Sun Mar-Oct, 10am-4pm Tue-Sun Nov-Feb) Just inland from the river, the Royal Palace boasted 350 rooms during the 16th-century reign of King Matthias. Today the palace is

THE DANUBE BEND & WESTERN TRANSDANUBIA VISEGRÁD

a mere shadow of its former self and has been only partly reconstructed. The handful of rooms that can be visited are mostly the royal suites centred on the Court of Honour and its Hercules Fountain, a replica of the original Renaissance piece. Take a peek at ancient ceramics, weaponry and household items in the small museum.

Moving from room to room, you'll discover more reconstructions and replicas: a cold and clammy royal bedchamber from the 1400s, a warmer kitchen, beautiful tile stoves, and, in the courtyard to the east, the Lion Fountain in red marble. Also of note is the petite St George's Chapel (1366), but once again, it's not original.

To find the palace from the Mahart ferry, walk south in the direction of the Nagymaros ferry about 400m, then turn left towards town to find Fő utca.

Solomon's Tower
TOWER

(Salamon Torony; ☑26-398 026; www.visegrad.hu; Salamon Torony utca; adult/concession 700/350Ft; ☺9am-5pm Wed-Sun May-Sep) North of the main town and just a short walk up Salamon Torony utca, 13th-century Solomon's Tower was once part of a lower castle, built during the reign of Béla IV and used to control river traffic. These days, the rather unsympathetically restored, stocky, hexagonal keep, with walls up to 8m thick, houses one of the castle's original Gothic fountains, along with five storeys of exhibits related to town history.

Nagy-Villám Lookout Tower
TOWER

(Nagy-Villám Kilátó; ☑26-397 099; www.kilato.hupont.hu; adult/concession 400/200Ft; ☺10am-6pm) There are some easy walks and hikes in the immediate vicinity of the Citadel – to the 377m-high Nagy-Villám Lookout Tower, for example. On a good day you can see Slovakia from the top of the highest hill in these parts.

🏃 Activities

Bobsled Track
ADVENTURE SPORTS

(Bob-pálya; ☑26-397 397; www.bobozas.hu; adult/3-14yr 450/350Ft; ☺10am-5pm Mon-Fri, to 6pm Sat & Sun) A 700m bobsled track, on which you wend your way down a metal chute while sitting on a felt-bottomed cart, is on the hillside below the lookout. Closed on rainy days. In winter it becomes a toboggan track.

🛏 Sleeping

Yurt Camping
CAMPGROUND $

(Jurta Kemping; ☑06 20 399 7002; www.mogyorohegy-erdeiiskola.hu/jurta-kemping; Mogyoróhegy; campsites per adult/child/tent 1150/900/1100Ft; ☺May-Sep) About 2km northeast of the citadel is this nicely situated campground near meadows and woods. It's ideal for cyclists and motorists, but if you don't have your own wheels, you'll find that it's far from the centre and the shuttle service is infrequent.

Hotel Honti
HOTEL $$

(☑26-398 120; www.hotelhonti.hu; Fő utca 66; hotel s/d 17,000/21,900Ft, guesthouse s/d 12,000/16,000Ft, campsites per person 1100Ft; ☀☎🌐) This friendly, please-everyone establishment has seven homey rooms in its guesthouse on quiet Fő utca and 23 in its chalet-style hotel facing Rte 11. Perks include the hotel's large garden and indoor pool and spa facilities, plus bicycles are also available for rent. There's a fairly basic camping ground next to the guesthouse, catering largely to motorists.

★Hotel Silvanus
HOTEL $$$

(☑26-398 311; www.hotelsilvanus.hu; s/d from €117/169; 🅿☎🌐) Up on a forested hillside, not far from the citadel, this is hands down the most memorable place to stay in Visegrád. Yes, some rooms are somewhat dated, but the views of the Danube are pretty special and there's an appealing outdoor pool and delightful spa. Staff are attentive and rates include half-board. One for romancing your sweetie.

Hotel Visegrád
HOTEL $$$

(☑26-397 034; www.hotelvisegrad.hu; Rév utca 15; s/d from €62/72; ☀@☎🌐) This flash four-star spa hotel opposite the Nagymaros ferry pier has 71 finely tuned rooms with all the trimmings as well as several pools (inside and out), a sauna, a steam room and treatments available. Staff are attentive but somewhat disorganised.

🍴 Eating

Don Vito Pizzeria
PIZZA $

(☑26-397 230; www.donvitovisegrad.hu; Fő utca 83; mains 990-2590Ft; ☺noon-10pm; 🚗) Don Vito is quite a joint for such a small town. Its collection of gangster memorabilia is as impressive as its selection of top-shelf liquor. But we particularly like its stone-baked pizzas.

Sirály   INTERNATIONAL $$

(☑26-398 376; www.siralyvisegrad.hu; Rév utca 15; mains 2200-4500Ft; ⊗noon-11pm; ⚡) Next door to the Hotel Visegrád (p172), but very much retaining its own identity, the 'Seagull' is a classy eatery popular with coach parties. It serves international and Hungarian favourites, as well as several good vegetarian dishes, from pearl barley and mushroom risotto to grilled vegies and salads.

Kovács-kert   HUNGARIAN $$

(☑26-398 123; www.kovacs-kertetterem.hu; Rév utca 4; mains 1990-2890Ft) This adorable restaurant just up from the Nagymaros ferry has a large photo menu covering a fine array of Hungarian standards. Its leafy terrace seating is a welcome relief in the warmer summer months. Try the catfish stew or the pork cutlets.

ℹ Information

Dunakanyar Takarékszövetkezet (Rév utca 9) ATM next to the Hotel Visegrád.

Post Office (Fő utca 77; ⊗8am-4pm Mon-Fri)

Visegrád Info (☑26-597 000; www.palotahaz. hu; Dunaparti út 1; ⊗10am-6pm Apr-Oct, to 4pm Tue-Sun Nov-Mar) Good source of local information.

Visegrád Tours (☑26-398 160; www.visegrad-tours.hu; Rév utca 15; ⊗8am-5pm) Inside the Hotel Visegrád (p172).

www.visegrad.hu A useful website.

ℹ Getting There & Away

BOAT

Mahart PassNave (p299) runs fast hydrofoils from Budapest to Visegrád and Esztergom between late April and late September, departing from Vigadó tér at 9.30am, arriving in Visegrád (4000Ft) at 10.30am and Esztergom (5000Ft) at 11am, making the return journey from Visegrád at 5.30pm.

It also runs slower scenic boat tours to Visegrád (2500Ft, 3½ hours) via Szentendre on weekends only in July and August, departing Vigadó tér at 10am. A 9am excursion boat runs from Vigadó tér to Visegrád via Vác, continuing to Esztergom (Tuesday to Sunday, April to August).

BUS

Buses are very frequent to/from Budapest's Újpest-Városkapu train station (745Ft, 1¼ hours, 39km), Szentendre (465Ft, 45 minutes, 25km) and Esztergom (560Ft, 45 minutes, 26km).

TRAIN

Trains run at least once hourly from Budapest-Nyugati to Nagymaros-Visegrád (1120Ft,

40 minutes), across the river from Visegrád proper. The hourly car ferry schedule is linked to train arrivals; the river crossing takes 10 minutes.

ℹ Getting Around

Car Ferry (☑26-398 344; per person/bicycle/car 420/420/1400Ft) Connects Nagymaros with Visegrád hourly between 6.20am and 8pm.

City-Bus (☑26-397 372; www.city-bus.hu; up to 8 people 2500Ft; ⊗9am-6pm Apr-Sep) Operates a taxi van service between the Mahart ferry pier opposite the Hotel Visegrád and the citadel, via the Nagymaros ferry pier.

Esztergom

☑33 / POP 27,990

Esztergom's massive basilica, sitting high above the town and Danube River, is an incredible sight, rising out of what seems like nowhere in a rural stretch of country. But Esztergom's attraction goes deeper than the domed structure: the country's first king, St Stephen, was born here in 975. It was a royal seat from the late 10th to the mid-13th centuries, as well as the seat of Roman Catholicism in Hungary for more than a thousand years. A picturesque town, packed with historic attractions, Esztergom makes a great day trip from Budapest and rewards those who linger longer.

History

Castle Hill (Vár-hegy), towering over the city centre, was the site of the Roman settlement of Solva Mansio in the 1st century AD, and it is thought that Marcus Aurelius finished his *Meditations* in a camp nearby during the second half of the 2nd century.

Prince Géza chose Esztergom as his capital, and his son Vajk (later Stephen) was crowned king here in 1000. Stephen founded one of the country's two archbishoprics at Esztergom and built a basilica.

Esztergom lost its political significance when King Béla IV moved the capital to Buda after the Mongol invasion in 1241. It remained the ecclesiastical seat, but Esztergom's capture by the Turks in 1543 interrupted the church's activities, and the city's archbishop fled to Nagyszombat (now Trnava in Slovakia). The church did not re-establish its base in this 'Hungarian Rome' until the early 19th century.

◉ Sights

★ Esztergom Basilica
CHURCH

(Esztergomi Bazilika; Map p176; ☑33-402 354; www.bazilika-esztergom.hu; Szent István tér 1; basilica free, crypt 200Ft, dome adult/concession 700/500Ft, treasury adult/concession 900/450Ft; ☺8am-6pm, crypt & treasury 9am-5pm, dome 9am-6pm) The largest church in Hungary is on Castle Hill, and its 72m-high central dome can be seen for many kilometres around. The building of the present neoclassical church was begun in 1822 on the site of its 12th-century counterpart, which was destroyed by the Turks. József Hild, who designed the cathedral at Eger, was involved in the final stages, and the basilica was consecrated in 1856 with a sung Mass composed by Franz Liszt. Highlights include the dome, treasury and crypt.

The grey church is colossal, measuring 114m long and 47m wide. Its highlight is the red-and-white marble Bakócz Chapel on the southwest side, which is a splendid example of Italian Renaissance stone carving and sculpture. The chapel escaped most – though not all – of the Turks' vandalism; note the smashed-in face of Gabriel and the missing heads of other angels above the altar. The altar painting by Michelangelo Grigoletti (1854) is said to be the world's largest painting on a single canvas.

On the northwest side of the church is the entrance to the basilica's treasury, an Aladdin's cave of vestments and church plate in gold and silver, studded with jewels. It is the richest ecclesiastical collection in Hungary.

The door to the right as you enter the basilica leads to the crypt, a series of eerie vaults down 50 steps with tombs guarded by monoliths representing Mourning and Eternity. Among those at rest here are Cardinal József Mindszenty and Csernoch János, the Archbishop of Esztergom. It's worth making the tortuous climb up to the dome for the outstanding views over the city. The 400 steps leading up to it are to the left of the crypt entrance and on the way you pass through the new Panorama Hall and cafe.

Castle Museum
MUSEUM

(Vármúzeum; Map p176; ☑33-415 986; www. mnmvarmuzeuma.hu; Szent István tér 1; tours adult 1500-2000Ft, tours concession 750-1000Ft, joint ticket with Balassa Bálint Museum 3400/1700Ft; ☺10am-6pm Tue-Sun) The Castle Museum is housed in the former Royal Palace, built mostly by French architects in the 12th century during Esztergom's golden age. The palace was largely destroyed by the Turks; today the structure is a combination of modern brickwork and medieval stone masonry. Entry is by tour only; the longest of the three (90 minutes) is particularly worthwhile as it takes in all the highlights, such as the ornate basilica, the views from the White Tower and the royal apartments.

Christian Museum
MUSEUM

(Keresztény Múzeum; Map p176; ☑33-413 880; www.christianmuseum.hu; Mindszenty hercegprímás tere 2; adult/concession 900/450Ft; ☺10am-5pm Wed-Sun Mar-Nov) The former Bishop's Palace, in the picturesque riverbank Watertown (Víziváros) district, houses the Christian Museum, which holds the finest collection of medieval religious art in Hungary. It contains Hungarian Gothic triptychs and altarpieces as well as later works by German, Dutch and Italian masters. The most prized pieces have QR barcodes, so smartphone users can enjoy more in-depth descriptions.

Among the museum's treasures is the sublime Holy Sepulchre of Garamszentbenedek (1480), a wheeled cart in the shape of a cathedral, with richly carved figures of the 12 Apostles and Roman soldiers guarding Christ's tomb. The sepulchre was used during Easter Week processions and was painstakingly restored in the 1970s.

Be sure to see Tamás Kolozsvári's Calvary altar panel (1427), which was influenced by Italian art; the late-Gothic *Christ's Passion* (1506) by 'Master M S'; the gruesome *Martyrdom of the Three Apostles* (1490) by the so-called Master of the Martyr Apostles; and the *Temptation of St Anthony* (1530) by Jan Wellens de Cock, with its drug-like visions of devils and temptresses. Audio guides are available for 500Ft, and guided tours in English for 5000Ft.

The fastest way to reach the museum from Castle Hill is to walk down steep Molnár sor, which can be accessed just north of the basilica.

Öziçeli Hacci Ibrahim Mosque
MOSQUE

(Dzsámi Múzeum és Kávézó; Map p176; ☑33-315 665; www.esztergomidzsami.hu; Berényi utca 18; ☺10am-5pm Tue-Sun) FREE This 400-year-old mosque was built in the 17th century, during the Ottoman occupation of Esztergom. In its later incarnations it served both as a granary and as a residence before becoming a museum that showcases its remarkable history. The *mihrab* (prayer niche facing

Mecca) is largely intact, and it is the only two-storey mosque in the whole of Hungary. Out back is a waterwheel; there was a well here during the Ottoman siege of Esztergom. Without water, the Hungarians surrendered. There's an appealing cafe downstairs, too.

Mária Valéria Bridge BRIDGE

(Map p176) Cross the bridge from Watertown over to Primate Island (Prímás-sziget) and to the southwest is the Mária Valéria Bridge, connecting Esztergom with the Slovakian city of Štúrovo. Destroyed during WWII, the bridge only reopened in 2002. The bridge's original Customs House (Vámház) is on the left as you cross.

Plague Pillar MONUMENT

(Map p176; Széchenyi tér) The erection of this monument was the town's way of giving thanks when a plague epidemic passed it by.

Balassa Bálint Museum MUSEUM

(Map p176; ☑33-412 584; www.balassa muzeum.hu; Pázmány Péter utca 13, Víziváros; adult/concession 1200/600Ft; ⊙9am-5pm Tue-Sun) This museum, in an 18th-century baroque building, has a small collection of black-and-white photos of the excavations of the town's castle, as well as a wealth of archaeological finds, a display of model boats and a collection of Hungarian coins through the ages.

Danube Museum MUSEUM

(Duna Múzeum; Map p176; ☑33-500 250; www. dunamuzeum.hu; Kölcsey utca 2; adult/concession 700/350Ft; ⊙9am-5pm Wed-Mon; ♿) This surprisingly interesting (and quite high-tech) museum has exhibits on all aspects of the history of Hungary's greatest river, including its mighty floods and how best to control them. With all the hands-on exhibits, it's a great place for kids.

🛏 Sleeping

Amadeus Vendégház GUESTHOUSE $

(Map p176; ☑06 70 944 7262; www.eszter-gomszallas.hu; Becket Tamás utca 17; s/d/tr 3500/7000/11,100; ☎) After you've finished huffing and puffing your way up the hill, you can congratulate yourself. The viewpoint just metres away from this cosy little guesthouse offers a superb vista of Castle Hill opposite. The three rooms have sloping roofs and private baths, and there's a shared kitchen downstairs for self-caterers. Very little English spoken. Cash only.

Gran Camping CAMPGROUND $

(Map p176; ☑06 30 948 9563, 33-402 513; www.grancamping-fortanex.hu; Nagy-Duna sétány 3; campsites per adult/child/tent/tent & car 1400/800/1300/1500Ft, bungalows from 16,000Ft, dm/d/tr 3000/10,000/13,000Ft; ⊙May-Sep; 🛜🏊) Small but centrally located on Primate Island, Gran Camping has space for 500 souls in various forms of accommodation (including a hostel with dormitory accommodation and posher air-conditioned bungalows), as well as a good-sized swimming pool.

⭐Szent Kristóf Panzió GUESTHOUSE $$

(Map p176; ☑33-416 255; www.szentkristofpan zio.com; Dobozi út 11; r/apt from 12,200/14,700Ft; ❄🛜) A stone's throw from the basilica, this central guesthouse is run by a kind host and is popular with cycling groups (there's secure storage in a garage). Rooms and apartments vary in size – the smallest doubles will see you consigned to the attic like Mr Rochester's mad wife – but all are spotless, with hardwood floors and flowery touches. Hearty breakfast included.

Alabárdos Panzió GUESTHOUSE $$

(Map p176; ☑33-312 640; www.alabardospanzio. hu; Bajcsy-Zsilinszky utca 49; s/d 9000/12,000Ft, apt from 18,000Ft; ❄🛜) This mustard-yellow landmark up a small hill isn't flashy, but it does provide neat and tidy rooms and apartments just below Castle Hill. The laundry room and big breakfast are pluses, but the location just off a main road won't thrill light sleepers.

Bazilika alatt Panzió GUESTHOUSE $$$

(Map p176; ☑33-312 672; www.bazilika.eu; Batthyány Lajos utca 7; s/d 18,300/21,900Ft; ❄🛜) Close to restaurants (useful, since breakfast is basic) and Esztergom's main attraction – the basilica – this guesthouse may not look like much from the outside, but it is thoroughly modern inside. Rooms are spacious and carpeted, staff are generally helpful, and there's even an on-site spa so cyclists can steam those tired muscles.

🍴 Eating

There are a dozen or so decent restaurants serving largely Hungarian specialities (with a couple of more-creative exceptions), mostly spread along Pázmány Péter utca, Batthyány Lajos utca and in the basilica area in general.

⭐Koriander FUSION $$

(Map p176; ☑33-315 719; Simor János utca 8; mains 2800-4300Ft; ⊙noon-9pm) Outwardly unprepossessing, inside Koriander blows

Esztergom

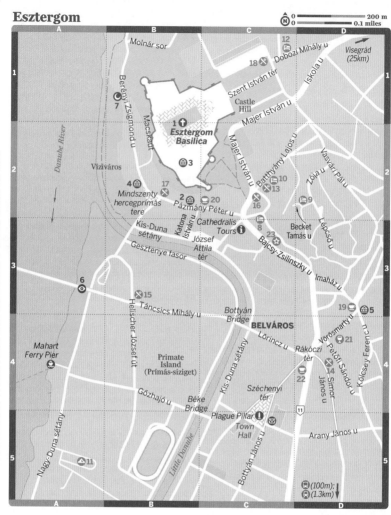

you away with some of the most daring dishes you're likely to taste in Hungary. So prepare yourself for the likes of pork belly with Coca-Cola sauce and duck breast with lavender and sour cherry sauce. Don't leave without trying the lightest ever cheesecake, made of purple potato and served with sea buckthorn sauce. Remarkable.

★ **Padlizsán**   HUNGARIAN $$
(Map p176; ☑ 33-311 212; Pázmány Péter utca 21; mains 2000-2500Ft; ☺ noon-10pm) With a sheer rock face topped by a castle bastion as the backdrop to its courtyard, 'Aubergine' has the most dramatic restaurant setting in Esz-

tergom. And its menu doesn't let the show down either, featuring modern Hungarian dishes (grilled perch, chicken with wild mushroom sauce). The dining room feels like an intimate parlour and there's soft live music most nights.

Csülök Csárda   HUNGARIAN $$
(Map p176; ☑ 33-412 420; www.csulokcsarda.hu; Batthyány Lajos utca 9; mains 1890-4300Ft) The 'Pork Knuckle Inn' – guess the speciality here – is a charming eatery that is popular with visitors and locals alike. It serves up good homestyle cooking, including a mean imam bayaldi (stuffed eggplant) for vegetarians,

Esztergom

and the portions are huge.There are some antique kitchen items on display here, too.

Prímás Pince   HUNGARIAN $$
(Map p176; ☑33-541 965; www.primaspince.hu; Szent István tér 4; mains 1290-4490Ft; ⊙10am-9pm Mon-Thu, to 10pm Fri & Sat, to 5pm Sun) In the cellars beneath the basilica you'll find some of Esztergom's most creative takes on Hungarian cuisine. We love the gooseberry soup with chicken and the savoury beef shank in a mustard and dark-beer emulsion. But the best thing here are the wines, carefully sourced from small wineries from around the country, many available by the glass.

Mediterraneo Vendégfogadó   HUNGARIAN $$
(Map p176; ☑33-311 411; www.facebook.com/MediterraneoVendegfogado; Primas Sziget 2; mains 2400-4600Ft; ⊙noon-10pm) In spite of the name, the dishes at this friendly restaurant tend to be Hungarian (unless you count the pasta). That said, the portions are generous, the likes of grilled perch-pike and lamb tend to be well-executed and the service is smooth.

Múzeumkert   HUNGARIAN $$
(Map p176; ☑33-404 440; www.muzeumkertet terem.hu; Batthyány Lajos utca 1; mains 2190-5490Ft; ⊙noon-10pm) This jack of all trades near the basilica is a restaurant, serving such classics as beef tartare and pork medallions, as well as a pizzeria and sophisticated cocktail bar. There's a delightful inner courtyard and wonderful, upbeat modern decor. Lovely place to spend an evening.

🍷 Drinking & Nightlife

Coffee shops are found around Széchenyi tér and there are a couple of lively local bars along nearby Vörösmarty utca and Bajcsy-Zsilinszky utca.

Kaleidoszkóp Ház   CAFE
(Map p176; ☑06 30 377 0891; www.kaleidosz kophaz.hu; Pázmány Péter utca 7; ⊙noon-9pm Tue-Sat, 4-9pm Sun) **FREE** This cafe-cum-cultural centre in Watertown, with mix-and-match furnishings, a steady stream of events and a shop selling a rare mix of must-have non-necessities, is one of the coolest spots in Esztergom. It's also the go-to place for the latest craft beers.

Pálinka Patika   CAFE
(Map p176; ☑06 20 551 2121; Széchenyi tér 25; ⊙10am-10pm) The main square location is good for people-watching and a handy spot for a post-sightseeing tipple. Besides jars of multiflavoured lemonades, try a beer or a sip from their wide range of *pálinkas* (fruit brandies).

Maláta Bar   BAR
(Map p176; ☑33-520 570; Vörösmarty utca 3; ⊙4pm-2am Sun-Thu, to 4am Fri & Sat) If you want to kick your heels up, head for this popular pub-bar with a retro Hungarian look (curios, 'antiqued' stuff, exposed brick walls) and canned music. It gets lively with locals way into the wee hours, but is a chilled-out spot for a beer during the day.

Café Trafó CAFE
(Map p176; ☏ 33-403 980; www.trafocafe.
hu; Vörösmarty utca 15; ⏰7am-2am Mon-Sat,
8am-midnight Sun) This cosy cafe-bar, housed
in a little glass house opposite the Danube Museum, has plenty of tree shade and
a large terrace for hot summer days. It's a
wonderful place to take a breather, sit back
and relax at any time.

☆ Entertainment

All In Music Cafe LIVE MUSIC
(Map p176; ☏ 33-311 028; http://hovamenjek.hu/
esztergom/all-in-music-cafe; Bajcsy-Zsilinszky utca
35; ⏰5-10pm Sun-Thu, to 1am Fri & Sat) Boasting
a large selection of wines and *pálinkas,* this
local hang-out, just down from the basilica,
stages DJs and live bands on Friday and Saturday nights.

ℹ Information

Cathedralis Tours (Map p176; ☏ 33-
520 260; www.cathedralistours.hu;
Bajcsy-Zsilinszky utca 26; ⏰9am-6pm Mon-Fri,
to noon Sat) This private travel agency is the
only place in town for information.
www.esztergom.hu A useful Hungarian website with English-language links.
OTP Bank (Rákóczi tér 2-4) Has a 24-hour ATM.
Post Office (Map p176; Arany János utca 2;
⏰9am-5pm Mon-Fri, to noon Sat) Enter from
Széchenyi tér.

ℹ Getting There & Away

BOAT
Sightseeing **Mahart PassNave** (Map p176;
www.mahartpassnave.hu; Nagy-Duna sétány)
boats and hydrofoils run from Budapest to
Esztergom via Visegrád between May and
September. The sightseeing boats depart Budapest's Vigadó tér at 9am, arriving in Esztergom
(4500Ft) at 2pm, heading back at 4.30pm.

Faster hydrofoils depart Budapest at 9.30am,
arriving in Esztergom (7500Ft) at 11am and
heading back at 5pm.

BUS & TRAIN
Esztergom has excellent bus connections.
The train station is 1.2km south of town; take
bus 1 or walk for 15 minutes. To get to Western
Transdanubia and points beyond, take a train to
Komárom.

WESTERN TRANSDANUBIA

Sopron
☏ 99 / POP 61,887

Hungary's 'most faithful city' (a reference
to the 1921 referendum when Sopron opt-
ed to stay part of Hungary rather than be
absorbed into Austria) has been around for
a while, first settled by the Celts, then the
Romans (as a trading spot along the Amber
Route from the Baltic Sea to the Adriatic
and Byzantium), then a succession of Germans, Avars, Slavs and Magyars. In recent
years, this little town also indirectly brought
about the most dramatic event of the late
20th century – the fall of the Iron Curtain.
Today it is the most beautiful town in western Hungary, its medieval Inner Town (Belváros) intact and its cobbled streets a pleasure to wander. And if that weren't enough,
it's also famous for its wine, surrounded as it
is by flourishing vineyards.

◎ Sights

★**Firewatch Tower** TOWER
(Tűztorony; Map p180; ☏ 99-311 327; www.
muzeum.sopron.hu; Fő tér; adult/concession
1200/600Ft; ⏰10am-8pm May-Sep, to 6pm Oct-

BUSES FROM ESZTERGOM

DESTINATION	PRICE	DURATION	KM	FREQUENCY
Budapest	930Ft	1¼hr	46	half-hourly
Szentendre	930Ft	1¼hr	50	hourly
Visegrád	930Ft	45min	26	hourly

TRAINS FROM ESZTERGOM

DESTINATION	PRICE	DURATION	KM	FREQUENCY
Budapest	1120Ft	1¼-1½hr	53	hourly
Komárom	1120Ft	1½hr	53	2 daily

Dec, to 6pm Tue-Sun Jan-Apr) A narrow spiral staircase of 116 steps leads to the summit of this 60m-high tower, from which trumpeters would warn of fire, mark the hour and watch for salespeople trying to smuggle in non-Sopron wine. Apart from taking in the all-encompassing view of the hills and the Inner Town from the top, you can also check out the excavated remains of the Amber Road and the Roman gate in the tower basement, along with parts of buildings from medieval Sopron.

Fidelity Gate   HISTORIC SITE

(Map p180; Fő tér) Fidelity Gate, at the bottom of the Firewatch Tower (p178), depicts 'Hungaria' receiving the kneeling *civitas fidelissima* (Latin for 'the most loyal citizenry') of Sopron, together with Sopron's coat of arms. It was erected in 1922 after Sopron's citizens rejected the offer of Austrian citizenship in a referendum.

Fő tér   SQUARE

(Main Square; Map p180) The oddly shaped Fő tér contains several museums, churches and monuments, including the massive Firewatch Tower, which can be climbed. In the centre of Fő tér is the 1701 Trinity Column.

★ Storno House   MUSEUM

(Storno Ház és Gyűjtemény; Map p180; ☑ 99-311 327; www.muzeum.sopron.hu; Fő tér 8; adult/concession Storno Collection 1000/500Ft, Boundless Story 700/350Ft; ☉ 10am-6pm Tue-Sun) Storno House, built in 1417, has an illustrious history: King Matthias stayed here in 1482–83, and Franz Liszt played a number of concerts here in the mid-19th century. Later it was taken over by the Swiss-Italian family of Ferenc Storno, chimney sweep turned art restorer, whose recarving of Romanesque and Gothic monuments throughout Transdanubia divides opinions to this day. Don't miss the Storno Collection, the family's treasure trove. The Boundless Story exhibition of local history is also worth a peek.

The highlights of the Storno Collection include a beautiful enclosed balcony with leaded windows and frescoes, an extensive collection of medieval weaponry, leather chairs with designs depicting the devil and dragons, and door frames made from pews taken from a nearby 15th-century church.

★ Fabricius House   MUSEUM

(Map p180; ☑ 99-311 327; http://portal.sopron. hu; Fő tér 6; adult/concession archaeological exhibition 900/450Ft, urban flats 900/450Ft;

☉ 10am-6pm Tue-Sun Apr-Sep, to 2pm Oct-Mar) This baroque mansion is divided into three sections. The archaeological exhibition covers Celtic, Roman and Hungarian periods of history, the standout artefact being the 1200-year-old Cunpald Goblet – don't miss the 'whispering gallery' either. The basement – a former Roman bathhouse – features impressive Roman sarcophagi and Scarbantia-era statues (including enormous statues of Juno, Jupiter and Minerva). Upstairs, the urban flats feature interior furnishings from the 17th and 18th centuries, with some elaborate davenports, travelling chests and magnificent tiled stoves.

Goat Church   CHURCH

(Kecsketemplom; Map p180; http://turizmus. sopron.hu/; Templom utca 1; adult/concession 800/400Ft; ☉ 10am-6pm Tue-Sun Apr-Oct, to 3pm Tue-Sun Nov-Mar) Built in the late 13th century, this mostly Gothic church gets its unusual name from the legend that the church had been built thanks to the treasure unearthed by a goatherd (hence the stone goat being cuddled by an angel on a pillar). The interior is mostly baroque, with a splendid red-marble pulpit in the centre of the south aisle. The church's Chapter Hall has fading frescoes and grotesque stone carvings – mainly animals with human heads – representing humankind's deadly sins.

Pharmacy Museum   MUSEUM

(Patikamúzeum; Map p180; ☑ 99-311 327; Fő tér 2; adult/concession 500/250Ft; ☉ 10am-2pm Tue-Sun Apr-Sep) Housed in a Gothic building just off the main square, the Pharmacy Museum features a 17th-century apothecary. This collection of curios comprises an assortment of ancient pharmaceutical tools, cures, books and gorgeous walnut furnishings. Look for oddities such as the amulet to ward off the evil eye and the hat against epilepsy.

Harrer Chocolate Factory   FACTORY

(Harrer Csokoládéműhely és Cukrászda; ☑ 99-505 904; www.harrercafe.com; Faller Jenő utca 4; adult/4-15yr 2990/2490Ft; ☉ 10am & 2pm daily by appointment) Sopron's answer to Willy Wonka's Chocolate Factory. The Austrian confectioner dynasty Harrer goes back four generations and aims to initiate you into the mysteries of pralines, truffles, flavoured chocolate and so much more. Visits to the factory (book in advance) involve a video on the production of chocolate and lots of chocolate tasting, be it dipping fruit into chocolate fountains, sampling Harrer's raw, dark,

Sopron

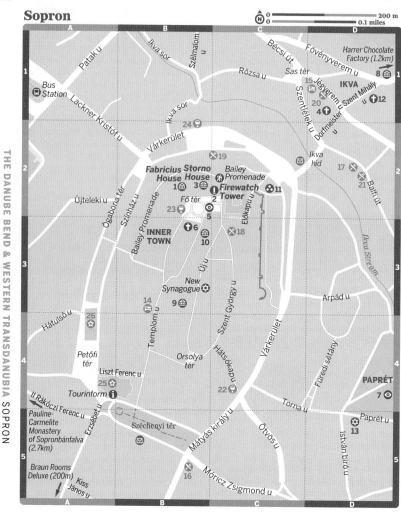

milk and flavoured chocolates, or sipping champagne alongside your truffles.

Old Synagogue
MUSEUM

(Ó Zsinagóga; Map p180; Új utca 22; adult/concession 700/350Ft; ⏰10am-8pm May-Oct) The Old Synagogue, built in the 14th century, contains two rooms, one for each sex (note the women's windows along the west wall). The main room contains a medieval 'holy of holies', with geometric designs and trees carved in stone, and some beautiful stained-glass windows. The inscriptions on the walls date from 1490. There's a reconstructed

mikvah (ritual bath) in the courtyard as well as a plaque commemorating the devastation of Sopron's Jewish community under the Nazis in 1944.

Új utca, on which the Old Synagogue stands, was known as Zsidó utca (Jewish St) until the Jews were evicted from Sopron in 1526, after being accused of plotting with Turks.

New Synagogue
JEWISH SITE

(Új Zsinagóga; Map p180; Új utca 11; ⏰10am-5pm) **FREE** Like the Old Synagogue (p180), the New Synagogue was also built in the 14th

Sopron

century; both are among the greatest Jewish Gothic monuments in Europe. The New Synagogue contains an exhibit on the Forgotten Sopronians – the 40 Jewish families that perished during WWII. Descriptions are in Hungarian only, but the enthusiastic curator tells their story in German and broken English.

Chapel of St James CHURCH
(Szent Jakab-kápolna; Map p180; Szent Mihály utca) Behind St Michael's Church is the Romanesque-Gothic Chapel of St James, the oldest structure in Sopron and originally an ossuary.

Holocaust Memorial MEMORIAL
(Map p180; Paprét utca) This Holocaust memorial, across the street from the derelict Orthodox synagogue, was erected with much political chest-beating in 2004. It features sculptures of jackets with the Star of David and a pile of shoes, which represent Auschwitz remains.

Synagogue JEWISH SITE
(Map p180; Paprét utca 14) Evidence of Sopron's Jewish past can be seen at the crumbling Orthodox synagogue east of the Inner Town, boarded up and falling into disrepair. A plaque explains that '1640 martyrs' were taken from here to Auschwitz on 5 July 1944.

Roman Ruins RUINS
(Szabadtéri rom; Map p180) As the plaque on the ground in Fő tér reminds you, Sopron

used to be an important stop along the Amber Road, and fragments of Sopron's Roman past – in the form of reconstructed Roman walls and outlines of 2nd-century buildings – can be found at the open-air ruins behind the city's town hall.

St Michael's Church CHURCH
(Szent Mihály-templom; Map p180; Szent Mihály utca) At the top of the Lővér Hills is St Michael's Church, built between the 13th and 15th centuries and featuring impressive gargoyles. Not much escaped the Stornos' handiwork when they 'renovated' St Michael's – they even added the spire. Check out the lovely polychrome Stations of the Cross (1892) in the churchyard and the large number of tombstones with German family names.

Church of the Holy Spirit CHURCH
(Szentlék-templom; Map p180; Dorfmeister utca; ⊙ hours vary) The interior of this 15th-century church is rather dark, but if you time your visit for midday, you'll be able catch a glimpse of some fine wall and ceiling frescoes by Dorfmeister, as well as a stupendously ornate altar.

House of the Two Moors HISTORIC BUILDING
(Két mór ház; Map p180; Szent Mihály utca 9) Fashioned from two 17th-century peasant houses, the House of the Two Moors and its ornate gate are guarded by two large statues.

Previously painted an exaggerated black to represent the darker-skinned Moors, they are now painted white.

🏃 Activities

Bailey Promenade
WALKING

(Map p180; ⊙ 9am-9pm Apr-Sep, to 6pm Oct-Mar) **FREE** The Bailey Promenade skirts the medieval walls of the Old Town and takes in ruins dating from the time when Sopron was a tiny Roman outpost known as Scarbantia.

🎉 Festivals & Events

Spring Days
CULTURAL

(⊙ Mar) Music, theatre, food and dance.

Sopron Festival Weeks
CULTURAL

(www.prokultura.hu; ⊙ mid-Jun–mid-Jul) All manner of concerts and theatrical performances, plus arts and crafts exhibitions, in Sopron's squares from mid-June to mid-July.

★ VOLT
MUSIC

(www.volt.hu; ⊙ early Jul) Hugely popular music festival, with 100,000 revellers rocking out to mostly Hungarian bands, but some international acts also.

Grape Harvest
WINE

(Soproni Borvidek; ⊙ late Sep) Wine tasting, music and folk dancing to celebrate the opening of the harvest season in late September.

🛏 Sleeping

There are several good hotels in and on the outskirts of the Old Town, plus guesthouses and pensions dotting the streets of the city centre and beyond. For a special experience, stay in a converted monastery on the outskirts of town.

★ Braun Rooms Deluxe
GUESTHOUSE $$

(☑ 06 70 300 6460; http://braun-rooms-deluxe-sopron.bedspro.com; Deák tér 15; s/d €30/38; ☀ ❄ �🔊) Halfway between the Old Town and the train station, this great place consists of just three spotless, super-comfortable doubles, with sunken bathtubs, climate control, coffee makers and murals on the walls. And if you want your teeth done, you're in an ideal location – right above a dental surgery.

Wieden Panzió
GUESTHOUSE $$

(Map p180; ☑ 99-523 222; Sas tér 13; s/d from 7800/10,900Ft; 🔊) This guesthouse is located in an attractive old town house a stone's throw from Inner Town. Rooms are spacious, bright and coloured in peaceful hues,

and bigger apartments are also an option. The downside is poor communication on the part of the owners.

★ Pauline-Carmelite Monastery of Sopronbanfalva
MONASTERY $$$

(Sopronbánfalvi Pálos-Karmelita; ☑ 99-505 895; www.banfalvakolostor.hu; Kolostorhegy utca 1; s/d/ste €84/128/164; 🔊) Having worn many hats over the centuries – home for coal miners, Carmelite nunnery, mental hospital, museum – this 15th-century monastery has now been sensitively restored as a beautiful hotel/retreat. The vaulted singles and light-filled doubles look out on to the forest. Upstairs there's an art gallery and a tranquil common space, the library. The refectory (p184) serves the best meals in Sopron.

★ Hotel Wollner
HOTEL $$$

(Map p180; ☑ 99-524 400; www.wollner.hu; Templom utca 20; s/d/tr from €75/90/110; ☀ 🔊) This refined family-run hotel offers 18 spacious and tastefully decorated rooms in a 300-year-old villa in the heart of the Inner Town. It has a unique tiered garden, in which the reconstructed medieval walls of the castle can be seen, and a romantic wine cellar where you can sample some of the region's celebrated vintages.

Erhardt Pension
GUESTHOUSE $$$

(Map p180; ☑ 99-506 711; www.erhardts.hu; Balfi út 10; s/d from 15,500/19,500Ft; 🔊) This great central spot comprises one of the best restaurants in town (p183), plus a handful of compact, homey rooms decked out in soothing creams and browns, complete with super-comfy mattresses. There are newer rooms also in a separate building.

🍴 Eating

Stubi Borozò
HUNGARIAN $

(Map p180; Balfi út 16; meals 750-1200Ft; ⊙ noon-9pm) This is very much a local place for local people, so it'll help if you speak German (or Hungarian). The goulash, hearty cabbage and potato stew, noodles with crushed poppy seeds and sugar, and other Hungarian daily specials are the best (and cheapest) in town and the portions are large.

Alcatraz
SANDWICHES $

(Map p180; Mátyás Király utca 1; sandwiches 390-440Ft; ⊙ 9am-6pm) We could make a joke about prison food here, but we won't. Suffice to say that it's an island of quick eats, such as stuffed baguettes, wraps and pizza slices, in

PANNONHALMA ABBEY

In a country filled with religious sites, nothing comes close to the hilltop Pannonhalma Abbey (Pannonhalmi főapátság; ☑96-570 191; www.bences.hu; Vár utca 1; adult/concession 2200/1100Ft; ⊗9am-4pm Tue-Sun Apr & Oct–mid-Nov, 9am-5pm daily Jun-Sep, 10am-3pm Tue-Sun mid-Nov–Mar) in terms of architectural splendour and historical significance.

Still a functioning monastery today, it was originally founded in 996 by monks from Venice and Prague, who came on the invitation of Prince Géza. Its creation marked the beginning of Christianity in Hungary; Géza's son, King Stephen, converted the pagan Magyars with the Benedictines' help. The monastery is an eclectic mix of architectural styles with its buildings razed, rebuilt and restored over the centuries. It served as a mosque during the Turkish occupation and as a refuge for Jews in autumn 1944 under the protection of the International Red Cross. Since the early 1990s, the brethren of the Pannonhalma Abbey have revived the monastery's age-old tradition of winemaking at the award-winning Archabbey Winery (☑96-570 222; www.apatsagipinceszet.hu; tours by appointment 1000Ft, with 3/5/7 wine tastings 2200/3000/4000Ft).

The centrepiece of the central courtyard is a statue of the first abbot, Asztrik, who brought the crown of King Stephen to Hungary from Rome, and a relief of King Stephen himself presenting his son Imre to his tutor Bishop Gellért. The main entrance to St Martin's Basilica (Szent Márton-bazilika), built in the early 12th century, is through the Porta Speciosa, a red limestone doorway comprising a series of arches.The fresco above the doorway depicts the church's patron, St Martin of Tours. To the right below the columns is probably the oldest graffiti in Hungary: 'Benedict Padary was here in 1578', it says in Latin.

Inside the pleasantly austere stone church, well-worn steps lead down into the 13th-century crypt. The red marble niche allegedly covers the wooden throne of St Stephen and a marble slab inscribed with 'Ottó 1912–2011' marks the burial spot of the heart of Otto von Habsburg – the last crown prince of Austria-Hungary and one of the leaders of Austrian anti-Nazi resistance (the rest of him is buried in Vienna).

In the cloister arcade, you'll notice the little faces carved in stone on the wall. They represent human emotions and vices, such as wrath, greed and conceit, and are meant to remind monks of the baseness and transitory nature of human existence. In the cloister garden a Gothic sundial offers a sobering thought: 'Una Vestrum Ultima Mea' (One of you will be my last).

The most beautiful part of the abbey is the neoclassical library built in 1836 by János Packh, who was involved in designing the Esztergom Basilica. It contains some 400,000 volumes – many of them priceless historical records – making it the largest private library in Hungary.

In the heart of Pannonhalma village, Borbirodalom (☑96-471 730; www.borbirodalom.hu; Szabadság tér 27, Pannonhalma; mains 1490-2590Ft; ⊗noon-10pm) has an extensive selection of wines from the nearby Pannonhalma-Sokoróalja region in its cellar, and a gourmet menu that includes game stew, roasted duck breast and goose liver.

Trains run from Budapest and Sopron to Győr; frequent buses connect Győr to Pannonhalma (465Ft; 30 minutes; 21km; half-hourly).

a town with very few such places, but don't expect to be wowed gastronomically.

★Erhardt   INTERNATIONAL $$
(Map p180; ☑99-506 711; www.erhardts.hu; Balfi út 10; mains 2990-4590Ft; ⊗11.30am-10pm Sun-Thu, to 11pm Fri & Sat; ☑) An excellent restaurant where a pleasant garden terrace, a wooden-beamed ceiling and paintings of rural scenes complement imaginative dishes such as paprika catfish with oyster mushrooms and crispy duck leg with cabbage noodles. There's an extensive selection of Sopron wines to choose from (also available

for purchase at its wine cellar), and the service is both informed and welcoming. If you happen to be sampling the local wines in the extensive wine cellar, your bed is just a stagger away in Erhardt Pension (p182).

Forum Pizzeria   PIZZA $$
(Map p180; ☑99-340 231; www.forumpizzeria.hu; Szent György utca 3; pizza 920-1920Ft) Though the menu at this popular pizzeria tries to be all things to all people (pasta, meat, fish, Mexican dishes), stick to wood-fired pizza as this is what they do best. The vaulted ceiling in the dining area makes you feel as if you're

eating in a church. No English spoken, so come prepared.

Graben INTERNATIONAL $$

(Map p180; ☑99-340 256; www.grabenetterem. hu; Várkerület 8; mains 2200-3690Ft; ☺8am-10pm) Located in a cosy cellar near the old city walls, Graben attracts a largely Austrian clientele with the likes of 'old man's steak', schnitzel, chicken cordon bleu and game dishes. Great flavours and friendly service; some English spoken. In summer its terrace spreads out over an inner courtyard.

Jégverem HUNGARIAN $$

(Map p180; ☑99-510 113; www.jegverem.hu; Jégverem utca 1; mains 890-3600Ft) The slogan of this rustic pension restaurant is 'The Restaurant for Guzzle-guts'. It is defined by its extensive, ambitious menu, portions large enough to satisfy a famished sumo wrestler and seriously inexpensive weekday lunch specials (940Ft) including the likes of sausage with fried mushrooms and chicken soup with liver dumplings.

★Sopronbánfalvi Pálos-Karmelita Kolostor FUSION $$$

(Pauline-Carmelite Monastery of Sopronbanfalva; ☑99-505 895; www.banfalvakolostor.hu; Kolostorhegy utca 2; mains 2750-6850Ft, tasting menus 7200Ft; ☺noon-3pm & 6-9pm; ☑) On the outskirts of Sopron, this monastery is home to the only fine dining restaurant in town and is worth the trip for a meal alone. Eating in the splendid vaulted dining room lends the meal a spiritual element and the food – from scallop ravioli with buttered shrimp sauce to venison with morels – is inspired and beautifully presented.

🍷 Drinking & Nightlife

The Sopron region is noted for its red wines, especially *kékfrankos* and *merlot,* and the white *tramini* is also worth a try. There a number of wine cellars scattered about the city where you can try the local tipple, but watch your intake if you don't want a massive *macskajaj* ('cat's wail' – Hungarian for 'hangover') the next day.

★Cezár Pince WINE BAR

(Map p180; ☑99-311 337; www.cezarpince. hu; Hátsókapu utca 2; ☺noon-midnight Mon-Sat, 4-11pm Sun; ☎) Atmospheric bar in a 17th-century cellar, where you can imbibe a wide selection of local wines while sharing large platters of cured meats, local cheeses, pâtés and salami.

TasteVino Borbár & Vinotéka WINE BAR

(Map p180; ☑06 30 519 8285; www.tastevino.hu; Várkerület 5; ☺noon-midnight Tue-Sat) This is a vaulted bar and wine shop all in one, where you can sample the best that Sopron's wineries have to offer and also purchase your tipples of choice.

Museum Cafe CAFE

(Map p180; ☑06 30 285 1177; www.museum cafesopron.hu; Előkapu utca 2-7; ☺10am-10pm Sun-Thu, to 2am Fri & Sat) This wonderful cafe on the 1st floor of the Firewatch Tower (p178) has stunning views through oversized windows and cutting-edge decor, and is surrounded by a lapidary of Roman and medieval finds. And it's not just about coffee here. There are also lemonades (try the passion fruit), wines and *pálinka* and, as blotter, sandwiches (550Ft to 880Ft) and cakes (250Ft to 690Ft).

Gyógygödör Borozó WINE BAR

(Map p180; ☑99-311 280; http://gyogygodor.hu; Fő tér 4; ☺10am-10pm Sun-Thu, to 11pm Fri & Sat) The incongruously cutesy wooden furniture looks out of place inside this stone cellar, but that shouldn't detract from the pleasure of sampling the extensive collection of Sopron wines and a couple of Sopron beers alongside inexpensive Hungarian dishes.

☆ Entertainment

Petőfi Theatre THEATRE

(Petőfi Színház; Map p180; ☑99-517 570; www. soproniszinhaz.hu; Petőfi tér 1) This beautiful theatre with National Romantic–style mosaics on the front facade features both contemporary plays and Hungarian and foreign drama.

Ferenc Liszt Conference & Cultural Centre PERFORMING ARTS

(Map p180; ☑99-517 517; www.prokultura.hu; Liszt Ferenc utca 1; ☺9am-5pm Mon-Fri, to noon Sat) This beautifully renovated venue facing Széchenyi tér contains a theatre, concert hall, Tourinform office, casino and restaurant, and hosts some of the most important musical and cultural events in Sopron.

ℹ Information

Main Post Office (Map p180; Széchenyi tér 7-8; ☺8am-5pm Mon-Fri, 9am-1pm Sat) There's also an Inner Town **branch** (Map p180; Várkerület 37; ☺8am-4pm Mon-Fri). **OTP Bank** (Várkerület 96/a) Handy ATM.

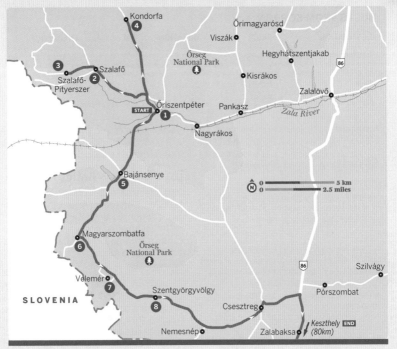

Driving Tour
Őrség National Park

START ŐRISZENTPÉTER
END KESZTHELY
LENGTH 140.5KM; EIGHT HOURS

If you lack the leisure to explore the national park on foot or by bike, take in the park's highlights on a day's driving tour. Begin your tour at ❶ **Őriszentpéter**, the 'capital' of Őrség National Park – an attractive village of thatched wooden dwellings scattered over several hills. Follow the road northwest for 2km towards Szalafő and stop at the remarkably well-preserved ❷ **Romanesque church** featuring a wonderful carved portal and an 18th-century altarpiece painted by a student of Franz Anton Maulbertsch. Continue 5km west to Szalafő-Pityerszer; the ❸ **Open-Air Ethnographical Museum** here is an excellent place to view traditional Őrség architecture. Built around a central courtyard, the U-shaped houses are very cute and have large overhangs, which allowed neighbours to chat when it rained.

Head back to Őriszentpéter and then north for 7.5km to tiny Kondorfa. In a restored traditional house you'll find ❹ **Vadkörte** (p186) – a folksy, kitsch restaurant specialising in Hungarian cuisine. After lunch, drive back to Őriszentpéter and carry on south for 8km along the E65 to ❺ **Bajánsenye**, a village famous for its delicious, locally sourced fish. Another 10km south brings you to ❻ **Magyarszombatfa** – an area that has for centuries been known for its pottery, and where the craft is still very much alive. If you don't catch the local potters in action, the 1760 Fazekasház (potter's house) has an excellent museum featuring some splendid unglazed containers and cooking vessels.

Head 7km southeast of Magyarszombatfa; in the forest on the edge of the village of ❼ **Velemér** there is a beautiful 13th-century church featuring frescoes by Austrian painter Johannes Aquilla, designed to be illuminated by the sun at certain times of year. Another 4km along, the Calvinist church at the village of **Szentgyörgyvölgy** has an absolutely splendid ceiling. Head east for 15km to join Hwy 86, turn south, then east into Hwy 75 and head east for another 80km until you reach your final destination of Keszthely.

BUSES FROM SOPRON

DESTINATION	PRICE	DURATION	KM	FREQUENCY
Balatonfüred	3130Ft	4hr	178km	daily
Esztergom	3410Ft	4hr	198km	daily
Győr	1680Ft	2-2½hr	87km	hourly
Keszthely	2520Ft	3hr	129km	4 daily

Tourinform (p170) Some information on Sopron and surrounds, including local vintners.

❶ Getting There & Away

BUS

There are regular buses to various destinations from the Sopron **bus station** (Map p180; Lackner Kristóf utca). See table below.

TRAIN

➜ There are express trains to Budapest (4735Ft, 2½ hours, 216km, six daily) and direct trains to Vienna's Haufbahnhof and Miedling (5000Ft, 1½ hours, up to 12 daily).

➜ The **train station** (Állomás utca) is a 10-minute walk from the heart of Sopron. Domestic train tickets can be bought from ticket machines, but tickets to Vienna must be purchased at the international office here. English is spoken at the information office.

Őrség National Park

Unspoilt nature and pure rural essence are the biggest drawcards of Őrség, Hungary's westernmost region, where the country converges with Austria and Slovenia in forest and farmland. Much of the region forms the boundaries of the 440-sq-km Őrség National Park, founded in 2002 and recently designated a European Destination of Excellence in recognition of the area's commitment to environmental and cultural sustainability. Besides the park's rich bird life, the villages here maintain a strong folk tradition, with local pottery enterprises going back some generations.

🏃 Activities

The park is a green belt of dense woods, peaceful meadows, rolling hills and slow streams, which makes it a grand place for hiking, cycling and horse riding. There are marked hiking trails that link many of Őrség's villages, including Őriszentpéter,

Szalafő, Velemér and Pankasz. Cartographia's 1:60,000-scale map *Őrség és a Göcsej* is a good reference for hikers.

🛏 Sleeping & Eating

Őriszentpéter has the best choice of accommodation, with several pensions and private rooms advertised along Városszer.

The information centre in Őriszentpéter can help with finding private accommodation in the villages.

Vadkörte HUNGARIAN **$$**
(☑ 94-393 879; www.vadkorte.hu; Alvég 7, Kondorfa; mains from 2500Ft) This adorable country inn at tiny Kondorfa, in the heart of Őrség National Park, has an excellent restaurant serving hearty seasonal cuisine with an emphasis on local ingredients, so expect robust stews with wild mushrooms, and seasonal berries and fruit in desserts. If you want to stay overnight, there are five spacious, pleasant rooms (single/double 5500/8800Ft) and two apartments to choose from.

❶ Information

Information Centre (☑ 94-548 034; http://onp.nemzetipark.gov.hu; Siskaszer 26/a, Őriszentpéter; ⊙ 8am-4.30pm Mon-Fri, 10am-3pm Sat-Sun mid-Jun–Aug, closed Sat & Sun Sep–mid-Jun) Őrség National Park's information centre is housed in the same building as Tourinform in Őriszentpéter at the turn-off to Szalafő. Tourinform can provide information on activities, as well as places to stay in the villages.

❶ Getting There & Away

➜ It's best to have your own transport with which to explore the region, as buses are infrequent and getting to the villages can be tricky.

➜ Őriszentpéter can be reached by bus from Sopron, though this requires changing buses in Szombathely and Zalaegerszeg. It can also be reached from Keszthely by changing buses in Ukk.

Lake Balaton & Southern Transdanubia

Best Places to Eat

➡ Zsolnay Restaurant (p212)

➡ Bistro Sparhelt (p193)

➡ Baricska Csárda (p193)

➡ Jókai Bisztró (p211)

➡ Régi Idők Udvara Skanzen és Étterem (p197)

➡ Paletta Keszthely (p203)

Best Places to Sleep

➡ Gombás Kúria Mansion (p192)

➡ Kora Panzió (p197)

➡ Adele Boutique Hotel (p210)

➡ Club Hotel Füred (p192)

➡ Bacchus (p203)

Why Go?

Extending roughly 80km like a skinny, lopsided paprika, at first glance Lake Balaton seems to simply be a happy, sunny expanse of opaque tourmaline-coloured water in which to play. But step beyond the beaches of Europe's biggest and shallowest body of water and you'll encounter vine-filled forested hills, a national park and a wild peninsula jutting out 4km, nearly cutting the lake in half. Oh, and did we mention Hungary's most famous porcelain producer and a hilltop fairy-tale fortress?

Then there's Southern Transdanubia, where whitewashed farmhouses with thatched roofs dominate a countryside that hasn't changed in centuries. Anchoring its centre is one of Hungary's most alluring cities, Pécs, where a Mediterranean feel permeates streets filled with relics of Hungary's Ottoman past and a head-spinning number of exceptional museums. Beyond, a clutch of medieval castles enchant and vineyard cellars beckon you to wine-taste your heart out.

When to Go
Pecs

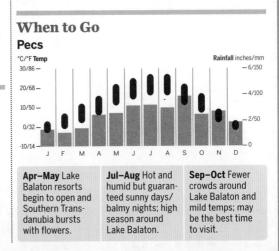

Apr–May Lake Balaton resorts begin to open and Southern Transdanubia bursts with flowers.

Jul–Aug Hot and humid but guaranteed sunny days/balmy nights; high season around Lake Balaton.

Sep–Oct Fewer crowds around Lake Balaton and mild temps; may be the best time to visit.

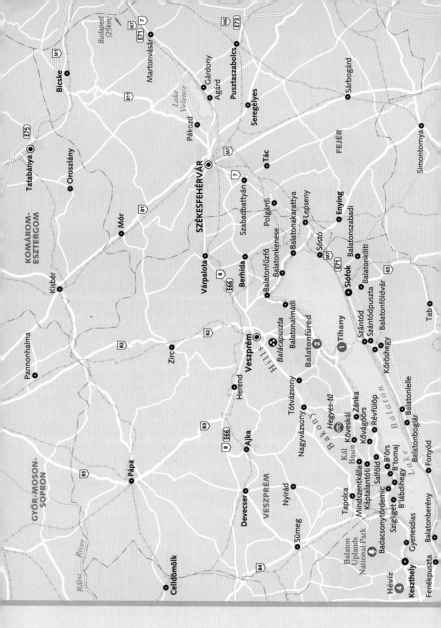

Lake Balaton & Southern Transdanubia Highlights

1 Tihany (p194)
Wandering the wild peninsula, poking around in the Abbey Church and sipping a home-brewed beer in Hungary's most picture-perfect lakeside village.

2 Balatonfüred (p190)
Sailing, paddleboarding, swimming and cycling in the Lake Balaton capital, then hitting lakeside restaurants and bars by night.

3 Pécs (p205)
Checking out the excellent museums, craft beer bars and coffee shops in this lively university town, plus marvelling at the greenish- and goldish-hued ceramics at the famous porcelain factory.

4 Hévíz (p203)
Taking a leisurely dip in the healing waters of Europe's largest thermal lake.

5 Busójárás
(p214) Seeing the devil masks at this wild Mohács festival and checking out the memorial of Hungary's historic defeat.

Paks

M6

6 E73

Tolna

M9

Sárköz Region

Bárányfok

Ócsény

Decs

Pörböly

Duna-Dráva National Park

55

56

E73

Danube River

Mohács

5

Mohács Historical Memorial Site

Sátorhely

Udvar

Villánykövesd

Villány

Nagyharsány

63

Sió River

Szekszárd

Szekszárd Hills

Bátaszék

TOLNA

65

Bonyhád

M6

Pécsvárad

6

Zengő (682m)

57

Palkonya

Villány Hills

Siklós

Harkány

61

Tamási

Komló

Mecsek Hills

Pécs

3

58

Máriagyüd

Adorjás

Kórós

Vajszló

BARANYA

Andocs

Dombóvár

Sásd

Abaliget

Orfű

Szentlőrinc

Sellye

Ormánság Region

61

Taszár

Zselic Region

67

Szigetvár

Drávaiványi

Lengyeltóti

Kaposvár

Szenna

6

Dráva River

Drávavölgye

67

SOMOGY

Marcali

E661

68

Nagyatád

E661

68

Barcs

CROATIA

Balatonszentgyörgy

Zalavár / Balaton Uplands National Park

E71

M7

Kápolnapuszta

61

Bélavár

Vizvár

Virovitica

20 km
10 miles

N

LAKE BALATON REGION

Balatonfüred

⏱ 87 / POP 13,082

Balatonfüred is not only the oldest resort on Lake Balaton's northern shore, it's also the most fashionable. In former days the wealthy and famous built large villas on its streets, and their architectural legacy can still be seen today. Yes, it's highly touristy, but it's an excellent place to base yourself on the lake, with endless lodging and dining options, and a superb tree-lined promenade along the shore where everyone goes for their pre- or postdinner stroll. The town also has the most stylish marina on the lake and is known for the thermal waters of its world-famous heart hospital.

History

The thermal water here, rich in carbonic acid, has been used as a cure for stomach ailments for centuries, but its other curative properties were only discovered by scientific analysis in the late 18th century. Balatonfüred was immediately declared a spa with its own chief physician in residence.

Balatonfüred's golden age was in the 19th century, especially the first half, when political and cultural leaders of the Reform Era (roughly 1825–48) gathered here in the summer; it was also the site chosen by István Széchenyi to launch the lake's first steamship, *Kisfaludy*, in 1846.

By 1900 Balatonfüred was a popular place for increasingly wealthy middle-class families to escape Budapest's heat. Wives would base themselves here all summer along with their children while husbands boarded the 'bull trains' in Budapest at the weekend. It is a sign of the times that even Balatonfüred has begun to modernise itself in the last couple of years.

⦿ Sights

Tagore Sétány AREA

(Lake Promenade; Map p191) The entire town seems to stroll the leafy lake-hugging promenade all day. It hides a number of statues, including a bust of Nobel Prize–winning poet Rabindranath Tagore in front of a lime tree that he planted in 1926 to mark his recovery from illness after treatment here. Diagonally opposite is a disturbing memorial: a hand stretching out of the water in memory of those who drowned when the *Pajtás* boat sank in 1954.

Gyógy tér SQUARE

(Cure Square; Map p191) This leafy square is home to the State Hospital of Cardiology. In the centre you'll encounter the **Kossuth Pump House** (1853), a natural spring that dispenses slightly sulphuric, but drinkable, thermal water. If you can ignore the water's pale-yellow hue, join the locals lining up to fill their water bottles.

Jókai Memorial Museum MUSEUM

(Jókai emlékmúzeum; Map p191; ☎ 87-950 876; www.furedkult.hu; Honvéd utca 1; adult/concession 1300/650Ft; ⊙ 10am-5pm Tue-Sun) The Jókai Memorial Museum is housed in the summer villa of the prolific writer Mór Jókai, just north of Vitorlás tér. Jókai churned out many of his 200 novels in his study here, under the stern gaze of his wife, the actress Róza Laborfalvi. The museum is filled with family memorabilia and period furniture. All the signage is in Hungarian; ask for the laminated English guide at the entrance.

Round Church CHURCH

(Kerek templom; Map p191; ☎ 87-343 029; Blaha Lujza utca 1; ⊙ services only) FREE Inspired by the Pantheon in Rome, the tiny neoclassical Round Church was completed in 1846. The *Crucifixion* (1891) by János Vaszary sits above the altar on the western wall and is the only notable thing inside.

Balaton Pantheon MONUMENT

(Map p191; Gyógy tér) The Balaton Pantheon has memorial plaques from those who took the cure at the town's famous hospital; the Bengali poet Rabindranath Tagore was one of them.

State Hospital of Cardiology HISTORIC BUILDING

(Állami Szívkórház; Map p191; Gyógy tér 2) The famed State Hospital of Cardiology and its hot springs is what put Balatonfüred on the map.

Vaszary Villa GALLERY

(Map p191; ☎ 87-950 876; www.vaszaryvilla.hu; Honvéd utca 2-4; adult/child 1800/900Ft; ⊙ 10am-6pm Tue-Sun) This beautifully restored villa (1892), once the residence of the Vaszarys, exhibits some works by the best-known family member, the painter János Vaszary, as well as a wonderful collection of arts and crafts from the 18th century.

Lóczy Cave CAVE

(Lóczy-barlang; Öreghegyi utca; adult/3-14yr 500/300Ft; ⊙ 10am-6pm Tue-Sun mid-Apr–Sep) Around 40m of this cave is accessible to the

Balatonfüred

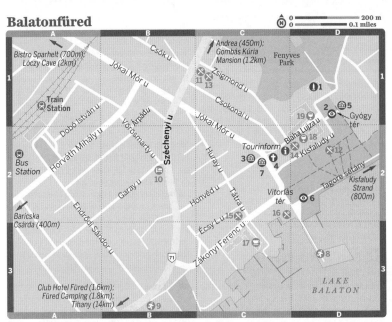

Balatonfüred

Sights
1 Balaton Pantheon	D1
2 Gyógy tér	D1
3 Jókai Memorial Museum	C2
4 Round Church	C2
5 State Hospital of Cardiology	D1
6 Tagore sétány	D2
7 Vaszary Villa	C2

Activities, Courses & Tours
8 Balaton Shipping Co Pleasure Boats	D3
9 Surf Pro Center	B3

Sleeping
10 Aqua Haz	B2

Eating
11 Arany Csillag Pizzéria	C1
12 Balaton	D2
13 Cafe Bergman	C1
14 Kedves Cukrászda	D2
15 Nem Kacsa	C2
16 Vitorlás	C2

Drinking & Nightlife
17 Karolina	C3
18 Kredenc Borbisztró	D2
19 Vivamus Borharapó	D1

public, and the highlight inside is the thick layers of limestone. It's located north of the old town centre. It's a cool 12°C year-round, so bring a warm top.

Activities

The 210km Balaton cycle path runs through Balatonfüred, and cycling around exploring the town along the water is a fine way to spend the day (but note that as soon as you head away from the lake it's all uphill). Rent bicycles from **Eco Bike** (06 20 924 4995, 06 70 264 2299; www.greenspark.hu; Széchenyi utca 8; per ½/1/2 days from 1900/2755/5655Ft; 9am–8pm) at the western end of the promenade.

Kisfaludy Strand   BEACH
(www.balatonfuredistrandok.hu; Aranyhíd sétány; adult/child 600/400Ft; 8.30am-7pm mid-Jun–mid-Aug, 8am-6pm mid-May–mid-Jun & mid-Aug–mid-Sep) Relatively sandy, this is the best of the three public beaches in Balatonfüred. There's a fairly tame zip line at the entrance

It's east of Tagore sétány (p190), 800m northeast of the pier along the footpath.

Surf Pro Center
WATER SPORTS

(Map p191; ☑06 30 936 6969; www.surfpro. hu; Széchenyi utca 10; ⊙9am-6pm Apr-Oct) Windsurfing gear (one hour/three hours 3500/8000Ft), stand-up paddleboards (one hour/day 2000/15,000Ft) and kayaks (one hour/day 1000/10,000Ft) are available to hire here. These guys also offer windsurfing lessons (5000Ft per hour).

Balaton Shipping Co Pleasure Boats
CRUISE

(Map p191; ☑87-342 230; www.balatonihajozas. hu; ferry pier; adult/concession 1800/800Ft) One-hour pleasure cruises depart several times a day from late April to early October from the central ferry pier, in addition to sunset cruises (adult/concession 2000/1100Ft).

🎭 Festivals & Events

Anna Ball
DANCE

(www.annabal.hu; Anna Grand Hotel; ⊙26 Jul) The annual Anna Ball has been a prime event on the Hungarian calendar since 1825. Even if you don't attend the ball it's worth joining the crowds gathering to watch the beautifully attired guests, and on the following day the ball queen parades around town in an elaborate horse and carriage. Concerts accompany the days around the ball.

🛏 Sleeping

Füred Camping
CAMPGROUND $

(☑87-580 241; http://balatontourist.hu; Széchenyi utca 24; campsite per adult/child/tent 1900/1200/4800Ft, bungalows/caravans from 21,000/29,500Ft; ⊙mid-Apr–early Oct; ▣) This is one of the largest camping grounds on the lake and can accommodate 3500 people. In addition to places to pitch your tent, there are bungalows (sleeping up to four) and caravans to rent. The property has direct access to the lake and a nice swimming pool with a slide for kids. The bathroom facilities are old.

Aqua Haz
PENSION $$

(Map p191; ☑87-342 813; www.aquahaz.hu; Garay utca 2; s/d/tr 9350/11,000/15,500Ft; ▣�) Family-run, mustard-yellow, three-storey house, conveniently located between the lake and the train/bus station. The operators go out of their way to make you feel right at home, most rooms feature bright balconies, and free bikes are available for tooling around town. Excellent breakfast.

Andrea
PENSION $$

(☑06 30 468 8824; www.facebook.com/Andrea pansio; Petőfi Sándor utca 44; r €50; ▣⏰�) An appealing mustard-yellow house that's just off the main road, but far enough away from it to not be disturbed by traffic. The 17 rooms are spick-and-span, with breezy balconies, and there's a small pool for guest use. Staff are friendly and the lake is a 10-minute walk away. The closest train station is Balatonarács.

⭐Club Hotel Füred
RESORT $$$

(☑06 70 458 1242, 87-341 511; www.clubhotelfured. hu; Anna sétány 1-3; r/ste from 22,100/60,000Ft; ⏰⏰⏰s) This stunner of a resort hotel, right on the lake, about 1.5km from the town centre, has 43 rooms and suites in several buildings spread over 2.5 hectares of parkland and lush gardens. There's an excellent spa centre with sauna, steam room and pool, but the real delight is the private beach at the end of the garden. Stellar service.

⭐Gombás Kúria Mansion
B&B $$$

(☑87-340 080; www.gombaskuria.hu; Arácsi út 94; r €57-75, apt €80-161; ▣⏰⏰s) In the foothills of Mt Thomas, this beautiful 18th-century residence has a vaulted cellar, a paddling pool for kids, a barbecue terrace and sunloungers in the tranquil garden. Gabor (the owner) is extremely helpful, rooms are spacious, and the apartments are a good bet for families, and it's a 15- to 20-minute walk from the lake.

🍴 Eating

Oodles of restaurant-bars line the waterfront; the majority are excellent for a beer or glass of local wine. The food tends to be rather samey and largely mediocre, though the fish will generally be fresh from the lake. Excellent Hungarian fare (and wine) is worth seeking out in the vineyards just east of the town.

Cafe Bergman
DESSERTS $

(Map p191; ☑87-341 087; Zsigmond utca 3; ⊙10am-7.30pm) Ignore the lakeside ice-cream stands and head uphill to this elegant cafe for scoops of the best ice cream in town (including local favourite, poppy-seed ice cream). Located on a quiet street, this is a relaxing escape from the crowds and has a lovely tree-shaded exterior terrace. In addition, it offers a handsome selection of cakes and sandwiches.

Kedves Cukrászda
CAFE $

(Map p191; ☑06 20 471 2073; www.facebook. com/KedvesCukraszda; Blaha Lujza utca 7; cakes from 280Ft; ⊙9am-7pm Sun-Thu, to 8pm Fri & Sat)

Join fans of Lujza Blaha and take coffee and cake at the cafe where the famous actress used to while away the hours when not in residence across the street. It's also appealing for its location, away from the madding crowds.

★**Nem Kacsa**   HUNGARIAN $$
(Map p191; ☑06 70 364 7800; www.facebook.com/nemkacsaetterem; Zákonyi Ferenc utca; mains from 3300Ft; ☺noon-11pm Wed-Sun) The gourmet stylings of chef Lajos Takács stand out against the town's largely mediocre offerings. The kitchen delivers beautifully crafted dishes featuring freshly grown produce from the farm it shares with the chef of Bistro Sparhelt. Duck stands out, but it's hard to go wrong with other meats or the homemade Italian pasta. Marina views and local wines seal the deal.

Vitorlás   HUNGARIAN $$
(Map p191; ☑06 30 546 0940; www.vitorlasetterem.hu; Tagore sétány 1; mains 2300-3900Ft; ☺9am-midnight) This enormous wooden villa sits right on the lake's edge at the foot of the town's pier. It's a prime spot to watch the yachts sail in and out of the harbour from the terrace while munching on Hungarian cuisine and sipping local wine. A fish dish is de rigueur here; we recommend the fiery catfish stew.

Balaton   HUNGARIAN $$
(Map p191; ☑87-481 319; www.balatonetterem.hu; Kisfaludy utca 5; mains 2190-6400Ft; ☺11am-11pm) This cool, leafy oasis amid all the hubbub is set back from the lake in a shaded park area. It serves generous portions of such Hungarian culinary delights as catfish soup and turkey stuffed with Camembert and prunes. There's an extensive fish selection.

Arany Csillag Pizzéria   PIZZA $$
(Map p191; ☑87-482 116; www.aranycsillagpizzeria.hu; Zsigmond utca 1; mains 1320-2880Ft; ☺noon-11pm Sun-Thu, to midnight Fri & Sat; ☑) A convivial pizza/pasta joint away from the flashy waterfront, Arany Csillag is a local favourite that attracts a mix of people from every age group. Its small shaded terrace fills up quickly in summer, so either come early (6ish) or reserve in advance.

★**Baricska Csárda**   HUNGARIAN $$$
(☑87-950 738; www.baricska.hu; Baricska dűlő; mains 3100-4900Ft; ☺noon-10pm Thu-Sun) If you only eat in one place in town, let it be here, under the trellises covered in creeping vines, among the vineyards. The setting is particularly magical in the evenings, and the dishes – catfish paprikash with cottage cheese noodles, smoked duck breast with red cabbage, and other Hungarian classics – are beautifully presented. Extensive list of local wines.

★**Bistro Sparhelt**   BISTRO $$$
(☑06 70 639 9944; http://bistrosparhelt.hu; Szent István tér 7; mains 2790-6390Ft; ☺noon-10pm Wed-Sun; ☑) Head inland from the lake to the town hall for a rare gastronomic treat. Chef Balázs Elek presides over a sleek, minimalist restaurant with a succinct, monthly changing menu, its dishes dictated by what's market-fresh. Expect to be treated to the likes of osso bucco with truffled mash, red crab with homemade noodles and venison with dumplings. Superb stuff.

🍷 Drinking & Nightlife

Kredenc Borbisztró   WINE BAR
(Map p191; ☑06 20 518 9960; www.kredencborbisztro.hu; Blaha Lujza utca 7; ☺noon-10pm Mon-Fri, 10am-midnight Sat & Sun) This family-run combination wine bar and bistro is a peaceful retreat near the lakefront. The menu is stacked with oodles of local wines and the owner is often on hand to thoughtfully recommend the best tipple according to your tastes. The wine bar sells bottles of everything they serve, plus an extensive selection of regional wines. Weekend DJ sets.

Vivamus Borharapó   WINE BAR
(Anna Grand Hotel Wine Bar; Map p191; ☑87-580 200; Gyógy tér 1; ☺11am-10pm) This atmospheric cellar below Anna Grand Hotel (p107) serves an excellent selection of local wines, along with meat-and-cheese plates.

Karolina   CAFE
(Map p191; ☑87-583 098; www.karolina.hu; Zákonyi Ferenc utca 4; ☺9am-11pm) One of the most popular places in town for a drink or a quick bite (dishes 1200Ft to 3100Ft), Karolina is a sophisticated cafe-bar with live music from 8pm on weekends. The interior, with its art nouveau wall hangings and subtle lighting, has a certain decadent air about it, while the terrace with sofas couldn't be more laid-back.

ℹ️ Information

Tourinform (Map p191; ☑87-580 480; www.balatonfured.info.hu; Blaha Lujza utca 5; ☺9am-7pm Mon-Sat, 10am-4pm Sun) is the main tourist office. www.balatonfured.hu and www.welovebalaton.hu are useful websites.

BUSES FROM BALATONFÜRED

DESTINATION	PRICE	DURATION	KM	FREQUENCY
Budapest	2520Ft	2-3hr	136	5-8 daily
Keszthely	1300Ft	1-1½hr	67	3 daily
Tihany	310Ft	30min	14	at least 15 daily

ℹ Getting There & Away

BOAT

From April to June and September to late October, at least four daily **Balaton Shipping Co** (Balatoni Hajózási Rt; ☑ 84-310 050; www.balatonihajozas.hu; Krúdy sétány 2, Siófok) ferries link Balatonfüred with Siófok and Tihany (adult/concession 1300/650Ft). Up to seven daily ferries serve these ports from July to August.

BUS

Buses leave from Balatonfüred's bus station (Map p191). Some services are more frequent in summer.

TRAIN

Trains travel from Balatonfüred to Budapest (2520Ft, 2½ hours, 132km, three daily).

ℹ Getting Around

Balatonfüred is small enough to get around on foot, but you can reach Vitorlás tér and the lake from the train and bus stations on buses 1, 1/a and 2; bus 1 continues on to Füred Camping (p192). There's also a local taxi service (☑ 06 20 954 9373).

Tihany

☑ 87 / POP 1383

The place with the greatest historical significance on Lake Balaton is Tihany, a peninsula jutting 5km into the lake. Tihany village, perched on an 80m-high plateau along the peninsula's eastern coast, is home to the celebrated Abbey Church and in the height of summer the church attracts so many people it's hard to find space to breathe. Visit the church but then escape the madness by wandering around the tiny town filled with lovely thatched-roof houses.

The peninsula itself is a nature reserve of hills and marshy meadows with an isolated, almost wild feel. Two inland basins are fed by rain and ground water: the Inner Lake (Belső-tó) is almost in the centre of the peninsula and visible from the village, while the Outer Lake (Külső-tó) to the northwest has almost totally dried up and is now a tangle of reeds. Both basins attract considerable bird life.

History

There was a Roman settlement in the area, but Tihany first appeared on the map in 1055, when King Andrew I (r 1046–60), a son of King Stephen's great nemesis, Vászoly, founded a Benedictine monastery here. The Deed of Foundation of the Abbey Church of Tihany, now in the archives of the Pannonhalma Abbey, is one of the earliest known documents bearing any Hungarian words – some 50 place names within a mostly Latin text. It's a linguistic treasure in a country where, until the 19th century, the vernacular in its written form was spurned – particularly in schools – in favour of the more 'cultured' Latin and German.

In 1267 a fortress was built around the church, and it was able to keep the Turks at bay when they arrived 300 years later. But the castle was demolished by Habsburg forces in 1702 and all you'll see today are ruins.

◉ Sights

★**Benedictine Abbey Church**　　　CHURCH
(Bencés Apátság Templom; Map p196; ☑ 87-538 200; http://tihany.osb.hu; András tér 1; adult/concession incl museum 1000/700Ft; ☺ 9am-6pm Apr-Sep, 10am-5pm Oct, 10am-4pm Nov-Mar) Built in 1754 on the site of King Andrew's church, this twin-spired, ochre-coloured church is Tihany's dominant feature. Don't miss the fantastic altars, pulpits and screens carved between 1753 and 1779 by an Austrian lay brother named Sebastian Stuhlhof, all baroque-rococo masterpieces in their own right. The remains of King Andrew I lie in a limestone sarcophagus in the atmospheric Romanesque crypt. The spiral swordlike cross on the cover is similar to ones used by 11th-century Hungarian kings.

Upon entering the main nave, turn your back to the sumptuous main altar and the abbot's throne and look right to the side altar dedicated to Mary. The large angel kneeling on the right supposedly represents Stuhlhof's fiancée, a fisherman's daughter who died in her youth. On the Altar of the Sacred Heart across the aisle, a pelican (symbolising Christ) nurtures its young (the faithful) with its own blood. The figures atop the pulpit beside it are the four doctors of the Roman Catholic church: Sts Ambrose, Gregory, Jerome and Augustine. The next two altars on the right- and left-hand sides are dedicated to Benedict and his twin sister, Scholastica; the last pair, a baptismal font and the Lourdes Altar, date from 1896 and 1900 respectively.

Stuhlhof also carved the magnificent choir rail above the porch and the organ with all the cherubs. The frescoes on the ceilings by Bertalan Székely, Lajos Deák-Ébner and Károly Lotz were painted in 1889, when the church was restored.

Admission includes entry to the attached Benedictine Abbey Museum.

Benedictine Abbey Museum   MUSEUM
(Bencés Ápátsági Múzeum; Map p196; András tér 1; adult/concession incl Abbey Church 1000/700Ft; ☻9am-6pm Apr-Sep, 10am-5pm Oct, 10am-3pm Nov-Mar) This museum, next door to the Abbey Church in the former Benedictine monastery, is entered from the church crypt. It features exhibits on Lake Balaton, liturgical vestments, religious artefacts, a handful of manuscripts and a history of King Andrew. A room is devoted to the appealing pastoral sketches by contemporary artist Dudás Jenő and in the gift shop you can buy four types of beer brewed by the abbey.

Lavender House   GALLERY
(Levendula Ház; Map p196; ☑87-538 033; www.levendulahaz.eu/; Tihany Major utca 67; adult/concession/3-14yr 1000/800/500Ft; ☻9am-7pm Jun-Aug, 9am-5pm May, 10am-5pm Sep, to 4pm Oct, Mar & Apr, to 3pm Sat & Sun Nov-Feb) On the shores of a little lake, this excellent visitor centre introduces you to the history and people of the Tihany peninsula – from its raging volcanic origins to present-day lavender production. There are hands-on activities for kids, as well as a maze and boardwalk overlooking the lake.

Visszhang-hegy   HILL
(Echo Hill; Map p196; Pisky sétány) You'll find Visszhang-hegy at the end of Pisky sétány. At one time, up to 15 syllables of anything shouted in the direction of the Abbey Church would bounce back but, alas, because of building in the area (and perhaps climatic changes) you'll be lucky to get three syllables nowadays. From Visszhang-hegy you can descend Garay utca and Váralja utca to the Inner Harbour and a small beach, or continue on to the hiking trails that pass this way.

Open-air Folk Museum   MUSEUM
(Szabadtéri Néprajzi Múzeum; Map p196; Pisky sétány 10; adult/concession 600/400Ft; ☻10am-6pm May-Sep) This cluster of folk houses with thick thatch roofs have been turned into a small outdoor museum.

🏃 Activities

Tihany is a popular recreational area with beaches on its eastern and western coasts and a big resort complex at its southern tip, where you can rent windsurfing and stand-up paddleboarding equipment. Designated cycling trails criss-cross the peninsula, and two-wheeled exploration is a fun thing to do.

★ Sail & Surf   WATER SPORTS
(Map p196; ☑06 30 227 8927; www.wind99.com; Rév utca 3, Club Tihany; windsurfer/stand-up paddleboard hire per hr €11/10, windsurfing lessons per hr €31; ☻8am-6pm May–mid-Oct) An excellent sailing and windsurfing centre offering private windsurfing lessons, along with stand-up paddleboard and windsurfer hire. The equipment is in top condition. Good English spoken.

Lavender Trail   HIKING
(Purple Trail) The longest of Tihany's three trails runs from the main street to the shore of Belső-tő Lake before skirting it, and then meanders northwest through the fields to Külső-tő Lake. Add an extra little loop by scaling the 232m-high Csúcs-hegy (Csúcs Hill), for panoramic Balaton views. Further north, the trail joins the main road, leading back to Tihany.

Legend Trail   HIKING
(Red Trail) The second-longest of the three trail loops that start in Tihany village, Red Trail starts at the church and meanders down to the ferry landing before heading up the coast and rising back to the village again.

Echo Trail   HIKING
(Green Trail) Hiking is one of Tihany's main attractions, and this is the smallest of the three colour-coded trail loops, taking in just the village. Following the Green Trail northeast of the village centre for an hour will bring you to the Russian Well (Orosz-kút) and the ruins of the Old Castle (Óvár) at 219m, where Russian Orthodox monks, brought to Tihany by Andrew I, hollowed out cells in the soft basalt walls.

The 232m-high Csúcs-hegy (Csúcs Hill), with panoramic views of Lake Balaton, is about two hours west of the church via the Red Trail. From here you can join up with the Yellow Trail originating in Tihanyi-rév,

Tihany

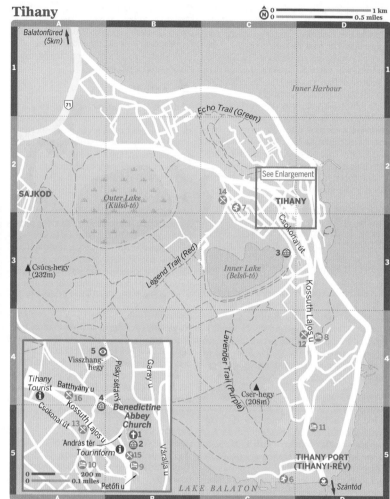

which will lead you north to the ruins of the 13th-century Apáti Church (Ápáti templom) and to Rte 71. From the church, it's possible to follow the Yellow Trail south till it crosses the Blue Trail near Aranyház, a series of geyser cones formed by warm-water springs and resembling (somewhat) a 'Golden Horse'. From here, you can take the Blue Trail north to the Inner Lake and on to the town centre.

Tihany Lovasudvar   HORSE RIDING
(Map p196; ☏ 06 20 231 3431; Kiserdőtelepi utca 10; 3hr rides 6000Ft; ☺ 8am-7.30pm Apr-Oct)

Horses are available for hire at the Tihany Lovasudvar, just north of the Inner Lake.

🛏 Sleeping

Accommodation in Tihany is somewhat limited and can be pricey during the summer. That said, it's a more appealing place to stay than nearby Balatonfüred. Many hotels are closed between mid-October or November and March or April. For private rooms (from 10,000Ft), consult Tihany Tourist (p198) or Tourinform (p198) or look for *Zimmer frei* (room for rent) signs.

Tihany

Centrum Vendégház GUESTHOUSE **$$**
(Map p196; ☑ 06 30 997 8271; www.centrum vendeghaz.hu; Petőfi utca 13; d 13,500-15,000Ft, tr/apt 18,000/21,000Ft; ❄) This family-run guesthouse offers simple but tastefully decorated rooms with polished wood floors in thatched houses a short hop from the main sights.

Kántás Panzió GUESTHOUSE **$$**
(Map p196; ☑ 87-448 072; www.kantas-panzio-tihany.hu; Csokonai út 49; r €46-52; ❄ ⚡) Kántás is an example of Tihany's cheaper accommodation; it's small and comfortable enough, with pleasant attic rooms (pricier ones have a balcony) above a restaurant. Views are across the Inner Lake.

⭐ **Kora Panzió** B&B **$$**
(Map p196; ☑ 06 20 944 3982; www.tihany kora.hu; Halász utca 56; r €60-80; ❄ ⚡ ⚒) A five-minute walk from the waterfront, this delightful B&B is drowning in flowers just off the side of the road towards Tihany village. The rooms are spotless, quiet and comfortable, there's a small pool for fending off the summer heat and the owners are delightful. Good English spoken and maps of Tihany provided.

Adler Hotel BOUTIQUE HOTEL **$$$**
(Map p196; ☑ 87-538 000; www.adler-tihany. hu; Felsőkopaszhegyi utca 1/a; r €65-72; apt €115; ❄ ⚡ ⚒) Large, whitewashed rooms; the more expensive come with balconies. The two-bedroom apartments are good for families and perks include a jacuzzi, sauna and restaurant (half-board available).

✗ Eating

Like the hotels, most restaurants close between mid-October or November and March or April. Most restaurants are also geared towards visitors and quality varies. That said, there are a couple of really good options.

⭐ **Levendula** ICE CREAM **$**
(Map p196; Kossuth Lajos utca 31; scoops 350Ft; ◷ 11am-6pm Mon-Fri, to 7pm Sat & Sun) The fame of 'Lavender' is spreading far and wide; there are four branches in Budapest already. Expect such interesting flavours as lavender and dark chocolate, Roquefort, gingerbread, Champagne, rose and many others. Dairy- and gluten-free available.

Rege Cukrászda CAFE **$**
(Map p196; ☑ 06 30 901 2077; www.regecukrász-da.hu; Kossuth Lajos utca 22; cakes from 400Ft; ◷ 10am-8pm Tue-Sun) From its high vantage point near the Benedictine Abbey Museum, this cafe has an unsurpassed view of Balaton. On a sunny day, there's no better place to enjoy coffee, cake and the sparkling lake.

⭐ **Régi Idők Udvara**
Skanzen és Étterem HUNGARIAN **$$**
(Map p196; ☑ 06 70 284 6705; http://tihanyi-etterem.tihanyinfo.com/; Batthyány utca 3; mains 1600-3200Ft; ◷ 11am-11pm) Part enchanted garden, part ethnography museum with farming implements all over the place, Tihany's best restaurant is as much a place to linger over a beer brewed on the premises as it is to eat. Though we urge you to eat: the smoked trout, the goose liver with egg barley and the spare ribs are all delicious, and the portions are generous.

Miska Pince Csárda   HUNGARIAN $$

(Map p196; ☑ 06 30 929 7350; www.miskacsarda.
hu; Kiserdőtelepi utca; mains 1900-2900Ft; ⊙ 11am-
11pm) Miska Pince is a cute thatch-roof cottage down near the banks of the Inner Lake.
It serves big portions of Hungarian cuisine
(we like the fisherman's soup and the venison
stew with gnocchi), and its secluded, sunny
terrace is just the place to escape the madding crowds up near the church.

Ferenc Pince   HUNGARIAN $$

(Map p196; ☑ 87-448 575; www.ferencpince.hu;
Cserhegy 9; mains from 2800Ft; ⊙ noon-11pm
Wed-Mon) Not only does the chef cook up a
Hungarian storm in the kitchen here, but
some of Tihany's best wine is served by the
very people who produce the stuff. The lovely open terrace offers expansive views of the
lake. Ferenc Pince is just under 2km south
of the Abbey Church. Our only quibble is the
lack of consistency, food-wise.

❶ Information

Tihany Tourist (Map p196; ☑ 87-448 481;
www.tihanytourist.hu; Kossuth Lajos utca
11; ⊙ 9am-6pm Jun-Aug, to 5pm May & Sep,
10am-4pm Apr & Oct) Organises accommodation and local tours.

Tourinform (Map p196; ☑ 87-448 804; www.
tihany.hu; Kossuth Lajos utca 20; ⊙ 9am-7pm
Mon-Fri, 10am-6pm Sat & Sun mid-Jun–mid-
Sep, 10am-4pm Mon-Fri mid-Sep–mid-Jun)
Marginally helpful main tourist office.

❶ Getting There & Away

Buses cover the 14km from Balatonfüred's bus
and train stations to and from Tihany up to 15
times daily (310Ft, 30 minutes). The bus stops
at both ferry landings before climbing to Tihany
village.

The Inner Harbour (Belső kikötő), where
ferries to/from Balatonfüred and Siófok dock,
is below the village. Tihany Port (Tihanyi-rév),
to the southwest at the tip of the peninsula, is
Tihany's recreational area. The Balaton passenger ferries (p194) from Balatonfüred and
elsewhere stop at Tihany from early April to
early October. Catch them at the Inner Harbour
ferry pier or at Tihanyi-rév.

❶ Getting Around

If you arrive by boat and you aren't keen to huff
it up the hill to the 80m-high village, a dinky,
wheeled **tourist train** (multiple rides adult/con-
cession 1000/600Ft, single ride 400/200Ft)
runs between the ferry terminal and the Abbey
Church (p194), every 30 minutes from May to
September.

Keszthely

☑ 83 / POP 19,910

Keszthely, a town of gently crumbling grand
town houses perched at the very western end
of Lake Balaton, is hands down one of the
loveliest spots to stay, far removed from the
tourist hot spots on the lake. You can dip in its
small, shallow beaches by day, absorb its lively
yet relaxed ambience by night and get a dose
of culture by popping into its handful of museums and admiring its historical buildings.
Whatever you do, don't miss the Festetics Palace, a lavish baroque home fit for royalty.

History

The Romans built a fort at Valcum (now
Fenékpuszta), around 5km to the south, and
their road north to the colonies at Sopron
and Szombathely is today's Kossuth Lajos
utca. The town's former fortified monastery
and Franciscan church on Fő tér were strong
enough to repel the Turks in the 16th century.

In the middle of the 18th century, Keszthely and its surrounds (including Hévíz)
came into the possession of the Festetics
family, who were progressives and re-
formers, very much in the tradition of the
Széchenyis. In fact, Count György Festetics
(1755–1819), who founded Europe's first agricultural college, the Georgikon, here in 1797,
was an uncle of István Széchenyi.

◉ Sights

Keszthely has a clutch of seven niche museums: the Erotic Panoptikum (p199), Toy
Museum (p199), Doll Museum (p199)
and more. Admission to each one costs from
500Ft but a combined ticket to all seven
costs 2500Ft.

If you're looking to visit the Festetics
Palace there are various combinations of
tickets you can purchase. A combined ticket (4200Ft) gives you access to the Palace,
Coach Museum (p201), Amazon House,
Hunting Museum, Model Railway Museum
(p201), Palm House and Aquarium. Cheaper combos are available and are worthwhile
if you want to see more than two attractions.

★ **Festetics Palace**   PALACE

(Festetics Kastély; Map p200; ☑ 83-312 194; www.
helikonkastely.hu; Kastély utca 1; Palace & Coach
Museum adult/6-26yr 2500/1250Ft; ⊙ 9am-6pm)
The glimmering white, 100-room Festetics
Palace was begun in 1745; the two wings were
extended out from the original building 150

years later. Some 18 splendid rooms in the baroque south wing are now part of the Helikon Palace Museum, as is the palace's greatest treasure, the Helikon Library, with its 100,000 volumes and splendid carved furniture.

Many of the decorative arts in the gilt salons were imported from England in the mid-1800s. The museum's rooms, each in a different colour scheme, are full of portraits, bric-a-brac and furniture, much of it brought from England by Mary Hamilton, a duchess who married one of the Festetics men in the 1860s. The library is known for its enormous collection of books, but just as impressive is the golden oak shelving and furniture carved in 1801 by local craftsman János Kerbl. Also worth noting are the Louis XIV Salon with stunning marquetry, the mirrored dining hall, the Long Gallery with paintings, the oaken staircase and the private chapel (1804).

Erotic Panoptikum   MUSEUM

(Map p200; ☑83-318 855; www.szexpanoptikum. hu; Kossuth Lajos utca 10; over-18s 800Ft; ☺9am-6pm) Full disclosure: this is an X-rated wax museum. Kind of tacky – yes. Fascinating – absolutely. The tiny subterranean space brings to 'life' lust and sex scenes from illustrated books about Renaissance erotic fiction by the likes of Voltaire, Rousseau and others. Think wax figures of women in bodices with their hooped skirts hiked up over their knees having kinky intercourse, women performing cunnilingus on women, and acrobatic orgies with extraordinarily real-looking private parts on vivid display.

It's a bit like seeing an up-close freeze-frame of a porn film with actors dressed up in medieval garb. Beyond the, er, action scenes, check out the sketches and paintings of erotica gracing the walls or the elaborate terracotta penis sculpture.

Toy Museum   MUSEUM

(Map p200; ☑83-318 855; www.szexpanoptikum. hu; Bakacs utca; 500Ft; ☺9am-6pm) Depending on what generation you're from, the exhibits at this wonderful place will either make you smile in remembrance or gawp in fascination. Ye olde prams nailed to the ceiling, creepy bug-eyed dolls, legions of teddy bears, Barbies, model cars and trains, doll's houses and old board games await. Look out for miniature washing machines and sewing machines, designed to prepare little girls for adulthood drudgery, and *Spitting Image*-style Margaret Thatcher and Ronald Reagan.

Doll Museum   MUSEUM

(Map p200; ☑83-318 855; www.szexpanopti kum.hu; Bakacs utca; 500Ft; ☺9am-6pm) This surprisingly absorbing museum showcases two floors' worth of dolls dressed in folk costumes from all parts of Hungary. On the ground floor, there's also a remarkable wooden seat carved from the roots of a yew tree (rather like a wooden version of the Iron Throne from *Game of Thrones*). On the top floor you'll find models of traditional houses and ornate doorways.

Georgikon Farm Museum   MUSEUM

(Georgikon Majormúzeum; Map p200; ☑83-311 563; www.elmenygazdasag.hu; Bercsényi Miklós utca 67; adult/concession 900/450Ft; ☺9am-5pm Tue-Sat Jun-Aug, to 4pm Mon-Fri Apr & Oct-Nov, to 5pm Mon-Sat May & Sep) Housed in several early-19th-century buildings of what was the Georgikon's experimental farm, this is the perfect museum for lovers of early industrial farming tools and farming techniques, with exhibits divided into separate trade and agriculture sections. Learn about the history of viniculture in the Balaton region and traditional farm trades such as those performed by wagon builders, wheelwrights and coopers. Highlights include 19th-cenury blacksmith tools and an enormous antique steam plough.

Fő tér   SQUARE

(Map p200) Fő tér, Kezthely's colourful main square, received a facelift in 2012 – the result is a traffic-free, pedestrian-friendly expanse of white cobblestone surrounded by lovely buildings, including the late-baroque Town Hall on the northern side, the Trinity Column (1770) in the centre and a former Franciscan church (Ferences templom; Map p200; Fő tér; ☺9am-6pm) in the park to the south.

Balaton Museum   MUSEUM

(Map p200; ☑83-312 351; www.balatonimuzeum. hu; Múzeum utca 2; adult/concession 900/450Ft; ☺9am-6pm) The Balaton Museum was purpose-built in 1928 and its permanent exhibits focus on the life and history of Lake Balaton. The Balaton aquarium showcases the lake's fish, while several interconnected rooms detail lake life and culture. Highlights include the exhibit on how bathing culture has evolved over the years (don't miss the 19th-century bathing suits!) and János Halápy's expressive paintings of Lake Balaton life – he is known for capturing the vibrant light and colours of the region.

Keszthely

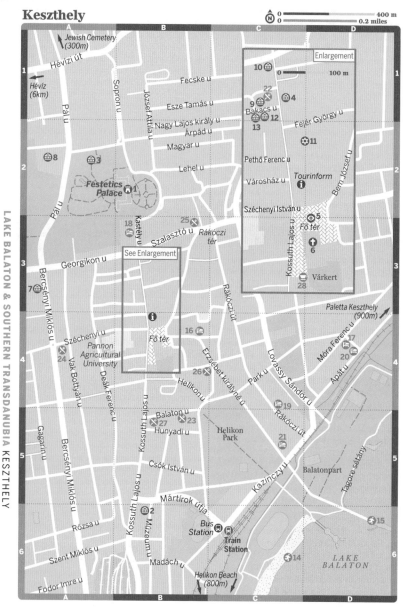

Snail Parliament   MUSEUM
(Map p200; ☏83-318 855; www.szexpanoptikum.
hu; Bakacs utca; 500Ft; ⊗9am-6pm) What do
you get when you take one woman's obsession, 14 years of loving labour, and 4.5 million snail shells? A 7m by 2.5m scale model

of Budapest's Parliament, that's what. While
it isn't quite the 'eighth Wonder of the World'
it's touted to be, the attention to detail is remarkable. The actual parliament building
took marginally longer to build: 17 years.

Keszthely

Synagogue SYNAGOGUE
(Map p200; Kossuth Lajos utca 20; ⊙5-6pm Fri) Before WWII Keszthely's Jewish community numbered 1000; at the end of the war it had dropped to 170. Today less than 40 Jews live in the town and attend services at the 18th-century baroque synagogue, located in a quiet courtyard off Kossuth Lajos utca (enter through the arched passageway just south of Fejér György utca). Visits to the synagogue and the Biblical Plant Garden are only possible during service times.

Jewish Cemetery CEMETERY
(Goldmark karoly utca 33; ⊙10am-4pm Sun-Fri) In addition to the synagogue (p201), evidence of the town's Jewish community can be found at the largely forgotten Jewish cemetery, north of the palace.

Torture Museum MUSEUM
(Map p200; 🖉83-318 855; www.szexpano ptikum.hu; Bakacs utca; 500Ft; ⊙9am-6pm) Complete with buckets of fake blood and distressed-looking mannequins demonstrating various forms of medieval torture, this small museum also features Hungary's most bloodthirsty monarch, Erzsébet, bathing in the blood of virgins.

Model Railway Museum MUSEUM
(Map p200; 🖉83-312 190; Pál utca; 1 museum adult/concession 1100/550Ft, combined tickets

1600/800Ft; ⊙9am-6pm) On the top floor of a former military building, this grin-inducing museum exhibits one of the world's largest mountain railway layouts. Trains whiz round a 40m-long railway network straight out of a picture book: one section contains the historic Vienna to Trieste train line and an awe-inducing section of Austrian mountains complete with tunnels; another goes through Nuremberg and a snow-covered rendition of the Black Forest. Further along are Lake Balaton towns, including amazingly detailed versions of their train stations.

Coach Museum MUSEUM
(Hintómúzeum; Map p200; 🖉83-314 194; www. helikonkastely.hu; Pál utca; incl in admission to Festetics Palace; ⊙9am-6pm) Behind Festetics Palace (p198) in a separate building is the Coach Museum, which is filled with coaches and sleighs fit for royalty. You may not know the difference between a gala coupe and a baroque hunting coach, but you will by the time you leave here.

Museum of Historical Wax Figures MUSEUM
(Historical Panoptikum; Map p200; 🖉83-318 855; www.szexpanoptikum.hu; Bekacs utca; 500Ft; ⊙9am-6pm) This is a surprisingly fun way to acquaint yourself with the who's who of Hungary's rulers, poets, clerics and military commanders. The eclectic collection includes Árpád, the leader of the Hungarian tribes in

the 9th and 10th centuries; St Stephen, Hungary's first king; St Margaret; János Hunyadi, the defeater of the Turks; and György Dózsa, who led a peasant revolt and was 'crowned' for his efforts on a red-hot throne. A parade of nun dolls awaits near the entrance.

Nostalgia Museum
MUSEUM
(Map p200; ☑ 83-318 855; www.szexpanoptikum. hu; Kossuth Lajos utca 1; adult/5-14yr 500/400Ft; ⊙9am-6pm) This treasure trove of ordinary objects ranging from 1800s antiques to 'retro' items is fun to poke around in, and before you know it, an hour has flown by. You will find anything from old barbershop tools, antique typewriters, Communist banners and vintage cameras to objects made from WWII cartridges, a reconstructed 1940s doctor's surgery, kerosene bicycle lamps and an array of phallic glassware.

Activities

The 210km Balaton cycle path passes through Keszthely, and a 4km path connects the town with Hévíz (home to Europe's largest thermal lake). Rent bicycles from Green-Zone (☑ 83-315 463; www.greenzonekeszthely.hu; Rákóczi utca 15; 3hr/6hr/1 day 800/1200/2000Ft; ⊙9am-6pm Mon-Fri, to 1pm Sat).

Helikon Beach
BEACH
(Helikon Strand; Map p200; adult/concession 500/350Ft; ⊙8am-7pm May–mid-Sep) Reedy Helikon Beach, north of City Beach, is good for swimming and sunbathing. It has a unique view of both the north and south shores of the lake.

City Beach
BEACH
(Városi Strand; Map p200; adult/concession 800/400Ft; ⊙8am-7pm May–mid-Sep) City Beach is OK for swimming or sunbathing, good for kids and close to the ferry pier. There's a pool with water slides, and a windsurfing and kitesurfing school open in summer. Windsurfing gear is available for rent (800Ft per hour).

Pleasure Cruise
CRUISE
(Map p200; ☑ 83-312 093; www.balatonihajozas. hu; ⊙adult/concession 1800/800Ft) From late April to early October you can take a one-hour pleasure cruise on the lake on Fridays and Saturdays.

Festivals & Events

Keszthelyfest
MUSIC
(http://keszthelyfest.balatonszinhaz.hu; ⊙Jul) A three-day musical extravaganza in the beginning of July, featuring bands from around Hungary, jazz performances and kids' events.

Wine Festival
WINE
(Festetics Palace, Music Pavilion; ⊙late Aug) Every summer brings the lovely two-day Wine Festival where local winemakers, restaurants and food purveyors sell their wares and bands perform anything from rock to pop to jazz concerts. There's a craft fair and children's events, too.

Sleeping

Tourinform (p204) can help find you find a private room if you're stuck.

Villa Sissy
PENSION $
(Map p200; ☑ 83-315 394; www.villasissy.hu; Erzsébet királyné utca 70; r/apt 5000/8000Ft; ☎) Sweet, quiet little pension in an old villa steps across from leafy Helikon Park. Simple rooms vary considerably: some have wood floors and stained-glass French doors, others dull carpet, but all feature small refrigerators. Some share bathrooms. The apartments are good value for families; the kitchen is shared.

★ Ilona Kis Kastély Panzió
PENSION $$
(Map p200; ☑ 83-312 514; Móra Ferenc utca 22; s/d/apt 9400/12,130/16,980Ft; ❈☎) Its pointy turrets covered in creepers, this delightful pension resembles a miniature castle. The rooms might be on the compact side, but some have balconies, while the apartments are positively spacious. A generous, varied breakfast is included. What sets this place apart is the attitude of its owners, who can't do enough to make their guests feel welcome.

Silatti Panzió
B&B $$
(Map p200; ☑ 06 20 217 1645; www.silatti.hu; Rákóczi út 72; r 16,350Ft; ☎⛵) This quiet, centrally located guesthouse offers a cluster of cosy rooms that vary in size; stay in a spacious one on the ground floor, or roost in the attic. There's a small outdoor pool and sauna, and breakfast is served on a sunny patio.

Párizsi Udvar
INN $$
(Map p200; ☑ 83-311 202; parizsiudvar@ freemail.hu; Kastély utca 5; d/tr/apt from 12,000/15,600/18,000Ft; ☎) There's no closer accommodation to the Festetics Palace than the 'Parisian Courtyard'. Rooms are a little too big to be cosy, but they're colourful, well kept and look on to a sunny and very leafy inner courtyard (a corner of which is taken over by a decent daytime restaurant and beer garden).

HÉVÍZ THERMAL LAKE
··

Fed by 80 million litres of thermal water daily, **Gyógy-tó** (Hévíz Thermal Lake; ☑83-342 830; www.spaheviz.hu; Dr Schulhof Vilmos sétány 1; 3hr/4hr/whole day 2600/3000/4500Ft; ◷8am-7pm Jun-Aug, 9am-6pm May & Sep, 9am-5.30pm Apr & Oct, 9am-5pm Mar & Nov-Feb) in Hévíz, 8km northwest of Keszthely, is an astonishing sight. The temperature averages 33°C and never drops below 22°C in winter, allowing bathing even when there's ice on the fir trees of the surrounding Park Wood. Just float, or indulge in every kind of thermal remedy, massage and scrub imaginable at the on-site indoor spa.

A covered bridge leads to the thermal lake's fin-de-siècle central pavilion, which contains a small buffet, sun chairs, showers, changing rooms and steps down into the lake. Catwalks and piers fan out from the central pavilion to sun decks and a second pavilion where massage treatments are offered. You can swim protected beneath the pavilions and piers or swim out into the lake and rest on wooden planks secured to the lake's bottom. There are some piers along the shore for sunbathing as well.

Buses bound for Hévíz (250Ft, 15 minutes) leave Keszthely every 30 minutes throughout the day.

Tokajer Wellness Panzió GUESTHOUSE **$$**
(Map p200; ☑83-319 875; www.pensiontoka jer.hu; Apát utca 21; r/f from 13,900/22,700Ft; ✴⊛⊛) Spread over three three-storey buildings in a quiet area of town, Tokajer has slightly dated rooms, but they're spacious and have balconies. Added extras include three pools, free use of bicycles and a fitness room. Wellness centre perks are the steam room, salt room, hot tub and Finnish and infra-red saunas.

Bacchus HOTEL **$$$**
(Map p200; ☑83-314 096; www.bacchushotel.hu; Erzsébet királyné útja 18; s/apt 13,300/26,000Ft, d 16,400-21,400Ft; ✴⊛) Bacchus' central position and immaculate rooms – each named after a grape variety – make it a popular choice with travellers. The 26 rooms, some with terraces, are simple but inviting with solid wood furnishings. Equally pleasing is its atmospheric cellar, which includes a lovely restaurant (p204) that has wine tastings. Bacchus indeed. The service, however, can be *Fawlty Towers*-esque on occasion.

✖ Eating

Margaréta HUNGARIAN **$**
(Map p200; ☑83-314 882; Bercsényi Miklós utca 60; mains 1990-3290Ft; ◷11am-10pm) Ask locals where they like to eat and one answer dominates: Margaréta. It's no beauty, but the wraparound porch and hidden backyard terrace heave in the warmer months, and the small interior packs them in the rest of the year. Food sticks to basic but hearty Hungarian staples. Weekday set lunches are a snip at 750Ft to 890Ft.

Korzó Café CAFE **$**
(Map p200; ☑83-311 785; Kossuth Lajos utca 7; cakes 390Ft; ◷9am-7pm) Korzó is one of the few cafes worthy of your attention on pedestrian Kossuth Lajos utca. It's a simple place with street seating, but the cakes are divine and the music thankfully not too intrusive.

Pizzeria Donatello PIZZA **$**
(Map p200; ☑83-315 989; www.donatellopizze ria.hu; Balaton utca 1; pizza 690-1230Ft; ☑) A student favourite that still manages to attract families and diners wanting a quick bite – it's always bustling. Pizzas are standard, though extra-crispy and topped with fresh vegetables and homemade sauce.

Park Vendéglő HUNGARIAN **$**
(Map p200; ☑83-311 654; Vörösmarty utca 1/a; mains 1590-3690Ft) The service can be a little haphazard here, but there's a pleasant garden terrace. Park serves the likes of pork medallions with garlic sauce and paprika catfish; quantity tends to trump quality. If at the end you can fit in a Drunken Monk, the house dessert, you're doing better than us.

Oasis VEGETARIAN **$**
(Map p200; ☑83-311 023; Rákóczi tér 3; meals from 600Ft; ◷11am-4pm Mon-Fri) This small vegetarian restaurant down the hill from the palace has buckets of good energy and healthy (if not terribly inspiring) daily menus during the midweek lunch-hour rush.

★Paletta Keszthely BISTRO **$$**
(☑06 70 431 7413; www.facebook.com/Palet taKeszthely; Libás Strand; mains 1700-3300Ft; ◷9am-11pm May-mid-Oct) On a summer

terrace by the marina, this appealing spot mixes international fare such as bouillabaisse and its signature Basalt Burger. The dishes on the succinct menu are well-executed and the staff are friendly and prompt.

Bacchus
HUNGARIAN $$

(Map p200; ☑83-378 566; www.bacchushotel.hu; Erzsébet királyné utca 18; mains 1890-2990Ft; ⊙11am-11pm) Oenophiles and foodies should head straight to this restaurant and wine mecca, which serves simple but lovingly prepared Hungarian fare including local faves like fish from Lake Balaton (the catfish with paprika curd-cheese pasta is wonderful). The subterranean restaurant's chunky furniture is made from old wine barrels and presses, while the vaulted cellar is *the* place for wine tastings.

Lakoma Étterem
HUNGARIAN $$

(Map p200; ☑83-313 129; Balaton utca 9; mains 1990-3200Ft; ⊙11am-10pm; ☑) With a good vegetarian and fish selection (trout with almonds, grilled perch-pike), meaty stews and roasts, plus a back garden that transforms itself into a convivial dining area in the summer months, it's hard to go wrong with Lakoma.

🍷 Drinking & Nightlife

The nightlife scene consists almost exclusively of tacky strip bars. Wine tastings are held in the Festetics Palace (p198) cellars in summer.

Pelso Café
CAFE

(Map p200; ☑83-315 415; Kossuth Lajos utca 38; ⊙8am-8pm; 🛜) This modern two-level cafe boasts a fantastic terrace overlooking the southern end of the main square. It does decent cakes, teas from around the world, and coffee concoctions (coffee and cake from

500Ft). But we like it best as a prime spot for an al fresco sundowner – the wine and beer list is small, but the vantage point is lovely.

ℹ Information

OTP bank (Kossuth Lajos utca 38) has an ATM.

Tourinform (Map p200; ☑83-314 144; www.keszthely.hu; Kossuth Lajos utca 30; ⊙9am-7pm mid-Jun–Aug, to 5pm Mon-Fri & to noon Sat Sep–mid-Jun) An excellent source of information on Keszthely and the west Balaton area. Brochures in English are available, and English is spoken. Bicycles for rent, too.

www.welovebalaton.hu A handy listings website.

ℹ Getting There & Away

AIR

Hévíz Balaton Airport (SOB; ☑83-200 304; www.hevizairport.com; Repülőtér 1, Sármellék), 15km southwest of Keszthely, serves Berlin, Dresden, Düsseldorf, Erfurt, Frankfurt, Hamburg, Leipzig and Moscow between April and November.

BusExpress (☑06 30 288 2320, 83-777 088; www.busexpress.hu) offers door-to-door services from the airport to Keszthely from €7 per person.

BUS

Keszthely is well served by buses. The main bus station is next to the train station, off Mártírok útja. Some buses, including those to Hévíz and Sümeg, can be boarded at the bus stops in front of the Franciscan church (p199) on Fő tér.

TRAIN

Keszthely has train links to Budapest and Balatonfüred. Most trains to/from Budapest go to Budapest Déli station, but occasionally they go to Budapest Keleti.

TRAINS FROM KESZTHELY

DESTINATION	PRICE	DURATION	KM	FREQUENCY
Balatonfüred	1490Ft (change at Tapolca required)	1½-2½hr	77	10 daily
Budapest	3705Ft	3hr	190	7 daily

BUSES FROM KESZTHELY

DESTINATION	PRICE	DURATION	KM	FREQUENCY
Budapest	3410Ft	2½-4hr	190	up to 9 daily
Hévíz	250Ft	15min	8	every 30 minutes
Pécs	2830Ft	3½hr	152	up to 4 daily
Veszprém	1490Ft	1¾hr	77	hourly

ⓘ Getting Around

Buses run from the train and bus stations to the **Franciscan church** (p199) on Fő tér, but unless there's one waiting on your arrival it's just as easy to make the 10-minute walk.

Taxi (☏ 06 30 777 5444; www.keszthelytaxi. hu) One of several taxi companies.

SOUTHERN TRANSDANUBIA

Pécs

⌨ 72 / POP 145,347

Blessed with a mild climate, an illustrious past and a number of fine museums and monuments, Pécs is one of the most pleasant and interesting cities to visit in Hungary. For its handful of universities, the nearby Mecsek Hills and the lively nightlife, many travellers put it second only to Budapest on their Hungarian 'must-see' list.

Lying equidistant from the Danube to the east and the Dráva to the south on a plain sheltered from the northern winds by the Mecsek Hills, Pécs enjoys a microclimate that lengthens the summer and is ideal for viticulture and fruit production, especially almonds. A fine time to visit is during a warm *indián nyár* (Indian summer), when the light seems to take on a special quality.

History

The Romans may have settled here for the region's fertile soil and abundant water, but it's more likely that they were sold by the protection offered by the Mecsek Hills. They called their settlement Sophianae, and it quickly grew into the commercial and administrative centre of Lower Pannonia. The Romans brought Christianity with them, and reminders of that can be seen in the early clover-shaped chapels unearthed here.

Pécs' importance grew in the Middle Ages, when it was known as Quinque Ecclesiae after the five churches dotting the town; it is still called just that – Fünfkirchen – in German. King Stephen founded a bishopric here in 1009, the town was a major stop along the trade route to Byzantium and Hungary's first university opened here in 1367. The 15th-century bishop Janus Pannonius, who wrote some of Europe's most celebrated Renaissance poetry in Latin, made Pécs his home.

The city walls – a large portion of which still stand – were in such poor condition in the 16th century that the Turks took the city with virtually no resistance in 1543. The occupiers moved the local populace out and turned Pécs into their own administrative and cultural centre. When the Turks were expelled almost 150 years later, Pécs was virtually abandoned, but still standing were monumental souvenirs that now count as the most important Turkish structures in the country.

The resumption of wine production by German and Bohemian immigrants and the discovery of coal in the 18th century spurred Pécs' development. The manufacture of luxury goods (gloves, Zsolnay porcelain, Angster organs, Pannonvin sparkling wine) would come later.

◉ Sights

Pécs has a considerable wealth of museums, ranging from contemporary art and fine porcelain to ethnography. The most important museums are concentrated along Káptalan utca, all in listed buildings, running east from Dóm tér to Hunyadi János út. The other major concentration of attractions lies east of Old Town, in the Zsolnay Cultural Quarter.

If you plan to visit more than two or three museums in Pécs purchase the Museum Pass (adult/student 4000/2000Ft), which gives you entry to the Csontváry Museum (p206), Zsolnay Porcelain Museum (p206), Victor Vasarely Museum (p206), Ethnographic Museum (p209), Modern Hungarian Gallery (p206) and Historical Museum (p209). The pass is valid for one day and can be purchased at any of the participating museums.

★**Széchenyi tér**   SQUARE
(Map p207) Surrounded by largely baroque buildings, Pécs' main square is the city's hub, great for people-watching. With the Mosque Church (p205) at the north end, the square is anchored by the Trinity Column in the centre. At the southern end the porcelain Zsolnay Fountain boasts a lustrous eosin glaze and four bull's heads; the fountain was donated to the city by the Zsolnay factory in 1892. The eosin creates an iridescent, metallic sheen that most people either love or hate.

★**Mosque Church**   MOSQUE
(Mecset templom; Map p207; ☏72-321 976; Hunyadi János út 4; adult/concession 1000/500Ft; ⊙9am-5pm Mon-Sat, 1-5pm Sun) The largest building from the time of the Turkish

LAKE BALATON & SOUTHERN TRANSDANUBIA PÉCS

occupation, the former Pasha Gazi Kassim Mosque (now the Inner Town Parish Church) dominates the main square in Pécs. Turks built the square mosque in the mid-16th century with the stones of the ruined Gothic Church of St Bertalan. The Catholics moved back in the early 18th century. The Islamic elements include windows with distinctive Turkish ogee arches, a *mihrab* (prayer niche), faded verses from the Koran and lovely geometric frescoes.

In the mazelike basement the remains of the six martyrs are interred, as well as the more recent remains of the city's more illustrious citizens. The painting above the gallery depicts the Turks' defeat. The mosque's minaret was pulled down in 1753 and replaced with a bell tower; bells are rung at noon and 7pm.

★ **Csontváry Museum**   MUSEUM
(Map p207; ☑72-310 544; www.jpm.hu; Janus Pannonius utca 11; adult/concession 1500/750Ft; ⊙10am-6pm Tue-Sun) This museum shows the major works of master 19th-century symbolist painter Tivadar Kosztka Csontváry (p125). Elements of postimpressionism and expressionism can be seen in such works as *East Station at Night* (1902), *Storm on the Great Hortobágy* (1903) and *Solitary Cedar* (1907). But arguably his best and most profound work is *Baalbeck* (1906), an artistic search for a larger identity through religious and historical themes.

★ **Victor Vasarely Museum**   MUSEUM
(Map p207; ☑06 30 873 8129; www.jpm.hu; Káptalan utca 3; adult/concession 1500/750Ft; ⊙10am-6pm Tue-Sun) This museum exhibits the work of the father of op art, Victor Vasarely. Symmetrical, largely abstract pieces are exhibited with clever illuminations that intensify the 3D experience and make it seem as if the works are bursting forth from the wall, though there have been arguments about whether or not this visual distortion represents what Vasarely had in mind. But overall the well-curated selection is evocative, eye-bending and just plain fun.

★ **Modern Hungarian Gallery**   MUSEUM
(Modern Magyar Képtár; Map p207; ☑72-891 328; www.jpm.hu; Papnövelde utca 5; adult/concession 700/350Ft; ⊙noon-6pm Tue-Sun) This gallery exhibits the art of Hungary from 1850 till today across several floors; works run the gamut from impressionist paintings to visually striking and even menacing contemporary installations. Pay special attention to the

works of Simon Hollósy, József Rippl-Rónai and Ödön Márffy. More abstract and constructionist artists include András Mengyár, Tamás Hencze, Béla Uitz and Gábor Dienes.

★ **Zsolnay Cultural Quarter**   NOTABLE BUILDING
(☑72-500 350; www.zskn.hu; adult/concession 4500/2500Ft; ⊙9am-6pm Apr-Oct, to 5pm Nov-Mar) The biggest project to evolve out of the 2010 Capital of Culture has been the Zsolnay Cultural Quarter, built on the grounds of the original Zsolnay Family Factory. Divided into four quarters (craftsman, family and children's, creative and university), it's a lovely place to stroll around. Highlights include the street of artisans' shops and the functioning Zsolnay Factory, which now takes up just a section of the grounds.

Zsolnay Factory   FACTORY
(Zsolnay utca 37, Zsolnay Cultural Quarter; adult/concession 1200/700Ft; ⊙10am-6pm Tue-Sun Apr-Oct, to 5pm Nov-Mar) Watch pieces of the legendary porcelain being created by hand.

Basilica of St Peter   CHURCH
(Szent Péter bazilika; Map p207; Dóm tér; adult/concession 1200/600Ft; ⊙9am-5pm Mon-Sat, 1-5pm Sun) The foundations of the neo-Romanesque four-towered basilica dedicated to St Peter date from the 11th century and the side chapels are from the 1300s, but the rest is as recent as 1881. The most interesting parts of the basilica's very ornate interior are the elevated central altar and four chapels under the towers and the crypt, the oldest part of the structure. Other highlights include the distinctive features of its four chapels.

The Chapel of Mary on the northwest side and the Chapel of the Sacred Heart to the northeast contain works by 19th-century painters Bertalan Székely and Károly Lotz. The Mór Chapel to the southeast has more works by Székely as well as magnificent pews. The Corpus Christi Chapel on the southwest side (enter from the outside) boasts a 16th-century red marble tabernacle, one of the best examples of Renaissance stonework in the country.

Zsolnay Porcelain Museum   MUSEUM
(Zsolnay Porcélan Múzeum; Map p207; ☑72-514 045; www.jpm.hu; Káptalan utca 2; adult/concession 1500/750Ft; ⊙10am-6pm Tue-Sun) The porcelain factory established in Pécs in 1853 was at the forefront of European art and design for more than half a century. Many of its majolica tiles were used to decorate

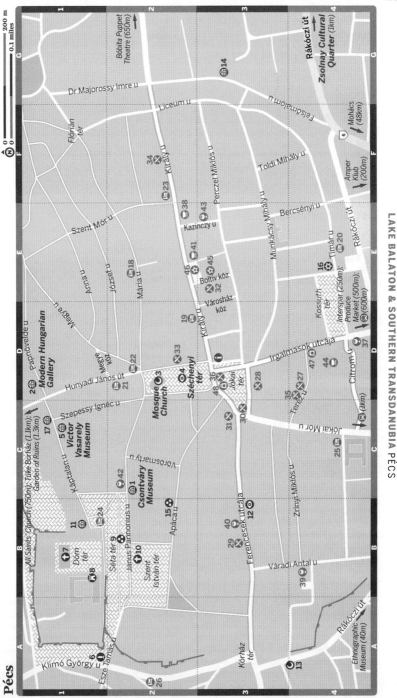

Pécs

Bóbita Puppet Theatre (650m)

Rákóczi út

Zsolnay Cultural Quarter (1km)

Dr Majorossy Imre u

Liceum u

Flórián tér

Felsőmalom u

Mohács (48km)

Amper Klub (200m)

Király u

Toldi Mihály u

Perczel Miklós u

Szent Mór u

Kazinczy u

Anna u

József u

Mária u

Bercsényi u

Munkácsy Mihály u

Megye u

Paprövelde u

Modern Hungarian Gallery

Hunyadi János út

Megye köz

Városház köz

Király u

Kossuth tér

Interspar (250m); Produce Market (500m); (600m)

Timár u

Rákóczi út

Szepessy Ignéc u

Mosque Church

Széchenyi tér

Jókai tér

Irgalmasok utcája

Citrom u

(1km)

Tüke Borház (1.1km); Garden of Ruins (1.3km)

Kaptalan u

Victor Vasarely Museum

Vörösmarty u

Teréz u

Jókai Mór u

All Saints' Church (750m)

Csontváry Museum

Janus Pannonius u

Apáca u

Ferencesek utcája

Zrínyi Miklós u

Dóm tér

Séta tér

Szent István tér

Váradi Antal u

Klimó György u

Esze Tamás u

Kórház tér

Rákóczi út

Ethnographic Museum (40m)

Pécs

buildings throughout the country, and it contributed to the establishment of a new pan-Hungarian style of architecture. Post-communism it's operational again, but contemporary Zsolnay can't hold a candle to the *chinoiserie* pieces of the late 19th century and the later art nouveau and art deco designs done in the lustrous eosin glaze.

Once the home to the Zsolnay family, several rooms here contain many original furnishings and personal effects.

All Saints' Church
CHURCH

(Mindenszentek temploma; ☑72-512 400; Tettye utca 14; ⊙ mass 7pm) The suburb of Budaiváros, to the northeast of Pécs' town centre, is where most Hungarians settled after the Turks banned them from living within the city walls; the centre of this community was the

All Saints' Church. The city's oldest church, it was originally built in the 12th century and reconstructed in Gothic style 200 years later.

All Saints was the only Christian church allowed in Pécs during the occupation and was shared by three sects – who fought bitterly for every square centimetre. Apparently it was the Muslim Turks who had to keep the peace among the Christians.

Synagogue
SYNAGOGUE

(Zsinagóga; Map p207; Kossuth tér; adult/concession 800/500Ft; ⊙ 10am-5pm Mon-Fri) Pécs' beautifully preserved 1869 Conservative synagogue is south of Széchenyi tér and faces renovated Kossuth tér. It was built in the Romantic style in 1869; a seven-page fact sheet, available in 11 languages, explains the history of the building and the city's Jewish population. Some 2700 of the city's Jews were deported to Nazi death camps in May 1944; only 150 Jews now live here. The pews hewn from Slavonian oak and the Angster organ are particularly fine.

Early Christian Tomb Chapel CHURCH
(Ókeresztény sírkápolna; Map p207; Szent István tér 12; adult/concession 600/300Ft; ⊙10am-6pm Tue-Sun) The early Christian tomb chapel, under renovation at research time, dates from about AD 350 and has frescoes of Adam and Eve and Daniel in the lion's den. Two Roman tomb (p209) sites are a little further south.

Hassan Jakovali Mosque MOSQUE
(Hassan Jakovali mecset; Map p207; Rákóczi út; adult/concession 1000/500Ft; ⊙10am-5.30pm Tue-Sun, closed for services 2.30-3.30pm Fri) Wedged between two modern buildings, this 16th-century mosque comes complete with a minaret and is still used for services. Inside there's a wonderful mirror room that reflects the floor tiles, plus an intact *mihrab* and a display on Ottoman history.

TV Tower TOWER
(☑72-336 900; www.tvtoronypecs.hu; adult/student/4-14yr 950/800/650Ft; ⊙9am-7pm Sun-Thu, to 8pm Fri & Sat) The 200m-tall TV tower sits atop the 535m summit of Misini hill. On a clear day, from the viewing platform you can see Pécs and its historic buildings, the ribbon of the Danube and the Mecsek Hills. Take bus 34.

Ferencesek utcája AREA
(Map p207) One of Pécs' most enjoyable pedestrian streets, Ferencesek utcája, runs east from Kórház tér to Széchenyi tér and boasts the magnificent baroque Franciscan Church dating from 1760 as well as a relic of the Turkish period: the rather low-key ruins of the 16th-century Pasha Memi Baths.

Cella Septichora Visitors Centre RUINS
(Cella Septichora látogató központ; Map p207; ☑72-224 755; www.pecsorokseg.hu; Janus Pannonius utca; adult/concession 1700/900Ft; ⊙10am-6pm Tue-Sun Apr-Oct, to 4pm Tue-Sun Nov-Mar) This Christian burial site illuminates a series of early Christian tombs that have been on Unesco's World Heritage list since 2000. The highlight is the so-called Jug Mausoleum, a 4th-century Roman tomb; its name comes from a painting of a large drinking vessel with vines.

Garden of Ruins SACRED SITE
(Romkert; Tettye) You can get a taste of the Mecsek Hills by walking northeast from the centre of Pécs to Tettye and the Garden of Ruins, what's left of a bishop's summer residence built early in the 16th century and later used by Turkish dervishes as a monastery.

Historical Museum MUSEUM
(Történeti múzeum; Map p207; ☑72-310 165; www.jpm.hu; Felsőmalom utca 9; adult/concession 700/350Ft; ⊙10am-2pm Tue-Sat) This absorbing museum traces Pécs' history across two floors of a former tannery, with period costumes and clothing, photos and exhibits walking you through the Turkish occupation, and explaining how coal mining in the area boosted the development of local factories, including Zsolnay Porcelain.

Roman Tomb Sites RUINS
(Map p207; ☑72-224 755; Apáca utca 8 & 14; adult/concession 450/250Ft; ⊙10am-5pm Tue-Sun) These two tomb sites contain 110 graves. The entire area – excavations have so far revealed 16 burial chambers and several hundred graves – is now a designated Unesco site. Closed for refurbishment at research time.

Bishop's Palace PALACE
(Püspöki palota; Map p207; ☑72-513 057; Szent István tér 23; adult/concession 2000/1000Ft; ⊙tours 10am, 2pm & 4pm Mon-Fri, hourly 9am-noon Sat Apr-Nov) The Bishop's Palace, dating to 1770, keeps very limited hours (access by tour), but have a look at the curious statue of Franz Liszt (Imre Varga; 1983) peering over the palace balcony.

Barbican TOWER
(Barbakán; Map p207; Esze Tamás utca 2; ⊙garden 7am-8pm May-Sep, 9am-5pm Oct-Apr) FREE Fronted by a lovely garden, the impressive circular barbican, the only stone bastion to survive in Pécs, dates from the late 15th century and was restored in the 1970s.

Ferenc Martyn Museum MUSEUM
(Map p207; ☑72-510 628; Káptalan utca 6; ⊙8am-6pm Mon-Fri) FREE Displays works by the Pécs-born painter and sculptor (1899–1986) and has previously hosted temporary exhibitions by Chagall, Dalí and others.

Ethnographic Museum MUSEUM
(Néprajzi Múzeum; Map p207; ☑72-315 629; www.jpm.hu; Rákóczi út 15; adult/concession 500/250Ft; ⊙10am-4pm Tue-Sat, to 6pm Sun) Showcases ethnic Hungarian, German and South Slav folk art in the region.

LAKE BALATON & SOUTHERN TRANSDANUBIA PÉCS

✨ Festivals & Events

Pécs Spring Festival CULTURAL
(www.pecsitavaszifesztival.hu; Mar) A month-long 'everything-but-the-kitchen-sink' event in late March.

International Culture Week THEATRE
(www.icwip.hu; ☉ Jul) The late-July International Culture Week is a thematic student festival that focuses on theatrical performances.

Pécs Days Heritage Festival CULTURAL
(www.pecsprogram.hu; ☉ Sep) This 10-day festival of dance and music in late September has a couple of wine-related events.

European Wine Song Festival MUSIC
(www.winesongfestival.hu; ☉ Sep) This late-September festival is Europe's only festival exclusively for male choruses.

🛌 Sleeping

In July and August more than a dozen of the city's colleges open up their doors to travellers; prices start at around 5000Ft for a dorm bed. Tourinform (p213) has the complete list.

Pilgrimage House GUESTHOUSE $
(Map p207; ☎72-513 057; http://pecsiegyhaz megye.hu/; Dóm tér 2; dm 5000Ft) A tranquil place next to the cathedral, Pilgrimage House is just that: a quiet place to bed down when you're not looking for major creature comforts. Rooms are segregated by gender and shared, and there's a communal kitchen for guest use. It's no-frills, but super-central and cheap. Book ahead.

Nap Hostel HOSTEL $
(Map p207; ☎72-950 684; www.naphostel. com; Király utca 23-25; dm €10-15, d €44; @ 🛜) This friendly hostel has three dorm rooms, with between six and eight beds each, and a double with washbasin on the 1st floor of a former bank (1885). One of the six-bed dorm rooms has a corner balcony, and there's a little garden at the rear. There's a large communal kitchen and great on-site bar (p213). Enter through the bar's main entrance.

Pollack Mihály Kollégium HOSTEL $
(Map p207; ☎72-513 680; Jókai Mór utca 8; dm from 2400Ft; ☉ Jul & Aug; 🛜) In July and August many of the city's colleges, including central Pollack Mihály College, open up their doors to travellers. Spartan dormitories with two to five beds.

★Szinbád Panzió PENSION $$
(Map p207; ☎72-221 110; www.szinbadpanzio. hu; Klimó György utca 9; s/d from €37/48; ❄🛜) A cosy, standard pension with excellent service and well-maintained, snug, wood-panelled rooms with cable TV, just outside the walls of Old Town. The warm welcome from the staff is much appreciated.

Hotel Főnix HOTEL $$
(Map p207; ☎72-311 680; www.fonixhotel.com; Hunyadi János út 2; s/d/ste 8000/13,000/14,000Ft; ❄🛜) The Főnix appears to be a hotel too large for the land it's built on and some of the 13 rooms and suites are not even big enough to swing, well, a phoenix in. Still, the welcome is always warm and the Mosque Church is within easy reach. The suite has a large open terrace.

Aranyhajó Fogadó HOTEL $$
(Map p207; ☎72-210 685; www.aranyhajo.hu; Király utca 3; s/d/tr from 11,000/15,000/18,000Ft; 🛜) Aranyhajó Fogadó claims to be Hungary's oldest hotel, and judging by the lovely, listed medieval building it's situated in, we're ready to believe it. The rooms are traditionally furnished and basic, but clean and very neat. It feels like a grandmother's home that could use a revamp, and air-con would be welcome in summer. Otherwise, it's central and good value.

★Adele Boutique Hotel BOUTIQUE HOTEL $$$
(Map p207; ☎72-510 226; www.adelehotel.hu; Mária utca 15; s/d/ste from €66/73/109; ❄🛜) Inside a 200-year-old heritage building with a granite portal, this delightful new boutique hotel has just 19 rooms and is well worth the splurge. The rooms – all creams and charcoals – are large and contemporary, the service is attentive and professional and breakfast is extensive and varied. It's very central, but doesn't suffer from street noise.

Hotel Arkadia BOUTIQUE HOTEL $$$
(Map p207; ☎72-512 550; www.hotelark adiapecs.hu; Hunyadi János út 1; s/d/tr 17,000/25,000/28,500Ft; ❄🛜) This minimalist bastion, spread across two structures, its common areas with polished steel, exposed brick and plenty of Corbusier cement furniture, is a firm student of Bauhaus. Rooms follow the same vein with lots of straight lines and solid colours, but thick throws and ample doses of natural light lend them a cosy vibe. Avoid the windowless rooms.

Diána Hotel
GUESTHOUSE $$$

(Map p207; ☑72-328 594; www.hotel diana.hu; Tímár utca 4/a; s/d/ste from 12,000/17,000/25,000Ft; ☒☎) This very central guesthouse offers 20 spotless rooms and two spacious suites, with comfortable kick-off-your-shoes decor. It's a great choice overlooking the synagogue, and staff are extra friendly.

✗ Eating

Pécs has an excellent dining scene, with varied offerings. There are a couple of restaurants in the Old Town that are particularly worth seeking out, as well as a worthy contender for the town's best restaurant at the Zsolnay Cultural Quarter.

★ Jókai Cukrászda
BAKERY $

(Map p207; ☑06 20 929 2025; www.facebook. com/jokaicuki/; Ferencesek utcája 6; cakes from 700Ft; ☉10am-9pm) The elaborate sweet creations – cheesecakes, pastries, eclairs – at this new bakery are the best in town, by a long shot. Even the macarons are Magyarised: try the poppy seed and blackcurrant ones.

Streat
BURGERS $

(Map p207; ☑06 30 880 0346; https://hu-hu. facebook.com/streatpecs; Király utca 35; burgers 700-1300Ft; ☉8am-8pm Mon-Fri, 9am-8pm Sat, 10am-4pm Sun) Putting a classy spin on casual munchies, this little place has a short and sweet menu of excellent homemade burgers (including pulled pork – our favourite) that attracts the young and trendy. There's a veggie burger for the non-carnivorous, too.

Produce Market
MARKET $

(Zólyom utca; sandwiches & sausages from 800Ft; ☉10am-6pm Tue-Sun) Pécs' excellent fruit and vegetable market is next to the bus station; food stalls lining the interior sell gut-busting sandwiches and sausages.

Giuseppe
ICE CREAM $

(Map p207; Ferencesek utcája 28; scoops 200Ft; ☉11am-8pm Mon-Fri, 2-8pm Sat & Sun) This place has been serving its very own Italian-style *lapátos fagyalt* (scooped ice cream) since 1992.

Interspar
SUPERMARKET $

(Nagy Lajos Király út, Árkád shopping centre; ☉7am-9pm Mon-Thu & Sat, to 10pm Fri, 8am-7pm Sun) Well-stocked supermarket in the basement of the shopping centre.

Mecsek
CAFE $

(Map p207; ☑72-315 444; Széchenyi tér 16; cakes from 395Ft; ☉9am-9pm) One of two cake shops on the main square serving gooey sweet delights and multiple gelato flavours.

Virág
CAFE $

(Map p207; ☑72-313 793; Széchenyi tér; cakes from 590Ft; ☉8am-10pm; ☑) A worthy contender for the 'best cakes and ice cream on the main square' title.

★ Bloff Bisztró
MEDITERRANEAN $$

(Map p207; ☑72-497 469; Jokai tér 5; mains 1600-3800Ft; ☉11am-1am) This (mostly) Balkan bad boy has quickly acquired a solid following in town. This may be partly to do with its super-central location, but we believe that the quality of their simple, satisfying dishes – fried fresh sprats with garlic and parsley, *cevap* (Balkan sausages), Sicilian-style monkfish – and the prompt, friendly service may have something to do with it.

★ Jókai Bisztró
HUNGARIAN $$

(Map p207; ☑06 20 360 7337; www.jokai bisztro.hu; Jókai tér 6; mains 1890-3580Ft; ☉11am-midnight) Arguably Pécs' best, a charming bistro with stylish decor overlooks Jókai tér – a seat on the terrace in summer is hot property. The menu is short, exceptionally well constructed and seasonal; dishes may include catfish stew with noodles and duck breast with cherry-port sauce. Most of the produce and meat is grown and reared by the restaurant.

Tex-Mex Mexikói Étterem
TEX-MEX $$

(Map p207; ☑72-215 427; www.tex-mex.hu; Teréz utca 10; mains 1800-2890Ft; ☉8am-10pm Tue-Sat; ☑) We know what you're thinking: 'Tex-Mex is Pécs? Pshaw!'. But this is the real deal: the enchiladas, burritos and fajitas are lovingly prepared using fresh ingredients. We don't know where they get their avocados, but their guacamole is spot on. We particularly like their Papa Chulo chimichangas.

Az Elefánthoz
ITALIAN $$

(Map p207; ☑72-216 055; www.elefantos.hu; Jókai tér 6; mains 2890-5900Ft, pizza 1100-3300Ft; ☑) With its enormous terrace and quality Italian cuisine, 'At the Elephant' is a sure bet for first-rate food in the city centre. The pizzas emerging from its wood-burning stove are the best in town and the atmosphere always manages to be elegant but unpretentious.

LAKE BALATON & SOUTHERN TRANSDANUBIA PÉCS

Aranykacsa
INTERNATIONAL $$

(Map p207; ☑72-518 860; www.aranykacsa.hu; Teréz utca 4; mains 1620-3690Ft; ☺11.30am-10pm Tue-Thu, to midnight Fri & Sat, to 4.30pm Sun) This wine restaurant takes pride in its silver service and venue; the Zsolnay Room evokes past grandeur. Formerly one of the town's best restaurants, the 'Golden Duck' has been resting on its laurels awhile, and it shows in the quality of its subpar signature duck dishes. The ambience is great, but don't expect to be gastronomically wowed.

★ Zsolnay Restaurant
HUNGARIAN $$$

(☑06 20 345 7000; http://zsolnayetterem.hu/; Zsolnay Vilmos utca 37; mains 2490-5990Ft; ☺11.30am-10pm Tue-Sat, to 5pm Sun) The star of the Zsolnay Cultural Quarter (p206), this stylish restaurant with crisp white linen is a worthy contender for Pécs' top dining spot. Creative dishes? Absolutely. Forest-mushroom-infused beef cheeks and raspberry soup stand out. Service? Professional and attentive; they'll carefully select the best wines to go with your dishes if you ask them to. Flawless.

Korhely Pub
HUNGARIAN $$$

(Map p207; ☑72-535 916; www.korhelypub.hu; Boltív köz 2; mains 2190-6890Ft; ☺11.30am-11pm) This outrageously popular *csapszék* (tavern) named 'Drunkard' has peanuts on the table, straw on the floor, a half-dozen beers on tap and a retro sorta-socialist/kinda–Latin American decor. It works. Having leapt on the *Game of Thrones* bandwagon, it serves epic portions of such delights as Ned Stark's Favourite, Sir Loin of Stripes and Deeractor's Cut. Meaty dishes predominate.

🍸 Drinking & Nightlife

Numerous pubs and bars line Király utca and the surrounding streets. Craft beer is very much a feature of the drinking scene, and you'll find excellent local wines and proper coffee, too. Pécs is a big university town; the nightlife is good, but don't expect everything to be heaving in summer, which is the low season in these parts.

★ Egylet Craft Beer Pub
CRAFT BEER

(Map p207; ☑06 20 350 8919; www.facebook.com/egylet; Ferencesek utcája 32; ☺11.30am-midnight Mon-Sat, to 10pm Sun) It's a rare phenomenon for a place to successfully wear three hats at once, yet Egylet manages it with flair. It's primarily a craft beer pub with 12 changing Hungarian brews on tap. It's also a terrific place for grilled meats (mostly Balkan – see

the map on the wall). To top it off, there's the excellent coffee. Full marks.

★ Pécsi Kávé
COFFEE

(Map p207; ☑72-951 586; www.facebook.com/pecsikave; Irgalmasok utca 6; ☺7am-8pm Mon-Fri, 9am-8pm Sat & Sun) Tucked away in a green courtyard is one of Pécs' best coffee spots. Inside, it's a quirky cross between a study space (complete with cute reading lights) and a bar, complete with old-fashioned weighing scales and bags of roasted beans. Knock back a ristretto or sip one of their glorious mint lemonades in the garden in warm weather.

★ Csinos Presszó
RUIN PUB

(Map p207; ☑06 30 357 0004; www.facebook.com/csinospresszo; Váradi Antal utca 8; ☺10am-midnight Mon-Thu, noon-2am Fri & Sat, noon-midnight Sun) Between the al fresco garden with mismatched furniture painted in bright pastels and the Christmas lights strung from the trees it's easy to see why Csinos packs in relaxed patrons. A small snack menu accompanies an inventive drinks menu (a number of the cordials are house-made) and in the afternoon it's also a prime spot to grab a coffee and press pause.

★ Amper Klub
CLUB

(☑06 20 667 8800; www.amperklub.hu; Czindery utca 6; ☺10pm-5am Fri & Sat) This big club has been revamped lately with a state-of-the-art sound system, and it features all-night DJ sets with illustrious guests working the decks. It attracts mainly 20something trendoids who boogie to the house and techno or sip cocktails and look pretty in the outdoor garden.

Karavella
CRAFT BEER

(Map p207; ☑06 30 953 3363; www.facebook.com/karavellapecs; Kazinczy utca 3; ☺2pm-midnight Sun-Thu, to 4am Fri & Sat) With a curiously boat-shaped wooden ceiling, this snug bar provides a safe haven for lovers of good beer. Apart from craft beers from all over Hungary, there are some international offerings and the bar staff are good at making suggestions. We have one for them: add some decent music and this bar will go straight from good to amazing.

Filter
COFFEE, WINE BAR

(Map p207; ☑06 30 222 7650; www.facebook.com/filtercafepecs; Színház tér; ☺10am-10pm Mon-Sat, to 8pm Sun) 'Drinking coffee is sexy' says the sign outside this thimble-sized place. We agree. Is this a cafe? A wine bar?

A bit of both, actually, with carefully chosen local wines by the glass, seriously good coffee, and a central location to hang out and people-watch.

Cooltour Café
CAFE

(Map p207; ☑72-310 440; http://cooltourcafe.hu; Király utca 26; ⊙11am-midnight Sun-Tue, to 2am Wed & Thu, to 3am Fri & Sat) Cooltour embodies so many cool things it's hard to choose what we love best. It's a ruin pub, yet it's open all day, making it fine for both coffee and snacks or cocktails and mellow chit-chat. It's on the main drag, but its rear garden feels like a secret spot. Occasional live music and parties in the evening.

Tüke Borház
WINE BAR

(☑06 20 317 8178; www.tukeborhaz.hu; Böckh János utca 39/2; ⊙4-10pm Thu & Fri, noon-10pm Sat, noon-7pm Sun) This wine bar tucked away in a stone house in the hills above Pécs offers a fantastic selection of local wines served by gracious and knowledgable staff. The vast terrace has panoramic views across the city and if you're feeling peckish, cold cuts and grilled meats are always on hand.

Nappali Bár
BAR

(Map p207; ☑72-585 705; www.facebook.com/nappali.bar; Király utca 23-25; ⊙10am-2am) Its outdoor seating filling up on lazy warm evenings, Nappali Bár is one of the hippest gathering spots in town for a coffee, breakfast or a glass of wine. Live music some nights.

Club 5 Music Pub
CLUB

(Map p207; ☑06 20 535 5090, 72-212 621; Irgalmasok utca 24; ⊙7pm-2am Tue-Thu, to 4am Fri & Sat) This hard-to-find basement bar transforms itself into a small (and very central) club on weekends.

Káptalani Borozó
WINE BAR

(Map p207; Janus Pannonius utca 8-10; ⊙10am-2am Mon-Sat, to midnight Sun) This funny little 'wine bar' opposite the Csontváry Museum has outdoor seating on a tiny terrace next to an early Christian site and serves white Cirfandli, a speciality of the Mecsek Hills, in spades. There's a story behind all those padlocks on the gate just down the street.

☆ Entertainment

Pécs is a city of culture. The list of theatres and concert venues is extensive for a place of its size, and most times of the year you can find something going on.

Chamber Theatre
THEATRE

(Kamaraszínház; Map p207; ☑72-512 660; www.pnsz.hu; Perczel Mór utca; tickets 1000-3000Ft) Intimate, experimental productions staged next door to the Pécs National Theatre.

Pécs National Theatre
THEATRE

(Pécsi nemzeti színház; Map p207; ☑72-512 660, box office 72-211 965; www.pnsz.hu; Színház tér 1; tickets 1000-2800Ft; ⊙box office 10am-5pm Mon-Fri, 1hr before performances Sat & Sun) Pécs is renowned for its opera company and the Sophianae Ballet, both of which perform at this theatre. Advance tickets can be purchased from the theatre's box office.

Bóbita Puppet Theatre
THEATRE

(Bóbit Bábszínház; Map p207; ☑72-210 301; www.bobita.hu; Felsővámház utca 50, in the Zsolnay Cultural Quarter; grand hall performances 1000Ft, cabin shows 900Ft, puppet museum 400Ft) Somewhere John Malkovich would be proud to perform, the Bóbita is not just for kids; there are shows aimed at adults only. There are also arts and crafts classes for kids.

🛍 Shopping

Sunday Flea Market
MARKET

(Vásár tér; ⊙5am-6pm) The Sunday flea market, about 3km southwest of the inner town on Megyeri út, attracts people from the countryside, especially on the first Sunday of the month. It's a great place to browse, or just hang out and enjoy the atmosphere (and good food).

ℹ Information

Tourinform (Map p207; ☑06 30 681 7195; www.iranypecs.hu; Széchenyi tér; ⊙8am-8pm Mon-Fri, 9am-8pm Sat, 10am-6pm Sun Apr-Oct, 8am-8pm Mon-Fri, 10am-6pm Sat & Sun Nov-Mar) Knowledgeable staff; copious information on Pécs and surrounds.

ℹ Getting There & Away

Pannon Volán Taxi (☑72-333 333) Reputable taxi company.

BUS & TRAIN

See the table for buses departing from Pécs' bus station. Up to nine direct trains daily connect Pécs with Budapest's Keleti station (4485Ft, three hours, 237km). Most destinations in Southern Transdanubia are best reached by bus.

ℹ Getting Around

➧ Buses 3 and 50 from the train station are good for the flea market.

BUSES FROM PÉCS

DESTINATION	PRICE	DURATION	KM	FREQUENCY
Budapest	3690Ft	4½hr	215	5 daily
Győr	4200Ft	4½hr	256	2 daily
Kecskemét	3410Ft	4¼hr	200	daily
Keszthely	2830Ft	3½hr	152	up to 4 daily
Mohács	930Ft	1¼ hr	48	up to 19 daily
Szeged	3690Ft	3½hr	207	2 daily

→ Bus 20A runs to the Zsolnay Cultural Centre.
→ Bus 35 serves the TV tower.
→ You can also order a local taxi.

Mohács

🖉 69 / POP 17355

Mohács is a sleepy little port on the Danube that wakes up only during the frenzied annual Busójárás festival (late February or March). But history buffs won't want to give this place a miss: it's a must-do for its significant role in Hungarian history. And last but not least, Mohács is an excellent place to start exploring the Mohács-Bóly White Wine Route.

⊙ Sights

Mohács Historical Memorial Site   MEMORIAL
(Mohácsi Történelmi Emlékhely; 🖉 06 20 918 2779, 69-382130; www.mohacsiemlekhely.hu; 1km off Rte 56; adult/concession 1500/1200Ft; ⊙9am-6pm Apr-late Oct, to 4pm late Oct-Mar) The defeat of the ragtag Hungarian army by the Turks at Mohács on 29 August 1526 was a watershed in the nation's history, its effects felt up to this day. With it came partition and foreign domination that would last almost five centuries. The small visitor centre is 6km southwest of town at Sátorhely, with clever images of the battle projected on the walls, a section with archaeological remains and wooden markers outside representing the Hungarian and Turkish sides.

Originally opened in 1976 to mark the 450th anniversary of the Mohács battle, the visitor centre is a fitting memorial to the dead over a common grave that was only discovered in the early 1970s.

Dorottya Kanizsai Museum   MUSEUM
(🖉69-306 604; www.kanizsaidorottyamuzeum. hu; Városház utca 1; adult/concession 1000/600Ft; ⊙10am-3pm Tue-Sat Apr-Oct) This lovely museum has a large collection of costumes worn by the Sokác, Slovenes, Serbs, Croats, Bosnians and Swabians who repopulated this devastated area in the 17th century. The distinctive grey-black pottery of Mohács also figures. More interesting is the surprisingly well-balanced exhibit devoted to the landmark 1526 battle against the Turks, with both sides getting the chance to tell their side of the story.

Busóház   MUSEUM
(🖉69-302 677; Kossuth Lajos utca 54; adult/concession 400/250Ft; ⊙9am-5pm Mon-Fri) If you can't make the Busójárás festival, just before Lent, Busóház is the place to come: it tells the story of the festival from its origins as a South Slav spring rite to a fancy-dress mummery directed at the erstwhile enemy, the Turks. The horrifying devils' and rams' head masks are on frightening display.

✦✧ Festivals & Events

★ Busójárás   CULTURAL
This pre-Lenten free-for-all carnival celebration takes place in late February or March. Men adorned with freakish, horned wooden masks (busós) parade through town (on the Sunday before Ash Wednesday) to scare off winter and welcome spring.

❶ Information

Tourinform (🖉69-505 515; www.mohacs.hu; Széchenyi tér 1; ⊙7.30am-5pm Mon-Fri, 10am-3pm Sat mid-Jun–mid-Sep, 8am-4pm Mon-Fri mid-Sep–mid-Jun) Located in the Moorish Town Hall in the centre of town, the tourist office has a leaflet of the Mohács-Bóly White Wine Route. It pinpoints about a dozen villages in the area where you can sample the local drop.

❶ Getting There & Away

Bus services from Mohács aren't as frequent as they are from other towns, but to Pécs (930Ft, 1¼ hours, 48km) there are up to 19 buses daily.

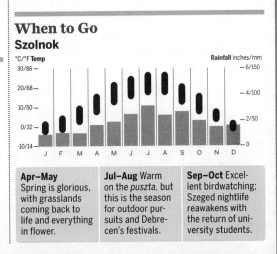

The Great Plain

Why Go?

Like the outback for Australians or the Wild West for Americans, the Nagyalföld (Great Plain) – also known as the *puszta* – holds a romantic appeal for Hungarians. Many of these notions come as much from the collective imagination as they do from history, but there's no arguing the spellbinding potential of big-sky country. The Hortobágy region is where the myth of the lonely *pásztor* (shepherd), the wayside *csárda* (inn) and Gypsy violinists – kept alive in literature and art – was born. The horse and herding show at Hortobágy National Park recreates this pastoral tradition, while Bugac is one of the best places in Hungary to learn about life on the plain. The Great Plain is also home to cities of graceful architecture and history. Szeged is a centre of art and culture, Kecskemét is full of art nouveau gems and Debrecen is the 'Calvinist Rome'.

Best Places to Eat

➡ Ikon (p220)

➡ Tiszavirág Restaurant (p238)

➡ Hortobágyi Csárda (p225)

➡ Malata (p237)

➡ Tepsi Gastropub (p229)

Best Places to Sleep

➡ Tiszavirág Hotel (p236)

➡ Fábián Panzió (p229)

➡ Régi Posta (p220)

➡ Sóvirág Vendégház (p225)

➡ Centrum Panzió (p219)

When to Go
Szolnok

°C/°F Temp
30/86 —
20/68 —
10/50 —
0/32 —
-10/14 —

Rainfall inches/mm
— 6/150
— 4/100
— 2/50
— 0

J F M A M J J A S O N D

Apr–May
Spring is glorious, with grasslands coming back to life and everything in flower.

Jul–Aug Warm on the *puszta*, but this is the season for outdoor pursuits and Debrecen's festivals.

Sep–Oct Excellent birdwatching; Szeged nightlife reawakens with the return of university students.

The Great Plain Highlights

1 Hortobágy National Park (p223) Birdwatching and sampling the namesake meat-filled pancake in a century-old inn.

2 Kecskemét (p225) Enjoying its wonderful art nouveau architecture and pretty pedestrian squares.

3 Szeged (p235) Taking to the Tisza in a boat and seeing this culture-filled town from an entirely new vantage point.

4 Kiskunság National Park (p232) Feeling the earth move under your feet as a Hungarian cowboy rides by

'five-in-hand' at the park's horse show.

5 Debrecen (p217) Marvelling at the grandeur of the city's iconic Great Church, Hungary's largest Protestant house of worship.

Debrecen

📍 52 / POP 203,000

Debrecen is Hungary's second-largest city, and its name has been synonymous with wealth and conservatism since the 16th century. Flanked by the golden Great Church and the historic Aranybika hotel, Debrecen's central square, Kossuth tér, sets the rather subdued tone for this city. During summer, frequent street festivals fill the pedestrian core with revellers, and old-town bars and nightclubs create a lively scene for night crawlers on weekends year-round. The array of museums and thermal baths in this 'Capital of the Great Plain' will keep you busy for a day or two, but then you'll want to take a day trip out to the *puszta* to explore natural wonders and see a cowboy show.

History

The area around Debrecen has been settled since earliest times. When the Magyars arrived late in the 9th century, they found a settlement of Slovaks here who called the region Dobre Zliem for its 'good soil'. Debrecen's wealth, based on salt, the fur trade and cattle raising, grew steadily through the Middle Ages and increased during the Turkish occupation; the city kept all sides happy by paying tribute to the Ottomans, the Habsburgs and the Transylvanian princes at the same time.

By the mid-16th century much of the population had converted to Protestantism and churches were being erected with gusto, earning the city the nickname 'Calvinist Rome'. Debrecen played a pivotal role in the 1848–49 War of Independence, and it experienced a major building boom in the late 19th and early 20th centuries.

◉ Sights

Just walking along Piac utca and down some of the side streets, with their array of neo-classical, baroque and art nouveau buildings, is a treat.

Great Church CHURCH
(Nagytemplom; 📞 52-412 694; www.nagytemplom.hu; Piac utca 4-6; adult/concession 500/400Ft; ⊙ 9am-6pm Mon-Fri, 10am-1pm Sat, noon-4pm Sun Jul & Aug, 9am-6pm Mon-Fri Apr-Jun, Sep & Oct, 10am-1pm Mon-Fri Nov-Mar) Built in 1822, the iconic Great Church accommodates 3000 people and is Hungary's largest Protestant house of worship. The nave is rather austere apart from the magnificent organ; climb the 210 steps to the top of the west clock tower for grand views over the city and the 4.6-tonne Rákóczi Bell. It was in the Great Church that Lajos Kossuth read the Declaration of Independence from Austria on 14 April 1849. There are several exhibition spaces inside the church.

Calvinist College LIBRARY
(Református Kollégium; 📞 52-614 370; www.reformatuskollegium.ttre.hu; Kálvin tér 16; adult/concession 900/500Ft; ⊙ 10am-4pm Mon-Fri, 10am-1pm Sat) North of the Great Church stands the Calvinist College, built in 1816 on the site of a theological college dating back to the mid-16th century. Downstairs there are exhibits on religious art and sacred objects (including a 17th-century chalice made from a coconut), and on the regimented school's history. Upstairs via a fabulous painted staircase is the 600,000-volume green pillared library and the bright, white oratory, where the breakaway National Assembly met in 1849.

This was also where Hungary's provisional government was declared towards the end of WWII in 1944.

Déri Museum MUSEUM
(📞 52-322 207; www.derimuz.hu; Déri tér 1; adult/child 2000/1000Ft; ⊙ 10am-6pm Tue-Sun) Folklore exhibits at the Déri Museum offer excellent insights into life on the plain and for the bourgeois citizens of Debrecen up to the 19th century. Mihály Munkácsy's mythical interpretations of the Hortobágy and his *Passion of Christ* trilogy take pride of place in a purpose-built gallery. The museum's entrance is flanked by four superb bronzes by sculptor Ferenc Medgyessy, a local boy who merits his own Memorial Museum (p218) in an old burgher house a short distance to the northeast.

Pászti Street Orthodox Synagogue SYNAGOGUE
(Pásti Utcai Orthodox Zsinagóga; 📞 06 30 846 1703, 52-415 861; http://dzsh.hu/en; Pászti utca 4-6; adult/child 1200/600Ft; ⊙ 8am-4pm Mon-Fri) This beautiful pink synagogue built in 1893 has undergone a complete renovation and is once again open to the public. There are the remains of a mikvah in the basement. In the courtyard is a Holocaust memorial bearing the names of local people murdered in Nazi concentration camps.

Debrecen

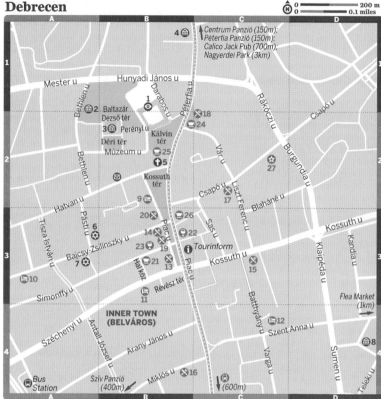

Status Quo Ante Synagogue SYNAGOGUE

(Status Quo Ante Zsinagóga; ☑52-415 861; Kápolnási utca 1) Debrecen had a Jewish population of 12,000 people up to the end of WWII. This Conservative synagogue, just south of Bajcsy-Zsilinszky utca, dates from 1909 and is once again in use.

Tímárház GALLERY

(Tanner House; ☑52-321 260; www.debrecenimuvkozpont.hu; Nagy Gál István utca 6; adult/child 400/200Ft; ☺10am-6pm Tue-Fri, 10am-2pm Sat) East of the city centre, the Tímárház is a folk-craft centre and workshop run by the Debrecen Cultural Centre, where potters, cheesemakers, weavers and carvers (but no tanners) do their stuff in rotation.

Centre of Modern
& Contemporary Art MUSEUM

(MODEM, Modern és Kortárs Művészeti Központ; ☑52-525 010; www.modermart.hu; Baltazár Dezső tér 1-3; adult/child 1800/900Ft; ☺10am-6pm Tue-Sun) Hungary's second-largest contemporary art gallery after the Ludwig Museum in Budapest, MODEM (as it is called) houses the country's most significant private art collection.

Ferenc Medgyessy
Memorial Museum MUSEUM

(Medgyessy Ferenc Emlékmúzeum; ☑52-413 572; www.derimuzeum.hu/en/for-visitors/permanent-exhibitions/ferencz-medgyessy-memorial-museum; Péterfia utca 28; adult/child 600/300Ft; ☺10am-6pm Tue-Sun) This memorial museum for local sculptor Ferenc Medgyessy is in an old burgher house to the northeast of the Déri Museum (p217); the museum entrance is flanked by four superb bronzes by the artist.

🏃 Activities

Aquaticum Thermal Baths THERMAL BATHS

(Aquaticum Termálfürdő; ☑52-514 174; www.aquaticum.hu; Nagyerdei Park 1; adult/child from

Debrecen

1900/1550Ft; ⊙7am-9pm) A massive facelift has turned the old thermal baths, with their pools filled with nonfiltered, purely mineral (read: muddy-coloured) waters, into pristine blue fountains of youth. Or at least that's what the bathers are hoping for. It's next door to the landmark Aquaticum Wellness Hotel (p222).

Aquaticum Debrecen Spa   SPA
(☑52-514 111; www.aquaticum.hu; Nagyerdei Park 1; adult/concession 3000/2450Ft; ⊙9am-7pm) The main attraction in Nagyerdei Park, north of the town centre, is Aquaticum, a huge complex of 'Mediterranean Adventure Baths' offering all manner of slides and waterfalls, spouts and grottoes within its pools – both indoors and out. Choose from a full menu of massages (from 1700Ft for 25 minutes) and other treatments.

🎉 Festivals & Events

Masquerade Carnival   CARNIVAL
(⊙Feb/Mar) Pre-Lenten festival just before Ash Wednesday that includes fancy-dress parties.

Spring Festival   PERFORMING ARTS
(⊙Mar-Apr) Comprehensive arts festival from mid-March to mid-April featuring music, theatre, exhibitions, films and literature.

Flower Carnival   PARADE
(www.iranydebrecen.hu/info/flower-carnival; ⊙Aug) The grandaddy of Debrecen's festivals, the week-long Flower Carnival held in mid-August includes a flowery float parade.

Wine & Jazz Festival   WINE, MUSIC
(⊙Aug) Good wine accompanied by good music for four days in early August.

🛏 Sleeping

Loads of dormitory accommodation is available in July and August; ask **Tourinform** (☑52-412 250; www.iranydebrecen.hu; Piac utca 20; ⊙9am-5pm Mon-Fri year-round, plus 9am-1pm Sat Jun-Aug) for details. Otherwise, Debrecen offers a wide range of accommodation choices, notably B&Bs.

★**Centrum Panzió**   GUESTHOUSE **$**
(☑52-442 843; www.panziocentrum.hu; Péterfia utca 37/a; s/d 7700/9200Ft; ❂🐾) Just north of the centre, the Centrum looks a little like your grandmother's house – if she collected Victorian bric-a-brac. Flowery odds and ends line the bright reception and public areas; some of the 25 large rooms (eg room 15) are out back, facing a long garden. All have both minifridge and microwave. Bike rental is available.

Szív Panzió   GUESTHOUSE **$**
(Heart Guesthouse; ☑52-322 200; www.szivpanzio. hu; Szív utca 11; s/d/apt 5800/7800/12,800Ft; ❂🐾) Staying at a guesthouse on a tree-lined street not far from the bus station helps make day trips a breeze, but the 'Heart Pension' is a bit away from the action. The 16 simple rooms have low-slung beds and well-stocked minibars; most face a large, quiet courtyard.

Péterfia Panzió
GUESTHOUSE $$

(☑52-418 246; www.peterfiapanzio.hu; Péterfia utca 37/b; s/d 8300/10,000Ft; ❋🛜) Natural-wood furniture fills this guesthouse's 19 comfy rooms, and the staff make you welcome by inviting you to relax in the very long back garden, where half of the guest rooms are located.

Belvárosi Panzió
GUESTHOUSE $$

(Downtown Guesthouse; ☑52-322 644; www.belvarosipanzio.hu; Bajcsy-Zsilinszky utca 60; s/d 7600/10,800Ft; 🛜) Bright, clean and modern, the 24-room 'Downtown' is less homey and more hotel-y than some others. Some 2nd-floor rooms have a balcony looking out onto a quiet street.

Stop Panzió
GUESTHOUSE $$

(☑52-420 302; stoppanzi@vnet.hu; Batthyány utca 18; s/d/tr 7300/9700/13,100Ft; 🛜) The dozen renovated rooms here fill up because they're the right price for the right location – in a courtyard off a cafe-lined pedestrian street. The brightly tiled, plant-filled lobby and the staff are welcoming. Parking is to the rear.

★ Régi Posta
BOUTIQUE HOTEL $$$

(☑52-325 325; www.regiposta.hu; Széchenyi utca 6; s/d 12,000/16,800Ft; 🛜) Located in one of the oldest buildings in Debrecen, a burgher house dating from the 1690s, the 'Old Post Office' (one of its many avatars over the centuries) is now a cute boutique hotel with a dozen entirely unique rooms. We love the rather incongruous Industrial and the 'fairy-tale' French Rooms. The Régi Posta almost feels like staying in the countryside. The destination restaurant has seating in both a cellar and, in the warmer months, an interior courtyard.

Aranybika
HOTEL $$$

(☑06 20 363 6121; www.hotelaranybika.com; Piac utca 11-15; s €47-70, d €55-77; ❋🛜🏊) This landmark art nouveau hotel has been *the* place to stay in Debrecen since 1915 but – alas – standards have fallen. Many of the 130 rooms still retain their drab carpets and plain, proletarian furnishings of a different era. Superior rooms have a bit more space than standard, though, as well as antique reproduction furniture. Room 333 is in a medieval-looking turret should you be looking for a little romance.

✖ Eating

Ikon Street
FAST FOOD $

(☑06 30 555 7754; www.ikonstreet.hu; Piac utca 11-15; dishes 990-1190Ft; ⊙11.30am-10.30pm Mon-Thu, 11.30am-5am Fri & Sat, 11.30am-9pm Sun)

Little sister to a big gourmet-feast palace of the same name just a block south, this hole-in-the-wall has cramped seating on two floors and does a brisk business selling to in-house and takeaway customers. The offerings are mostly burgers (including vegie and chicken varieties) and a range of different *kolbászok* (sausages).

Bonita Bisztró
ITALIAN $

(☑52-216 816; www.bonitabistro.com; Piac utca 21; pasta 1200-1590Ft, pizza 1000-1700Ft; ⊙noon-10pm) This upbeat pasta and pizza restaurant, with more than two dozen of the former on offer and almost four dozen of the latter, is as central as you could hope for.

Gilbert Pizzeria
PIZZA $

(☑52-537 373; www.gilbert.hu; Kálvin tér 8; pizza & pasta 990-1250Ft; ⊙10am-10pm Sun-Thu, 10am-11pm Fri & Sat; 🖉) Some of the cheapest (if not the best) pizza in town awaits in an interior courtyard just off the main square. A substantial number of the 50 choices are vegetarian.

Fruit & Vegetable Market
MARKET $

(Csapó utca; ⊙5am-3pm Mon-Sat, 5-11am Sun) This small market is right in the city centre.

Csokonai Étterem
HUNGARIAN $$

(☑52-410 802; www.csokonaisorozo.hu/eng; Kossuth utca 21; mains 2290-3990Ft; ⊙noon-11pm) In a vaulted cellar, the sharp service, excellent Hungarian specialities and a terrace with live music all help to create one of Debrecen's most welcome eating experiences. Csokonai also serves good pasta dishes (1700Ft to 2290Ft).

Flaska Vendéglő
HUNGARIAN $$

(☑06 30 998 7602, 52-414 582; http://flaska.hu; Miklós utca 4; mains 1368-3690Ft; ⊙11.30am-10pm Sun-Thu, 11.30am-11pm Fri & Sat) You can't miss the giant red flask jutting out from the wall – a landmark in these parts – and you shouldn't skip the food either. Poultry and pork top the Hungarian menu; try the authentic Debrecen-style stuffed cabbage (1200Ft) and the Gundel *palacsinta* (pancakes filled with chocolate and nuts; 640Ft) for dessert.

★ Ikon
INTERNATIONAL $$$

(☑06 30 555 7766; www.ikonrestaurant.hu; Piac utca 23; mains 1990-4490Ft; ⊙11.30am-11pm Mon-Sat) One of the best restaurants in town, Ikon commands a prominent position on the main square, but with its trimmed-down decor and classily clad wait staff, it remains discreet and upscale. Enjoy such inventive dishes as beetroot risotto with grilled goat's cheese (2300Ft) and rabbit cooked in *lecsó* (a sauce of tomatoes, vegetables and paprika). Five-/six-course tasting menus are 6500/9999Ft.

Régi Vigadó
HUNGARIAN $$$

(☑ 52-514 189; www.regivigado.hu; Nagyerdei Park 1; mains 1890-3990Ft; ☉ 10am-11pm Sun-Thu, 10am-midnight Fri & Sat) Wedged between the Aquaticum Wellness Hotel and thermal baths in Nagyerdei Park is this gourmet restaurant housed in a lovely old theatre. Try the catfish stew and sweet roasted duck. There's also a good selection of Hungarian *pálinka* (fruit brandy).

Belga
INTERNATIONAL $$$

(☑ 52-536 373; http://belgaetterem.hu; Piac utca 29; mains 1790-3990Ft; ☉ 10am-midnight Sun-Thu, 10am-2am Fri & Sat; ☑) More international than Belgian, this restaurant with a beer-hall atmosphere serves many fish and lacto-ovo vegie dishes; a good choice for those eschewing meat.

🍸 Drinking & Nightlife

Streetside-cafe tables sprout like the flowers in spring; any of those on the pedestrian squares, and several along pedestrian Simonffy utca and Hal köz, are good places to sip your fill. Piac utca is home to several bars and clubs that change beat with the speed of summer lightning. Pick up a copy of the monthly *Debreceni Korzó* (Debrecen Promenade) for listings.

DiVino
WINE BAR

(☑ 06 20 480 6574; www.debrecen.divinoborbar. hu; Piac utca 18; ☉ 5pm-midnight Mon-Thu, 5pm-3am Fri & Sat) A branch of the massively popular wine bars in Budapest, DiVino has a dizzying range of Hungarian wines, which you can sample by the 0.15cL glass (650Ft to 2400Ft). It's a wonderful and easy (and potentially dangerous) way to gain some insights into Hungarian wine.

Volt Egyszer
CAFE

(☑ 06 70 386 6825; www.facebook.com/Voltegyszer-196863703817700; Piac utca 16; ☉ 7am-9pm Mon-Fri, 9am-9pm Sat, 10am-8pm Sun) 'Once Upon a Time' is a delightful retro-style cafe near the main square serving Italian coffee along with sandwiches (560Ft) and homemade cakes (from 420Ft).

Cut & Coffee
CAFE

(☑ 52-747 312; www.facebook.com/cutandcoffee; Hal köz 3/a; ☉ 8am-10pm Mon-Fri, 9am-10pm Sat,

---

THE PUSZTA: FROM FOREST TO TREELESS PLAIN

Half a millennium ago, the Great Plain was not a treeless steppe but forest land at the constant mercy of the flooding Tisza and Danube Rivers. The Turks felled most of the trees, destroying the protective cover and releasing the topsoil to the winds; villagers fled north or to the market towns and *khas* (settlements under the sultan's jurisdiction). The region had become the *puszta* ('deserted' or 'abandoned') and home to shepherds, fisher folk, runaway serfs and outlaws. You'll find few fortifications on the Great Plain; the Turks demanded they be destroyed as part of the agreement of retreat. In the 19th century regulation of the rivers dried up the marshes and allowed for methodical irrigation, paving the way for intensive agriculture, particularly on the Southern Plain, but flooding still occurs to this day.

2-10pm Sun) No one cares more (and can tell you as much) about their coffee: its provenance, in-house roasting time and temperature, how to drink it and so on. And they've trained a lot of the baristas working in the area. Blotter choices include sandwiches (590Ft to 690Ft) and cakes (450Ft).

Drazsé Bár
COCKTAIL BAR

(☑ 52-322 222; www.facebook.com/drazsebar; Simonffy utca 1/b; ☉ 10am-midnight Mon-Thu, 10am-2am Fri & Sat, 10am-10pm Sun) The 'Sugar-coated Pill', with its attractive yellow and black decor, mezzanine seating and terrace, is a great choice for a sundowner just off Piac utca. Cocktails start at 900Ft and wraps and sandwiches (from 890Ft) are available should you require blotter.

Karakter 1517
CAFE

(☑ 52-614 186; www.nagytemplom.hu; ☉ noon-6pm Mon-Sat) Directly behind the Great Church (p217) and run by same, this glassed-in cafe and bookshop with ancient bits and bobs excavated from the area is a comfortable spot for something warm after touring the nearby museums and religious buildings.

Calico Jack Pub
PUB

(☑ 52-455 999; www.calicojackpub.hu; Bem tér 15; ☉ 9am-midnight) A classic setting for drinking *sör* (beer) just north of the centre, with an interior done up like a late-19th-century sailing vessel (look for our mate Jack climbing the mast). Extensive beer selection and menu (mains 2450Ft to 2990Ft) and a large outdoor terrace.

Gara Cukrászda   CAFE

(☑52-311 618; www.garacukraszda.hu; Kálvin tér 6; cakes 380-550Ft; ☺9am-7pm) Debrecen's pre-eminent cafe and cakeshop since 1988, Gara has some of the best cakes and ice cream (made with real fruit and loads of it) outside Budapest.

☆ Entertainment

Roncs Bár   LIVE MUSIC

(☑52-688 050; www.roncsbar.hu; Csapó utca 27; ☺11am-midnight Mon & Tue, to 2am Wed & Thu, to 4am Fri & Sat, to 10pm Sun) A ruin bar that would do Budapest proud, the 'Wreck' has random old stuff – guitars, bikes, a disintegrating light aircraft – strewn both within a large covered courtyard and a cool pub, where spirits flow freely. There's live music at 8pm on Friday and Saturday and a great menu of burgers, gyros and wraps. Weekday set lunch is 880Ft.

🛍 Shopping

Flea Market   MARKET

(Vágóhíd utca; ☺7am-1pm Wed-Sun) The colourful flea market attracts a motley group of hawkers selling everything from socks to live animals. It's served by buses 15 and 30 from the train station.

ℹ Information

Ibusz (☑52-415 555; www.ibusz.hu; Révész tér 2; ☺9am-5pm Mon-Fri) Travel agency; rents private apartments.

Main Post Office (Hatvan utca 5-9; ☺7am-7pm Mon-Fri, 8am-noon Sat)

OTP Bank (Piac utca 45-47; ☺7.45am–6pm Mon, to 5pm Tue-Thu, to 4pm Fri) Has an ATM.

Tourinform (p219) The very helpful tourist office in the town hall has more information than you can carry about the whole region.

ℹ Getting There & Away

In general, cities to the north and northwest are best served by train. For points south, use the bus or a transfer combination.

BUS & TRAIN

Buses are quickest if you're going direct to the destinations listed in the table. Trains leave from Debrecen for Satu Mare, Romania (three hours, 106km) at 9.12am and 3.12pm. You have to transfer in Záhony to get to Csap (Čop; 120km) in Ukraine. The night train from Budapest to Moscow stops here just after 4am.

ℹ Getting Around

Tram 1 is ideal both for transport and sightseeing; the new Tram 2 less so. From the train station, Tram 1 runs north along Piac utca to Kálvin tér and then carries on to Nagyerdei Park, where it loops around for the same trip southward. Tickets are 300Ft from newsagents and 400Ft from the driver. Most other city transport can be caught at the southern end of Petőfi tér. Trolleybuses 3 and 5 link the bus and train stations.

BUSES FROM DEBRECEN

DESTINATION	PRICE	DURATION	KM	FREQUENCY
Eger	2520Ft	2½hr	130	8 nonstop daily
Gyula	2520Ft	2½hr	128	5 nonstop daily
Miskolc	1860Ft	2hr	99	hourly nonstop daily
Nádudvar	745Ft	1hr	39	hourly nonstop daily
Szeged	3950Ft	4½hr	229	3 nonstop daily

TRAINS FROM DEBRECEN

DESTINATION	PRICE	DURATION	KM	FREQUENCY
Budapest	3950Ft	2hr	221	hourly
Hajdúszoboszló	370Ft	15min	20	half-hourly
Hortobágy	840Ft	50min	42	hourly
Nyíregyháza	930Ft	40min	49	half-hourly
Tokaj	1680Ft	1½hr	81	hourly

Hortobágy National Park

📷 52 / POP 1450

Hortobágy National Park lies 40km west of Debrecen. At its centre is the tiny village of Hortobágy, once celebrated for its sturdy cowboys, inns and Gypsy bands. You can see the staged recreation of all this, complete with traditionally costumed *csikósok* (cowboys) at a *puszta* horse show. But you'll want to explore more of the 810-sq-km national park and wildlife preserve – home to hundreds of birds, as well as plant species that are usually found only by the sea. Unesco added the park to its World Heritage list in 1999.

◎ Sights

A combination ticket allowing entry to most of Hortobágy's museums is available for adult/child 1500/800Ft. There are two open-air zoos in the national park south of Hortobágy village.

Máta Stud Farm
FARM

(Mátai Ménes; 📷 06 70 492 7655, 52-589 369; www.hortobagy.eu/hu/matai-menes; Hortobágy-Máta; adult/child 2600/1400Ft; ⊙10am, noon & 2pm mid-Mar–Oct, plus 4pm Apr–mid-Oct) Staged it may be, but the 1½-hour *puszta* show at the 300-year-old Máta Stud Farm, 3km north of Hortobágy village, *is* Hungarian. You get to ride in a horse-drawn wagon train across the prairie, making stops to peer into the pens of *racka* sheep, see great grey cattle grazing, witness semi-wild horses herded and watch Hungarian *csikósok* perform tricks, including 'five-in-hand' galloping, standing balanced on the back of the two rear horses, with three more reined in front.

To get to the stud farm on foot, cross the train tracks from the station and find the path through the brush (to the right). This well-worn track through the fields, over the river and past the now-closed Hortobágy Club Hotel cuts the walk to 1.5km, down from 3km if you follow the road. Buy tickets at the cafe Nyerges Presszó (p225) and have a look at the Carriage Exhibition near the main entrance.

Carriage Exhibition
MUSEUM

(Szekérkiállítás; Hortobágy-Máta; ⊙9am-7pm May-Sep, to 6pm Apr & Oct, to 4pm Nov-Mar) Housed in a thatched cottage by the main entrance of the Máta Stud Farm, this small exhibition presents a dozen traditional carriages and coaches that were once prevalent on the Great Plain.

Nine-Hole Bridge
BRIDGE

(Kilenclyukú-híd) The Nine-Hole Bridge, built in 1833 and spanning the marshy Hortobágy River, is the longest – and certainly the most sketched, painted and photographed – stone bridge in the country. Just in front stands the still-operating roadside inn Hortobágyi Csárda (p225).

Bird Park & Clinic
WILDLIFE RESERVE

(Madárpark és Kórház; 📷52-369 181; www.madarpark.hu; Petőfi tér 6; adult/child 1000/800Ft; ⊙9am-6pm Apr-Oct, 9am-4pm Nov-Mar) Get up close with ailing feathered friends as they convalesce at the Bird Park & Clinic. Walk through the 'hospital' section of this sanctuary (including an operating room), among ambling storks in the park and into an aviary with hawks. Fidgety kestrels stay behind one-way glass. Kids can learn about conservation from simple displays before they head for the playground.

World of Cranes Exhibition
MUSEUM

(Darvak Világa; 📷52-589 321; www.hnp.hu; Petőfi tér 9; ⊙9am-6pm Jul & Aug, to 5pm May, Jun & Sep, shorter hours Oct-Apr) Upstairs at the Hortobágy National Park Visitor Centre (p225), this exhibition tells the story of cranes on the plains, particularly about their annual migration in October when between 60,000 and 100,000 common cranes stop over.

Herder Museum
MUSEUM

(Pásztormúzeum; 📷52-369 040; Petőfi tér 1; adult/child 1500/800Ft; ⊙9am-6pm Jul & Aug, 8am-5pm May, Jun & Sep, 10am-4pm Mar, Apr, Oct & Nov) Housed in an 18th-century carriage house across from the landmark Hortobágyi Csárda, this museum illustrates life on the plains for shepherds, swineherds and cowboys in the 19th century. Tickets include entry to the Round Theatre, Hortobágy Inn Museum and World of Cranes exhibition.

Hortobágy Inn Museum
MUSEUM

(Hortobágyi Csárda Múzeum; 📷52-589 010; www.hortobagy.eu; Petőfi tér 1; adult/child 500/250Ft; ⊙9am-6pm Jul & Aug, shorter hours mid-Jan–Jun & Sep-Nov) As you'll discover at the small Hortobágy Inn Museum inside the Hortobágyi Csárda, the inn dates to 1781 and is one of the original eating houses used by salt traders on their way from the Tisza River to Debrecen. The inns provided itinerant Roma fiddlers with employment; Gypsy music and *csárdak* (inns) have been synonymous ever since.

THE GREAT PLAIN HORTOBÁGY NATIONAL PARK

BIRDWATCHING IN HORTOBÁGY NATIONAL PARK

With its varied terrain and water sources, the patchwork Hortobágy National Park, established in 1973 and Hungary's oldest, has some of the best birdwatching in Europe. Indeed, more than 340 species (of the continent's 530) have been spotted here, including many types of grebe, heron, shrike, egret, spoonbill, stork, kite, warbler, eagle and kestrel. The great bustard, one of the world's largest birds, standing 1m high and weighing in at 20kg, has its own reserve, with limited access to humans. Some 160 species nest here.

Ask the Hortobágy National Park Visitor Centre (p225) about the occasional local weekend birdwatching tours, too. October is a great month to visit; between 60,000 and 100,000 common cranes stop over on the Hortobágy plain during their annual migration. The World of Cranes (p223) is one of the exhibitions in the visitor centre.

Park passes, available from the visitor centre, allow entry to three restricted 'demonstration areas' – nature trails, in reality – within driving distance (adult/concession 1000/600Ft), including the trail around the Hortobágy Great Fishponds (p224).

Round Theatre   MUSEUM
(Körszín; ☑52-369 025; Petőfi tér; adult/child 500/250Ft; ☺9am-6pm Jul & Aug, 8am-5pm May, Jun & Sep, 10am-4pm Mar, Apr, Oct & Nov) FREE The Round Theatre has a small exhibit on Hortobágy traditional crafts and a gift shop.

Puszta Animal Park   ZOO
(Pusztai Állatpark; ☑52-701 037; www.pusztaial latpark.hu/hu; off Hwy 33; adult/child 600/300Ft; ☺9am-6pm mid-Mar–Oct, 10am-4pm Nov–mid-Mar) The Puszta Animal Park, 2km south of the Nine-Hole Bridge, with its weird and wonderful animals, is a fun place for kids of all ages. Here you'll see the rare breeds of the *puszta* up close: the heavy-set long-horned grey cattle, the curly-haired *mangalica* pig and the *racka* sheep, whose corkscrew-like horns are particularly devilish.

Hortobágy Wild Animal Park   ZOO
(Hortobágyi Vadaspark; ☑52-589 321; www.hnp. hu/vadaspark; Hortobágy-Malomháza; adult/child 1600/1000Ft; ☺9am-6pm Jul & Aug, 9am-5pm May, Jun & Sep, 10am-4pm mid-Mar–Apr & Oct) Located about 7km south of Hortobágy village, this zoo hosts animals that lived on the *puszta* before it was farmed: wolves, jackals, wild horses, vultures, pelicans and more. Visitors are transported by 'safari bus', which departs hourly from the Hortobágy National Park Visitor Centre between 9am and 4pm.

🏃 Activities

Hortobágy Great Fishponds   BIRDWATCHING
(Hortobágy Nagyhalastó; off Hwy 33; 3 trails adult/ concession 1000/600Ft; ☺10am-5pm mid-Jun–Aug, 10am-6.30pm Sat & Sun Apr–mid-Jun, Sep & Oct) Among the most interesting areas in Hortobágy National Park are these fishponds 7km to west of the village, where you can walk along interpretive trails and climb a watchtower to see the amazing amount of aquatic birdlife that inhabits this 20-hectare swath.

Horse Riding   HORSE RIDING
(Hortobágy-Máta; per hr 4500Ft) It is possible to ride horses at the Máta Stud Farm, but you must book a minimum of two days in advance. Beginners must stay in the corral but experienced riders can gallop into the sunset across the *puszta*. Carriage-driving lessons are also available (30,000Ft per hour).

⚜ Festivals & Events

National Gulyás Competition & Shepherd's Meeting   RODEO
(Országos Gulyásverseny és Pásztortalálkozó; ☺May-Jun) Cattle herdsmen test their skills in competition, with a competition for cooking *gulyás* (a thick beef soup cooked with onions and potatoes) thrown in.

Hortobágy Equestrian Days   RODEO
(Hortobágyi Lovasnapok; ☺Jul) Equestrian events over three days in Máta.

Hortobágy Bridge Fair   FAIR
(Hortobágyi Hídi Vásár; www.hnp.hu; ☺Aug) This century-old fair held in Hortobágy around St Stephen's Day (20 August) has dance, street theatre, folklore performances, local dishes and the occasional horse and pony for good measure.

⛏ Sleeping

Ask Tourinform (p225) about private rooms in the area (from 4000Ft per person).

Hortobágy Inn GUESTHOUSE **$**
(Hortobágyi Fogadó; ☑ 06 30 286 6793; Kossuth utca 1; s/d 3500/7000Ft; ⊘ Apr-Oct) This bare-bones inn is still begging for an update but it is the most central place to stay. The 10 basic rooms come with balconies and there's a bar on-site.

Ökotúra Vendégház GUESTHOUSE **$$**
(☑ 52-369 075; www.okotura.hu; Borsós utca 12; campsite per person/tent/caravan 1000/1000/3000Ft, s/d/tr 6000/10,000/12,000Ft; ☏) This guesthouse and campground is just over 2km east of the village off Rte 33. The 19 rooms are large, bright and spotlessly clean with wood-laminate floors; they look onto a large, open green space that accommodates campers from April to October. There's a kitchen here, too.

★ **Sóvirág Vendégház** GUESTHOUSE **$$$**
(☑ 52-369 130, 06 30 849 9772; www.sovirag vendeghaz.hu; Czinege János utca 52-53; s/d 14,000/17,000Ft; ❄☏) This attractive chalet-like guesthouse about 2.5km east of the village on the road to Debrecen is surrounded by a huge garden with large sitting area and barbecue. The six rooms are generously proportioned and most have a balcony or terrace. There's a small spa with sauna and jacuzzi and the welcome could not be warmer.

✕ **Eating**

Pizza Sfera PIZZA **$**
(☑ 06 30 555 4759; Petőfi tér; mains 1450-1600Ft; ⊘ 7am-midnight) This central place does Hungarian main courses but most people come to the Sfera for the pizza (1190Ft to 1450Ft).

★ **Hortobágyi Csárda** HUNGARIAN **$$**
(☑ 52-589 010; www.hortobagy.eu; Petőfi tér 1; mains 1990-2390Ft; ⊘ 8am-10pm Apr-Aug, to 8pm Sep–mid-Nov) This is Hungary's most celebrated roadside inn, built at the end of the 18th century. Sit back and admire the Hortobágy kitsch taking up every place on the walls; Gypsy violinists often play as you tuck into your game dishes or *bogrács gulyás* (beef soup served in a small kettle; 1340Ft). Don't miss the famous *Hortobágyi palacsinta* (pancakes; 1290Ft) as an appetiser.

🍷 **Drinking & Nightlife**

Nyerges Presszó CAFE
(☑ 06 70 492 7655, 52-589 369; ⊘ 9am-6pm) At the Máta Stud Farm (p223), get info and buy your tickets for its horse show here at the cafe Nyerges Presszó, which serves hot and cold drinks opposite the stables.

ℹ️ **Information**

Hortobágy National Park Visitor Centre (Hortobágyi Nemzeti Park Látogatóközpont; ☑ 52-589 321; www.hnp.hu; Petőfi tér 9; ⊘ 9am-6pm Jul & Aug, to 5pm May, Jun & Sep, shorter hours Oct-Apr) Stop here to get an overview of the flora and fauna of the region, both from the helpful staff and the excellent exhibitions.

Post Office (Kossuth utca 2; ⊘ 8am-noon & 12.30-4pm Mon-Fri)

Takarékszövetkezet (Petőfi tér 3; ⊘ 7.30am-4pm Mon, to 3pm Tue-Thu, to 2pm Fri) Bank in the shopping complex, with an ATM.

Tourinform (☑ 52-589 000; hortobagy@tourinform.hu; Petőfi tér 9; ⊘ 9am-6pm Jul & Aug, to 5pm May, Jun & Sep, shorter hours Oct-Apr) Shares the same space and hours as the visitor centre.

ℹ️ **Getting There & Away**

Buses stop on both sides of the main road (Rte 33) near the Hortobágyi Csárda. The train station is to the northeast at the end of Kossuth utca.

Six buses stop daily at Hortobágy village on runs between Debrecen (745Ft, 40 minutes, 38km) and Eger (1680Ft, 1¾ hours, 90km). A couple of buses connect daily with Hajdúszoboszló (1120Ft, 1¼ hours, 57km).

Hortobágy is on the main train line linking Debrecen (840Ft, 50 minutes, 42km), Tiszafüred (650Ft, 40 minutes, 31km) and Füzesabony (1300Ft, 1¼ hours, 61km), served by up to a dozen trains daily. For Eger, connect at Füzesabony.

Kecskemét

☑ 76 / POP 111,700

Lying halfway between the Danube and the Tisza Rivers in the heart of the southern Great Plain, Kecskemét is a city ringed with vineyards and orchards that don't seem to stop at the limits of this 'garden city'. Indeed, Kecskemét's agricultural wealth was used wisely – it was able to redeem all its debts in 1832 – and today it boasts some of the finest architecture of a small city in Hungary. Along with colourful art nouveau and Secessionist architecture, its fine museums and the region's excellent *barackpálinka* (apricot brandy) attract. And Kiskunság National Park, the *puszta* of this part of the plain, is right at the back door. Day-trip opportunities include hiking in the sandy, juniper-covered hills, a horse show at Bugac or a visit to one of the region's many horse farms.

⊙ Sights

Kecskemét is a city of multiple squares that run into one another without definition. Walking northeast into Szabadság tér, for example, you'll pass the 17th-century Calvinist church (p228) and adjoining Calvinist New College (p228) from 1912, a later version of the Hungarian Romantic style that looks like a Transylvanian castle and is now a music school.

Town Hall
ARCHITECTURE

(☎76-513 513; Kossuth tér 1; ⊙by arrangement) The sandy-pink, stepped-roof Town Hall (1895) was designed by Ödön Lechner. With a mixture of art nouveau/Secessionist and folkloric elements, Lechner produced a uniquely Hungarian style. The exterior tilework is from the renowned Zsolnay porcelain factory in Pécs, and the carillon chimes out works by Ferenc Erkel, Kodály, Mozart, Handel and Beethoven just after noon, 6pm and 8pm. The floral ceilings and frescoes of Hungarian heroes in the Ceremonial Hall (Díszterem) were painted by Bertalan Székely. Other beautiful examples of this architectural style are the restored Otthon Cinema (p228), on the corner of pedestrian Görögtemplom utca, and the Ornamental Palace (p227).

Great Church
CHURCH

(Nagytemplom; ☎76-487 501; Kossuth tér 2; ⊙noon-7pm Mon, 6am-7pm Tue-Sun) The late-baroque Great Church, dedicated in 1806, dominates Kossuth tér, the southeasternmost of the main squares. The interior is quite sombre. Large tablets on the front honour (from left to right) a mounted regiment of Hussars that served in WWI; citizens who died in the 1848–49 War of Independence; and the Kecskemét victims of WWII. The 73m-tall tower offering views of the city's sun-bleached rooftops is no longer open to the public.

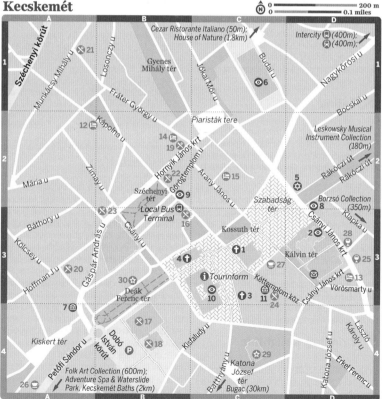

Kecskemét

Ornamental Palace
ARCHITECTURE

(Cifrapalota; Rákóczi út 1) The masterful art nouveau Ornamental Palace, which dates from 1902, has multicoloured majolica tiles decorating its 'waving' walls. The palace contains the Cifrapalota Art Gallery, with a large and important collection of 19th- and 20th-century Hungarian art. But visit mainly to view the aptly named Decorative Hall (Díszterem) and its amazing stucco peacock, bizarre Secessionist windows and more colourful tiles.

Cifrapalota Art Gallery
GALLERY

(Kecskeméti Képtár; ☑ 76-480 776; www.museum. hu/kecskemet/keptar; adult/concession 700/ 350Ft; ☺ 10am-5pm Tue-Sun) This art gallery in the art nouveau Ornamental Palace contains upwards of 20,000 works by 19th- and 20th-century Hungarian painters, and is one of the largest collections in the nation.

House of Science & Technology
JEWISH SITE

(Tudomány és Technika Háza; ☑ 76-322 788; www. titbkkm.microsystem.hu; Rákóczi út 2; adult/child 500/250Ft; ☺ 8am-4pm Mon-Fri) A Moorish-looking structure dating from 1871, this was once a synagogue and is now used for conferences and both temporary and permanent exhibitions, including one of plaster copies of 15 statues by Michelangelo.

Museum of Hungarian Naive Artists
MUSEUM

(Magyar Naiv Müvészek Múzeuma; ☑ 76-324 767; www.museum.hu/kecskemet/naivmuzeum; Gáspár András utca 11; adult/child 450/250Ft, with Toy Museum & Workshop 600/300Ft; ☺ 10am-5pm Tue-Sun Mar-Oct) Arguably the city's most interesting museum and one of the few of its kind in Europe, the Museum of Hungarian Naive Artists contains works with lots of folksy themes, but the warmth and craft of Rozália Albert Juhászné's work, the druglike visions of Dezső Mokry-Mészáros and the bright and comical paintings of András Süli should hold your attention.

Something extra special is the work of István Kada – a Hungarian Grandma Moses – and János Balázs, whose glass paintings are Magritte-like. Keep an eye out for weavings by Anna Kiss and woodcarvings by Pál Gyursó.

Toy Museum & Workshop
MUSEUM

(Szórakaténusz Játékmúzeum; ☑ 76-481 469; www.szorakatenusz.hu; Gáspár András utca 11; adult/child 450/250Ft, with Museum of Hungarian Naive Artists 600/300Ft; ☺ 10am-5pm Tue-Sun Mar-Oct, to 4pm in winter) This museum has a large collection of rather spooky 19th- and early-20th-century dolls. Also in the rows of glass cases are wooden trains and board games. The museum organises events and classes for kids on Saturday. It's next to the Museum of Hungarian Naive Artists.

THE GREAT PLAIN KECSKEMÉT

Kecskemét

Bozsó Collection
MUSEUM

(Bozsó Gyűjtemény; ☑ 76-324 626; www.bozso.net; Klapka utca 34; adult/child 800/500Ft; ☺ 10am-6pm Thu-Sun) This collection of period furniture, folk art, religious items and clocks amassed by the pack-rat painter János Bozsó (1922–98) is massive and endlessly fascinating, but best of all is the delightful pretty cottage (1776) on a quiet street that houses part of it.

Leskowsky Musical Instrument Collection
MUSEUM

(Leskowsky Hangszergyűjtemény; ☑ 76-486 616; www.hangszergyujtemeny.hu; Rákóczi út 15; adult/child 1000/750Ft; ☺ 10am-5pm Tue-Sun) In a new location on leafy Rákóczi út, this private collection traces the development of music-making over the centuries. Of the 150 instruments on display from five continents most are stringed, but there are also flutes and accordions. All instruments can be played.

Folk Art Collection
MUSEUM

(Népi Iparművészeti Gyűjtemény; ☑ 76-327 203; www.nepiiparmuveszet.hu; Serfőző utca 19/a; adult/child 600/300Ft; ☺ 10am-5pm Tue-Sat Mar-Dec & Oct, to 4pm Jan & Feb) A dozen rooms of a 200-year-old brewery are crammed with embroidery, weaving, woodcarving, furniture, agricultural tools and textiles at the Folk Art Collection, the grandaddy of all Kecskemét museums. Styles from across the entire region are represented and a few local handicrafts are for sale at the reception. It's located about 1.5km southwest of Kossuth tér.

Otthon Cinema
ARCHITECTURE

(Széchenyi tér 4) The restored Otthon Cinema, on the corner of pedestrian Görögtemplom utca, is a beautiful example of art nouveau/Secessionist architecture mixed with folkloric elements.

Calvinist New College
ARCHITECTURE

(Református Újkollégium; Szabadság tér 7) Now a music school, the Calvinist New College was built in 1912 in the late Hungarian Romantic style and looks like a Transylvanian castle.

Calvinist Church
CHURCH

(Református Templom; Szabadság tér) This Calvinist church in Szabadság tér dates to the 17th century.

Market
MARKET

(Jókai Mór utca; ☺ 6am-noon Tue-Sun) One of the liveliest on the Great Plain, Kecskemét's market to the north of the centre is worth a trip, but get there as early as you can to see it at its animated best.

Franciscan Church of St Nicholas
CHURCH

(Szent Miklós Ferences Templom; ☑ 76-497 025; Lestár tér) On the eastern side of Kossuth tér is the Franciscan Church of St Nicholas, dating in part from the late 14th century. It was shared by squabbling Catholics and Protestants during the Turkish occupation until 1564.

Zoltán Kodály Institute of Music Education
MUSEUM

(Kodály Zoltán Zenepedagógiai Intézet; ☑ 76-481 518; www.kodaly-inst.hu; Kéttemplom köz 1; adult/child 150/100Ft; ☺ 10am-6pm) The world-renowned music institute, established in 1975, occupies the baroque monastery behind the Franciscan church. There's a small exhibit inside devoted to the life and work of the eponymous founder-composer (1882–1967).

✈ Activities

Adventure Spa & Waterslide Park
WATER PARK

(Élményfürdő és Csúszdapark; ☑ 76-417 407; www.csuszdapark.hu; Csabay Géza körút 2; adult/child 1600/1200Ft; ☺ 9am-8pm Jun–mid-Sep) Kecskemét's main summer attraction is this huge water park 3km southwest of the centre, which is loaded with fun things for the kids – five pools and slides, including a six-lane one, ball courts, grassy park etc.

Kecskemét Baths
SPA

(Kecskeméti Fürdő; ☑ 76-500 320; www.kecskemetifurdo.hu; Csabay Géza körút 5; adult/concession 3600/3000Ft; ☺ 6am-9pm) A year-round, rather extravagant complex with thermal baths, swimming pools, full spa facilities and every wellness treatment known to man, woman or child.

✦ Festivals & Events

Kecskemét Apricot Brandy & Wine Festival
WINE

(Kecskeméti Barackpálinka és Bor Fesztivál; www.hirosagora.hu; ☺ Jun) Vintners and distillers from around the country set up tasting booths on the town squares of Kecskemét.

Hírős Week Festival
MUSIC

(Hírős Hét Fesztivál; http://hiros7.hu; ☺ Aug) Seven days of folk- and pop-music concerts in mid-August.

🛏 Sleeping

Tourinform (p231) has a list of summer college accommodation. In addition, Kecskemét offers a range of accommodation options at all budget levels.

Jam Pub
GUESTHOUSE **$**

(☑06 30 950 5147; www.facebook.com/Jampub1; Beniczky Ferenc utca 1; s/d from 2500/5000Ft; ✱❄🕏) If you like the idea of crashing just above where you spent the night bending your elbow, book one of the nine rooms above this raucous pub (and club at the weekend). The rooms have sloping ceilings and are basic at best, but they are clean and the price is certainly right.

Klárá Lővei College
HOSTEL **$**

(Lővei Klárá Kollégium; ☑76-486 977; www.kefo.hu; Piaristák tere 4; s/d 4000/8000Ft; ☺mid-Jun–Aug; ❄) The most central and friendly of Kecskemét's summer college accommodation, this dormitory has basic rooms with twin beds and (mostly) en suite bathrooms.

★ Fábián Panzió
GUESTHOUSE **$$**

(☑76-477 677; www.panziofabian.hu; Kápolna utca 14; s €30-35, d €35-45; ✱❄🕏) We love, love, love this 10-room guesthouse on a quiet street that looks onto an inner courtyard garden. Four of the rooms are upstairs in the terraced main building; they're smaller and a bit cheaper than the six at nose level with flowers and trees. If the friendly service doesn't keep you coming back, the homemade biscuits and jam at breakfast will.

The world-travelling family that owns the place seem to know exactly what their guests want, with local restaurant menus and travel brochures to peruse.

Pálma Hotel
HOTEL **$$**

(☑76-321 045; www.hotelpalma.hu; Arany János utca 3; s 6850-9650Ft, d 10,300-12,800Ft; ✱❄🕏) As central in Kecskemét as you could possibly want, the Pálma has 40 simple guest rooms in two modern buildings. The more expensive ones are on the 1st floor and have TV, fridge and air-conditioning. Cheaper rooms are upstairs and have sloping ceilings, but are quiet and bright. Free self-service laundry facilities are available.

Granada Hotel
HOTEL **$$$**

(☑76-503 130; http://granadahotel.hu; Harmónia utca 12; s/d from €66/75; ✱@🕏❄🕏) Wellness (indoor swimming pool, sauna, treatments) and sport (tennis, soccer, minigolf) are the reasons to stay at this 86-room resort several kilometres from the centre. But the location near the M5 makes a good base for those with a car that want to tour the region and return to cool and contemporary comfort.

✖ Eating

Max
PIZZA **$**

(☑76-321 600; www.maxpizzeria.hu; Széchenyi tér 9; mains 1600-1950Ft; ☺10am-11pm Mon-Wed, 10am-midnight Thu-Sat, 10am-10pm Sun) This cosy place with a small courtyard claims to be a cafe, a restaurant and a pizzeria and perhaps it is. But most come for the pasta (1320Ft to 1840Ft) and pizza (1100Ft to 1990Ft), which many locals will tell you is the best in town.

Főzelékház Étterem
HUNGARIAN **$**

(☑06 20 439 4101, 76-321 206; Deák Ferenc tér 6; mains 460-790Ft; ☺10am-6pm Mon-Fri, 10am-2pm Sat) This simple eatery hiding in the middle of a shopping centre is just the place to try Hungarian soul food, including the eponymous *főzelék*, twice-cooked vegetables often served with sliced meat. The two-course set menu is a steal at 790Ft.

Aranyhomok Gyorsétterem
FAST FOOD **$**

(☑06 20 479 9199; Kossuth tér 3; mains 590-990Ft; ☺7am-midnight Sun-Thu, to 2am Fri & Sat) Locals love the quick and tasty self-service cafeteria on the ground floor of the city's largest central hotel.

Italia Pizzeria
PIZZA **$**

(☑06 20 947 6847, 76-327 328; www.italiapizzeria.hu; Hornyik János körút 4; pizza 1090-1950Ft; ☺8am-11pm) Italia is a little short on atmosphere, but it does a roaring trade with students from the nearby colleges. A full menu also includes pasta dishes (990Ft to 1690Ft) and meat mains (1540Ft to 2290Ft). Set lunch is just 1150Ft.

★ Tepsi Gastropub
INTERNATIONAL **$$**

(☑76-508 558; www.tepsipub.hu; Kéttemplom köz 7; mains 1150-5900Ft; ☺noon-11pm Tue & Wed, noon-midnight Thu-Sat) Our favourite new place to eat in the centre, Tepsi has pushed the Kecskemét dining scene into the 21st century with its simple, clean decor and a menu with things like *lepény*, Hungarian-style savoury pies stuffed with cheese or meat (try the one with brisket), and organic Charollais beef steak. But best are the gourmet burgers (1490Ft to 2550Ft).

Kisbugaci Csárda
HUNGARIAN **$$**

(☑06 30 968 6350, 76-322 722; www.kisbugaci.hu; Munkácsy Mihály utca 10; mains 1700-3800Ft; ☺11am-11pm Mon-Sat, noon-4pm Sun) This *csárda* trades on folksy charm, with its wooden benches, plates on the wall and Gypsy music. But the food, which comes in huge meaty portions, holds its own. Try the *Erdélyi flekken* (Transylvanian barbecue) or the *betyárpörkölt* (thief's stew).

Cezar Ristorante Italiano ITALIAN $$

(☑76-328 849; www.clubcaruso.hu; Kaszap utca 4; ⊗noon-11pm Tue-Sat, noon-4pm Sun) Italian-owned and operated, Cezar serves dishes made with ingredients almost entirely sourced in Italy. The minestrone and tomato and mozzarella salad are out of this world. The choice of pizza (1290Ft to 1990Ft) and pasta dishes (1800Ft to 3900Ft) is huge, but don't be frightened off by the gargantuan sizes of the main courses, as they do half-portions.

Kecskeméti Csárda HUNGARIAN $$

(☑76-488 686; www.kecskemeticsarda.hu; Kölcsey utca 7; mains 2600-5500Ft; ⊗noon-10pm Mon-Sat, to 4pm Sun) This place goes over the top with its rustic fishing gear on the walls and costumed wait staff. But the food is good, there's a large open courtyard and live music on the weekend. Unusual for a *csárda*, the wine selection is very good.

Rozmaring HUNGARIAN $$$

(☑76-509 175; www.rozmaringbisztro.hu; Mária utca 1; mains 1990-4290Ft; ⊗8am-11pm Mon-Fri, 11am-11pm Sat, 11am-3pm Sun; ☑) Artistic presentations are standard at this silver-service restaurant in a new location, whether you order the catfish stew or the chicken breast with prunes and goose liver (both 2490Ft). This is modern Hungarian done right.

Géniusz INTERNATIONAL $$$

(☑76-497 668; www.facebook.com/Géniusz-Kávéház-Étterem-194569090588212; Kisfaludy utca 5; mains 2700-4300Ft; ⊗9am-11pm Mon-Sat; ☑) This is business-account territory but not for nothing as the rather inventive menu changes seasonally, and options might include stuffed trout with almonds or Thai chicken. Decent vegetarian choices too. Weekday set lunches are 1250Ft and 1500Ft.

🍷 Drinking & Nightlife

Vincent CAFE

(☑06 30 570 0518; www.facebook.com/vincent cukraszda; Szabadság tér 6; ⊗8am-10pm Mon-Thu, 8am-midnight Fri, 9am-midnight Sat, 9am-10pm Sun) We've always tended to avoid the eating and drinking outlets on Szabadság tér like the plague but we make an exception for our favourite, Vincent. It serves excellent coffee and is a decent place for such a central (read touristy) location.

Black Cat Pub BAR

(☑06 30 997 7875; Csányi János körút 6; ⊗8am-10pm Mon-Wed, 8am-midnight Thu, 8am-2am Fri, 10am-2am Sat, 10am-10pm Sun) The Black Cat – more a bar than a pub – offers an alternative night on the town.

Wanted Söröző PUB

(☑76-434 815; www.facebook.com/wanted kecskemet; Csányi János körút 4; ⊗4pm-midnight Mon-Sat) This Western-themed pub just down from the Ornamental Palace is where Kecskemét's young bloods congregate.

Jakó Cukrászda CAFE

(☑76-505 949; www.jakocukraszda.com; Petőfi Sándor utca 7; ⊗9am-8pm) This is where locals go in season for ice cream and cake (190Ft to 550Ft) when they are trying to avoid tourist-rammed Szabadság tér.

⭐ Entertainment

Kecskemét is a city of music and theatre; cultural festivals are on nearly year-round. Ask Tourinform (p231) for the list it prepares annually.

József Katona Theatre THEATRE

(Katona József Színház; ☑76-501 174; www. kecskemetikatona.hu; Katona József tér 5; ⊗box office 9am-6pm Mon-Fri) This attractive 19th-century theatre named after the eponymous local boy who brought new life to Hungarian theatre stages dramatic works, as well as operettas and concerts.

Kecskemét Cultural & Conference Centre PERFORMING ARTS

(Kecskeméti Kulturális és Konferencia Központ; ☑76-503 880; www.efmk.hu; Deák Ferenc tér 1) The cultural centre sponsors some events and is a good source of information.

ℹ️ Information

House of Nature (Természet Háza; ☑76-482 611; www.knp.hu; Liszt Ferenc utca 19; ⊗9am-4pm Tue-Fri, 10am-2pm Sat Apr-Oct, 9am-4pm Mon-Fri Nov-Mar) Ask about birding and other tours at Kiskunság National Park's main office in Kecskemét, or check its website.

Ibusz (☑76-486 955; www.ibusz.hu; Korona utca 2, Malom Centre; ⊗10am-7pm Mon-Sat) In the central shopping plaza; helps with apartment rental.

Main Post Office (Kálvin tér 10; ⊗7am-7pm Mon, 8am-7pm Tue-Fri, 8am-noon Sat)

OTP Bank (Korona utca 2, Malom Centre; ⊗7.45am-6pm Mon, 7.45am-5pm Tue-Fri, 8am-

BUSES FROM KECSKEMÉT

DESTINATION	PRICE	DURATION	KM	FREQUENCY
Baja	2200Ft	2hr	111	5 nonstop daily
Budapest	1830Ft	1¼hr	84	hourly nonstop
Debrecen	4620Ft	6hr	240	6 daily with 1 change
Eger	3410Ft	4hr	186	2 nonstop daily
Gyula	2830Ft	3½hr	143	2 nonstop daily
Pécs	3410Ft	3½hr	200	3 nonstop daily
Szeged	1680Ft	2hr	88	hourly nonstop

noon Sat) Foreign exchange and ATM; in the central shopping centre.

Tourinform (☑ 76-481 065; www.visit-kecskemet.hu; Kossuth tér 1; ☉ 8.30am-5.30pm Mon-Fri, 9am-1pm Sat May-Aug, 8.30am-4.30pm Mon-Fri Sep-Apr) In the northeastern corner of City Hall.

❶ Getting There & Away

The intercity bus and train stations are opposite one another at József Katona Park, a 10-minute walk northeast along Nagykőrösi utca from Szabadság tér.

BUS & TRAIN

Kecskemét is on the train line linking Nyugati train station in Budapest (3105Ft, 1½ hours, 106km) with Szeged (1830Ft, 1¼ hours, 85km) at least hourly. To get to other towns north and east, you must change at Cegléd (650Ft, 30 minutes, 33km).

❶ Getting Around

Buses 1 and 15 link the intercity bus and train stations with the **local bus terminal** on Széchenyi tér. For the water parks/spas, buses 5 and 22 are good. Rent bicycles at **Tourinform** (p231) for 1000/3000Ft per hour/day.

Kiskunság National Park

Kiskunság National Park, established in 1975, consists of nine 'islands' of land totalling about 50,000 hectares. Much of the park's alkaline ponds, dunes and grassy 'deserts' are off-limits to casual visitors.

The easiest place to get up close with Kiskunság National Park's environmentally fragile area and see its famous horse herds go through their paces is at Bugac (population 2685), on a sandy steppe 30km southwest of Kecskemét.

◉ Sights

Herder Museum MUSEUM
(Pásztormúzeum; ☑ 76-575 112; www.museum.hu/bugac/pasztormuzeum; Nagybugac 135; ☉ 10am-5pm May-Sep) FREE Board a horse-driven carriage (extra charge), drive or walk the 1.5km along a sandy track to the Herder Museum, a circular structure designed to look like the horse-driven dry mills once so prevalent on the Great Plain. It's filled with stuffed fauna and shepherds' implements – carved wooden pipes, embroidered fur coats and a tobacco pouch made from a gnarled old ram's scrotum.

🏃 Activities

Ask about birding and other tours at the Kiskunság National Park's main office, the House of Nature (p230) in Kecskemét, or check its website.

Somodi Tanya HORSE RIDING
(☑ 06 30 953 0987, 76-377 095; www.somoditanya.hu; Fülöpháza; horse riding/carriage training per hr 4500/8000Ft) It's not possible for visitors to ride horses at Bugac. If you want to mount your own steed you'll have to head for this ranch at Fülöpháza, some 50km northwest of Bugac, where along with riding possibilities there is accommodation and a very good restaurant.

🍴 Sleeping & Eating

Most people visiting Kiskunság National Park and attending the cowboy show do so as a day trip from Kecskemét so have accommodation there.

Karikás Csárda HUNGARIAN $$
(☑ 06 30 416 6439, 76-575 112; www.bugacpuszta.hu; Nagybugac 135; mains 2000-4000Ft; ☉ 10am-9pm Jul-Sep, to 8pm May & Jun) The food is

THE GREAT PLAIN KISKUNSÁG NATIONAL PARK

DON'T MISS

HIKING IN KISKUNSÁG NATIONAL PARK

There are several nature and educational hiking trails in the park's vicinitiy, with explanatory signposting in English, where you can get out and see this amazing ecosystem of dunes, bluffs and swamps. The circular 2km Juniper Trail (Boróka Sáv), behind the stables, is an interpretive track that leads you to the edge of the juniper forest and sandy hills, which is a restricted area. You can take an offshoot trail to a nearby tower for a better look before heading back.

surprisingly good at the entirely kitschy Karikás Csárda, next to the park entrance. The *gulyás* (beef goulash soup; 1100Ft) is hearty and the accompanying folk-music ensemble will get your foot tapping on the large and shady terrace.

☆ Entertainment

Cowboy Show   HORSE RACING

(Csikósbemutató; www.bugacpuszta.hu; adult/child 1900/1400Ft, with carriage ride 3600/2600Ft; ⊙12.15pm May-Sep) The highlight of a trip to the Kiskunság National Park is the chance to see the *puszta* cowboy show at Bugac. In addition to making noble Nonius steeds perform tricks that most dogs would be disinclined to do, the *csikósok* (cowboys) crack their whips and race one another bareback.

The cowboys also ride 'five-in-hand' – a breathtaking performance in which one *csikós* gallops five horses around the field at full tilt while standing on the backs of the rear two.

❶ Getting There & Away

Getting to the park and the cowboy show without your own vehicle is difficult. There's an 11am bus from Kecskemét to Bugac (745Ft, one hour, 37km) but it won't get you there in time for the 12.15pm show. (Buses before that leave at an ungodly 5.25am on weekdays and 6.30am at the weekend.) An alternative but complicated way to go is to take the hourly train to Kiskunfélegyháza (615Ft, 16 minutes, 25km) at 9.11am and then the hourly bus to Bugac (370Ft, 30 minutes, 18km). A taxi will cost a whopping 9600Ft.

Szeged

📞 62 / POP 162,600

It's hard to name the single thing that makes Szeged such an appealing city. Is it the shady, gardenlike main square with all the park benches or the abundant streetside-cafe seating in a pedestrian area that seems to stretch on forever? Maybe it's the interesting architecture of the palaces in the old town. Then again, it could be the year-round cultural performances and lively university-town vibe (students marched here in 1956 before their classmates in Budapest did). Szeged – a corruption of the Hungarian word *sziget* (island) – sits astride the Tisza River, with a thermal-bath complex and park opposite the old town. Another thing that makes the city unique is the unusual Szeged accent in Hungarian (eg 'e' is pronounced as 'ö'), which sounds strange in a country with so few dialectical differences.

◉ Sights

Votive Church   CATHEDRAL

(Fogadalmi templom; 📞 62-420 157; www.szeged idom.hu; Dóm tér; ⊙6.30am-7pm Mon-Sat, 7.30am-7pm Sun) The twin-towered Votive Church is a disproportionate brown-brick monstrosity that was pledged after the flood in 1879 but not completed until 1930. About the only things worth seeing inside are the gigantic organ with 9040 pipes, the cupola covered in frescoes and the choir. To climb the tower, enter via the Votive Church Exhibition Centre.

Votive Church Exhibition Centre   MUSEUM

(Fogadalmi Templom kiállítótér; 📞 62-420 157; www.szegedidom.com; Dóm tér; adult/child 1000/600Ft; ⊙9am-5pm Tue-Sun) This new exhibition space opened in the crypt of the Votive Church below Dom tér in 2016. It examines the history of the cathedral and the surrounding square. It also displays liturgical objects and church plate moved from the nearby Diocesan Museum & Treasury. This is also where you enter to climb one of the church's twin towers (287 steps).

Reök Palace   ARCHITECTURE

(Reök Palota; 📞 62-541 205; www.reok.hu; Tisza Lajos körút 56; ⊙10am-6pm Tue-Sun) The Reök Palace is a mind-blowing green-and-lilac art nouveau structure, built in 1907, that looks like a decoration at the bottom of an aquarium. It's been polished up to regain its original lustre in recent years and now hosts regular photography and visual-arts exhibitions.

New Synagogue
SYNAGOGUE

(Új Zsinagóga; ☑62-423 849; www.zsinagoga. szeged.hu; Jósika utca 10; adult/concession 500/250Ft; ☺10am-noon & 1-5pm Sun-Fri Apr-Sep, 9am-2pm Sun-Fri Oct-Mar) The recently renovated art nouveau New Synagogue, designed by Lipót Baumhorn in 1903, is the most beautiful Jewish house of worship in Hungary, if not the world. It is still in use, though the community has dwindled from 8000 before WWII to about 500 people today. Dominating the enormous blue-and-gold interior is the cupola, decorated with stars and flowers (representing infinity and faith) and appearing to float heavenward.

Other notable features inside include the tabernacle of carved acacia wood, the metal fittings and the stained glass by Miksa Róth.

Serbian Orthodox Church
CHURCH

(Görögkeleti Szerb ortodox templom; ☑06 30 484 8778, 62-426 091; Dóm tér; adult/child 400/300Ft; ☺by appointment 8am-5pm) The Zopf-style Serbian Orthodox church in Dóm tér, dating from 1778, has a fantastic iconostasis: a central gold 'tree', with 70 icons hanging from its 'branches'.

Ferenc Móra Museum
MUSEUM

(☑62-549 040; http://moramuzeum.hu; Roosevelt tér 1-3; adult/concession 1890/1290Ft; ☺10am-6pm Tue-Sun year-round, also to 8pm Thu May-Sep) The erstwhile Palace of Education (1896) now houses this excellent museum containing a colourful collection of folk as well as traditional trades from greater Szeged, a natural history section called 'We Have Only One Earth', and an extensive collection of works by Hungarian artists including József Rippl-Rónai and Mihály Munkácsy. The high entrance fee allows entry to the permanent collection and often excellent temporary exhibitions.

Castle Museum & Lapidarium
MUSEUM

(Varmúzeum és kőtár; ☑62-549 040; Stefánia sétány 15; adult/child 300/200Ft; ☺by appointment 10am-6pm Tue-Sun) After the 1879 flood claimed many of the walls of Szeged's riverfront castle built around 1240, the city demolished the rest. Behind the Ferenc Móra Museum you can see ongoing excavations of the foundation and ancient subterranean walls at this small gallery displaying archaeological finds. Seek admission at the museum.

Dóm tér
SQUARE

'Cathedral Square' contains Szeged's most important monuments and buildings, including the Votive Church (p232), and is the centre of events during the annual summer festival.

National Pantheon
MONUMENT

(Nemzeti Emlékcsarnok; Dóm tér) The National Pantheon – statues and reliefs of more than 100 notables running along an arcade around three sides of Dóm tér – is a crash course in Hungarian art, literature, science and history. Even the Scotsman Adam Clark, who supervised the building of Budapest's Chain Bridge, wins a place, but you'll look forever for any sign of a woman.

St Demetrius Tower
TOWER

(Dömötö-torony; Dóm tér) The Romanesque Demetrius Tower in Dóm tér is the city's oldest structure and is all that remains of a church erected here in the 12th century. It can be visited on a group tour only from the Votive Church Exhibition Centre (p232).

Heroes' Gate
HISTORIC SITE

This gate was erected in 1936 in honour of Miklós Horthy's White Guards, who were responsible for 'cleansing' the nation of 'reds' after the ill-fated Republic of Councils in 1919.

Pick Salami &
Szeged Paprika Museum
MUSEUM

(Pick szalámi és Szegedi paprika múzeum; ☑06 20 980 8000; www.pickmuzeum.hu; Felső Tisza-part 10; adult/child 980/740Ft; ☺3-6pm Tue-Sat) Between the two bridges spanning the Tisza is this museum with two floors of exhibits showing the methods of salami production and the cultivating, processing and packaging of Szeged's 'red gold'. It's a lot more interesting than you might think and you even get samples of both salami and paprika.

Gróf Palace
HISTORIC BUILDING

(Gróf Palota; Tisza Lajos körút 20) This lovely Secessionist office building with floral mosaics was completed in 1913.

Former Jewish
Community Centre
JEWISH SITE

(Zsidó Hitközség; Gutenberg utca 20) Among the buildings of interest in Szeged's one-time Jewish quarter is this former Jewish community centre built in 1902, which once served as an old-age home.

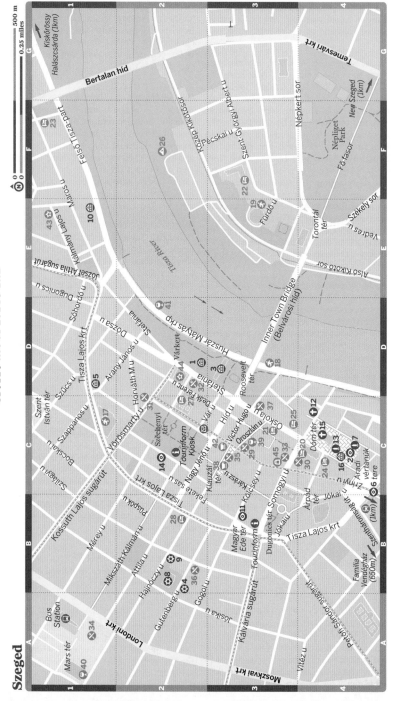

Szeged

Szeged

THE GREAT PLAIN SZEGED

Town Hall ARCHITECTURE
(Városház; Széchenyi tér 10) On the west side of the Széchenyi tér is the neobaroque town hall, built in 1883, with its bizarre, top-heavy tower and colourful tiled roof.

Old Synagogue JEWISH SITE
(Ózsinagóga; Hajnóczy utca 12) There are a few buildings of interest in Szeged's former Jewish quarter, including the neoclassical Old Synagogue, built in 1843. It now houses theatre workshops. The interior is in a bad state of repair.

🏃 Activities

Napfényfürdő Aquapolis WATER PARK
(☑62-566 488; www.napfenyfurdoaquapolis.com; Torontál tér 1; adult/child 4900/2500Ft; ☺6am-10pm, outdoor pools 9am-8pm May-Sep) Across the Tisza in New Szeged (Újszeged) is this positively enormous spa and water park with all manner of pools inside and out, basins with thermal water, saunas, steam rooms and treatment centres. Flanking the complex is New Szeged Park (Újszegedi Liget), a great

place for walking and biking. There's a small public beach on the river bank.

Anna Baths SPA
(☑62-553 330; www.szegedsport.hu/intez menyek/anna-furdo; Tisza Lajos körút 24; adult/child 1650/1350Ft; ☺6am-8pm) The lovely cream-coloured Anna Baths were built in 1896 to imitate the tilework and soaring dome of a Turkish bath. Rich architectural detail surrounds all the modern saunas and bubbly pools you'd expect. There's a fountain spouting free thermal drinking water in front of the building.

Boat Cruise BOATING
(Hajókirándulás; ☑62-402 302, 06 20 230 8817; www.hajokirandulas.hu; Roosevelt tér; adult/child 1200/900Ft; ☺3pm Tue-Fri, 11am, 1pm & 3pm Sat & Sun May-Sep) See Szeged from a different vantage point altogether by taking a boat cruise departing down from Roosevelt tér just next to the Inner Town Bridge. The excursion lasts an hour and takes you northward to where the Maros flows into the Tisza and then southward past the old town.

✿ Festivals & Events

Szeged Wine Festival   WINE
(Szegedi Borfesztivál; www.szegediborfesztival.hu;
☺May) A 10-day wine-oriented extravaganza
in mid-May.

Rose Festival   FLOWER
(Rózsafesztivál; www.rozsaunnep.hu; ☺Jun)
Three-day flower festival in late June, with
new breeds on display as well as parades
and entertainment.

★ Szeged Open-Air Festival   MUSIC
(Szegedi Szabadtéri Játékok; ☑62-541 205; www.
szegediszabadteri.hu; ☺Jul & Aug) The Szeged
Open-Air Festival held in Dom tér in July
and August is the largest festival in Hungary outside Budapest. The outdoor theatre in
front of the Votive Church seats some 6000
people. Main events include an opera, an operetta, a play, folk dancing, classical music,
ballet and a rock opera.

International Tisza Fish Festival   FOOD & DRINK
(Nemzetközi Tiszai Halfesztivál; www.halfesztival.
hu; ☺Sep) Three-day festival celebrating
Szeged's most iconic comestible in early
September.

🛏 Sleeping

As one of Hungary's largest cities, Szeged
offers a full range of accommodation from
pensions and hostels – Tourinform (p239)
has a full list of summer college accommodation – to boutique and business hotels.

Szeged Beach Camping   CAMPGROUND $
(Szegedi Partfürdő Kemping; ☑62-430 843; www.
szegedcamping.hu; Középkikötő sor 1-3; campsite
per person/tent 1490/590Ft, bungalow for 2/3/4
9900/12,900/15,900Ft; ☺May-Sep; 🛜🏊) Looking a bit like a public park, this large grassy
camping ground is on the banks of the Tisza.
It has sites for 700 happy campers, volley-
ball courts and a grassy beach. Bungalows
on stilts, containing both rooms and apartments (with kitchens), are also available.

István Apáthy College   HOSTEL $
(Apáthy István Kollégium; ☑62-545 896; www.
apathy.szote.u-szeged.hu; Apáthy utca 4; dm/s/d
4200/8700/9800Ft; @🛜) Strong feelings
about the Apáthy? This supremely central
option offers pretty bare-bones dormitory accommodation. More than 200 rooms
are available in July and August, but only a
handful – in fact, three – throughout the rest
of the year. There are communal kitchens
and a laundry room on each floor.

Familia Vendégház   GUESTHOUSE $$
(Family Guesthouse; ☑62-441 122; www.
familiapanzio.hu; Szentháromság utca 71; s/d/
tr 7500/11,000/14,000Ft; ❄🛜) Families and
international travellers often book up this
family-run guesthouse with contemporary,
if nondescript, furnishings in a great old-
town building close to the train station. The
two-dozen rooms have high ceilings, lots
of wood and brick walls, and loads of light
from tall windows. Air-conditioning costs an
extra 500Ft.

Illés Hotel   GUESTHOUSE $$
(☑06 20 927 2642, 62-315 640; www.illespanzio-
vadaszetterem.hu; Maros utca 37; d Mon-Fri
13,900Ft, Sat & Sun 15,900Ft; ❄🛜🏊) The
cheery facade of this former mansion now
calling itself a hotel stands in stark contrast
to its 14 rooms' dark-wood veneers and woven rugs. The courtyard garden with pool
is quite pleasant, though. Walk 10 minutes
southwest to the city centre or take a rental
bike (per day 1500Ft). There's a cellar restaurant here specialising in game.

★ Tiszavirág Hotel   BOUTIQUE HOTEL $$$
(☑62-554 888; http://tiszaviragszeged.hu; Hajnóczy utca 1/b; s/d/ste €80/90/140; ❄🛜) Wow.
Our favourite new boutique hotel in Szeged
is a jaw-dropper. Set in a historic townhouse built by a wealthy goldsmith in 1859,
it counts 12 rooms, many with original features and all with fabulous modern artwork.
There's a new wing too, separated from the
old one by a splendid glass-enclosed inner
courtyard perfect for lounging.

The in-house spa is state of the art, with
a salty 'sea-climate' room. The hotel restaurant (p238) is one of the finest in Szeged.

Art Hotel Szeged   BUSINESS HOTEL $$$
(☑06 30 697 4681, 62-592 888; www.arthotel
szeged.hu; Somogyi utca 16; s/d/ste
17,950/21,750/32,000Ft; ❄🛜) Business travellers love this upbeat 71-room hotel for its
ubercentral location just off Somogyi utca
and its large underground garage. We love
the primary colours, the neon and the interesting artwork strewn here and there.
Rooms are generously proportioned and
some bathrooms have tubs. The centrepiece
of the fitness centre is a hot tub facing the
Votive Church.

Dóm Hotel Szeged   BOUTIQUE HOTEL $$$
(☑62-423 750, 06 30 834 8883; http://dom
hotelszeged.info; Bajza utca 6; s/d/apt from
23,900/27,900/47,000Ft; ❄@🛜) A welcome

addition to Szeged's top-end accommodation scene is this smart and very central 16-room boutique hotel. There's a small wellness centre with jacuzzi, sauna and massage, a popular in-house restaurant and a 21st-century underground car park accessed by lift. But the main draw is the extremely helpful multilingual staff for whom no request is too much.

Mozart Hotel
BOUTIQUE HOTEL $$$

(☑62-800 040; www.mozarthotel.hu; Oskola utca 16; s 15,500-20,500Ft; d 17,500-22,500Ft; ✳🐕) This elegant, peachy (as in the colour), but understated 15-room hotel just north of Dóm tér is attractively furnished in retro-style furniture and adorned with portraits of the Viennese composer (the owner is a big fan). The back terrace is a good place to relax and the bar small but convivial.

Tisza Hotel
HOTEL $$$

(☑06 30 636 7975, 62-478 278; www.tiszahotel.hu; Széchenyi tér 3; s/d/ste €48/60/102; ✳🐕) An old communist-era neon sign still lights the way at Szeged's old-world hotel. But while the public areas may drip with crystal chandeliers and gilt mirrors, many of the 51 guest rooms are quite boxy, small and somewhat frayed. Go for a superior room if budget allows; they are generally larger, brighter and a lot airier.

Hotel Forrás
HOTEL $$$

(☑62-566 466; www.hotelforras.hunguesthotels. hu; Szent-Györgyi Albert utca 16-24; s/d €110/147; ✳🐕🏊) This enormous hotel on the doorstep of the Napfényfürdő Aquapolis water park (entry included in the room price) in New Szeged counts 196 large rooms, mostly with balconies. The preference for orange, chocolate, tan and purple is rather masculine, but somehow works. As bowlers from way back, we love the four fully equipped lanes just begging for a strike. Bikes are available for rent (1000Ft per day).

🍴 Eating

When visiting Szeged make sure you try one of the celebrated local edibles including Pick salami and its own type of local paprika that marries very well with spicy Szegedi halászlé (Szeged fish soup).

Boci Tejivó
FAST FOOD $

(☑62-423 154; http://bocitejivoszeged.hu; Zrínyi utca 2; dishes 335-800Ft; ⏰6am-10pm Mon & Tue, to 11pm Wed & Thu, 24hr Fri & Sat, 9am-10pm Sun; 🐕) This is a very modern take on an old-fashioned idea – the 'milk bar' so popular during socialist times. Though not vegetarian there are dozens of meatless dishes – cheese and mushroom omelettes, noodles with walnuts or poppyseed, and anything with the ever-popular túró (curd), especially túrógombóc (curd dumplings; 650Ft).

Pizza e Pasta
PIZZA $

(☑06 30 351 8336; www.pizza-pasta.hu; Oskola tér 6; pasta 1190-2490Ft, pizza 1090-2490Ft; ⏰11am-10pm) Taking pride of place on Szeged's most attractive square, Pizza e Pasta serves, well, just that, and is said to be the best in town.

Market
MARKET $

(Márs tér; ⏰4am-6pm Mon-Fri, 4am-3pm Sat & Sun) One of the liveliest markets on the Great Plain; near the bus station.

★ Malata
BURGERS $$

(www.facebook.com/malatakezmuves; Somogyi utca 13; mains 1190-3000Ft; ⏰2-11pm Mon-Thu, 2pm-1am Fri, noon-1am Sat, noon-11pm Sun) This great new hipster hang-out is part ruin garden, part pub/cafe and counts upwards of two dozen craft beers on tap and by the bottle. The food is mostly gourmet burgers (1450Ft to 1850Ft) though not exclusively so; order and pay at the bar. In winter and rain, sit in the colourful cafe with upended umbrellas dangling from the ceiling.

Kiskőrössy Halászcsárda
SEAFOOD $$

(☑62-555 886; www.kiskorossyhalaszcsarda.hu; Felső Tisza-part 336; mains 1540-4350Ft; ⏰11am-11pm Sun-Thu, 11am-midnight Fri & Sat) Housed in a traditional fisherman's cottage with a terrace on the banks of the Tisza a few kilometres east of the centre, this excellent fish restaurant is an atmospheric place to sup. Have one of the many fish soups on offer, a whole roasted pike with garlic or fillet of carp, and watch the boats go by.

To reach the 'fish csárda' take trolleybus 9 to Etelka sor then walk 300m east along Felső Tisza-part.

Classic Cafe
SERBIAN $$

(☑62-422 065; www.classiccafe.hu; Széchenyi tér 5; mains 2590-3300Ft; ⏰10am-11pm Mon-Thu, 10am-midnight Fri & Sat, 11am-10pm Sun) This welcoming Serbian place with its lovely inner-courtyard garden (fine for a quiet drink, too) serves up grills like csevap (spicy meatballs of beef or pork) and pljeskavica (meat patties).

Taj Mahal
INDIAN $$

(📋 06 30 337 0142, 62-452 131; www.tajmahal szeged.hu; Gutenberg utca 12; mains 1550-2800Ft; ⊙ 11am-11pm Mon-Sat, noon-10pm Sun; 🍴) This pleasantly authentic Indian restaurant is just metres from the New Synagogue. If you get a hankering for a curry or a spot of tandoor, this is the place to come. There are up to 10 vegetarian dishes (1250Ft to 1550Ft) on offer as well.

Vendéglő A Régi Hídhoz
HUNGARIAN $$

(📋 62-420 910; www.regihid.hu; Oskola utca 4; mains 1600-3900Ft; ⊙ 11.30am-11pm Sun-Thu, 11am-midnight Fri & Sat) For an authentic Hungarian meal that won't break the bank, head for 'At the Old Bridge', a traditional restaurant with all the favourites and a great terrace just a block in from the river. It's a great place to try *Szögedi halászlé* (1700Ft), Szeged's famous fish soup.

★ Tiszavirág Restaurant
HUNGARIAN $$$

(📋 62-554 888; http://tiszaviragszeged.hu; Hajnóczy utca 1/b; mains 2900-4500Ft; ⊙ noon-3pm & 6-10pm Tue-Sat) Probably the best restaurant in Szeged, the eatery of the Tiszavirág Hotel (p236) serves beautifully presented international and modernised Hungarian dishes like *hurka* (black pudding) with caramelised apple and pine nuts and paprika duck-liver pâté. The selection of Hungarian wine by the glass is excellent and the service both friendly and efficient. The decor is simple but elegant, with great lighting.

Bistorant
INTERNATIONAL $$$

(📋 62-555 566; http://bistorant.hu; Oroszlán utca 8; mains 1150-4970Ft; ⊙ 11am-10pm Mon & Tue, to 1am Wed-Sat, to 8pm Sun) This very stylish and very comfortable basement restaurant and wine bar has an ever-changing menu that includes everything from *sous vide* dishes to pasta (1150Ft to 2650Ft) and grills. Two-/three-/four-course set lunches are 1290/1490/1990Ft. There's a cafe on the ground floor and a lovely back courtyard too.

Kajak Bistro
INTERNATIONAL $$$

(📋 62-547 988; www.portroyal.hu; Stefánia utca 4; mains 1980-3980Ft; ⊙ 10am-10pm Sun-Thu, 10am-midnight Fri & Sat) The leafy terrace of this interesting place facing the National Theatre is enough reason to make this restaurant your destination on a warm summer evening. Add to that the fact that in any season the modern kitchen turns out tasty traditional dishes, international faves and vegie

options, and you have a winner. Two-/three-course set lunches are 1290/1590Ft.

🍷 Drinking & Nightlife

Virág Cukrászda
CAFE

(📋 62-559 967; www.facebook.com/viragcukraszdaeskavehaz; Klauzál tér 1; ⊙ 9am-9pm) For coffee, ice cream and cakes (355Ft to 650Ft), check out the celebrated 'Flower Cakeshop', established in 1922, which has tables inside and on the square, and a museum-quality Herend coffee machine. The Virág outlet opposite the square at No 8 is for stand-up service and takeaway.

John Bull Pub
PUB

(📋 62-484 217; www.johnbullpubszeged.hu; Oroszlán utca 6; ⊙ 11am-1am) This place does a grand 'English pub' imitation, with mock 'Turkey' carpets, proper pints (seven beers on tap) and bar stools, and there's a full menu (mains 1850Ft to 3950Ft). Its garden courtyard, which backs onto a former synagogue, is a welcome respite.

Sing Sing
CLUB

(📋 62-420 314; www.sing.hu; Mars tér, C Pavilion; ⊙ 11pm-5am Wed, Fri & Sat) This long-established warehouse club near the bus station is still party central at the weekend and hosts theme nights.

Tisza Dokk
CLUB

(www.tiszadokk.hu; Huszár Mátyás rakpart; ⊙ 10am-1am Sun-Thu, 10am-5am Fri & Sat) This bar-cum-dance-club sitting on a dock on the Tisza at the bottom of Arany János utca attracts Szeged's beautiful people with its streamlined decor and lighting, sophisticated music and excellent cocktails.

A Cappella
CAFE

(📋 62-559 966; http://acappella.atw.hu; Kárász utca 6; ⊙ 7am-10pm) This giant, two-storey sidewalk cafe overlooking Klauzál tér has a generous choice of frothy coffee concoctions, ice creams and cakes (345Ft to 660Ft).

☆ Entertainment

Your best source of entertainment information in this culturally active city is Tourinform (p239): ask for the *Programme* they prepare annually.

Jazz Kocsma
LIVE MUSIC

(📋 06702509279; www.facebook.com/jazzkocsma; Kálmány Lajos 14; ⊙ 5pm-midnight Tue-Thu, 5pm-2am Fri & Sat) The kind of small, basement music club that no self-respecting university

BUSES FROM SZEGED

DESTINATION	PRICE	DURATION	KM	FREQUENCY
Debrecen	3950Ft	5hr	230	3 nonstop daily
Gyula	2830Ft	3½hr	152	6 nonstop daily
Hódmezővásárhely	560Ft	half-hour	26	hourly nonstop
Mohács	3130Ft	3hr	153	4 daily with 1 change
Ópusztaszer	560Ft	half-hour	28	hourly nonstop
Pécs	3410Ft	3½hr	192	7 nonstop daily

TRAINS FROM SZEGED

DESTINATION	PRICE	DURATION	KM	FREQUENCY
Békéscsaba	1860Ft	1¾hr	97	hourly nonstop
Budapest	3705Ft	2½hr	191	hourly nonstop
Hódmezővásárhely	650Ft	40min	31	hourly nonstop
Kecskemét	1680Ft	1hr	85	hourly nonstop

town would be without. Gets pretty crowded during the academic year for live music on Friday and Saturday nights. Things slow down in summer, but it's still worth searching out for a drink.

Szeged National Theatre THEATRE
(Szegedi Nemzeti Színház; ☑ 62-479 279, box office 62-557 714; www.szinhaz.szeged.hu/sznsz; Deák Ferenc utca 12-14) This theatre, where operas, ballet and classical concerts are staged, has been the centre of cultural life in Szeged since 1886.

🛍 Shopping

Alexandra BOOKS
(☑ 62-540 967; www.alexandra.hu; Kölcsey utca 4; ⊙ 9am-6pm Mon-Fri, 9am-1pm Sat) This branch of the nationwide chain of bookshops has some titles in English as well as a good selection of maps. There's a cafe on the 1st floor.

Magyar Pálinka Háza DRINKS
(☑ 06 30 929 5403; www.magyarpalinkahaza.hu; Zrínyi utca 2; ⊙ 9am-7pm Mon-Fri, 9am-2pm Sat) The 'Hungarian Pálinka House' has a large selection of fruit brandies on sale as well as other libations.

ℹ Information

Budapest Bank (Klauzál tér 2; ⊙ 8am-5pm Mon, 8am-4pm Tue-Thu, 8am-3pm Fri) With ATM.

Kigyó Patika (☑ 62-574 174; Klauzál tér 1; ⊙ 8am-9pm Mon-Sat, 8am-8pm Sun) Pharmacy with extended hours.

Main Post Office (Széchenyi tér 1; ⊙ 8am-8pm Mon, 8am-7pm Tue-Fri, 8am-noon Sat)

Tourinform (☑ 62-488 690; www.szeged tourism.hu; Dugonics tér 2; ⊙ 9am-5pm Mon-Fri year-round, plus 9am-1pm Sat Apr-Oct) This exceptionally helpful office is tucked away in a courtyard near the university. There is a seasonal **Tourinform kiosk** (⊙ 8am-8pm Jun-Sep) in Széchenyi tér.

ℹ Getting There & Away

The main **train station** (Indóház tér) is south of the city centre on Indóház tér. The **bus station** (Mars tér), to the west of the centre, is on Mars tér, within easy walking distance via pedestrian Mikszáth Kálmán utca.

BUS & TRAINS

Buses also head for Nagylak (1115Ft, 1½ hours, 54km) on the Romanian border, where you can catch buses to Arad and points beyond. Buses run to Novi Sad (2510Ft, 3½ hours) in Serbia at 2.30pm daily, and to Subotica (1200Ft, 1½ hours) three to four times daily.

Szeged is on several rail lines, including a main one to Budapest's Nyugati train station. You have to change at Békéscsaba for Gyula. Southbound trains leave Szeged for Subotica (1500Ft, two hours, 48km) in Serbia twice daily.

ℹ Getting Around

Trams 1 and 2 (320Ft) from the train station will take you north to Széchenyi tér. From the bus station catch bus 71a or 72a or trolleybus 5 for New Szeged. Rent bikes at **Tourinform** for 1000/3000Ft per hour/day.

Northern Hungary

Best Places to Eat

➜ Macok Bistro & Wine Bar (p250)

➜ Toldi Fogadó Restaurant (p255)

➜ 1552 (p249)

Best Places to Sleep

➜ Hotel Senator Ház (p249)

➜ Gróf Degenfeld Castle Hotel (p254)

➜ Hollóköves Guesthouses (p243)

➜ Toldi Fogadó (p253)

➜ Baráth Vendégház (p258)

Why Go?

Forested hiking trails, superb wine regions, traditional folk culture and hilltop castle ruins beckon you to what are called the Northern Uplands. In a country as flat as a *palacsinta* (pancake), these foothills of the Carpathians soar above most of Hungary. After exploring Bükk National Park on foot, why not sample the spectacular red wines of Eger or the honey-sweet whites of Tokaj?

As reminders of far too many battles won and lost, ageing castles and evocative ruins punctuate the landscape. This is also a land where the Palóc people hold strong in traditional villages such as Hollókő. If you want to experience village life – steeped in folk culture, replete with horse-drawn carts, dirt roads and tiny wooden churches – the Bereg region in the northeast is the place to go.

When to Go
Eger

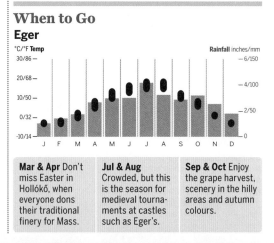

Mar & Apr Don't miss Easter in Hollókő, when everyone dons their traditional finery for Mass.

Jul & Aug Crowded, but this is the season for medieval tournaments at castles such as Eger's.

Sep & Oct Enjoy the grape harvest, scenery in the hilly areas and autumn colours.

Northern Hungary Highlights

1 Eger (p244) Savouring the unequalled jewel of the Northern Uplands, celebrated for its legendary wine, baroque architecture and easy-going temperament.

2 Hollókő (p242) Spending the night and listening to the silence in this tiny village where folk art and tradition live on.

3 Tokaj (p252) Tasting the famous 'wine of kings and the king of wines' in this picturesque little town.

4 Szatmárcseke (p258) Trying to crack the code on the boat-shaped grave markers at the village cemetery.

5 Tákos (p257) Marvelling at the patterns of the painted wooden interior in its 'peasants' cathedral'.

HOLLÓKŐ

🗺 32 / POP 330

The Cserhát Hills may not be graced with soaring peaks (none of them is higher than 650m), but they are cloaked in a rich folk-culture tapestry belonging to the Palóc people. Hollókő (Raven Rock), a two-street village nestled in a tranquil valley, is the epicentre. What sets Hollókő apart is its restored 13th-century castle and the architecture of the so-called Old Village (Ófalu), where some 67 houses and outbuildings have been on Unesco's World Heritage list of cultural sites since 1987. The village has burned to the ground many times since the 13th century (most recently in 1909), but the residents have always rebuilt their houses exactly to plan in traditional wattle and daub.

◉ Sights

The folk architecture of the Old Village is the main attraction. Stroll down one cobblestone street and up the other, past whitewashed houses with carved wooden porches and tiled roofs. Few people live in the Old Village any more, preferring the more modern accommodation of the New Village, which you'll pass on the way here.

Buy a Village Walk Ticket (Faluséta Jegy; adult/child 3000/2000Ft) from the Küszöb Information Office; this paper bracelet will grant entry to several attractions, including the castle, as well as free samples of wine and cheese.

Hollókő Castle   CASTLE

(Hollókői Vár; 🗺 06 60 508 2454; adult/child 900/600Ft; ⊙10am-5.30pm mid-Mar–Oct) Hollókő Castle commands a striking view of the surrounding hills from 365m-high Stalk Hill (Szár-hegy). Climb to the top of the pentagonal keep to look out across fields and forested hills without a trace of human occupation. Exhibits inside focus on weaponry and heraldry. There's a rather bogus mock-up of a medieval banquet from the time of the castle's inception.

The fortress was built at the end of the 13th century and strengthened 200 years later. Captured by the Turks, it was not liberated until 1683 by the Polish king Jan Sobieski (r 1674–96). It was partially destroyed after the War of Independence early in the 18th century but the shell is intact. Reach it via signposted paths from the top of the parking lot and the western end of Kossuth utca.

Church of St Martin   CHURCH

(Szent Márton Templom; Kossuth utca) The focus of the village's spiritual and social life, this adorable wooden church is on the corner where Petőfi út, the Old Village's 'other' street, branches off from Kossuth út. Built as a granary in the 16th century and sanctified in 1889, it is a fairly austere affair both inside and out.

Village Museum   MUSEUM

(Falumúzeum; 🗺 32-379 255; Kossuth utca 82; adult/child 250/100Ft; ⊙10am-6pm mid-Mar–Oct) This award-winning museum contains the usual three rooms of a Hungarian peasant house, stuffed with local folk pottery, painted furniture and embroidered pillows. In the backyard there's an interesting carved wine press dating from 1872.

Palóc Doll Museum   MUSEUM

(Palóc Babamúzeum; 🗺 06 30 394 4424; Kossuth utca 96; adult/child 350/150Ft; ⊙10am-5pm mid-Mar–Oct) This museum exhibits more than 200 porcelain dolls in traditional costumes from all across Hungary.

Guzsalyas   MUSEUM

(🗺 06 30 508 2454; Kossuth utca 94; ⊙10am-6pm mid-Mar–Oct) This museum of traditional clothing takes a detailed look at the step-by-step process of preparing such fabrics as wool and linen.

Postal Museum   MUSEUM

(Postamúzeum; 🗺 06 30 435 3893; Kossuth utca 80; adult/child 500/250Ft; ⊙10am-6pm Tue-Sun Apr-Oct) The Postal Museum is a branch of the one in Budapest. Only for keen philatelists.

Country House   MUSEUM

(Tájház; 🗺 06 70 201 5546; Kossuth utca 99; adult/child 400/250Ft; ⊙10am-5pm daily mid-Mar–Oct, Sat & Sun Nov–mid-Mar) The Country House contains an exhibition devoted to nature.

🏃 Activities

There are some gentle walks into the hills and valleys of the 140-hectare landscape protection reserve to the west and south of Hollókő castle. Cserhát, the 1:60,000 map (No 8; 1350Ft) from Cartographia, will help you plan your route..

🎎 Festivals & Events

Hollókő Easter Festival   RELIGIOUS

(Hollókői Húsvéti Fesztivál; www.holloko.hu; ⊙Mar/Apr) Traditional costumes and folk traditions welcome in spring at this Hollókő festival.

Castle Days

SPORTS

(Várjátékok; ☺ May/Jun, Aug) Medieval tournaments take place at Hollókő Castle at Whitsunday/Pentecost (late May or June) and St Stephen's Day (20 August).

Vintage Festival

WINE

(Szüreti Mulatság; ☺ late Sep) Revelry to mark the end of the grape harvest in late September.

🛏️ Sleeping

There are quite a number of private rooms in the New Village charging from 4000Ft per person.

⭐Hollóköves Guesthouses

HOMESTAY $$

(Hollóköves Vendégházak; ☎ 06 20 325 8775; www.holloko.hu/hu/szallashely; s/d 7000/14,000Ft) Up to nine traditional houses that could easily double as folk museums are available for rent throughout the Old Village. Some of the whitewashed cottages with dark beams have antiques and curios – hand-carved beds, hanging lanterns, washbasins – and others are plainer. All have fully equipped kitchens and modern bathrooms.

Tugári Vendégház

GUESTHOUSE $$

(☎ 32-379 156, 06 20 379 6132; www.holloko-tugarivendeghaz.hu; Rákóczi út 13; r 9500-11,500Ft; 🐾) This old cottage with four attractive rooms in the New Village is charmingly traditional. Cheerful owners Ádám and Tünde provide electric kettles in every room and will deliver a breakfast basket to your door for 1500Ft. Two rooms have en suite bathrooms; two are down the hall. One apartment has its own kitchen; the other three rooms share a common one.

Ádám is also a driver guide with two cars (including an East German Trabant) and can take you on tour in Hollókő and places further afield, such as Eger and Gödöllő.

Castellum Hotel Hollókő

HOTEL $$$

(☎ 06 30 286 7014; www.hotelholloko.hu; Sport utca 14; r €120-135; 🅿️@🛜🏊) This flashy new hotel on a hill up from the town parking lot counts 68 large and modern rooms with some Hollókő designs (lest you forget where you are) and wonderful views over the Cserhát Hills. There's a swimming pool, wellness centre and a children's play area. The restaurant serves buffet-style meals. Great for comfort but perhaps not local atmosphere.

🍴 Eating

Places to eat close early here, so plan accordingly. There's a small grocery store called Támásek Boltja (József Attila utca 4; ☺ 7am-4pm Mon-Sat, 8-11am Sun) on the road to the municipal car park.

Kalácsos

BAKERY $

(☎ 06 30 576 2652; Kossuth utca 70; ☺ 10am-6pm mid-Mar–Oct) This wonderful little bakery sells bread and both savoury and sweet baked goods, including *hókifli*, crescent-shaped pastries filled with nuts, plum or apricot.

Muskátli Vendéglő

HUNGARIAN $$

(☎ 32-379 262; www.muskatlivendeglo.hu; Kossuth utca 61; mains 2000-2200Ft; ☺ 11am-7pm Wed-Fri, to 5pm Sat & Sun) The traditional dishes at this cottage restaurant are the best in the village. The flower-bedecked courtyard down in the back garden is a positive delight in the warmer months but is often booked out by groups.

Vár Étterem

HUNGARIAN $$

(☎ 32-379 029; Kossuth utca 93-95; mains 1850-2500Ft; ☺ 11am-6pm Tue-Sun, to 10pm in summer) This eatery offers covered outside dining in the warmer months but closes early otherwise.

🍸 Drinking & Nightlife

There are a couple of cafes and at least one uninviting pub in Hollókő but they don't exactly burn the candle at both ends here.

Hollóköves Kávézó

CAFE

(☎ 06 20 626 2844; Kossuth utca 50; ☺ 8.30am-5.30pm) This new, very upbeat coffee house has seating on a large terrace overlooking Kossuth út and the Old Village.

🛍️ Shopping

Bercsényi Pottery Workshop

ARTS & CRAFTS

(Bercsényi Fazekas műhely; ☎ 06 70 456 7116; www.bercsenyifazekas.hu; Kossuth utca 65; ☺ 10am-6pm) This is the only place in Hollókő where ceramic pots and plaques are made and fired on-site, in a workshop below the store.

Gazduram Cheese Shop

CHEESE

(Gazduram Sajtbotja; ☎ 06 20 242 5441; Petőfi út 3; ☺ 9am-5pm mid-Mar–Oct) This wonderful new shop sells homemade yoghurt and various types of sheep and cow's milk cheese, including a braided smoked yellow variety called *parenyica*. The fresh goat's cheese flavoured with garlic is excellent.

❶ Information

ATM (Kossuth út 50) Between the grocery store and Hollókőves Kávézó (p243).

Küszöb Information Office (Küszöb Információs Iroda; 🗷 32-579 010; www.holloko. hu; Kossuth Lajos utca 68; ⊗8am-4pm Apr-Oct, 11am-3pm Nov-Mar) Very helpful tourist office next to the town parking lot.

Post Office (Kossuth út 72; ⊗8am-2.30pm Mon-Fri)

❶ Getting There & Away

One direct bus a day at 3.15pm heads from Budapest (1860Ft, 2¼ hours, 90km) to Hollókő; it returns at 5am weekdays, and 4pm Saturday and Sunday. Otherwise you must change in Szécsény (370Ft, 25 minutes, 17km, up to five daily). To reach Balassagyarmat (740Ft, one hour, 36km) you must also change there. The bus stops on Kossuth utca at Dósza György utca. From there walk downhill to the Old Village.

EGER

🗷 36 / POP 54,500

Filled with beautifully preserved baroque buildings, Eger (pronounced 'egg-air') is a jewellery box of a town with loads to see and do. Explore the bloody history of Turkish occupation and defeat at the hilltop castle, climb an original Ottoman minaret, listen to an organ performance at the colossal basilica, or relax in a renovated Turkish bath. Then spend time traipsing from cellar to cellar in the Valley of Beautiful Women, tasting the celebrated Eger Bull's Blood (Egri Bikavér) and other local wines from the cask. Flanked by northern Hungary's most inviting range of hills, the Bükk, Eger also provides nearby opportunities for hiking and other outdoor excursions..

◉ Sights

★**Eger Castle**   FORTRESS
(Egri Vár; Map p246; 🗷 36-312 744; www.egrivar. hu; Vár köz 1; castle grounds adult/child 800/400Ft, incl museum 1600/800Ft; ⊗exhibits 10am-5pm Tue-Sun May-Oct, 10am-4pm Tue-Sun Nov-Apr, castle grounds 8am-8pm May-Aug, to 7pm Apr & Sep, to 6pm Mar & Oct, to 5pm Nov-Feb) Climb up cobbled Vár köz from Tinódi Sebestyén tér to reach the castle, erected in the 13th century after the Mongol invasion. Models, drawings and artefacts like armour and Turkish uniforms

in the Castle History Exhibition, on the 1st floor of the former Bishop's Palace (1470), painlessly explain the castle's story. On the eastern side of the complex are foundations of the 12th-century St John's Cathedral. Enter the castle casemates (p244) hewn from solid rock via the nearby Dark Gate.

Below the Bishop's Palace a statue of local hero István Dobó takes pride of place in Heroes' Hall (guided visits only). The terrace of the renovated Dobó Bastion offers stunning views of the town; it now hosts changing exhibits. Have a look at the creepy dungeon nearby. Other attractions cost extra, including the hokey Panoptikum (Waxworks; adult/concession 500/350Ft) and two 3D films (eight and 15 minutes; one/two films 300/600Ft). Alternatively, you can just wander the castle grounds, which are also open Monday, when most exhibits are closed.

Castle Casemates   HISTORIC SITE
(Kazamata; Map p246) Beneath Eger Castle are casemates hewn from solid rock. Part of them is open to the public, accessible via the Dark Gate in the eastern part of the complex and containing displays and some high-tech videos. To go deeper down you must join a tour with a Hungarian-speaking guide included in the general admission price, or pay 800Ft extra for an English-language guide.

Dobó Bastion   HISTORIC SITE
(Dobó Bástya; Map p246) The terrace of the renovated Dobó Bastion (1549), which collapsed in 1976, offers stunning views of the town; it hosts changing exhibits (adult/concession 500/300Ft) from time to time.

Dobó István tér   SQUARE
(Map p246) Statues of István Dobó and his comrades-in-arms routing the Turks fill Eger's main square, which has been totally revamped in recent years. To the south is the splendid Minorite church. Just north of and visible from the square is the 40m-tall minaret (p247).

★**Minorite Church of
St Anthony of Padua**   CHURCH
(Páduai Szent Antal Minorita Templom; Map p246; Dobó István tér 6; suggested donation 300Ft; ⊗9am-5pm Tue-Sat, 9.30am-5.30pm Sun) On the southern side of Eger's main square stands this church, built in 1771 by Bohemian architect Kilian Ignaz Dientzenhofer and one of the most glorious baroque buildings in the world. The altarpiece of the Virgin Mary and

St Anthony of Padua is by Johann Lukas Kracker, the Bohemian painter who also created the fire-and-brimstone ceiling fresco in the Lyceum library.

Lyceum HISTORIC BUILDING
(Líceum; Map p246; ☑ 36-520 400; http://uni-esz terhazy.hu/hu/egyetem/kultura/liceum; Eszterházy tér 1) Directly east of Eger Basilica is the Zopf-style Lyceum (1765), now headquarters of the Károly Eszterházy University of Applied Sciences. It contains a priceless historical library on the 1st floor of the south wing. Above that and spread over several floors is the so-called Magic Tower), a 'popular science centre' that will surprise and delight both adults and children.

★Lyceum Library LIBRARY
(Liceumi Könyvtar; Map p246; ☑ 36-520 400 ext 2214; Eszterházy tér 1, Lyceum; adult/child 1000/500Ft; ☺ 9.30am-1.30pm Tue-Sun Mar & Apr, 9.30am-3.30pm Tue-Sun May-Sep, by appointment Oct-Feb) This awesome 60,000-volume all-wood library on the 1st floor of the Lyceum's south wing contains hundreds of priceless manuscripts, medical codices and incunabula. The *trompe l'oeil* ceiling fresco painted by Bohemian artist Johann Lukas Kracker in 1778 depicts the Counter-Reformation's Council of Trent (1545–63), with a lightning bolt setting heretical manuscripts ablaze. It was Eger's – and its archbishop's – response to the Enlightenment and the Reformation.

Magic Tower MUSEUM
(Varásztorony; Map p246; ☑ 36-520 400 ext 2279; www.varasztorony.hu; Eszterházy tér 1, Lyceum; adult/child 1300/1000Ft; ☺ 9.30am-5.30pm May-Aug, 9.30am-3.30pm Tue-Sun mid-Mar–Apr, Sep & Oct, 9.30am-1pm Fri-Sun Nov–mid-Dec & Feb–mid-Mar) Attractions in the so-called Magic Tower above the Lyceum are spread over several floors and include an Astronomy Museum on the 6th floor of the east wing containing 18th-century astronomical equipment, a Magic Hall of interactive experimental devices, a planetarium with regularly scheduled shows and a panorama terrace. On the 9th floor is the astonishing camera obscura, the 'eye of Eger', designed in 1776 to spy on the city in real time and entertain townspeople. It still does.

Astronomy Museum MUSEUM
(Csillagászati Múzeum; Map p246; ☑ 36-520 400 ext 2279; www.varazstorony.ektf.hu; Eszterházy tér 1, Lyceum; adult/student 1300/1000Ft; ☺ 9.30am-5.30pm May-Aug, 9.30am-3.30pm Tue-Sun mid-Mar, Apr, Sep & Oct, 9.30am-1pm Fri-Sun Nov–mid-Dec & Feb–mid-Mar) The Astronomy Museum, on the 6th floor of the east wing of the Lyceum, contains 18th-century astronomical equipment, a planetarium with scheduled shows and an observatory. Climb two more floors up to the observation deck for a great view of the city and then up one more to try out the 1776 camera obscura, the 'eye of Eger'.

Eger Basilica CHURCH
(Egri Bazilika; Map p246; ☑ 36-420 970; www.eger-bazilika.plebania.hu; Pyrker János tér 1; suggested donation 300Ft; ☺ 7am-7pm Mon-Sat, 1-7pm Sun) A highlight of the town's amazing architecture is Eger Basilica. This neoclassical monolith was designed in 1836 by József Hild, the same architect who later worked on the cathedral at Esztergom on the Danube Bend. The half-hour organ concert (p250) is a good time to visit, when the ornate altars and soaring dome create interesting acoustics.

City Under the City HISTORIC SITE
(Város a Város Alatt; Map p246; ☑ 36-310 832, 06 20 961 4019; www.varosavarosalatt.hu; Pyrker János tér; adult/concession 1000/500Ft; ☺ 9am-6pm Apr-Sep, 10am-4pm Oct-Mar) To the right of the main steps up to Eger Basilica is the entrance to the former archbishop's cellars. A guided history-oriented tour on the hour leads you through the caverns and takes 45 minutes. Take a jumper (sweater); it's 12°C down there.

Kossuth Lajos Utca STREET
(Map p246) Kossuth Lajos utca is a fine and leafy street lined with such architectural gems as the former Orthodox synagogue, built in 1893, and the former neoclassical synagogue (p246), dating from 1845. You'll pass several outstanding baroque and Eclectic buildings along the way as well, including the county hall, with its fine wrought-iron work, and the rococo Provost's Palace (p246).

County Hall NOTABLE BUILDING
(Megyeháza; Map p246; Kossuth Lajos utca 9) Kossuth Lajos utca boasts dozens of baroque and Eclectic gems, including the delightful County Hall, with a wrought-iron grid above the main door portraying (from the left) Faith, Hope and Charity by Henrik Fazola, a Rhinelander who settled in Eger in the mid-18th century. Walk down the passageway, and

Eger

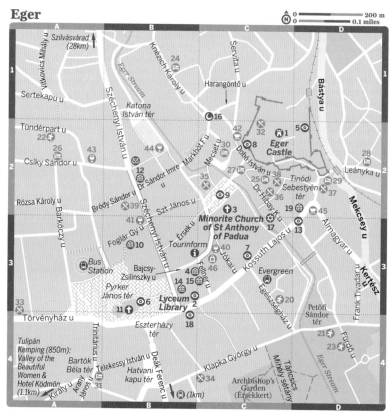

you'll see more of his magnificent works –
two baroque wrought-iron gates that have su-
perseded the minaret as the symbol of Eger.

The one on the right shows the seal of Heves County at the top and has a comical figure
on its handle. The more graceful gate on the
left is decorated with flowers and grapes.

Provost's Palace
NOTABLE BUILDING
(Kisprépositi palota; Map p246; Kossuth Lajos utca
4) The wrought-iron balcony and window
grilles of this rococo building were the work
of master craftsman Henrik Fazola.

Neoclassical Synagogue
JEWISH SITE
(Map p246; Dr Hibay Károly utca 7) The erstwhile neoclassical synagogue dating from
1845 is now partly renovated and functions
as a theatre.

Sándor Ziffer Gallery
GALLERY
(Ziffer Sándor Galéria; Map p246; ☎36-785
027; Kossuth Lajos utca 17; adult/concession

500/250Ft; ⏰11.30am-7pm Tue-Sun) This gallery is housed in the former Orthodox synagogue, built in 1893 and named after the
painter Sándor Ziffer (1880–1962). It has
rotating exhibitions. To reach it from Dobó
István tér, cross the little Eger Stream to
Tinódi Sebestyén tér and turn south onto
Kossuth Lajos utca.

Eger Archbishop's Palace
HISTORIC BUILDING
(Egri Érseki Palota; Map p246; ☎36-517 356;
www.egriersekipalota.hu; Széchenyi István utca
3; adult/child 1800/900Ft; ⏰10am-6pm Tue-
Sun Apr-Sep, 10am-4pm Tue-Sun Oct-Mar) This
splendid 18th-century structure contains
two very rich collections. On the ground
floor is the Ecclesiastical Collection. Don't
miss the scale mode of the basilica from
1832. The 1st floor now houses the Eger Art
Gallery, recently moved from the castle.

Here too are rooms furnished as they
would have been when the archbishop

Eger

lived here: the Decorative Hall (Díszterem) is a show-stopper, and there are portraits of bishops going back to the 1th century.

Ecclesiastical Collection · MUSEUM
(Egyházi Gyűjtemény; Map p246; ☑36-517 356; www.egriersekipalota.hu; Széchenyi István utca 3, Eger Archbishop's Palace; adult/child 1800/900Ft; ◎10am-6pm Tue-Sun Apr-Sep, 10am-4pm Tue-Sun Oct-Mar) The Ecclesiastical Collection, in the Eger Archbishop's Palace, consists of priceless vestments, church plate and liturgical objects.

Eger Art Gallery · GALLERY
(Művészeti Galéria; Map p246; ☑36-517 356; www.egriersekipalota.hu; Széchenyi István utca 3, Eger Archbishop's Palace; adult/child 1800/900Ft; ◎10am-6pm Tue-Sun Apr-Sep, 10am-4pm Tue-Sun Oct-Mar) This collection of fine art that once hung in Eger Castle contains works by Canaletto and Ceruti, among others.

Minaret · ISLAMIC SITE
(Map p246; ☑06 70 202 4353; www.minaret eger.hu; Knézich Károly utca; 300Ft; ◎10am-6pm May-Sep, 10am-5pm Apr & Oct) This 40m-high minaret, topped incongruously with a cross, is one of the few reminders of the Ottoman occupation of Eger. Nonclaustrophobes can brave the 97 narrow spiral steps to the top for the awesome view.

Kepes Institute · GALLERY
(Kepes Intezet; Map p246; ☑36-420 044; www. kepeskozpont.hu; Széchenyi utca 16; adult/child 1200/600Ft; ◎10am-6pm Tue-Sat) This unusual gallery exhibits the work of Hungarian-born American artist and designer György Kepes, who is celebrated for – among other things – his light installations.

☀ Activities

★ Turkish Bath · SPA
(Török Fürdő; Map p246; ☑36-510 552; www. egertermal.hu; Fürdő utca 3-4; 2½hr session adult/

DON'T MISS

WINE TASTING IN THE VALLEY OF THE BEAUTIFUL WOMEN

You can taste Eger's famous wines at many places around town, including at restaurants at the base of the castle and in commercial cellars like Fúzio Wine Bar & Cellar (p250) and István Cellar. But why bother drinking in town when you can do the same in the cellars of the evocatively named Valley of the Beautiful Women (Szépasszony-völgy Hétvége)? Here, more than two dozen *pincék* (cellars) have been carved into the horseshoe-shaped rock. For an average of 100Ft you can have a one-decilitre taste of a range of reds, such as Bull's Blood, and whites, such as *olaszrizling, leányka* and *hárslevelű*. The choice of wine cellars can be a bit daunting, so walk around and have a look yourself. (Hint: the ones on the west side have big terraces and better seating; the east cellars are busier.) They're not to be missed.

The valley is a little over 1km southwest across Rte 25, off Király utca. Catch one of the vans, including those from Evergreen (Map p246; ☑ 06 20 388 6241; Egészségház utca; 800Ft; ☺10am-5pm Apr-Oct), from Egészségház utca south of Kossuth Lajos utca. A taxi costs about 1200Ft.

child 2200/1500Ft; ☺4.30-9pm Mon & Tue, 3-9pm Wed & Thu, 1-9pm Fri, 9am-9pm Sat & Sun) Nothing beats a soak and steam at this historic spa, which has a bath dating to 1617 at its core. A multimillion-forint renovation has added six pools, saunas, steam room and a hammam (Turkish bath). Various kinds of massage and treatments are also available.

Eger Bike   CYCLING
(Map p246; ☑ 06 20 503 9922, 06 70 564 3388; www.egerbike.hu; Egészségház utca 11; 6hr/day/week 2000/3000/10,000Ft; ☺9am-5pm Mon-Fri, 9am-1pm Sat) This outfit just north of the Archbishop's Garden rents bicycles by the half-day, day and week.

Eger Thermal Baths   SPA
(Egri Térmalfürdő; Map p246; ☑ 36-510 558; www.egertermal.hu; Petőfi tér 2; adult/child 1900/1600Ft, swimming pool only 900Ft; ☺6am-7pm Apr-Sep, 9am-6pm Oct-Mar) After strolling in the Archbishop's Garden (Érsékkert), once the private reserve of papal princes, you can further unwind at these thermal baths. Admission gains you access to a variety of pools, including bubbling massage pools and a castle-themed kids' pool, and other recreational and spa features spread over 5 hectares.

István Cellar   WINE
(Map p246; ☑ 36-313 670; www.koronahotel.hu; Tündérpart utca 5, Hotel Korona; wine tasting 2200-7500Ft; ☺2-6pm Tue-Sat by appointment) You can sample Eger's famous wines at many locations around town, including in the István Cellar at the Hotel Korona, and a couple of places at the base of the castle (Tourinform has an extensive list).

✦ Festivals & Events

Spring Festival   PERFORMING ARTS
(Tavaszi Festivál; ☺Apr) Concerts, puppet shows, exhibitions and more over two weeks in April.

Egri Bikavér Festival   WINE
(Egri Bikavér Ünnep; www.eger.hu; ☺Jul) Four July days devoted to Eger's iconic wine.

Castle Merrymaking Historical Festival   SPORTS
(Végvári Vigasságok Történelmi Fesztivál; ☺Aug) Three days of medieval games and shenanigans in August.

Valley of the Beautiful Women Weekend   MUSIC
(Szépasszony-völgy Hétvége; ☺Sep) Three days of popular music (and wine) in the Valley of the Beautiful Women.

🛏 Sleeping

Tourinform (p251) publishes a booklet of accommodation available, not only in the city (including private rooms) but in the surrounding area. It also has a list of colleges offering cheap dormitory accommodation from June to August.

Agria Retur Vendégház   GUESTHOUSE $
(Map p246; ☑ 36-416 650; www.returven deghaz.hu; Knézich Károly utca 18; s/d/tr 4200/7600/10,600Ft; @🛜) You couldn't receive a warmer welcome than the one you'll get at this guesthouse near the minaret. Walking up three flights of stairs, you enter a cheery communal kitchen/eating area central to four mansard rooms. Out the back is a huge garden with tables and a barbecue at

your disposal. Just read the fan mail on the wall.

Imola Hostel
HOSTEL $

(Leányka úti Kollégium; Map p246; ☑36-520 430; www.imolanet.hu/imolahostel; Leányka út 2; s/d 3650/6850Ft; ❄@🛜) This former college dormitory has been modernised, and comfortable beds and large desks now fill quite smart twin rooms. Each floor shares a kitchen and a computer with internet.

Tulipán Kemping
CAMPGROUND $

(☑06 70 385 1166; www.tulipancamping.com; Szépasszonyvölgy utca 71; campsite per person/tent/caravan 800/900/1600Ft, bungalow for 4/5 6000/10,000Ft) Many of the caravan and tent sites at Tulipán Kemping are in an open, shadeless field. But you're surrounded by vineyards and just stumbling distance from the wine cellars of the Valley of the Beautiful Women. The bungalow is just a cabin, with no bath or kitchen.

Dobó Vendégház
GUESTHOUSE $$

(Map p246; ☑06 20 442 3849, 36-421 407; www.dobovendeghaz.hu; Dobó István utca 19; s/d/tr 10,500/15,900/22,500Ft; 🛜) Tucked away along one of the old town's pedestrian streets just below Eger Castle, this lovely little hotel has seven spick-and-span rooms, some with balconies. Check out the museum-quality Zsolnay porcelain collection in the breakfast room.

Szent Kristóf Panzió
GUESTHOUSE $$

(Map p246; ☑06 20 436 7877; www.stkristof panzioeger.hu; Arany János utca 1; d/tr 8900/11,900Ft; 🛜) This guesthouse, just south of the basilica and on the way to the Valley of the Beautiful Women, has eight rather small but comfortable rooms with fridge. Ceilings slope but that's the price you pay for staying in an old building. We like the round turreted room on the corner.

★ Hotel Senator Ház
BOUTIQUE HOTEL $$$

(Senator House Hotel; Map p246; ☑36-320 466; www.senatorhaz.hu; Dobó István tér 11; s/d €57/64; ❄@🛜) Eleven warm and cosy rooms with traditional white furnishings fill the upper floors of this delightful 18th-century inn on Eger's main square. The ground floor is shared between a quality restaurant and a reception area stuffed with antiques and curios.

Imola Udvár Hotel
APARTMENT $$$

(Map p246; ☑36-516 180; www.imolaudvar haz.hu; Tinódi Sebestyén tér 4; s/d/ste 16,000/19,900/25,000Ft; ❄🛜) With six sleek and stylish apartments under the very nose of the castle, this is where you'll want to stay if you're looking for a central location and the freedom to prepare your own meals. Kitchens come fully equipped.

Hotel Ködmön
RESORT $$$

(☑36-413 172; www.szepasszonyvolgy.eu; Szépasszonyvölgy utca 1; r €92-125; ❄@🛜🏊) If you like the idea of staying out in the Valley of the Beautiful Women, choose this relatively new, modern-design resort hotel with 20 rooms. Awaken to a view of the vineyards and then take advantage of its fully equipped wellness centre. There's a popular *csárda* (Hungarian-style inn) opposite.

✖ Eating

Lining the entry path to the Valley of the Beautiful Women are 10 food-stand-like eateries, with waiters who come to your covered picnic table with menus at which you point (mains 1200Ft to 2200Ft). There are also several *csárdák* among the wine cellars to choose from.

Il Padrino
PIZZA $

(Map p246; ☑06 20 547 9959, 36-786 040; www.padrinopizza.hu; Fazola Henrik utca 1; pizza 990-2190Ft; ⊙11am-10pm) This little hole in the wall is hidden away in a narrow street just up from the landmark former Neoclassical Synagogue. It's worth a look though as it serves the best premium Italian pizza in Eger. Salads (990Ft to 1290Ft) too. Limited seating both inside and out.

Agria Park
INTERNATIONAL $

(Map p246; ☑36-512 401; www.agriapark.hu; Törvényház utca 4; mains 750-1200Ft; ⊙10am-8pm Mon-Sat, to 6pm Sun) Chinese, Hungarian and Greek self-service restaurants are among your choices on the top floor of the Agria Park shopping centre west of the basilica.

★1552
HUNGARIAN $$

(Map p246; ☑06 30 869 6219; www.1552.uu; Egri Vár; mains 1690-3390Ft; ⊙11am-11pm) With a name like this, the stunning new 1552 has just got to be up in the castle. The upscale menu, created by Budapest-trained chef Matyás Hegyi, offers largely New Hungarian cuisine, with a polite nod to the losers way back in 1552: a handful of Turkish-inspired dishes are available as well.

With seating in a stylish dining room as well as on a large terrace facing the central courtyard, 1552 is a welcome addition to the castle's many attractions.

NORTHERN HUNGARY EGER

Senator Ház Restaurant INTERNATIONAL $$
(Map p246; ☑36-320 466; www.senatorhaz.hu;
Dobó István tér 11; mains 2000-3200Ft; ☺noon-
11pm) Seats in the antique-filled dining room
of this charming hotel are coveted, but the
outdoor ones are the hot seats of Eger's main
square. Try the kohlrabi cream soup with
baguette chips (900Ft), the mushroom ra-
violi with pecorino cheese (1300Ft) and the
smoked local trout (2800Ft).

Fő Tér HUNGARIAN $$
(Main Square; Map p246; ☑36-817 482; http://
fotercafe.hu; Gerl Matyas utca 2; mains 1490-4190Ft;
☺10am-10pm) With a prominent position on
Dobó István tér opposite the Minorite church,
'Main Square' adds a bit of colour to Eger's
dining scene, and boasts a fine terrace with
a tented roof open in summer and glassed-in
during the colder months. The food is Hungarian with a contemporary taste.

Szantofer Vendéglő HUNGARIAN $$
(Map p246; ☑36-517 298; www.szantofer.
hu; Bródy Sándor utca 3; mains 1400-2500Ft;
☺11.30am-10pm) Choose this renovated eat-
ery for hearty, home-style Hungarian fare.
The cosy inside dining room shows off its
nice wine collection but the covered court-
yard with aquarium out the back is perfect
for escaping the summer heat. Two-course
weekday lunches are a snip at 890Ft.

Palacsintavár CREPERIE $$
(Pancake Castle; Map p246; ☑36-413 980; www.
palacsintavar.hu; Dobó István utca 9; mains 1950-
2350Ft; ☺noon-11pm Tue-Sat, to 10pm Sun) Pop
art and a fascinating collection of antique
cigarettes still in their packets line the walls
in this eclectic eatery. Savoury *palacsinta*
– pancakes, for lack of a better word – are
served with an abundance of fresh vegetables and range in flavour from Asian to
Mexican. There's a large choice of sweet ones
(from 1790Ft) too. Enter from Fazola Henrik
utca.

★ Macok Bistro & Wine Bar HUNGARIAN $$$
(Macok Bisztró és Borbár; Map p246; ☑36-516
180; www.imolaudvarhaz.hu/en/the-macok-bisztro-
wine-bar.html; Tinódi Sebestyén tér 4; mains 2190-
4900Ft; ☺noon-10pm Sun-Thu, to 11pm Fri & Sat)
This stylish eatery at the foot of the castle,
with its inventive menu and excellent wine
cellar, has been named among the top dozen
restaurants in Hungary, and who are we to
disagree? We'll come back in particular for
the foie gras *brûlée* (1890Ft) and the roasted
rabbit with liver 'crisps' (2870Ft). There's a

lovely dining-room courtyard with a water
feature.

Fehérszarvas Vadásztanya HUNGARIAN $$$
(Map p246; ☑36-411 129; www.feherszarvas
etterem.hu; Klapka György utca 8; mains 2700-
5050Ft; ☺11.30am-midnight Mon-Sat, to 6pm Sun)
With its game specialities, cellar setting and
trophies throughout, the 'White Deer Hunt-
ers' Farm' is really a place to enjoy in season
– autumn and winter. Cold fruit soups and
goose-liver pâté are particular specialities –
to be enjoyed in the warmer months too.

🍷 Drinking & Nightlife

The open-air tables at the wine cellars of the
Valley of the Beautiful Women are among
the best places to drink in warm weather.
They offer wine by the carafe in addition to
the decilitre servings.

★ Fúzio Wine Bar & Cellar WINE BAR
(Map p246; ☑06 20 852 5002; www.galtibor.hu/
fuzio-borbar.html; Csiky Sándor utca 10; ☺4-10pm
Wed & Thu, 4-11pm Fri, 11am-11pm Sat, 11am-3pm
Sun) This rather precious wine bar in the cellars of master vintner Tibor Gal has tastings
and serves wine by the glass and bottle. A
large, comfortably furnished space with seating in a central court just up from the city
centre, Fúzio underscores how up to date the
Hungarian wine industry has become.

Bíboros CLUB
(Map p246; ☑06 70 199 2733; www.facebook.
com/biboroseger; Bajcsy-Zsilinszky utca 6; ☺11am-
3am Mon-Fri, 1pm-3am Sat, 3pm-midnight Sun)
A subdued ruin bar by day, the 'Cardinal'
transforms into a raucous dance club late in
the evening; the cops at the door most weekend nights are a dead giveaway. Enjoy.

Egri Pasa Sátra CAFE
(Eger Pasha's Tent; Map p246; ☑36-363 806;
www.egripasasatra.com; Dobó István utca 40;
☺10am-midnight Mon-Sat, to 10pm Sun Mar-Dec)
Cool or what? This cafe/drinks bar just below the castle's Dobó Bastion is in a huge
Turkish-style tent – a marquee really – with
copper coffee and teaware, *sofra* (those
low-lying tables so popular in the Near East)
and carpets also from that region. Remove
your shoes before entering – under pain of
death if not.

Club Leonardo CLUB
(Map p246; ☑06 30 345 1622; www.facebook.
com/ClubLeonardoEger; Klapka György utca 8;
☺6pm-midnight Tue-Thu, 10pm-3am Fri & Sat)

BUSES TO EGER

DESTINATION	PRICE	DURATION	KM	FREQUENCY
Debrecen	2520Ft	2¾hr	130	6 nonstop daily
Gyöngyös	1170Ft	1hr	52	hourly nonstop daily
Kecskemét	3130Ft	4hr	166	2 nonstop daily
Miskolc	1300Ft	1½hr	68	8 nonstop daily
Szeged	3950Ft	5½hr	234	2 nonstop daily
Szilvásvárad	560Ft	40min	29	hourly nonstop daily

In the basement of the Hotel Korona, the Leonardo is a drinks venue during the week and a popular dance club at the weekend; it attracts a professional and well-dressed crowd.

Cortado Gastrobar COCKTAIL BAR
(Map p246; ☑ 36-526 434; www.facebook. com/cortadoeger; Foglár György utca 2; ⊙ 10am-midnight Sun-Thu, to 2am Fri & Sat) As much a Latin cocktail bar as a cafe (with Has Bean Bolivian and Ethiopian coffee) and a place for fancy burgers (1890Ft to 2490Ft), Cortado Gastrobar is great for kicking back after a hard day's sightseeing. Cocktails are 980Ft to 1590Ft.

Marján Cukrászda CAFE
(Map p246; ☑ 36-312 784; http://marjancukraszda. hu; Kossuth Lajos utca 28; ⊙ 9am-10pm Jun-Sep, to 7pm Oct-May) Linger over coffee and sweets (cakes are 200Ft to 600Ft) on the big terrace south of Tinódi Sebestyén tér (formerly Dózsa György tér), just below the castle.

Hippolit CLUB
(Map p246; ☑ 06 20 340 1041; www.hippolit. hu; Katona István tér 2; ⊙ 10pm-5am Wed & Sat) Eger's classic club, where the dance floor doesn't heave but buckles until the wee hours twice a week to mainstream and classic favourites. It's below the southern end of the covered *piac csarnok* (market hall).

☆ Entertainment

For cultural programs, especially music concerts, check out the listings in the free *#Eger* guide.

🛍 Shopping

Lira Magvető Könyvesbolt BOOKS
(Map p246; ☑ 36-517 757; www.lira.hu/hu/ bolthalozat/eger1; Bajcsy-Zsilinszky utca 4; ⊙ 9am-6pm Mon-Fri, to 1pm Sat) Small bookstore with a selection of English titles and maps.

ℹ Information

OTP Bank (Széchenyi István utca 2; ⊙ 7.45am-5pm Mon, to 4pm Tue-Fri) Has an ATM.

Post Office (Map p246; Széchenyi István utca 22; ⊙ 7am-7pm Mon, 8am-7pm Tue-Fri, 8am-noon Sat)

Tourinform (Map p246; ☑ 36-517 715; www. eger.hu; Bajcsy-Zsilinszky utca 9; ⊙ 8am-6pm Mon-Fri, 9am-1pm Sat & Sun Jul & Aug, 8am-5pm Mon-Fri, 9am-1pm Sat May, Jun, Sep & Oct, 8am-5pm Mon-Fri Nov-Apr) Helpful office that promotes both the town and areas surrounding Eger.

ℹ Getting There & Away

BUS

The only bus that goes through the Bükk Hills via Felsőtárkány to Miskolc leaves on Sunday at 9.10am.

TRAIN

Eger's main train station is on Vasút utca, south of the Archbishop's Garden. To reach the city centre, walk north on Deák Ferenc utca and then head along pedestrian Széchenyi István utca, Eger's main drag. The Egervár train station, which serves Szilvásvárad and other points northeast, is on Vécseyvölgy utca, about a five-minute walk north of Eger Castle.

Up to seven direct trains a day connect to/from Budapest's Keleti train station (2905Ft, two hours, 120km). Otherwise, Eger is on a minor train line linking Putnok and Füzesabony, so you have to change at the latter for Miskolc (1490Ft, 1½ hours, 74km) or Debrecen (2200Ft, 2½ hours, 120km). Catch the train to Szilvásvárad (420Ft, one hour, 30km) from Egervár station.

ℹ Getting Around

From the main train station, buses 11, 12 or 14 will drop you off at the city centre or at the bus station (Map p246).

NORTHERN HUNGARY EGER

TOKAJ

📱 47 / POP 4300

The world-renowned sweet wines of Tokaj (*toke*-eye) have been produced here since the 15th century. Today Tokaj is a picturesque little town of old buildings, nesting storks and wine cellars, offering plenty of opportunities to sample its famous tipple. And lying at the confluence of the Bodrog and Tisza Rivers, it provides ample options for recreation as well. Tokaj is just one of 28 towns and villages of what is called the Tokaj-Hegyalja, 70-sq-km vine-growing region that produces wine along the southern and eastern edges of the Zemplén Hills.

◉ Sights

The bells of the two churches on Kossuth tér make for an especially sonorous Sunday morning.

World Heritage Wine Museum   MUSEUM
(Világörökségi Bormúzeum Tokaj; Map p254; 📱47-552 050; www.bormuzeum.eu; Serház utca 55; adult/concession 1000/500Ft, combined ticket with the Tokaj Museum 1500/600Ft; ⊙9am-5pm Tue-Sun Jun-Oct, 10am-5pm Tue-Sun Nov-May) This ambitious museum has comprehensive coverage of Tokaj and the Hegyalja region and its wines. But it doesn't stop there, with a high-tech look at the half-dozen other World Heritage wine regions in Europe (Italy, France and Portugal). And there's very little you won't know about coopers and barrel-making after a visit here.

Great Synagogue   JEWISH SITE
(Nagy Zsinagóga; Map p254; 📱47-552 000; Serház utca 55; ⊙by appointment) The 19th-century Eclectic Great Synagogue, which was used as a German barracks during WWII, is once again gleaming after a total reconstruction. It is now used as a conference and cultural centre; seek entry via the Ede Paulay Theatre (p254).
There's also a large Orthodox Jewish cemetery in Bodrogkeresztúr, 6km northwest of Tokaj.

Tokaj Museum   MUSEUM
(Tokaji Múzeum; Map p254; 📱47-352 636; www.tokajimuzeum.hu; Bethlen Gábor utca 7; adult/concession 800/400Ft, combined ticket with World Heritage Wine Museum 1500/600Ft; ⊙9am-5pm Tue-Sun Jun-Oct, 10am-5pm Tue-Sun Nov-May) The Tokaj Museum, in an 18th-century mansion built by Greek wine traders, leaves nothing unsaid about the history of Tokaj and the Hegyalja region. There's also a superb collection of Christian liturgical art, including icons, medieval crucifixes and triptychs, Judaica from the former Great Synagogue, and temporary exhibits by local artists. There's also an old wine cellar with exhibits below the museum.

Church of the Sacred Heart   CHURCH
(Jézus Szíve Templom Tokaj; Map p254) This central Catholic church was built in 1912.

🏃 Activities

Rákóczi Cellar   WINE
(Rákóczi Pince; Map p254; 📱06 30 436 5767, 47-352 408; www.rakoczipince.hu; Kossuth tér 15; ⊙11am-6pm) Head to the 600-year-old Rákóczi Cellar for wine tasting and a tour. Bottles of wine mature underground in the long cave-like corridors (one measures 28m by 10m).

Erzsébet Cellar   WINE
(Map p254; 📱06 20 802 0137; www.erzsebetpince.hu; Bem út 16; ⊙10am-6pm by appointment) This small, family-run affair usually needs to be booked ahead. Tasting six Tokaj/Aszú wines costs 3600/8000Ft.

Hímesudvar   WINE
(Map p254; 📱47-352 416; www.himesudvar.hu; Bem utca 2; ⊙10am-6pm) Hímesudvar is a 16th-century wine cellar with a shop for tastings, northwest of the town centre.

Benkő Borház   WINE
(Benkő Winehouse; 📱06 20 920 9844, 47-353 607; www.benkoborhaz.hu; Szerelmi Pincesor; ⊙10am-7pm by appointment) This is one of several small cellars that line Hegyalja utca, off Bajcsy-Zsilinszky utca, at the base of the vine-covered hill above the train station.

Kékcápák   CANOEING
(📱47-353 227; www.turak.hu; Malom utca 11) Canoeing routes and camping in northeastern Hungary, with transport to/from Tokaj included.

River Boat Tours   BOATING
(Map p254; 📱06 20 971 6564, 47-552 187; www.tokaj-info.hu; Hajókikötő; adult/child 1200/900Ft; ⊙11am & 3pm May-Oct, plus 11am & 5pm Sat & Sun Jun-Aug) From May through October, hour-long sightseeing boat tours ply the Tisza and Bodrog waters. Board at the pier just south of the Tisza Bridge.

Vízisport Turistaház Boat Rentals   BOATING
(Map p254; 📱47-552 187; www.tokaj-info.hu; Horgász utca 3; per 4hr/day canoe 700/1000Ft,

WINE TASTING IN TOKAJ

Private cellars (pincék) and restaurants for wine tastings are scattered throughout town. Start with 100mL glasses; you may swallow more than you think! If you're serious, the correct order is to move from dry to sweet: *furmint,* dry Szamorodni, sweet Szamorodni and then the Aszú wines. The last, dessert-like wines have a rating of four to six *puttony* (a measure of how much of the sweet essence of noble rot grapes has been used). A basic flight of three/six Tokaj wines costs from 1500/3500Ft; an all-Aszú tasting of four wines can run between 4100Ft and 6500Ft.

The grandaddy of tasting places is the 600-year-old Rákóczi Cellar (p252), where bottles of wine mature in long corridors (one measures 28m by 10m). Erzsébet Cellar (p252) is a smaller, family-run affair that usually needs to be booked ahead. There's also tasting (four wines, 1800Ft) at their Tokaj Coffee Roasting Company cafe (p255). The most friendly of the central tasting places is Hímesudvar (p252). Smaller cellars line Hegyalja utca, off Bajcsy-Zsilinszky utca, at the base of the vine-covered hill above the train station, including Benkő Borház (p252).

kayak 1000/1500Ft, bicycle per 4hr 1000Ft; ⊙8am-8pm) You can rent canoes, kayaks and bicycles from Vízisport Turistaház; enquire inside the restaurant Halra Bor (p255).

Tutajos Beach SWIMMING
(Map p254; ☑06 20 220 2112; www.tutajos beach.hu; Strand utca; adult/child 700/500Ft; ⊙9am-7pm Jun-Aug) There's a grassy riverfront beach for swimming at Tutajos Beach Camping, across the Tisza Bridge from town.

✯ Festivals & Events

Tokaj Wine Festival WINE
(Tokaji Borfesztivál; ⊙Jun) This three-day wine festival in early June attracts oenophiles from far and wide.

Tokaj-Hegyalja Vintage Days WINE
(Tokaj-Hegyaljai Szüreti Napok; ⊙Sep/Oct) This three-day festival marks the end of the regional harvest season in late September and early October.

🛏 Sleeping

Private rooms on offer along Hegyalja utca are convenient to the train station and surrounded by vineyards. Bring lots of mosquito repellent if you're camping along the river.

Huli & Bodrog Panzió GUESTHOUSE $
(Map p254; ☑06 20 465 5903; www.hulipanzio. hu; Rákóczi Ferenc út 16; s 6000-8000Ft, d 8000-11,000Ft; ❄🏠) A sunny yellow colour covers both the walls and the flowered duvets in down-to-earth rooms spread across the 1st floor of a popular counter-service restaurant (mains 1100Ft to 1600Ft). The 12 rooms in the Huli wing aren't huge and decor is basic;

choose one of the seven more up-to-date ones in the Bodrog wing. All rooms have small fridges; air-con costs 1500Ft.

Vaskó Panzió GUESTHOUSE $
(Map p254; ☑06 70 315 8481, 47-352 107; www.vaskopanzio.hu; Rákóczi Ferenc út 12; s/d 5500/8000Ft; ❄🏠) The very central Vaskó has 11 tidy rooms with window sills bedecked with flower pots. It's above a private wine cellar and the proprietor can organise tastings.

Tutajos Beach Camping CAMPGROUND $
(Map p254; ☑06 20 220 2112; Strand utca; per person/tent/caravan 1100/1300/2500Ft, bungalow d 6000Ft; ⊙Apr-Oct) Shady tent sites and basic bungalows are adjacent to a beach with boat rental. Showers cost 100Ft for three minutes.

Tokaj Vár HOTEL $$
(Map p254; ☑47-353 743; www.tokaj varhotel.hu; Bajcsy-Zsilinszky út 5; s/d/ste 13,500/15,500/20,500Ft; ❄🏠) This rather boxy 21-room hotel southwest of the centre has nevertheless raised the bar on accommodation in Tokaj and is probably the most comfortable place to lay your head. Rooms are large and modern and many face a quiet inner courtyard. The hotel also owns a couple of wine cellars in nearby Bodrogkeresztúr and can organise tastings.

★ Toldi Fogadó GUESTHOUSE $$$
(Toldi Inn; Map p254; ☑47-353 403; www.toldi fogado.hu; Hajdú köz 2; d 16,900Ft; ❄@🏠🍴) An excellent and central choice is this 13-room inn in the heart of Tokaj. Most rooms look onto a quiet *köz* (lane) so sleep is

Tokaj

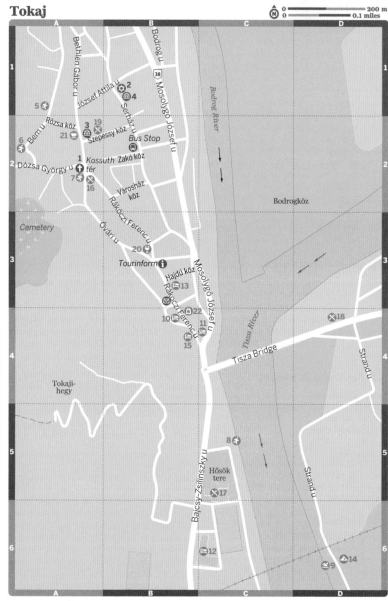

guaranteed. The long, narrow indoor pool is a welcome respite from the summer heat and the spa boasts a sauna, steam room and jacuzzi. Excellent in-house restaurant.

★ **Gróf Degenfeld Castle Hotel**   HOTEL **$$$**
(☑ 47-580 400; www.hotelgrofdegenfeld.hu; Terézia kert 9, Tarcal; s/d €100/110; ❄ @ ☎ ☒) Set in a converted castle, this plush hotel full of chandeliers and over-the-top decor counts 21 attractive rooms and suites boasting all

Tokaj

the amenities. There's a heated outdoor pool, tennis courts and fitness centre as well as an elegant restaurant and wine cellar.

✘ Eating

There are a lot of budget and fast-food places along the river southwest of the Tisza Bridge.

Halra Bor SEAFOOD $
(Map p254; ☎47-552 187; http://tokaj-info.hu/en/halra-bor-restaurant; Horgász utca 3; mains 1000-2690Ft; ⊙noon-9am) This riverside restaurant with its back terrace looking in the general direction of the Tisza is a cheap and cheerful option among Tokaj's rather limited selection of eateries.

Market MARKET $
(Map p254; ⊙7am-3pm Mon-Sat) This market is a good place to stock up on picnic supplies.

Bacchus HUNGARIAN $
(Map p254; ☎06 20 352 8730; www.borostyan bacchus.hu; Kossuth tér 3; mains 1300-1800Ft; ⊙9am-8pm) Head for this simple little eatery on the main square under two mini lindens for lunch or early dinner. It serves the usual Hungarian staples as well as pizza (950Ft to 1400Ft).

Bonchidai Csárda SEAFOOD $$
(Map p254; ☎06 20 584 1758, 47-352 632; www. hollandrt.hu/tokaj-bonc-top.htm; Bajcsy-Zsilinszky utca 21; mains 1600-3800Ft; ⊙10am-10pm) Nine types of *halászlé* (fish soup) are just the beginning of the offerings made from the water's bounty here. Sit on the large terrace overlooking the recreational boat pier on the Tisza River (with your back to the car park) or inside the rustic fish house.

Toldi Fogadó Restaurant HUNGARIAN $$$
(Map p254; ☎47-353 403; www.toldifogado.hu; Hajdú köz 2; mains 1950-3380Ft; ⊙11am-10pm; ✎) A lovely restaurant offering quasi-fine dining down a small *köz* (lane) off the main drag, Toldi excels at fish dishes (try the catfish) but also has some excellent duck dishes (duck leg with *lecsó*, a kind of ratatouille) and a generous selection of vegetarian mains.

Tokaj Hotel Restaurant HUNGARIAN $$$
(Map p254; ☎47-352 344; www.tokajhotel.hu; Rákóczi Ferenc út 5; mains 1500-3800Ft; ⊙7-10pm) This hotel restaurant specialises in game – as you might have guessed from all the trophies on the walls. Sit in the main dining room or on the pretty back terrace.

☕ Drinking & Nightlife

Just look around for the nearest *borozó* (wine bar) to sate your thirst.

Tokaj Coffee Roasting Company CAFE
(Map p254; ☎06 20 266 4455, 47-552 008; www.tokajcoffee.com; Bethlen Gábor utca 10; ⊙9am-7pm Sun-Thu, 9am-8pm Fri & Sat) This is one of those nouveau cafes that takes its coffee very seriously (and its cakes too, judging from the oh-so-homemade taste; 300Ft to 450Ft). They also do tastings: four wines for 1800Ft.

NORTHERN HUNGARY TOKAJ

Cafe Műhely Borbár WINE BAR

(Map p254; ☑06 20 454 1188; Rákóczi Ferenc út 40; ☺2pm-midnight) A very stylish wine bar that's just the place to sate your thirst, should you want to try Tokaj's vintages in a relaxed atmosphere.

Shopping

Wine, wine and more wine – from a 10L plastic jug of new Furmint to a bottle of six-*puttony* Aszú – is available in shops and cellars throughout Tokaj. One of the better central places is Borostyán (Map p254; ☑06 20 263 1316; www.borostyanbacchus.hu; Rákóczi Ferenc út 11; ☺2-10pm). There's also a shop with a high-end selection at the Rákóczi Cellar (p252).

Information

OTP Bank (Rákóczi Ferenc út 37; ☺8am-4pm Mon, 8am-2.30pm Tue-Thu, 8am-1pm Fri) Has an ATM.

Post Office (Map p254; Rákóczi Ferenc út 24; ☺8am-6pm Mon, 8am-4pm Tue-Fri, 8-11am Sat)

Tourinform (Map p254; ☑06 70 388 8870; www.tokaj-turizmus.hu; Serház utca 1; ☺9am-6pm Mon-Fri, 10am-6pm Sat, 10am-2pm Sun Jun-Aug, 9am-4pm Mon-Fri, 10am-2pm Sat & Sun Sep-May) Just off Rákóczi Ferenc út; a helpful office distributing brochures and organising weekend 'wine bus' tours.

Getting There & Away

Bus travel in the Zemplén Hills requires frequent changes and careful timing; few buses run daily, though you can reach Debrecen (1830Ft, two hours, 85km) via Nyíregyháza (800Ft, 40 minutes, 32km) twice a day and Sárospatak (800Ft, 50 minutes, 32km) two to three times daily. Buses (Map p254) arrive and depart from Serház utca, east of Kossuth tér.

Tokaj's train station is 1.2km south of the town; walk north for 15 minutes along Baross Gábor utca and Bajcsy-Zsilinszky utca to Rákóczi Ferenc út. Up to 16 trains a day head west through Miskolc (1550Ft, one hour, 56km) to Budapest Keleti (4605Ft, 2¾ hours, 238km), and east through Nyíregyháza (650Ft, 35 minutes, 32km) to Debrecen (1830Ft, one hour, 81km). If you want to travel north to Sárospatak (1120Ft, 1½ hours, 54km), change at Mezőzombor or Szerencs.

Getting Around

Cycling is an excellent way to get around Tokaj, and the Hegyalja region in general – especially if you're wine tasting. Many lodgings can arrange rental in this bike-friendly town (including **Vízisport Turisztaház**; p252) or rent from **Tourinform**.

BEREG REGION

Folksy blue and red painted flowers enliven the walls of a church in Csaroda, a kerchief-clad grandmother sits by the fence in Tákos selling her needlework, and row after row of boat-shaped wooden grave markers stand sentinel in Szatmárcseke. The pleasures of Hungary's northeast are simple and rural. Regular flooding of the Tisza and Szamos Rivers cut Bereg off from the rest of Hungary, and isolation discouraged development and preserved traditional ways of life.

Bring your sense of adventure; the simple life is not always so simple. Each small village has only one sight, and the woman who keeps the church key may not be home. It might be best to base yourself in the region's only sizeable town, Vásárosnamény. And remember that having your own transport is key, as a negligible number of buses connect the villages.

Sleeping & Eating

There is no shortage of guesthouses and homestays in the villages of the Bereg region.

Most lodgings will prepare you up to three meals a day. Expect to pay about 2500Ft for full board.

Getting There & Away

It's very difficult to reach all the Bereg villages by public transport. Consider renting a car. Up to six weekday-only buses linking Vásárosnamény with Tákos (250Ft, 15 minutes, 10km) continue to Csaroda (310Ft, 20 minutes, 13km). Up to nine weekday buses serve Tarpa (465Ft, 40 minutes, 20km). To get to Szatmárcseke, you must change in Fehérgyarmat (840Ft, 1¼ hours, 40km, nine daily), but runs are few and far between. For all these buses expect a maximum of four on Saturday and perhaps two on Sunday.

Vásárosnamény

☑45 / POP 8760

Vásárosnamény was once an important trading post on the Salt Road, which ran from the forests of Transylvania via the Tisza River and across the Great Plain to Debrecen. Today it's a nondescript little town, but it is the region's only sizeable town and offers the closest city services for Bereg villages.

⊙ Sights

Bereg Museum   MUSEUM
(☑ 45-470 638; www.beregi-muzeum.hu; Szabadság
tér 26; adult/child 400/200Ft; ☺ 8.30am-4.30pm
Tue-Fri, 8am-4pm Sat & Sun Apr-Oct, 8am-4pm Mon-
Fri Nov-Mar) Inside Tomcsány Manor (1728),
this museum contains an excellent collection
of Bereg cross-stitch, pottery, iron stoves and
painted Easter eggs. A whole room is dedicated to how local textiles are woven. There's
a large collection of liturgical objects and
church plate.

🏃 Activities

Szilva Thermal Baths   SPA
(☑ 45-470 180; www.szilvafurdo.hu; Beregszászi
út 1/b; adult/child 1500/1100Ft; ☺ 9am-8pm)
The one outdoor and four indoor pools at
these impressive modern thermal baths are
a short distance southeast of the centre.

Atlantika Waterpark   WATER PARK
(Atlantika vízividámpark; ☑ 45-570 112; www.ter
malfurdo.hu/furdo/atlantika-vizividampark-145;
Gulácsi út 56; adult/child 2500/2000Ft; ☺ 9am-
6pm mid-Jun–Aug, Sat only Sep) Some 2km
east of Vásárosnamény across the Rte 41
bridge in Gergelyiugornya, near the free
Tisza-part (Tisza bank) beach and opposite the camping ground Diófa Kemping,
is this large water park with 10 pools and
10 slides.

🛏️ Sleeping & Eating

Several holiday homes have rooms and apartments for rent on Gulácsi út and Tiszavirág
sétány in the Gergelyiugornya area across
the Tisza River southeast of the centre.

From June through August food stands
and bars open on the banks of the Tisza.

Bereg Apartments   COTTAGE $
(☑ 06 30 469 7252; www.beregapartman.com;
Sólyom sétány, Gergelyiugornya; per person 2500Ft;
☺ Apr-Sep; 🐾) This small cluster of holiday
homes in Gergelyiugornya, some 2km southeast of Vásárosnamény centre and overlooking the Tisza, counts eight small cottages on
stilts for two to three people (all with small
kitchens), and a larger apartment for six
people. Bikes cost 3000Ft per day; canoes
and kayaks can be rented from the beach
just steps away.

Diófa Kemping   CAMPGROUND $
(☑ 06 30 469 7252; www.diofakemping.hu;
Gulácsi út 71; campsite per person/tent/car-
avan 1000/1000/1500Ft, bungalow for 2/4

7000/14,000Ft; @) Not only does this small
camping ground have a fitness room and
sauna, it's right across the street from the
Atlantika Waterpark. Pitch your tent in the
field or bunk in an above-average bungalow.
There's a decent restaurant here too (mains
1300Ft to 2200Ft).

Hunor Hotel   HOTEL $$
(☑ 06 30 372 4770; www.hunorhotel.eu; Szabadság
tér 25; s/d 9000/11,000Ft; 🐾🏊) This flash new
hotel on the main square has added 41 mod-
ern rooms to Vásárosnamény's accommo-
dation inventory and they are comfortable
enough, with retro-style beds and fake bear
skins (recalling the owner's passion for big-
game hunting). There's a spa with jacuzzi and
sauna, a swimming pool and an excellent in-
house restaurant (mains 1090Ft to 3190Ft).

Winkler Ház Panzió   GUESTHOUSE $$
(☑ 45-470 945; www.winklerhaz.hu; Rákóczi utca
5; s/d 7000/9000Ft; 🐾🏠) This cute little
guesthouse is a very comfortable place to
stay in Vásárosnamény. Handwoven neutral
textiles are the highlight of its 13 pleasantly
plain (think brown and beige) guest rooms;
each has a minibar. The restaurant is tops in
town and especially popular at lunch (mains
1700Ft to 2700Ft).

ℹ️ Information

OTP Bank (Szabadság tér 28-31; ☺ 8am-4.30pm
Mon-Fri) Opposite the Bereg Museum; with ATM.

Tourinform (☑ 06 70 363 1628, 45-570 206;
www.vasarosnameny.hu; Szabadság tér 9;
☺ 8am-4.30pm Mon-Fri) The friendly staff here
will help you plan your rural excursions.

ℹ️ Getting There & Away

Eight daily trains connect with Nyíregyháza
(1120Ft, 1½ hours, 59km). Reaching Bereg villages by bus can be difficult. Up to six weekday-only
buses linking Vásárosnamény with Tákos (250Ft,
15 minutes, 10km) continue to Csaroda (310Ft,
20 minutes, 13km). Up to nine weekday buses
serve Tarpa (465Ft, 40 minutes, 20km). To get
to Szatmárcseke, you must change in Fehérgyarmat (840Ft, 1¼ hours, 40km, nine daily), but
runs are few and far between. For all these buses
expect a maximum of four on Saturday and
perhaps two on Sunday.

Tákos

A village must for anyone interested in folk
art, Tákos is 10km northeast of Vásárosnamény on Rte 41.

The 18th-century wattle-and-daub Calvinist church (Tákosi Református Templom; ☑ 06 70 222 1996; www.takos.hu; Bajcsy-Zsilinszky utca 25,; 300Ft; ☺ 7am-7pm) has a spectacularly painted coffered ceiling of blue and red flowers, a partly beaten-earth floor and an ornately carved 'folk baroque' pulpit sitting on a large millstone. Outside the church, which villagers call the 'Barefoot Notre Dame of Hungary', stands a perfectly preserved bell tower (1767). The keeper of the keys to this 'peasants' cathedral' lives at Bajcsy-Zsilinszky utca 20.

The Provincial House (Tákosi Tájház; ☑ 06 70 603 8267, 06 20 216 7319; www.takos.hu; Bajcsy-Zsilinszky utca; ☺ 8am-4.30pm Mon-Fri, 8am-1.30pm Sat) FREE, opposite the church, sells works by local craftspeople and local plum jam.

Down the road from the Calvinist church is the delightful guesthouse Baráth Vendégház (☑ 06 70 330 4209; www.barathvendeghaz.atw.hu; Bajcsy-Zsilinszky utca 27; s/d 3000/4000Ft).

Csaroda

A lovely Romanesque church (Csarodai Román Templom; ☑ 06 20 444 7624; www.csaroda.hu; Kossuth utca 2; adult/child 300/250Ft; ☺ 10am-6pm Mon-Fri Mar-Oct) from the late 13th century stands in the village of Csaroda, 3km east of Tákos. A wonderful hybrid, it has Western- and Eastern-style frescoes (some from the 14th century), as well as some fairly crude folk murals (1647) and pews decorated with birds. The nearby wooden bell tower is of a more recent vintage.

You can find repose in these peaceful rural surrounds at the three-room Székely Vendégház (☑ 06 30 261 9497; www.szekelyvendeghaz.info; József Attila utca 48; s/d 3500/7000Ft). There's more than a little rustic appeal at this long, yard-oriented former traditional peasant house, with its thick whitewashed walls, dark wood, chunky furniture and red geraniums in the windows. All rooms are en suite and there's a communal kitchen. More central (and commercial) is flower-bedecked guesthouse Julianna Vendégház (☑ 06 30 643 2512; www.juliannavendeghaz.honlapom.com; Kossuth Lajos utca 15; s/d 3000/6000Ft), opposite the church. It has four lovely rooms and is surrounded by a large, well-tended garden. Breakfast/dinner is available for 500/1000Ft.

Tarpa

A bit more of a town than other Bereg region villages, with actual shops, Tarpa lies 13km southeast of Csaroda. It's known for its plum products, but one of Hungary's last examples of a working, horse-driven, 19th-century dry mill (Tarpai Szárazmalom; ☑ 06 20 358 2938; Árpád utca 36, Tarpa; adult/child 300/150Ft; ☺ by appointment) can also be seen here. Nearby is a decorated Calvinist church (Tarpai Református Templom; Kossuth utca 13, Tarpa; ☺ 8am-noon Mon-Fri) FREE.

On a bend in the river, Tivadar (www.tivadar.hu), 5km south of Tarpa, is a quiet little beachfront settlement with alternative lodgings, a campsite and an eatery or two. A good choice here is the flash guesthouse Kuruc Vendégház (☑ 06 70 334 9083; www.kurucvendeghaz.hu; Táncsics utca 14, Tivadar; s/d 5000/10,000Ft; ❄), which is newer than its traditional style suggests and has five comfortable rooms, a big garden and a swimming pool. It rents bikes as well, which is the perfect way to get around in these parts.

Szatmárcseke

This village is the site of a famous cemetery (Szatmárcsekei Temető; Táncsics utca; ☺ 24hr) FREE with intriguing prow-shaped grave markers. To get here from Tarpa, cross at the Tivadar, turn east and carry on another 7km northeast.

The 1200 carved wooden markers that resemble up-ended prows are unique in Hungary; the notches and grooves represent a complicated language detailing marital status, social position and so on. No one knows how the tradition (which is still carried on today) started, but scholars generally agree it's not Finno-Ugric (ancestral Hungarian). One of the stone markers in the cemetery is that of native son Ferenc Kölcsey (1790–1838), who wrote the lyrics to *Himnusz*, the Hungarian national anthem.

The Szatmár Fogadó (☑ 06 20 468 7882, 06 70 387 2593; www.facebook.com/Szatmár-Fogadó-382332928462511; Petőfi út 7; dm/s/d 1500/3500/7000Ft) on the main road at the turning to the cemetery has six rooms, and hearty meals from 2500Ft.

Understand Budapest & Hungary

Budapest & Hungary Today

There have been some good, bad and ugly developments here recently. A national election has returned the old guard with more power than ever. The economy splutters along but there have been some improvements. And the country has unveiled a series of new attractions – from an ambitious contemporary art museum in Debrecen to a restored synagogue in Szeged and mosque in Esztergom. And then there's Budapest's ambitious bid for the 2024 Summer Olympics.

Best on Film

Dollybirds (*Csinibaba;* 1997) Comedy/satire about a contest to cross over the Iron Curtain.

Zimmer Feri (1998) Jokes about German tourists on the Balaton.

Moszkva tér (2001) End-of-communism comedy with kids.

A Kind of America (*Valami Amerika;* 2002) Flimflam film man from the USA.

Children of Glory (*Szabadság, Szerelem;* 2006) The 'blood in the water' water-polo match of 1956.

Best in Print

Prague (Arthur Phillips; 2002) Mixed-up young American does Budapest.

Ballad of the Whiskey Robber (Julian Rubenstein; 2005) Hockey-player-cum-bank-robber on the lam.

Twelve Days: The Story of the 1956 Hungarian Revolution (Victor Sebestyen; 2007) Day-by-day account of the Uprising.

The Invisible Bridge (Julie Orringer; 2010) Epic saga of a Hungarian Jewish family during WWII.

Enter Stage Right

Prime Minister Viktor Orbán was returned to power for a third term in April 2014, garnering just 45% of the vote and 133 seats. But a series of changes in the election laws – including halving the number of MPs and allowing gerrymandering – transformed this into a two-thirds parliamentary mandate. Orbán has morphed from the liberal he was in the 1990s to an authoritarian. 'Viktátor' (as he is sometimes called in the opposition press) has been accused at home and abroad – often by EU officials – of excessive nationalism, of politicising the judiciary and the central bank, and of stirring up ethnic tensions and suppressing media freedom.

Fun & Games

Meanwhile in Budapest's bars and clubs, the band plays on. Clubs – especially the outdoor 'garden' ones – heave throughout the week in summer, 'ruin pubs' (a Budapest phenomenon that has been imitated elsewhere but never feels quite the same) are filled to the brim and everyone wants just one last shot of pálinka (fruit brandy). And the fun and games are not just nocturnal ones. Budapest continues to be the undisputed nerve centre of live 'escape games', an innovative pastime in which teams of players are locked into a set of rooms – often in disused apartment blocks – and attempt to set themselves free by working through a series of complex riddles. The choice of venues is amazing – now well over 100 – and there's a wealth of different games on offer.

The Economy: Good News at Last

There's good news on the economic front. Until a few years ago, one of the biggest headaches for Hungarian homeowners (and the economy) was that a large percentage of outstanding mortgages remained in foreign currencies (largely Swiss francs), costing a fortune in local currency to repay. But the government finally came to the rescue, curing the nation's foreign exchange loan hangover when it agreed with banks to convert up to €9 billion of these mortgages into forints at the then-market rate. Inflation was at less than 1%, and the unemployment rate of 5.5% had been almost halved by the end of 2016, the lowest it had been in Hungary since the regime change in 1989. Also, encouragingly, tighter fiscal policy and stronger GDP growth led the three credit-rating agencies – Fitch Ratings, Standard & Poor's and Moody's – to upgrade Hungary to investment grade from sub-investment grade (also known as 'junk'), where it had languished for a few years.

Tourism: From Quantity to Quality

And in tourism the news is good too. The focus has now turned from quantity to quality: boutique hotels are popping up everywhere, not just in Budapest; world-class restaurants can be found as easily in Szeged and Pécs as they can in the capital; superior thermal retreats are replacing dated eyesores well past their use-by date; and the number of new attractions – museums, renovated houses of worship, water parks – is growing in leaps and bounds.

Despite the rising tide of commercialism, Hungary's roots remain firmly entwined with its folk traditions, as a trip outside Budapest to many other parts of the country will attest. Thankfully Hungary has held on to the one factor that makes it special – being Hungarian. That means different things to different people, but the good thing is that Magyarország likes to be different. It's been that way for centuries – it's not going to change now.

POPULATION: 9.82 MILLION (BUDAPEST 1.7 MILLION)

AREA: 93,030 SQ KM (BUDAPEST 525.2 SQ KM)

GDP: US$265 BILLION

GDP GROWTH: 1%

INFLATION: LESS THAN 1%

UNEMPLOYMENT: 5.5%

if Hungary were 100 people

71 would live in towns and cities
29 would live in rural areas

belief systems
(% of population)

37 Roman Catholic
12 Calvinist
2 Lutheran
2 Greek Catholic & Greek Orthodox
1 Jewish
46 Other

population per sq km

HUNGARY — BUDAPEST

= 105 people

History

Hungary's impact on Europe's history has been far greater than its present size and population would suggest. Hungarians – who call themselves the Magyar – speak a language and form a culture unlike any other in the region, which has been both a source of pride and an obstacle for more than 1100 years. Yet, despite endless occupations and wars, the Hungarians have retained their own identity without shutting themselves off from the world.

Early Inhabitants

The Carpathian Basin, in which Hungary lies, has been populated for at least half a million years. Bone fragments found at Vértesszőlős, about 5km southeast of Tata in western Hungary, in the 1960s are believed to be that old. Stone Age pottery shards and bone-tipped arrowheads have been found at Istállóskő Cave near Szilvásvárad in northern Hungary.

Indo-European tribes from the Balkans stormed the Carpathian Basin in horse-drawn carts in about 2000 BC, bringing with them copper tools and weapons. After the introduction of the more durable metal bronze, horses were domesticated, forts were built and a military elite was developed.

The Corvinus Library of Hungarian History (www.hungarianhistory.com) is a font of all knowledge and an excellent first step in exploring the nation's past; the links to related topics – from language to painting – are very useful.

Over the next millennium, invaders from the west (Illyrians, Thracians) and east (Scythians) brought iron, but it was not in common use until the Celts arrived at the start of the 4th century BC. They introduced glass and crafted some of the fine gold jewellery that can still be seen in museums (eg the Ferenc Móra Museum in Szeged).

The Roman Conquest

The Romans conquered the area west and south of the Danube River in about 35 BC; two dozen years later they were in the Danube Bend. By AD 10 they had established the province of Pannonia, which would later be divided into Upper (Superior) and Lower (Inferior) Pannonia. The Romans introduced writing, viticulture and stone architecture, and established garrison towns and other settlements, the remains of which can still be seen in Óbuda (Aquincum in Roman times), Szombathely (Savaria), Pécs (Sophianae) and Sopron (Scarbantia).

TIMELINE	AD 106	Late 430s	896–98
	Roman Aquincum in today's Óbuda becomes the administrative seat of the province of Pannonia Inferior and a fully fledged colony less than a century later.	Aquincum offers little protection to the civilian population when the Huns burn the colony to the ground, forcing the Romans and other settlers to flee.	Nomadic Magyar tribes set up camp in the Carpathian Basin, with five of the seven original tribes settling in the area that is now Budapest.

The Great Migrations

The first of the so-called Great Migrations of nomadic peoples from Asia reached the eastern outposts of the Roman Empire early in the 3rd century AD. Within two centuries, however, they were forced to pull out of Pannonia by the Huns, whose short-lived empire had been established by Attila. Other Germanic tribes occupied the region for the next century and a half until the Avars, a powerful Turkic people, gained control of the Carpathian Basin in the late 6th century. They in turn were subdued by the Frankish king Charlemagne in 796 and converted to Christianity. By that time the Carpathian Basin was virtually unpopulated, except for groups of Turkic and Germanic tribes on the plains and Slavs in the northern hills.

The Magyars were so skilled (and brutal) as archers on horseback that a common Christian prayer during the early Middle Ages was 'Save us, O Lord, from the arrows of the Hungarians.'

The Magyars

The origin of the Magyars is a complex issue, not helped by the similarity (in English) of the words 'Hun' and 'Hungary', which are *not* related. One thing is certain: Magyars are part of the Finno-Ugric group of peoples who inhabited the forests somewhere between the middle Volga River and the Ural Mountains in western Siberia and began migrating as early as 4000 BC.

By about 2000 BC population growth had forced the Finnish-Estonian branch of the group to move westward, ultimately reaching the Baltic Sea. The Ugrians migrated from the southeastern slopes of the Urals into the valleys, and switched from fishing, hunting and gathering to primitive farming and raising livestock, especially horses. The Magyars' equestrian skills proved useful half a millennium later when climatic changes brought drought, forcing them to move north to the steppes.

On the plains, the Ugrians turned to nomadic herding. After 500 BC, by which time the use of iron had become widespread among the tribes, some of the groups moved westward to the area of Bashkiria in central Asia. Here they lived among Persians and Bulgars and began referring to themselves as Magyars (from the Finno-Ugric words *mon*, 'to speak', and *er*, 'man').

After several centuries another group split away and moved south to the Don River under the control of the Turkic Khazars. Here they lived among different groups under a tribal alliance called *onogur* (or '10 peoples'), thought to be the derivation of the word 'Hungary'. The Magyars' last migration before the so-called conquest *(honfoglalás)* of the Carpathian Basin brought them to what modern Hungarians call the Etelköz, the region between the Dnieper and lower Danube Rivers above the Black Sea.

Although Hungarians are in no way related to the Huns, Attila remains a very common given name for males in Hungary today.

The Conquest of the Carpathian Basin

In about 895 and under attack, seven tribes under the leadership of Árpád, the chief military commander *(gyula)*, struck out for the Carpathian Basin. They crossed the Verecke Pass in today's Ukraine three years later.

1000	1241-42	1458-90	1514
Stephen (István in Hungarian) is crowned 'Christian King' of Hungary at Esztergom on Christmas Day; he is canonised as St Stephen in 1083.	Mongols sweep across Hungary, reducing the national population by up to a half and killing some 100,000 people in Pest and Óbuda alone.	Medieval Hungary enjoys a golden age under the enlightened reign of King Matthias Corvinus and Queen Beatrix, daughter of King Ferdinand I of Naples.	A peasant uprising is crushed, with 70,000 people executed, including leader György Dózsa, who dies on a red-hot iron throne fitted with a scalding crown.

Known for their ability to ride and shoot, the Magyars began plundering and pillaging on their own, taking slaves and amassing booty. Their raids took them as far as Spain, northern Germany and southern Italy, but in 955 they were stopped in their tracks by German king Otto I at the battle of Augsburg.

This and subsequent defeats forced them to form an alliance with the Holy Roman Empire. In 973 Prince Géza, the great-grandson of Árpád, asked Emperor Otto II to send Catholic missionaries to Hungary. Géza was baptised in his capital, Esztergom, as was his son Vajk, who took the Christian name Stephen (István). When Géza died Stephen ruled as prince but on Christmas Day in the year 1000 he was crowned 'Christian King' Stephen I.

> If you'd like to learn more about the nomadic Magyars, their history, civilisation and/or art, go to http://ancientmagyar-world.tripod.com, which also offers a number of useful and interesting links.

King Stephen I & the House of Árpád

Stephen set about consolidating royal authority by expropriating the land of the independent-minded clan chieftains and establishing a system of counties (megyék) protected by fortified castles (várak). Stephen shrewdly transferred much land to loyal (mostly German) knights. He also sought the support of the church and established 10 episcopates, two of which – Kalocsa and Esztergom – were made archbishoprics. When Stephen died in 1038, Hungary was a nascent Christian nation, increasingly westward-looking and multi-ethnic.

The next two and a half centuries – the extent of the Árpád Dynasty – were marked by dynastic intrigues and relentless struggles between rival pretenders to the throne, which weakened the young nation's defences against its powerful neighbours. In the mid-13th century the Mongols swept through Hungary, burning it virtually to the ground and killing an estimated one-third to one-half of its two million people. The Árpád line died out at the start of the next century with the death in 1301 of Andrew III, who left no heir.

> The Will to Survive: A History of Hungary by Bryan Cartledge, a former British diplomat, is one of the best all-round general histories of Hungary.

Medieval Hungary

The struggle for the Hungarian throne after the fall of the House of Árpád involved several European dynasties, with the crown first going to Charles Robert (Károly Róbert) of the French House of Anjou in 1307.

In the following century an alliance between Hungary and Poland gave the latter – with the pope's blessing – the Hungarian crown. When Vladislav I (Úlászló), son of the Polish Jagiellonian king, was killed fighting the Turks at Varna in 1444, János Hunyadi, a Transylvanian general, was made regent. His decisive victory over the Turks at Belgrade (Nándorfehérvár in Hungarian) in 1456 had checked the Ottoman advance into Hungary for 70 years and assured the coronation of his son Matthias (Mátyás), the greatest ruler of medieval Hungary.

1526	1541	1686	1795
Hungary is soundly defeated by the Ottomans at the Battle of Mohács and young King Louis is killed; the ensuing Turkish occupation lasts more than a century and a half.	Buda Castle falls to the Ottomans; Hungary is partitioned and shared by three separate groups: the Turks, the Habsburgs and the Transylvanian princes.	Austrian and Hungarian forces backed by the Polish army liberate Buda from the Turks; peace is signed with the Ottomans at Karlowitz (now in Serbia) 13 years later.	Seven pro-republican Jacobites, including the group's leader Ignác Martonovics, are beheaded at Vérmező (Blood Meadow) in Buda for plotting against the Habsburg throne.

Through his military exploits Matthias (r 1458–90), nicknamed 'the Raven' (Corvinus) from his coat of arms, made Hungary one of Central Europe's leading powers. Under his rule the nation enjoyed its first golden age.

But while Matthias busied himself with centralising power for the crown and being a good king, he ignored the growing Turkish threat. Under his successor, Vladislav II (Úlászló; r 1490–1516), what had begun as a crusade in 1514 turned into a peasant uprising against landlords under György Dózsa.

The revolt was brutally repressed by Transylvanian leader John Szapolyai (Zápolyai János), and 70,000 peasants, and Dózsa himself, were tortured and executed. The retrograde Tripartitum Law that followed codified the rights and privileges of the barons and nobles and reduced the peasants to perpetual serfdom.

The Battle of Mohács

The defeat of the ragtag Hungarian army by the Ottoman Turks at Mohács in 1526 is a watershed in Hungarian history. On the battlefield south of the small town in Southern Transdanubia, a relatively prosperous and independent medieval Hungary died, sending the nation into a tailspin of partition, foreign domination and despair that would last for centuries.

It would be unfair to put all the blame on the weak and indecisive teenage King Louis II (Lajos). Bickering among the nobility and the brutal response to the peasant uprising had severely diminished Hungary's military power, and there was virtually nothing left in the royal coffers. By 1526 Ottoman sultan Suleiman the Magnificent (r 1520–66) had occupied much of the Balkans and was poised to march on Buda.

Unwilling to wait for reinforcements from Transylvania under his rival John Szapolyai, Louis rushed south with an army of just over 25,000 and was thrashed in less than two hours. Among the estimated 18,000 dead was the king himself, who drowned while trying to retreat across a marsh.

Turkish Occupation

After the Turks returned and occupied Buda Castle in 1541, Hungary was divided into three parts. The central section, including Buda, went to the Turks, while parts of Transdanubia in the west and what is now Slovakia were governed by the Austrian House of Habsburg and assisted by the Hungarian nobility based at Bratislava (Hungarian: Pozsony). The principality of Transylvania prospered as a vassal state of the Ottoman Empire. This arrangement would remain in place for more than a century and a half.

Ottoman power began to wane in the 17th century. Buda was liberated from the Turks in 1686 after a 77-day siege, and an imperial army under Eugene of Savoy wiped out the last Turkish army in Hungary at the Battle of Zenta (now Senta in Serbia) 11 years later.

Eclipse of the Crescent Moon (Géza Gárdonyi, 1901) is a Boy's Own–style page-turner that tells the story of the siege of Eger by the Turks in 1552 and an orphaned peasant boy who grows up to become one of the greatest (fictional) heroes in Hungarian history.

1848–49	1867	1896	1918
During the War of Independence, poet Sándor Petőfi dies fighting, Lajos Batthyány and 13 of his generals are executed for their roles and Lajos Kossuth goes into exile.	The Act of Compromise creates the Dual Monarchy of Austria (the empire), based in Vienna, and Hungary (the kingdom), with its seat at Budapest.	The millennium of the Magyar 'conquest' of the Carpathian Basin is marked by a major exhibition in City Park that attracts four million people over six months.	Austria-Hungary loses WWI in November and its political system collapses; Hungary declares itself a republic under the leadership of Count Mihály Károlyi.

The Habsburgs

The expulsion of the Turks did not result in independence, and the policies of the Catholic Habsburgs' Counter-Reformation and heavy taxation further alienated the nobility. In 1703 the Transylvanian prince Ferenc Rákóczi II assembled an army of *kuruc* forces against the Austrians at Tiszahát in northeastern Hungary. The rebels 'dethroned' the Habsburgs as the rulers of Hungary in 1706 but were defeated five years later.

Hungary was now a mere province of the Habsburg Empire. Under Maria Theresa (r 1740–80) and her son, Joseph II (r 1780–90), Hungary took great steps forward economically and culturally. But Joseph's attempts to modernise society by dissolving the all-powerful (and corrupt) monastic orders, abolishing serfdom and replacing 'neutral' Latin with German as the official language of state administration were opposed by the Hungarian nobility, and he rescinded many orders on his deathbed.

Liberalism and social reform found their greatest supporters among certain members of the aristocracy, including Count György Festetics (1755–1819), who founded Europe's first agricultural college at Keszthely on Lake Balaton, and Count István Széchenyi (1791–1860), a true Renaissance man, who advocated the abolition of serfdom and returned much of his own land to the peasantry. But the radicals, dominated by the dynamic lawyer and journalist Lajos Kossuth (1802–94), demanded more immediate action.

Habsburg Emperor Joseph II was called the 'hatted king' because he was never actually *crowned* within the borders of Hungary.

The 1848–49 War of Independence

The Habsburg Empire began to weaken as Hungarian nationalism strengthened early in the 19th century and certain reforms were introduced, including a law allowing serfs alternative means of discharging their feudal service obligations and increased Hungarian representation in the Council of State in Vienna. The reforms were too limited and too late. On 15 March 1848 a group calling itself the Youth of March, led by the poet Sándor Petőfi, took to the streets of Pest with hastily printed copies of the Twelve Points to press for more radical reforms and even revolution.

In September 1848 Habsburg forces launched an attack. The Hungarians hastily formed a national defence commission and moved the government seat to Debrecen, where Kossuth was elected governor-president. In April 1849 the parliament declared Hungary's full independence and 'dethroned' the Habsburgs again.

The new Habsburg emperor, Franz Joseph (r 1848–1916), took action immediately. He sought the assistance of Tsar Nicholas I, who obliged with 200,000 troops. Weak and vastly outnumbered, the rebel troops were defeated by August 1849. Martial law was declared and a series of brutal reprisals ensued. Kossuth went into exile. Habsburg troops then went around the country systematically blowing up castles and fortifications lest they be used by resurgent rebels.

In what must be one of the oddest footnotes in Hungarian history, Napoleon Bonaparte entered Hungarian territory and spent the night of 31 August 1809 in the northwestern city of Győr, which was near a battle site.

1919	1920	1939	1944
Béla Kun's Republic of Councils, the world's second communist government after the Soviet Union's, lasts for five months until Kun is driven into exile by the Romanian army.	Treaty of Trianon carves up much of Central Europe, reducing Hungary's territory by almost two-thirds and enlarging the ethnic Hungarian populations in Romania, Yugoslavia and Czechoslovakia.	Nazi Germany invades Poland; Britain and France declare war on Germany two days later but Hungary remains neutral for two years when it joins the Axis led by Germany and Italy.	Germany invades and occupies Hungary; most Hungarian Jews, who had largely been able to avoid persecution under strongman Miklós Horthy, are deported to Nazi concentration camps.

The Dual Monarchy

Hungary was again merged into the Habsburg Empire as a conquered province. But disastrous military defeats by the French and then the Prussians in 1859 and 1866 pushed Franz Joseph to the negotiating table with liberal Hungarians under the leadership of reformer Ferenc Deák.

The result was the Act of Compromise of 1867, which created the Dual Monarchy of Austria (the empire) and Hungary (the kingdom) – a federated state with two parliaments and two capitals: Vienna and Budapest. This 'Age of Dualism', which would carry on until 1918, sparked an economic, cultural and intellectual renaissance in Hungary, culminating with a six-month exhibition in 1896 celebrating the millennium of the Magyars' arrival in the Carpathian Basin. But all was not well in the kingdom. The working class had virtually no rights and the situation in the countryside remained almost medieval. Despite an 1868 law protecting their rights, minorities under Hungarian control were under increased pressure to 'Magyarise'.

WWI & the Republic of Councils

On 28 July 1914, a month to the day after the assassination of Archduke Franz Ferdinand, heir to the Habsburg throne, by a Bosnian Serb in Sarajevo, Austria-Hungary declared war on Serbia and entered WWI allied with the German Empire. The result was disastrous, with widespread destruction and hundreds of thousands killed on the Russian and Italian fronts. After the armistice in 1918 the fate of the Dual Monarchy – and Hungary as a multinational kingdom – was sealed with the Treaty of Trianon.

A republic under the leadership of Count Mihály Károlyi was established but the fledgling republic would not last long. Rampant inflation, mass unemployment, the occupation of Hungary by the Allies, dismemberment of 'Greater Hungary' and the success of the Bolshevik Revolution in Russia all combined to radicalise much of the Budapest working class.

In March 1919 a group of Hungarian communists under a former Transylvanian journalist named Béla Kun seized power. The so-called Republic of Councils (Tanácsköztársaság) set out to nationalise industry and private property, but Kun's failure to regain the 'lost territories' brought mass opposition to the regime and the government unleashed a reign of 'red terror' around the country. In August Romanian troops occupied the capital, and Kun fled to Vienna.

The Horthy Years & WWII

In March 1920 parliament chose a kingdom as the form of state and – lacking a king – elected as its regent Admiral Miklós Horthy. He embarked on a 'white terror' – every bit as brutal as Béla Kun's red one – that attacked social democrats, communists and Jews for their roles in supporting the Republic of Councils. Though the country had the remnants

HISTORY THE DUAL MONARCHY

A Hungarian expression recalls the Turkish occupation: *Hátravan még a feketeleves* ('Still to come is the black soup'), suggesting something painful or difficult is on the cards. After a meal the Turks would serve their Hungarian guests an unknown beverage – coffee – which meant it was time to talk about taxes.

1945	1949	1956	1958
Budapest is liberated by the Soviet army in April, a month before full victory in Europe, with three-quarters of its buildings and all of its bridges in ruins.	The communists, now in complete control, announce the formation of the 'People's Republic of Hungary'; Stalinist show trials of 'Titoists' and other 'enemies of the people' begin.	Budapest is in flames after riots in October; Hungary briefly withdraws from the Warsaw Pact and proclaims its neutrality but the status quo is restored and János Kádár installed as leader.	Imre Nagy and others are executed by the communist regime for their role in the uprising and buried in unmarked graves in Budapest's New Municipal Cemetery.

of a parliamentary system, Horthy was all-powerful, and very few reforms were enacted.

Everyone agreed that the return of the 'lost territories' was essential for Hungary's development. Hungary obviously could not count on the victorious Allies to help recoup its land; instead, it sought help from the fascist governments of Germany and Italy.

Hungary's move to the right intensified throughout the 1930s, though it remained silent when WWII broke out in September 1939. Horthy hoped an alliance would not mean actually having to enter the war, but Hungary joined the German- and Italian-led Axis, declaring war on the Soviet Union in June 1941. The war was as disastrous for Hungary as WWI had been, and Horthy began secret discussions with the Allies.

When Hitler caught wind of this in March 1944 he dispatched the German army. Ferenc Szálasi, the leader of the pro-Nazi Arrow Cross Party, was installed as prime minister and Horthy was deported to Germany.

The Arrow Cross Party arrested thousands of liberal politicians and labour leaders. The puppet government introduced anti-Jewish legislation similar to that in place in Germany, and Jews, who lived in fear but carried on under Horthy, were rounded up into ghettos. From May to July of 1944, less than a year before the war ended, some 450,000 men, women and children – 60% of Hungarian Jewry – were deported to Auschwitz and other labour camps, where they starved to death, succumbed to disease or were brutally murdered.

Hungary now became an international battleground for the first time since the Turkish occupation, and bombs began falling on Budapest. Fierce fighting continued in the countryside, but by Christmas Day 1944 the Soviet army had encircled Budapest. By the time Germany had surrendered in April 1945, many of Budapest's homes, historical buildings and churches had been destroyed. The vindictive retreating Germans blew up Buda Castle and knocked out every bridge spanning the Danube.

> John Lukacs' classic *Budapest 1900: A Historical Portrait of a City and Its Culture* is an illustrated social history presenting the Hungarian capital at the height of its *fin de siècle* glory.

The People's Republic of Hungary

When free parliamentary elections were held in November 1945, the Independent Smallholders' Party received 57% of the vote. But Soviet political officers, backed by the occupying army, forced three other parties – the Communists, Social Democrats and National Peasants – into a coalition. Two years later in a disputed election held under a complicated new electoral law, the Communists declared their candidate, the oafish Mátyás Rákosi, victorious. The following year the Social Democrats merged with the Communists to form the Hungarian Workers' Party.

Rákosi, a big fan of Stalin, began a process of nationalisation and unfeasibly rapid industrialisation at the expense of agriculture. Peasants were forced into collective farms and all produce had to be delivered to state

1968	1978	1988	1989
Plans for a liberalised economy are introduced in an attempt to overcome the inefficiencies of central planning but are rejected as too extreme by conservatives.	The Crown of St Stephen is returned to Hungary from the USA, where it had been held at Fort Knox in Kentucky for safekeeping since the end of WWII.	János Kádár is forced to retire in May after more than three decades in power; he dies and is buried in Budapest's Kerepesi Cemetery the following year.	The electrified fence separating Hungary and Austria is removed in July; communist power is relinquished; the Republic of Hungary is declared in October.

warehouses. A network of spies and informers exposed 'class enemies' (such as Cardinal József Mindszenty) to the secret police, the ÁVO (ÁVH after 1949). Up to a quarter of the adult population faced police or judicial proceedings. Stalinist show trials became the norm and in August 1949 the nation was proclaimed the 'People's Republic of Hungary'.

After Khrushchev's denunciation of Stalin in 1956, Rákosi's tenure was up and the terror began to abate. Executed apparatchiks were rehabilitated, and such people as the former Minister of Agriculture Imre Nagy, who had been expelled from the party for suggesting reforms, were readmitted. By October of that year murmured calls for a real reform of the system – 'socialism with a human face' – could be heard.

The 1956 Uprising

The nation's greatest tragedy – an event that rocked communism, shook the world and pitted Hungarian against Hungarian – began on 23 October, when some 50,000 university students assembled at Bem tér in Buda, shouting anti-Soviet slogans and demanding that Imre Nagy be named prime minister. That night a crowd pulled down the colossal statue of Stalin near Heroes Sq, and shots were fired by ÁVH agents on another group gathering outside Hungarian Radio. Hungary was in revolution.

The following day Nagy formed a government, while János Kádár was named president of the Central Committee of the Hungarian Workers' Party. Over the next few days the government offered amnesty to all those involved in the violence, promised to abolish the ÁVH and announced that Hungary would leave the Warsaw Pact and declare itself neutral.

At this, Soviet tanks and troops crossed into Hungary and within 72 hours began attacking Budapest and other urban centres. Kádár had slipped away from Budapest to join the Russian invaders; he was now installed as leader. Fierce street fighting continued for several days – when it was over, 25,000 people were dead. Then the reprisals began. About 20,000 people were arrested and 2000 – including Nagy and his associates – were executed. Another 250,000 refugees fled to Austria.

Hungary Under Kádár

After the revolt, the ruling party was reorganised as the Hungarian Socialist Workers' Party, and Kádár began a program to liberalise the social and economic structure based on compromise. He introduced market socialism and encouraged greater consumerism. By the mid-1970s Hungary was light years ahead of any other Soviet-bloc country in its standard of living, freedom of movement and opportunities to criticise the government. It was 'the happiest barrack in the camp', wags said, and the so-called Hungarian model attracted much Western investment.

Paul Lendvai's lively *The Hungarians: A Thousand Years of Victory in Defeat* takes a look at why Hungarians have contributed so disproportionately, relative to their numbers, to modern sciences and arts.

Miklós Jancsó's 1967 film *Csend és Kiáltás* (Silence and Cry) is a political thriller about a 'red' who takes refuge among politically suspicious peasants after the overthrow of Béla Kun's Republic of Councils in 1919.

HISTORY THE 1956 UPRISING

1990	1991	1994	1999
The centrist MDF wins the first free elections in 43 years in April; Árpád Göncz is chosen as the republic's first president in August.	The last Soviet troops leave Hungarian soil in June, two weeks ahead of schedule; parliament passes the first act dealing with the return of property seized under communist rule since 1949.	Socialists win a decisive victory in the general election and form a government under Gyula Horn for the first time since the changes of 1989.	Hungary becomes a fully fledged member of NATO, along with the Czech Republic and Poland; NATO aircraft heading for Kosovo begin using Hungarian air bases.

But the Kádár system of 'goulash socialism' was incapable of dealing with such 'unsocialist' problems in the 1980s as unemployment, soaring inflation and the largest per-capita foreign debt in the region. Kádár and the 'old guard' refused to hear talk about party reforms. In June 1987 Károly Grósz took over as premier and Kádár retired.

Renewal & Change

Throughout the summer and autumn of 1988, new political parties were formed and old ones resurrected. In January 1989 Hungary, seeing the handwriting on the wall as Mikhail Gorbachev launched his reforms in the Soviet Union, announced that the events of 1956 had been a 'popular insurrection' and not a 'counter-revolution'. In June some 250,000 people attended the reburial of Imre Nagy and other victims of 1956 in Budapest.

The next month Hungary began to disassemble the electrified wire fence separating it from Austria. The move released a wave of East Germans holi-daying in Hungary into the West and the opening attracted thousands more.

German director Rolf Schübel's romantic drama *Ein Lied von Liebe und Tod* (Gloomy Sunday, 1999) is set in a Budapest restaurant just before the Nazi invasion and revolves around the song 'Gloomy Sunday', which was so morose it supposedly had people com-mitting suicide en masse in Budapest.

The Republic of Hungary Reborn

The communists had no choice but to agree to surrender their monopoly on power, paving the way for free elections the following March. On 23 Octo-ber 1989, the 33rd anniversary of the 1956 Uprising, the nation once again became the Republic of Hungary. The 1990 vote was won by the centrist Hungarian Democratic Forum (MDF), which advocated a gradual transition to full capitalism. Hungary had changed political systems almost in silence.

In coalition with two smaller parties – the Independent Smallholders and the Christian Democrats (KDNP) – the MDF provided Hungary with sound government during its painful transition to a free-market economy. Those years saw Hungary's neighbours to the north (Czechoslovakia) and south (Yugoslavia) split along ethnic lines, and Prime Minister József Antall did little to improve Hungary's relations with Slovakia, Romania and Yugo-slavia by claiming to be the 'emotional and spiritual' prime minister of the large Magyar minorities in those countries. He died in December 1993 and was replaced by interior minister Péter Boross.

In the May 1994 elections the Socialist Party, led by Gyula Horn, surpris-ingly won an absolute majority in parliament. Árpád Göncz of the SZDSZ was elected for a second five-year term as president in 1995.

The Road to Europe

After its dire showing in the 1994 elections, the Federation of Young Demo-crats (Fidesz), which until 1993 had limited membership to those aged un-der 35 in order to emphasise a past untainted by communism and privilege, moved to the right and added the extension 'MPP' (Hungarian Civic Party) to its name to attract the support of the burgeoning middle class. In the 1998 elections, during which it campaigned for integration with Europe,

2004	2006	2008	2010
Hungary is admit-ted to the EU along with nine other new member-nations, including neighbouring states Slovakia and Slovenia, with Romania following three years later and Croatia in 2013.	Socialist Ferenc Gyurcsány is re-elected as prime minister; Budapest is rocked by rioting during the 50th anniversary cel-ebrations of the 1956 Uprising.	The government loses a key referendum on health-care reform; the SZDSZ quits the coalition, leaving the socialists to form a minority government; Hungary is particularly hard hit by the world economic crisis.	Fidesz-MPP wins a 52% majority in general elections; Viktor Orbán resumes the premier-ship and governs with a two-thirds majority of 263 of 386 seats.

Fidesz-MPP won by forming a coalition with the MDF and the conservative Independent Smallholders. The party's youthful leader, Viktor Orbán, was named prime minister. The electorate grew increasingly hostile to Fidesz-MPP's strongly nationalistic rhetoric and unseated the government in April 2002, returning the MSZP, allied with the SZDSZ, to power under Prime Minister Péter Medgyessy, a free-market advocate who had served as finance minister in the Horn government. In August 2004, amid revelations that he had once served as a counterintelligence officer, Medgyessy resigned and Sports Minister Ferenc Gyurcsány of the MSZP was named premier. Hungary became a fully fledged member of NATO in 1999 and, with nine so-called accession countries, was admitted into the EU in May 2004.

At Home at Last

Reappointed prime minister in April 2006 after the electorate gave his coalition 55% of the vote, Gyurcsány began a series of austerity measures to tackle Hungary's budget deficit, which had reached a staggering 10% of GDP. But in September, just as these unpopular steps were put into place, an audiotape recorded shortly after the election at a closed-door meeting of the prime minister's cabinet had Gyurcsány confessing that the party had 'lied morning, noon and night' about the state of the economy since coming to power and now had to make amends. Gyurcsány refused to resign, and public outrage led to a series of demonstrations near the Parliament building in Budapest, culminating in widespread rioting that marred the 50th anniversary of the 1956 Uprising.

After that, violent demonstrations became a not-infrequent feature on the streets of Budapest and other large cities. The radical right-wing nationalist party Jobbik Magyarországért Mozgalom (Movement for a Better Hungary) has been at the centre of many of these demonstrations and riots.

Gyurcsány led a feeble minority government until general elections in 2010 when Fidesz-MPP won a majority of 52% in the first round of voting and joined forces with the Christian Democratic People's Party (KDNP) to rule with a two-thirds majority in parliament.

Hungary's most recent appearance on the world stage came in 2011 when it assumed presidency of the EU Council. A new constitution came into effect at the start of 2012.

In the April 2014 national elections, the first since constitutional changes reduced voting to a single poll and the number of MPs from 386 to 199, Fidesz took almost 45% of the vote and 133 seats, returning Orbán to the premiership. Orbán was clearly in charge once again but 'Viktátor', as the opposition press nicknamed him, was frequently criticised for strong-armed tactics and abuse of power. At the time of research Orbán was still at the helm but his ship did not appear to be on course.

The Minister of Culture in Béla Kun's short-lived Republic of Councils was one Bela Lugosi, who fled to Vienna in 1919 and eventually made his way to Hollywood, where he achieved fame as the lead in several *Dracula* films.

Szabadság, Szerelem (Children of Glory, 2006) by Krisztina Goda is the simplified (but effective) history of the 1956 Uprising, as seen through the eyes of a player on the Olympic water-polo team and his girlfriend, who is one of the student leaders.

HISTORY AT HOME AT LAST

2011	2012	2014	2015
In its most high-profile role on the European stage to date Hungary assumes the presidency of the EU council; a new Constitution of Hungary is ratified.	The new and very controversial Constitution of Hungary, deleting the word 'republic' from the country's official name, goes into effect.	Prime Minister Viktor Orbán is returned to power, with his Fidesz party handily winning 133 of 199 parliamentary seats.	In a bid to stop the flow of migrants from crossing through its territory, Hungary builds a barrier along its borders with Serbia and Croatia.

The Arts

Hungarian art has been both stunted and spurred on by pivotal historical events. King Stephen's conversion to Catholicism brought Romanesque and Gothic art and architecture, while the Turkish occupation nipped Hungary's Renaissance in the bud. The Habsburgs opened the doors wide to baroque influences. The arts thrived under the Dual Monarchy, through Trianon and even under fascism. Under communism much money was spent on classical music and 'correct' theatre. Under current economic conditions funding for the arts is being slashed.

Painting & Sculpture

For Gothic art, have a look at the 15th-century altarpieces done by various masters at the Christian Museum (p174) in Esztergom. The Bakócz Chapel in Esztergom Basilica (p174) and the Royal Palace (p171) at Visegrád contain exceptional examples of Renaissance sculpture and masonry.

The finest baroque painters in Hungary were the 18th-century artists Franz Anton Maulbertsch and István Dorffmeister, who decorated many churches with frescoes and murals The ornately carved altar in the Benedictine Abbey Church (p194) in Tihany is a masterpiece of baroque woodcarving.

The saccharine Romantic Nationalist school of heroic paintings, best exemplified by Bertalan Székely (1835–1910) and Gyula Benczúr (1844–1920), gave way to the realism of Mihály Munkácsy (1844–1900), the 'painter of the *puszta*'. See his work at the Déri Museum (p217) in Debrecen. The greatest painters from this period were Tivadar Kosztka Csontváry (1853–1919), who has been compared with Van Gogh, and József Rippl-Rónai (1861–1927), the key exponent of Secessionist painting in Hungary. For the former's work visit the Csontváry Museum (p206) in Pécs. The Hungarian National Gallery (p46) in Budapest has a large collection of paintings by Rippl-Rónai.

Hungary's favourite artists of the 20th century included Victor Vasarely (1908–97), the so-called father of op art, and the sculptor Amerigo Tot (1909–84). There are museums dedicated to the former in both Pécs and Budapest. For an idea of where fine art is in Hungary today, visit the Ludwig Museum of Contemporary Art (p91) in Budapest or Debrecen's new Centre of Modern & Contemporary Art (p218).

Folk Art

From the beginning of the 18th century, as segments of the Hungarian peasantry became more prosperous, ordinary people tried to make their world more beautiful by painting and decorating clothing and everyday objects. Thus, Hungary has one of the richest folk traditions in Europe and, quite apart from its music, this is where the country has come to the fore in art.

Three groups of people stand out for their embroidery, the acme of Hungarian folk art: the Palóc of the Northern Uplands, especially around the village of Hollókő; the Matyó from Mezőkövesd near the city of Miskolc; and the women of Kalocsa on the Great Plain. Also impressive are the waterproof woollen coats called *szűr*, once worn by herders on the Great Plain, which were masterfully embroidered by men using thick, 'furry' yarn.

The yellow ochre that became the standard colour for all Habsburg administrative buildings and many churches in the late 18th century – ubiquitous throughout Hungary – is called 'Maria Theresa yellow'.

Though a commercial site, Folk-Art-Hungary (www.folk-art-hungary.com) is a good introduction and primer to embroidery and other textile folk art by artisans in Hollókő, Kalocsa and Mezőkövesd.

Folk pottery is world-class here and no Hungarian kitchen is complete without a couple of pairs of matched plates or shallow bowls hanging on the walls. There are jugs, pitchers, plates, bowls and cups, but the rarest and most attractive are the *írókázás fazékok* (inscribed pots), usually celebrating a wedding day, or produced in the form of animals or people, such as the *Miskai kancsó* (Miska jugs), not unlike English Toby jugs.

Most people made and decorated their own furniture in the old days, especially cupboards for the *tiszta szoba* (parlour) and *tulipán ládák* (trousseau chests with tulips painted on them).

One art form that ventures into the realm of fine art is ceiling and wall folk painting. Among the best examples of the former can be found in churches, especially in villages like Tákos and Csaroda in the Bereg region of northern Hungary.

THE ARTS MUSIC

The difficulty and subtlety of the Magyar tongue has always excluded outsiders from Hungarian literature in the original, prompting the poet Gyula Illyés (1902–83) to write: 'The Hungarian language is at one and the same time our softest cradle and our most solid coffin.'

Music

One person stands head and shoulders above the rest: Franz (or, in Hungarian, Ferenc) Liszt (1811–86). He established the Liszt Music Academy (p85) in Budapest and liked to describe himself as 'part Gypsy'. Some of his works, notably his 20 *Hungarian Rhapsodies,* do in fact echo the traditional music of the Roma people.

Ferenc Erkel (1810–93) is the father of Hungarian opera, and two of his works – the nationalistic *Bánk Bán,* based on József Katona's play of that name, and *László Hunyadi* – are standards at the Hungarian State Opera House (p77).

Imre Kálmán (1882–1953) was Hungary's most celebrated composer of operettas. *The Gypsy Princess* and *Countess Marica* are two of his most popular works and standard fare at the Budapest Operetta (p150).

Béla Bartók (1881–1945) and Zoltán Kodály (1882–1967) made the first systematic study of Hungarian folk music, travelling together and recording throughout the Magyar linguistic region of today's Romania and Hungary in 1906. Both incorporated some of their findings in their music – Bartók in *Bluebeard's Castle,* for example, and Kodály in the *Peacock Variations.*

Pop music is as popular here as anywhere – indeed, Hungary has one of Europe's biggest pop spectacles, the annual Sziget Festival (p102). It boasts more than 1000 performances over a week and attracted an audience of just under 500,000 people in 2016.

Folk Music

When discussing folk music, it's important to distinguish between 'Gypsy' music and Hungarian folk music. Gypsy music is schmaltzy and based on tunes called *verbunkos* played during the Rákóczi independence wars of the 18th century. At least two fiddles, a bass and a cymbalom (a curious stringed instrument played with padded beaters) are de rigueur. You can hear this music at almost any fancy hotel restaurant in the country or get hold of a recording by Sándor Déki Lakatos and his band.

Hungarian folk musicians play violins, zithers, hurdy-gurdies, bagpipes and lutes on a five-tone diatonic scale. Watch out for Muzsikás, Marta Sebestyén, Ghymes (a Hungarian folk band from Slovakia), and the Hungarian group Vujicsics that mixes elements of South Slav music. Another folk musician with eclectic tastes is the Paris-trained Beáta Pálya, who combines such sounds as traditional Bulgarian and Indian music with Hungarian folk.

Roma – as opposed to Gypsy – music is different altogether, and traditionally sung a cappella. Some modern Roma music groups – Kalyi Jag (Black Fire) from northeastern Hungary and the newer Ando Drom (On the Road) and Romanyi Rota (Gypsy Wheels) – have added guitars, percussion and even electronics to create a whole new sound.

Franz Liszt was born in the Hungarian village of Doborján (now Raiding in Austria) to a Hungarian father and an Austrian mother, but never learned to speak Hungarian fluently.

Dance

Táncház (literally 'dance house') is an excellent way to hear Hungarian folk music and to learn traditional dance, and they're good fun and relatively easy to find, especially in Budapest (eg at the Aranytíz House of Culture (p150) or the Municipal Cultural House (p149)). You'll rarely – if ever – encounter such traditional dances as the *karikázó* (circle dance) and *csárdas* (inns) outside the capital these days.

Hungary has ballet companies in Budapest, Pécs and Szeged (contemporary), but the best by far is based in the western city of Győr.

For a complete and up-to-date listing of the times, dates and places of *táncház* meetings and performances in Budapest and elsewhere in Hungary in English, check out www.tanchaz.hu.

Literature

Sándor Petőfi (1823–49) is Hungary's most celebrated and widely read poet, and a line from his work *National Song* became the rallying cry for the 1848–49 War of Independence. A deeply philosophical play called *The Tragedy of Man* by Imre Madách (1823–64), published a decade after Hungary's defeat in that war, is still considered the country's greatest classical drama.

After Hungary's loss in 1849 many writers looked to Romanticism for inspiration: winners, heroes and knights in shining armour became popular subjects. Petőfi's comrade-in-arms, János Arany (1817–82), wrote epic poetry (including the *Toldi Trilogy*) and ballads. Another friend of Petőfi, the prolific novelist and playwright Mór Jókai (1825–1904), gave expression to heroism and honesty in such accessible works as *The Man with the Golden Touch* and *Black Diamonds*. A perennial favourite, Kálmán Mikszáth (1847–1910), wrote satirical tales such as *The Good Palóc People* and *St Peter's Umbrella*, in which he gently poked fun at the gentry in decline.

Zsigmond Móricz (1879–1942) was a very different type of writer. His works, in the tradition of Émile Zola, examined the harsh reality of peasant life in Hungary in the late 19th century. His contemporary Mihály Babits (1883–1941), poet and editor of the influential literary magazine *Nyugat* (West), made the rejuvenation of Hungarian literature his lifelong work.

Two 20th-century poets are unsurpassed in Hungarian letters. Endre Ady (1877–1919), sometimes described as a successor to Petőfi, was a reformer who ruthlessly attacked Hungarians' growing complacency and materialism, provoking a storm of protest from right-wing nationalists. The work of socialist poet Attila József (1905–37) expressed the alienation felt by individuals in the modern age; his poem *By the Danube* is brilliant even in translation. József ran afoul of both the underground communist movement and the Horthy regime in the 1930s. Tragically, he threw himself under a train near Lake Balaton at the age of 32. The crisp style of Sándor Márai (1900–89) has encouraged worldwide interest in Hungarian literature.

Among Hungary's most important contemporary writers are György Konrád (1933–) and Péter Nádas (1942–); two titans – Imre Kertész (1929–2016) and Péter Esterházy (1950–2016) – died within months of one another in 2016. Konrád's *A Feast in the Garden* (1985) is an almost autobiographical account of a Jewish community in a small eastern Hungarian town. *A Book of Memoirs* (1986) by Nádas traces the decline of communism in a style reminiscent of Thomas Mann. In the *End of a Family Story* (1977), Nádas uses a child narrator as a filter for the adult

In Anthony Minghella's film *The English Patient* (1996), when László Almásy (Ralph Fiennes) plays a Hungarian folk song on the phonograph for Katharine Clifton (Kristin Scott Thomas), the voice you hear is that of Marta Sebestyén singing 'Szerelem, Szerelem' (Love, Love).

experience of 1950s communist Hungary. Esterházy's partly autobiographical *Celestial Harmonies* (2000) painted a favourable portrait of the protagonist's father. His later *Revised Edition* (2002) was based on documents revealing that his father had been a government informer during the communist regime.

Novelist and Auschwitz survivor Kertész won the Nobel Prize for Literature in 2002, the first time a Hungarian had gained that distinction. Among his novels available in English are *Fatelessness* (1975), *Fiasco* (1988), *Kaddish for an Unborn Child* (1990), *Liquidation* (2003) and *Dossier K* (2006). Works by Hungary's foremost female contemporary writer, the late Magda Szabó (1917–2007), include *Katalin Street* (1969), *Abigail* (1970) and *The Door* (1975), a compelling story of a woman writer and the symbiotic relationship she has with her peasant housekeeper.

Making a big splash in literary circles both at home and abroad these days is the novelist and screenwriter László Krasznahorkai, who writes demanding postmodernist novels (*Satantango*, 1985; *The Melancholy of Resistance*, 1988; *War and War*, 1999; *Seiobo There Below*, 2008). In 2015 he was awarded the Man Booker International Prize, the first Hungarian author to receive that distinction.

Hungarian Literature Online (www.hlo.hu) leaves no page unturned in the world of Hungarian books, addressing everyone from writers and editors to translators and publishers, with a useful list of links as well.

THE ARTS CINEMA

Cinema

For classic Hungarian films look out for works by Oscar-winning István Szabó *(Sweet Emma, Dear Böbe, The Taste of Sunshine)*, Miklós Jancsó *(Outlaws)* and Péter Bacsó *(The Witness, Live Show)*. Other favourites are *Simon Mágus,* the surrealistic tale of two magicians and a young woman in Paris, from Ildikó Enyedi, and her *Tender Interface,* about the brain drain from Hungary after WWII.

Péter Timár's *Dollybirds* is a satirical look at life – and film production quality – during communism. *Zimmer Feri*, set on Lake Balaton, pits a young practical-joker against a bunch of loud German tourists; the typo in the title is deliberate. Timár's *6:3* takes viewers back to that glorious moment when Hungary defeated England in football. Gábor Herendi's *A Kind of America* is the comic tale of a film-making team trying to profit from an expatriate Hungarian who pretends to be a rich producer.

Of more recent vintage is Hungarian-American director Nimród Antal's *Kontroll*, a high-speed romantic thriller set almost entirely in the Budapest metro in which assorted outcasts, lovers and dreamers commune. Kornél Mundruczó's award-winning *Delta* is the brooding tale of a man's return to his home in Romania's Danube Delta and his complex relationship with his half-sister.

Films that that use pivotal events in Hungarian history as backdrops are *Children of Glory* by Krisztina Goda, which recounts the 1956 Uprising through the eyes of a player on the Olympic water-polo team; Ferenc Török's *Moszkva tér,* the comic tale of high-school boys in 1989 oblivious to the important events taking place around them; and *And Son of Saul*, a poignant debut film by László Nemes in which a prisoner at Auschwitz tries to give a dead child he takes to be his son a proper burial. It won the Oscar for Best Foreign Language Film in 2016.

The 26th American president, Theodore Roosevelt, enjoyed the novel *St Peter's Umbrella* by Kálmán Mikszáth so much that he insisted on visiting the ageing novelist during a European tour in 1910.

Art Nouveau Architecture

Art nouveau architecture (and its Viennese variant, Secessionism) is Budapest's signature style, and examples can be seen throughout the city. Its sinuous curves, flowing, asymmetrical forms, colourful tiles and other decorative elements stand out like beacons in a sea of refined and elegant baroque and mannered, geometric neoclassical buildings. It will have you gasping in delight.

The Beginning & the End

Above Elephant House, Budapest Zoo (p94)

Art nouveau was an art form and architectural style that flourished in Europe and the USA from 1890 to around 1910. It began in Britain as the Arts and Crafts Movement founded by William Morris (1834–96), which stressed the importance of manual processes and attempted to create a new organic style in direct opposition to the imitative banalities spawned by the Industrial Revolution.

The style soon spread to Europe, where it took on distinctly local and/or national characteristics. In Vienna a group of artists called the Secessionists lent its name to the more geometric local style of art nouveau architecture: Sezessionstil (Hungarian: Szecesszió). In Budapest, the use of traditional facades with allegorical and historical figures and scenes, folk motifs and Zsolnay ceramics and other local materials led to an eclectic style. Though working within an art nouveau/Secessionist framework, this style emerged as something that was uniquely Hungarian.

But fashion and styles changed as whimsically and rapidly at the start of the 20th century as they do today, and by the end of the first decade art nouveau and its variants were considered limited, passé, even tacky. Fortunately for the good citizens of Budapest and us, the economic and political torpor of the interwar period and the 40-year 'big sleep' after WWII left many art nouveau/Secessionist buildings beaten but standing – a lot more, in fact, than remain in such important art nouveau centres as Paris, Brussels, Nancy and Vienna.

Apart from Sezessionstil in Austria and Szecesszió in Hungary, art nouveau (from the French 'new art') is known as Jugendstil in Germany, Modern in Russia, Modernisme in Catalonia and Stile Liberty in Italy.

Budapest Makes Its Mark

The first Hungarian architect to look to art nouveau for inspiration was Frigyes Spiegel, who covered traditional facades with exotic and allegorical figures and scenes. At the northern end of VI Izabella utca at No 94 is the restored **Lindenbaum apartment block** (Map p86; VI Izabella utca 94; ⊡trolleybus 72, 73), the first in the city to use art nouveau ornamentation, including suns, stars, peacocks, flowers, snakes, foxes and long-tressed nudes.

IN PURSUIT OF THE FINEST

One of the joys of exploring the so-called 'Queen of the Danube' is that you'll find elements of art nouveau and Secessionism in the oddest places. A street with a unified image is a rarity in Budapest; keep your eyes open and you'll spot bits and pieces everywhere and at all times. The following are our favourite 'hidden gems':

Bedő House (p82) Emil Vidor, 1903

Berzenczey utca Apartment Block (Map p92; IX Berzenczey utca 18; ⓂM3 Klinikák, ⊡4, 6) Ödön Lechner, 1882

City Park Calvinist Church (Map p86; VII Városligeti fasor 7; ⓂM1 Kodály körönd) Aladár Arkay, 1913

Dob utca Primary School (Map p86; VII Dob utca 85; ⊡4, 6) Ármin Hegedűs, 1906

Egger Villa (Map p96; VII Városligeti fasor 24; ⓂM1 Bajza utca) Emil Vidor, 1902

Elephant House, Budapest Zoo (p94) Kornél Neuschloss-Knüsli, 1912

Institute of Geology (p278) Ödön Lechner, 1899

Léderer Mansion (Map p86; VI Bajza utca 42; ⓂM1 Bajza utca) Zoltán Bálint & Lajos Jámbor, 1902

National Institute for the Blind (Map p96; XIV Ajtósi Dürer sor 39; ⓂM1 Bajza utca) Sándor Baumgarten, 1904

Philanthia (p56) Kálmán Albert Körössy, 1906

Sonnenberg Mansion (Map p86; VI Munkácsy Mihály utca 23; ⓂM1 Bajza utca) Albert Körössy, 1904

Thonet House (p56) Ödön Lechner, 1890

Török Bank House (Map p74; V Szervita tér 3; ⓂM1/2/3 Deák Ferenc tér) Henrik Böhm & Ármin Hegedűs, 1906

Vidor Villa (Map p96; VII Városligeti fasor 33; ⓂM1 Bajza utca) Emil Vidor, 1905

ÖDÖN LECHNER. ARCHITECT EXTRAORDINAIRE

Ödön Lechner (1845–1914) has been nicknamed 'the Hungarian Gaudí' because, like the Catalan master, he took an existing style and put his own spin on it, creating something new and unique for his time and place. Hungary has submitted five of his masterpieces, including the **Museum of Applied Arts** (p89), the **Royal Postal Savings Bank** (p77) and the **Institute of Geology** (Map p96; XIV Stefánia út 14; ⊠1), for inclusion in Unesco's World Heritage list.

Lechner studied architecture at Budapest's József Trade School, the precursor to the University of Technology and Economics (BME) in Buda, and later at the Schinkel Academy of Architecture in Berlin. At the start of his career, Lechner worked in the prevailing styles, and there were few indications that he would leave such an indelible mark on his city and his era. The firm he formed in 1869 received a steady flow of commissions in Pest during the boom years of the 1870s but, like everyone else, he worked in the popular and all-too-common historicist and neoclassical styles.

Lechner spent the years 1875 to 1878 in France working under the architect Clément Parent on the renovation and redesign of chateaux. At this time he was also influenced by the emerging style of art nouveau.

After his return to Budapest Lechner began to move away from historicism to more modern ideas and trends. A turning point in his career was his commission for **Thonet House** (p56) on Váci utca, his innovative steel structure that he covered with glazed ceramics from the Zsolnay factory in Pécs. More ambitious commissions followed, including the Museum of Applied Arts and the Institute of Geology. But not all was right in the world of Hungarian art nouveau. Lechner's Royal Postal Savings Bank building, now often seen as the architect's *tour de force,* was not well received when it was completed in 1901 and Lechner never really worked independently on a commission of that magnitude again.

The master of the style, however, was Ödön Lechner: his most ambitious work in Budapest is the Museum of Applied Arts (p89). Purpose built as a gallery and completed in time for the millenary exhibition in 1896, the museum was faced and roofed in a variety of colourful Zsolnay ceramic tiles, and its turrets, domes and ornamental figures lend it an Eastern or Mogul feel. His crowning glory (though not seen as such at the time), however, is the sumptuous Royal Postal Savings Bank (p77), a Secessionist extravaganza of floral mosaics, folk motifs and ceramic figures just off Szabadság tér in Lipótváros and dating from 1901.

The Liszt Music Academy (p150), completed in 1907, is interesting not so much for its exterior as for its interior decorative elements. There's a dazzling art nouveau mosaic called *Art Is the Source of Life* by Aladár Kőrösfői Kriesch, a leader of the seminal Gödöllő Artist Colony, on the 1st-floor landing, and some fine stained glass by master craftsman Miksa Róth, whose home and workshop in central Pest is now a museum (Miksa Róth Memorial House; p95). In the music academy take a look at the grid of laurel leaves below the ceiling of the main concert hall, which mimics the ironwork dome of the Secession Building (1897–1908) in Vienna, and the large reflecting sapphire-blue Zsolnay ball finials on the stair balusters.

The Danubius Hotel Gellért (p105), designed by Ármin Hegedűs, Artúr Sebestyén and Izidor Sterk in 1909 but not completed until 1918, contains examples of late art nouveau, notably the thermal spa with its enormous arched glass entrance hall and Zsolnay ceramic fountains in the bathing pools. The architects were clearly influenced by Lechner but added other elements, including baroque ones.

Very noteworthy indeed is the arcade near V Ferenciek tere called Párisi Udvar (p56), built in 1909 by Henrik Schmahl. The design contains myriad influences – from Moorish Islamic and Venetian Gothic architecture to elements of Lechner's own eclectic style. At the time of research it was being turned into a luxury hotel.

The Art Nouveau European Route website (www.artnouveau.eu) is among the most comprehensive on the art nouveau heritage of Europe.

The Wines of Hungary

Wine has been made in Hungary since at least the time of the Romans. It is very much a part of Hungarian culture, but only in recent years has it moved on from the local tipple you drank at Sunday lunch or the overwrought and overpriced thimble of rarefied red sipped in a Budapest wine bar to the all-singin', all-dancin', all embracin' obsession that it is today.

Choosing Wine

Wine is sold by the glass or bottle everywhere – at food stalls, wine bars, restaurants, supermarkets and 24-hour grocery stores – and usually at reasonable prices. Old-fashioned wine bars ladle out plonk by the *deci* (decilitre, or 0.1L), but if you're into more serious wine, you should visit one of Budapest's excellent wine bars, such as DiVino Borbár (p141), Doblo (p143), Kadarka (p145) or Palack Borbár (p138). Good wine restaurants include Klassz (p133), Borkonyha (p125) and Fióka (p119). Among speciality

Above Winery in Badacsony (p283)

Hungary's Wine Regions

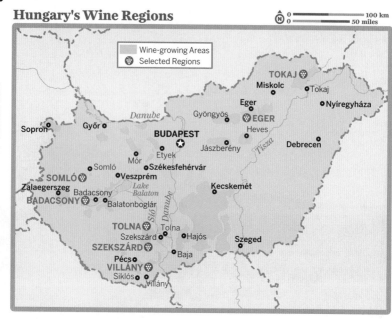

wine shops are those in the Bortársaság (p152) chain and the Malatinszky Wine Store (p155).

When choosing a Hungarian wine, look for the words *minőségi bor* (quality wine) or *különleges minőségi bor* (premium quality wine), Hungary's version of the French quality regulation *appellation d'origine contrôlée*. On a wine label the first word indicates the region, the second the grape variety (eg Villányi *kékfrankos*) or the type or brand of wine (eg Tokaji Aszú, Szekszárdi Bikavér). Other important words that you'll see include *édes* (sweet), *fehér* (white), *féledes* (semisweet), *félszáraz* (semi-dry or medium), *pezsgő* (sparkling), *száraz* (dry) and *vörös* (red).

Very roughly, anything costing more than 2000Ft in the shops is a serious bottle of Hungarian wine. Pay more than 3000Ft and you'll be getting something very fine indeed.

A good website for Hungarian wines is www.bortarsasag.hu. It appraises vintners and their vintages and lists prices from the Bortársaság (Budapest Wine Society), Hungary's foremost wine club and retail wine chain. Other good sites include www.winesofa.eu, https://budapestwinesnob.wordpress.com and http://tokajwineregion.com.

Wine Regions

Hungary is divided into seven major wine-growing regions. In the west are Észak Dunántúl (Northern Transdanubia), Balaton, Sopron and Dél-Pannonia (Southern Transdanubia). In the east are Felső-Magyarország, Tokaj and Duna ('Danube'), encompassing parts of the Great Plain. Subdivisions range in size from tiny Somló in Transdanubia in the west, to the vast vineyards of the Kunság on the southern Great Plain, with its sandy soil nurturing more than a third of the vines grown in the country.

It's all a matter of taste but the most distinctive and exciting Hungarian red wines come from Eger in the Northern Uplands; the cooler climate and limestone bedrock make elegant, complex reds more akin to Burgundy than Bordeaux. In Southern Transdanubia the reds from Villány are more rustic, not unlike some Italian reds, while those from Szekszárd, are softer and subtler. The best dry whites are produced around Lake Balaton's northern shore and in Somló, though the latest craze is for bone-dry, slightly tart *furmint* from Tokaj, which also produces the world-renowned sweet wine. If you're looking for sparkling wine *(pezsgő)* go for Hungaria Extra Dry. Other excellent sparkling wines are Kreinbacher from Somló and Szent Tamás Furmint Pezsgő from Tokaj.

Tokaj

The volcanic soil, sunny climate and protective mountain barrier of the Tokaj-Hegyalja (Tokaj Uplands) region in northern Hungary make it ideal for growing grapes and making wine. Tokaj wines were exported to Poland and Russia in the Middle Ages and reached the peak of their popularity in Europe in the 17th and 18th centuries.

Tokaj dessert wines are rated per the number – now from four to six – of *puttony (butts,* or baskets for picking) of sweet Aszú grapes added to the base wines. These are grapes infected with 'noble rot', the *Botrytis cinera* mould that almost turns them into raisins on the vine.

For Tokaji Aszú, one name to look out for is István Szepsy; he concentrates on both the upscale six-*puttony* type and the Esszencia – so sweet and low in alcohol it's hardly even wine. His Szepsy Cuvée, aged in stainless-steel barrels for a year or two (against the usual five for Tokaji Aszú), is a complex, elegant blend comparable to Sauternes. That said, Zoltán Demeter's version is almost pushing Szepsy aside in terms of quality. Other names to watch out for are Hétszőlő, Gróf Degenfeld, Erzsébet Pince, Disznókő and Pendits.

Tokaj also produces less-sweet wines, including dry Szamorodni (an excellent aperitif) and sweet Szamorodni, which is not unlike an Italian *vin santo;* for the latter try Disznókő's version). Of the five grape varieties grown here, *furmint* and *hárslevelű* (Linden Leaf) are the driest. Some Hungarian wine experts believe Tokaj's future is in dry white wine, with sweet wines just the icing on the cake. They say that dry *furmint*, with a flavour recalling apples, has the potential to become the best white wine in the country. Try it from any of the following vineyards: Oremus, Tinon, Szent Tamás and Béres.

Vintage has always played a more important role in Tokaj than elsewhere in Hungary. Though it is said that there is only one truly excellent year each decade, the wines produced in 1972, 1988, 1999, 2000, 2003, 2006, 2009 and 2013 were all superb.

Eger

Flanked by two of the Northern Uplands' most beautiful ranges of hills and on the same latitude as Burgundy in France, Eger is the home of the celebrated Egri Bikavér (Eger Bull's Blood). By law, Hungarian vintners must spell out the blend of wine on their label; the sole exception is Bikavér, though it is usually a blend of *kékfrankos* (Blaufränkisch) mixed with other

A MATCH MADE IN HEAVEN

The pairing of food with wine is as great an obsession in Hungary as it is in France. Everyone agrees that sweets like strudel go very well indeed with a glass of Tokaji Aszú, but what is less appreciated is the wonderful synergy that this wine enjoys with savoury foods like foie gras and such cheeses such Roquefort, Stilton and gorgonzola. A bone-dry *olaszrizling* from Badacsony is a superb accompaniment to any fish dish, but especially the *fogas* (pike-perch) indigenous to Lake Balaton, while dry Tokaj *furmint* goes well with river fish like *harcsa* (catfish). Villány *sauvignon blanc* is excellent with creamy and salty goat's cheese.

It would be a shame to 'waste' a big wine like a Vili Papa Cuvée from Eger on Hungarian staple dishes like *pörkölt;* instead try a *kékfrankos* or Szekszárd *kadarka.* Cream-based dishes stand up well to late-harvest *furmint* and pork dishes are nice with new *furmint* or any type of red, especially *kékfrankos.* Try *hárslevelű* with poultry.

reds, sometimes *kadarka*. Bikavér producers to watch out for are Tibor Gál, Nimród Kovács and István Toth; the last's Bikavér easily compares with any of the 'big' reds from Villány and is said to have set the standard for Bull's Blood in Hungary. Look out for *kékfrankos* and *merlot* from János Bolyki.

Two excellent tomes on Hungarian wines are Robert Smyth's *Hungarian Wine: A Tasting Trip to the New Old World* and Miles Lambert-Gócs' *Tokaj Wine: Fame, Fate, Tradition*. Others include the rather, er, sober *The Wines of Hungary* (Alex Liddell) and the flashier, colourful *Hungary: Its Fine Wines & Winemakers* (David Copp).

Eger's signature grape is *pinot noir;* try the versions from Tibor Gál and Vilmos Thummerer, whose vintages have been on par with the *premiers crus* from Burgundy. The latter's Vili Papa Cuvée, a blend of *cabernet franc, cabernet sauvignon* and *merlot,* is a monumental wine aged in new wood, with fleshy fruit flavours.

You'll also find several decent whites in Eger, including *leányka* (Little Girl), *olaszrizling* (Italian *riesling*) and *hárslevelű* from Debrő. Recently vintners have introduced a white blend called Egri Csillag (Star of Eger) to develop a brand along the same lines as red Egri Bikavér. It's light- to medium-bodied, fresh and easy drinking but complex. Try it from Thummerer, Böjt or Szent Andrea.

Villány

Villány, in Hungary's warm south and on the same latitude as Bordeaux in France, is especially noted for red wines: Blauer Portugieser (once known as Kékoportó here), *cabernet sauvignon, cabernet franc* and *merlot*. The region has also been experimenting in *pinot noir* in recent years. Red wines here are almost always big-bodied, Bordeaux-style and high in tannins.

Among the best vintners in Villány is József Bock, whose Royal Cuvée is a special blend of *cabernet franc, pinot noir* and *merlot*. Other ones to watch out for are Heumann (Evelyne and Erhard), Bence Bodor, Márton Mayer and Alajos Wunderlich. Wines to try from this region include Attila Gere's elegant and complex *cabernet sauvignon* or his Solus *merlot* as well as Ede and Zsolt Tiffán's elegant and complex Blauer Portugieser and *cabernet franc*.

WHAT'S NEW
....
Hungary has for some time now been moving away from technology-driven wine production to *terroir*-based cultivation and vineyard-specific bottling. Let's face it – anyone with
the money and know-how can produce a decent *cabernet* or *chardonnay*. What people
are looking for now is wine that speaks of the region and the soil – the *terroir*. There's
even talk of introducing village denomination. Until recently these phenomena occurred
only in Tokaj and Villány; they're now becoming the norm in places like Badacsony on the
northern shore of Lake Balaton. Most vintners now produce their own premium *cuvée*
(blend) – often named after themselves, such as Gere's eponymous Attila. And some
winemakers have adopted biodynamic cultivation methods, such as Pendits in Tokaj.

Szekszárd

Mild winters and warm, dry summers combined with favourable loess
soil help Szekszárd in Southern Transdanubia to produce some of the
best affordable red wines in Hungary, and they are becoming increasingly popular throughout the land. They are not like the big-bodied reds of
Villány, but softer and less complex, with a distinct spiciness, and easy to
drink. In general, they are much better value too.

The premier grape here is *kadarka*, a late-ripening variety produced
in limited quantities. The best *kadarka* is made by Ferenc Takler and Pál
Mészáros. *Kadarka* originated in the Balkans – the Bulgarian *gamza* grape
is a variety of it – and is a traditional ingredient here in making Bikavér, a
wine usually associated with Eger. In fact, many wine aficionados in Hungary prefer the Szekszárd's 'Bull's Blood'; try Zoltán Heimann's version.

Ferenc Vesztergombi produces some excellent Szekszárd *merlot* and
kékfrankos; try La Vida *merlot* as well. *Syrah* from Takler is making
quite a splash in Szekszárd. Tamás Dúzsi is one of the finest producers of
rosé; sample his *kékfrankos* rosé.

Badacsony

Badacsony is named after the 400m-high basalt massif that rises like a
bread loaf from the Tapolca Basin along the northwestern shore of Lake
Balaton. Wine has been produced here for centuries and the region's signature *olaszrizling*, especially produced by Huba Szeremley and Ambrus
Bakó, is among the best dry white wine for everyday drinking available
in Hungary. It's a straw-blond *welschriesling* high in acid that is related
to the famous Rhine vintages in name only. Drink it young – in fact, the
younger, the better. The most reliable *chardonnay* is from Ottó Légli on
Balaton's southern shore.

The area's volcanic soil gives the unique, once-threatened *kéknyelű*
(Blue Stalk) wine its distinctive mineral taste; it is a complex tipple of very
low yield that ages well; Szeremley's version and one produced by Endre
Szászi are reliable. Jásdi is another big-name producer of quality Badacsony white wines (such as Nagykúti *chardonnay* and Csopaki *rizling*).

> Louis XIV
> famously called
> Tokaj 'the wine
> of kings and the
> king of wines',
> while Voltaire
> wrote that 'this
> wine could be
> only given by the
> boundlessly good
> God'!

Somló

Somló is a single volcanic dome and the soil (basalt talus and volcanic
tuff) helps to produce wine that is mineral-tasting, almost flinty. The
region boasts two indigenous grape varieties: *hárslevelű* and *juhfark*
(Sheep's Tail). Firm acids give 'spine' to this wine, and it reaches its peak
in five years. Excellent producers of Somlói *juhfark* are Kreinbacher and
Károly Kolonics. Imre Györgykovács' *olaszrizling* is a big wine with a
taste vaguely reminiscent of burnt almonds. His *hárslevelű* is a golden
wine, with a tart, mineral finish.

The Hungarian People

Most of Hungary's 10 million people are Magyars, an Asiatic people of obscure origins who do not speak an Indo-European language and who found their way to the Carpathian Basin in the late 9th century. The only cousins Hungarians have are the far-flung Finns and the Estonians. Much of Hungarian culture and nationalism has been formed by an almost paranoid fear of being swallowed by neighbouring countries.

A Polite Formality

Hungarians are not uninhibited people like the extroverted Romanians or the sentimental Slavs. Forget about the impassioned, devil-may-care, Gypsy-fiddling stereotype – it's just that. Hungarians are a reserved and somewhat formal people. They are almost always extremely polite in social interactions, and the language can be very courtly. But while all this civility certainly oils the wheels that turn a sometimes difficult society, it can be used to keep 'outsiders' (both foreigners and other Hungarians) at a distance.

When the Italian-American Nobel Prize–winning physicist Enrico Fermi (1901–54) was asked whether extraterrestrial beings existed, he replied: 'Of course they do…[and] they are already here among us. They are called Hungarians.' He had worked with Hungarian scientists on the so-called Manhattan Project, which led to the development of the atomic bomb.

Penchant for the Blues

Himnusz, Hungary's national anthem, describes Hungarians as a people 'long torn by ill fate', and the overall mood here is one of *honfibú*, literally 'patriotic sorrow' but with a penchant for the blues with just enough hope to keep most people going. This mood certainly predates communism. In the early 1930s a song called *Szomorú Vasárnap* (Gloomy Sunday) reportedly so depressed many ordinary Budapesters that whenever it was played, they would rush to jump off a nearby bridge. Also called 'the Suicide Song', it has been covered in English by many artists, including Billie Holiday, Sinéad O'Connor, Marianne Faithfull and Björk. It *is* a real downer.

Scientific Minds

Hungary is a highly cultured and educated society, with a literacy rate of more than 99% among those 15 years of age and older. The nation's contributions to specialised education and the sciences have been far greater than its present size and population would indicate. A unique method of music education devised by the composer Zoltán Kodály (1882–1967) is widespread and Budapest's Pető Institute, founded by András Pető (1893–1967) in 1945, has a very high success rate in teaching children with cerebral palsy to walk. Albert Szent-Györgyi (1893–1986) won the Nobel Prize in 1937 for his discovery of vitamin C. Georg von Békésy won the Nobel Prize in 1961 for his research on the inner ear and Eugene Paul Wigner received it two years later for his research in nuclear physics. Both Edward Teller and Leo Szilard worked on the so-called Manhattan Project, which led to the development of the atomic bomb.

Lifestyle

If Kovács János and his wife, Kovácsné Szabó Erzsébet, invite you home for a meal, be flattered. By and large, Hungarians meet their friends outside the home at cafes and restaurants. If you do go along, bring a bouquet of flowers or a bottle of good wine.

You can talk about anything under the sun in the Kovács *háztartási* (Kovács household) – from religion and politics to whether their language is more difficult than Japanese and Arabic – but money is a touchy subject. Traditionally, the discussion of wealth – or even wearing flashy bling and clothing – was considered gauche. Though it's almost impossible to calculate (with the 'black economy' being so widespread and significant), the average monthly salary at the time of research was about €900 – but after taxes and social security deductions, only half of that went home.

For a list of people who you may or may not have known were Magyar get hold of *Eminent Hungarians* by Ray Keenoy.

Like more than two-thirds of all Hungarians, the Kovács live in a town but retain a connection with the countryside, having access to a hut in a wine-growing region. Friends have a more coveted *nyaralóház* (summer cottage) by the lake. During *szüret* (grape harvest), they head for the hills and probably attend a *disznótor*, which involves the slaughtering of a pig followed by a party.

There's not much gay or lesbian life in the countryside unless you take it with you; both communities keep a low profile outside Budapest. Since 2009 Hungary has allowed registered partnerships *(bejegyzett élettársi kapcsolat)*, which offer almost all the benefits of marriage, except adoption, to same-sex couples. However, same-sex marriage is prohibited by the Hungarian constitution, which was rewritten in 2011 under Prime Minister Viktor Orbán.

Life expectancy in Hungary is very low by European standards: just over 72 years for men and 79 for women. Kovács Jánosné can expect to outlive Kovács János by almost seven years (but that might have something to do with the amount of alcohol János puts away).

Drinking is an important part of social life in a country that has produced wine and fruit brandies at least the time of the Romans. Consumption is high at an annual 13.3L of alcohol per person, putting it within the top half-dozen heaviest-drinking countries in the world. Alcoholism here may not be as visible to the outsider as it is in, say, Russia, but it's here nonetheless; official figures suggest that as much as 20% of the population abuse alcohol in some form. And it must be said that even social drinking is not always a happy affair and can often end (willingly) in tears. Indeed, Hungarians have an expression for this bizarre arrangement: *sírva vigadni*, or 'to take one's pleasure sadly'.

Multiculturalism

In the 2011 census, just under 84% of those counted identified themselves as Hungarians (Magyars), followed by Roma (3.1%), Germans (1.3%), Slovaks (0.3%), Romanians (0.3%) and Croats (0.2%). The rest did not declare their ethnicity. The number of Roma is officially put at around 310,000 people, but some believe the figure is twice as high, and members of the Roma community itself put the number at closer to 800,000.

For the most part, ethnic minorities in Hungary aren't discriminated against and their rights are inscribed in the constitution. Yet this has

WHERE THE FIRST COME LAST

In a practice unknown outside Asia, Hungarians reverse their names in all usages, and their 'last name' (surname) always comes first. For example, John Smith is never János Kovács but Kovács János, while Elizabeth Taylor is Szabó Erzsébet.

Most titles also follow the structure: Mr John Smith is Kovács János úr. Many women follow the practice of taking their husband's full name. If Elizabeth was married to John, she might be Kovács Jánosné (Mrs John Smith) or, increasingly popular among professional women, Kovácsné Szabó Erzsébet.

not stopped the occasional attack on nonwhite foreigners, a rise in anti-Semitism and the widespread discrimination against Roma.

In the summer of 2015, at the height of the European refugee crisis, Hungary was the first country in Eastern Europe to build a barrier along its borders to stop the flow of what it called migrants. In an October 2016 government referendum, 98% of those voting rejected an EU initiative to relocate about 1300 refugees to Hungary. On the surface that may appear to suggest that Hungarians – at least those who vote – are anti-foreigner. But voter turnout was very low (just 40%), which made the referendum invalid, and many people who did vote spoiled their ballots. And in the period preceding the construction of the fence, thousands of volunteers assisted refugees both along the highways to Austria and at the Keleti train station (the main point of assembly in Budapest) with food, water and bedding.

The Roma

The origins of the Gypsies (Hungarian: *cigány*), who call themselves the Roma (singular Rom) and speak Romani, a language closely related to several spoken in northern India, remain a mystery. It is generally accepted, however, that they began migrating to Persia from India sometime in the 10th century and had reached the Balkans by the 14th century. They have been in Hungary for at least 500 years, and they officially number around 310,000, although that figure could be higher.

Though traditionally a travelling people, in modern times the Roma settled down in Hungary and worked as smiths and tinkers, livestock and horse traders, and as musicians. As a group, however, they are chronically underemployed and have been the hardest hit by economic recession (statistically, Roma families are twice the size of *gadje*, or 'non-Roma' ones).

Unsettled people are often persecuted in one form or another by those who stay put, and Hungarian Roma are no exception. They are widely despised and remain the scapegoats for everything that goes wrong in certain parts of the country, from the rise in petty theft and prostitution to the loss of jobs. Though their rights are inscribed in the constitution, along with those of other ethnic minorities, their housing ranks among the worst in the nation, police are regularly accused of harassing them and, more than any other group, they fear the revival of extreme nationalism as promulgated by the right-wing Jobbik party, which has 24 seats in parliament.

You will probably be shocked at what even educated, cosmopolitan Hungarians say about the Roma and their way of life. Learn the truth from Budapest-based Romedia Foundation (http://romediafoundation. org), whose remit is to use media as a tool to bring about social change.

Religion

Hungarians tend to have a much more pragmatic approach to religion than most of their neighbours; it has even been suggested that this generally sceptical view of matters of faith has led to Hungary's high rate of success in science and mathematics. Except in villages and on the most important holy days (Easter, the Assumption of Mary and Christmas), churches are never full. The Jewish community in Budapest on the other hand, has seen a great revitalisation in recent years, mostly due to an influx of Chasidic Jews from the USA and Israel.

Of those Hungarians declaring religious affiliation in the most recent census, about 53% said they were Christians, with Roman Catholics making up the bulk at 37%, followed by Reformed (Calvinist) Protestant at 11% and Evangelical (Lutheran) Protestant at 2.2%. There are also small Greek Catholic and Orthodox (2.7%) and other Christian (1%) congregations. Hungary's Jews (not all practising) number around 100,000, down from a pre-WWII population of about 750,000.

Culture Shock! Hungary: A Guide to Customs & Etiquette by Zsuzsanna Ardó goes beyond the usual anecdotal information and observations offered in this kind of book and is virtually an anthropological and sociological study of the Magyar race.

Outdoor Activities

Hungary has a lot to offer fresh-air fiends, from excellent hiking, canoeing, kayaking, horseback riding, hiking and fishing, to more contemplative pursuits. The country's many varied ecosystems make it a good birding destination, while spas and thermal springs are great for postactivity unwinding.

Horse Riding

There's a Hungarian saying that the Magyars were 'created by God to sit on horseback' – just look at any statue of Árpád. Most stables that we recommend offer follow-the-leader treks up to scenic spots, but the emphasis is usually on lessons. English riding and saddles are the preferred style. Book ahead.

The nonprofit **Hungarian Equestrian Tourism Association** (Magyar Lovas Turisztikai Szövetség, MLTSZ; Map p92; ☑06 20 578 7600; www.mltsz. hu; I Aranyhal utca 4, Budapest; Ⓜ M3/4 Kálvin tér) classifies stables countrywide and has full information on riding facilities and tours. See too the Hungarian National Tourist Office website and its helpful *Hungary on Horseback* brochure.

Look for good schools around the Lake Balaton region, including the Kál Basin, Tihany and Siófork. Riding a white Lipizzaner horse through the wooded hills of Szilvásvárad is the stuff of dreams.

> Nonius horses, bred at Máta near Hortobágy, have been raised in Hungary since 1671.

Birdwatching

Some 398 of Europe's 530-odd bird species have been sighted in Hungary, and spring and autumn are always great for birdwatching (May and October, especially). Huge white storks nesting atop chimneys in eastern Hungary are a striking sight from May through October.

There are dozens of excellent birding sites in Hungary, but the grassy, saline steppe, large fish ponds and marshes of the Hortobágy (p223) and Kiskunság (p231) National Parks are some of the best. Look for birds of prey, egrets, herons, storks, bee-eaters and rollers. In October up to 100,000 common cranes and geese stop on the plains as they migrate south.

The wooded hills of Bükk National Park near Eger hold woodpeckers and other woodland birds year-round; April to June sees the most activity in the reed beds of the shallow, saline Lake Fertő, while autumn brings white-fronted and bean geese. Freshwater lakes Tisza and Öreg-tó are prime sites for wading birds and waterfowl.

For a guided outing, go to the expert: Gerard Gorman, author of *The Birds of Hungary* and *Birding in Eastern Europe*. He owns and operates **Probirder** (www.probirder.com), an informational website and guide service out of Budapest. Fixed tours take in the woodland birds of the Bükk Hills and sites on the Great Plain and typically last a week. **Hungarian Bird Tours** (☑+44 7774 574 204; www.hungarianbirdtours.com) operates similar woodland and plains tours from a base near Eger. For both companies, three-night tours cost €380 to €470 and seven-night tours are €870 to €1050.

> Find out about the conservation of the rare imperial eagle (*Aquila heliaca*), a globally threatened Eurasian bird species, with a world population of only a few thousand breeding pairs, at www.imperial eagle.hu.

Cycling

Hungary counts some 2200km of cycle tracks, with thousands more kilometres of relatively quiet country roads. Three **EuroVelo** (www.euro velo.org) routes sponsored by the **European Cycling Federation** (www. ecf.com) cross Hungary, including the new so-called Iron Curtain Trail (Route 13). Many cities, including Budapest, Szeged, Kecskemét and Esztergom, have dedicated bike lanes. The Danube Bend is among the best areas to explore on two wheels. In the Lake Balaton region a 200km track circles the entire lake.

Bicycles are banned from motorways as well as national highways 0 to 9. On certain train lines, bicycles can be transported in special carriages for 235Ft per 50km travelled.

Local tourist offices are good sources of information about suggested routes, and some routes are posted on the Hungarian National Tourist Office website. Frigoria publishes the very useful guide *Hungary Cycling Atlas*, which outlines 100 tours, with places of interest and service centres listed in several languages. **Happy Bike** (www.happybike.hu) organises ambitious week-long cycle tours of Lake Balaton and the Danube Bend. **Velo-Touring** (www. velo-touring.hu) has a great selection of multinight trips in all regions, from a seniors-friendly Southern Transdanubia wine tour (€1559) lasting nine days to an eight-day spa-and-wine tour in the Tokaj region (€659). **Eco-tours** (www.ecotours.hu) has cycle trips with camping through Transdanubia (six days, €580), the Zemplén Hills (five days, €480) and around Balaton (three days, €250).

The Danube Cycleway, by John Higginson, maps the 2875km-long riverfront route along the Danube from Donaueschingen near Basel in Germany through Slovakia and Hungary and to the river's mouth in the Black Sea.

Canoeing & Kayaking

Many of Hungary's more than 4000km of waterways are navigable by *kajak* (kayak) or *kenu* (canoe) from April to September. The most famous long-haul routes course from Rajka to Mohács (386km) on the Danube and from Tiszabecs to Szeged (570km) on the Tisza River. Rentals are available at tourist centres in places such as Tiszafüred and Tokaj.

Ecotours (p288) leads week-long Danube River canoe and camping trips for about €600 (tent rental and food extra), as well as shorter Danube Bend and Tisza River trips. Tokaj-based Kékcápák (p252) organises four-day trips on the smaller rivers in north and eastern Hungary.

Hiking

The forests of the Bükk Hills near Eger are the best in Hungary for serious trekkers; much of the national park there is off-limits to cars. The Mátra and Zemplén Hills, to the east and west respectively, also offer hiking possibilities. There are good short hikes in the forests around Visegrád, Esztergom and Budapest, too.

Cartographia (www.cartographia.hu) publishes two-dozen hiking maps of the hills, plains and forests of Hungary. On all hiking maps, paths appear as a red line and with a letter indicating the colour-coding of the trail. Colours are painted on trees or the letter of the colour in Hungarian appears on markers: 'K' for *kék* (blue), 'P' for *piros* (red), 'S' for *sárga* (yellow) and 'Z' for *zöld* (green).

Fishing

Hungary's lakes and sluggish rivers are home to pike, perch, carp and other coarse fish. You'll see locals fishing in waterways everywhere, but Lake Balaton and Tiszafüred are particularly popular. You'll need a national fishing licence valid for a year as well as a local one issued for the day, week or year for your area. You can usually buy local ones at tackle shops, anglers' clubs and fishing associations. The **National Federation of Hungarian Anglers** (MOHOSZ; ☏1-248 2590; www.mohosz.hu; XII Korompai utca 17, Budapest) sells national licences.

Survival Guide

Directory A–Z

Accommodation

Hungary has a wide range of accommodation. Book a couple of months in advance if you're planning on visiting Budapest, Lake Balaton or the Danube Bend in July or August.

Camping These range from private sites with few facilities to large caravan campgrounds with swimming pools.

Hostels Inexpensive, prevalent in Budapest, and with lots of backpacker facilities.

Hotels Anything from socialist-era brutalist architecture to elegant five-star places, quirky boutique hotels and converted castles.

Pensions, inns and B&Bs Many are cosy, family-run places with all the facilities of a small hotel.

Private homes and apartments Book a room or the whole place (usually) with English-speaking hosts.

Booking Services

Camping One of the best resources for finding a campsite in a particular part of the country is en.camping.info; another good website is www.camping.hu.

Farmhouses For information contact **Tourinform** (☏from abroad 36 1 438 80 80; www.tourinform.hu; ⊙8am-8pm Mon-Fri), or the **Association of Hungarian Rural & Agrotourism** (FATOSZ; Map p86;☏1-352 9804; www.fatozs.eu; VII Király utca 93; ▯trolleybus 70, 78) or the **Centre of Rural Tourism** (Map p86;☏1-788-9932; www.falutur.hu; VII Dohány utca 86; ▯4, 6) in Budapest.

Hostels The Hungarian Youth Hostel Association (www.miszsz.

hu) lists a number of places across the country associated with Hostelling International (HI), but not all HI-associated hostels provide discounts to HI card-holders. Useful websites for online booking include www.hostelworld.com and www.hihostels.hu.

Pensions, Inns & B&Bs A useful website is www.panzio.lap.hu.

Camping

Camping grounds are the cheapest places to stay. Campgrounds range from small, private sites with few facilities to large, fully equipped sites that accommodate camper vans and have restaurants on their premises. On average, you'll end up paying around 1100Ft per tent, plus another 1300Ft per person on top of that, but it could be significantly more on Lake Balaton in the height of summer.

Most camping grounds open from April or May to September or October, and some offer simple bungalows (üdölőházak or faházak) from around 4000Ft to around 21,500Ft; book ahead in summer. A Camping Card International (www.campingcardinternational.com) will sometimes get you a discount of up to 10%. Camping 'wild' is prohibited in Hungary.

Farmstays

'Village tourism' means an introduction to the rural

PRICE RANGES

The following price ranges refer to a double room with bathroom in high season. Unless otherwise stated, breakfast is included in the price.

Budapest

€ less than 15,000Ft

€€ 15,000Ft–30,000Ft

€€€ more than 30,000Ft

Provinces

€ less than 9000Ft

€€ 9000Ft–16,500Ft

€€€ more than 16,500Ft

lifestyle by staying at a farm-house. Most of the places are truly remote, however, and you'll usually need your own transport, as well as some relevant language skills.

Hostels

The youth hostel (*ifjúsági szállók*) scene in Budapest has exploded in the last half-decade, leaving back-packers with a massive array of options. However, in the rest of Hungary quality hostels are still fairly rare.

In a Budapest hostel dormitory beds cost between 3000Ft and 4000Ft per person, doubles 6000Ft to 8000Ft; prices drop considerably in the countryside. A HI card sometimes gets you a small discount. Many hostels, particularly the ones in the capital, come with a plethora of services – from laundry and tour bookings to free wi-fi, guest kitchen and more.

Hotels

Hotels, called *szállók* or *szállodák*, run the gamut from luxurious five-star palaces to the run-down old socialist-era hovels that still survive in some towns, and the star rating may not always paint an accurate picture of a hotel's facilities.

As a rule of thumb, two-star hotels usually have rooms with a private bathroom, whereas one-star places offer basic rooms with shared facilities; prices start from around 9000Ft. Three stars and up (from around 15,000Ft) and you're usually looking at TV and telephone as extras; some come with saunas and/or a pool. Four- and five-star hotels (from around 30,000Ft to 40,000Ft) tend to have a gym and spa, and most hotels apart from the cheapest tend to have their own restaurant. A buffet breakfast is usually included in the price at the cheaper

> ### BOOK YOUR STAY ONLINE
>
> For more accommodation reviews by Lonely Planet authors, check out http://lonelyplanet.com/hotels/. You'll find independent reviews, as well as recommendations on the best places to stay. Best of all, you can book online.

hotels, whereas at the top-end ones you may end up paying extra. Then there are the 'wellness hotels' which make the most of Hungary's thermal waters and come equipped with spas offering a variety of treatments – from pampering packages to medical treatments aimed at rheumatism, asthma and more.

For the big splurge, or if you're romantically inclined, check out Hungary's network of castle hotels (*kastély szállók*) or mansion hotels (*kúria szállók*).

PENSIONS, B&BS & INNS

Privately run pensions (*panziók*), B&Bs and inns (*fogadók*) have been springing up like mushrooms over the past decade. Some are really just little hotels in all but name, charging from about 11,000Ft for an en-suite double. They are usually modern and clean, and often have an attached restaurant, a sauna and maybe even a pool. Others are cosy, family-run B&Bs and offer great value for money, as they tend to have all the facilities of a hotel (TV, wi-fi) in the same price range as well as the personal touch of an owner who really cares about the clientele.

Private Rooms

Hungary's 'paying-guest service' (*fizetővendég szolgálat*), or homestay, essentially means a simple room in a private house, with facilities shared with the owner/family. It's inexpensive – around 4500Ft to 8000Ft per night (7000Ft to

10,000Ft in Budapest) – but the lack of facilities and the advent of pensions, Air B'n'B and other easily booked private accommodation, where listings and (usually English-speaking) hosts are rated by users, means that it's neither very widespread nor popular. Most Tourinform offices don't keep a list of private rooms in the region, but it's worth inquiring about if you're short of other options. In resort areas look for houses with signs reading '*szoba kiadó*' or '*Zimmer frei*', advertising private rooms in Hungarian or German.

University Accommodation

From 1 July to 20 August (or later) and sometimes during the Easter holidays, Hungary's cheapest rooms are available at vacant student dormitories, known as *kollégium* or *diákszálló*, where beds in double, triple and quadruple rooms start as low as 2700Ft per person. There's no need to show a student or hostel card, and facilities are usually basic and shared.

Customs Regulations

The usual allowances apply to duty-free goods purchased outside the EU:

➡ 200 cigarettes, 50 cigars or 250g of loose tobacco

➡ 2L of wine and 1L of spirits

➡ 50mL of perfume

➡ 250mL of eau de toilette

You must declare the import/export of any currency exceeding the sum of €10,000.

When leaving the country, you are not supposed to take out valuable antiques without a 'museum certificate', which should be available from the place of purchase.

Discount Cards

Hungary Card

Those planning on travelling extensively in the country might consider buying a **Hungary Card** (www.hungarycard.hu), which comes in three denominations (basic/standard/plus 5000/8000/12,000Ft). Depending on the denomination, benefits may include free admission to many museums nationwide; a 50% discount on a number of return train fares and some bus and boat travel, as well as other museums and attractions; up to 20% off selected accommodation; and 25% off the price of the Budapest Card. Cards are available at Tourinform offices nationwide.

Regional Cards

A number of regions in Hungary offer region-specific discount cards. These include, among others, the Budapest Card, Balaton Card and Badacsony Card.

Student & Youth Cards

The **International Student Identity Card** (ISIC; www.isic.org; 2610Ft) gives students many discounts on certain forms of transport, and cheap admission to museums and other sights. If you're aged under 26 but not a student, you can apply for ISIC's **International Youth Travel Card** (IYTC; 2050Ft) or the **Euro<26 card** (2500Ft) issued by the **European Youth Card Association** (EYCA; www.eyca.org), both of which offer the same discounts as the student card.

Electricity

Type E
230V/50Hz

Embassies & Consulates

Selected countries with representation in Budapest (where the area code is 1) are listed here. The opening hours indicate when consular or chancellery services are available, but be sure to confirm these times before you set out as they change frequently. The nearest embassies representing Australian and New Zealand citizens are in Vienna, Austria.

Austrian Embassy (1-479 7010; www.bmeia.gv.at/botschaft/budapest.html; VI Benczúr utca 16; 9-11am Mon-Fri; M1 Bajza utca)

Canadian Embassy (1-392 3360; www.hungary.gc.ca; II Ganz utca 12-14; 8.30am-4.30pm Mon-Thu, 8am-1.30pm Fri; 19, 41)

Dutch Embassy (1-336 6300; www.netherlandsembassy.hu; II Kapás utca 6-12; 9am-4.30pm Mon-Fri; 17)

French Embassy (1-374 1100; www.ambafrance-hu.org; VI Lendvay utca 27; 9am-12.30pm Mon-Fri; M1 Hősök tere)

German Embassy (1-488 3567; www.budapest.diplo.de; I Úri utca 64-66; 9am-noon Mon-Fri, 1-3.30pm Sat; 16, 16A, 116)

Irish Embassy (1-301 4960; www.embassyofireland.hu; V Szabadság tér 7, Bank Center, 6th fl, Platina Tower; 10am-12.30pm & 2.30-4.30pm Mon-Fri; 15, 115)

Serbian Embassy (1-322 9838; www.budapest.mfa.gov.rs; VI Dózsa György út 92/a; 10am-1pm Mon-Fri; M1 Hősök tere)

South African Embassy (1-392 0999; www.dirco.gov.za/budapest; II Gárdonyi Géza út 17; 8am-noon & 1-5pm Mon-Thu, 8am-12.45pm Fri; 11, 111)

UK Embassy (1-266 2888; http://ukinhungary.fco.gov.uk/en; V Harmincad utca 6; 10am-4pm Mon-Thu, to 2pm Fri; M1 Vörösmarty tér)

US Embassy (1-475 4400; https://hungary.usembassy.gov; V Szabadság tér 12; 8am-5pm Mon-Fri; M3 Arany János utca)

Food & Drink

Hungary has an ever-increasing range of eating options, particularly in Budapest. In most places, it's fine to book on the day or not book at all; for fine dining in Budapest, book a week or two ahead.

➡ **Restaurants** Range from cheap Hungarian to refined sushi and Michelin-starred fine-dining establishments.

➡ **Vendéglő** Regional restaurants typically serving inexpensive homestyle cooking.

➡ **Cafes** Open during the daytime, these are great for coffee, cake and light (and sometimes substantial) meals.

➡ **Csárda** Typically rustic places serving large portions of Hungarian cuisine, often accompanied by Gypsy music.

AMREST KÁVÉZÓ KFT.

1138 BUDAPEST

DUNAVIRÁG UTCA 2-6 3 ep. 2 em.

SBX Astoria

1088 Budapest

Rákóczi út 1-3.

ADÓSZÁM: 14126444-2-41

NYUGTA

C99 WhiMocShakenEspT

1 DB * 1 090 Ft/DB 1 090

A99 Cup+LidFlatT

1 DB * 0 Ft/DB 0

ÖSSZESEN: **1 090 Ft**

BANKKÁRTYA .... 1 090 Ft

Rendelési Típus:	Take Away
Értékesítőhely:	Starbucks Coffee
Alkalmazott Azonosító:	100018
Felszolgáló:	Caleb L
Bizonylatszám / CHK Szám:	2158

AmRest

CC/: 308033

Toilet code/: 1456

NYUGTASZAM: 1217/00051

2022.08.20. 12:17

NAV Ellenőrző kód:E88C3

APA20700146

Gay & Lesbian Travellers

There have been a couple of violent far-right demonstrations recently in response to Budapest's Gay Pride parades, and Hungarian society maintains largely conservative views, but attitudes are slowly changing. There's good gay nightlife in Budapest (but not elsewhere in Hungary) and Budapest was also the venue for EuroGames 2012 – Europe's largest gay-friendly sporting event.

Háttér Gay & Lesbian Association (☑1-238 0046; www.hatter. hu) Has an advice and help line operating daily.

Labrisz Lesbian Association (☑1-252 3566; www.labrisz.hu) Has info on Hungary's lesbian scene.

Health

Good travel health depends on your predeparture preparations, your daily health care while travelling and the way you handle any medical problem that develops while you are on the road. Hungary is an easy country to travel around, with ready access to medication (though if you require prescription medication, it's best to bring your own) and few health hazards.

Before You Go
HEALTH INSURANCE

➡ If you're an EU citizen, a European Health Insurance Card (EHIC), available from health centres, covers you for most medical care. It will not cover you for nonemergencies or emergency repatriation. Citizens from other countries should find out if there is a reciprocal arrangement for free medical care between their country and Hungary.

➡ In Hungary, foreigners are entitled to first-aid and ambulance services only when they have suffered

an accident and require immediate medical attention; follow-up treatment and medicine must be paid for.

➡ If you do need health insurance while travelling, find out in advance if your insurance plan will make payments directly to providers or reimburse you later for overseas health expenditures. The former option is generally preferable, as it doesn't require you to pay out of pocket in Hungary, but if you have to claim later, make sure you keep all documentation.

VACCINATIONS

Hungary doesn't require any vaccination of international travellers, but the World Health Organization (WHO) recommends travellers be covered for diphtheria, tetanus, measles, mumps, rubella and polio, regardless of their destination.

In Hungary
AVAILABILITY & COST OF HEALTH CARE

➡ Medical care in Hungary is generally up to the standards of most Western countries and good for routine problems but not complicated conditions. Treatment at a *rendelő intézet* (public outpatient clinic) costs little, but doctors working privately will charge much more. Very roughly,

a consultation in an *orvosi rendelő* (doctor's surgery) costs from 8000Ft while a home visit is from around 12,000Ft.

➡ Most large towns and all of Budapest's 23 districts have a *gyógyszertár* or *patika* (rotating 24-hour pharmacy). A sign on the door of any pharmacy will help you locate the closest one.

➡ Emergency dental care is easy and inexpensive to obtain as many Hungarian towns feature an abundance of dentists.

INSECT BITES & STINGS

Tick-borne encephalitis, a serious infection of the brain spread by *kullancs* (ticks), which burrow under the skin, is a common problem in parts of Hungary. Vaccination is advised for campers and hikers, particularly in Transdanubia and the Northern Uplands between May and September.

Lyme disease is another tick-transmitted infection not unknown in Central and Eastern Europe. The illness usually begins with a spreading rash at the site of the tick bite and is accompanied by fever, headaches, extreme fatigue, aching joints and muscles, and mild neck stiffness. If untreated, these symptoms usually resolve themselves over several weeks, but over subsequent weeks or months disorders of the nervous system, heart and joints might develop. Protect yourself by wearing trousers and long-sleeved shirts when hiking in forests.

Mosquitoes are a real scourge around Hungary's lakes and rivers in summer, so make sure you're armed with a DEET-based insect repellent and wear long-sleeved shirts and long trousers around sundown.

SEXUAL HEALTH

The number of people registered as having AIDS or being HIV positive in Hungary is relatively low (around 1100), though Hungarian epidemiologists estimate the actual number of those infected with HIV to be around 3000 or more. That number could multiply substantially as Budapest claims the less-than-distinguished title of 'sex industry capital of Eastern and Central Europe'. An AIDS line to contact in Budapest is the **Anonymous AIDS Association** (☏1-466 9283; www.anonimaids.hu; XI Karolina út 35/b; ☏5-8pm Mon & Wed, 9am-noon Tue & Fri; ☏61).

TAP WATER

Tap water in Hungary is safe to drink.

Insurance

➡ A travel insurance policy to cover theft, loss and medical problems is a good idea. There is a wide variety of policies available, so check the small print.

➡ If you need to make a claim regarding a loss or theft of possessions, you will need to produce a police report and proof of value of items lost or stolen.

➡ Worldwide travel insurance is available at www.lonelyplanet.com/travel-insurance. You can buy, extend and claim online anytime – even if you're already on the road.

TIPPING

Gratuities in Hungary are commonplace.

➡ **Bars** 30Ft to 50Ft per drink at the bar; if drinks are brought to your table, 10% of total.

➡ **Hairdressers** 10% of haircut price is appropriate.

➡ **Hotels** 500Ft for luggage, 200Ft to 300Ft per day for housekeeping.

➡ **Petrol stations & thermal spas** Attendants expect some loose change.

➡ **Restaurants** For decent service 10%, up to 15% in more upmarket places; 12.5% service often included in the bill.

➡ **Taxis** Round up the fare.

In Budapest and other locations frequented by tourists, many restaurants now automatically add a gratuity of about 10% to the bill. Ask if you're not sure whether service is included. Elsewhere, the way you tip in restaurants is unusual: you never leave the money on the table – that is considered rude – but instead you tell the waiter how much you're paying in total. If the bill is 3600Ft, you're paying with a 5000Ft note and you think the waiter deserves a gratuity of about 10%, tell the waiter you're paying 4000Ft or that you want 1000Ft back.

Internet Access

Hungary is a wired country.

➡ Many libraries in Hungary have free (or almost free) terminals.

➡ Internet cafes are rapidly becoming obsolete with the proliferation of smartphones and easy access to free wi-fi hot spots.

➡ Almost all hostels and hotels offer internet and/or wi-fi, mostly free but sometimes for a small surcharge.

➡ Free wi-fi is also available at major airports, and the majority of restaurants and cafes (particularly in Budapest).

Legal Matters

Those violating Hungarian laws, even unknowingly, may be expelled, arrested and/or imprisoned. Penalties for possession, use or trafficking of illegal drugs in Hungary are severe, and convicted offenders can expect long jail sentences and heavy fines.

There is a 100% ban on alcohol when driving and it is taken very seriously. Police conduct routine roadside checks with breathalysers and if you are found to have even 0.005% of alcohol in your blood, you could be fined up to 300,000Ft on the spot; police have been known to fine for less than that, so it's best not to drink at all. In the event of an accident, the drinking party is automatically regarded as guilty.

Maps

Hungary's largest map-making company, Cartographia, publishes a useful 1:450,000-scale sheet map of the country, as well as maps of all the main cities and towns, widely available in kiosks. Its 1:250,000 *Magyarország autó-atlasza* (Road Atlas of Hungary) is indispensable if you plan to do a lot of travelling in the countryside by car. Bookshops in Hungary generally stock a wide variety of maps, or you can go directly to the **Cartographia** (Map p78; ☑1-312 6001; www.cartographia. hu; VI Bajcsy-Zsilinszky út 37; ⏰9am-5pm Mon-Fri; Ⓜ M3 Arany János utca) outlet in Budapest.

Cartographia also produces national, regional and hiking maps (average scales 1:40,000 and 1:60,000), as well as city plans (1:11,000 to 1:20,000). Smaller companies such as **Topográf** (www. topograf.hu) and **Magyar Térképház** (www.terkephaz. hu) also publish excellent city and specialised maps.

Money

ATMs

➡ All major banks have ATMs and most ATMs accept cards issued outside Hungary. ATMs are plentiful, particularly in Budapest and larger towns.

➡ Some of the ATMs at branches of Országos Takarékpénztár (OTP), the national savings bank, give out 20,000Ft notes, which can be difficult to break.

➡ There's a proliferation of Euronet ATMs dispensing both forint and Euros, particularly in tourist hotspots. They offer comparatively poor exchange rates and visitors are better off using the ATMs of major banks instead.

Credit & Debit Cards

Credit cards, especially Visa, MasterCard and American Express, are widely accepted in Hungary, and you'll be able to use them at many restaurants, shops, hotels, car-rental firms, travel agencies and petrol stations. At train and bus stations it's possible to use them if you purchase tickets from ticket machines rather than ticket counters. Many banks give cash advances on

---

---

major credit cards but charge both a fee and interest.

A good alternative to credit cards are preloaded cash cards such as the **Travelex Cash Passport** (www. travelex.com): load it up with funds before departure and then withdraw funds in local currency as you travel.

Currency

➡ The Hungarian currency is the forint (Ft). There are coins of 5Ft, 10Ft, 20Ft, 50Ft, 100Ft and 200Ft. Notes come in seven denominations: 500Ft, 1000Ft, 2000Ft, 5000Ft, 10,000Ft and 20,000Ft.

➡ Prices in shops and restaurants are uniformly quoted in forint. Many hotels and guesthouses give their rates in euros. In such cases you can usually pay in either euros or forint, though we recommend you pay in forint as the euro exchange rate is likely to be unfavourable.

➡ It's always prudent to carry a little foreign cash – preferably euros or US dollars – in case you can't find an ATM nearby.

Money Changers

For the best rates, change money at banks rather than moneychangers.

Taxes & Refunds

ÁFA, a value-added tax of up to 27%, is levied on all new goods in Hungary. It's usually included in the price

---

but not always. Visitors are not exempt, but non-EU residents can claim refunds for total purchases of at least 52,001Ft on one receipt, as long as they take the goods out of the country (and the EU) within 90 days.

The ÁFA receipts (available from where you made the purchases) should be stamped by customs at the border, and the claim has to be made within 183 days of exporting the goods. You can then collect your refund – minus commission – from the VAT desk in the departure halls of Terminals 2A and 2B at Ferenc Liszt International Airport in Budapest, and at branches of the IBUSZ chain of travel agencies at the land border crossings.

Opening Hours

See p17 for information regarding typical opening hours in Hungary.

Post

The **Hungarian Postal Service** (Magyar Posta; www.posta.hu) is reasonably reliable, but at the post offices service can be slow, so buy your bélyeg (stamps) at newsagents to beat the crowds.

Postcards or letters sent within Hungary cost 135/115Ft, while postcards or letters within/outside Europe cost 305Ft/355Ft. At post offices, look for the window marked with the symbol of an envelope.

To send a parcel, look for the sign 'Csomagfeladás' or 'Csomagfelvétel' at post offices, but it's best not to send anything of value by regular post. If absolutely necessary, opt for registered post and ask for an *ajánlott levél* form to fill in; you keep the stamped form while the package is marked with an ID number.

Hungarian addresses start with the name of the recipient, followed on the next line by the postal code and city or town, and then the street name and number. The postal code consists of four digits. The first one indicates the city, town or region (eg '1' is Budapest, '6' is Szeged), the second and third are the district, and the last is the neighbourhood.

Public Holidays

Hungary celebrates 10 *ünnep* (public holidays) each year.

New Year's Day 1 January

1848 Revolution/National Day 15 March

Easter Monday March/April

International Labour Day 1 May

Whit Monday May/June

St Stephen's/Constitution Day 20 August

1956 Remembrance Day/ Republic Day 23 October

All Saints' Day 1 November

Christmas holidays 25 & 26 December

Safe Travel

➜ Pickpocketing is common at popular tourist sights, inside foreign fast-food chains, near major hotels and in flea markets. Sometimes pickpockets work together, with one distracting you by running into you and then apologising profusely – as an accomplice takes off with the goods.

➜ Thefts from rental vehicles are not uncommon. Don't leave anything of value, including luggage, inside the car.

➜ This is a rare occurence these days, but occasionally waiters may make a 'mistake' when tallying the bill, or add service to the bill and then expect an additional tip. If you think there's a discrepancy, ask for the menu and check the bill carefully.

➜ There are isolated incidents of taxi drivers, particularly in Budapest, taking advantage of passengers unfamiliar with local currency – switching large denomination notes for smaller ones and demanding

extra payment. Only ever take taxis from reputable companies and make sure you know exactly how much cash you're handing over. Reputable ones include **Budapest Taxi** (☎1-777 7777; www.budapesttaxi.hu) and **Fő Taxi** (☎1-222 2222; www.fotaxi.hu).

Telephone

Hungary has extensive mobile phone network coverage. Public phones can be used to make domestic and international calls, though they are rapidly becoming obsolete with the advent of cheap mobile phone calls, Skype and other VOIP services.

Mobile Phones

➜ The three main mobile phone providers are: **Telenor**, **T-Mobile** and **Vodafone**.

➜ Call and SMS rates are now standardised across the board and an increasing number of service providers include the use of other countries' networks in home tariffs.

➜ You can also purchase a rechargeable or prepaid SIM card from any of the three providers, but check first with your service provider, as it may be possible to get an even cheaper rate with your own home network.

Local & International Calls

➜ All localities in Hungary have a two-digit telephone area code, except for Budapest, which has just a '1'.

➜ To make a local call, dial the phone number (seven digits in Budapest, six elsewhere).

➜ For an intercity landline call within Hungary and whenever ringing a mobile telephone, dial ☎06, followed by the area code and phone number.

➜ Cheaper or toll-free numbers start with ☎06 40 and ☎06 80, respectively.

PRACTICALITIES

➜ **Newspapers** Budapest has two English-language newspapers: the *Budapest Times* (online only) with good reviews and opinion pieces, and the biweekly *Budapest Business Journal*.

➜ **Radio** Magyar Radio has three main stations: MR1-Kossuth (107.8FM; jazz, talkback and news); MR2-Petőfi (94.8FM; popular music); and MR3-Bartók (105.3FM; classical music). Sláger FM (103.9FM) is a good mix of local and international pop music, and Rádió C (88.8FM) addresses issues concerning the Roma people.

➜ **TV & DVD** Like Australia and most of Europe, Hungary uses PAL, which is incompatible with the North American and Japanese NTCS system.

➜ **Weights & Measures** Hungary uses the metric system.

➡ To make an international call, dial ☎00, then the country code, the area code and the number.

➡ The country code for Hungary is ☎36.

Phonecards

You can make domestic and international calls from public telephones; they take either coins or phonecards. Phonecards issued by **NeoPhone** (www.web.neophone.hu) come in values of 1000Ft, 2000Ft, 5000Ft and 10,000Ft and are available from post offices and newsstands. Other discount phonecards such as **No Limits** (www.nolimits. hu) also offer good rates for international calls.

Time

Hungary lies in the Central European time zone and is one hour ahead of GMT. Clocks are advanced by one hour on the last Sunday in March and set back on the last Sunday in October. The 24-hour clock is used.

Toilets

➡ Public toilets in Hungary are relatively common but often in poor condition.

➡ A fee of 200Ft to 300Ft is typically payable.

Tourist Information

Hungarian National Tourist Office Has a chain of some 130 tourist information bureaus called **Tourinform** (☎from abroad 36 1 438 80 80; www. tourinform.hu; ⊘8am-8pm Mon-Fri) across the country. They are usually the best places to ask general questions and pick up brochures – and can sometimes provide more comprehensive assistance.

EMERGENCY NUMBERS	
Hungary country code	☎36
Ambulance	☎104
Europe-wide emergency number For English-, German- and French-speakers	☎112
Fire	☎105
Police	☎107

Budapest Tourism (www. budapestinfo.hu) produces plenty of handy information about the capital and its attractions.

Travellers with Disabilities

Hungary has made great strides in recent years in making public areas and facilities more accessible to the disabled. Wheelchair ramps, toilets fitted for the disabled and inward opening doors, though not as common as they are in Western Europe, do exist, and audible traffic signals for the blind are becoming commonplace in the cities.

For more information, contact the **Hungarian Federation of Disabled Persons' Associations** (MEOSZ; Map p70; ☎1-388 2387; www. meoszinfo.hu; III San Marco utca 76; ⊘8am-4pm Mon-Fri).

Download Lonely Planet's free Accessible Travel guide from http://lptravel.to/AccessibleTravel.

Visas

See p16 for visa requirement information.

Volunteering

➡ AIESEC (www.aiesec.org) run volunteer programmes in Hungary of varying lengths in the education, literacy and sustainable living fields.

➡ United Way Hungary (www.unitedway.hu) take on volunteers looking to work with children for three months or longer.

➡ Alternatively, backpackers from European countries looking to linger in Budapest are often able to do volunteer work in hostels in exchange for accommodation.

Women Travellers

Women should not encounter any particular problems while travelling in Hungary besides some mild local machismo. If you do need assistance and/or information, ring the **Women's Line** (NANE; ☎06 40 630 006; www. nane.hu; ⊘10am-6pm Mon & Wed, to 2pm Fri).

Work

There's a high demand in Hungary for foreign employees in the IT and telecommunications fields, as well as English teachers. It is relatively straightforward to apply for a job in these fields if you're an EU citizen; citizens of other nationalities, however, can only be employed if the company they wish to work for can prove that they can't find a Hungarian to do the job. www.jobsinbudapest. eu and www.budapestjobs. net are useful sites if you're after a professional posting in the capital.

Transport

GETTING THERE & AWAY

Entering Hungary

Border formalities with Austria, Slovenia and Slovakia are virtually nonexistent. However, one may only enter or leave Hungary via designated border crossing points during opening hours if travelling to/from Croatia, Romania, Ukraine or Serbia, especially since, in the wake of the Syrian refugee crisis, a controversial border wall now stretches along Hungary's border with Serbia and Croatia. For the latest on border formalities, check www.police.hu.

Passport

To enter Hungary everyone needs a valid passport or, for many citizens of the EU, a national identification card.

Air

Airports & Airlines

INTERNATIONAL AIRPORTS

International flights land at **Ferenc Liszt International Airport** (BUD; ☑1-296 7000; www.bud.hu), 20km southeast of Budapest. Flights to/from Schengen countries use Terminal 2A, while Terminal 2B serves non-Schengen countries. Between April and November, **Hévíz-Balaton Airport** (SOB; ☑83-200 304; www.hevizairport.com; Repülőtér 1, Sármellék) receives flights from Berlin, Düsseldorf and Frankfurt, among other German destinations, as well as Moscow, and is located 15km southwest of Keszthely near Lake Balaton.

Malév Hungarian Airlines, the national carrier, was liquidated due to bankruptcy in 2012.

Land

Hungary is well connected with all seven of its neighbours by road and rail, though most transport begins or ends its journey in Budapest.

Timetables for both domestic and international trains and buses use the 24-hour system. Also, Hungarian names are sometimes used for cities and towns in neighbouring countries on bus and train schedules.

Border Crossings

If crossing into Hungary from Croatia, Serbia, Romania or Ukraine, you may have to alight from the bus or train at the border. If driving, you may only enter Hungary via designated border crossing points during opening hours if travelling to/from Croatia, Romania, Ukraine or Serbia, especially since, in the wake of the Syrian refugee crisis, a controversial border wall now stretches along Hungary's border with Serbia and Croatia. There are no border stops or checks when entering from Austria, Slovenia and Slovakia. For the latest on the border situation, check www.police.hu.

Bicycle

➡ It is entirely possible to bring a bicycle into the country aboard select train services that come with bicycle cars; bicycle tickets are usually inexpensive.

ARRIVING IN BUDAPEST

Ferenc Liszt International Airport (Budapest) (BUD; ☑1-296 7000; www.bud.hu) Buses run around the clock from the airport to the Kőbánya-Kispest metro station. The airport shuttle does door-to-door drop-offs (around €22 to central Budapest), while taxis cost from around 5650Ft.

Keleti, Nyugati & Déli train stations (Budapest) All three stations are on metro lines of the same name; trams and/or night buses call when the metro is closed.

Népliget & Stadionok bus stations (Budapest) Both are on the M3 metro line and served by trams 1 and 1A.

→ Eurolines buses transport bicycles to Budapest from various destinations, including Vienna, Zagreb, Venice and Florence; bicycle tickets cost €9, irrespective of the route; advance bookings are advisable.

Bus

→ Crossing the continent by bus is cheapest. Most international buses are run by **Eurolines** (www.eurolines.com) and link with its Hungarian associate, **Volánbusz** (⏱1-382 0888; www.volanbusz.hu).

→ The **Eurolines Pass** (www.eurolines.com/en/eurolines-pass/) allows unlimited travel between 51 European cities, including Budapest. Sample prices for high season include €320/270 for over/under 26 years old for 15 days and €425/350 for 30 days.

Car & Motorcycle

Drivers and motorbike riders will need the vehicle's registration papers, liability insurance and an international driver's permit in addition to their domestic licence.

Train

Hungary is well connected to neighbouring countries, with international services arriving and departing at least once a day.

MÁV (Magyar Államvasutak, Hungarian State Railways; ⏱1-349 4949; www.mavcsoport.hu) (Hungarian State Railways) links up with the European rail network in all directions. Its trains run as far as London (via Munich and Paris), Stockholm (via Hamburg and Copenhagen), Moscow, Rome and Istanbul (via Belgrade). Almost all international trains bound for Hungary arrive and depart from Budapest's Keleti station; Déli handles trains to Croatia, Slovenia, Bosnia and Herzegovina, and Serbia.

The **Thomas Cook European Timetable** (www.europeanrailtimetable.co.uk), updated monthly and available from Thomas Cook outlets, is the train-lover's bible, with a complete listing of train schedules, supplements and reservations information. **The Man in Seat 61** (www.seat61.com) can also help you plan your train journey across Europe.

CLASSES, COSTS & RESERVATIONS

→ Seat reservations are required for international destinations, and are included in the price of the ticket.

→ Tickets are normally valid for 60 days from purchase and stopovers are permitted.

→ On long hauls, sleepers are almost always available in both 1st and 2nd class, and couchettes are available in 2nd class.

→ Not all express trains have dining or even buffet cars; make sure you bring along snacks and drinks as vendors can be few and far between.

→ All prices quoted are full-price, one-way, 2nd-class fares; 1st-class seats are around 50% more expensive than 2nd class.

→ Substantial discounts to a number of European capitals are available on tickets purchased more than three days in advance. Due to limited seating, book early to take advantage of the savings.

TRAIN PASSES

Inter Rail (www.interrail.eu) Global Pass covering 30 European countries; can be purchased by European nationals or residents of at least six months. Sample costs for an adult/under-26 travelling 2nd class:

→ five days within a 15-day period: €264/200

→ 10 days within a month: €374/292

→ 22 continuous days: €484/374

1st-class Global Passes tend to cost at least €150 more per pass than 2nd-class Global Passes.

Eurail (www.eurail.com) Global Pass gives non-European citizens unlimited travel in 28 European countries, including Hungary. Sample costs for an adult/under-26 travelling 2nd class:

→ five days within a month: €459/300

→ 15 days within two months: €903/589

→ 3 months' continuous travel: €1609/1048

Eurail Select Passes Allow you to pick combinations of two, three or four neighbouring countries; passes are valid for five, six, eight or 10 days within two months.

River

Mahart PassNave (Map p74; ⏱1-484 4013; www.mahartpassnave.hu; V Belgrád rakpart; ☺9am-4pm Mon-Fri; 🚊2) runs

---

CLIMATE CHANGE & TRAVEL

Every form of transport that relies on carbon-based fuel generates CO_2, the main cause of human-induced climate change. Modern travel is dependent on aeroplanes, which might use less fuel per kilometre per person than most cars but travel much greater distances. The altitude at which aircraft emit gases (including CO_2) and particles also contributes to their climate change impact. Many websites offer 'carbon calculators' that allow people to estimate the carbon emissions generated by their journey and, for those who wish to do so, to offset the impact of the greenhouse gases emitted with contributions to portfolios of climate-friendly initiatives throughout the world. Lonely Planet offsets the carbon footprint of all staff and author travel.

daily hydrofoil services on the Danube River between Budapest and Vienna (5½ to 6½ hours) from mid-May to late September. Adult one-way/return fares for Vienna are €99/125. For the return journey, consult **Mahart PassNave Wien** (☎01 72 92 161, 01 72 92 162; Handelskai 265, Reichsbrücke pier, Vienna) in Vienna.

GETTING AROUND

Hungary's domestic transport system is efficient, comprehensive and inexpensive. Towns are covered by a system of frequent buses, trams and trolleybuses.

The majority of Hungary's towns and cities are easily negotiated on foot. There are no scheduled flights within Hungary; it's small enough to get everywhere by train or bus within the span of a day.

EU citizens over the age of 65 travel for free on all public transport.

Menetred (www.menet rendek.hu) has links to all the timetables: bus, train, public transport and boat.

Train Reasonably priced, with extensive coverage of the country.

Car Handy for exploring the wilder corners of Hungary.

BUS CONNECTIONS

Eastern Europe

From Budapest's Népliget station there are good bus connections with destinations in Croatia, Romania, the Czech Republic and Poland, among others. Services to Croatia operate between mid-June and mid-September. Prices fluctuate depending on day and time of departure.

Sample destinations and prices include the following:

DESTINATION	COST	TIME (HR)	FREQUENCY
Bratislava	3400Ft	3	2 daily
Dubrovnik	10,000Ft	14	Fri mid-Jun–mid-Sep
Poreč	11,000Ft	11½	Fri mid-Jun–mid-Sep
Prague	6000Ft	7¼	3 daily
Pula	11,000Ft	9½	Fri mid-Jun–mid-Sep
Rijeka	10,000Ft	8	Fri mid-Jun–mid-Sep
Kraków	5000Ft	7	Tue, Wed, Fri & Sun
Sofia	12,900Ft	13½	up to 3 daily
Split	14,000Ft	12¾	Fri mid-Jun–mid-Sep
Subotica (Szabadka)	3900Ft	4½	daily

Western Europe

From Népliget station there are buses to many cities across Western Europe. Prices fluctuate depending on day and time of departure.

DESTINATION	COST	TIME (HR)	FREQUENCY
Amsterdam	19,900Ft	22¼	daily
Athens	24,000Ft	23½	Wed, Fri & Sun
Berlin	18,900Ft	4¾	Thu & Sat
Düsseldorf	18,900Ft	18½	Mon & Fri
Frankfurt	17,900Ft	14¼	daily
London	20,900Ft	28¼	Wed & Fri
Paris	20,900Ft	21¾	Mon, Wed & Fri
Rotterdam	19,900Ft	23½	Mon, Thu, Fri & Sun
Venice	11,900Ft	9¾	Wed, Fri & Sun
Vienna	5800Ft	3	up to 6 daily
Zürich	26,900Ft	15	Wed & Sat

Bus Cheaper and often faster than trains. Useful for more remote destinations not served by trains.

Air

There are no scheduled flights within Hungary. Hungary is small enough to get everywhere by train or bus within the span of a day.

Bicycle

➡ Hungary offers endless opportunities for cyclists: challenging slopes in the north, much gentler terrain in Transdanubia, and flat though windy (and hot in summer) cycling on the Great Plain.

➡ In Hungary's cities, the cycle-path network is being extended all the time; there's a proliferation of designated cycle lanes in Budapest in particular.

➡ Bicycle hire is readily available. Outside the tourist hot spots, your best bets are camping grounds, resort hotels and – very occasionally – bicycle repair shops.

➡ Bicycles are banned from all motorways and national highways with a single digit, and bikes must be equipped with lights and reflectors.

➡ Bicycles can be taken on many trains (look for the bicycle symbol on the timetables) at 25% additional cost, and can also be taken on boats, but not on buses.

Boat

From April to late October the Budapest-based **Mahart PassNave** (Map p74; ☎1-484 4013; www.mahartpassnave.hu; V Belgrád rakpart; ☺9am-4pm Mon-Fri; ☒2) runs excursion boats on the Danube from Budapest to Szentendre, Vác, Visegrád and Esztergom and, between May and September,

hydrofoils from Budapest to Visegrád, Nagymaros, Esztergom and Komárom.

From spring to autumn, 23 ports around Lake Balaton are well served by passenger ferries of the **Balaton Shipping Company** (www.balatonihajozas.hu).

Bus

Hungary's **Volánbusz** (☎1-382 0888; www.volanbusz.hu) network comprehensively covers the whole country. In Southern Transdanubia and many parts of the Great Plain, they are far quicker and more direct than trains, as is the case for short trips around the Danube Bend or Lake Balaton areas.

Budapest has separate long-distance bus stations (*távolságiautóbusz pályaudvar*) and local stations (*helyiautóbusz pályaudvar*). Outside the capital the stations are often found side by side or in the same building. Arrive early to confirm the correct departure bay or *kocsiállás* (stand), and check the individual schedule posted at the stop itself; the times

shown can be different from those shown on the *tábla* (main board).

Some larger bus stations have luggage lockers or else left-luggage rooms that generally close early (around 6pm). The left-luggage offices at nearby train stations keep much longer hours.

Tickets are purchased directly from the driver. There are sometimes queues for intercity buses, so arrive around 30 minutes before departure. Buses are reasonably comfortable and have adequate leg room. On long journeys there are rest stops every two or three hours.

Bus Costs

Bus ticket costs are calculated according to distance:

FARE	DISTANCE
250Ft	up to 10km
370Ft	15-20km
1300Ft	60-70km
2200Ft	100-120km
3690Ft	200-220km
4660Ft	280-300km

TRANSPORT AIR

DECIPHERING BUS TIMETABLES

Posted bus timetables can be horribly confusing for non-Hungarians. Here's a guide to some essential words and symbols:

➡ *Indulás:* departures

➡ *Érkezés:* arrivals

➡ Numbers one to seven in a circle refer to the days of the week, beginning with Monday

➡ D *naponta:* daily except Saturday

➡ M *munkanapokon:* working days

➡ O *szabadnapokon:* Saturday

➡ + *munkaszüneti napokon:* Sunday and holidays

➡ I *iskolai napján:* school days

➡ *hétköznap:* weekdays

➡ *szabad és munkaszünetes napokon:* Saturday, Sunday and holidays

➡ *szabadnap kivételével naponta:* daily except Saturday

➡ *munkaszünetes nap kivételével naponta:* daily except holidays

Car & Motorcycle

Driving in Hungary is useful if you're exploring the remotest rural corners of the country; trains and buses take care of the rest.

Automobile Associations

In the event of a breakdown, the so-called **Yellow Angels** (Sárga Angyal; call ☏188, 24 hours) of the **Hungarian Automobile Club** (Magyar Autóklub; ☏1-345 1800; www. autoklub.hu; IV Berda József utca 15, Budapest; Ⓜ M3 Újpest

Városkapu) are the people to call, as they do basic car repairs free of charge if you belong to an affiliated organisation such as AAA in the USA, or AA in the UK.

For 24-hour information on traffic and public road conditions around Hungary, contact **Útinform** (☏1-336 2400; www.kozut.hu). In the capital, ring Főinform.

Hire

➡ You must be at least 21 years old and have had your licence for a year to hire a car.

➡ Drivers under 25 sometimes have to pay a surcharge.

➡ All of the big international firms, such as **Avis** (☏1-318 4240; www.avis.hu; V Arany János utca 26-28; ☺7am-6pm Mon-Fri, 8am-2pm Sat & Sun; Ⓜ M3 Arany János utca) and **Europcar** (☏1-505 4400; www.europcar.hu; V Erzsébet tér 7-8; ☺8am-6pm Mon & Fri, to 4.30pm Tue-Thu, to noon Sat; Ⓜ M1/2/3 Deák Ferenc tér), have offices in Budapest, and there are scores of local companies throughout the country.

TRAIN CONNECTIONS

Eastern Europe

Budapest's Keleti station has services to the following destinations in Romania, Croatia, Slovakia, the Czech Republic, Ukraine and Russia. Note that the Moscow service goes via Kyiv (25 hours) and Lviv (15 hours).

DESTINATION	COST	TIME (HR)	FREQUENCY
Belgrade via Subotica	€15	8	3 daily
Cluj-Napoca	€35	7¼	2 daily
Košice via Miskolc	€16	3½	2 daily
Ljubljana (change at Kelenföld)	€39	9	daily
Moscow via Lviv and Kyiv	€271	30	daily
Prague via Bratislava	€19	6¼	up to 6 daily
Sofia	€126	21½	daily
Timişoara	€29	5	4 daily
Warsaw	€29	10	2 daily
Zagreb	€29	6	daily

Western Europe

Budapest has connections to the following destinations:

DESTINATION	COST	TIME (HR)	FREQUENCY
Berlin via Dresden, Prague and Bratislava	€39	11½	daily
Frankfurt (change in Dresden, Munich or Vienna)	€60	10¼-11½	3 daily
Munich via Salzburg	€49	9½	6 daily
Venice (change in Vienna)	€67	19	daily
Vienna	€19	3	12 daily
Zürich	€72	11-12	2 daily

Insurance

➡ Third-party liability insurance is compulsory in Hungary. If your car is registered in the EU, it is assumed you have it. Other motorists must show a Green Card or buy insurance at the border.

➡ All accidents should be reported to the police immediately.

➡ Any claim on insurance policies bought in Hungary can be made to Allianz Hungária (☑06 40 421 421; www.allianz.hu) in Budapest. It is one of the largest insurance companies in Hungary and deals with foreigners all the time.

Road Conditions

Roads in Hungary are generally good – in some cases excellent nowadays – and there are several basic types.

There are now nine motorways and eight express roads, preceded by an 'M'. National highways (dual carriageways) are designated by a single digit without a prefix and fan out mostly from Budapest. Secondary/tertiary roads have two/three digits.

Driving in Hungary – particularly in Budapest – can be quite trying. Overtaking on blind curves, tailgating, making turns from the outside lane, running stop signs and lights, and jumping lanes in roundabouts are everyday occurrences.

Many cities and towns have a confusing system of one-way streets, pedestrian zones and bicycle lanes. Parking is an issue in Budapest. You are required to 'pay and display' when parking your vehicle – parking discs, coupons and stickers are available at newsstands, petrol stations and, increasingly, automated ticket machines. In smaller towns and cities a warden collects 200Ft or so for each hour you plan to park. In Budapest, parking on the street costs between around 200Ft and 440Ft per hour, depending on the neighbourhood.

Hitching

Hitching is never entirely safe in any country and we don't recommend it. Travellers who decide to hitch are taking a small but potentially serious risk. Hitching is legal everywhere in Hungary except on motorways. Though it isn't as popular as it once was (and can be difficult), the road to Lake Balaton sees hitching in the holiday season.

Local Transport

➡ Urban transport is well developed in Hungary, with efficient bus (and, in many cities and towns, trolleybus) services. It usually runs from about 5.30am to 9pm in the provinces and a little longer in the capital.

➡ You'll probably make extensive use of public transport in Budapest, but little (if any) in provincial towns and cities. Most places are manageable on foot, and bus services are not all that frequent. Generally, city buses meet incoming long-distance trains; hop on to anything waiting outside when you arrive and you'll get close to the city centre.

➡ You must purchase transport tickets (around 280Ft to 320Ft) at newsstands or ticket windows beforehand and validate them once aboard. Travelling without a ticket (or 'riding black') is an offence; you'll be put off and fined on the spot.

Boat

Budapest and Lake Balaton have ferry systems.

Bus

Buses are the mainstay of public transport in most villages, towns and cities in Hungary. They are a cheap and efficient way of getting to further-flung places.

Metro

Budapest is the only city in Hungary with a metro; it is convenient and extensive.

ROAD RULES

➡ You must drive on the right-hand side of the road.

➡ Speed limits for cars and motorbikes are consistent throughout the country and strictly enforced: 50km/h in built-up areas; 90km/h on secondary and tertiary roads; 110km/h on most highways and dual carriageways; and 130km/h on motorways. Exceeding the limit will earn you an on-the-spot fine of up to 300,000Ft.

➡ Seat belts are compulsory for the driver and all passengers.

➡ Using a hand-held mobile phone while driving is prohibited.

➡ Headlights must be on at all times outside built-up areas. Motorcyclists must illuminate headlights too, but at all times and everywhere. Helmets are compulsory.

➡ There is a 100% ban on alcohol when you are driving, and this rule is strictly enforced.

➡ Hungary's motorways may only be accessed with a motorway pass or *matrica* (vignette), to be purchased beforehand from petrol stations and post offices. The cost of passes depends on the class of vehicle (see www.autopalya.hu for more details); prices start from 2975Ft for 10 days and 4780Ft for a month.

Taxi

Taxis are plentiful on the streets of most Hungarian cities. Unscrupulous drivers are common, particularly in the capital, so it's best to call a reputable taxi company rather than hail a taxi in the street. If you do hail a taxi, make sure it has the company name on the side and that the meter is switched on. Make sure you know exactly how much cash you're handing over, as switching large denomination notes for small ones and then demanding extra payment is an occasional scam. Flag fall varies, but a fare between 6am and 10pm is from 320Ft (in Budapest from 450Ft), with the charge per kilometre 280Ft in Budapest and somewhat less elsewhere.

Tram

Hungary's larger cities – Budapest, Szeged, Miskolc and Debrecen – have the added advantage of a tram system. The capital also has a suburban railway known as the HÉV.

Train

MÁV (☎1-444 4499; www.mav csoport.hu) operates clean, punctual and relatively comfortable (if not ultramodern) train services with free wi-fi. Budapest is the hub of all the main railway lines, though many secondary lines link provincial cities and towns. There are three main stations in Budapest, each serving largely (but not exclusively) destinations from the following regions:

Keleti (Eastern Railway) station Northern Uplands and the Northeast

Nyugati (Western Railway) station Great Plain and Danube Bend

Déli (Southern Railway) station Transdanubia and Lake Balaton All train stations have left-luggage offices, some of which stay open 24 hours. You sometimes have to pay the fee (around 400/600Ft per small/large locker per day) at another office or window nearby, which is usually marked *pénztár* (cashier).

Some trains have a carriage especially for bicycles; on other trains, bicycles must be placed in the first or last cars. You are able to freight a bicycle for 25% of a full 2nd-class fare.

Departures and arrivals are always on a printed timetable: yellow is for *indul* (departures) and white for *érkezik* (arrivals); fast trains are marked in red and local trains in black. The number (or sometimes letter) next to the word *vágány* indicates the platform from which the train departs or arrives.

Classes

➡ InterCity (IC): the fastest and most comfortable in Hungary; only stops in major towns/cities. Reservations mandatory.

➡ *Gyorsvonat* and *sebesvonat* ('fast trains', indicated on the timetable by boldface type, a thicker route line and/or an 'S'): stop more frequently. Cheaper than IC trains by around 10%.

➡ *Személyvonat* (passenger trains or 'snail trains'): stop at every city, town, village and hamlet along the way. Only use for short hops. Most domestic links between smaller towns normally offer 2nd-class services only.

Reservations

On Hungarian domestic trains, seat reservations are compulsory on intercity express services (indicated by an 'R' in a circle or square on the timetable) or available without needing to book (just a plain 'R').

IC trains normally levy a supplement that depends on the distance travelled on the train. It is now easy to purchase train tickets (with express train supplements included) online; you just have to set up an account with the main train website (http:// elvira.mav-start.hu), purchase the ticket online and then collect it at the train station from a ticket machine using the reference number you receive upon purchase. You can also

buy tickets directly from ticket machines. Passengers holding a ticket of insufficient value must pay a fine. If there is no ticket counter or ticket machine at the departure station, the express train supplement can be purchased on board the train for the whole journey without penalty.

Special Trains

Twenty-four *keskenynyomközű vonat* (narrow-gauge trains; http://kisvasut.hu/) pass through many wooded and hilly areas of the country. They are usually taken as a return excursion by holidaymakers, but in some cases can be useful for getting from A to B (eg Miskolc to Lillafüred and the Bükk Hills).

An independent branch of MÁV runs vintage *nosztalgiavonat* (steam trains) in summer, generally along the northern shore of Lake Balaton (eg from Keszthely to Tapolca via Badacsonytomaj) and along the Danube Bend from Budapest to Szob or Esztergom. For information, contact **MÁV Nostalgia** (☎1-238 0558; www.mavnosztal gia.hu) at Keleti train station.

Train Passes

The One Country pass from **Eurail** (www.eurail.com), available to non-European residents only, costs US$171/244 for five/eight days of 1st-class travel in a month and US$114/161 for youths in 2nd class. Children six to 14 pay half.

The **InterRail** (www.inter rail.eu) One Country Pass offers 1st- and 2nd-class travel available for three, four, six or eight days within a month to non-Hungarian European residents.

MÁV (☎1-444 4499; www. mavcsoport.hu) has a START Klub Card that gives you 50% off all tickets for 2nd-class travel (though not prebooked tickets); it costs 14,900/24,900Ft for those under 26 for six/12 months and 19,900/34,900Ft for those over 26.

Language

Hungarian is a member of the Finno-Ugric language family; it is related very distantly to Finnish and Estonian. There are approximately 14.5 million speakers of Hungarian.

Hungarian is easy to pronounce, and if you read our coloured pronunciation guides as if they were English, you'll be understood. The stressed syllables are indicated with italics. The symbol ˉ over a vowel (eg ā) means you say it as a long vowel sound. Note that eu is pronounced as in 'her' (without the 'r'), ew as i but with rounded lips, and zh as the 's' in 'measure'. The apostrophe (') indicates a slight y sound. If you see double consonants like bb, dd or tt, draw them out a little longer than you would in English. Polite and informal forms are included where relevant, indicated with the abbreviations 'pol' and 'inf'.

BASICS

Hello.	Szervusz. (sg)	ser·vus
	Szervusztok. (pl)	ser·vus·tawk
Goodbye.	Viszont-látásra. (pol)	vi·sawnt·laa·taash·ro
	Szia. (inf sg)	si·o
	Sziasztok. (inf pl)	si·os·tawk
Yes./No.	Igen./Nem.	i·gen/nem
Please.	Kérem. (pol)	kay·rem
	Kérlek. (inf)	kayr·lek
Thank you.	Köszönöm.	keu·seu·neum
You're welcome.	Szívesen.	see·ve·shen

WANT MORE?

For in-depth language information and handy phrases, check out Lonely Planet's *Hungarian Phrasebook*. You'll find it at **shop.lonelyplanet.com**, or you can buy Lonely Planet's iPhone phrasebooks at the Apple App Store.

Excuse me.	Elnézést kérek.	el·nay·zaysht kay·rek
Sorry.	Sajnálom.	shoy·naa·lawm
How are you?		
Hogy van/vagy? (pol/inf)		hawd' von/vod'
Fine. And you?		
Jól. És Ön/te? (pol/inf)		yāwl aysh eun/te
What's your name?		
Mi a neve/neved? (pol/inf)		mi o ne·ve/ne·ved
My name is ...		
A nevem ...		o ne·vem ...
Do you speak English?		
Beszél angolul? (pol)		be·sayl on·gaw·lul
Beszélsz angolul? (inf)		be·sayls on·gaw·lul
I don't understand.		
Nem értem.		nem ayr·tem

ACCOMMODATION

Where's a ...?	Hol van egy ...?	hawl von ed' ...
campsite	kemping	kem·ping
guesthouse	panzió	pon·zi·āw
hotel	szálloda	saal·law·do
youth hostel	ifjúsági szálló	if·yū·shaa·gi saal·lāw

I'd like to book a ... room, please.	Szeretnék egy ... szobát foglalni.	se·ret·nayk ed' ... saw·baat fawg·lol·ni
single	egyágyas	ed'·aa·dyosh
double	duplaágyas	dup·lo·aa·dyosh
twin	kétágyas	kayt·aa·dyosh

How much is it per ...?	Mennyibe kerül egy ...?	men'·nyi·be ke·rewl ed' ...
night	éjszakára	ay·so·kaa·ro
person	főre	fēū·re

DIRECTIONS

Where's (the market)?
Hol van (a piac)? hawl von (o *pi*·ots)

What's the address?
Mi a cím? mi o tseem

How do I get there?
Hogyan jutok oda? haw·dyon yu·tawk aw·do

Can you show me (on the map)?
Meg tudja mutatni meg *tud*·yo *mu*·tot·ni
nekem (a térképen)? ne·kem (o *tayr*·kay·pen)

EATING & DRINKING

I'd like to *Szeretnék* se·ret·nayk
reserve a *asztalt* os·tolt
table for ... *foglalni ...* fawg·lol·ni ...

(eight) *(nyolc)* (nyawlts)
o'clock *órára* *aw*·raa·ro

(two) *(két) főre* (kayt) *fēū*·re
people

The menu, please.
Az étlapot, kérem. az ayt·lo·pawt *kay*·rem

What would you recommend?
Mit ajánlana? mit o·yaan·lo·no

Do you have vegetarian food?
Vannak önöknél von·nok eu·neuk·nayl
vegetáriánus ételek? ve·ge·taa·ri·aa·nush ay·te·lek

I'd like..., please.
Legyen szíves, le·dyen see·vesh
hozzon egy... hawz·zawn ej...

Cheers! (to one person)
Egészségére! (pol) e·gays·shay·gay·re
Egészségedre! (inf) e·gays·shay·ged·re

Cheers! (to more than one person)
Egészségükre! (pol) e·gays·shay·gewk·re
Egészségetekre! (inf) e·gays·shay·ge·tek·re

Please bring the bill.
Kérem, hozza a kay·rem *hawz*·zo o
számlát. saam·laat

Key Words

bar	*bár*	baar
bottle	*üveg*	ew·veg
breakfast	*reggeli*	reg·ge·li
cafe	*kávézó*	kaa·vay·zāw
cold	*hideg*	hi·deg
dinner	*vacsora*	vo·chaw·ro
glass	*pohár*	paw·haar
hot	*forró*	fawr·rāw
lunch	*ebéd*	e·bayd
restaurant	*étterem*	ayt·te·rem
warm	*meleg*	me·leg

Meat & Fish

beef	*marhahús*	*mor*·ho·hūsh
chicken	*csirke*	*chir*·ke
fish	*hal*	hol
meat	*hús*	hūsh
pork	*disznóhús*	*dis*·nāw·hūsh
turkey	*pulyka*	*puy*·ko
veal	*borjúhús*	*bawr*·yū·hūsh

Fruit & Vegetables

apple	*alma*	*ol*·mo
banana	*banán*	bo·naan
carrot	*sárgarépa*	*shaar*·go·ray·po
cherry (sour)	*meggy*	mejj
fruit	*gyümölcs*	*dyew*·meulch
grape	*szőlő*	*sēū*·lēū
mushroom	*gomba*	*gawm*·bo
orange	*narancs*	*no*·ronch
peach	*őszibarack*	*ēū*·si·bo·rotsk
spinach	*spenót*	*shpe*·nāwt
vegetables	*zöldség*	*zeuld*·shayg

Numbers

1	*egy*	ed'
2	*kettő*	*ket*·tēū
3	*három*	*haa*·rawm
4	*négy*	nayd'
5	*öt*	eut
6	*hat*	hot
7	*hét*	hayt
8	*nyolc*	nyawlts
9	*kilenc*	*ki*·lents
10	*tíz*	teez
20	*húsz*	hūs
30	*harminc*	*hor*·mints
40	*negyven*	*ned'*·ven
50	*ötven*	*eut*·ven
60	*hatvan*	*hot*·von
70	*hetven*	*het*·ven
80	*nyolcvan*	*nyawlts*·von
90	*kilencven*	*ki*·lents·ven
100	*száz*	saaz
1000	*ezer*	e·zer

Other

butter	*vaj*	voy
cheese	*sajt*	shoyt
egg	*tojás*	taw·yaash
honey	*méz*	mayz
pepper	*bors*	bawrsh
salt	*só*	shāw
sugar	*cukor*	tsu·kawr

Drinks

apple juice	*almalé*	ol·mo·lay
beer	*sör*	sheur
champagne	*pezsgő*	pezh·geu
coffee	*kávé*	kaa·vay
fruit juice	*gyümölcslé*	dyew·meulch lay
milk	*tej*	tey
orange juice	*narancslé*	no·ronch·lay
red wine	*vörösbor*	veu·reush bawr
soft drink	*üdítőital*	ew·dee·tēū·i·tal
tea	*tea*	te·o
water	*víz*	veez
white wine	*fehér bor*	fe·hayr bawr

EMERGENCIES

Help!
Segítség! · she·geet·shayg

Go away!
Menjen el! · men·yen el

Call the police!
Hívja a rendőrséget! · heev·yo o rend·ēūr·shay·get

Call a doctor!
Hívjon orvost! · heev·yawn awr·vawsht

I'm lost.
Eltévedtem. · el·tay·ved·tem

I'm sick.
Rosszul vagyok. · raws·sul vo·dyawk

I'm allergic to ...
Allergiás vagyok ... · ol·ler·gi·aash vo·dyawk ...

Where are the toilets?
Hol a véce? · hawl o vay·tse

SHOPPING & SERVICES

Where's a/an ...?	*Hol van ...?*	hawl von ...
shopping centre	*egy bevásár-lóközpont*	ed' be·vaa·shaar-láw·keuz·pawnt
super-market	*egy élelmi-szeráruház*	ed' ay·lel·mi·ser·aa·ru·haaz

Signs

Bejárat	Entrance
Kijárat	Exit
Nyitva	Open
Zárva	Closed
Felvilágosítás	Information
Tilos	Prohibited
Toalett/WC	Toilets
Férfiak	Men
Nők	Women

I want to buy ...
Szeretnék venni ... · se·ret·nayk ven·ni ...

Can I look at it?
Megnézhetem? · meg·nayz·he·tem

Do you have any others?
Van másmilyen is? · von maash·mi·yen ish

How much is this?
Mennyibe kerül ez? · men'·yi·be ke·rewl ez

That's too expensive.
Ez túl drága. · ez tūl draa·go

Do you have something cheaper?
Van valami olcsóbb? · von vo·lo·mi awl·chāwbb

There's a mistake in the bill.
Valami hiba van a számlában. · vo·lo·mi hi·bo von o saam·laa·bon

ATM	*bank-automata*	bonk·o·u·taw·mo·to
internet cafe	*Internet kávézó*	in·ter·net kaa·vay·zāw
post office	*posta-hivatal*	pawsh·to·hi·vo·tol
tourist office	*turista-iroda*	tu·rish·to·i·raw·do

TIME & DATES

What time is it?
Hány óra? · haan' āw·ra

It's (one/10) o'clock.
(Egy/Tíz) óra van. · (ed'/teez) āw·ra von

Half past (10).
Fél (tizenegy). · fayl (ti·zen·ed')

At what time ...?
Hány órakor ...? · haan' āw·ro·kawr ...

At (10).
(Tíz)kor. · (teez)·kawr

yesterday	*tegnap*	teg·nop
today	*ma*	mo
tomorrow	*holnap*	hawl·nop

morning	reggel	reg·gel
afternoon	délután	dayl·u·taan
evening	este	esh·te

Monday	hétfő	hayt·fēū
Tuesday	kedd	kedd
Wednesday	szerda	ser·do
Thursday	csütörtök	chew·teur·teuk
Friday	péntek	payn·tek
Saturday	szombat	sawm·bot
Sunday	vasárnap	vo·shaar·nop

January	január	yo·nu·aar
February	február	feb·ru·aar
March	március	maar·tsi·ush
April	április	aap·ri·lish
May	május	maa·yush
June	június	yū·ni·ush
July	július	yū·li·ush
August	augusztus	o·u·gus·tush
September	szeptember	sep·tem·ber
October	október	awk·tāw·ber
November	november	naw·vem·ber
December	december	de·tsem·ber

TRANSPORT

Public Transport

Which ... goes (to Budapest)?	Melyik ... megy (Budapestre)?	me·yik ... med' (bu·do·pesht·re)
bus	busz	bus
train	vonat	vaw·not
metro line	metró	met·rāw
tram	villamos	vil·lo·mawsh
trolleybus	trolibusz	traw·li·bus

When's the ... (bus)?	Mikor megy ... (busz)?	mi·kawr med' ... (bus)
first	az első	oz el·shēū
last	az utolsó	oz u·tawl·shāw
next	a következő	o keu·vet·ke·zēū

| A ... ticket to (Eger). | Egy ... jegy (Eger)be. | ed' ... yej (e·ger)·be |

| one-way | csak oda | chok aw·do |
| return | oda-vissza | aw·do·vis·so |

What time does it leave?
Mikor indul? — mi·kawr in·dul

What time does it get to (Eger)?
Mikor ér (Egerbe)? — mi·kawr ayr (e·ger·be)

Is it a direct route?
Ez közvetlen járat? — ez keuz·vet·len yaa·rot

Please tell me when we get to (Eger).
Kérem, szóljon, amikor (Eger)be érünk. — kay·rem sāwl·yawn o·mi·kawr (e·ger)·be ay·rewnk

Is this taxi available?
Szabad ez a taxi? — so·bod ez o tok·si

Please take me to (this address).
Kérem, vigyen el (erre a címre). — kay·rem vi·dyen el (er·re o tseem·re)

Please stop here.
Kérem, álljon meg itt. — kay·rem aall·yawn meg itt

Driving & Cycling

I'd like to hire a/an ...	Szeretnék egy ... bérelni.	se·ret·nayk ed' ... bay·rel·ni
bicycle	biciklit	bi·tsik·lit
car	autót	o·u·tāwt
motorbike	motort	maw·tawrt

| LPG | folyékony autógáz | faw·yay·kawn' o·u·tāw·gaaz |
| unleaded | ólommentes | āw·lawm·men·tesh |

Is this the road to (Sopron)?
Ez az út vezet (Sopronba)? — ez oz út ve·zet (shawp·rawn·bo)

Where's a petrol station?
Hol van egy benzinkút? — hawl von ed' ben·zin·kūt

I need a mechanic.
Szükségem van egy autószerelőre. — sewk·shay·gem von ed' o·u·tāw·se·re·lēū·re

The car/motorbike has broken down.
Az autó/A motor elromlott. — oz o·u·tāw/o maw·tawr el·rawm·lawtt

I have a flat tyre.
Defektem van. — de·fek·tem von

I've run out of petrol.
Kifogyott a benzinem. — ki·faw·dyawtt o ben·zi·nem

GLOSSARY

ÁEV – Állami Erdei Vasutak (State Forest Railways)

ÁFA – value-added tax (VAT)

Avars – a people of the Caucasus who invaded Europe in the 6th century

ÁVO – Rákosi's hated secret police in the early years of communism; later renamed ÁVH

bélyeg – stamp

BKV – Budapest Közlekedési Vállalat (Budapest Transport Company)

borozó – wine bar; any place serving wine

büfé – snack bar

centrum – town or city centre

Copf – a transitional architectural style between late baroque and neoclassicism

csárda – a Hungarian-style inn or restaurant

csikós – 'cowboy' from the *puszta*

cukrászda – cake shop or patisserie

Eclectic – an art and architectural style popular in Hungary in the Romantic period, drawing from sources both indigenous and foreign

élelmiszer – grocery shop or convenience store

érkezés – arrivals

eszpresszó – coffee shop, often also selling alcoholic drinks and snacks; strong, black coffee; same as *presszó*

étkezde – canteen that serves simple dishes

étterem – restaurant

fasor – boulevard, avenue

forint (Ft) – Hungary's monetary unit

főzelék – a traditional way of preparing vegetables, where they're fried or boiled and then mixed into a roux with milk

gulyás or **gulyásleves** – a thick beef soup cooked with onions and potatoes and usually eaten as a main course

gyógyfürdő – bath or spa

gyógyszertár – pharmacy

gyorsvonat – fast trains

gyűjtemény – collection

ház – house

hegy – hill, mountain

helyiautóbusz pályaudvar – local bus station

HÉV – Helyiérdekű Vasút (suburban commuter train in Budapest)

híd – bridge

HUF – international currency code for the Hungarian forint

Huns – a Mongol tribe that swept across Europe under Attila in the 5th century AD

Ibusz – Hungarian national network of travel agencies

ifjúsági szálló – youth hostel

indulás – departures

kastély – manor house or mansion (see *vár*)

kemping – campground

képtár – picture gallery

khas – towns of the Ottoman period under direct rule of the sultan

kocsma – pub or saloon

kolostor – monastery or cloister

könyvesbolt – bookshop

könyvtár – library

kórház – hospital

körút – ring road

köz – alley, mews, lane

központ – centre

lángos – deep-fried dough with toppings

lekvár – fruit jam

lépcső – stairs, steps

liget – park

Mahart – Hungarian passenger ferry company

Malév – Hungary's national airline

MÁV – Magyar Államvasutak (Hungarian State Railways)

mihrab – Muslim prayer niche facing Mecca

MNB – Magyar Nemzeti Bank (National Bank of Hungary)

műemlék – memorial, monument

Nagyalföld – the Great Plain (same as the *puszta*)

nosztalgiavonat – vintage steam train

nyitva – open

nyugat – west

önkiszolgáló – self-service

óra – hour, 'o'clock'

orvosi rendelő – doctor's surgery

pálinka – fruit brandy

palota – palace

pályaudvar – train or railway station

panzió – *pension,* guesthouse

patika – pharmacy

pénztár – cashier

piac – market

pince – wine cellar

pörkölt – stew

presszó – same as *eszpresszó* (coffee shop; strong, black coffee)

puszta – literally 'deserted'; other name for the Great Plain (see *Nagyalföld*)

puttony – the number of 'butts' of sweet *aszú* essence added to other base wines in making Tokaj wine

racka – sheep on the Great Plain with distinctive corkscrew horns

rakpart – quay, embankment

sebesvonat – swift trains

Secessionism – art and architectural style similar to Art Nouveau

sétány – walkway, promenade

skanzen – open-air museum displaying village architecture

söröző – beer bar or pub

strand – grassy 'beach' near a river or lake

sugárút – avenue

szálló or **szálloda** – hotel

személyvonat – passenger trains that stop at every city, town, village and hamlet along the way

sziget – island

színház – theatre

szoba kiadó – room for rent

táncház – folk music and dance workshop

templom – church

tér – town or market square

tere – genitive form of *tér* as in Hősök tere (Square of the Heroes)

turul – eagle-like totem of the ancient Magyars and now a national symbol

u – abbreviation for *utca* (street)

udvar – court

út – road

utca – street

utcája – genitive form of *utca* as in Ferencesek utcája (Street of the Franciscans)

útja – genitive form of *út* as in Mártíroká útja (Street of the Martyrs)

város – city

vendéglő – a type of restaurant

vonat – train

zárva – closed

Zopf – German and more commonly used word for *Copf*

ALTERNATIVE PLACE NAMES

On many bus and train timetables, Hungarian names are used for cities and towns in neighbouring countries. Many of these are in what once was Hungarian territory, and the names are used by the Hungarian-speaking minorities who live there. You should be familiar with the more important ones (eg Pozsony for Bratislava, Kolozsvár for Cluj-Napoca, Bécs for Vienna).

ABBREVIATIONS

(C) Croatian, (E) English, (G) German, (H) Hungarian, (R) Romanian, (S) Serbian, (Slk) Slovak, (Slo) Slovene, (U) Ukrainian

Baia Mare (R) – Nagybánya (H)

Balaton (H) – Plattensee (G)

Belgrade (E) – Beograd (S), Nándorfehérvár (H)

Beregovo (U) – Beregszász (H)

Brașov (R) – Brassó (H), Kronstadt (G)

Bratislava (Slk) – Pozsony (H), Pressburg (G)

Carei (R) – Nagykároly (H)

Cluj-Napoca (R) – Kolozsvár (H), Klausenburg (G)

Danube (E) – Duna (H), Donau (G)

Danube Bend (E) – Dunakanyar (H), Donauknie (G)

Debrecen (H) – Debrezin (G)

Eger (H) – Erlau (G)

Eisenstadt (G) – Kismárton (H)

Esztergom (H) – Gran (G)

Great Plain (E) – Nagyalföld, Alföld, Puszta (H)

Hungary (E) – Magyarország (H), Ungarn (G)

Kisalföld (H) – Little Plain (E)

Komárom (H) – Komárno (Slk)

Košice (Slk) – Kassa (H), Kaschau (G)

Kőszeg (H) – Güns (G)

Lendava (Slo) – Lendva (H)

Lučenec (Slk) – Losonc (H)

Mattersburg (G) – Nagymárton (H)

Mukačevo (U) – Munkács (H)

Murska Sobota (Slo) – Muraszombat (H)

Northern Uplands (E) – Északi Felföld (H)

Oradea (R) – Nagyvárad (H), Grosswardein (G)

Osijek (C) – Eszék (H)

Pécs (H) – Fünfkirchen (G)

Rožnava (Slk) – Rozsnyó (H)

Satu Mare (R) – Szatmárnémeti (H)

Senta (S) – Zenta (H)

Sibiu (R) – Nagyszében (H), Hermannstadt (G)

Sighişoara (R) – Szegesvár (H), Schässburg (G)

Sopron (H) – Ödenburg (G)

Štúrovo (Slk) – Párkány (H)

Subotica (S) – Szabadka (H)

Szeged (H) – Segedin (G)

Székesfehérvár (H) – Stuhlweissenburg (G)

Szombathely (H) – Steinamanger (G)

Tata (H) – Totis (G)

Timişoara (R) – Temesvár (H)

Transdanubia (E) – Dunántúl (H)

Transylvania (R) – Erdély (H), Siebenbürgen (G)

Trnava (Slk) – Nagyszombat (H)

Uzhhorod (U) – Ungvár (H)

Vienna (E) – Wien (G), Bécs (H)

Villánykövesd (H) – Growisch (G)

Wiener Neustadt (G) – Bécsújhely (H)

Behind the Scenes

SEND US YOUR FEEDBACK

We love to hear from travellers – your comments keep us on our toes and help make our books better. Our well-travelled team reads every word on what you loved or loathed about this book. Although we cannot reply individually to your submissions, we always guarantee that your feedback goes straight to the appropriate authors, in time for the next edition. Each person who sends us information is thanked in the next edition – the most useful submissions are rewarded with a selection of digital PDF chapters.

Visit **lonelyplanet.com/contact** to submit your updates and suggestions or to ask for help. Our award-winning website also features inspirational travel stories, news and discussions.

Note: We may edit, reproduce and incorporate your comments in Lonely Planet products such as guidebooks, websites and digital products, so let us know if you don't want your comments reproduced or your name acknowledged. For a copy of our privacy policy visit lonelyplanet.com/privacy.

OUR READERS

Many thanks to the travellers who used the last edition and wrote to us with helpful hints, useful advice and interesting anecdotes:

Ann-Marie Vinde, Cem Hasanoglu, Cloud Downey David Kozma, David Smallwood, Dora Szkuklik, Ellen de Jong, Emlyn Thomas, Gaybrielle Gordon, George & Linda Moss, John Baxter, John Prideaux, Kate Stenberg, Krisztina Bolla, Megan Tortorelli, Nadine Xi Chen, Neil Atkinson, Patrick Condren, Peter Lowthian, Peterjon Cresswell, Queenie Szeto, Rosemarie Folk, Sandra Carstens, Saul Robinson, Sophie Wenger-Cortellesi, Sue Pon, Tim & Evelyne Johns, Victoria Izz.

WRITER THANKS

Steve Fallon

In Budapest, thanks to Bea Szirti, Judit Maróthy and faithful correspondent Virág Vántora for their very helpful suggestions. Gábor and Carolyn Banfalvi and Péter Lengyel showed me the correct wine roads to follow; Tony Láng and Balázs Váradi the political paths. Once again, Michael Buurman opened his flat, conveniently located next to the Great Synagogue; co-author Anna Kaminski was a pleasurable dining companion. A tip of the hat to Zsuzsi Fábián in Kecskemét for help and hospitality. *Nagyon szépen köszönöm mindenkinek!* As always, I'd like to dedicate my share of this to partner Michael Rothschild, with love and gratitude.

Anna Kaminski

A big thank you to Brana, for entrusting me with the most beguiling parts of Hungary, to fellow scribe Steve for all the help and advice on the road, and to everyone who helped me along the way. In particular: András Török, Sándor, Virag, Gabor, Petra, and Julia in Budapest, Kimo and family for the repeated warm welcome in Sopron, the awesome paddleboarding outfit on Lake Balaton and Matthias in Pécs.

ACKNOWLEDGEMENTS

Climate map data adapted from Peel MC, Finlayson BL & McMahon TA (2007) 'Updated World Map of the Köppen-Geiger Climate Classification', Hydrology and Earth System Sciences, 11, 1633–44.

Cover photograph: Fishermen's Bastion, Budapest, Michele Falzone/AWL ©

THIS BOOK

This 8th edition of Lonely Planet's *Budapest & Hungary* guidebook was researched and written by Steve Fallon and Anna Kaminski. The previous two editions were also written by Steve and Anna, along with Neil Bedford, Lisa Dunford, Sally Schafer and Caroline Sieg. This guidebook was produced by the following:

Destination Editor Brana Vladisavljevic

Product Editors Joel Cotterell, Anne Mason

Senior Cartographer David Kemp

Book Designer Gwen Cotter

Assisting Editors Imogen Bannister, Michelle Bennett, Nigel Chin, Anne Mulvaney, Charlotte Orr, Alison Ridgway

Assisting Cartographer Hunor Csutoros

Cover Researcher Naomi Parker

Thanks to Bruce Evans, Kirsten Rawlings

Index